QUICK AND EASY DIY

READER'S DIGEST

QUICK AND EASY DIY

Helpful hints

Time-saving tips

Ingenious solutions

Tricks of the trade

THE READER'S DIGEST ASSOCIATION (PTY) LIMITED, CAPE TOWN

QUICK AND EASY DIY

Editors
Rod Baker, Joseph Gonzalez,
Robert V. Huber

Art Editors
Carol Nehring, Augusta Prohn

Writers
Thomas Christopher
Mark Feirer
Wade A. Hoyt
Laura Tringali

Researchers
Pat Brennan
Taryn James
Frances le Roux
Willard Lubka

Artists
Sylvia Bokor
Ron Chamberlain
Mario Ferro
Don Mannes
Robert Steimle
Linda Stevenson

Consultants
Charles Avoles
Roy Barnhart
Steven Beatty
J. Bodenstein
Bob Buteyn
Dave Corton
Phil Englander
Dora Galitzki
Allan R. Hildenbrand
Thor Johanneson
George Lambert
Jim McCann
Tim McCreight
Steve Miller
Americo Napolitano
Kathleen Poer
Evan Powell
Meryl Prichard-O'Rourke
Dee Quigley
Brad Reen
Vernon Robins
Mark Russo

Jenny Simpson
Stanley H. Smith, Ph.D.
Jay Stein
Paul Weissler
Tom Zera

Acknowledgments
The acknowledgments that appear on page 384 are hereby made a part of this copyright page.
First edition copyright © 1997 The Reader's Digest Association South Africa (Pty) Limited, 130 Strand Street, Cape Town 8001.

All rights reserved. No part of this book may be reproduced, translated or stored in a retrieval system or transmitted in any form or by any means, electronic, electrostatic, magnetic tape, mechanical photocopying, recording or otherwise, without permission in writing from the publishers.

Reader's Digest and the Pegasus logo are registered trademarks of The Reader's Digest Association Inc of Pleasantville, New York, USA.

ISBN 1-874912-47-5

Warning
All do-it-yourself activities involve a degree of risk. Skills, materials, tools, and site conditions vary widely. Although the editors have made every effort to ensure accuracy, the reader remains responsible for the selection and use of tools, materials, and methods. Always obey local bylaws and regulations, follow manufacturers' operating instructions, and observe safety precautions. In the case of electrical or plumbing work, and where both disciplines are combined, for example, in geysers, certain work is not permitted by the homeowner. Do not attempt any repair, adaptation or other work on such installations, but call a suitably qualified and licensed contractor.

The publishers cannot accept any responsibility for any act or omission arising from consulting this book.

QUICK AND EASY DIY

Like it or not, all of us need to get to grips with the thousand-and-one jobs that always need to be done around the home—from dripping taps to broken tiles, and even roof repairs.

And no matter how good you get at it, there's always more to learn.

That's the object of this book from Reader's Digest: a wonderful collection of DIY hints and tips specifically designed to make your home maintenance quicker, easier—and cheaper.

They say that the best way to learn is from experience—and in this book we've pooled the collective experience of hundreds of DIY experts to give you, the home handyman and woman, a perfect tool for a perfect job... every time.

Enjoy doing it yourself.

How to use this book

Quick And Easy DIY contains 12 chapters. The first three cover the home workshop: tools, organization, and hints and tips on how to improve your skills.

The next five chapters deal with your home, and are followed by a chapter on your garden.

Chapter 10 deals with your car and garage, and then we're back in the home and garden with Household Hints—a bonanza of solid suggestions that are just too good to leave out.

Finally, we discuss Travel and Sports, because no matter how much we enjoy our workshop or garden, we all enjoy going on holiday. The section on sports has a number of very useful tips dealing with outdoor activities.

In addition to the hints and tips, you'll find dozens of special boxes that will help you work more safely, keep your home in good repair, and select the best tools for the job. A variety of longer, step-by-step features shows you the best way to perform basic do-it-yourself tasks.

CONTENTS

CHAPTER 1
BASIC TOOLS AND EQUIPMENT

Drills and drill bits 9
Screws and screwdrivers 12
Hammers and nails 15
Staplers 18
Spanners and pliers 19
Cutting and shaping tools 20
Handsaws 21
Keeping tools sharp 22
Power tool safety 24
Power sanders 25
Routers and router bits 26
Portable saws 28
Table saws 30
Measuring tools 32
Marking tools 34
Layout tools 35
Clamps and vices 36
Supplies and equipment 38
Ladders 44
Tool care and storage 46

CHAPTER 2
WORKSHOP ORGANIZATION

Workshop basics 49
The workbench 52
Other workshop furniture 54
Workshop storage 56
Workshop cleanup 62
Work gear and personal cleanup 64

CHAPTER 3
WORKSHOP SKILLS

Wood basics 67
Measuring 68
Marking 69
Laying out 70
Drilling 72
Chiselling and planing 73
Sawing 74
Routing 78
Joining wood 79
Sanding 80
Clamping 84
Glueing 88
Finishing wood 90
Metalworking 94
Working with glass 98
Working with plastics 100

CHAPTER 4
HOUSEHOLD STORAGE

Passages and entrances 103
Bedrooms and living areas 104
Kitchen 106
Bathrooms 110
Laundry area 112
Home office 113
Shelves 114
Cupboards 118
Children's rooms 122
Sports equipment 123
Attic and garage 124

CHAPTER 5
HOME IMPROVEMENTS

Wall repair 129
Wallboard installation 132
Wall trim 134
Wall framing 135
Wall panelling 136
Ceilings 137
Floors 138
Floor coverings 140
Ceramic tiles 142
Windows 144
Doors 146
Soundproofing 148
Weatherproofing 150
Walls, floors and columns 156
Cladding and wood preservation 158
Walls 160
Roofs 162

CHAPTER 6
PAINT AND WALLCOVERINGS

Working with paint 167
Brushes 170
Rollers and spray guns 172
Choosing and buying paint 174
Preparing a room for painting 176
Painting walls and ceilings 179
Windows, doors, and stairs 180
Decorative painting 182
Painting a house exterior 184
Paint cleanup and storage 188
Preparing to hang wallcoverings 190
Hanging wallcoverings 192

CHAPTER 7
HOME SYSTEMS

Electrical tools and testers 199
Safety first 200
Electrical system basics 202
Working with wiring 204
Expanding circuits 206
Lamps and fixtures 208
Low-voltage and fluorescents 210
Plumbing basics 211
Pipes 212
Valves and taps 214
Baths, showers, and more taps 216
Toilets and drains 218
Geysers 220
Solar power 222
Home cooling 224
Home security 226

CHAPTER 8
HOUSEHOLD REPAIRS

Repairing furniture 233
Fixing furniture surfaces 238
Stripping furniture 242
Varnishing and staining furniture 246
Painting and antiquing furniture 248
Spray-painting furniture 250
Appliance repair tips 252
Refrigerators and freezers 256
Dishwashers and stoves 258
Washing machines and dryers 260
Electronic equipment 262

CHAPTER 9
YARD AND GARDEN

Planting a garden 265
Landscaping 268
Handling weeds, insects,
    and animals 270
Easier gardening 272
Establishing a lawn 273
Lawn care and maintenance 274
Trees and shrubs 276
Yard and garden tools 280
Outdoor power tools 282
Setting posts 284
Building and repairing fences 286
Building and restoring decks 288
Masonry and concrete 290
Repairing masonry and concrete 292
Garden improvements 293
Seasonal chores 297
Swimming pools 298

CHAPTER 10
CAR AND GARAGE

Tools and equipment 303
Changing the motor oil and
    oil filter 304
Tune-up 306
Cooling and exhaust systems 308
Transmission, steering, and
    suspension 310
Tyres 312
Wheels and brakes 314
Electrical system 316
Fuel system 318
Paint touch-up 319
Keeping up appearances 320
Storage, restraints, and security 322
Winter tips 324
Garage 326

CHAPTER 11
HOUSEHOLD HINTS

Curtains and blinds 329
Picture frames 330
Picture hanging 331
Childproofing your home 332
Eliminating household odours 336
Pets 337
Container gardening 338
Freshly cut flowers 339
Braais 340
Fireplaces 341
Christmas decorations and wraps 342
Controlling household pests 344
Moving heavy objects 345
Household moving 346
Simple solutions 350

CHAPTER 12
TRAVEL AND SPORTS

Travel tips 357
Sports equipment 360
Boats 362

Directory 364
Index 366
Acknowledgments 384

CHAPTER 1

BASIC TOOLS AND EQUIPMENT

DRILLS AND DRILL BITS 9
SCREWS AND SCREWDRIVERS 12
HAMMERS AND NAILS 15
STAPLERS 18
WRENCHES AND PLIERS 19
CUTTING AND SHAPING TOOLS 20
HANDSAWS 21
KEEPING TOOLS SHARP 22
POWER TOOL SAFETY 24
POWER SANDERS 25
ROUTERS AND ROUTER BITS 26
PORTABLE SAWS 28
TABLE SAWS 30
MEASURING TOOLS 32
MARKING TOOLS 34
LAYOUT TOOLS 35
CLAMPS AND VICES 36
SUPPLIES AND EQUIPMENT 38
LADDERS 44
TOOL CARE AND STORAGE 46

DRILLS AND DRILL BITS

Drilling basics

Hold it right ▲
To drill a straighter hole and avoid breaking a bit, hold the drill so that the force you exert helps push the bit straight into the wall. Place the palm of your hand in line with the chuck, extending your index finger along the drill body. Pull the trigger with your second finger.

Keep it level
Newer power drills might have one or two built-in levels to help you drill accurately. To upgrade an older drill, cut the hooks off a mason's line level and attach it to the top of the drill with tape. ▼

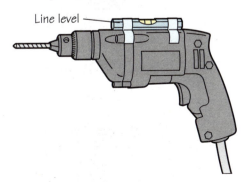

Line level

Hole starters
To keep the bit from skating around when you are starting a hole in wood and most materials, draw cross marks where you want to drill. Then use a centre punch to dimple the cross marks. For ceramic tile, make an X with a carbide masonry bit or put the X on some masking tape stuck on the tile. ▼

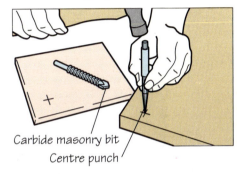

Carbide masonry bit
Centre punch

How deep?
When drilling to a precise depth, mark the depth on the bit with a piece of masking tape. Cut the piece a little long and stick the overlapping ends together to make a flag. When the right depth is reached, the flag will brush away the debris.

The right-size bit
Suppose you need to drill a clearance hole for a bolt or screw, but you don't have a drill gauge at hand. Use the fastener itself and the drill's chuck to gauge the right bit diameter. Chuck the fastener lightly into the drill; then remove it without changing the chuck setting. Try shanks of various bits until one fits snugly.

Replacing a drill chuck
If you find that the chuck jaws of your trusty old electric drill don't hold bits tightly enough, replace the old chuck with a new one of the same size, 10 mm for example. If the old one needs a key, you may be able to replace it with a keyless type. Removing the old is easy: apply some penetrating oil inside the chuck, place the drill on your workbench, and insert the key so that it is parallel with the bench top. Next, follow the steps shown below. To mount a keyless chuck, follow the directions on the package. Finally, lightly lubricate the new chuck's jaws and work it back and forth until it operates smoothly. ▼

Use a ball-peen hammer to strike the key with a solid blow so that the key will turn in an anticlockwise direction.

Next, unscrew the old chuck, using pliers (locking or slip-joint) if necessary. Screw on the new chuck.

To lock a new keyed chuck in place, insert the chuck key and tap the key lightly in a clockwise direction.

DRILLS AND DRILL BITS

More basics

Straight bits

A bent bit is likely to break and damage your work. Because bits bend easily (especially the thinner ones), test them for straightness before use and discard any bent ones. To test a bit, roll it slowly with your fingertips on a flat surface. If the bit wobbles, it's bent. Or place the bit against a straightedge and look for gaps between the two surfaces. ▼

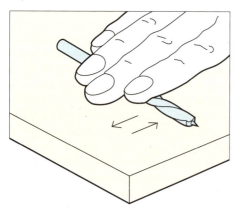

Pointed bits

Brad point

When drilling wood, use a brad-point bit instead of a common twist bit. The little spur on the tip of a brad-point bit cuts cleanly into the wood and keeps the bit from skating around when you start the hole or from drifting if the bit hits a knot.

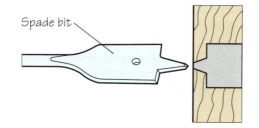

Spade bit

Splinter-free drilling ▲

Drilling a hole completely through stock leaves a rough, splintery edge where it exits. To make a clean hole, look (don't feel) for the point of the bit as it pierces the back side of the work. Pull out the bit, and using the little hole as a centring guide, drill from the back. This method works with spade, auger, Forstner, and brad-point bits.

Metal tips

Use a high-speed steel (HSS) bit for drilling metal. To protect the bit and keep the drill and its bit from overheating, lubricate the surface with plenty of light machine oil. If you need to drill a large-diameter hole (12 mm or larger) in thick metal, work up to the desired diameter in stages: first 5 mm, then 8 mm, and so on.

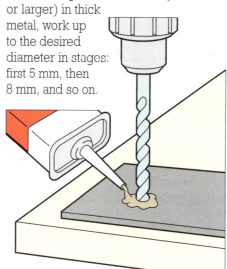

The hard stuff

For drilling tile, concrete, and masonry, use a masonry bit with a carbide tip. When drilling into concrete, start with a small hole, then enlarge it. A hammer drill does the job best—by pounding the spinning bit into the surface, it makes your work much easier. If drilling through a tile, however, don't use the hammer function—the tile may shatter.

Wall hang-ups

Drilling into a plastered wall often damages the wall's surface and leaves a mess on the floor. To avoid both problems, tape an open paper bag or coffee filter under the location of the new hole, with the tape over the spot you intend to drill into. When you've finished drilling, peel off the tape and empty and reuse the dust catcher.

Another dust catcher

Here's how to keep the dust from falling all over the floor or into your eyes when you drill into a ceiling. Simply drill through the centre of a plastic coffee tin lid, leave the lid on the drill bit, and drill the hole. Any size lid will do; clear plastic ones allow you to see the bit as you drill. The top of an aerosol can works well too.

Neat and clean

Here's the pitch
Used on some woods, a bit becomes coated with wood resin. If this is allowed to build up, it will dull the bit. To clean a bit, lay it on newspaper and spray it with oven cleaner. (Or, to contain the fumes, you can put the bit inside a plastic bag and then spray.) Let the bit soak for about 20 minutes, and then wipe it clean with a rag.

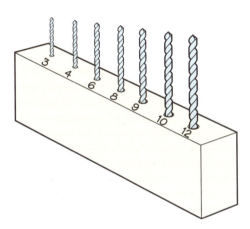

Bit holder ▲
To keep drill bits from bumping against other tools or against each other, and thereby losing their cutting edge, don't store them loose. You can either buy a bit holder for a few rands at a hardware store or improvise your own with a compartment or niche for each bit. To make the holder shown above, drill different-size holes in a block of wood and label each hole with the size of the bit it will hold. If you always keep the bits in their proper places in the holder, they will stay sharp and be easy to find.

Put a cork on it
Protect the business end of expensive bits such as brad-point, spade, and Forstner bits by screwing a piece of cork onto the end of each bit. The cork, which should have a diameter slightly larger than the bit, will protect the bit's lead-in point and the cutting spurs.

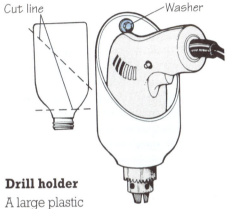

Drill holder
A large plastic bottle makes a handy holder for your drill. Cut off the bottom and the top of the bottle as shown, and attach it to the wall with screws and washers. You can also make a power tool holder out of a 200 mm length of 100 mm diameter PVC pipe. Cut a notch into the top rim to accommodate the tool's handle.

Another hang-up
To hang your drill on a pegboard hook, insert a screw eye into the chuck and tighten it.

BUYING A DRILL

A good basic electric drill has a 10 mm chuck, a variable-speed reversing (VSR) capability and a hammer action. Such a drill accepts bits with shanks up to 10 mm and lets you control how fast you drill. Buy the best, most powerful model you can afford. Be sure that the drill fits comfortably in your hand.

Cordless drills are very convenient, but they are usually slower and less powerful than the plug-in type and of course require recharging (from 15 minutes to several hours). As a result, you may opt to use a plug-in drill and a cordless one in combination.

Cordless drills come in three categories: screwdrivers, light drills, and full-size drill/drivers. The first type lives up to its name, and not much more. The second kind is more powerful and is easy to handle overhead. However, a charge powers only 10 minutes or so of drilling time and the built-in recharger is slow. Full-size drill/drivers have more features than the light drills, usually have a detachable battery, and are powerful enough to handle most drilling jobs, yet are good at driving screws. If you buy a second battery pack, you can use one while the other is recharging, and drill as long as you wish.

SCREWS AND SCREWDRIVERS

Handling with care

Treat it right
By using a screwdriver for a job it is not designed for, you risk damaging the tool and injuring yourself. Do not use a serviceable screwdriver as a prise bar, chisel, hole punch, scraper, or paint stirrer. If you must use a screwdriver for one of these tasks, choose an old one that's already damaged.

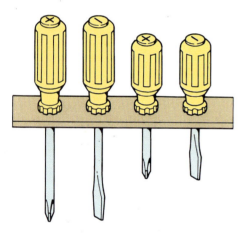

This end up ▲
To protect your screwdrivers and make it easy to find the size you're looking for, store them with their handles up. If your screwdrivers are not colour-coded, you can make identification even easier by marking the tops of the handles with a minus sign for slot screwdrivers or with a plus sign for Phillips screwdrivers. Either write the sign with indelible ink on a piece of tape and attach it to the top of the handle, or burn the sign into the handle with a soldering iron.

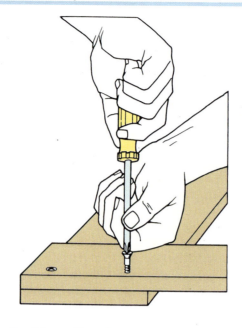

Avoiding slips ▲
▷ When driving a screw, always hold the screwdriver blade in the screw slot. If you hold the work as you drive the screw, the blade can easily slip out of the slot and injure your hand.
▷ In selecting a screwdriver, be sure that the tip fits the slot perfectly. If the tip is too big or too small, the blade will slip out of the slot.
▷ A screwdriver with a damaged (rounded) tip or edges can slip and injure you or damage the work. Similarly, a screwdriver that has a split or broken handle can cause injury.
▷ Keep screwdriver handles clean. A greasy handle can easily slip out of your hand.
▷ Never use a screwdriver near live wires or for electrical testing.
▷ Do not use pliers to increase the torque (turning power) of a screwdriver. Use a wrench for this purpose, and only with square-shank screwdrivers.

Smoother driving

Holding power
Before driving a screw, dip the tip of the screwdriver blade into a small mound of scouring powder or dig it into a cone of carpenter's chalk. The coating of chalk or cleanser will help the tip stay in the screw slot.

Magnetic tip
To start screws in tight places, use a magnetized screwdriver. You can either buy a factory-magnetized screwdriver or magnetize one yourself by dragging its shaft over a magnet several times in one direction. To prevent the charge from draining out of a magnetized screwdriver, keep it away from other metal objects. A home-magnetized screwdriver should hold its charge for about a week. To demagnetize the tool, just drag the shaft over the magnet in the opposite direction.

Lube job
You'll have an easier time driving a screw if you first pull its threads across a bar of soap, beeswax, floor wax, or lip balm. Dipping a screw into linseed oil before driving not only eases the job, it also protects the screw from rust.

Getting a grip

Another way to start screws in difficult places is to push the screw through the sticky side of a piece of adhesive tape, insert the screwdriver into the slot, and wrap the tape around the blade of the screwdriver. Or try dabbing a little rubber cement on the screwhead.

Sticky side

Hammer time

Despite the rule that says you should never hit a screw with a hammer, a few light taps when a screw is almost in place causes the wood fibres to compress and slant downward against the screw threads. As the screw is given its final tightening, it will get a better bite.

Brass screws

Brass screws make attractive but fragile fasteners. Because the metal is soft, a screwdriver can damage the slot or break the screw. To avoid this problem, drill a pilot hole, pick a steel screw the same size as the brass one, and drive it into the hole. Then remove the steel screw, lubricate the threads of the brass one with soap, and drive it into place.

Set in shellac

To keep a screw from being loosened by vibrations, dab shellac underneath the screwhead. If it's necessary to remove the screw later on, you can break the shellac film by pressing firmly on the screwdriver as you turn it. (When working with shellac, follow the manufacturer's safety instructions.)

SCREWDRIVERS

Having the right screwdriver makes most jobs a lot easier. A basic screwdriver set includes standard slot-tip and cross-tip (Phillips) drivers in various shaft lengths and blade sizes. Larger sets may also include a few star-shaped Torx and Pozidriv screwdrivers, handy when repairing household appliances and cars. The Pozidriv head is similar to the Phillips head but has a square end instead of a pointed tip. If you plan to work with many different screw types and sizes, consider buying a set of tips that fit just one handle.

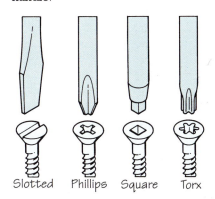
Slotted   Phillips   Square   Torx

Buyer's guide. Buy only the best screwdrivers, never the cheap kind. The best tools have handles made of butyrate or other strong plastic, and strong steel blades that are rough-finished or ridged to resist slippage. Cheap screwdrivers are likely to be made of steel that is softer than many fasteners. Choose screwdrivers that feel comfortable in your hand. You may find that a triangular handle or one that has deep ridges is easiest to grip and turn. As you shop, keep in mind that the larger the handle, the more torque (turning power) you can bring to bear on the screw.

Power drivers. The proliferation of power screwdrivers coincides with the widespread use of hardened drywall screws instead of wood screws. (The drywall screw has a deeply cut Phillips head that is ideal for power driving.) The most basic type of power driver is the pocket-size cordless screwdriver which, although slow, is convenient for driving any type of small screw. A drill/driver is essentially a drill, typically cordless, that has a variable-speed trigger to adjust the drill's torque or a low-speed setting for screwdriving. Remember, when driving screws, going slower gives more control.

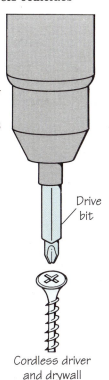
Drive bit

Cordless driver and drywall screw

SCREWS AND SCREWDRIVERS

Reusing and adapting

Renew-a-screw
Removing and reseating a slotted, Pozidriv or Phillips-head screw often results in a damaged head, especially if your screwdriver's blade didn't fit the screwhead in the first place. If you don't have a replacement screw on hand, try restoring the old screw by running a hacksaw along the slot (or slots in the case of a Phillips or Pozidriv head) to deepen it. If you're repairing a screw out of its hole, put it in a vice between two wood scraps. This way you'll avoid injury and protect the threads. ▼

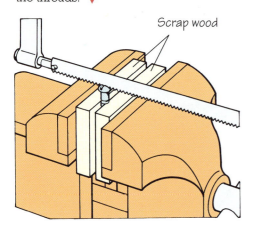

Scrap wood

Converting Phillips-head screws
Suppose you need to seat or remove a Phillips-head screw and you have only a slotted screwdriver on hand. Use a hacksaw to extend one of the slots in the screwhead so that it goes all the way across the screw. Again, if the screw is out of its hole, make sure to hold it in a vice, not in your fingers.

Unclog it
To remove a screw when its slot is clogged with paint, first use a scratch awl to dig out the paint from the slot.

Keeping track
When disassembling a piece that needs to be repaired or moved, thread the screws into the edge of a strip of corrugated cardboard. Then tape the strip to one of the larger parts. To make reassembly easier, write notes about the screws' positions on the strip of cardboard.

Golf tee trick
To restore a worn or stripped screw hole, plug it with several glue-covered toothpicks, a piece of dowel, or a wooden golf tee. Fill the hole with glue and insert the plug. When the glue has set, cut off the excess plug. You'll then be ready to drill the pilot hole and drive the screw. ▼

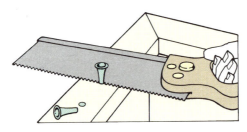

Stuck screws

Break it up
Winning the war against stuck screws usually depends on breaking up the layer of corrosion (grime and rust) that develops around the head. Before you try to force the offending screw, spray it with a lubricant such as penetrating oil. If you don't have a lubricant on hand, try using a little vinegar, lemon juice, or carbonated cooldrink (the fizz does the work). Allow some time for the lubricant to do its job; then help break the bond by tapping a hammer on the area surrounding the screw.

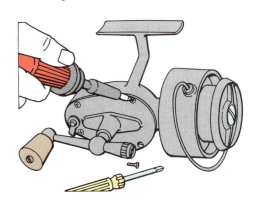

Hot metal ▲
If you still can't get that screw out of a metal object, lubricate the screw as described above and then heat it with a soldering iron or a gas torch. (An iron works well on the thin metal of home appliances but you'll need a gas torch if the screws are large and the metal thicker.) The heat makes the lubricant thinner, so it can seep into the threads. While the screw is still hot, tap the area lightly around the screw with a hammer.

14 / Basic Tools and Equipment

HAMMERS AND NAILS

Basic tips

Swing time

Everyone bends a nail now and then. To reduce your chances of doing so, try to drive a nail home with the fewest possible hammer blows—no more than three or four. Hold the hammer's handle at its end, not in the middle, and swing your arm like a clock pendulum, keeping your wrist stiff during the swing. Always wear eye protection.

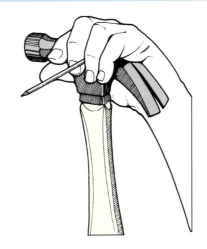

Another nail starter ▲

Grasp the hammerhead in your fist as shown, and hold the nail firmly between your fingers and against the side, or cheek, of the hammer. To start the nail, rap the nail point against the work.

No more smashed fingers

Holding a small nail or a brad when you start it often results in pain. To keep your fingertips out of harm's way, stick the nail through one end of a folded sheet of stiff paper. Using the paper as a holder, drive in the nail. Before finally seating the nail, tear the paper away. The teeth of a comb, tweezers, or needle-nose pliers can also serve as nail holders. ▼

Protective cover

Here's a way to shield a work surface from an accidental hammer blow when you're driving in finishing nails. Simply drive the nail through a hole in a scrap of pegboard with 5 mm holes. As you near the surface, remove the pegboard and use a nail set to sink the nail. ▼

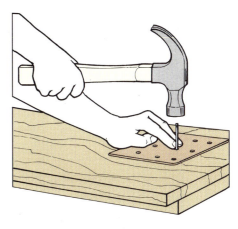

Cushion the blow

Need to tap a joint together without marring the wood? Convert your hammer into a mallet by slipping a rubber furniture leg tip over the hammer's striking face. Or cut an X in an old tennis ball and slip the ball over the hammer's face.

Directory assistance

When hammering indoors, use a pair of thick telephone books as a work surface. The books will not only protect the surface but also deaden the sound. (And if you're working on a messy project, you can tear out the pages of the book and use them to catch spills.)

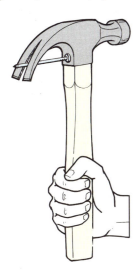

One-handed start ▲

Starting a nail with one hand allows you to hold on to the work or to the side of a ladder with your free hand; it also makes it much easier to drive a nail in a hard-to-reach place. One way to do this is to wedge the nail tightly in the claw of your hammer, with the nailhead against the base of the hammerhead. Swing the hammer, claw side first, to start the nail; then lift the hammer off the nail and drive it in the usual way.

HAMMERS AND NAILS

Easy driving

Pilot holes
Driving a nail into hardwood is easier if you drill a pilot hole first, just as you would for a screw. If you don't have the right drill bit, nip off the head of a nail that is the same size as the nail you are going to use, and drive it into the wood a little way. ▼

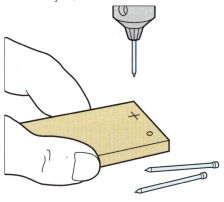

Fast driver
Another strategy for easing nails into hardwood is to lubricate the nails. Beeswax, lubricating (household) oil, even lip balm, all work well. If your hammer has a wooden handle, you can drill a hole in the handle end and fill it with beeswax or lip balm. ▼

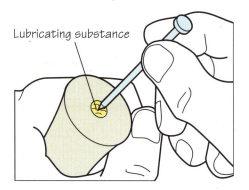

Lubricating substance

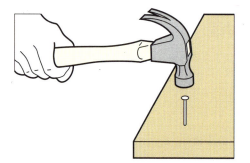

No more split wood ▲
To keep wood from splitting when you drive a nail into it, blunt the point of the nail slightly. Turn the nail so that the point faces up, and tap it with a hammer. Then try to drive the nail into the soft, lighter areas of the wood, not the darker, and harder, grain lines.

Nail attractor
Glue a small magnet to the end of your hammer handle. When you want to pick up a few nails, just stick the handle into your nail container or apron pocket.

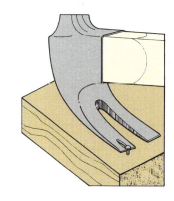

Mini-claw ▲
To pull nails too small for the claw of your hammer to grip, create a miniature nail puller by filing a V-shaped notch into one claw tip. A triangular-shaped needle file will do the job nicely.

Versatile nail-pulling wedge
To get just the right leverage under the hammerhead when you're pulling a nail, make a nail-puller block like the one shown below from a scrap piece of wood. Cutting the piece at about a 35° angle will give you a great deal of flexibility. ▼

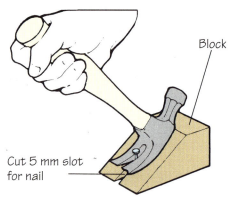

Block

Cut 5 mm slot for nail

Care and handling

Put on a smooth face
A good-quality hammer will perform well for years. But with use—and abuse—its face will become nicked and gouged. When that happens, you can restore the hammer's face by lightly filing it smooth. Make sure the outer edge of the face remains bevelled so that it is less likely to leave hammer marks on the work.

Sharp claws
The claw, that handy nail puller, may need restoration too. When the claw becomes damaged, restore the ends and the inside edges of the V with a flat metal file. Deepen the point of the V with a triangular file.

Stronger by far

When joining two pieces of wood, instead of driving them in straight, drive them in at opposing angles. You will achieve a much stronger join as the nails will not be able to pull loose, which they might if driven in at right angles.

Handle remedies

If your hammer's wooden handle is loose, put it in a jar of linseed oil for an hour. The wood fibres swell in the oil, making for a snugger fit. If a handle cracks or breaks, replace it or discard the hammer. To attach a new handle, first shape it to fit. Then coat the handle tip with 5-minute epoxy, tap it into the hammerhead, drive in the end wedges, and let the epoxy cure for 24 hours.

Hammer hold

Make your nail apron do double duty as a convenient holder for your hammer. Drill two holes in a suitable PVC pipe coupling and thread one of the apron strings through the holes. ▼

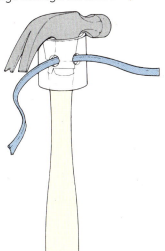

HAMMERS

Most types of hammer come in a variety of head weights and handle lengths. Handles made of wood, tubular steel (with a rubber grip), or fibreglass absorb shock well, are comfortable to hold, and provide a good grip. The head should be cleanly forged (not cast) of quality steel. The face of a hammer intended for general use should be smooth and have slightly bevelled edges. A textured face clings to nails and is best for long nailing sessions. However, a textured face will mar the work surface. A smooth face, found on peen hammers, mallets, and sledges, is designed to strike either a work surface or other tools, such as a cold chisel or a punch.

Curved-claw hammer

Claw hammers. The basic household hammer is a 450 g curved-claw hammer. For rough construction work, choose a heavier straight claw, called a ripping hammer, which has heads up to 750 g. For lighter work, use a light 340 g hammer.

Ball-peen hammer   *Cross-peen hammer*

Peen hammers. Instead of a claw, these hammers have a second striking surface, called a peen. The rounded ball peen is used to bend and shape soft metal. The hammer used by cabinetmakers has a long, thin cross peen to start a brad and a flat face to drive a nail. A bricklayer's hammer has a flat end to settle masonry into place and a long chisel-like face to score bricks before they're cut.

Bricklayer's hammer

Carpenter's mallet

Rubber mallet

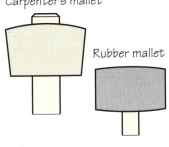

Mallets and sledges. To strike woodworking chisels and assemble wood parts, use a carpenter's mallet. Assemble other projects and pound out dents in metal with a rubber mallet. Sledgehammers (not shown) have solid steel heads weighing from 3,6 to 6,3 kg. Long-handled heavy sledges are used for demolition work, such as breaking up concrete. The lighter, short-handled type is used to drive stakes and spikes into place.

Basic Tools and Equipment / 17

STAPLERS

Staple gun operation

Quick screen fix
A staple gun makes short work of small household repairs. For example, to repair a screen that has pulled out of its wood frame, staple the screen to the frame, folding a hem as you go. Doubling over the screen makes the fastening stronger and reduces the chance that the wires will unravel and work loose again. ▼

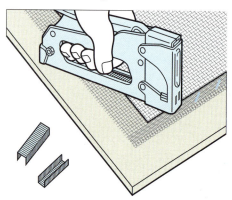

A better angle
When stapling fabric or screen mesh to a surface, place the staples at an angle to the weave or mesh. This way the staple has more material to grip, making the attachment more secure. ▼

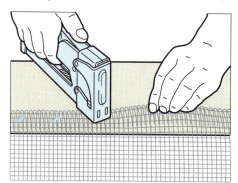

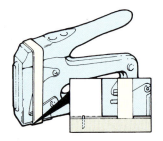

Temporary stapling ▲
Some fastening jobs, such as stapling plastic sheets over a window, are meant to be temporary. Here's a way to make staple removal hassle-free. Slip a heavy-duty rubber band around the staple gun as shown. The rubber band acts as a spacer, leaving the staples sticking up slightly so that they are easy to remove with a staple remover. This method also keeps the staples from cutting through very thin materials.

Specialized tasks

For stereo, phone and power flex
Here's a quick, neat way to safely and firmly attach flex along various surfaces in the workshop and elsewhere. You will need only a staple gun and cloth tape available from a haberdasher or supermarket. Loop the tape around the flex, place the staple gun on it, so that it holds the tape firmly, push it hard up against the flex and staple the tape to the surface. Cut the tape 5 mm from the staple.

Hammer tacker
This handy tool is great for attaching a vapour barrier, insulation, and roofing and builder's felt. A hammer tacker is useful for any job that does not require great accuracy of placement. The tacker also makes it easier to work overhead and is kinder to arm muscles and hands than a regular stapler. To set a staple, just strike the tacker. If you do a lot of stapling, a power stapler is a worthwhile investment. ▼

COMMON STAPLES

LEG LENGTH	USE
6 mm	Light upholstering, such as valances and shades
8 mm	Heavy upholstering, draperies, thin insulation
10 mm	Light insulation, weatherstripping, roofing papers, wire mesh, electrical wire
12 mm	Carpet underfelt, canvas, felt stripping
14 mm	Insulation board, roofing felt, cupboard

SPANNERS AND PLIERS

Techniques

Pliers or spanner?
Always turn a nut with a spanner. Using pliers for this purpose will round the edges of the nut and make it even harder to remove later on. If necessary, hold the bolt with pliers, but turn the nut with a spanner.

Turn it right ▲
When using an adjustable spanner, pull on the handle so that the stronger, fixed side of the jaw is applying pressure, rather than the weaker adjustable side. Before you turn the spanner, be sure that the jaws are holding the nut tightly.

Padded jaws
If you're using pliers on an easily scratched surface, such as chrome, brass, or plastic, be sure to pad the jaws. Either wrap them with adhesive tape, or snip the fingers off an old leather glove and slip these "sleeves" over the jaws.

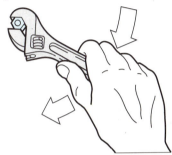

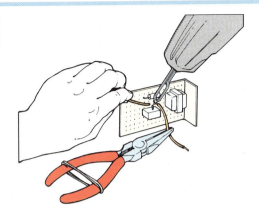

A third hand ▲
Long-nose locking pliers act as a third hand that can grip small objects while you assemble, solder, or clamp them. You can convert ordinary pliers into a mini-vice by slipping a rubber band over the handle. The rubber band will keep the pliers' jaws clamped closed while you work.

Working with bolts

Small nut
Positioning a small nut in a tight place often involves a certain amount of fumbling. To facilitate matters, wrap a strip of double-sided carpet tape around the end of your finger. Use the tape to pick up the nut and hold it in place on the end of the bolt. Then turn the bolt to secure the nut.

Extra reach
Screw a nut onto a dowel with a turn or two, when you have to place it in a spot beyond your reach. Turn the bolt onto the nut and simply pull the dowel away.

Hard to reach, easy to fit ▲
Threading a washer and nut onto a bolt in a blind spot can be awkward. The job will be much easier if you glue the washer and nut together. Apply a drop of glue from a hot-glue gun where the washer and nut meet, but be sure to keep the glue off the threads. When the glue has set, thread the nut.

Another nut trick
When you need to remove a nut and the only open-end spanner you have is too large for it, simply insert a coin or washer between the spanner and the nut. The gap will be filled, a tight fit achieved and you'll be able to turn the nut without any further problems. ▼

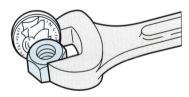

Homemade lock washer
If you don't have a lock washer to secure a nut, wrap a rubber band or a layer of plastic film around the threaded end of the bolt and tighten the nut. As the nut tightens, the material runs into its threads, locking the nut into place.

Basic Tools and Equipment / 19

CUTTING AND SHAPING TOOLS

Files and rasps

Get into shaping

Single-cut

Double-cut

Rasp

A single-cut file has parallel rows of ridged teeth that smooth and sharpen metal. A double-cut file has a second, crossing, set of parallel ridges; it removes metal and wood stock rapidly. A rasp has individual teeth ridges and gives a rough cut on wood and soft metals; the bigger the teeth, the coarser the finish. You can use a bastard file for a coarse finish, a second-cut file for a medium to coarse finish and a smooth file for a fine finish. Generally, the bigger the job, the longer the file. A large file removes a lot of stock quickly, while a small file removes less stock but gives you more control. Most jobs require only an all-purpose flat file. But if you are enlarging a round or contoured shape, use a round or half-round file. If you're working on rectangular holes or corners, use a square file, and for acute internal angles, a taper (triangular) file. ▼

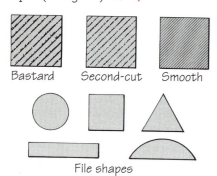
Bastard   Second-cut   Smooth

File shapes

Get a handle on it

For safety and better control, make sure a file has a handle on its tang before you use it. Some handles screw onto the tang. Others are held by friction. In the latter case, insert the tang into the handle, hold it vertically, and rap the handle on a firm surface to seat the file. Don't strike the file or the handle with a hammer.

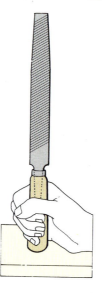

One-way stroke

Files cut only on the push stroke, never on the return. To avoid dulling the teeth, lift the tool off the work surface at the end of the push stroke.

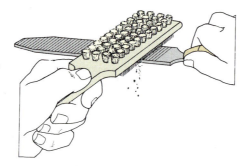

Card sharp ▲

If your file glides over the work without cutting the surface, clean the file teeth with a special wire brush called a file card. To use the card, run the wire bristles over the file, parallel to the grooves of the file teeth.

Chisels and planes

Easy glider

To make a plane glide across a surface, rub the soleplate with a bit of candle. Buff well to spread a thin, even coating. Warming the sole with a hairdryer first will make the job easier.

Tray organizer

Nothing dulls chisel blades faster than bumping into other tools. Either store them individually in a kitchen utensil tray, or, if you wish to put more than one chisel in a compartment, add a layer of cotton or bubble packing between tools.

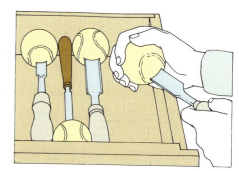

Guard duty ▲

Another way to keep chisels away from other tools is to protect the ends with inexpensive plastic chisel covers. You can also make your own chisel protectors out of slit tennis balls or hollowed-out pieces of cork.

Plane rest

To protect the cutting edge of a plane when it is not in use, set it down on its side or rest it on a block of polystyrene. To store the plane, secure a block of polystyrene to the tool with a couple of sturdy rubber bands.

HANDSAWS

Sharp ideas

The right way to hold a saw
Instead of gripping the handle with all four fingers around it, extend your index finger and place it against the handle as though you were pointing along the saw blade. You'll have better control and cut a straighter, truer line. ▼

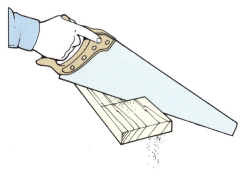

Don't gum it up
Sawing resinous softwoods such as pine clogs saw teeth with a gummy buildup that soon makes the saw seem dull. To remove the resin, apply oven cleaner (see p 27). To keep the sticky stuff from adhering in the first place, spray silicone on the teeth. Or try running a bar of soap or some candle wax across them.
Note: Saws treated this way should be used only for construction work, not for finished pieces.

Keeping your (hacksaw) teeth clean
If you cut soft metals with a hacksaw, the saw's teeth will soon clog. You can avoid this problem by using a blade with bigger teeth, slowing down your strokes (so the metal doesn't melt), and pushing down more gently on the saw.

THE RIGHT SAW

For most "around-the-house" jobs you can probably get away with owning just two handsaws: a hacksaw for metal and a general-purpose, or combination, saw that will make cross-grain and ripping (with the grain) cuts in wood. If, however, you are going to be doing any joinery, you will probably need a tenon saw as well. This saw has a thick rib along its top edge to keep the blade rigid. For even finer work, a dovetail saw may be required. The more teeth a saw blade has (they are still referred to in Imperial terms of teeth per inch—tpi), the smoother—and slower—the saw cuts. In addition, the teeth of tenon saws and dovetail saws are set to make a narrow kerf and so are useful in making tightly fitting joints.

Bow saws. Most of us who live in houses will at some time face the task of trimming trees, and one of the best tools for this job is the bow saw. It is designed specially for the coarse cutting of logs, and dry, green or seasoned wood. The narrow replaceable blade is held under tension by the bow and has pegged teeth and gullets which allow for cutting in both directions. The narrow blade keeps friction to a minimum but waxing the blade before use will ease the task even more. But beware of jamming it if the branch twists as it begins to break at the cut line.

How dull
How can you tell if a saw is dull *before* you use it? Check the teeth closely to see if the points are rounded and the cutting edges show wear. (Use a magnifying glass to inspect fine-tooth saws.) If the saw appears dull, take it to your hardware shop for resharpening. ▼

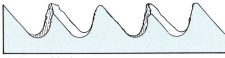
Dull saw blade

Sharp saw blade

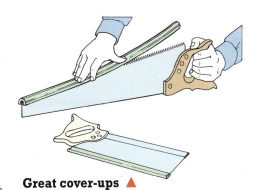

Great cover-ups ▲
When you store handsaws, be sure to cover the cutting teeth. An economical protector is a section of old garden hose that has been slit along its length. You can also use a section of rigid foam or a couple of slip-on spines from a plastic report cover.

KEEPING TOOLS SHARP

DIY sharpening

On edge

Dull tools are dangerous and inefficient. Save time and money by learning how to sharpen the blades of simple hand tools like chisels, planes, knives, and shears (see facing page; for tips on sharpening large garden tools, see p 281). However, let a professional sharpen tools that have complex or contoured cutting edges, such as router and drill bits, handsaws, and circular saw blades. The same applies to tools with hardened (carbide-tipped and diamond-coated) surfaces.

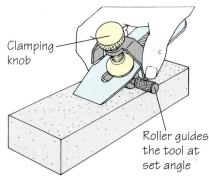

Clamping knob

Roller guides the tool at set angle

Honing guide ▲

This handy device holds the tool you are sharpening at the correct angle. Insert the tool into the guide, squaring the blade to the stone; then adjust the angle setting (the method varies from guide to guide) and tighten the clamp.

Homemade strop

Need a honing strop to give a fine finish to the edges of newly sharpened tools? Just cut off a 150 mm length of an old leather belt and glue it onto a board. Add a little oil if necessary.

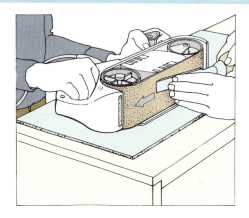

Substitute bench grinder ▲

You can use a belt sander, fitted with a worn 100-grit aluminium oxide belt, to rough-grind a tool. Have a helper hold the sander on its side on a mat of foam carpet padding, angling it if necessary so the belt will turn freely. Put on safety goggles. Hold the tool against the belt, pointing it in the direction of the belt's movement. Otherwise, the tool will catch dangerously on the belt.

Abrasive block

You can make a honing tool by glueing a piece of silicon carbide paper to a wood block. Clamp the block in a vice, and draw the blade along it a few times to give the final touch to a sharpened tool or to touch up a cutting edge. ▼

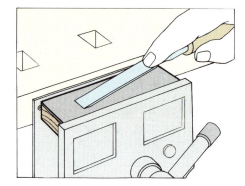

HOW TO SHARPEN

To restore the original bevel, or angle, of a tool, a flat stone or a honing rod (for long blades) will suffice. To remove a nick and to do rough grinding, you'll need a bench grinder. To detect nicks—and to check your progress in restoring the edge—examine both sides of the tool under a magnifying glass.

Chisel and plane angles range between 15° and 30°. Some tools have a narrow secondary bevel at the tip that is 5° greater than the primary one. This secondary bevel slows the dulling of the blade. (Its width varies from 2 mm to a micro bevel.)

Using a bench grinder. Before mounting a wheel, test it for cracks: Insert an old screwdriver into the wheel's centre hole. Hold the wheel in the air and tap it in several places with the handle of another screwdriver. If it rings, the wheel is intact; if it thuds or rattles, discard it.

The grinding technique shown at right is for rough sharpening or removing nicks. In either case, be sure that the tool doesn't overheat and lose its temper.

Caution: Wear safety goggles and use the wheel guard and eye shield. Never grind on the side of a wheel unless it is designed to be used that way. Keep the tool rest 2 mm from the wheel. For more on power tool safety, see p 24.

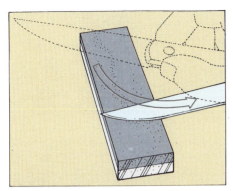

Sharpen a dull knife on a coarse stone first; then finish on a fine stone. Move the blade to the right as you pivot and pull it. Repeat on the other side of the blade, pushing it away as you pivot. Stroke alternate faces the same number of times. Keep the angle and pressure consistent.

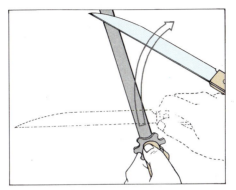

Use a honing rod for long-bladed knives. Holding the rod motionless, begin with the heel of the blade near the rod handle. Move the length of the blade along the rod in an arcing motion. Stroke each side equally. Keep the blade angle and the pressure constant.

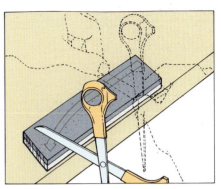

Scissor blades have a secondary bevel that can be sharpened. Place the bevel on the stone, and pull the blade toward you and slightly to the right. Use a pulling motion only.

When sharpening a chisel or a plane iron, use the stone's coarse side first. Rub the primary bevel back and forth a few times. Move the tool across the stone so the stone will wear evenly. To create a secondary bevel, raise the tool slightly and rub again on the fine side. To remove the raised burr, turn the tool over and gently rub the flat side.

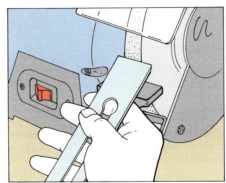

To sharpen a chisel or a plane blade on a bench grinder, set the tool rest so it supports the blade at the correct angle. Hold the blade, bevel side down and square to the wheel, with your forefinger against the tool rest. Keep the metal cool by repeatedly dipping it in water. Use a medium-grit wheel; then finish on a stone.

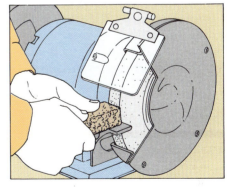

When the wheel of a bench grinder becomes clogged with foreign material or gouged from use, it needs to be cleaned, or dressed. One way to do this is to run a silicon carbide stick over the face of the wheel; the stick will clean and flatten the face, exposing new grit. Or use a hooded star wheel dresser.

Basic Tools and Equipment / 23

POWER TOOL SAFETY

Plugging in

Join the pros
Some of the major power tool manufacturers sell two lines of tools—one that is for professional use and another for the do-it-yourselfer. Professional tools are usually more powerful, heavier, and more costly. But they are also safer for an experienced do-it-yourselfer—and are usually worth the money, especially if they will be used a lot.

Amps of power
When you are shopping around for a power tool, don't rely on the boldly promoted power rating as an indicator of the tool's capabilities. Such ratings may be less than accurate. Instead, compare how many amperes each tool's motor draws—the more amperes, the more powerful the tool. If the amperage isn't listed on the tool's packaging, check the nameplate on the tool itself. For more on power tools and ampere measures, see p 43.

Go ahead and blow it
Sawdust is the enemy of all power tool motors. It accumulates inside the motor, around the motor housing, and in the motor vents. Vacuum debris from the housing and from the vents every month or so. Or blow it out with compressed air, using either an air compressor or tinned air, available at photography supply stores. (Be sure to wear eye protection.) If you fail to keep the vents open and the housing free of sawdust, your tools are likely to overheat.

AVOIDING ACCIDENTS

Whenever you use a power tool, make safety your main concern. Following are general power tool safety rules; for more tool-specific tips, see pp 22, 26, and 31.

Read, understand, and follow the directions in the owner's manual. Use a tool only for the jobs for which it is designed. Don't force a tool or otherwise cause its motor to overheat.

Analyze the job environment. Never operate a tool in a damp, wet, or fume-filled atmosphere. Keep your workspace well lit, well ventilated, and free of clutter.

Dress safely. Don't wear jewellery or loose clothing. Keep long hair tied back. Wear the appropriate safety gear (p 65).

Evaluate your mood. If you are out of sorts, ill, or taking a medication that could affect your alertness or judgment, postpone the job.

Think before you act. Know the consequences of every move you make. This will slow you down at first, but after a while knowing what's safe—and what's not—will become second nature to you.

Concentrate on the job. Don't talk to anyone while you work, and keep children and pets away. Focus on what you are doing at that moment, not on the next step.

Take your time. Hurrying and taking short cuts are major causes of workshop accidents.

Maintain your balance. Wear nonslip footwear, and make sure your footing is secure. Grip a portable tool firmly. Don't reach too far with a tool or work with it held over your head; stand on a sturdy stepladder instead.

Listen to the sound of the motor. If a tool makes an unfamiliar noise or vibration, turn it off and unplug it.

Attach that plug safely ▶
If you have to connect a 3-pin plug to a power tool's cord, ensure the green-and-yellow wire goes on the large earth pin. Then ensure that the brown (live) and blue (neutral) wires are attached to the correct pins. The latter two wires must be connected correctly. Look for the markings on the plug.

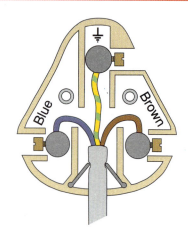

POWER SANDERS

Sanding alternatives

Make a stand
Sanding small pieces with a portable sander is awkward, if not impossible. The stand shown below is designed to hold a sander upside down so that you can hold a workpiece against it. To create the cutout for the sander, make a wire template that fits around the sander body, outline it on the board, and cut the hole with a jigsaw. Go over the edges with a rasp until the sander fits snugly. Make the frame deep enough so that the sander doesn't touch the workbench. To reduce vibration, attach strips of foam insulation on the bottom of the frame and the edges of the opening. ▼

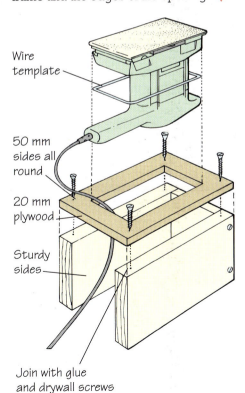

Wire template
50 mm sides all round
20 mm plywood
Sturdy sides
Join with glue and drywall screws

Random orbiter
Next time you're in the market for a power sander, take a look at a random-orbit sander. Like its cousin the orbital sander, the random orbiter moves the abrasive in tight little circles—but the circles in this case are random, moving first one way, then another, then another. As a result, the sander removes stock faster and doesn't leave those telltale little circles on your finished piece.

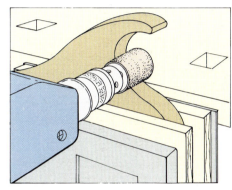

Sanding drill ▲
Tired of hand-sanding curved edges and other tight or hard-to-reach spots? Try a sanding drum attachment on your drill. Some models take special self-stick abrasive paper, others a custom cylindrical sanding sleeve. As you sand, hold the drill so that the drum smooths the surface uniformly.

Abrasive advice

Put it on tape
To strengthen sandpaper and sanding belts and keep them from tearing, apply duct or masking tape to the back. Write the grit on the tape; on a sanding belt, mark the direction of rotation as well.

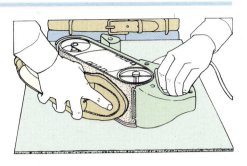

Prolonged life ▲
Sanding belts are expensive and quickly clog up. To remove buildup, place the sander on its side, angling it slightly if necessary so the belt turns freely. Hold the bottom of an old crepe-soled shoe or a belt-cleaning stick against the moving belt near the rear wheel. You can also use the handle of an old toothbrush, running it from one side of the belt to the other. (The plastic melts and picks up fragments from the paper.) Place the sander on a piece of foam carpet padding to help hold it steady.

Put it away
To store sheet abrasives, stick them on a clipboard and hang it on a hook. To help a sanding belt keep its shape and prevent unwanted creases, hang it on a pegboard hook covered with an old paint roller or a length of PVC pipe.

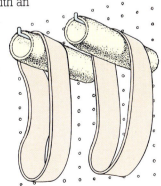

Basic Tools and Equipment / 25

ROUTERS AND ROUTER BITS

Setting up

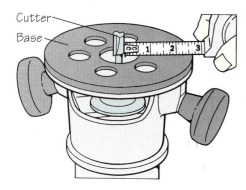

Measure for straightedge guide ▲
A straightedge clamped in place on the work serves as a guide for cutting dadoes or grooves and for trimming or squaring imperfect edges. The trick to setting the guide accurately is to measure from the edge of the cutter to the outside edge of the router base. Measure the same distance on your workpiece; clamp the straightedge tightly in place.

Get a grip
When you insert a bit into the collet, push it in all the way. Then before you tighten the collet, withdraw the bit slightly, about 3 mm. This enables the collet to get a good grip on the bit and makes it easier to remove the bit.

Plan a path
Before turning on the router, make sure its path is clear, with no small fasteners or nails lying around. To avoid tripping when working on a large piece, check that the area where you will walk is clear, and work away from the cord.

Router tables

Table talk
A router becomes more versatile and easier to use when installed on a router table. Look for a bench-top model that will accept nearly all routers, has a smooth-working adjustable fence, and has a see-through blade guard.

Router table switch
Even though a router table is very useful, reaching the switch under the table can be awkward. If you are handy with things electrical, you can solve the problem by installing a foot-control switch from a sewing machine on your router. That way both hands are free to handle the workpiece.

Homemade mount
Instead of buying a router table, you can make one from a piece of 20 mm plywood and clamp it to your workbench.

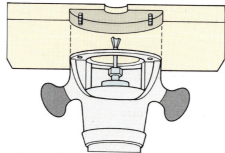

1. Rout a 10 mm deep recess in one side of the plywood, using the router baseplate as a template. Then cut a hole for the bit in the middle of the recess. Next, unscrew the baseplate, place the router in the recess, and attach it to the plywood base with several countersunk screws.

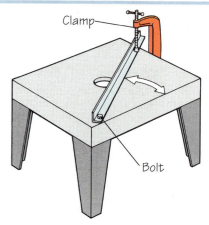

Quick guide ▲
Here's an easy-to-adjust fence for all routing jobs (except edge routing). Loosely bolt an aluminium angle to one corner of the table. Clamp the other end to the table at the desired position. To adjust the fence, pivot it and reclamp.

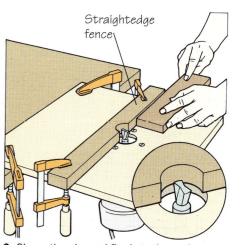

2. Clamp the plywood firmly to the workbench. Make a straightedge fence for the table, cutting an opening to accept the bit (inset). On narrow work, use a push stick to move the work safely past the bit. To make workpieces slide more smoothly, glue a piece of hardboard on top of the plywood.

Putting things away

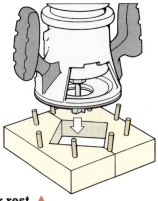

Router rest ▲

After you switch off a router, it takes a while for the bit to stop turning. If placed on its side, a router can roll around. So build this simple stand so that you can rest the router upright. Cut V-shapes into two pieces of wood to make an opening for the spinning bit; then glue the pieces together. Draw the outline of the baseplate on the stand and insert 50 mm dowels at an angle around the circumference line.

Toothbrush tip ▲

To remove resin buildup on a bit, spray it with oven cleaner, scrub it as needed with a toothbrush, and rinse it in water. Wear gloves and safety goggles.

BUYER'S GUIDE

A router with a 600 watt motor can do most jobs and will last a lifetime. Try handling some models in the store. Look for one that can be switched on and off while both hands hold the tool. Check for balance and weight by running it along the edge of a surface.

Router bits. Consider investing in the more expensive carbide-tipped bits. Carbide-tipped bits can rout hard- and softwoods, plastic, and manufactured woods; they stay sharp for hundreds of uses. Less expensive machined-steel bits can't be used on manufactured wood and require frequent resharpening.

Basic shapers. Shown here are the most commonly used router bits. A rabbeting or other edge-shaping bit usually comes with a guide, called a *pilot*. The pilot of a machined-steel bit spins as fast as the bit and tends to burn the work. A carbide-tipped bit has a ball-bearing pilot that rotates much more slowly and will not harm the work. Bits that make an inner groove (straight, V-shaped, corebox, and dovetail) have no pilots.

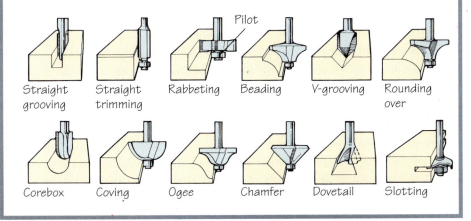

Straight grooving · Straight trimming · Rabbeting · Beading · V-grooving · Rounding over
Corebox · Coving · Ogee · Chamfer · Dovetail · Slotting

Protect those bits ▶

To protect router bits from bumping into other tools and each other—and to store them so they are easy to find—line a small cardboard box or workbench drawer with rigid foam or foam rubber. Cut out recesses in the liner to create a resting place for each bit. A light coating of oil on each will stop any rust.

PORTABLE SAWS

Circular saws

The right blade
Two kinds of circular saw blades will see you through just about any job. The first should be a general-purpose combination blade with 20 to 24 teeth; the other should be a fine cutting blade with about 40 teeth. Both blades should be carbide-tipped.

Cutting metal
If you plan to cut metal, use a special metal-cutting blade—and brace yourself for a shower of sparks. To ensure safety, wear hearing protectors, and goggles or a full face mask and work far away—say 15 m—from sawdust, flammable liquids, and anything else that is likely to catch fire. Don't try to saw metal unless your saw has a metal blade guard; a plastic guard will melt.

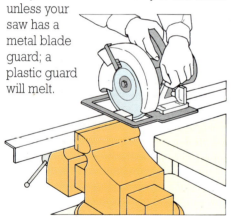

Permanent marker
The cuts you make with a circular saw will be more accurate if you mark the cutting line on the front of the saw's baseplate. Do it with paint or use an indelible felt-tip marker.

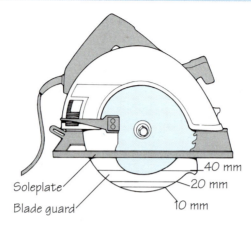

Measuring circular saw cuts ▲
Here's how to set your circular saw's cutting depth without having to pull out a measuring tape every time. Mark 10 mm, 20 mm and 40 mm blade depth measurements on the saw's blade guard with an indelible felt-tip marker. Then just line up the bottom of the saw's soleplate with the appropriate mark.

Clever with cord
Drape the cord over your shoulders. It will then move with you and be less likely to catch on anything. Remember: always work away from your cord, never towards it. Also make sure before starting any job that no other tools, wood or other items are in a position to catch on the cord. Even a slight tug on the cord can cause the tool to wander, ruining the job.

Wax works
Want your saw to glide as it cuts? Rub a block of candle wax on the underside of its baseplate. If you first heat the surface slightly with a hair dryer, the wax will coat the area more completely.

Jigsaws

Cutting curves
When you need to cut a curve with a small radius use a purpose-designed narrow blade. But be careful—the thinner it is, the easier it is to break.

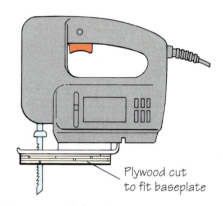

Put more teeth into it ▲
As a jigsaw blade makes its "sewing machine" up-and-down motion, only a few of the teeth do the actual cutting. With use, these teeth become dull and the blade useless. You can extend the life of a blade by adding a piece of plywood to the baseplate. This auxiliary baseplate should be at least as thick as the length of the saw stroke. Use your jigsaw to cut a notch in the plywood to accept the blade. Then outline and cut the plywood to fit the metal baseplate. Sand, finish, and wax the plywood to make it as smooth as the original metal plate. (It will also guide the blade and keep it from wandering as much.) Mount the plywood base with double-sided tape or hot glue. When the blade wears in the new spot, remove the base and change the blade.

Cleaning and storing

Oven cleaner
Sawing a lot of pine causes resin to build up on saw blades, making even sharp teeth seem dull. To clean a blade, spray it with oven cleaner. For easy application, suspend a circular blade on a dowel and hang it inside a cardboard box. Because oven cleaner fumes are toxic, close the flaps of the box for the 10 to 20 minutes it takes to loosen the deposit. Then wash the blade off with soap and warm water, dry it, and coat it with a lubricant to prevent corrosion. ▼

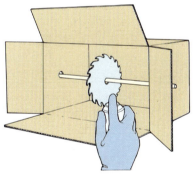

Soaking tin
To clean saw blades by soaking in acetone or turpentine, you'll need a shallow tin with a lid to contain the fumes, rubber gloves, and something for handling the blade. You can recycle a biscuit tin and cover it with aluminium foil. Or cut off the bottom of a plastic 20 litre container and use it as your soaking tray. Use a piece of scrap plywood to cover it while in use.

Capping saw teeth
When you have finished for the day, store your unmounted circular saw blades (and table and radial arm saw blades) so that the teeth stay sharp and won't injure anyone. You can make your own saw cover by slitting a length of garden hose or a section of an old inner tube. Other possibilities include stacking saw blades in a round plastic pie or cake container (put cardboard spacers between the blades). Or slip them into old record album covers (one blade in each sleeve). If you use album covers, be sure to reinforce the covers' edges with strong tape, because the teeth will cut the cardboard.

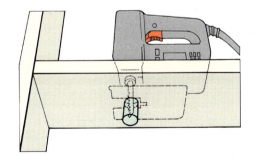

Shelf insert ▲
To store a jigsaw upright on a shelf, cut a hole through the shelf to accept the blade. Protect the blade by glueing a length of tubing to the underside of the shelf. Then just rest the saw on the shelf, hanging the cord on a nearby hook.

JIGSAWS

When selecting a new jigsaw, try one with an orbital action rather than one with only a simple up-and-down movement. The orbital action, which moves the teeth into the work on the cutting stroke and away from it on the return stroke, cuts quickly and cleanly.

To make the most of a jigsaw, you need to buy the right blades. Here's a sample of what's available: (A) a hollow-ground blade for fine cuts; (B) a double-sided blade that can back out of tight spots; (C) a flush-cutting blade that makes straight cuts flush to a wall or other obstruction (it's too wide to cut a curve); (D) a knife-edge for leather and carpeting; (E) a carbide-grit abrasive (riff) blade to cut hard materials such as ceramic tiles; and (F) a metal-cutting blade that will work on aluminium, steel, and pipe with walls 3 mm thick, or on metal plate and sheet.

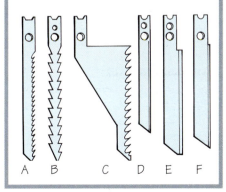

TABLE SAWS

Tips and tricks

Room to work
Setting up your table saw? If you'll be working with 1,22 x 2,44 m sheets of plywood, allow enough free room for them around the saw. For ripping, you'll need at least 3 m at the front of the saw and 2,5 m at the rear. For crosscutting, leave 2,5 m on each side of the blade.

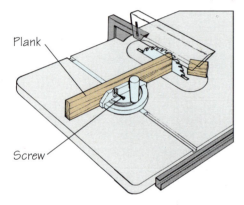

Mitre gauge guide ▲
When you're crosscutting, a mitre gauge places the work at the proper angle to the blade. However, the gauge doesn't show you exactly where the blade is going to cut, nor does it provide enough support to cut long pieces. To make a cut-off guide that will provide added support, attach a 22 x 69 mm plank permanently to your mitre gauge so that it extends from the edge of the saw to just beyond the path of the blade. Make a pass to cut off the excess. The cut end will mark the exact cut-off point of your saw. To keep the work from shifting as it comes into contact with the blade, glue a piece of coarse sandpaper along the full length and width of the plank's face. The paper's grit will grip the workpiece.

Parallel and square ▶
To ensure a proper rip cut and avoid kickback, align your table saw blade so it is parallel to the fence and square to the table. Here's a way to check that the blade is aligned properly: Measure the distance between the blade and the fence at both the front and the back. The measurements should be the same. Adjust the fence if necessary. Set the blade and the mitre gauge to 0° and test-cut a piece of scrap wood. Turn one piece upside down and place the cut ends together. If the pieces match perfectly, the blade is aligned correctly.

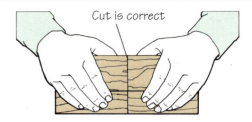

Make a height gauge
Here's a jig that will help you adjust the height of your saw blade quickly and precisely. Take a scrap piece of plywood and cut accurate notches in 3 mm steps, alternating sides as you cut (this way, each notch is 6 mm higher than the one below it). Mark the heights on the jig. To set the blade, place the gauge over it and raise it until it just touches the exact cut-off point of your appropriate notch in the gauge. **Caution:** Unplug the saw when you're adjusting the blade.

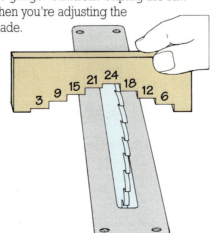

Improvements

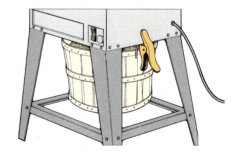

Collecting dust ▲
Ripping wood on a table saw generates a great deal of sawdust. Here are two ways to collect most of the larger sawdust particles as they fall: Attach a large plastic bag to the underside of the table saw with clothes pegs or duct tape. Or mount a large basket inside the saw apron, holding it in place with two spring clamps through the handles. These dust catchers are easy to empty and remount, but, for safety reasons, unplug the saw before doing so.

Wax your table
To keep the metal surface of your table saw free from rust—and help the work move smoothly as you cut—apply clear floor wax to the surface.

Bumpers for fence guides
Cover those metal fence guides that protrude beyond the saw base. Slit a pair of tennis balls and fit them over the ends. You'll save yourself many a bruise and avoid causing a head or eye injury to a child. ▼

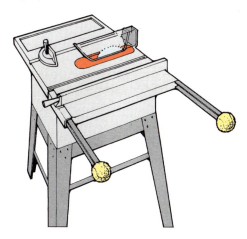

Seeing red ▲
As a graphic reminder to keep your fingers and hands away from the blade of your table saw (and any other stationary power saw, for that matter), paint the area around the blade a bright red. First make a new table insert and paint it red. Then paint 100 mm in front of and behind the blade. Be sure to mask the fence and any other areas you don't want painted. If you decide to give the treatment to the work surface of your radial arm saw, paint three bands—on the 90° position and the positions for 45° on either side of it.

Hang the accessories
As you accumulate accessories for your table saw, you'll appreciate having them all within easy reach. One way to organize accessories is to hang them on a piece of 6 mm pegboard attached to two side legs of the table saw. Drill holes in the legs and mount the pegboard with machine screws and nuts.

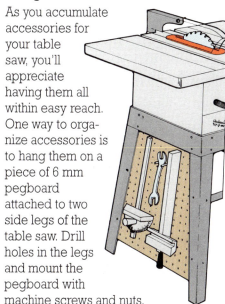

Push sticks and feather boards
When you're ripping stock, you need to guide the board accurately while keeping your fingers from coming too close to the blade. Using a push stick on small pieces keeps fingers at a safe distance (at least 75 mm away). To brace the work, clamp a feather board to the saw table so that it is in front of the blade (side pressure next to the blade would cause it to bind in the cut). Adjust the splitter to keep the cut open.

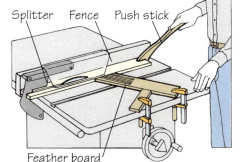

Splitter Fence Push stick
Feather board

POWER SAWS

▷ Always let the saw reach its full speed before you do any cutting.
▷ Keep all levers and clamps tight.
▷ Support both the work and the waste when cutting.
▷ Keep your fingers away from the saw blade.
▷ Always wear protective gear for your eyes and ears.
▷ Feed the work against the rotation of a stationary saw's blade.

Table saws
▷ Never remove the blade guard.
▷ Never reach behind a moving saw blade.
▷ Set the blade so that it protrudes about 3 to 6 mm above the work.
▷ Use push sticks, as shown at left.
▷ Hold the widest portion of the board you are ripping against the fence. Feed the work until it is completely clear of the blade.
▷ Never cut freehand.
▷ Use either the fence or the mitre gauge—never both at once.

Radial arm saws
▷ Stay out of the path of the blade.
▷ When ripping, use a push stick and the antikickback mechanism.

Band saws
▷ Follow the manual's guidelines on the proper speed, rate of feed, and turning radius for each blade.
▷ Keep the blade guide 5 mm above the work.

For more on power tool safety, see p 24.

MEASURING TOOLS

Home rules

Give credit where it's due
If you ever want to estimate the length of an item but you don't have a measure available, the solution is simple. Your credit card can be used as a rough and ready measure for a variety of stock items on sale in hardware stores. Credit cards are 85 mm long by 54 mm wide and their magnetic strip on the back is 11 or 12 mm wide. That makes it very useful when confirming that the p.a.r. (planed all round) timber you intend buying really is 22 mm thick—or 44 mm wide. The security hologram on some cards is 20 mm wide—which is also a useful measure. Measure the features on your credit card and decide which ones you may be more likely to use. Then bear them in mind next time you need to check a dimension, but have no tape measure or rule to hand.

Painted numbers
Have you noticed that the numbers and graduation marks etched in metal measuring tools become hard to read after a while? You don't need to replace the tools when that happens. Instead, paint them white and wipe off the excess paint while it is wet. The numbers and marks will be easy to read again. On aluminium tools, use black paint.

For good measure
Rather than discard an old tape measure, snip off a section about 100 mm long and keep it in your wallet. This portable ruler is especially handy for checking the size of small items in hardware stores.

Make your floor work for you ▶
Cutting timber to size is much easier if you have an oversize ruler painted on your workshop floor. Begin at one wall and draw lines every 100 mm, numbering the lines as you go. Use a ruler to find the intermediate lengths between the floor markings. To protect the marks, paint them with a clear sealer. You can also use floor markings showing angles to speed marking of timber, including large sheets, prior to cutting.

BE YOUR OWN RULER

If you need a tape measure or a ruler and there's none to be had, take a cue from our ancestors and use your body to estimate distances from 20 mm to 2 m or more. The illustrations below give some approximate measurements and their traditional names. To achieve more exact guidelines, measure your own fingers, hands, limbs, etc. (Be sure you are fully extended when you do so.) Memorize the results and you're ready to go. ▼

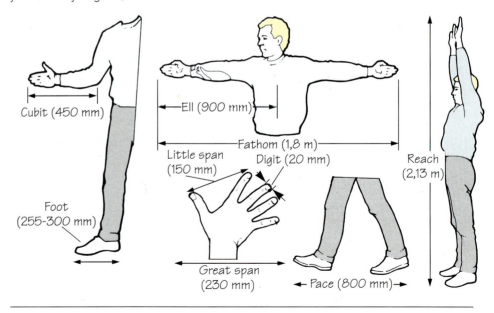

Mounted measure

For quick and easy measuring, glue a metal rule to your workbench. If you glue a smaller rule to your toolbox, you'll find that measuring as you work is always a snap.

Quick and easy transfers

Because an incorrect measurement can ruin a project, transferring it accurately is critical. If you don't have the right measuring tool handy, slip a hose clamp around a dowel and tighten the screw until the clamp fits snugly. Then slide it to the required position and tighten the screw to lock it in position. You can even colour-code a number of clamps to give you a number of measurements.

Magnetic measurer

You can also use a scrap piece of metal to transfer a measurement. Mark the place with a small rectangular or square magnet. It will clamp onto the metal and stay there as long as needed.

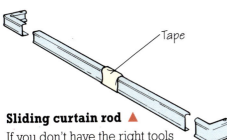

Sliding curtain rod ▲

If you don't have the right tools to measure an inside dimension, press a sliding curtain rod into service. Cut off the elbows of the rod, extend it to fit the space, wrap tape around the point where the sections of the rod overlap to keep them from sliding out of position, then remove the rod and measure it. To measure smaller inside dimensions, cut the rod down.

Dip straw

Here's a simple, accurate, and spill-proof way to measure out a small amount of stain or other liquids. Dip a plastic straw into the liquid just deep enough to get the amount needed. Then place a finger on the open end to hold the liquid in the straw. Keep your finger on the straw while you take it to its new destination. You can even mark frequently used measures on the straw and then discard it at the end of the job.

Hammer gauge

If one hand holds the hammer and the second hand holds the nail, how do you gauge the distance between nails without using a third hand to measure? Let your hammer be a measuring tool. Insulation tapes of different colours can be used to show the distances at which you wish to position the nails. Painted bands can be used for more permanent marking of gaps you often use, such as 200 mm and 300 mm.

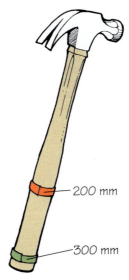

Tape tricks

Wax tape

Pros use a steel tape because it gives an accurate measurement and retracts at the touch of a button. To protect the numbers and keep the action smooth, coat the tape with a little candle wax; then buff it thoroughly with a cloth. ▼

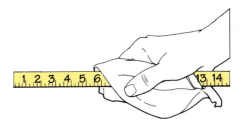

Taking notes

You'll always have a place to jot down measurements if you stick a self-adhesive label to the side of your tape measure. Either replace the label when you're done or erase the marks and reuse it.

Add a little, take a little

The hook of a metal tape gets in the way of a measurement that starts in the middle of a surface. To obtain a very accurate result in this case, try starting your measurement down the tape a little, for example at the 20 mm mark. Subtract the 20 mm later on. Use the same adjustment every time so that you get used to it.

MARKING TOOLS

Sharp and snappy

Sandpaper sharpener

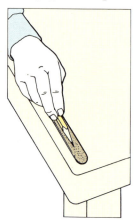

A sharp pencil is indispensable for making precise layouts. One way to keep your pencils sharp at all times is to tape or hot-glue a strip of medium-grit sandpaper or an emery board to your workbench or a nearby wall. To sharpen a pencil, just rub the point back and forth a few times against the abrasive surface. To achieve the chisel-shaped point that's best for marking wood, sand only the opposite sides of the point.

Another one-handed sharpener

You can also hot-glue a small plastic pencil sharpener to the underside of your workbench. Position the sharpener over a rubbish bin to catch the shavings.

Chalk talk

The coloured chalk used for snapping lines is highly visible, but it can be hard to remove from porous surfaces such as brick and unfinished wood. To make cleanup easier in such cases, an extra chalk box filled with talcum powder is just what you need. The white powder is almost as visible as chalk on dark-coloured surfaces and is easy to remove. On lighter surfaces, however, the white can be hard to see.

Snap line holder

When snapping a chalk line, both ends of the line must be anchored while the line is snapped. On wood, tie the line around a nail driven into one end of the stock or panel. Or cut a saw kerf and hook the string in the kerf.

Mechanical compass

To avoid having to resharpen and reposition the little pencil in a compass over and over again, substitute a mechanical pencil for the wood one. You'll have a durable marking tool that needs no sharpening and little adjusting. All you have to do to get a fresh point is push down on (or twist) the end.

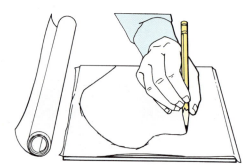

Draw anywhere ▲

Ceramic tiles, glass, and metal are hard to mark. One solution is to cover the area to be marked with a tape that's easy to peel off, such as artist's tape, or with a sheet of contact adhesive paper such as shelf liner. This way you'll be able to draw your cutting lines. Leave the tape or contact paper in place until you've finished cutting.

Unconventional tools

Circle chain

A length of chain is a handy aid when drawing circles. Drive the tip of a nail into the centre of your circle and use this nail as a pivot point. Slip the end of the chain over the nail, insert the point of a pencil at the desired radius and draw the circle. For the most accurate results keep the pencil perpendicular and the chain taut. ▼

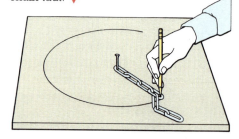

Pegboard circle

A 50 mm wide strip of pegboard makes a great substitute trammel—a tool used to mark large circles—because the board's holes offer a variety of radii. To use your pegboard trammel, first locate the pivot point by fastening one end of the board to the workpiece with a screw. Use a screw that fits the hole, but leave it a little loose so that the strip can pivot freely. Place a pencil in the appropriate hole and rotate the pegboard to draw an arc or circle. ▼

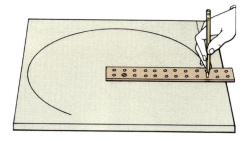

34 / Basic Tools and Equipment

LAYOUT TOOLS

Improvisations

On a roll
If you don't have a level, you can still check your workpiece. Place a marble in the middle of the unit and at various positions along the work surface. If it doesn't roll in any direction, your work is level.

Here's the pitch
Align your work to a specific angle or pitch like this: assemble a right-angle triangle from three lengths of wood clamped together, with the angle opposite the right angle being the pitch you require when the other two sides are vertical and horizontal respectively. Using a spirit level and your triangle you will be able to establish the correct pitch time and again.

Plumb bob impostor
If you don't have a plumb bob handy, try using a chalk line box as a substitute. Secure the hook end of the chalk line and extend the string; then mark the spot, using the tapered bottom end of the chalk box as a reference. ▼

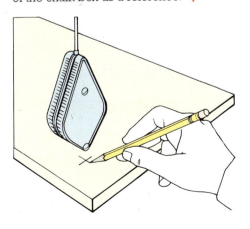

Checking up

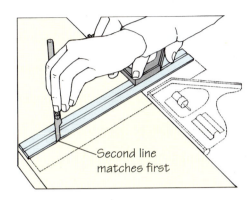

Second line matches first

Test for square ▲
Every so often, it's a good idea to test your combination square to see if it is true. Place the tool on a straight board and draw a line along the square's blade. Then turn the square over, place the blade at the line, and draw a line; if the lines match, the square is true.

Protect your tools

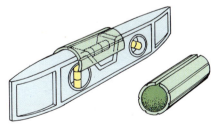

Bubble cover ▲
Those little glass vials in a level can be easily broken. To protect the glass, cut 75 mm lengths of garden hose and slit them lengthwise. Between jobs slip the covers over the vials.

On the level
Always check a level before you buy it, and test it periodically afterward. To make the test, place the level on the floor or on a table, mark where you've placed it, and note the bubble positions on the vials. Then rotate the level, end for end, align it on the same spot, and note the reading. Finally, turn the level over top to bottom, and make a final reading. All three readings should be the same. If your level has tiny screws, you can adjust them to true the level. If there are no screws and the level isn't true, replace it. ▼

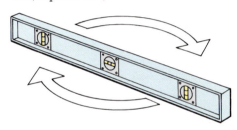

Hanging square
The best way to ensure the accuracy of a square year after year is to take good care of the tool. Try not to drop it and always hang it on the wall when you're not using it. To hang your square, take a piece of wood and either bevel one edge at a 45° angle or cut a thin groove to accept the square. Nail the strip securely to the wall. ▼

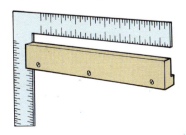

CLAMPS AND VICES

Clamp improvements

Recycled film caps

A tight G-clamp can mar a work surface. To protect your projects, hot-glue caps from plastic 35 mm film containers to the G-clamp jaws. When you no longer need the caps, just pop them off.

Magnetic pads

Ever wish you had a third hand when fitting protective wood blocks between a workpiece and steel pipe-clamp jaws? Magnets fitted into the blocks can make the job easier. Cut recesses in the blocks so the magnets will be flush with the surface; then glue the magnets in place with epoxy.

Red flag

The ends of long bar and pipe clamps often stick out during a clamping job. To avoid bumping into them, drape a brightly coloured rag over the end of each clamp. That way you won't hurt yourself or tear your clothing. ▼

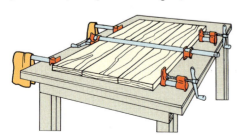

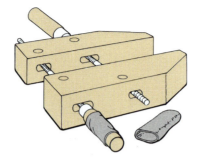

Turning point ▲

If you have trouble getting enough torque (turning pressure) on the smooth handles of a hand-screw clamp, stretch a length of bicycle tube over the handle. The tube will go on easily if you dust the inside with talcum powder.

Squeeze-out protection

To keep your clamps free from rust and dried glue, rub them with paraffin or floor wax. The coating gives moisture resistance and allows you to easily chip off any gobs of glue. ▼

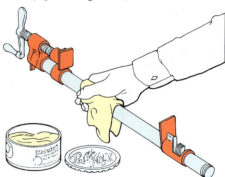

Vice advice

Vice cushions

To keep a vice from marring wood or other soft material, make two wood cushions the same size as the jaws of the vice. To hold the cushions in place, attach magnetic strips to them with construction adhesive.

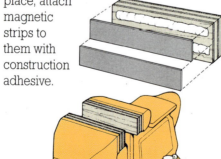
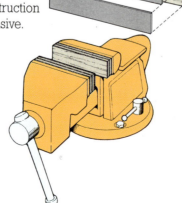

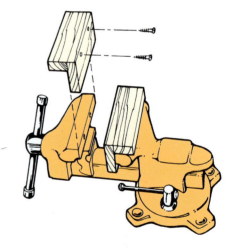

Shield a vice ▲

Another way to protect a work surface from the jaws of a bench vice is with a pair of wood shields. The ones shown here are easy to make out of four pieces of scrap wood glued and screwed together to form L-joints.

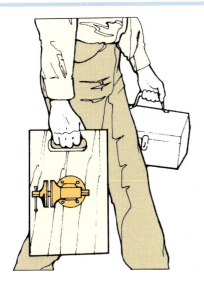

You *can* take it with you ▲

Have you ever been away from your workshop and needed a vice? Here are two ways to take the vice to the job. Bolt a 75 mm vice to a breadboard-size piece of plank with a cutout handle. This size board is heavy enough to keep things steady. Or bolt a 44 x 44 mm block of wood to the end of your toolbox. Then when you need to support a workpiece on a small job, clamp a 75 mm vice onto the wood block. ▼

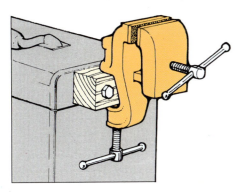

USER-FRIENDLY CLAMPS

Clamps make great assistants. Many home workshops are stocked with G-clamps, spring clamps, pipe clamps, and hand screws, but there are other types to meet just about any job. Some of the handiest are shown below.

Bar clamps

Quick-Grip bar clamp

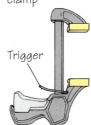

Trigger

A *Quick-Grip bar clamp* can be set one-handed. To move the jaws or release the clamp, pull its trigger. To close the clamp, squeeze its grip. Removable pads protect the work surface.

Aluminium bar clamp

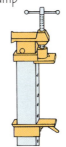

Lightweight *aluminium bar clamps* work as well as, or even better than, steel bar clamps. The lighter weight makes a large glue-up easier to move, and the aluminium won't leave glue stains.

Cam-action bar clamp

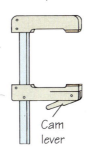

Cam lever

Try a *cam-action bar clamp* for light-duty jobs. To set one, slide the movable jaw to the work; lock it in place by turning the cam lever so that it is perpendicular to the bar of the clamp.

Speciality clamps

Band clamp

Choose a *band clamp* when you need to hold irregularly shaped pieces together, and when you are working with interlocking joints (such as those in a chair).

Deep-throat G-clamp

Use *deep-throat G-clamps* to apply pressure to the centre of wide pieces. These clamps come in a variety of sizes, and they are fairly inexpensive.

Edge clamp

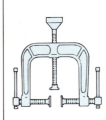

When you need to hold an edging, such as trim, moulding, or laminate, in place, use an *edge clamp*. As you set it, make sure that all the screws are applying equal pressure.

SUPPLIES AND EQUIPMENT

Glues

Economical refills
If you use a lot of carpenter's or other glue, buy it in large quantities. You'll save money and avoid the hassle of running out of glue in the middle of a job. To dispense the glue, use old sauce or mustard squeeze bottles with twist-seal nozzles or flip-top caps. Be sure to remove the labels and clearly mark the bottle with its new contents.

Slick tip
Have you ever struggled to get a stuck cap off a tube of glue? If so, here's an easy fix. Dab a little petroleum jelly on the tip before replacing the cap; the jelly will keep the glue from sticking.

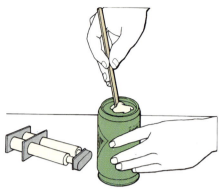

Cool it ▲
To keep epoxy from setting too quickly in warm weather or in a hot workshop, turn over a cold unopened tin of cool-drink and mix the ingredients in the recessed bottom of the tin. The cold aluminium will slow the setting process, and the recess in the tin makes a fine mixing bowl.

Removable adhesive
Inexpensive wall adhesive has many uses in the workshop. Use it to secure a screw on the tip of a screwdriver, or hold nuts and washers together, and to stick up assembly instructions and notes for yourself. In many situations it's a good substitute for tape or staples.

Carpet scrap applicator
Cleaning brushes that have been used to apply contact cement is a terrible job. So, instead of throwing away brush after brush, make a reusable applicator out of scrap wood. Attach a handle to a 100 x 100 mm scrap and just staple a fresh piece of carpet to the block for each new job.

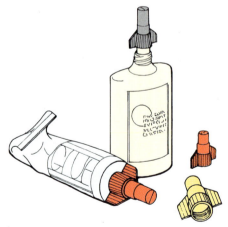

Top substitute ▲
Wire connectors, sold at hardware and electrical supply stores, make good substitute caps for glue bottles or tubes. Keep several sizes of connector on hand and you won't have to waste time searching for misplaced caps.

Other adhesives

Cement collar
When applying contact cement, keep the rim of the cement tin clean by covering it with an aluminium foil collar. The foil will catch the drips and prevent gummy buildup. Once the job is done, discard the foil; the lid will sit tightly in place. ▼

Storing adhesives

An upside-down trick
Storing glue bottles and tubes upside down keeps the contents ready to pour. To make a holder for your glue bottles, drill holes through an existing shelf in your workshop. Another option is to drill holes in an offcut and attach it to the wall.

Hang tubing

Here's a clever solution to a common workshop storage problem. Since plastic squeeze tubes of contact cement and caulk don't lie flat and can't be stacked, try hanging them up. Cut a piece of duct tape about 50 mm long and trim its width to that of the tube. Stick one end on the bottom of the tube; then fold it in half over the tube, pinching the sticky sides together. Punch a hole through the tape and hang it on a nail or on a pegboard hook.

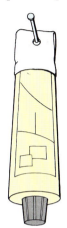

Glue gun holder

The hot dripping tip of a glue gun can be a safety hazard. To keep it out of harm's way, put it in this handy holder made by mounting a spring-metal broom clip on a small piece of scrap timber. To catch the drips, screw a small jar lid on the holder. ▼

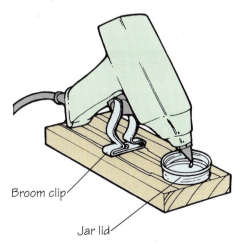

Broom clip
Jar lid

DISPOSING OF HAZARDOUS WASTE

Products containing solvents or other ingredients that carry cautionary warning labels (such as flammable, reactive, and corrosive) are likely to be classified as hazardous waste. Before you buy such a product, try to find a safer (water-base) substitute. If none is available, buy only as much of the product as you reckon you will use. If you are unsure of how to dispose of a material, contact your nearest government health department or your municipal health department. The table below outlines some general guidelines for workshop materials. See p 301 for disposal of automotive waste.

TYPE OF WASTE			
Contact cement, solvent-base*		♦	▲
Contact cement, water-base		♦	
Degreasing chemicals			▲
Glue, adhesive, and sealants, solvent-base			▲
Glue, adhesive, and sealants, water-base		♦	
Kerosene		▼	
Paint, PVA (water-base)		♦	
Paint and varnish stripper (alkaline)	●		
Paintbrush cleaner, phosphate	●		
Paintbrush cleaner, solvent			▲
Paint remover or thinner (residue)			▲
Paints, oil (enamel) and rust-inhibiting			▲
Polish, furniture (solvent-base)			▲
Rust remover, phosphoric acid	●		
Wood finishes (polyurethane, oil, varnish)			▲
Wood preservative			▲

● Dilute small amount with plenty of water and pour down the drain. For large amount or if you have a septic tank, recycle or treat as hazardous waste.

♦ Allow to evaporate away from people and pets, or solidify with absorbent material, such as cat litter. Double-wrap in plastic; discard with rubbish.

▼ Recycle at a special centre set up for the purpose, or treat as hazardous waste.

▲ Do not discard this hazardous waste. Contact your municipal health department or your nearest government health department for instructions.

*Wrap and discard applicators when dry. Any unused cement is hazardous waste.

SUPPLIES AND EQUIPMENT

Putty and filler

Airless container ▲
Filler and putty dry out quickly when exposed to the air. To slow the drying, use a putty knife to transfer the material into a small plastic bag. Squeeze the bag to remove all of the air, which will speed drying if it is left in the bag. Seal the bag and then cut a small hole in one corner. To dispense the material, just squeeze the bag as if you were decorating a cake. When the job is done, twist the corner closed and secure it with a twist tie or a clothes peg. Store the closed bag in the original container.

Wood filler facts
When filling a large hole, don't fill it in one operation as the wood filler will probably crack as it dries. It's better to build up the filler in a series of layers, allowing each layer ample time to dry thoroughly. Overfill a hole a little and sand it down to obtain a super finish.

Steel wool and brushes

Magnetic attraction
Small particles of steel wool can collect on a workpiece and even become airborne as metal dust. To contain metal particles and avoid breathing metal dust, wrap a small or medium-size magnet in the wad of steel wool. As you work, periodically wipe off the magnet. When the job is done, run it over the work to remove any remaining metal particles. Always wear a dust mask when working with steel wool.

For tight spots
How can you rub steel wool effectively in a tight corner or in a groove? Cut off the end of a bicycle's plastic or rubber handlebar grip. Then stuff a piece of steel wool tightly into the opening, leaving a knot of the stuff protruding. The handle enables you to apply pressure—and protects your hands. ▼

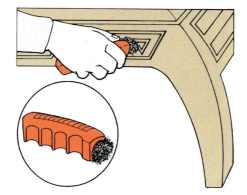

Adjust a brush
Here's a way to convert an ordinary paintbrush into a light-duty scrub brush: simply wrap the bristles securely with masking tape. The closer the tape is to the bristles' tips, the stiffer the brush will be.

Wire brush renewal
The front section of a wire brush always wears out before the rest. To rejuvenate a worn brush, clamp it upside down in a vice and saw about 25 mm off the brush along with the worn bristles. Another option is to snip off bent or damaged edges with a wire cutter. Cut them diagonally so the ends will be sharp. Wear eye protection when cutting.

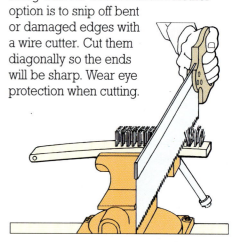

Oil

About spouts
To reduce the flow of oil from a spout, you need to make the opening smaller. One way to do this is to dab a little fingernail polish over the tip. When the polish is dry, reopen the spout by poking it with a pin.

Straw applicator
You can extend the reach of an oil spout by taping a straw from a broom, or a length of wire, to it. In either case, the oil will follow the straw or wire to the intended spot. It's a great way to apply oil to those awkward places.

Knives in the workshop

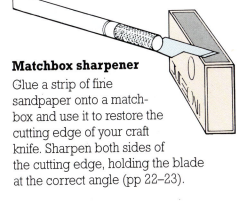

Matchbox sharpener
Glue a strip of fine sandpaper onto a matchbox and use it to restore the cutting edge of your craft knife. Sharpen both sides of the cutting edge, holding the blade at the correct angle (pp 22–23).

Quick-change artist
Ever wished there was an easier way to change the blade in your utility knife? Take a look in hardware stores and home centres for knives that will do so with the push of a button and a twist of the wrist. No more messing around with a screwdriver and then trying to line up the halves of the knife so that it works properly again.

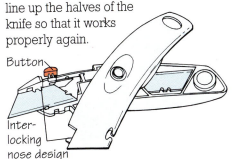

Sharp storage ideas
If you need to use razor blades on a job, use a matchbox as a temporary carrying case. Back in your workshop, you can store your razor blades in slots cut into a small scrap piece of polystyrene packing material—and keep it out of reach of children.

Plans and instructions

Write your own
If you are tackling a job that doesn't come with its own instructions, take a few minutes to write your own before you begin. It also helps to make your notes on an oversize pad of paper, such as the flip charts you see in conference and meeting rooms. Available at office supply stores, flip charts provide all the room you need to write instructions and draw plans and diagrams. For easy viewing, mount the pad on a nail in a workshop wall.

Blow it up
Ever strained to see the fine print and small details of assembly instructions? A trip to a photocopier that can enlarge your original is in order. By enlarging hard-to-read instructions, you can work without spectacles or eyestrain.

Sheer protection
Protect plans, drawings, and instructions with clear self-adhesive plastic. They stay clean and dry, won't tear with use, and are easy to roll up. If necessary, you can make notes on the plastic with a grease pencil. To erase the marks, just rub them with a cloth.

Hang 'em high
Instead of leaving instruction sheets on your workbench, where they can get lost, torn, or badly soiled, separate the pages and tape them at eye level to the wall just above your work area.

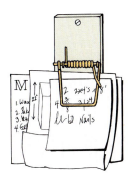

Mousetrapping ▲
Mount a spring-type mousetrap to your workshop wall with screws and you'll have a sturdy holder for your plans. Before you mount the trap, however, remove the bait holder.

Handy manuals
Can't find your owner's manual when you need it? Keep the manuals for all your power tools in one place. Punch holes in them and use a three-ring binder in which to store them, or use a magazine storage file. You can make your own file by cutting off one end of a large detergent box as shown. Make it a habit to put the manual for a new tool in your special storage place as soon as you finish reading it.

Basic Tools and Equipment / 41

SUPPLIES AND EQUIPMENT

Buckets

Recycled plastic buckets
Large plastic buckets have a multitude of uses. If you have a swimming pool, or know someone with one, the large ones in which pool chemicals are sold are ideal for other uses, particularly as they have fitted lids. But be sure you empty the bucket after each use and store it where a child can't get at it. There have been cases of toddlers falling into nappy buckets and drowning.

Heavy load
When you are carrying a heavy load in a bucket, the container's thin handle can cut painfully into your hand. Slipping an open-ended spanner onto the handle as shown is kinder to your hand and steadies the load. Some hose on the handle also works well.

Leaky buckets
To find the exact location of a bucket leak, turn on a small table lamp, remove the shade, and place the bucket upside down over it. The light will shine through the hole.

Hole repairs
To make a temporary patch over a small hole in a plastic bucket, fill the hole from both sides with pure silicone caulk. (The caulk layers adhere to each other better than to plastic.) Or drip candle wax over the hole. The wax plug will stay intact, however, only if the bucket is filled with cold water—hot water will melt the wax.

Ropes

Rope saver
To keep a rope from fraying where it rubs against something, slip a length of rubber hose over it at the point of contact. Hold the hose in place with knots tied on either side of it.

No more unravelling
The ends of a length of rope will not unravel if you dab them with either silicone sealant, liquid (air-dry) rubber, or vinyl coating.

Untangle that mess
Don't struggle with a snarled string, rope, or cord. Begin untangling it by gently pulling outward all around the edges of the snarl. As the tangled mass becomes bigger and looser, the loops will be easier to untangle and you won't be faced with a lot of tight knots to undo.

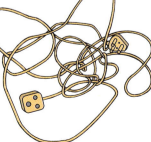

Extension cords

Cord keeper
Extension cords stay tangle-free when kept in a large bucket. Near the bottom of the pail, cut or drill a hole large enough so that the cord's pronged end can pass through it. Then coil the rest of the cord into the bucket. The cord will come out easily when pulled. Plug the ends of the cord together when it's not in use. You can use the space in the centre of the coil to carry tools to a work site.

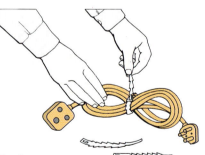

Just one more
If you want to store your cords flat—and keep them organized—coil or loop the cord as shown above. Then tie the centre of the cord tightly with cable tie or with a plastic "key lock" tie. To hold very long cords, join two or more plastic ties together.

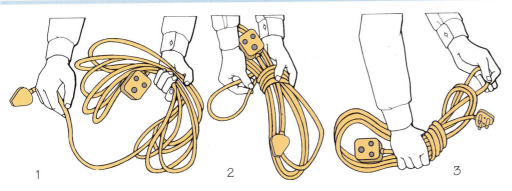

1   2   3

Coil and hang ▲

Here are three quick steps to coiling and hanging a long extension cord. Hold the end of the cord in one hand. With the other hand, loop it back and forth in figure-eights (1). When the cord is coiled, take a single loop and wrap it twice around one end of the coil (2). Finally, insert that same loop through the centre of the smaller coil opening and pull it tight (3). To store the cord, hang this loop on a large nail or peg.

Preventing a sudden disconnect ▶

Does the plug of your lawnmower or edge trimmer tend to pull out of the extension cord when you are moving around a lot? You can keep this from happening with any similar portable power tool by tying the ends of the two cords together in a simple knot.

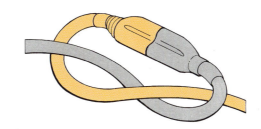

THE RIGHT EXTENSION CORD FOR THE TOOL

The conductor of an extension cord determines how much current it can safely carry. (The larger the wire's diameter, the greater its current-carrying capacity.) Measures of current are amperage and wattage. Look for these ratings on the cord and on the tool's specifications plate; the cord ratings should be equal to or greater than those of the tool. **Note:** If a cord seems hot, or is over 15 m long, choose the next larger wire diameter.

WIRE DIAMETER	AMP RATING	WATT RATING	TYPICAL TOOL TO USE
0,75 mm	5–8	960	Small drill, belt sander, reciprocating saw
1,0 mm	8–12	1 440	Router, circular saw
1,5 mm	12–15	1 800	Small table saw
2,5 mm	15–20	2 400	Large table saw, radial arm saw, band saw

Lights and torches

In tight places

To drive a screw in a dark corner, attach a little pen-light to the shaft of your screwdriver. You'll be able to see the screw-head easily.

A point of light

Create a light for small jobs in tight places by plugging a night-light into a household extension cord. You'll be able to move this little light about as required—and you can add a hook for greater versatility.

Prop it up

Turn a pair of pliers into a torch stand. Place the torch in the pliers' jaws and prop it up at the required angle. To hold the jaws tightly around the torch, place a rubber band around the handles of the pliers.

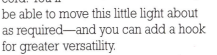

LADDERS

Extension ladders

Hand over hand
To raise an extension ladder, place its feet at the base of the wall. Starting at the top, walk the ladder up, hand over hand, until it is vertical. Then pull its feet out from the wall, extend the ladder to the height you want it, lock the extension, and set the feet of the ladder at a 75° angle—you should be able to stand with your toes against the feet of the ladder, your arms and back straight, and your hands on the rungs at shoulder height (below). To move a ladder, lower it, hand over hand, and carry it parallel to the ground. ▼

Ground support
If you've ever tried to use a ladder on soft ground, you know that the ladder's feet will sink as soon as you start to climb. To keep the legs from sinking, set them on a piece of 20 mm plywood that is at least 200 mm deeper and wider than the ladder. The board spreads the load over a greater area.

Padded ends
The best ladders have padded ends that protect the surfaces they lean against. If your ladder lacks pads, buy rubber ones or make your own by wrapping rags around the ends and tying them with elastic cord. Still another option is to cover the ends with thick socks, heavy-duty work gloves or pieces of car tyre inner tube.

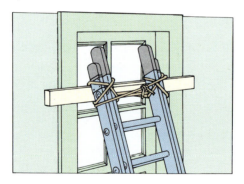

Window treatment ▲
When a job calls for you to rest the top of your ladder in the centre of a window opening, you run the risk of damaging the sill or breaking the glass. To avoid problems, attach a stout beam securely to the top rung of the ladder so that the board spans the opening and rests on the window frame or wall on both sides. The beam also makes a handy rest for a bucket or two (see p 45).

Tie one on
When using a ladder as a way to get to and from the roof, tie the ladder to a handy roof truss. A gust of wind can knock over an unsecured ladder, damaging whatever is in its path and leaving you stranded. You should never rest the ladder directly on the gutters.

Customizing ladders

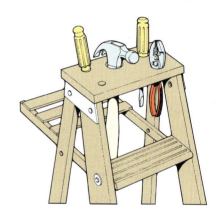

Tools at hand ▲
Tired of climbing up and down a stepladder to retrieve fallen tools? Just drill some holes in the top step of the ladder to hold the tools you use the most.

Basket case
To turn your ladder's shelf into a handy tool and equipment holder, use an elastic cord to fasten a plastic household basket to the shelf.

Shoe cleaner
Clean shoes mean surer footing on a ladder. Staple or glue a strip of scrap carpet to the bottom rung of your ladder, and use it to wipe the soles of your shoes each time you climb the ladder.

More on treads
To improve traction on ladder steps, glue strips of sandpaper to the steps. Another way to slip-proof them is to paint them and then sprinkle a layer of sand into the wet paint. When the coating dries, you'll have a nice gritty surface to step on.

Keep it closed
A simple hook-and-eye fastener will keep a wooden stepladder closed while you're carrying or storing it. Screw the hook into one leg and the eye into the other leg, directly across from the hook. If you have a metal stepladder, keep the legs closed with a belt or length of rope.

Bucket holder ▲
Keep a paint tin or small bucket within easy reach on an extension ladder by hanging it on a length of broom handle or plastic water pipe extending from one of the ladder's hollow rungs. The pole should be about 600 mm longer than the width of the ladder; notch it at both ends to keep the bucket in place.

Storage

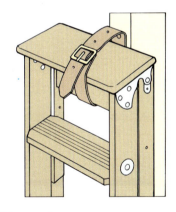

Car carrier ▲
How do you get a rented extension ladder home if you don't have a roof-rack? One solution is to pad the top of the car with a couple of blankets and then use ratchet belt ties to secure the load. The belts can pass between the doors and the roof without damaging the rubber door seal. Tie on a couple of red caution flags and be sure the ladder is secure before you drive away.

Theft protection
Never store a ladder outside or in an unlocked garage. A burglar may use it to reach a window that would otherwise be out of reach. If you have to leave a ladder out, chain it securely to a tree.

Compact ladder
If you don't have room to store an extension ladder, buy a multipurpose articulated ladder. It unfolds to make an extension ladder and, though fairly expensive, it is versatile and can also be used as a sawhorse, for example.

Steady as you go ▲
Keeping your balance while standing on a ladder is of utmost importance. A metal towel rack fastened to the top step of the ladder makes a convenient handrail for steadying yourself.

Buckle up ▲
When it's time to store a ladder, don't just lean it against the wall—it can easily fall over. A better way is to attach an old leather belt to the wall and wrap it around the ladder's top step. Or mount a stepladder vertically on a pair of pegs securely fastened to the wall. Hang an extension ladder horizontally on pegs spaced no more than 1,8 m apart.

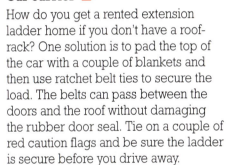

Basic Tools and Equipment / 45

TOOL CARE AND STORAGE

Better boxes

Toolbox organizer
Use magnets to hold your favourite flat tools, such as wrenches and pliers, against the inside lid of your toolbox. Purchase magnets of various sizes and of sufficient strength to hold the tools, and hot-glue the magnets to the inside lid of the box.

Handy storage
A bread bin or old lunch box will comfortably hold all the tools you need for small jobs around the house. Such containers are also good for keeping a duplicate set of your favourite and most-used hand tools in a place other than your workshop. Having the right tools close at hand may keep you from putting off needed repairs.

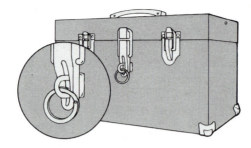

Keyless lockup ▲
To keep curious small children out of your toolbox, secure its lock hasp with a spring-steel key ring rather than using a lock. This way, you can childproof the toolbox (little hands are not strong enough to remove the key ring) without having to carry around another key.

Tool cushion
Line the bottom of your toolbox with felt, scrap carpeting, or bubble wrap. The padding will protect the tools and help reduce noise when you handle them.

Tool toting tips

Pick some pockets
A jacket or vest with lots of pockets, like those worn by photographers, can help you organize and hold small tools, fasteners, and other items you need on a job. Beware of carrying sharp items in the pockets, however.

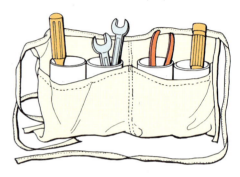

Pockets for tools ▲
Use empty jam tins, cooldrink tins, or short lengths of 50 mm plastic pipe to transform the deep, wide pockets of a nail pouch into convenient carriers for wrenches, pliers, and screwdrivers. If you use tins, remove their tops and bottoms. Glue or tape the cylinders together to stop them shifting about, and put them into the pouches to create dividers. The tools are also held upright, making them easier to grab.

Tool roll-up
A good way to store drill bits, chisels and files is in a segmented pouch sold with spanner sets. If you don't have one, make one from a piece of sturdy cloth folded and sewn in half lengthways with subdivisions sewn into it as shown in the nail pouch hint, above.

Multipurpose box ▶
This simple plywood toolbox doubles as a step for reaching high places or as a portable mini-workbench/sawhorse. Make the box 450 mm high, 600 to 750 mm wide, and just deep enough to accommodate a sturdy plastic cutlery tray. (Use the tray for storing small tools, bits, and fasteners.) Using a jigsaw, make cutouts for carrying the unit.

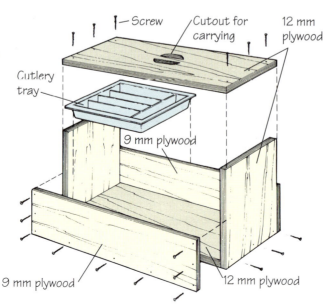

46 / Basic Tools and Equipment

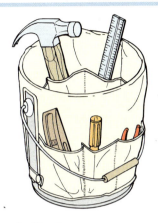

Bucket belts ▲

Turn a plastic bucket into a handy carrier by fitting it with a sturdy tool "belt". It is made in similar fashion to the tool roll-up on the facing page. In this case, however, there will be pockets facing each other so that when the "belt" is in position, it saddles the rim of the bucket, the pockets hanging on the inside and outside of the bucket sides, as in the illustration. There's lots of room to store a range of items.

Keeping track

Tag time

Before lending a tool, write your name on a stick-on label and affix it to the handle. The label will serve as a reminder to the borrower to return the tool when the job is done.

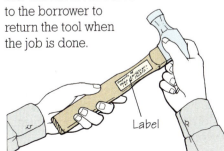

Label

Permanent ID

Another way to identify your tools permanently (and discourage thieves in the process) is to engrave your name on them with an electric etcher.

Show your colours

If you are working with a partner on a job and are using similar tools, code them with coloured tape so there'll be no mix-ups at the end of the day. Using reflective tape provides another advantage: a mislaid tool is easier to spot by day and, with a torch, by night.

Rust busting

A little prevention

Moisture in the air invites rust, and if moist air gets into a toolbox, it corrodes the tools. One way to keep the air in your toolbox dry is to drop in some packets of silica gel, sold at hardware stores and craft shops or available free in the packaging of new products. Once the silica gel becomes saturated, renew the packets by placing them near a lit 60-watt light bulb for 15 minutes.

And some more on prevention

Other effective moisture absorbers that will keep the contents of your toolbox rust-free are a handful of mothballs and a cube of camphor (sold in small packs at local pharmacies). Camphor loses its effectiveness after about six months, so you'll have to replace the cube twice a year.

The brush-off

If your tools do become corroded, you'll find that a wire brush is useful for scrubbing off the rust. To make your own sturdy brush, all you need is a strip of window screening and a screw cap from a bottle of laundry detergent. First, make a fringe of wire "bristles" at one edge of the screening by cutting two or three rows of horizontal wire strands. Then roll up the screening tightly, secure it with wire, and wedge it firmly into the cap.

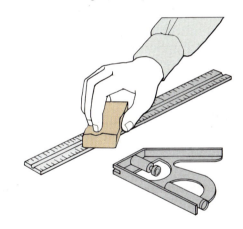

Wonder sponge ▲

Those scourer sponges for the kitchen work well when you need to clean and polish metal that's become dirty and corroded. To clean a tool, just rub the surface and wipe off the dust. You can use the sponge dry or wet (with water, oil, or detergent). After cleaning the metal, rinse off the tool, dry it well and spray it with a rust preventer.

CHAPTER 2
WORKSHOP ORGANIZATION

WORKSHOP BASICS 49
THE WORKBENCH 52
OTHER WORKSHOP FURNITURE 54
WORKSHOP STORAGE 56
WORKSHOP CLEANUP 62
WORK GEAR AND PERSONAL CLEANUP 64

WORKSHOP BASICS

Creature comforts

Foot ease
Here's relief from tired feet and legs: cover the floor in front of your workbench with a scrap of low-pile carpet. Besides providing cushioning, it prevents a major cause of leg discomfort—the transfer of body heat from legs and feet to cold concrete. And it cleans easily with a vacuum. Or you could use some motor vehicle rubber floor mats to form a walkway along the floor in front of your workbench. Even cheap mats will last for years.

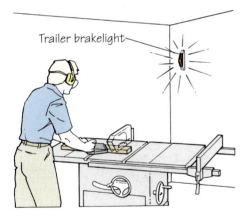

Home alone ▲
Can't hear the doorbell in your workshop? Buy a 12-volt trailer brakelight at a motor spares shop and connect it to the doorbell wiring at the point where its wires run closest to your workshop. Install it at eye level so that it will catch your attention whenever someone rings the bell. In the case of your telephone, Telkom can install a telephone set with a light that flashes when a call comes in.

Attention getter
Family members can also call you to come to dinner or to the phone by "ringing" a trailer brakelight. Just hook it to a separate doorbell transformer and to a doorbell button inside the house. It's a lot safer than getting an unexpected tap on your shoulder while you're running a machine.

It's not the heat
If your workshop is damp, install a dehumidifier. In addition to making life more comfortable for you, it will keep tools from rusting, prevent timber from swelling, and speed the drying of glue, paint, and other finishes.

Clearing the air
To rid your workshop of fine dust particles and noxious fumes, it's essential to have good cross-ventilation. If your workshop has two facing windows, open one and place a fan in the other so that it blows air out. If there is only one window, consider installing an exhaust fan in the wall opposite it.

Chilly workshop?
Give it a quick warm-up by installing an infrared heat lamp over your workbench. It will warm your hands and tools so that you can work on cool days.

Warm and safe
Of course you'll wear an old sweater or jersey on a cool day, but ensure you choose a garment that is reasonably tight-fitting, and in reasonable repair. A flapping sleeve or loose piece of cloth can be caught by a power tool.

Extended work season
Is your workshop in an unfinished, unheated garage? By insulating it, you can use the space for the greater part of the year and increase your comfort in both hot and cold weather. Give priority to the roof, where most heat is lost or gained. Staple fibreglass batts, vapour barrier down, between the joists or rafters, or install a ceiling of wallboard and lay insulation between the joists. ▼

Save steps
Take a cue from kitchen designers and set up your workshop in an efficient triangle that puts the workbench, tool storage, and assembly areas all within easy reach of one another. Set up your timber storage, and wood-cutting and wood-shaping tools the same way. ▼

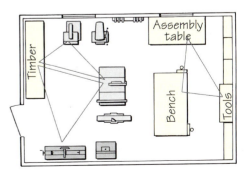

WORKSHOP BASICS

Noise control

Workshop door sealants
Keep both noise and dirt out of the rest of the house by sealing the gaps around your workshop door. Self-adhesive foam strip attached along the edges of the frame will cut out a lot of noise. You can also attach acoustical tiles on its inner surface. If your garage doubles as a workshop, insulating your garage door in the same manner will help reduce the noise levels outside.

Seal that gap!
Sound can be likened to a liquid in one sense: wherever there's a gap, sound will get through. So seal every gap when sound-proofing your workshop. Inner surfaces to doors, door frames and window frames should all be sealed for the best results. When sealing doors, don't forget to add felt or a weatherstrip to the foot of the door.

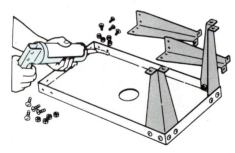

Glue rattling parts together ▲
To silence a freestanding piece of workshop equipment, take apart its base, stand, or cabinet. As you reassemble the piece, apply a bead of silicone sealant wherever metal parts meet. This will bond the parts and keep them from vibrating against one another.

Clamp down on vibes
Reduce the noisy vibrations of a benchtop power tool by putting a rubber pad or carpet scrap under each tool leg and clamping the tool to the bench.

Shedding light

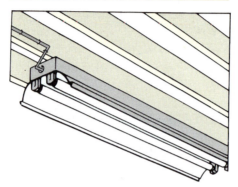

General illumination ▲
Replace overhead incandescent bulbs with fluorescent fixtures, which are more economical to operate, last longer, and give an even, diffused light. Have an electrician install the units over major work areas. Choose 1,2 m units or, for a large workshop, 2,4 m ones.

Reflected glory
To improve visibility in your workshop, paint wall and ceiling areas white or a light colour (the lighter, the better, as it will reflect natural and artificial light).

Make short work of shadows
Every now and then we drop some item which, of course, rolls out of sight under the workbench. Beat the problem with a small mirror and direct light where you need it. Use a small polished steel mirror, available through stockists of hiking and camping equipment.

Workbench lighting
A folding-arm lamp is perfect for close work. But having it clamped on the workbench edge can limit its usefulness. To put the lamp wherever you need it, remove the lamp bracket or heavy base and drill holes at various points in the bench top for the lamp to fit into. You can add holes when and where needed.

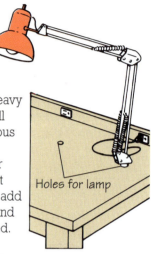

Holes for lamp

Mobile light
Clip-on lamps with reflectors also provide a flexible source of light for close work. If you don't have a shelf that you can attach them to, mount a wood strip on the wall above your workbench. This arrangement will let you light your work from many different angles or from two angles at once. ▼

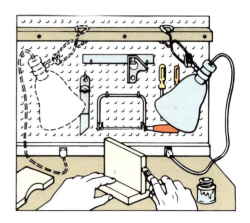

50 / Workshop Organization

Prevent popping lights
Flying debris produced by power tools can shatter a hot light bulb. Keep the light source out of the most likely path of any flying debris.

Power supply

Dust off
Keep your workshop's electrical outlets from becoming sawdust-clogged fire hazards. Cap unused sockets with plug-in "childproof" plastic covers. Or install the outdoor weatherproof type that snaps shut when a socket is not in use.

Cord hangers
Use clip-on clothes pegs to keep power cords out of your way. Screw or glue them to overhead joists or strategic spots. Or, for a hanger that lets a cord move without chafing it, slit a short length of old garden hose diagonally. Open the slit to tack the hanger in place and to insert or remove the cord. ▼

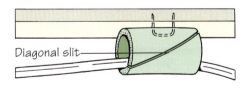
Diagonal slit

Convenient outlets
A multi-outlet power strip installed under the front edge of your workbench provides a handy place to plug in power tools while keeping cords out of your way. Use one with individual switches for each socket and a circuit breaker to prevent overloads, and make sure it is rated to handle the maximum amperage that you will use on it.

Power where you need it
For easy access to electricity, mount a multi-outlet power strip on a board and drive a few nails into joists at strategic points. You can then hang the board where needed. You should also position a few slit-hose hangers, like the one shown below left, at intervals between the nails or hooks and the outlets so that you can keep the extension cord out of the way while working. The turn button keeps the board out of the way if you need it in the same spot for a while. ▼

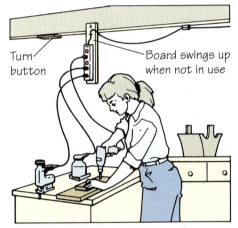
Turn button
Board swings up when not in use

Rewiring?
A well-planned electrical system helps you make the most of your workshop, but an incorrectly installed one can be very dangerous. Have an electrician install a subpanel near the workshop to control all workshop circuits, so you can easily turn off all power to the workshop if necessary. By placing the subpanel near the workshop, you also won't have far to go should an emergency require you to turn off the power as quickly as possible. A good place is right outside the door where another member of the family can turn it off if you cannot.

AVOID SHOCK

Here are some simple ways to cut electrical risks in your workshop:

ELR's. Have all the circuits in your workshop connected to an earth leakage relay. If there is a power leakage, an ELR switches the power off almost instantly, fast enough to keep you from receiving a life-threatening shock.

Cords and plugs. Replace frayed or cracked cords and plugs. Damaged cords are extremely dangerous and should be replaced immediately. Never try to fix a cord with electrical tape. Keep cords from underfoot and away from the work area as much as possible. Always use heavy-duty cords rated to handle more current than your tools will draw (see chart, p 43). Avoid octopus outlets and spaghetti tangles.

Grounding. If you have a metal workbench, have it grounded to reduce the chances of a shock from shorted equipment. An electrician can earth it by running a wire from the bench to an electrical subpanel or other metallic electrical conduit.

Extension cords. Avoid using them. But if you have to, then make sure they are all three-core and exceed the rating of the tools you use. Finally, avoid stepping on cords, it could damage them.

Workshop Organization / 51

THE WORKBENCH

AN ALL-PURPOSE BENCH

No workbench is ideal for everyone, but this sturdy, easily assembled design will fit many needs. It has two shelves for power tools and room for a workshop vacuum underneath. It measures 1 676 mm long, 610 mm deep, and 915 mm high. Feel free to modify it to fit your needs.

Materials: You'll need five 3,66 m lengths of 44 x 96 mm SA pine, two 1 220 x 2 440 mm sheets of 9 mm commercial plywood, 45 and 70 mm screws, wood glue, and 50 mm nails.

Assembly: First, screw together the frames for the top and the two shelves, and screw the legs to them. Then screw on the side and back bottom frame pieces, the shelf ends and shelves, and the side and back panels. Tack one top piece to the frame, spread wood glue on it, and screw the other sheet to it and the frame. Predrill holes for all screws.

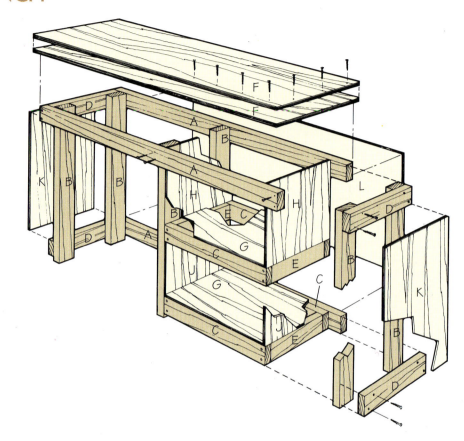

Cutting guides

Plywood (1 220 x 2 440 mm sheets)

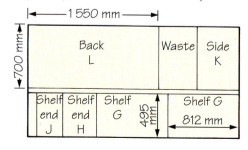
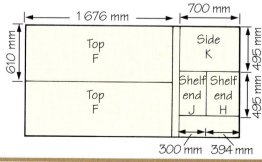

52 / Workshop Organization

Side view

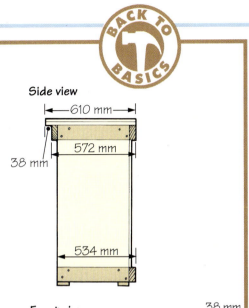

Front view

44 x 96 mm (1,62 m lengths)

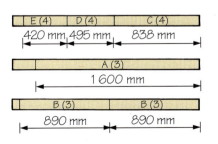

Bench amenities

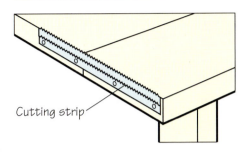

Handy cutter ▲
Tack a cutting strip from a foil or plastic wrap box to your workbench and use it to cut tape and cords. An old hacksaw blade will also work. Mount the cutter on an edge that's easily accessible but where you're unlikely to brush against it.

Hooked in place
If your bench tends to move when you are working on it, attach each end to a wall stud with a hook and eye.

Sprout a leaf
Add extra length to your workbench when you need it, with a removable extension leaf. Cut a piece of plank to fit along the edge. Drill matching 10 mm holes, 150 mm deep, in the leaf and the bench edge. Then fit 10 mm steel rods, 300 mm long, in the holes.

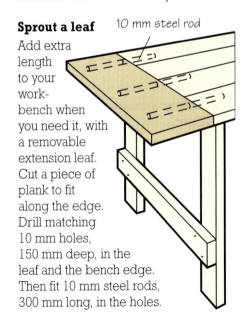

Flip-top bench top
Another way to extend your work surface is to have hinged flip-up flaps where needed. Use brackets of your choice to brace them when in use.

Bench top savers

Roll-on protection
To avoid staining your bench top with paint, mount an old window shade on one end. When you're ready to paint, just pull out the shade and hook it to the other end. Let it dry before rerolling. ▼

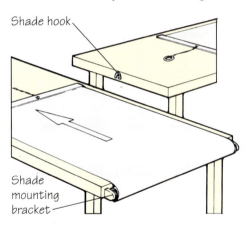

Cheap resurfacing
For a smooth surface that can take a lot of punishment, tack 6 mm hardboard over your bench top and seal it with pure varnish. When it becomes pitted, just flip it over or replace it. Also use a scrap of thick plank as a cutting and drilling board.

Mat top
Don't mar your project on a rough, battered bench top. Cover the work area with a rubber bath mat or carpet scrap.

OTHER WORKSHOP FURNITURE

Sawhorse savvy

Soft saddle
The saw-chewed top rails of most sawhorses can scratch finished wood or furniture. To provide a non-marring surface, cover the rails with scrap carpeting. Even better, make a cap for each sawhorse from two lengths of 22 x 69 mm and a 22 x 96 mm length of pine as shown, and cover its top with carpet. Then you can slip the caps on the sawhorses whenever you need them. ▼

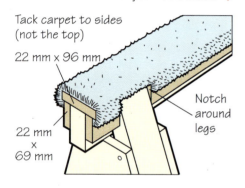

Tools at your fingertips
Add a tool tray between the legs of your sawhorse. Make a shallow box, a 22 x 96 mm frame with a plywood base, and attach it to cross braces running between each pair of legs. Put the tray on just one sawhorse so the pair will still stack.

Instant measure
Fix an old tape measure blade to the side of your sawhorse's top rail. It's most useful when you're cutting. Level with the end of the tape, drill a hole in the top surface. A peg placed in it will act as a stop when measuring wide pieces.

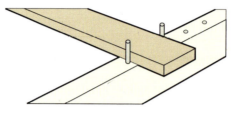

Sawhorse dogs ▲
To hold your work in place on sawhorses, drill a series of nail holes along each top rail. Measuring from a hole near the rail's centre, make the distance to each hole correspond to a standard timber measure—22, 44, 69 mm and so on (see chart, p 67). At most, you'll need to apply light hand pressure to steady a piece. Keep the nail on a string for easy access.

Knock-down horses
Here's a way to make knock-down sawhorses. Cut four legs out of SA pine, 44 x 96 mm, cutting an angled rebate in each for the top rail. For better grip, line the inner surfaces of each rebate with rubber from an inner tube. Attach a hinged brace to each pair of legs as in the illustration, cutting a slot for the end in the opposing leg. Join the legs with 100 mm hinges. When you push the brace down to lock the legs, the "jaws" close, gripping the top rail.

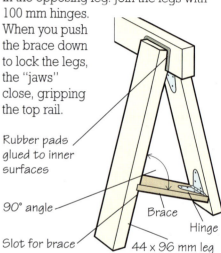

Build your own ▶
Here is a design for a strong sawhorse with the load bearing directly on the legs. There are no nails in the top rails to damage your saw blade, and the slot between the rails serves as a built-in handle for easy carrying. The sawhorse is made entirely from 44 x 96 mm lengths, and all ends are cut square or at a 17½° angle.

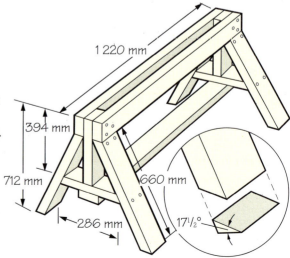

54 / Workshop Organization

Sawhorse substitute

No sawhorse? Your stepladder can often provide instant support for sawing, sanding, planing, or painting timber. Simply lay the ladder on its side, open its legs, and get to work as shown.

Relieve your aching back

When oversize projects force you out onto the driveway or patio, don't keep stooping to retrieve drills, saws, rulers, pencils, and other items from the ground. Instead, take along this fold-up tool table. Made of 12 mm plywood, the table is bench height when set up but only 100 mm deep when collapsed. ▼

610 mm square top. Battens around upper edges prevent items rolling off table

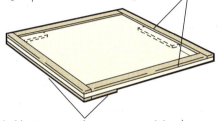

Nail battens under top to position base

Versatile pieces

Extra reach

Need to hold a wider piece in your portable workbench? Make four extension pieces from 22 x 44 mm pine. At one end of each piece, drill a hole and glue in a dowel that fits in the bench dog hole on the bench. At the other end of each piece, drill a hole for the bench dog.

Bench dog
22 x 44 mm extension
Dowel

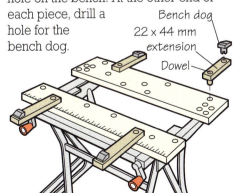

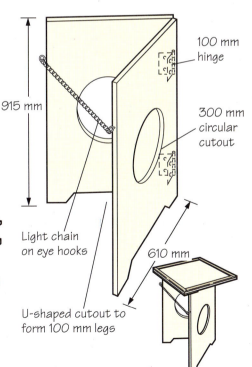

915 mm
100 mm hinge
300 mm circular cutout
Light chain on eye hooks
610 mm
U-shaped cutout to form 100 mm legs

SAFETY FIRST

FIGHTING FIRE

In a home workshop, a fire extinguisher is more essential than any piece of furniture. Get one that can handle the most common types of fires: wood and paper, flammable liquid, and electrical. Locate it in a highly visible, easily accessible place away from volatile substances, preferably near an exit. Check periodically to make sure it's fully charged. Install a smoke alarm as well. Keep flammable paints and solvents in sealed containers in a locked metal cabinet near the exit. Don't store them near any flame source or in a living area or confined space with little airflow. Use two foot-operated flip-lid rubbish bins—one for sawdust and wood chips and the other for oily and solvent-soiled rags. Empty both bins frequently. (For more on the proper disposal of hazardous workshop waste materials, see p 39.)

WORKSHOP STORAGE

Free organizers

Instant order
Get your workshop shipshape fast by storing everything you can in cardboard boxes of the same size. Cut off the tops, label the boxes by general categories such as "plumbing" and arrange them alphabetically on shelves. Boxes about 300 mm in height, width, and depth work well. Boxes for photocopier paper are ideal and they can be obtained from stationers and office supply stores.

Recycled dish rack
Turn that old vinyl-coated wire dish rack into storage racks. Use bolt cutters and pliers to cut and bend the rack into the sizes and shapes you need. The long sides of a dish rack make convenient wall racks for hanging tools and supplies. Turn the bottom and ends into a portable table rack by bending the cut wire ends at the bottom and fitting them into holes in wood dowels as shown. ▼

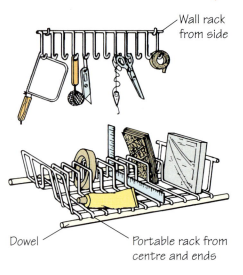

Wall rack from side

Dowel

Portable rack from centre and ends

Serving up hardware
Turn discarded cupcake pans (or other items with a projecting top lip) into pull-out shelves for tools or fasteners. Mount the trays in a box made of plywood with grooves routed in the sides so that the trays can slide in and out of the box. Or, instead of routing grooves, tack thin strips to the sides. ▼

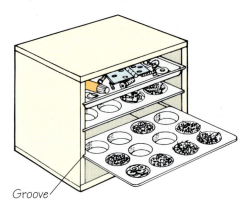

Groove

Pegboard lore

Put it everywhere
Don't limit your use of pegboard to workshop walls. Mount it on the inside of cabinet doors and on the sides of your workbench and cabinets. Thinner board is fine for hand tools but thicker board is better for heavier items. (For advice on installing pegboard, see p 127.)

Hook security
Pegboard hooks can come loose and get lost but you can prevent that by putting a dab of hot glue on the ends that hook into the board. If you need to move the hook, a light tug will usually free it. If necessary, you can soften the glue with a heat gun.

Outline reminder
You'll always return tools to their proper places on pegboard if you outline each tool with a wide felt-tip marker. Or put up tool silhouettes cut out of coloured adhesive plastic sheets.

Drawer magic

Protect your toes
To avoid pulling a heavy drawer out too far and spilling its contents, paint lines on the drawer edges to indicate how far it can be safely pulled out. Also attach a wood block on the back that will catch on the frame. Pivot the block and make one end longer than the other. That way it will hang vertically but you can turn it aside to take out the drawer. ▼

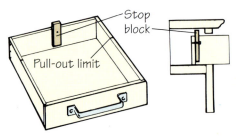

Stop block

Pull-out limit

Stronger pull
Does the handle on a tool-laden drawer keep pulling off? Replace it with a garage door handle secured with bolts going through the drawer front. Put a flat washer, then a lock washer, on each bolt before tightening the nut. ▼

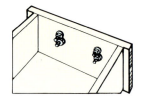

Garage shelves

Open stud wall?

Narrow shelves installed between open studs in a garage workshop are ideal for storing tins of paint, jars of fasteners, and supplies. Secure the shelves with 60 mm drywall screws going through predrilled holes in the studs and into the shelf ends; stagger the shelves in adjacent spaces. ▼

Deeper shelves on studs ▲

To store larger items in the space between studs, install 16 mm plywood shelves supported by wooden brackets. When making a bracket, cut the diagonal support's ends at a 45° angle; attach both pieces to the stud and to each other with 60 mm drywall screws. Mount a bracket on every other stud for a moderate load, on every stud for heavier loads. Notch the shelves to fit around the studs, and attach them to the brackets with 38 mm drywall screws.

UTILITY SHELVING

Great for workshops, this freestanding four-shelf, 290 mm deep storage unit can be up to 2,5 m high and up to 915 mm wide. To make it, you need five 2,5 m lengths of 44 x 44 mm pine, two 1,8 m lengths of 20 x 290 mm pine, one 2,5 m length of 20 x 100 mm pine, and two 2,5 m lengths of 20 x 44 mm pine. Use 38 mm screws to assemble the unit.

1 Clamp four of the 44 x 44 mm lengths together. Mark the overall length of the legs and the position of each cleat across all four pieces. Cut the legs to size.

2 From the remaining 44 x 44 mm length, cut cleats that are the same length as the shelves' depth. Align each cleat on a marked line and attach it to the legs with 38 mm screws.

3 Cut the shelves to the length you want. With the end frames on edge, use 38 mm screws to secure the shelves to the cleats. Stand the unit up and check that it's level and square.

4 Cut and attach the 20 x 100 mm brace across the back from the top shelf to the bottom shelf and add the 20 x 44 mm braces to both sides. Use 38 mm screws to secure.

WORKSHOP STORAGE

Handy hand tools

Easy-reach holder
Make a tool holder out of scrap wire mesh. Form the mesh into the shape shown below by bending it over the edge of a board, and attach it to the wall with screws and washers. A 10 mm square mesh holds a variety of tools, and it won't collect dust! ▼

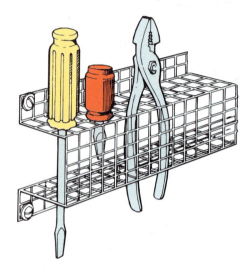

Holding power
Screw a magnetic knife-holder strip to the front edge of a shelf. These strips can hold a wide variety of workshop items and provide extra storage space on a shelf that may be too crowded for anything else.

Wrap those brushes
Paintbrushes, when rolled up in some newspaper, remain dust-free and their bristles don't splay out when drying.

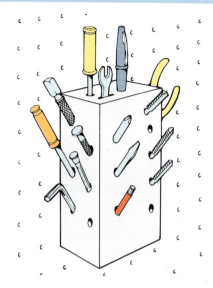

Small tool organizer ▲
Mount a block of polystyrene above your workbench and press punches, bits, knives, screwdrivers, and other such tools into it to keep them handy. Take foam used as packing material and replace it when it becomes more and more battered or pitted with holes.

Tool belt
Tack an old leather or strong canvas belt along the edge of a shelf to hold tools. As you nail it, leave small loops in the belt for tools to slip into. ▼

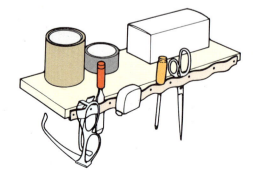

Handle holder
Chest handles are great for hanging large tools, such as hammers and hand axes. Mount the handles on a plywood backing, putting them upside down so that the handles stick out from the wall. You can also mount them vertically in pairs about 600 mm apart. A dowel slipped between them can be used to store extension cords.

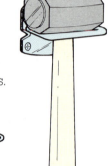

Orderly power tools

Power tower
To keep power tools handy, build a tall, narrow box out of 16 mm plywood. Then attach carpet scraps between the sides to form soft cradles for your tools.

58 / Workshop Organization

Concentrated power

Put your most frequently used power tools on a solidly mounted shelf over your workbench. Cut slots along the back for your power saws, and drill 25 mm holes along the front for your drill, power driver, and router. ▼

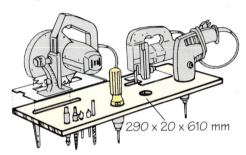
290 x 20 x 610 mm

In the wall

Another way to keep tools close at hand yet out of the way, and still avoid taking up too much valuable space, is to install a narrow shelf unit 100 mm deep. Make the shelves out of 20 x 100 mm pine and glue them on 22 x 44 mm cleats, angled slightly downwards toward the wall to keep the tools from falling. Cutouts for particular tools will hold them even more securely. ▼

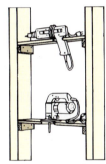

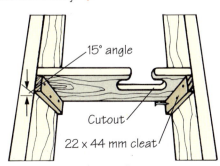
15° angle
Cutout
22 x 44 mm cleat

Ready supplies

String out

Make a dispenser for string by cutting off the bottom half of a 2 litre plastic bottle. Then mount the top half upside down on the wall with the string coming out of the bottle neck. A large coffee tin also works well with a hole in the lid.

All-in-one tape dispenser

A toilet paper holder mounted on a workshop wall or on a workbench makes a great dispenser for rolls of various types of tape used in the workshop. For easy cutting, tie scissors to the dispenser with a length of string.

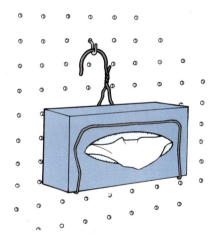

Quick wipes ▲

Facial tissues are great for quickly cleaning up water, oil, and glue and for wiping your hands when the phone rings. To make a holder for a box of tissues, bend a wire coat hanger as shown and hang it on a hook or a nail.

FIRST-AID KITS

An inexpensive and essential safety item for any workshop is a well-stocked first-aid kit. Buy one at a local pharmacy, and mount it where it is easy to see and reach. A standard kit will include gauze, antiseptic, bandages, elastic and adhesive tape, cotton swabs, eye drops, tweezers, and scissors. Latex gloves and an instant cold pack are also useful. Make sure the container closes tightly to keep out dirt and dust.

When working with paint, solvents, strippers, or chemicals with an eye-hazard warning, keep a bottle of eyewash solution handy. If chemical gets into your eyes, use the solution immediately. If a chemical irritates your skin, wash it off with water.
Note: A first-aid kit is for minor injuries only. Get prompt medical attention for a serious injury such as a deep cut or puncture or a head blow. Also see a doctor if eye irritation persists after washing.

Workshop Organization

WORKSHOP STORAGE

Nuts 'n nails

Self-identification
Here's an easy way to label boxes of nails, screws, and other fasteners: just attach a sample of each item to the outside of its box with a hot-glue gun. You'll be able to see at a glance what you have in stock and where it is.

Recycled labels
If you store screws or other fasteners in small glass jars, cut the label from the package the item was purchased in and slip it into the jar before filling it. Hold the label, face outwards, against the inside of the jar as you pour in the fasteners so that the details will be clearly visible through the glass.

Great cheap parts bins
Use rectangular plastic containers to make bins for screws, bolts, nuts, and other small items. Cut each container as shown with scissors or a utility knife; make a simple wooden frame to hold the bins. ▼

Spill preventer
Put a magnet in a container of small items such as screws or brads. This way, the metal pieces will bind together in a ball around the magnet and won't spill out if you accidentally knock over the container. If a few items do scatter, use the magnet to pick them up. For inexpensive magnets, remove the magnetic strip from an old refrigerator seal. You can break it into any lengths you need.

Nut rings
Store nuts and washers on metal shower-curtain rings hung from pegboard hooks. (The ring's pear shape and latching action allow for secure storage.) Hang nuts and washers of similar size on their own ring, so that you can find the right size quickly. ▼

Ready-made storage modules
Plastic electrical boxes, either single or double size, are just right for storing small items like fasteners. The boxes are inexpensive, and they stack or fit neatly side by side. Just make sure to remove any flanges or "wings" meant for attaching the boxes to studs.

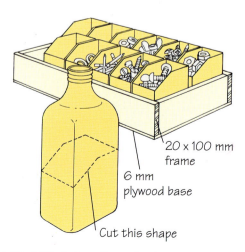

20 x 100 mm frame
6 mm plywood base
Cut this shape

Neat nail organizers ▲
Large plastic bottles with a section of their tops cut out make great nail bins. When the bottles are stored on their sides, the weight of the nails keeps them from rolling. Off the shelves, the bottles can stand upright, and their handles make for easy carrying to a job site.

Workbench catch-all
Don't let nuts, bolts, and other leftovers clutter your workbench. Bolt a cake tin or its lid under a shelf (the bolt being positioned off-centre). Swing it out and drop your odds and ends into it as you work. Occasionally sort through it to separate the useful from the useless. ▼

60 / Workshop Organization

Under-shelf storage

Make the most of your workshop shelf space by storing nails, nuts, and other fasteners in jars attached to the underside of a shelf. To mount the jars, simply screw their lids to the bottom of the shelf (place a washer under each screwhead for better security). ▼

Stand-up storage

Fill a sturdy cardboard box with sawed-off shipping tubes (or scraps of large-diameter PVC pipe) and use it to organize all those short pieces of mouldings, pipes and dowels.

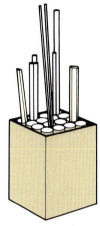

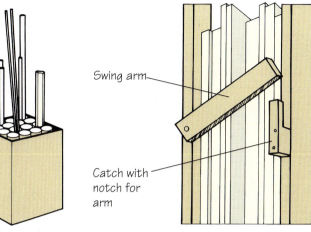

Retreads

Tie a series of old car tyres to overhead joists and use them to hold long pieces of timber and pipe. You can also lay old tyres flat on the floor or ground to provide a pallet that will keep timber and plywood sheets high and dry.

Easy-reach timber ▲

Store wood between two planks fixed to the wall and keep them safely contained with a swinging arm which slots into a simple catch. The arm should be at about waist height but you can add a second lower down for shorter pieces.

Timber and long goods

Gutter shelving

Inexpensive rain gutters provide convenient, surprisingly strong, storage for mouldings, lightweight timber, pipes, and other long, thin items. Mount four lengths of pine on the wall, attach gutter brackets and snap in the gutters. Use the brackets alone as hooks for garden hoses, extension cords, and wire coils. ▼

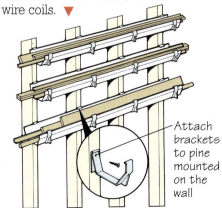

Timber overhead ▲

Keep timber out of the way with these "inverted T" racks. Bolt two to the bottom of your garage roof trusses; space them about 1,5 m apart to support 2,4 m lengths of timber. To avoid straining the trusses, limit stored pieces to the equivalent of 20 lengths of 50 x 100 mm pine and distribute the load evenly.

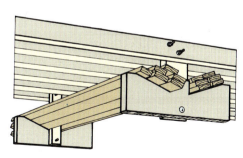

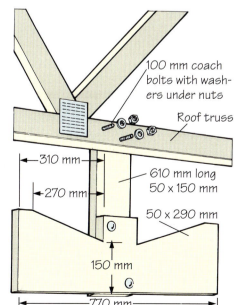

Workshop Organization / 61

WORKSHOP CLEANUP

Picking up small items

Nuts and bolts scoop
Get small items like screws, nuts and bolts back into their containers quickly with a scoop made from a square plastic bottle or jug that has a handle. Use kitchen shears to cut off the bottom half of the jug at an angle as shown. ▼

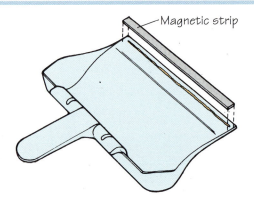

Magnetic strip

Magnetic sweep ▲
Glue a flexible magnetic strip from an old refrigerator door seal onto the edge of a dustpan. Small screws, nails and other items that may be reusable will cling to the strip when you empty the pan after sweeping up.

Magnetic bagger
Here's an easy way to pick up spilled washers, nuts, or nails: drop a bar magnet into a plastic sandwich bag. The spilled items will stick to the magnet through the plastic. Then turn the bag inside out and pour the items back into their container. Similarly, to clean up small metallic filings, put plastic wrap around a magnet, sweep it over the work area, then fold the wrap over the filings and discard it.

Dust busting

Brush it off
No vacuum readily at hand? Trim the frayed bristles from an old paintbrush and use it to sweep fine sawdust or filings from your bench top or to clean out blind corners on a drill press or lathe. Also, keep a child's broom handy for sweeping around stationary tools, workbench legs, and other tight spots you can't reach with a regular broom.

Blow it away
If you have a spare hair dryer, use it to blow away dust, dirt and shavings in the shop; to dry sweaty hands before handling new timber; and to speed the drying of paint touch-ups.

Enclose it
Before undertaking a large, messy sanding or sawing job, tape plastic sheets to the floor around the work area to contain the debris. Cleaning up the area afterwards is then a simple task taking only a few minutes.

Trap it
To capture fine airborne dust when sawing or sanding, mount a filter from an air conditioner on the air intake side of a box fan, using tape, wire, or a rubber stretch cord to secure it. Put the fan next to your work area, blowing away from you. Vacuum the filter when it becomes filled with dust. If the filter doesn't fit the fan casing, make a simple frame from offcuts. ▼

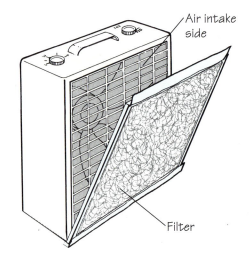

Air intake side

Filter

Recycle it
Save the sawdust from your workshop projects. It will come in handy for soaking up grease, oil, paint, or other spills. You can also use it to rub glue off your hands or mix it with carpenter's glue to make a wood filler.

Vacuuming

Thrifty timesaver

Extend the life of your workshop vacuum filter and avoid having to clean it frequently. Cut off the legs of an old pair of pantihose, tie the cut ends as shown, and then stretch the waistband top over the filter. The suction won't be affected, and you can clean the pantihose by simply rinsing it.

Easy-empty vacuum

To avoid the mess of emptying a vacuum, line the vacuum canister with a large plastic rubbish bag (fold the bag over the canister rim so the top holds the bag in place). To empty the vacuum, all you need to do is take the bag out.

Long reach

If the crevice tool on your vacuum isn't long enough to reach the accumulated sawdust behind your cabinets, make your own extra-long crevice vacuum attachment using a piece of PVC pipe that will fit the hose on your cleaner. Gently heat and flatten one end of the tube and connect it to the hose. Secure it with tape if necessary.

THE WORKSHOP VACUUM

Tools of the Trade

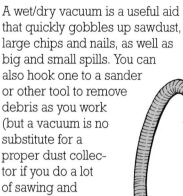

A wet/dry vacuum is a useful aid that quickly gobbles up sawdust, large chips and nails, as well as big and small spills. You can also hook one to a sander or other tool to remove debris as you work (but a vacuum is no substitute for a proper dust collector if you do a lot of sawing and sanding).

Power and performance. Luckily, most brand name units sold in home centres and department stores are adequate for a home workshop. For the average workshop, a vacuum with a capacity of 60 litres or so a minute should be adequate for most tasks.

Tank body. Plastic is the most common material and is fine for most workshops. It has the advantages of being lightweight, rust-proof, and dent-resistant. Steel, used on some models, is durable and less prone to damage from heat or solvents but might rust if you live anywhere near the coast. However, some of the substances used in workshops could harm a plastic body, or a metal one for that matter, so don't use the vacuum to clean up if there is a possibility that this could ever happen.

Fumes and flames. When cleaning up a spill, bear in mind that the vacuum exhaust may distribute fumes which could be harmful or inflammable. Ventilate the workshop and avoid using any tools until the air is completely clear.

Filter type. If you usually vacuum dry debris only, a pleated paper cartridge filter provides more surface area for dust, reducing the number of filter cleanings. But the pleats are hard to clean when the dust is wet or caked. If you do a lot of wet pickup, a flat paper (or foam) filter is better. A "cage" of 10 mm mesh taped over the end of the nozzle will stop it picking up large items that could block it or the pipe.

Attachments. A large-diameter hose is handy for picking up sawdust and chips, a small one for picking up nails and heavy particles. Some large-hose units have adaptors to accept small hoses. Extension wands, a floor nozzle, and a crevice tool are essential.

WORK GEAR AND PERSONAL CLEANUP

Work clothes

Take it off
Never wear a watch, ring, neck chain, or other piece of jewellery when working with a power tool. Mount a brightly coloured hook over your workbench to hold these items. The hook will remind you to take them off when you come into the workshop, and you'll always know where you put them.

Extended life
Reinforce knees, elbows, bottoms of pockets, and other areas on work clothes subject to heavy wear by putting iron-on patches on their undersides. Coat the edges of pockets with clear fingernail varnish to prevent fraying.

Glove hanger
Can't ever find your work gloves when you need them? Use a binder clip (available from office supply stores) to hang them on a nail in a shelf, or on a pegboard hook in full view. ▼

Binder clip

Coming to grips
Rub clear silicone sealant onto the palms of your work gloves. Once the sealant cures you'll be able to get a much firmer grip with the gloves.

Safety gloves
Fine sawdust can make your fingers slip when you are working with a power tool. To avoid this, wear household latex gloves with nonslip palms. Put talcum powder inside the gloves to ensure easy removal. To cut down on the likelihood of your slipping on a dust-strewn floor, wear rubber-soled shoes.

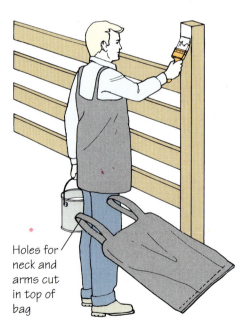
Holes for neck and arms cut in top of bag

Instant aprons ▲
Keep some plastic refuse bags in your workshop to use as aprons for messy chores. Cut neck and arm holes in the bottom of a bag, pull it over your head and start work. When finished, break the straps, step out of the bag and discard it.

Easy-on, easy-off apron
Tired of fumbling to tie your apron behind your back? Extend the straps so that they are long enough to pass around your waist completely and be tied either at the side or at the front. Just ensure that they are not so long that they pose a danger when working with tools.

Eyewear

No more broken glasses
Do your reading glasses keep falling out of your shirt pocket when you bend over? Attach a removable metal clip from a ballpoint pen to one of your glasses' stems. Position the clip so that it catches comfortably in your pocket, and use pliers to gently squeeze it on. ▼

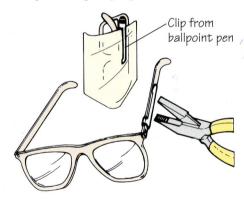
Clip from ballpoint pen

A clearer view
Fine sawdust tends to stick to safety glasses because of the static electricity that builds up in dry workshop air. To cut static and remove dust, wipe the surface of your safety glasses with a used laundry antistatic sheet—so that it won't scratch or smear the surface of the glasses.

Face-shield wrap

To keep your plastic face shield clean and scratch-free, cover the front with clear plastic wrap. It won't affect your vision, and when it gets dirty, you can just peel it off and replace it. ▼

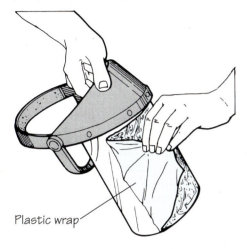
Plastic wrap

Quick spray and wipe

Keeping your safety goggles crystal clear takes only a matter of seconds if you just equip your workbench with a bottle of window cleaner and a roll of paper towels.

Keeping clean

Skin protection

Before beginning a messy job, give your exposed skin a light coat of petroleum jelly. It keeps paint or grease from getting into pores and washes off with soap. Rubbing undiluted liquid soap on your hands and letting it dry will also repel grease. To keep dirt from collecting under your fingernails, scrape your nails over a bar of soap first.

PROTECTIVE GEAR

Store your safety goggles, ear protectors and respirator on a foam head made for displaying hats and wigs (a store that sells these items may be willing to give you an old foam head or the name of a supplier). Put the head in a prominent place in your workshop and it will serve as a constant reminder to use your safety gear. Here are some tips on selecting safety gear.

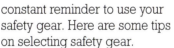

Eye protectors. Don't rely on ordinary spectacles to guard your eyes. Wear special protective safety glasses with side shields, or safety goggles which can be worn over your regular spectacles. For full face protection, wear a face shield.

Ear protectors. Earmuffs are easier to take off and put on than earplugs and harder to misplace. Hardware dealers and gunshops stock a wide range of ear protectors of both types.

Respiratory protectors. Look for a respirator with changeable dual cartridges to filter out specific types of toxic dust and fumes, such as when spray-painting. For ordinary tasks, use disposable dust masks.

Hand, foot and body protectors. Heavy-duty leather gauntlets and stout shoes can prevent injury when welding or working with heavy items, and always wear clothing that covers torso and legs for total safety.

Safe and effective cleaner ▶

Clean your greasy or paint-stained hands with vegetable oil. It's inexpensive and works well. More importantly, it won't irritate your skin or be absorbed, as are solvents. Put the vegetable oil into a plastic spray bottle; that way, you can just spray it on your hands and it won't spill. Laundry prewash and shampoo for oily hair are also good grease busters.

Vegetable oil

Workshop Organization / 65

WORKSHOP SKILLS

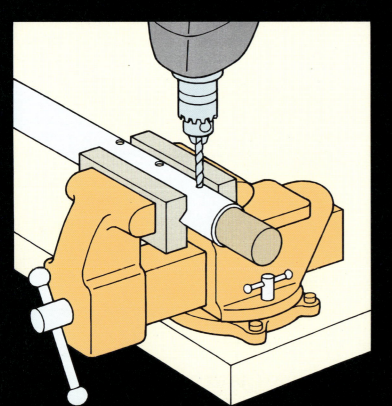

WOOD BASICS 67
MEASURING 68
MARKING 69
LAYING OUT 70
DRILLING 72
CHISELLING AND PLANING 73
SAWING 74
ROUTING 78
JOINING WOOD 79
SANDING 80
CLAMPING 84
GLUEING 88
FINISHING WOOD 90
METALWORKING 94
WORKING WITH GLASS 98
WORKING WITH PLASTICS 100

WOOD BASICS

Buying wood

Numbers game
When buying timber, you'll find that the actual dimensions are smaller than those specified. That's because timber is sold by "nominal size"—the size it is when it's cut at the mill. After planing and shrinkage, however, the actual size is a bit smaller. You may also find that the actual sizes can vary from region to region—so select your wood carefully.

Nominal size (mm)	Actual size (mm)
16 x 50	13 x 44
16 x 75	13 x 69
19 x 50	16 x 44
19 x 150	16 x 144
25 x 50	22 x 44
38 x 38	32 x 32
38 x 114	32 x 108
50 x 50	44 x 44
76 x 76	69 x 69

Think thick
The table above gives a selection of timber sizes and most often you will find that the actual size is as stated above. Nevertheless, when checking lengths for warping and knots, also check the cross-sections of each to ensure they are all correct. Some may differ.

It's all in the colour
If ever you run out of timber when engaged on a project, take a small sample of the wood along when buying extra lengths. This will ensure you will get a good colour match. You might also be able to match the grain more closely, which can be important on some items. Check the sizes carefully before buying.

Resuscitating old timber
Before throwing old timber away, or burning it in the fireplace or braai, consider reusing it. First remove any nails. Fill the nail holes with wooden toothpicks or matchsticks dipped in wood glue. If a knot falls out, glue it back in with wood glue.

Warped

Is it straight?
If one side of a piece of timber dries faster than another, the wetter side may develop a hump, or crown. To detect warping, sight along the length of the board. A slight crown is to be expected, but reject any board that has a very pronounced one. Also check for cracks, stains, splits and other damage.

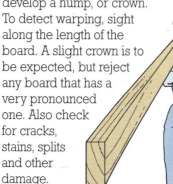

Stacking it up
To ensure air circulation and minimize warping, store timber off the ground and separate the layers with small dry 22 x 22 mm strips of pine. Position these at each end of the stack and at intervals of 450 mm along the stack's length for support.

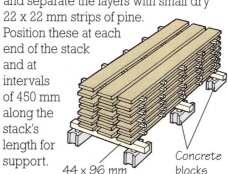

44 x 96 mm — Concrete blocks

Get rid of that warp
Place a warped plank, concave side down, on wet grass on a sunny day. The ground moisture on the concave side of the board and the sun's heat on the convex side may straighten the board in four hours to four days. If one end is more warped than the other, weight it down with a heavy rock.

Getting a handle on it

Hammer carrier
Carrying a full sheet of plywood (or wallboard or panelling) can be awkward at best, but a claw hammer can help. Hook the claws under the bottom edge of the plywood, near the centre of the sheet. The hammer handle makes a convenient carrying grip. Use your free hand to steady the load.

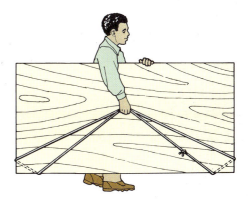

All tied up ▲
Another way to carry a sheet of plywood is with a length of rope tied into a loop. Slip it over the two bottom corners of the plywood sheet. Grasp the middle sections of the loop with one hand and steady the board with the other.

Workshop Skills / 67

MEASURING

How wide is it?

Boxed in
If you don't have a folding rule with a metal extension bar, you can still accurately measure inside a drawer or similar workpiece by using a retractable tape measure and a combination square. Place the square against one corner. Starting at the opposite corner, measure the remaining distance with the tape measure. Add the two measurements for the total width. ▼

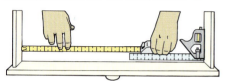

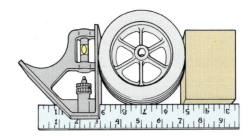

Too round for rules? ▲
Finding the exact diameter of a round object isn't that tricky. Place the object against a straightedge rule and between two blocks or other items with true straight edges. Then just read the diameter on the rule (the distance between the blocks). You can create variations of this gauge with a mix of try squares, framing squares, and combination squares.

Squared straight

Bright idea
If you're not sure that an edge is straight, place it against a known straightedge and hold the two pieces up to a light. If the light shines through, the edge isn't straight. To straighten it, shave off the high spots with a file, sander, or plane.

Get it square
When making a rectangular object, such as a drawer, check that it is actually square. Here's how: First measure across the workpiece diagonally from corner to corner. Then measure the opposite diagonal. If the two measurements match, the workpiece is square.

Gauging depth

Blind hole
Improvise a depth gauge for blind holes or recesses with a bolt and two nuts. With the nuts on the bolt, place the bolt in the hole. Twist the nuts down to the surface of the work. To hold the measure in place, tighten the top nut to the bottom one. A butterfly nut with wings downwards will allow depth measurement of large holes.

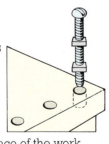

Rubber gauge
A gauge for measuring tyre treads can also be used by the woodworker. Use the gauge to check the depth of blind holes and shallow recesses.

Deep down
Use a combination square to determine the depth of a recess. Making sure the blade is free to slide, rest the square on a flat edge of the work. Adjust the blade to the depth of the recess, then lock the blade in place using the thumbscrew. Besides measuring the recess, you can use the square to transfer the depth dimension to other workpieces. ▼

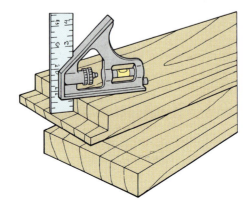

Another angle
To make sure that a right angle is true, use the 3:4:5 method of triangulation. For example, to check a corner for squareness, measure 3 m along one wall and 4 m along the other. If the distance between the two end points is 5 m, the corner is square. To create a right angle, tack two strings where you want the right angle to be. Measure out two legs of a triangle so that one is 3 m and the other is 4 m. Position the two legs so that the distance between their end points is 5 m. Just work in multiples of 3, 4 and 5, as in the illustration, and you will always achieve a perfect right angle.

MARKING

Chalk it up

Back to school
To identify parts when assembling a project, use white or yellow blackboard chalk. It's easy to sand off, and chalk doesn't leave a hard-to-remove impression the way a pen or pencil can. Use additional colours for big projects.

Snappy line
When marking out anything with a chalk line, first remove excess chalk from the line by snapping it on the ground. Then you'll be ready to stretch the line over the material and snap it as usual. The result will be a crisp line.

Plumb bobbing
A windy day can make it difficult to use a plumb bob. To keep the bob from swinging around, sink the weighted end in a bucket of water. (The bob shouldn't touch the side or the bottom of the bucket.) Since you can't align the work directly against the plumb bob cord, measure the distance between the work and the cord at the top and bottom. If they are aligned, the measurements will be the same.

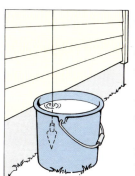

In the round

Centre finder
To find the centre of a circle, clamp a combination square to a framing or try square. The combination square should be set against the latter so that its rule intersects the inside corner of the framing square at 45°. Slide the device over the work until both sides of the framing square rest against it. Using the rule of the combination square as a guide, draw a pencil line on the work; rotate the work and draw a second line. The intersection of the lines marks the centre. You can also make a plywood jig. Cut out a right angle in the plywood; then attach a straightedge to it with screws, creating a 45° angle. Use the jig in the same way as the one above.

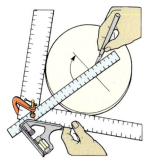

Cylindrical trick
To mark equal distances around a cylinder, measure the circumference with a strip of paper; then lay the paper flat and mark off equal segments with a compass (see right). Wrap the paper around the cylinder, tape down the end, and transfer the marks.

Dividing rules

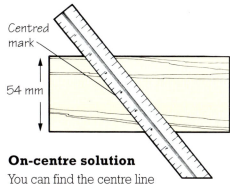

On-centre solution
You can find the centre line of an odd-size board without having to divide unwieldy fractions. Place a rule or measuring tape diagonally across the board with an even-numbered mark on each of the board's two edges. The midway point between these two numbers accurately locates the centre of the board.

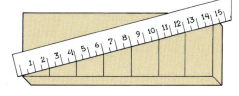

Equal time ▲
To mark equal segments, angle a ruler across the work. Place the beginning of the ruler on one edge of the work, and adjust the angle so that a centimetre mark divisible by the number of segments needed lies at the other end of the work. For example, to divide the work into 7 segments, let the ruler measure 14 cm; then mark every 2 cm.

Walk this way
Another way to mark equal segments is with dividers or a compass. Set the points at the desired distance; then walk the dividers along a straightedge by swinging one point in front of the other.

Workshop Skills / 69

LAYING OUT

Got it straight?

Let your finger do the work ▲

When scribing a straight line near the edge of a board, use your finger as a guide (but the edge of the board must be straight). Hold the pencil between your thumb and first finger, rest your middle finger's tip lightly on the edge of the board and then slide your hand along the board by adjusting your arm at the elbow and shoulder and keeping the wrist steady. With just a little practice your finger will soon be gauging straight lines.

Easy marker

This simple marking gauge can be made out of an offcut. Drill a series of holes at measured intervals along the length of the prong; make the holes large enough to accommodate a pencil point. Butt the head of the device against the work, and slide it along to mark the line. More holes can be drilled as and when needed.

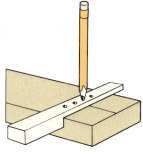

That versatile square

A combination square is an accurate aid for marking straight lines. Adjust the blade to the desired length, and position the square along the edge of the wood. Set the pencil at the end of the blade and pull the two toward you in a smooth motion. If you have problems keeping the pencil steady, file a notch into the end of the blade; it should be just wide enough to accommodate the pencil point. ▼

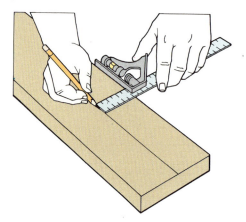

Down the centre

Use this jig to mark the centre of your work without first measuring. You'll need four 6 mm dowels and a block of wood at least 50 mm wide and 200 mm long (longer if you're working with material more than 150 mm wide). Mark centre lines (p 69) down the length and across the width of the block on both faces. Drill a hole wide enough for a pencil through the centre of the block. On one face drill two dowel holes on the longer centre line, 25 mm in from each end; on the other face drill two holes on the same line, centred 25 mm on either side of the pencil hole. Glue dowels into the holes. To use the jig, insert a pencil and place the jig over the work, with the dowels pressed tightly against the board's edges.

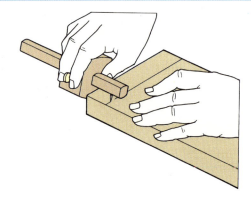

No more bumpy lines ▲

When you're using a marking gauge, it's not unusual for the scribe to be a little wavy near the edge of the wood. (The reason is that as the body of the gauge passes the edge of the wood, the pin may jump.) Instead of pulling or pushing the gauge all the way to the end of the work, stop just short of it—about 10 mm. Reposition the gauge so that the pin is at the end of the wood; then push or pull it until the two scribed lines meet.

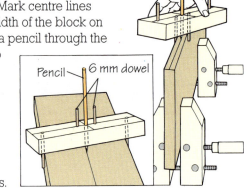

Going round in circles

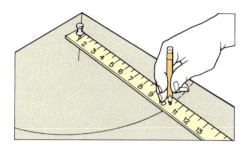

Double-duty plastic rule ▲
If your compass isn't large enough to make the circle or arc you need, try using a plastic rule. Drill a hole large enough for a push pin at the 1 cm mark. Then drill holes for a pencil point at the distances you need along the rule. When you're ready to use this homemade compass, insert a pin through the hole at the 1 cm mark and into the work. The rule will pivot at the push pin. (Because the pivot is set at the 1 cm mark, make sure you add 1 cm to your measurements.)

Adjustable rod
A standard curtain rod is ideal for creating a large adjustable compass. Bend the ends down as in the illustration. Cut it in two, and tape a large nail securely to one end as the pivot. Tape a pencil to the other end. Clamp the two sections together at the radius you need and scribe your circle.

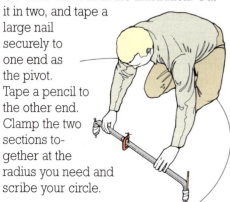

Irregularities

For the perfect fit
To fit together two objects, one of which is irregularly shaped (for instance, a lipped cabinet against a wall with moulding), use a compass. Set the point on the wall and the pencil point on the cabinet. With a slow, steady motion and without varying the distance between the compass legs, follow the original contour with the point. The pencil will trace the shape onto the work.

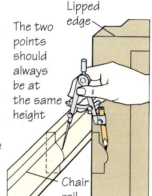

The two points should always be at the same height

Lipped edge

Chair rail

Shape it with solder
Bendable wire solder can become the perfect contour gauge, especially when you're making duplicates of odd shapes. Place the solder against the irregular object and push it in to fit the contour. Then position the bent solder on the workpiece and trace the contour onto it.

Dressmaker's trick
To transfer patterns—especially curved ones—to wood, slip a sheet of dressmaker's tracing paper between the work and the pattern. Then use a tracing wheel to copy the pattern onto the work. The radiating points on the wheel will pierce the pattern and press against the tracing paper, leaving a dotted ink line on the work.

Save your pattern
Often-used woodworking patterns soon become frayed and worn. To preserve your patterns, use the originals to make longer-lasting templates. Suitable materials include cardboard, thin plywood, hardboard, and acrylic plastic sheeting, which is easy to shape with most woodworking tools. An extra advantage to the clear acrylic template is that you'll be able to see the work under the template and know exactly where the pattern will fall—which means you can avoid knots and select sections that have better-looking grain.

Make it larger (or smaller)
A three-sided drafter's rule is the tool you need to reduce or enlarge objects or patterns. To make your own version of a drafter's rule, make several photocopies of a 300 mm ruler, scaled at various ratios such as 25, 50, 75, 100, 125, 150 and 175 per cent. Cut out the rules and glue them to two four-sided sticks—one with decreasing ratios, the other with increasing ratios. Use the 100 per cent rule to measure the object or pattern that you wish to copy; then look for the measurement on the rule with the desired ratio. Wrap the rulers in clear self-adhesive film to protect the surfaces.

Workshop Skills / 71

DRILLING

Bull's eye

Making the curve

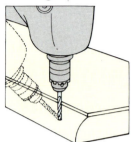

Drilling a hole on a curved surface, such as moulding, can be tricky because the bit has a tendency to wander. To keep the bit centred, first use an awl to punch a hole where you plan to drill. Then start drilling the hole with the bit perpendicular to the surface; once the bit takes, swing it gradually to the proper angle.

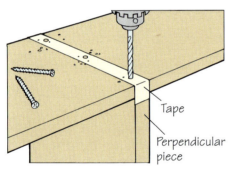

At the joint ▲

Masking tape is an ideal guide for drilling into dado and butt joints. The tape should be the same width as the end of the workpiece (for example, a shelf or a partition in a stereo cabinet) that butts against the face of the other workpiece. Lay the tape across the work with the ends overhanging and lining up with the perpendicular piece. Mark the hole locations on the tape and begin drilling. When you remove the masking tape, you'll find that the wood will be less chipped than usual.

Groovy jig ▶

Here's how to make a handy two-in-one jig for guiding drill bits. Cut a V-groove in each end of a scrap block of wood. One groove should be at a 90° angle for drilling perpendicular holes; the other one at another commonly used angle, such as 45°. Use the jig to start the drill bit at the desired angle; then remove it to continue drilling.

Shelf help

Drilling holes for shelf pins is a snap with this handy hole-spacing template. Cut a strip of pegboard three to five holes wide and long enough to cover the height of the work. To avoid drilling too many holes, cover every other row of holes with tape. Because the lowest shelf normally starts 200 mm from the bottom, you can also cover the bottom 200 mm of holes with tape. Label the top end of the template so you don't accidentally position it the wrong way around. Secure the template flush to the edge of the work with spring clamps. Then start drilling through the centre strip of holes.

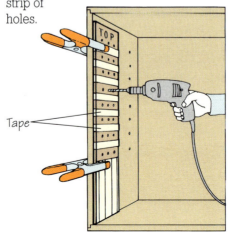

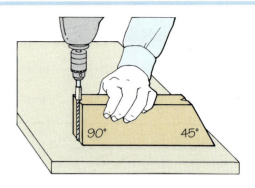

Hole truth

A bit of a trick

When drilling through some woods and all plywood, the bit may chew up the exit hole unless you drill the hole partway from both sides. A faster and neater method is to back up the work with a piece of scrap wood. The bit will chew up the scrap, not the work.

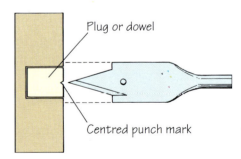

Hole in a hole ▲

Centring a drill bit can be difficult when you're enlarging an existing hole. The solution is to first fill the hole with a same-size dowel or plug (which you can make with a hole saw). Punch the centre of the dowel or plug with an awl; then use the punch mark to centre the spade bit for the larger hole.

CHISELLING AND PLANING

Chisel it away

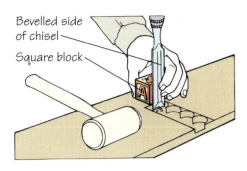

Hold it straight ▲
To create a neat cut when making a dado, mortise, or dovetail, the chisel must be held perpendicular to the wood. One way to guide the chisel is to hold a square block against the blade (with the chisel's bevel toward the waste). Or try clamping a board with a straight edge along the chisel line.

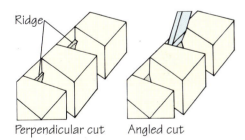

Another angle ▲
Perpendicular chisel cuts to remove waste in dovetail joints rarely line up at the halfway point where the cuts meet from the two opposite sides. Ridges that jut out at the halfway point require a separate removal step. To avoid this extra step, after making the first initial cuts along the marking lines with the chisel perpendicular to the work, continue the remaining cuts with the blade angled away from the waste slightly.

Plane sense

It's just scribble
It's hard to know if you've missed a spot after planing a large surface. Here's one way to be sure. Before you start planing, scribble on the surface with a pencil. As you plane, the scribbling will disappear. Repeat this step for additional passes.

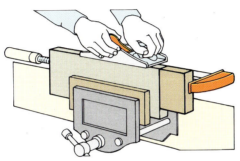

No more splinters ▲
To keep the end of a workpiece from splintering as it's being planed, clamp a block of scrap wood to the end. The height of the scrap should be the same as the height of the work.

Knotty solution
If there's a knot close to an edge that you want to plane, try holding the plane at an angle. The slicing action you get from an angled blade yields a better cut than a standard pass.

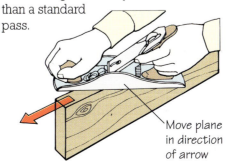

Holding block
When planing a long board, you may find that the clamps interfere with the plane. To avoid having to reposition the clamps, make two V-shaped holding blocks, and clamp the blocks rather than the workpiece. With the clamps out of the way, you can plane the work without encountering any interference.

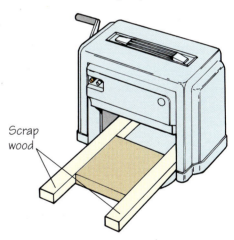

Too small for a planer? ▲
Here's how to plane short pieces of timber in a thickness planer. Hot-glue scrap wood to each side of the work, with the bottom faces of all three pieces flush. After planing, tap the pieces of scrap wood to break them off the work. To plane stock under 10 mm thick, use mirror tape to attach the stock to a scrap board wider and at least 20 mm longer than the work. (The scrap must be of a uniform thickness and free of warps.)

SAWING

Avoiding splinters

Here's the bad side
Cutting plywood across the grain can create a splintered edge on one side of the board. This won't matter as long as you have a good side and a bad side on the workpiece. The trick is to cut on the correct side. Here are the rules: good side facing up for a handsaw, table saw, and radial arm saw; good side facing down for a circular saw and jigsaw.

Haven't got a bad side?
If both faces of the plywood are intended as good sides, you have two options. One is to first make a deep score line with a sharp knife on both faces of the wood. This will ensure a cleaner saw cut and prevent the saw from leaving a ragged edge. The other option (which doesn't always work) is to apply masking tape on both faces of the board where you intend to cut. Mark your cut line on the tape. After you make the cut, peel off the strips of tape.

Circular saw

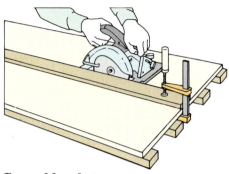

Ground level ▲
Forget about struggling with sheets of plywood on sawhorses. Here are three ways to cut plywood on the floor:
▷ Support the plywood on two or more lengths of 22 x 44 mm.
▷ Put another piece of plywood under the one you're cutting, and set your saw depth so that the blade just barely grazes the lower sheet.
▷ Set your saw so that the blade doesn't go all the way through; then break apart the two pieces and clean up the cut edges with a bit of sandpaper.

Handsaw

Guidance ▶
To ensure a straight cut, use a guide to keep the saw vertically straight and make frequent visual checks of the blade. A block of 75 x 75 mm wood cut straight and square will suffice as a guide for short cuts. For a guide for long cuts in thin plywood, clamp a length of 44 x 44 mm wood along the cutting line.

Deep thoughts
This depth gauge will help you cut saw kerfs to a specific depth. First measure the desired depth from the tips of the saw teeth up on both sides of the saw blade; then draw lines parallel to the teeth, again on both sides of the blade. Position strips of wood with a straight edge along the guidelines, straight edges facing down. Secure the strips to the blade with a pair of spring clamps or G-clamps. Saw until the edges of the depth gauge meet the work surface.

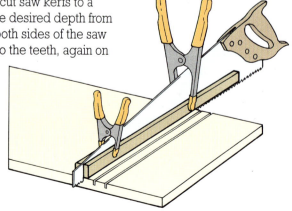

Binding kerf
A circular saw blade tends to catch the work when the kerf behind it closes up. Keep the kerf from binding the blade by inserting a wood shim or other small object into the kerf. When making longer cuts, slide the shim closer (but not too close) to the blade as you progress.

74 / Workshop Skills

Easy measuring

For those of you who have to cut several boards to the same length, here's a way to speed up the job. Cut one end of each board square; butt those ends against a straightedge nailed to your bench. On one board, measure and mark the desired length minus the distance between the saw blade and the end of the shoe; clamp a straightedge at this mark, extending it across all the boards. Now you can make one pass. ▼

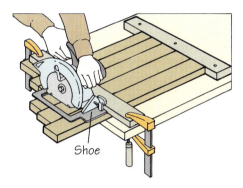
Shoe

Kerf bender

Bending wood is as easy as making a series of straight kerfs with your circular saw, using a square to guide the cuts. There's no rule of thumb about how far apart or how deep to cut the kerfs. Practise on scrap first. For tighter bends, space the kerfs more closely, but don't make them too deep or they will be visible from the opposite side. Before bending the wood, briefly soak it in hot water.

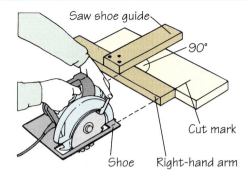
Saw shoe guide • 90° • Cut mark • Shoe • Right-hand arm

Seeking guidance ▲

If you plan to cut a lot of wood to the same length, give this jig a try. Use any scrap pieces of wood with straight and squared edges. Join the two pieces with glue and screws, making sure they are set at an exact right angle. Make the right-hand arm of the guide slightly longer than the distance from the circular saw blade to the left edge of the saw's shoe. Your first pass with the guide will cut off the arm's extra length. When you're ready to use the guide, line up the right end of the guide with the cut mark on the wood.

Jigsaw

Take an iron to it

It takes more than a pencilled line and good intentions to cut a straight line with a jigsaw. For long cuts, use a length of 20 mm angle iron as a straightedge guide. Clamped along the measured mark, the angle iron will guide the blade along the cut line and will keep the blade perpendicular to the work.

Supporting role

To support the work while using a jigsaw, clamp it to your workbench so that the area you are cutting juts past the edge of the bench. Or support the work on blocks made from scrap wood that is thicker than the length of your blade. As you reach the end of a cut, the work can collapse toward the cut and bind the blade. To prevent this from happening, slide additional blocks under the work after you cut halfway through it. Make sure the path for the saw blade avoids the bench and blocks.

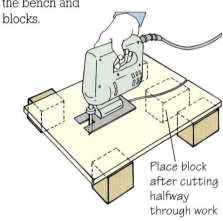
Place block after cutting halfway through work

Taking the plunge

To start a cut in the centre of the wood —not at an edge—without drilling a hole first, tilt the saw, resting the front of its shoe on the work; then, with the saw on medium speed, slowly and firmly lower the blade into the wood.

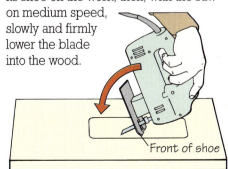
Front of shoe

Workshop Skills / 75

SAWING

Mitre saw

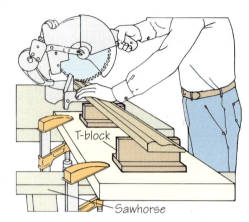
T-block — Sawhorse

Supporting role ▲
If you don't have a helper around to support long pieces of wood, make a couple of T-blocks. They'll support the work whether you're working on a table or on the floor. If your mitre saw is set up in a permanent area, you can nail or screw the T-blocks in place.

Ending repetition
If you have to cut a series of workpieces to the same length, try avoiding repetitive measuring and marking by using a stop block. To raise the stop block to the correct height, nail it to another block of the same thickness as the bed of the mitre saw. Clamp the block in place.

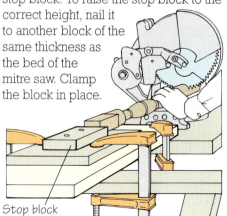
Stop block

On the wide side
Here's how to trick your mitre saw into making a wider cut: slide a piece of scrap wood under the workpiece. This raises the work so that a wider part of the blade will reach it.

Table saw

Ripping fun
To rip an uneven board straight when neither edge is true, nail a straight board on top of it. Use the straight board as a guide to run against the rip fence; the newly cut edge of the uneven board will then be true.

Straightedge
Double-headed nail is easy to remove

Narrow escape
To safely cut a narrow board, fasten a wider board to its edge with hot glue. After the cut is complete, break the boards apart; there'll be no damage.

Tall order ▶
To create a raised panel for a door, make a tenon or cut a slot into the end of a board, using this jig to make a smoother, more controlled cut. The jig is designed to straddle the rip fence of a table saw. Make the jig out of scrap wood and plywood, and size it to fit your needs—the jig's face can be smaller or larger, depending on the project. The jig should slide snugly and smoothly on the fence. Secure the work to the jig with G-clamps or other small clamps.

Mighty mitre jig
With this jig on your table saw, you'll cut perfect mitre angles every time. To guide the jig, fit two strips of wood into the mitre gauge grooves in the saw's table; then glue a 16 mm plywood base to the top of the strips and square the base to the table. Cut a slot for the blade partway through the base. Mark a 45° angle from both sides of the blade slot; screw two wood blocks with straight edges along these lines. Glue sandpaper strips to the outside edges of the wood blocks to keep the work from moving about. ▼

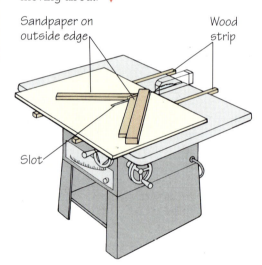
Sandpaper on outside edge — Wood strip — Slot

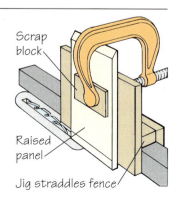
Scrap block — Raised panel — Jig straddles fence

Radial arm saw

Stop action
Controlling the depth of the blade cut is easy with this depth stop. Lower the blade to the desired height, measure the distance between the column castings, and cut a piece of scrap wood to that measurement. Place the wood between the castings and hold it in place with a hose clamp. ▼

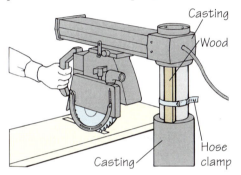

Narrow rip
To rip a thin strip of wood or avoid getting your fingers too close to the blade, clamp a straightedge guide to the wood. The guide should slide along the front edge of the saw's table. With this setup the blade won't hang far out on the arm, which reduces cutting accuracy. ▼

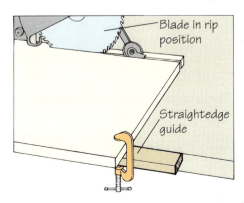

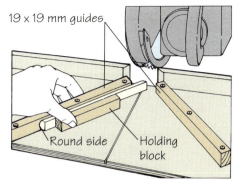

Mind your mitres ▲
This jig allows you to cut accurate mitres on rounded stock or moulding. Screw two guides to a plywood base at opposite 45° angles to the saw blade. Place the rounded stock against the guide that will give you the desired mitre angle. Press a square holding block against the stock, and make the cut. The holding block will keep the piece upright and will also prevent it from creeping out of place while it's being cut.

Band and scroll saws

Blade aid
If the band saw blade slips off the wheel when you try to replace it, use masking tape to hold it in place temporarily. Tape the blade to the top wheel; then slip it around the lower wheel and tighten it in place. Remove the tape.

Super duping
When cutting duplicate parts on a band or scroll saw, stack the parts together, using double-sided tape between the pieces to hold them in place. The whole stack can then be cut without any worry about the pieces moving.

Veneer
To make clean band or scroll saw cuts in thin sheets of veneer or metal, layer the work between two pieces of plywood. To indicate the position of the work, set the work on the bottom layer; then mark and drill holes through the plywood at each corner of the work. Dab hot-melt glue along each edge of the work, and place the second piece of plywood on top. (Or tape the plywood layers together.) Flip over the assembly; using the holes as a guide to the corners of the work, mark the cutting lines or glue a cutting pattern to the plywood.

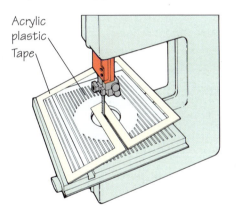

Work jam ▲
Small pieces can drop into the band saw table slot and jam against the blade. To keep this from happening, cut a sheet of 3 mm acrylic plastic the same dimensions as the saw table. Drill a 6 mm hole in the plastic where the blade will be located; then cut a slot from the back edge of the plastic to the hole. Anchor the plastic to the saw's table with strips of double-sided tape down the centre and around all four edges. Besides reducing the clearance around the blade, it also provides a smooth work surface. For a larger blade, drill a larger hole.

Workshop Skills / 77

ROUTING

Router rules

Which way to go?
When it comes to moving a router, the basic rule is: left to right as you face the cut. When making an interior cut, move the router clockwise. For perimeters, move it anticlockwise. If you're using a router table (in which case the router is mounted upside down), move the work from right to left. ▼

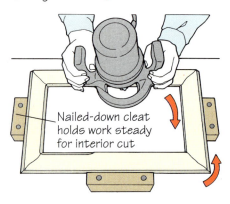
Nailed-down cleat holds work steady for interior cut

Five easy solutions
Here are simple solutions to common router problems:
▷ Burned edges: Move the router faster; check for a dull bit.
▷ Chatter marks: Move the router slower over the wood; check for a dull bit.
▷ Corner tearouts: Rout the end grain first, then remove splinters by routing the sides; instead of one pass, make your cut in two or three passes.
▷ Uneven depth of cut: Tighten the router's depth adjustment and collet; replace the collet if it is worn.
▷ Router straining: Don't rout a surface to its full width or depth in one pass. Increasing the cutting depth by 3 mm with each pass makes the task easier.

Shaping the work

Look! No clamps
This friction board may solve the problem of clamps in your router's path. Attach a block of wood to one end of a length of plywood. Spread white glue on the plywood, lay medium-grit sandpaper on it, and set the board upside down until the glue dries. Then hook the block over the edge of the worktable or hold it in a vice. The friction from the sandpaper will hold your work in place.

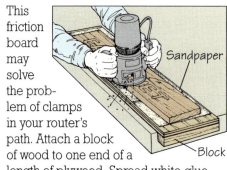

Dado jig
Make a T-square by screwing together two pieces of straight wood at a perfect right angle. Clamp the jig to a piece of scrap, and rout with the bit you plan to use, creating a dado in it. To use the jig, mark the work where you want a dado, and clamp the jig in place so that the dado is lined up with the mark. Use this jig only with the same router and the same size bit, set to the same depth.

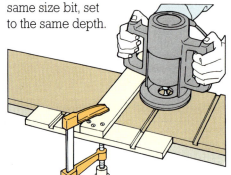

Tipping over the edge
When routing along a narrow edge, the router base can tip and create an uneven profile. For more control, clamp or hot-glue a straight board along the edge of the work.

Straight board

Again and again
If you are making a number of duplicate shapes with a router, you can simplify the job by using the original pattern to make a template out of 6 mm thick hardboard. Cut the workpiece to about 1 mm outside the layout line. Then nail the template to the bottom side of the workpiece, and rout off the excess with a ball-bearing bit designed for trimming plastic laminate.

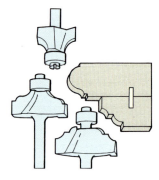

Combining bits ▲
Even if you own a complete set of bits, you don't have to settle for predesigned shapes. To increase the variety and style of the edges you make, try combining two or more bits.

JOINING WOOD

Edge, mitre, and tenon

An edgy solution
The table saw is the best tool for cutting straight glueing edges. If a table saw isn't available, first glue together the sections to be joined. When the glue has completely dried, cut the pieces apart with a circular saw, making sure the blade runs down the centre of the glued seam. The blade will remove a bit of the wood from each edge; even if the cut wavers, the edges will vary the same amount and will butt together perfectly.

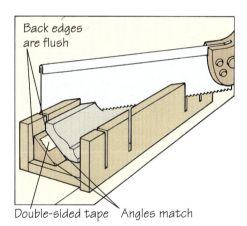

How to mitre a cornice ▲
Here's an aid to prevent a cornice from slipping in a mitre box. Cut one edge of a suitable scrap block at an angle that matches that of the cornice. Put double-sided tape along the cut edge, or glue a strip of sandpaper onto it. Trim the block so that its back edge is flush with the back edge of the cornice. Set the latter on the angled edge of the block. Hold it and the block against the mitre box as you saw. The tape or sandpaper will grip the cornice. To clamp the cornice, see p 84.

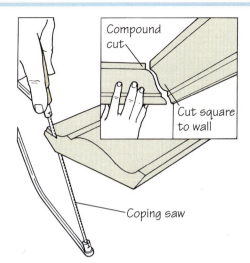

Coping a joint ▲
To install a cornice at an inside corner, you will have to make a compound cut. First cut one piece to fit flush against the wall. Then make a 45° inside mitre cut on the end of the other piece. With a coping saw, cut along this profile at the face of the trim, undercutting the edge about 30°. With practice, you'll get it to fit, creating a neat coped joint.

Binding tenon
To find out where a tenon is binding in a mortise, tape a piece of carbon paper over the tenon and drive it into the mortise until it binds. When you remove the tenon, you'll find a smudge on it that indicates where the joint is binding.

Joining with dowels

To the point
Mount an old pencil sharpener on your workshop wall and use it not only to sharpen pencils but also to chamfer dowels for joining wood workpieces.

Just a flute
A fluted dowel holds better in wood because it allows more glue to surround it. Make your own flutes on cheaper plain dowels by crimping the dowels with the serrated jaws of your pliers.

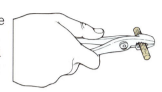

It goes in but won't come out
When test-fitting a dowel joint, the fit may be so snug that you can't pull the joint apart. To prevent this, use test dowels. Make them by cutting a slot into each end at right angles (use a dovetail saw or small backsaw). Test fit, then use regular dowels to assemble the joint.

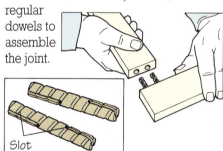

A better butt
Increase the strength of a butt joint by driving the screw through a dowel. Drill a hole for a 15 mm dowel so that it cuts across the path of the screw that will be driven into the end grain of one of the workpieces. Glue the dowel into the hole. When the glue has dried, drive in the screw and sand or cut the dowel flush to the surface. On wider joints, use more dowels.

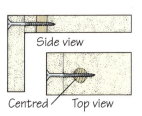

SANDING

Handling the paper

Curling clues
Sandpaper will curl up and crack if it's left lying around. To keep the paper from curling, place a weight on it. Or store the paper in the freezer so that heat and humidity won't affect the adhesive holding the abrasive to the paper.

Flexing paper
Sandpaper is usually stiff and brittle, making it tough to fold and likely to leave scuff marks on the work surface. To make the paper more flexible, pull it, with the grit side up, back and forth over the edge of a table or workbench.

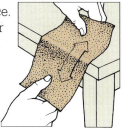

Hack it up
If you cut a lot of sandpaper, here's one way to save time and effort. Screw a hacksaw blade to the edge of a piece of plywood; the teeth should point up and jut above the plywood. For a fence, glue or screw a straightedge or ruler along one side of the plywood. Draw lines at often-used intervals for easy measuring. ▼

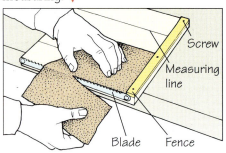

TYPES OF SANDPAPER

Sandpaper (more properly, abrasive paper) is available in a bewildering number of types. Here are some choices and the jobs that they best suit.

SANDPAPER	CHARACTERISTICS	USES
Aluminium oxide (bonded to paper)	Familiar light brown paper with tough, durable synthetic grains.	Good general-purpose sandpaper for the money.
Aluminium oxide (bonded to pad)	Bonded to a pad, this aluminium oxide abrasive can be rinsed and used a number of times, wet or dry. Fast-cutting and long-lasting but expensive.	Good for woodworking.
Emery	This has a fine natural abrasive bonded to a cloth backing. Grit described in words ("fine"), not numbers (see below).	Used for polishing metal.
Garnet	Reddish in colour. Garnet grains fracture during use, exposing fresh, sharp cutting edges; cuts quickly but wears quickly too.	Good all-purpose abrasive, particularly for hand-sanding.
Silicon carbide	Black wet or dry paper; has hardest grit and removes material very quickly. Can be wet with water or oil to keep it from gumming up. Available only in fine grits.	Ideal for very fine sanding, such as between coats of varnish and other finishes. Hard enough to sand metal.

GRADES OF SANDPAPER

Sandpaper is classified by a number reflecting the size of the grit particles on it. Higher numbers indicate smaller grains for finer sanding. Here are the common grades of sandpaper with their grit numbers and uses.

GRIT	TEXTURE	USE
50 – 60	Coarse	Rough sanding and shaping; removing paint.
80 – 100	Medium	Intermediate sanding after rough sanding; sanding on previously painted surfaces.
120–150	Fine	Final sanding before applying finish.
160–240	Very fine	Smoothing primer and paint.
280–320	Extra-fine	Smoothing between undercoats.
360–400	Superfine	Wet-sanding varnish or lacquer for ultrasmooth finish.

HAND-SANDING

Sanding can make or break a wood project's appearance. Even perfect-looking factory-planed wood needs hand-sanding to open the grain and promote even staining. A final hand-sanding is also essential to remove the tiny swirl marks left by oscillating power sanders. For professional-looking results, follow these tips:

Use the right grit size. Depending on the smoothness of the surface, start with 60-grit paper (for example, on work that has been cut on a table saw or run through a jointer or planer). Progress through finer grits, such as 80, 100, and 120, without skipping any steps. Your first, coarsest sanding should flatten high spots. Subsequent sandings should replace larger scratches with finer ones. Where to stop depends on the work. In general, sand surfaces to be painted to 120 grit, sand fine objects to be stained and varnished to about 150. An ultrasmooth oiled finish may require even finer grits and a longer progression, such as 120, 150, 180, and 220, then polishing with 400 wet-or-dry paper and oil.

Sand with the grain. Sanding at an angle to the grain leaves scratches that are difficult to remove. Overlap sanding strokes and apply equal pressure on both forward and backward strokes. Sand across the grain only when you want to remove a large amount of wood; then follow up by thoroughly sanding with the grain.

Use a sanding block. With a flat backing, sandpaper can remove bumps and span low spots. Buy a sanding block or fit a half sheet of paper around a 20 x 100 x 100 mm wood block. Don't use your fingers on flat surfaces—the sandpaper will follow any irregularities in the wood, leaving a wavy surface.

Don't sand out gouges and dents. You'll get wide, shallow, very noticeable craters. Instead, fill any deep scratches with wood putty; try raising dents with a steam iron (p 239).

Use a sanding block to ensure flat sanding, but take care not to let the block go more than halfway off the end of the workpiece, or it'll round the edge.

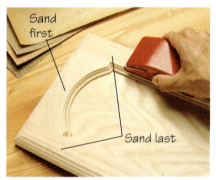

Avoid cross-grain scratches on pieces that butt at an angle by first sanding the piece with its ends set to the adjacent pieces, then the pieces with free ends.

A sanding sponge is a good alternative for sanding rounded or irregularly shaped pieces. You can also use a sponge for sanding wet surfaces.

Wet-sand between coats of varnish to produce a very smooth satin finish. Use 400- or 600-grit wet or dry silicon carbide paper on a block with water or oil.

SANDING

Odd shapes and sizes

Mopping about
For sanding walls and ceilings before painting, or for smoothing wallboard joints, you can buy a pole sander—or you can make one from your sponge mop. Remove the sponge, wrap a sheet of sandpaper around a block of wood the same size as the sponge and attach it to the mop. The frame will hold the paper to the block. You can also use a wider block for greater coverage. ▼

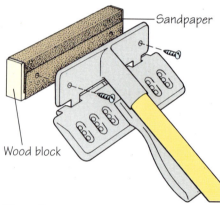

Shapely paper
You need to use sandpaper with a firm supportive backing when sanding a flat surface, but not if you have to sand any curved shapes. Then you can shape sandpaper with your fingers or the palm of your hand to match the contour of a rounded or irregularly shaped surface. To sand a long turning, such as a chair leg, wrap the sandpaper around the wood (make sure the ends overlap) and slide the paper up and down. For shorter sections on a curve, hold a strip of sandpaper at both ends and run it back and forth over the area as if you were shining a shoe.

A crooked deck
If a sanding sponge isn't handy when you need to smooth a curved surface, improvise one with a deck of playing cards. Wrap sandpaper around the deck, hold it on edge, and press it firmly against the surface. The cards will conform to the shape of the work and sand it evenly.

Matching curves
To smooth curved indentations, cut a short piece of old garden hose and make a slit down its length. Wrap sandpaper around the hose and tuck the ends into the slit. For smaller grooves, wrap the sandpaper around a wooden dowel, or fold it and fit the crease into the groove; apply pressure alternately on each side of the groove. For larger surfaces, wrap sandpaper around a cylindrical plastic container. When smoothing long mouldings, loop and staple a length of sandpaper so that it slips over your hand like a mitt.

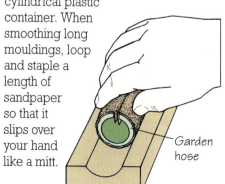

Not just a nail file ▲
Intricate cuts and small, hard-to-reach places can be easy to sand if you use emery boards; they're easily handled and provide two sanding grits. Glue other grades onto them if necessary.

Sticky fingers, longer reach
Sand hard-to-reach areas by attaching a small piece of double-sided tape to your fingertip. Stick a small square of sandpaper onto it. You'll have a good feel for the surface you're sanding and greater control over the work. You can also try this: sew a square of Velcro to the end of one finger of a glove and attach small squares to it as necessary. Sanding discs use this backing so cut up one or two in fine and medium grades.

Holding the work

Padded workbench
To keep the bottom of a workpiece from being scratched while you're sanding the top, use a rubber-backed carpet scrap as a pad for your workbench. When you've finished sanding, clean the carpet with a vacuum cleaner.

Against the grit 1
When sanding small parts, it's easier to rub the part against the sandpaper than vice versa. To make the job even easier, fasten the sandpaper onto a sturdy base with spring clips. ▼

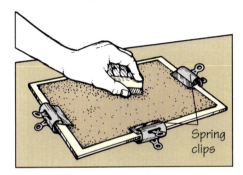

Against the grit 2
To rub pieces against sandpaper, cover a block of wood with sandpaper, using a rubber band to secure the edges. Then hold the block in a vice.

On a stick
Another way to sand small items is to dab hot glue on the back of the piece and stick it on the end of a dowel. Hold the work by the dowel while sanding. To unstick the piece, pop the assembly into the freezer for a few minutes. The cold will quickly free the workpiece.

Power-sanding

Snagging stockings
A problem with power sanders is they don't tell you when the job is done. To test for smoothness, slip a pantihose over your hand and pass it lightly over the work in the direction of the grain. Rough spots will snag the material.

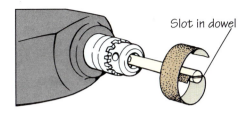

Creating a flap ▲
To sand the inside of a hole that is too small for a drum sander, make a flap sander with a 150 mm length of 10 mm dowel. Using a thin saw blade, cut a slot in one end of the dowel. Chuck the opposite end into a drill, and slip a strip cut from a sanding belt into the slot. With the slotted end of the dowel facing you, wrap the strip clockwise around the dowel. The grit side of the strip should now be on the outside; if it is, hot-glue the strip in the dowel.

Take a belt to it
Here's a way to keep the edges of a project from being rounded off by your belt sander. Take pieces of scrap wood of the same thickness as the work and secure them to both ends of the work, flush to its surface. Tack the scrap pieces in place with nails or clamp them on, making sure the clamps won't interfere with the sander. The sander will round off the scrap, not the work.

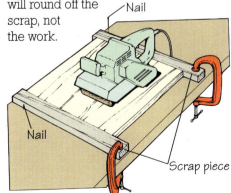

Recycling sanding discs
When sanding a painted surface, the discs become clogged and glazed long before they wear out. To get more life out of a disc, apply a coat of semi-paste water-soluble paint remover to the encrusted area. Let the remover stand on the disc until the paint has softened; then wash it off.

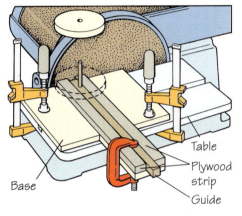

Sanding circles ▲
Sanding of wheels and other circular objects is easy with this custom-made disc sander jig. First, make a T-shaped base using 16 mm plywood. Cut a piece of wood to be used as a guide, and drill a hole in one end for a dowel. Centre the guide on the base; then nail or glue 16 mm plywood strips along each side of the guide, creating a channel. The guide should be held firmly in place yet be able to slide smoothly in the channel. Glue a dowel into the hole in the guide. To use the jig, clamp the base to your disc sander table. After you place the work on the dowel, adjust the guide so the work sits snugly at the disc; clamp it in place. Make sure the work sits on the left side of the disc.

CLAMPING

The basics

Dos and don'ts
Here are some pointers to keep in mind when you're clamping:
▷ Don't rely on clamps to make good a poorly fitting joint. Glue and pressure may hold things together for a while, but in the long run the joint will fail. Plane or sand the pieces until they fit properly.
▷ Before applying glue, test-fit the parts. Preset the clamps so they're ready to apply pressure with just a few twists.
▷ Never force a clamp or use a wrench to tighten it. If the clamp isn't strong enough, use a bigger one or add another clamp next to it.
▷ Too much clamping pressure can squeeze all the glue out of the joint and compress the wood fibres. Too little pressure can result in a glue line that is too thick and therefore weak. An even ridge of glue between clamped parts, at the top and the bottom, indicates proper pressure.
▷ Leave the clamps on for the recommended length of time. Most glues specify a minimum clamping time.

Spreading pressure
Clamp heads exert a cone-shaped area of force. To distribute pressure over a wider area (and to protect the work from damage), place scrap wood or angle irons between the work and the clamp heads.

Scrap wood spreads pressure

G-clamp

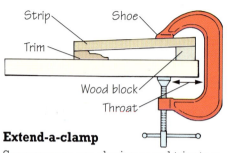

Strip, Shoe, Trim, Wood block, Throat

Extend-a-clamp
Suppose you are glueing wood trim to a flat workpiece and your G-clamp can't reach the joint because it has a shallow throat. Here's a way to increase the clamp's reach using only a strip of wood and a block of wood that's thicker than the trim. Place the block near the edge of the workpiece, position the strip under the clamp shoe so that it spans the gap between the block and the trim, and clamp down. The strip will transfer pressure to the joint.

Coupled... for a job
If a workpiece is too wide for one G-clamp to span it and you have no suitable substitute, combine two G-clamps as shown. This trick will work well in situations that require only light clamping pressure. Don't try it if you need to apply heavy pressure.

No more bouncing ball
It isn't easy to hold a curved, irregular piece tightly in a mitre box. An ordinary soft rubber ball can provide a good way around this problem. Cut off a piece of the ball to create a flat area, and glue a film canister cap to the opposite side. Place the cut side of the ball against the workpiece and the clamp head in the cap. Clamp the ball and workpiece securely in place. The ball will conform to fit any shape and won't scratch the work.

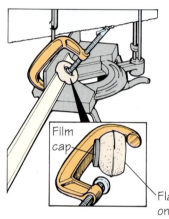

Film cap, Flat face cut on ball

On edge
If you don't have an edge clamp and tape isn't suitable for the job, use shims with a G-clamp. Drive wedge-shaped shims between the edge piece and the back of the clamp until they fit snugly. ▼

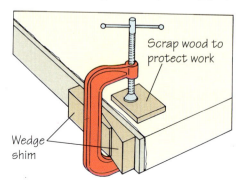

Scrap wood to protect work, Wedge shim

Hand screw

Jaw lineup

Mark the handles on your hand screw to quickly set the jaws parallel. With the jaws closed and parallel, apply a narrow paint line or other mark down the centre of each hand grip. No matter how wide apart the jaws are set, if you keep the lines in the same relationship to each other, the jaws will be parallel. Keep in mind that the jaws can also be set at an angle if the job calls for it.

Working together

Use pairs of hand screws to hold oddly placed pieces together, as shown at right. If you don't have a woodworker's vice,  use a combination of hand screws, bar clamps, and G-clamps to hold a workpiece for planing, sanding, chiselling, or shaping. A setup like the one below will allow you to work without interference from the clamps. ▼

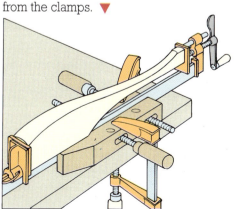

Pipe clamp

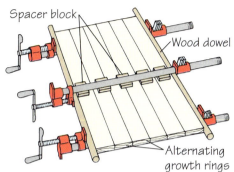

No warpage here ▲

Here are a few tricks for glueing strips edge to edge. When you glue up boards that will form an overhanging surface, such as a tabletop on a pedestal, set the boards with the growth rings alternating up and down. To hold any glue-up, stagger pipe clamps above and below the workpiece, adding spacer blocks to keep the clamp pressure in line with the boards. If the clamp jaws are longer than the thickness of the work, angle them so that they make more contact with the work. Or place a wood dowel lengthwise on each side of the work to redirect the clamping force.

Clamping a trapezium

To clamp shapes with unequal parallel sides, such as a chair seat frame, you'll have to create right-angle clamping surfaces. Place scrap wood against the two parallel edges as shown; this allows the clamps to seat properly and to apply pressure at the proper angle.

Custom-made block

Round or elliptical edge pieces, which are common in tabletops, can be clamped together with the help of a block that fits snugly around the workpiece. You can also make blocks to match other unusual shapes. If you have trouble steadying the block while applying the clamp, hot-glue it in place and break it off when you've finished. ▼

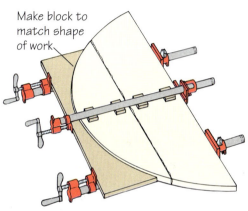

Hold the door

Secure a door in a vertical position for planing or mortising by using pipe clamps or hand screws. Stagger the pipe clamps, alternating left and right, along the bottom edge of the door. ▼

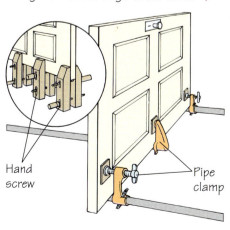

CLAMPING

Makeshift clamps

Spring clamp look-alikes
Here are two substitutes for a spring clamp: large battery clips from an old damaged jumper cable will accept work up to about 38 mm thick, and the spring clip on the end of a clothes hanger will hold a small workpiece. The jaws of some hanger clips are padded with felt strips that will protect your work from marring.

Mousetrap technology
You can turn a mousetrap into a strong, versatile, wide-grip clamp. Prise off the bait holder and cut off the hold-down side of the base before applying the other half to the work.

Gun clamp
A caulk gun is ideal for applying light pressure to small pieces. Place the work between pieces of scrap wood, and then position the assembly between the jaws of the gun. The scraps protect the work and provide a flat surface for even pressure. To apply pressure to the work, squeeze the trigger.

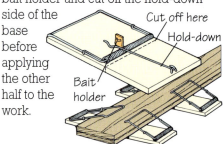

Rubber-band clamps
Sometimes clamps just don't work well for glueing small or irregularly shaped objects. To hold such pieces together, keep a variety of large rubber bands in your workshop.

It will work at a stretch
Rubber cords are an ideal substitute for band clamps. Because the cords are not adjustable, keep a variety of sizes in stock. You can combine short cords to make longer ones. Wrap long cords around small pieces several times or in a figure 8.

From the garage
An ordinary hose clamp, like one found on a motorcar hose, is just right for clamping a cracked or split wooden leg or spindle. This clamp is inexpensive, comes in a variety of sizes, and provides good uniform pressure when tightened. Slip a piece of cloth or vinyl under the band to prevent marring.

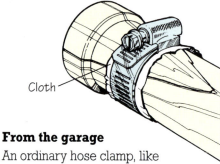

Big mouth
For a longer reach, you can extend the jaws on a pipe clamp. In two wood blocks, drill holes large enough for the pipe to fit through; then carve out jaws to concentrate the pressure. Use rubber bands to secure the blocks to the clamp heads as shown, and slip the assemblies onto the pipe.

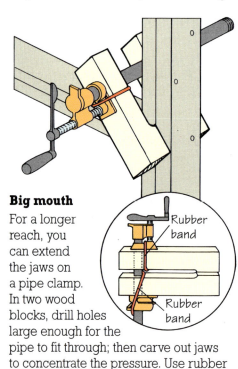

86 / Workshop Skills

Homemade clamps

Bag it

When you need to clamp irregular shapes, hold them together with a sandbag. For small fragile items, use a small plastic bag filled with sand. Use larger sand-filled bags for big items. For outdoor projects, try plastic bags or containers filled with water.

Tourniquet a frame

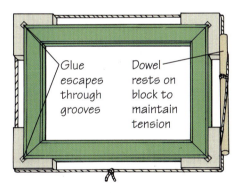

Holding mitred corner pieces together is simple with this tourniquet clamp. Make four L-shaped corner blocks. Rout or chisel grooves on the outer edges to guide the twine, and make vertical grooves at the inside corners to allow excess glue to escape. Place the blocks in position and run twine around the perimeter. To exert pressure, wrap a dowel or stick in the twine and twist it.

Holding a scarf

Here's an easy way to spread pressure evenly along a scarf joint. When you cut off the ends of the work, save the triangular scrap pieces. When you're ready to clamp, place the scraps between the work and the clamp as shown. ▼

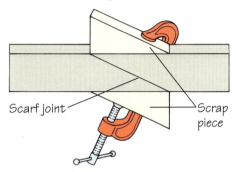

Edgy situation

If you run out of clamps in the middle of a project, you can make your own out of scrap timber. Screw one block to each end of a length of board that's slightly longer than the workpiece. Attach each block with only one screw so that it will pivot into alignment. Cut two wedge-shaped pieces of wood, and drive them between one of the blocks and the workpiece for a tight hold. ▼

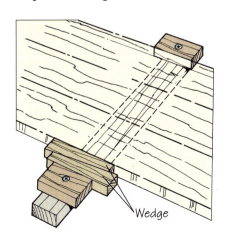

H-frame

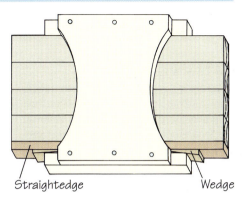

This jig is ideal for glueing two or more boards edge to edge (the long legs of the frame will apply equal pressure along the boards). The jig is easy to make out of offcuts and 16 mm plywood. To reduce the weight of the frame, cut the plywood as shown. Wedges pushed between the straightedge and the jig exert the necessary clamping pressure.

Extending the top

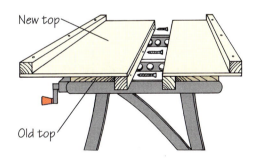

By building a larger top for your portable workbench, you can use it to clamp large objects. Make the new top out of 16 mm plywood and four lengths of 30 x 30 mm pine. One side of the new top should be slightly wider than the underlying side of the old top; the other side should be about twice as wide. Attach both sides of the new top to the original top with screws, as shown.

Workshop Skills / 87

GLUEING

Applying glue

Wait for it to dry
When using water-base glue on a joint, allow adequate time for it to set before painting or varnishing the unit. Enamel paint or varnish will seal the wood and prevent the glue setting properly, and the joint might come apart later, causing an injury. Bear in mind that glue may take longer to set in cool or damp weather and you should allow extra time in such conditions.

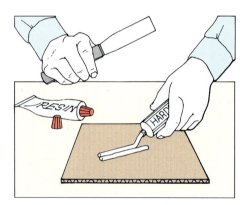

Epoxy mix-up ▲
For a strong epoxy bond, you must mix resin and hardener in equal parts. An easy way to gauge the proportions is to squeeze out the resin and hardener in parallel lines of equal width and length.

Dry run
Here's a good way to tell when glue has dried. At the same time you apply glue to your work, glue together two scrap pieces of the same material as the work. Test the scraps to determine when the work is dry. If the glue label lists a specific length of drying time, you can jot it down on the wood as a reference.

Make it hot
When applying hot glue to a large area, you may find that the glue is setting too fast. To slow down the setting time, try warming the work with a heat gun. Or put the work out in the sun for a while. After the glue has set, you can scrape off any excess with a utility knife.

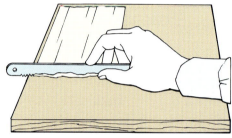

Spreading the glue ▲
A broken hacksaw blade spreads glue quickly over a large, flat area. The teeth let the glue flow easily and keep it to a smooth, even depth throughout.

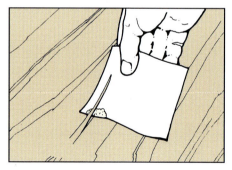

Slivery move ▲
To glue down a wood sliver, dab a spot of glue on the top side of a piece of paper. Slip the paper under the sliver; then pull the paper out, making sure that the glue coats the underside of the sliver. Tape or clamp the sliver in place until the glue dries; then sand the area.

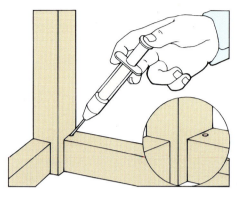

Sure-shot injector ▲
A medical syringe from your pharmacy is ideal for injecting glue into narrow places, such as in a hole made to reach a loose tenon. After filling the syringe barrel, insert the plunger and hold it upward while you depress it. This will expel air bubbles and prevent the glue from drying out. To store glue in the syringe, use a plastic needle protector to stop the glue drying.

A tight squeeze
As model makers know, toothpicks or dental picks are great for applying glue in tight areas with precise control. ▼

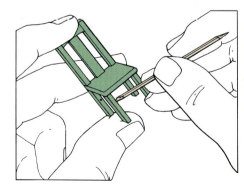

Excess glue

Oozing cure

If you can keep squeezed-out glue off the edges of the wood you're clamping, you'll avoid the bother of removing excess glue later. Here's a trick that will save you time and effort. Before glueing the pieces, clamp them together and apply tape over the joint. Slit the tape along the joint with a utility knife; then remove the clamps. Apply the glue and reclamp the pieces. This way the glue will ooze onto the tape rather than the wood. Once the glue has set, peel off the tape. ▼

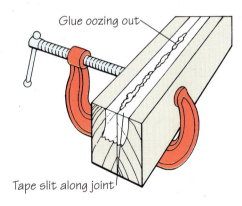

Give it some room

As you make a mortise-and-tenon or a dowel joint, leave extra space at the bottom of the recess. Excess glue will drain there instead of squeezing out of the joint. Chamfer the top edges of the holes for the same effect. There is another option as well—drilling a tiny hole from the far side of the joint will provide an escape route for excess glue. If it is 1 or 2 mm only, it will be almost invisible when filled.

No sticky clamps here

To avoid getting glue on your clamps, place two layers of wax paper strips between the clamp and the work. Make convenient-size strips by cutting a roll of wax paper into 100 mm sections; then, when you need the paper, rip off the appropriate lengths. If you run out of wax paper, cut a plastic bag into strips and use them instead. ▼

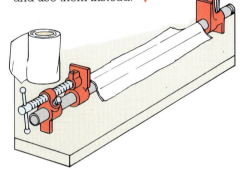

Cleaning up

Sip it up

A drinking straw is a handy instrument for removing excess glue from an inside corner. Slightly crease one end of the straw so that it fits into the corner. The glue will move up the straw as you push it along the joint. ▼

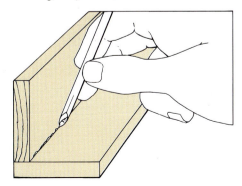

Take it off

Because dried glue won't take stain, it's important to remove any excess before it dries. Use a wet cloth to wipe off water-base glues. To avoid leaving behind a film of glue, rinse out the cloth periodically and make the final wipe with a well-rinsed cloth. (To remove non-water-base glues, use the appropriate solvent.) Sanding will take care of whatever glue residue may remain.

Too late for wiping

If squeezed-out glue has dried to a semi-hard state, use a putty knife to scrape it off. If the glue has dried completely, use a paint scraper to remove it. After scraping, sand the area to eliminate all remaining traces of glue. ▼

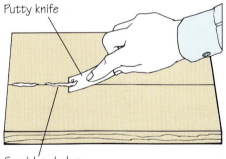

Splotchy job

Before applying a finish, make sure you really have removed all the glue. By wetting the surface with mineral spirits or a lacquer thinner, any glue splotches will show up clearly. (They will stay light-coloured while the rest of the area darkens.) Remove the glue from those spots so that they won't mar your finish. It's best to remove water-base glue when it is still wet, so keep a damp cloth handy when glueing.

Workshop Skills / 89

FINISHING WOOD

Filler

For all those guitarists
Save your old plastic guitar plectrums. Their flexibility makes them ideal for applying putty to nail holes and small nicks in woodwork. ▼

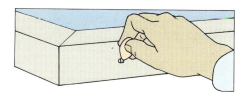

Knotty putty
To fill nail holes in knotty pine, mix raw sienna–coloured acrylic or dry powder paint with wood putty. Make about four mixtures, varying in shades from very light to dark brown. Apply the shades to match the knotty wood. For nail holes in regular unknotted wood, make your own filler by mixing sawdust from the wood with white glue.

Open pores
If you want a high-gloss smooth finish in an open-grained wood like oak, walnut, or mahogany, fill the pores with paste filler. (For a satin or more natural finish, the filler isn't needed.) For a light stain, apply a mixture of the stain and filler. For a dark stain, apply coats of the stain until it's a shade or two lighter than desired; apply the filler mixture as a final coat. Use a plastic card to spread the filler mixture; hold the card with a long side flexed on the wood. Spread the filler diagonally across the grain in each direction, then back and forth with the grain. Scrape off any excess filler with the card. Let the filler dry; then sand it.

From the container

Pour away
Here's how to avoid making a mess when pouring finish, thinner, or any other liquid from an oblong container: Just make sure you hold the tin so that the opening is at the top. The liquid will leave the container in a steady stream.

Nutty stain mixer
When you open a tin of wood stain, drop two medium-size steel nuts into it. Then each time you use the stain, shake the tin to thoroughly stir the contents. (Never do this in a glass jar.) You'll be able to hear when the pigments are no longer sitting at the bottom of the tin. Don't try this trick with varnish. Shaking or stirring varnish can create air bubbles that can ruin the finish.

A different filter
Have you run out of paint filters for removing impurities from thinners and light finishing oils, and you don't want to make a special trip to the store? Instead of a filter, use a clean disposable paper dust mask—it's a perfect substitute.

Out of the kitchen
These two kitchen tools are ideal for removing a small amount of liquid from a large container: A gravy ladle is handy for scooping up stain. A turkey baster is ideal for transferring mineral spirits and other solvents. (But if the baster has a plastic tube, first test it to make sure the solvent doesn't soften the tube.)

Applying the finish

Oily hands ▲
Your hands secrete natural oils that can mark unfinished wood. To protect the work, rub sawdust between your hands before handling the stock. The sawdust will draw out and absorb the excess oil. Repeat the procedure every so often.

Finish off those chipboard ends

One can get a good result on chipboard surfaces, but the ends of panels often pose a problem because they're so rough. But you can get a smooth result by spreading woodfiller on the edges and working it well into the fibres. Then sand with fine sandpaper to smooth it before applying paint or varnish

Layer by layer

For professional results, follow this work sequence when staining and varnishing: Before starting the job, use scrap wood to test how the stain and varnish will colour the wood. When you're ready to begin the sequence, apply the stain; then follow with the sealer and the coats of varnish. Sand the workpiece after sealing it and between coats of varnish. To prevent warping, make sure you finish every side—even bottoms and backs. This helps keep moisture from entering the wood.

Pour it in

Fitting a brush into a deep recess can be difficult at best. To make the job easier, thin the finish to one-half or one-third of its strength; then pour it into the recess. The thinned finish is less likely to drip. Swirl the finish around to cover the bottom and sides, then pour the excess back into the container. For complete coverage, repeat the process.

The dark end

When finishing a new wood project, treat the end grain last to keep it from staining darker than the rest of the work. Brush turpentine, paint thinner, or mineral spirits onto the end grain just before applying the stain.

Safe finish

To finish wood projects that will hold food or are likely to be chewed on by young children, use mineral oil, salad oil (walnut oil is best), or other non-toxic finish. Check with an authority if in any doubt about a product's suitability.

Bright idea ▲

After applying a finish to wood, you'll want to know if you've missed any spots. Here's the best way to check: Examine the work at a 45° angle while shining a bright light on it. The wet finish will reflect the light; missed spots will show up as dull areas.

ABOUT FINISHES

▷ Buy flammable liquids, such as tung oil, varnish, and thinners, in quantities that are just enough to do the job.

▷ Their vapours can ignite, so store flammable liquids in tightly sealed containers, away from the work area and heaters and out of reach of children.

▷ Keep a fire extinguisher in your work area. Never smoke in this area or near flammable liquids.

▷ Solvent-base liquids are a skin irritant; wear chemical-resistant rubber gloves when using them.

▷ Items soaked in natural oil-base finishes (tung oil, linseed oil, gel stains, and wipe-on finishes) can ignite or explode if exposed to air and then confined. Before disposing of brushes, cloths, and other materials exposed to one of these finishes, hang them from a line outside, away from children and pets, until they are dry.

▷ To dispose of leftover finishes, see p 39.

FINISHING WOOD

Equipment

Make it tacky
Use a tack rag to remove dust from a workpiece before applying the first coat of stain or finish, and between coats. You can make your own tack rag out of cheesecloth, an old cotton nappy, or any other lint-free cotton cloth. Dip the cloth in turpentine and wring it out. Then drizzle a small amount of varnish or polyurethane from a stirring stick onto the cloth, and knead the cloth to distribute the finish. The cloth should be able to pick up dust without leaving any finish. To avoid spontaneous combustion, store the rag in a tightly sealed tin.

Absorbent stockings
A rag used to apply a stain may leave lint particles all over the work. To avoid this problem, use discarded nylon stockings or pantihose as an applicator. The material leaves a lint-free finish and also absorbs less stain than some cloth applicators. ▼

Store them for later
Don't let your stain rags dry out in the middle of a project. When you finish for the day, store them in an empty stain tin. Be sure the lid seals the tin tightly, both to keep the rags from drying out and to prevent spontaneous combustion. The rags can be used for a quick touch-up without having to be dipped in the stain again.

Off the cuff
Tired of having stain or finish drip down your arm as you apply it overhead? Wear a long rubber glove on your working hand. Turn up the cuff a few centimetres and stuff it with toilet paper. The paper will catch the drips and absorb them, so you won't have to worry about spills when you lower your arm.

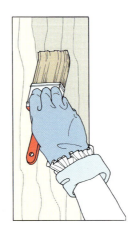

Loose bristles
Brushes lose bristles when first used. Before using a brush for the first time, soak it in the finish for 30 minutes; then clean it and let it stand overnight. The dried finish in the ferrule will bond the bristles. To remove any bristles that do come loose, wait for the finish to dry; then pick them out with a knife.

Miniature brush
To apply finishes in hard-to-reach areas, such as crevices on mouldings, recycle an old soft-bristle toothbrush.

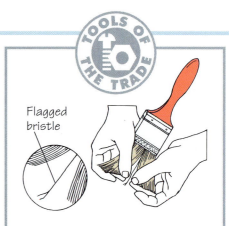

Flagged bristle

THE RIGHT BRUSH

One key to a successful finishing job is picking the right brush—or, more to the point, the right bristle—for the type of finish you'll be applying.

For oil varnish and polyurethane, use a brush with natural China bristles (black or white hog hairs). Look for long supple flagged or tapered bristles and a chiselled profile.

For water-base finishes, use synthetic-bristle brushes. (Natural bristles lose their shape in water.) Avoid flagged bristles; they can make the finish foam.

Always look for the best brush you can find. A good-quality brush is worth its price. Select one with a stainless steel ferrule; it won't leave rust marks.

Before dipping a brush in finish, soak it in the appropriate solvent; then squeeze it out. Make sure you clean the brush and reshape the bristles as soon as you've applied the finish.

Neatness counts

Bring out the Yellow Pages
Open up an old telephone book or catalogue and use it as a work surface for small finishing jobs. As the pages get messy, just rip them out and toss them away—it will take quite some time to use up all those pages.

Knob work
Finishing drawer knobs can be a messy proposition. Here's a way to keep your fingers free of finish by using the screw that secures the knob to the drawer. Fit the screw to the knob; then hold the screw with a clothes peg while you apply the finish. When the job is done, balance the assembly in an upright position on a flat surface until the finish dries.

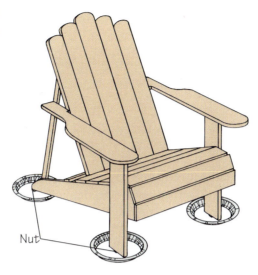

Leg rests ▲
For rot-free legs on outdoor chairs, soak them in wood preservative. To let the preservative soak in, stand the chair in disposable aluminium pie plates with a nut under each leg. Pour preservative into the plates and let the legs soak overnight. (The nuts raise the legs just enough for the preservative to soak in.)

Give it a lift
When applying finish to table or chair legs, keep the legs from sticking to the work surface by slipping washers under them. The diameter of the washers must be smaller than the diameter of the legs.

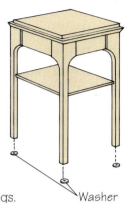

It's a hold-up
This contraption will allow you to elevate a small project off the work surface while you finish it. Cut 6 mm dowels into 100 mm lengths and sharpen both ends in a pencil sharpener. Push the dowels into a base made of foam insulation and rest the workpiece on them. Make sure you use enough so that the work doesn't tip over. ▼

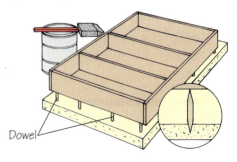

Suspended on nails
Here's a way to cut drying time when you're finishing (or painting) a door. Drive 75 mm nails into the top and bottom of the door, and then rest the nails on sawhorses. After you apply the finish on one side, flip the door over (use the nails as handles with a helper at the other end) and apply the finish to the other side. Both sides will dry at the same time. If you're working in a dusty area, use this method to suspend the work with one finished side facing down until it dries.

For those forgetful folks
Prepare for future touch-ups or refinishing jobs by keeping a record of your work. Before applying the finish, stick a label or glue a bit of paper to an inconspicuous area of the project. Record the type of wood, stain, and finish you used, and the date. The finish you apply over the paper will hold it in place.

METALWORKING

Clean holes

Sandwich time
To avoid rough or bent edges when you're drilling a hole in sheet metal, clamp the metal between two pieces of scrap wood and drill through the assembly. This trick will produce clean holes whether you use a portable drill or a drill press. It will also produce clean lines when you're cutting sheet metal with a hacksaw or jigsaw.

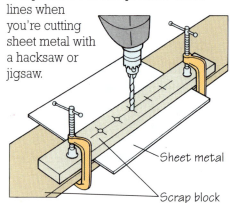

Removing burrs
Even if you've drilled a hole in sheet metal without sandwiching it in scrap wood, you can still get a clean hole. Just twirl a countersink bit in the hole a few times to remove the burrs. ▼

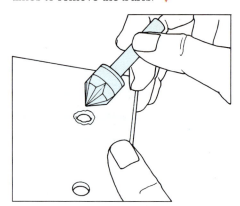

No more wandering bit
When drilling in metal, as in other materials (p 9), you can keep the drill bit from wandering off centre by dimpling the surface with a centre punch. Don't forget to add light motor oil to the hole to keep the bit from overheating (p 10). Lubrication will also speed cutting time and keep the bit from becoming dull.

Drilling deep
A good way to keep the bit lubricated when drilling in thick metal is to form a wall out of modelling clay around the area to be drilled, thus creating a circular dam. Fill the dam with light machine oil. Keep extra oil on hand to replenish the dam as needed.

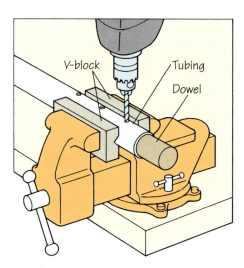

Straight through ▲
To drill holes in tubing, secure it in V-blocks clamped in a vice. Insert a dowel inside the tubing to reinforce the thin walls and to guide the bit straight through to the other side. Punch a small depression in the tube wall to stop the bit skidding off the surface.

On file

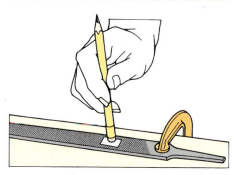

Too small for a vice ▲
Sometimes you may want to file a piece of metal that is too small to grip in a vice or to hold with your fingers. The solution is to move the piece against the file with an eraser-tipped pencil. Clamp or hold the file firmly on a work surface.

Cover up
While you are using a file, the unused side can mar your work. To protect the work from scratches, cover the file's unused side with tape.

Chalky filler
Soft metals, such as aluminium, copper and brass, clog the teeth of some files. To reduce clogging, first rub talcum powder or a piece of chalk across the file teeth. The powder keeps the metal from caking up and allows the chips to be cleaned out easily with a file card.

Clean up

Never blow on a file to remove metal particles. They might wind up in your eyes and cause serious injury. If you don't have a file card, remove the filings from the file by pressing putty or masking tape onto the cutting surface. When you pull the putty or tape off the file, the particles will come off too.

Saw power

Nick a notch

Before making a hacksaw cut, create a starting notch for the blade by nicking the workpiece at the cut line with a file. The notch will act as a guide, preventing the blade from slipping. (On a round piece of metal, use a three-cornered file to cut a V-shaped notch.)

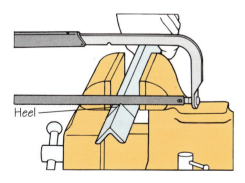

Cut the heel

When cutting a steel angle with a hacksaw, secure the angle in a vice with the heel end up. This way, the hacksaw will cut both sides of the angle at the same time. And because more saw teeth are in contact with the work, the resulting cut will be smoother and more accurate.

Stop that annoying chatter

When cutting steel, aluminium or brass plate in a bench vice, the free end lets out a noisy chatter or screech with every stroke of a hacksaw. To stop the racket, wrap the free end of the workpiece in a wet towel or cloth. This will dampen the offending vibrations and calm your nerves too.

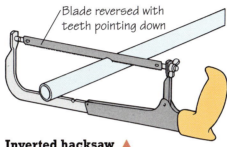

Inverted hacksaw ▲

If you have a hacksaw job to do but no room to use the saw, here's a way around your problem. Simply remove the blade and reinsert it in an inverted position. This trick is especially handy when cutting an overhead pipe.

Oily cut ▶

Aluminium and other soft metals are best cut with a jigsaw that is equipped with a fine-tooth blade. To keep the teeth on the blade from clogging, apply light machine oil along the cut line. The oil will also keep the blade cooler and sharper.

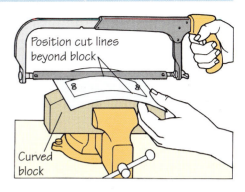

A rectangular hole ▲

It's possible to make a rectangular inside cut in sheet metal with a hacksaw without cutting in from the edge. First saw a curve in a block of scrap wood. Clamp the wood, curved edge up, in a vice. Mark cut lines on the sheet metal, make two holes in the waste area and hold the workpiece in place with two pushpins. The sheet will be bent, with its centre highest. Make the two cuts along the length of the block. Then remove and reposition the work to make the last two saw cuts.

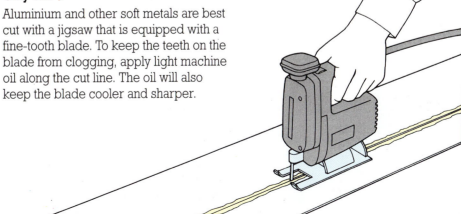

METALWORKING

Fastener facts

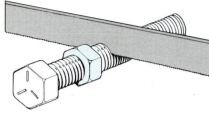

Customized bolt ▲
If a bolt is too long for the intended job, you can cut it to size with a hacksaw; but first put a nut onto the bolt past the cut mark. Unscrewing the nut after cutting cleans the threads and removes any burrs at the cut end. To make the newly cut bolt even easier to thread, bevel the end with a grinder or file.

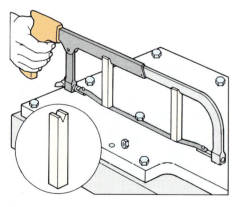

Flush cut ▲
With slight adaptations to a hacksaw, you can cut a bolt or screw flush to the work. Notch one end of two 85 mm long pieces of scrap wood. Loosen the saw blade and rotate it until the teeth point sideways. Place the wood pieces between the saw frame and the turned blade, and tighten the blade. The wood will push the blade down slightly below the saw frame, letting you make the cut.

Rusted nut and bolt
One way to remove a rusted nut and bolt is to apply penetrating oil (p 14). To keep the oil where it will do the most good, build a circular dam around the nut with wood putty or modelling clay. The dam not only holds the oil, it lets you soak the whole nut.

Take a hack at it
Here's how to remove a rusted nut without damaging the threads of the bolt. Use a hacksaw to make a starting cut in the nut, parallel to one of its faces; then split the nut with a cold chisel. (Make sure you wear safety glasses when doing this.) Now it's a simple job to remove the nut.

Too loose for comfort?
To keep nuts and bolts from coming loose, apply a small dab of clear silicone caulk on the bolt threads before you tighten the nut. For added insurance, smear a large dab of silicone caulk over any exposed threads. Once it's dry, the fasteners won't be able to work loose; but if you have to remove them, the caulk will easily peel off.

Sheet metal

Make it clear
Before marking metal with a scriber or awl, run a dark-coloured, wide-tipped felt marker over the area to be scribed. The scribe marks will show up more clearly against the dark background.

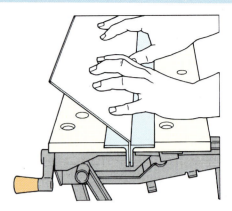

Homemade brake ▲
Turn your portable workbench and two pieces of metal angle into a homemade bending brake. The metal angles should have sharp 90° edges so that the sheet metal creases evenly. Place the angles in the workbench as shown. Start the fold by hand; then finish it by pounding the metal with a hardwood block and mallet for a sharp crease. If you don't have a portable workbench, use G-clamps to clamp the angles together.

Get the dents out
Here are two ways to remove dents from metal objects. Hold the object against a sandbag and gently flatten out the raised side of the dent with a mallet. Or hold the face of a sledgehammer firmly against the dent and tap out its raised side with the flat face of a ball-peen hammer. The thinner the metal, the lighter the taps.

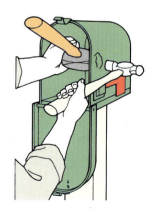

Soldering

Spool control
Chasing a runaway spool of solder can be a nuisance, especially if it rolls off the table and onto your foot first. To keep the solder from rolling about, bend out one rim of the spool. ▼

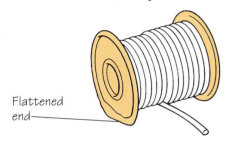

Flattened end

Dispensing solder
Clear plastic pill containers make excellent dispensers for thin wire solder. Just slip a coil of the solder into the container, pierce a hole in the cap, feed the solder through the hole, and snap the cap in place. Now all you have to do is pull out the solder as you need it. A plastic tape dispenser can also hold wire solder. Wind the wire around the empty spool, place it in the dispenser, and feed it through a hole drilled just below the serrated edge. (Break off the serrated edge to avoid cutting yourself on the teeth.)

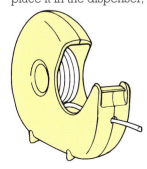

Cut to size
Join small parts more neatly with wire solder by first flattening it with a hammer and then cutting the solder with tin snips into three or more fine strands. ▼

Close quarters
If you have to solder two joints right next to each other, clamp a wet sponge over the first joint before soldering the second one. This will prevent heat from the soldering iron from reaching and loosening the first joint.

Resting place
Finding a place to put a hot soldering iron so it won't roll away or damage something can be tricky. One solution is to make a stand for the soldering iron out of a sturdy metal coat hanger by bending it as shown below. ▼

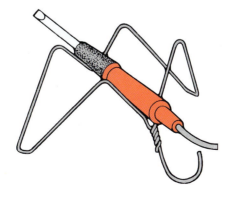

A clean tip
To ensure proper performance, it's important to keep the tip of your soldering gun or iron clean and bright at all times. Here's how to improvise your own tip cleaner. Stuff a pad of fine steel wool inside a shallow metal tin, such as a tuna fish or cat food tin, and crimp its edges. The crimped edges hold the steel wool in place, and they can also serve as a rest for the soldering iron. ▼

Clean tip by rubbing it against steel wool

Soldering iron

A chilling problem
When you're soldering outdoors on a cold day, the solder will get cold and draw heat away from the soldering iron. To remedy this problem, hammer the solder into a thin ribbon. It will melt almost instantly.

Wet cloth philosophy
When soldering copper plumbing pipes and fittings, keep a wet cloth handy to wipe the joint clean. After soldering the joint, wrap the cloth around it and turn the cloth with a twist of the wrist. This will not only result in a neater joint by removing excess solder; it will also fill any tiny holes in the solder, resulting in a more leakproof joint. While wiping the joint, be careful not to touch the hot pipe with your hand.

WORKING WITH GLASS

The equipment

Tape it down
To keep a metal straightedge from slipping when you cut glass, run a strip of thin double-sided tape along the cut line. Then lay the straightedge on the tape and make the cut with the glass cutter. The tape will keep the straightedge stationary.

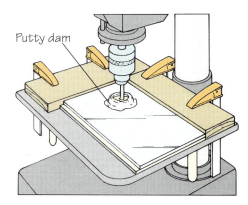

Here's a special bit ▲
Before installing handles, hinges, and other hardware in glass, you may have to drill a hole in the glass. For holes up to 10 mm in diameter, use a special spade-shaped glass bit in a drill press or hand drill. Surround the spot where you'll be drilling with a dam made out of putty. Fill the dam with turpentine, and run the drill slowly. For larger holes, use a circle cutter or have the job done by a glass supplier. Drill no closer than 25 mm to the edge of the glass. As always when handling glass, make sure you wear goggles and heavy gloves while you work.

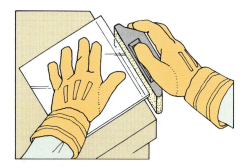

Smooth finish ▲
Rough edges can be smoothed with a silicone carbide stone or silicone carbide sandpaper supported with a block (p 81). Lubricate the edge with mineral spirits; lightly stroke the stone or block along the edge in one direction.

Supportive putty
Repairing a broken glass object, such as a champagne goblet, is easier if you support the pieces with putty while the glue sets. Because the putty will have to be positioned in several spots, test-fit the clean glass pieces on the putty before applying the glue. Use an epoxy adhesive specified for glass. ▼

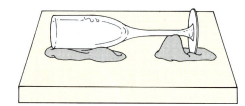

Wheel protection
A spectacle case is the perfect storage container for a glass cutter. To cushion the wheel and retard rust, wrap a piece of oil-moistened cotton cloth around the cutter's head when it's not in use.

Safety glass

Plastic and glass sandwich
Laminated glass consists of a layer of plastic sandwiched between two layers of glass. To cut it, score and run both faces of the glass, using a length of wire instead of a larger round object under the glass (see facing page). Heat the exposed plastic along the score with a heat gun until it is pliable, pull the glass far enough apart to insert a razor knife, and cut the plastic along the score.

Wired glass
To cut safety glass that has wire mesh embedded in it, place the glass on a workbench with the wire mesh closer to the bench top (the mesh is closer to one face of the glass than the other). Score this type of glass in the same way as you would regular glass (facing page); then snap the glass down over the round object until the wires are severed. If any wires poke out, just snip them off.

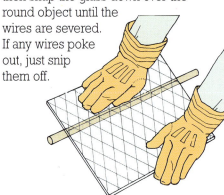

Tempered glass warning
While ordinary glass is easy to work, tempered glass (which you may find in a door, for instance) is a much stronger glass. Do not attempt to cut, drill, or smooth the edges of this type of glass.

CUTTING GLASS

Thicknesses and types of glass vary, so ask a retailer which glass is best for your application. Because large pieces are difficult to cut, work with smaller pieces at first.

Getting ready. Work on a flat surface, preferably a workbench or plywood. Clean the glass before you start. Lay out the cut with a marking crayon, glass-marking pencil, or china marker. To make the cut, you'll need a straightedge and a glass cutter. Use a sharp cutter; one with a carbide wheel will stay sharp longer. Lubricate the cutter and the cut line with mineral spirits or with equal parts of light machine oil and kerosene.

Score, then run. Cutting glass isn't cutting at all; it's controlled breaking. The process has two parts: scoring a line with the glass cutter, and running the cut along the score, which is known as breaking out the score. Score curved shapes around a wooden pattern. Break out a slight curve as you would a straight line. For a sharp curve, score extra radial lines and remove one piece at a time. Smooth all edges by rubbing them with a sharpening stone.

Caution: When handling glass, wear goggles and heavy gloves. Dispose of the shards in a closed container or wrap them in paper; then discard.

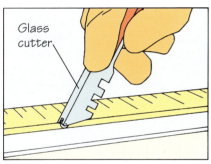

Make a single, fast, uniform stroke. A crackling sound means correct pressure. White flakes mean too much.

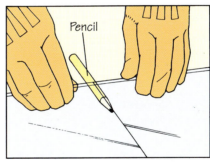

Run the cut by placing a round object at the edge of the glass under the score. Exert slight downward pressure.

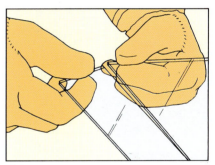

Small pieces and strips can be broken out by holding the glass on both sides of the score line and bending down.

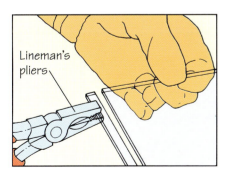

Narrow strips should be handled with lineman's or flat-jaw pliers. Bend the strip down to break out the score.

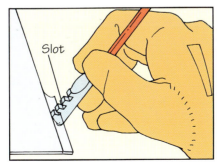

Nibble away at small pieces that don't break on the line, using pliers or the slots on the cutter.

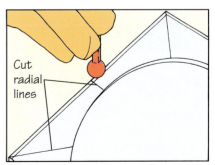

Curved cuts are run by turning the piece upside down and tapping with a cutter or pushing with a gloved thumb.

WORKING WITH PLASTICS

Special tools

Drill bit tip
Plastic laminate and acrylic tend to chip when drilled with standard twist bits. To avoid this problem, try rounding the tip of a standard twist bit and slowly blunting its two cutting edges on a grinder. Before drilling, make sure you clamp the plastic in place with a backing of scrap wood and don't apply too much pressure when making the hole.

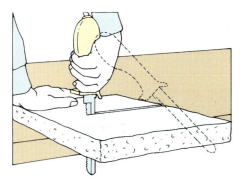

From the kitchen ▲
A kitchen electric carving knife is just the tool you need to make clean cuts in foam rubber or in rigid foam insulation. If you want to make a straight cut, mark the cutting line with a straightedge and marking pen. Place the material on a firm work surface, with the cutting line overhanging the edge of the surface by 25 mm or more. Begin the cut as you would a cut with a handsaw, starting with the knife at a 45° angle. Draw the knife about 50 mm into the foam; then straighten it until the blade is perpendicular to the work. For round or shaped cuts, hold the material on edge in a vice. With the cutting line facing you, make the cut with the blade facing down. Rotate the work as you go.

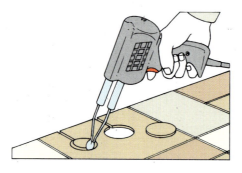

Some like it hot ▲
Some soldering guns come with a cutting tip that lets you cut plastics such as acrylic, vinyl, and expanded polystyrene. They're handy for cutting floor tiles to fit around water and heating pipes and door thresholds. To determine how fast to move the tip and how much pressure to apply, first practise cutting on scrap material.

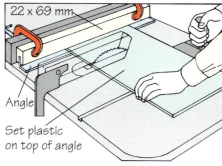

Under the fence ▲
Thin material, such as plastic laminate, can easily slip underneath the rip fence of a table saw. The next time you need to rip such thin stock, use this device. Cut a piece of 22 x 69 mm pine to the length of your fence; make a groove down the centre of one edge of the piece. Then glue a 19 x 19 mm aluminium angle into the groove, using epoxy adhesive. Use G-clamps to hold the guide in place while sawing.

Give it a lift
You can cut plastic tubing even if you don't have a pipe cutter. Instead, use a mitre box and a hacksaw. To raise small-diameter tubing high enough for the saw to cut through it, place a block of scrap wood under it. Clamp the scrap wood to the work surface to hold it and the mitre box in place. ▼

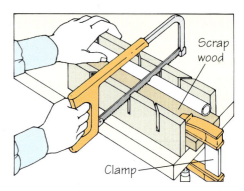

Acrylic

A cushioning point
It's possible to lay out circles on acrylic with a compass or dividers without leaving centrepoint marks in the work. At the centre of the circle build up a cushioned area with a few layers of masking tape. Just make sure the point doesn't go through all the layers of tape and into the acrylic.

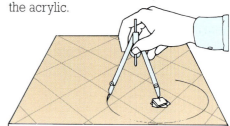

Clear cutting

To make the cutting line more visible on acrylic, apply a strip of masking tape along the area of the cut and mark the cutting line on the tape. Not only will the line stand out, but chipped edges will be kept to a minimum.

Old stuck paper

If you store acrylic for a long time with the protective paper still on it, the adhesive may dry out and make it tough to take off the paper. To make removal easier, soak the acrylic in isopropyl alcohol or kerosene. After peeling off the paper, remove any remaining adhesive with alcohol or kerosene on a soft cloth.

Gritty toothpaste

Because toothpaste is a mild abrasive, it's ideal for removing scratches in acrylic plastic. After removing the scratch, buff the area with a clean cloth.

Sheet laminate

Orderly fashion

When laminating a splashback, there's an order that makes the job easier. First laminate and trim the ends, then the front, and finally the top. Don't trim the top piece, however, until the splashback has been mounted; the back edge may have to be shaped to fit the wall (p 71).

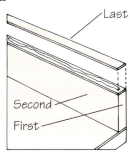

Placement aids ▲

To position sheet laminate on a substrate, you'll need spacers to keep the adhesive-covered surfaces apart until the two materials are properly aligned. You can use wooden dowels or cardboard strips, or you can snake a piece of rope or an extension cord down the length of the work. When the laminate is in the right position, start at one end and pull out one dowel at a time, or gradually remove the rope, as you press the laminate in place.

The other side

Here's a time-saving way to apply plastic laminate to both sides of a door, shelf, or other workpiece, at almost the same time. Drive four nails into your workbench so the workpiece can rest on them. Then spread the contact cement on the workpiece, turn it over, rest it on the nails and coat the other side. Once the cement reaches the correct tackiness, laminate the top side; then turn the door over and laminate the other side. When turning the workpiece over after laminating one surface, putting paper on the head of each nail will save having to remove glue from the laminate, and prevent scratches.

Exposed edges

If moisture penetrates the unsealed edges of a countertop, the laminate will separate from the chipboard base. To prevent moisture penetration, seal the exposed underside of the countertop (especially at the front edge) with a clear polyurethane.

Solid-surface material

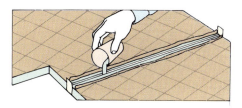

At the seam ▲

When joining solid surfacing material, set the pieces 3 mm apart. (And offset the seam from the corner to avoid placing stress on it.) To keep the adhesive from running, apply masking tape under the seam and up the ends.

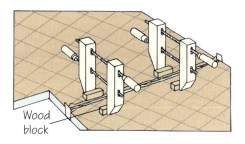

Gripping blocks ▲

If you don't have clamps long enough to hold the pieces while the adhesive dries, attach temporary blocks on each side of the seam with hot-melt glue. Clamp as shown, but not too tight. After the adhesive dries, tap off the blocks.

CHAPTER 4

HOUSEHOLD STORAGE

PASSAGES AND ENTRANCES 103
BEDROOMS AND LIVING AREAS 104
KITCHEN 106
BATHROOMS 110
LAUNDRY AREA 112
HOME OFFICE 113
SHELVES 114
CUPBOARDS 118
CHILDREN'S ROOMS 122
SPORTS EQUIPMENT 123
ATTIC AND GARAGE 124

PASSAGES AND ENTRANCES

Passage walls

Overhead shelving

Long passage walls are often overlooked as a source of storage space. Extra-wide passages can accommodate floor-to-ceiling shelving, but be sure to leave at least about a metre of floor space clear so as not to impede the traffic flow. In a narrower passage, install a single open shelf about 300 mm below the ceiling. Use it to store seldom-used items or to display decorative ones.

Not for kitchens only

If the passage is wide enough, kitchen wall cabinets—set on the floor and covered with a shallow countertop and/or hung on the wall—are a suitable alternative to floor-to-ceiling shelves.

Cupboard organizers

Moisture control

This shoe rack allows air to circulate around wet shoes and boots, while the underlying tray makes cleanup easy. The rack is a 22 x 44 mm pine frame fitted with 10 mm dowels. Make the frame large enough so that it fits over the aluminium or plastic tray. (Coated wire shelving is a simpler, if homelier, substitute for the wood rack.) ▼

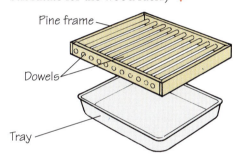

Winter wear storage

Store gloves and caps on this wire rack installed on the back of a passage cupboard door. Straighten a wire coat hanger and feed it through three screw eyes mounted on the door. Once the wire is past the middle eye, start sliding clothes pegs onto it. To secure the rack, bend the wire around the screw eyes at each end.

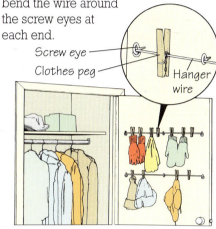

Heavy-duty entrance

Ideal for the smallholder ▶

An entrance room to a home on a smallholding will give family members a place to leave wet or muddy items of clothing. When planning the room:
▷ Consider enlarging a back-door pantry or partitioning a porch or garage.
▷ If possible, put a door at each end to make the room an energy-saving, dirt-blocking airlock.
▷ Design the room to meet the needs and activities of all family members and make sure it is positioned at the busiest entrance, where it will be needed most.

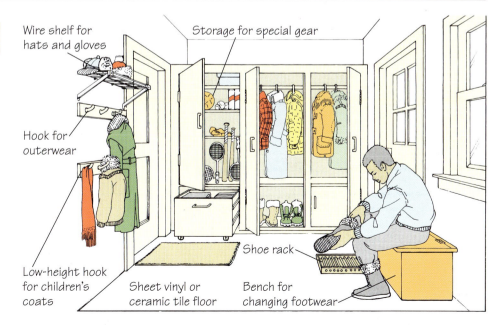

Household Storage

BEDROOMS AND LIVING AREAS

Simple shelves

Shelves where you need them

One of the areas we often don't use for shelves is above a bed, but a simple assembly like the one shown in the illustration is easy to make and will provide lots of easy-to-reach storage and display space. Make the unit from 22 x 290 mm SA pine and attach it to the wall. You will need about 8 m of timber if the unit is to be about a metre high and have a single shelf below the top. For additional shelves or height, adapt your material requirements accordingly. The completed unit should allow the bed to be slid in and out easily when making it up every morning. A reading light can be attached to the unit if necessary. ▼

Hidden tapes ▲

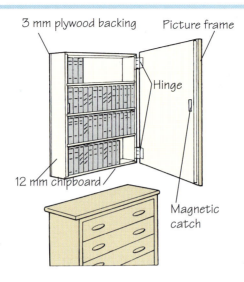

A wall-mounted cabinet, concealed by a favourite painting or block-mounted print, is great for storing video or music cassettes. Make the cabinet frame and the shelves out of 12 mm chipboard. Match the width and length of the cabinet to the dimensions of the picture frame; the cabinet's depth depends on the items being stored. Use 3 mm plywood to make the cabinet back. The picture frame or block-mounted print is hinged to the cabinet on one side and held shut by a magnetic catch.

Fold-away shelves

Shelves are a basic necessity in homes and workshops, and no matter how many we install, we often run out of space. There are, nevertheless, those times when a fold-away shelf can be a real boon. For example, a shelf mounted on the rear wall of the house may be used only every so often for repotting seedlings. For the rest of the time, it may be a nuisance. In such instances, install a folding shelf which can be collapsed out of the way when not required. A range of folding brackets is available from hardware dealers and can be attached to the wall quickly and easily.

Back-of-door hideaway

The back of cupboard and other interior doors is an untapped storage resource just waiting to be used. You can hang a full-length mirror on the back of a door, pepper it with clothes hooks, or use it to mount shelves or a tall, slender cabinet for the odd little items that don't fit elsewhere. (For more back-of-door storage ideas, see pp 103, 111, and 112.) Some of these space savers, however, can add a good deal of weight to the door. So, if you intend adding substantially to the load on a door's hinges, it's a good idea to install a third or even fourth hinge to ensure that the door will operate properly. You will ease any strain on the hinges, anyway, by ensuring that heavier items are always placed closest to the hinge side of the shelves with lighter items being placed towards the outer (lock) side. You might also have to consider reinforcing the door as a whole with a sheet of plywood or hardboard if its construction is too flimsy for the extra load.

Window seat ▶

Create extra seating and storage space along a window wall by lining the wall beneath the window with sturdy low cabinets. Install a plywood platform over the cabinets, and top it off with cushions. Edge the platform with moulding for a finished look.

Bedtime storage

Bed box ▶

If you're thinking about building a platform bed, consider one that rests not on drawers but on a deep box built of 16 mm chipboard. Even though you have to remove the mattress and lift off the top of the box to get at it, the space under the bed is ideal for storing cumbersome items, family heirlooms and other bits and pieces that you prefer to conceal or seldom use.

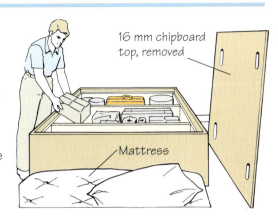

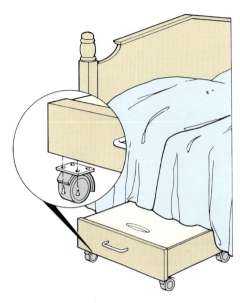

Recycled drawers ▲

Give new life to old dresser drawers as under-the-bed storage bins. Fasten small casters to their bases and use them to store seasonal clothes, extra blankets, and more. To keep out dust, add a hinged 6 mm plywood top to each drawer. If you don't have old ones on hand, second-hand furniture dealers and pawnshops may have units from which you can use the drawers. You can also buy easy-to-assemble drawers which can be adapted as required.

Head room

When buying a new bed, look for a headboard with shelves or shallow cabinets built into it. This type of bed not only provides convenient storage space, it makes efficient use of available bedroom floor space by eliminating the need for night tables.

Drawer organizers

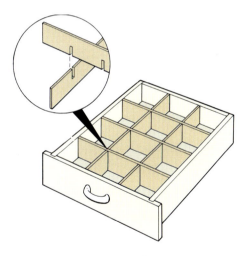

Divide and contain ▲

Create compartments in a shallow drawer by notching and joining strips of 3 mm hardboard or plywood. Clamp the crosspieces together and cut the slots all at once so they'll align exactly. Ensure you achieve a snug fit so that small items can't slip under the strips.

See-through dividers

Drawer dividers may also be made from 6 mm sheet acrylic (have the retailer cut the pieces to size, or cut them yourself). Butt the pieces together in whatever arrangement you desire; then bond the joints with acrylic solvent. (For more on working with acrylic, see pp 100–101.)

Sliding tray

Here's a way to increase the usable space in a deep drawer. Make a box of plywood or chipboard and support it on runners glued or screwed securely to the sides of the drawer. The tray should be about half the drawer's width or length so that you can slide it aside for easy access to the bottom of the drawer. Or make the tray full length and add handles for easy removal. ▼

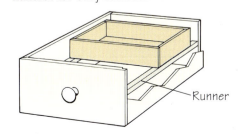

KITCHEN

Built-in units

Looking up ▶
The space between the tops of kitchen cabinets and the ceiling is ideal for storing pots, pans and serving dishes or for displaying baskets, plants, and ornamental pieces. To make the most of this space, install simple storage boxes made out of 12 mm chipboard. Build as many boxes as necessary to fill this space, butt them together and cover the joints and any exposed edges with strips of moulding or veneer of your choice.

Wall mart
One way to increase kitchen storage space is to install a shallow pantry on the wall. It need be deep enough only for items such as pet food, tinned goods and other items of this size, so SA pine or meranti 144 mm wide will be ample for most needs. Fit a couple of narrower doors rather than a single large door that may block the way when open. Such a pantry can be installed even in the entrance to a kitchen and still provide a great deal of storage space.

Hide that rubbish
Unsightly rubbish bins and bags can be a thing of the past if you install swing-out bins like the ones below. A simple frame is attached to a door hinged at the bottom and a stay is attached to the top edge to prevent the door falling open. This idea can be adopted to store laundry.

Cupboards to spare? ▲
If you have an under-used cupboard in or near the kitchen, why not turn it into a playroom? Simply decorate the walls with bright colours, install shelves and a desk, add a stool, toy bin, and wastebasket, and hook the door open. Your children can play close by, but not underfoot, while you work in the kitchen.

Trial run

Before equipping your kitchen with an island or any permanent cabinet, mark its location on the floor with masking tape or place a large box in the area to see how the installation will affect traffic flow. Rethink the layout if you continually overstep the lines or bump into the box.

Table in a drawer

Are you short of kitchen counter space? A removable insert of chipboard or plywood, cut to fit the top of a drawer, becomes an extra work surface when you need it. Storage space in the drawer is not affected. ▼

Counters and shelves

Inset cutting board

Make better use of your counter space by setting a cutting board into it. Use sink rim edging to keep the board flush with the countertop. For quick food cleanup, cut a slot in the cutting board and place a rubbish bin below it. ▼

Hideaway tables

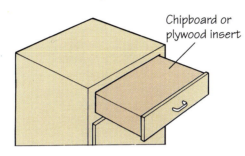

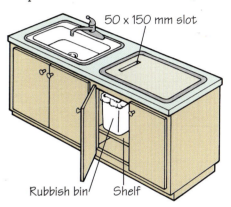

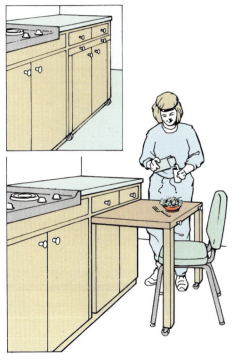

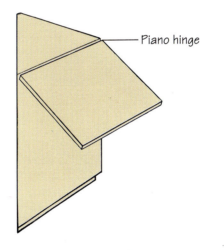

Disappearing act ▲

Even a tiny kitchen can accommodate this custom-made pull-out table. When not in use, the top and legs (mounted on casters) slide into slots cut into the base cabinet. The legs and front edge of the table are faced to match the cabinets. Storage space is virtually unaffected.

Kitchen swinger ▲

A swing-out top can be attached to the end of a kitchen counter and swung up when required. A piano hinge is used to attach the swinging top to the counter and is positioned so that the surface of the counter and that of the top are flush when the latter is deployed. Drop legs or pull-out supports hold the top in position when it is in use. Install the former if the top has to bear heavy loads.

Add-a-shelf

A slide-in shelf of 16 mm chipboard is a good way to organize the space below a sink. Determine the height of the shelf (allowing room for the trap), and cut two side supports to that height. Cut the shelf 6 mm shorter than the inside width of the cabinet. Attach the shelf to the supports with 50 mm screws; slide the unit into place. ▼

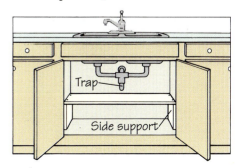

Household Storage / 107

KITCHEN

Racks and dispensers

Lid holder
Keep pot lids handy with these simple wooden racks. The unit is made of pine. The crosspieces are 22 x 22 mm square battens. ▼

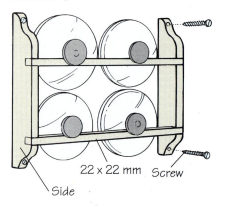

Suspended stemware
Protect fragile wine glasses by hanging them from this under-the-cabinet rack. Cut the openings with a plunge router or jigsaw and use 30 mm screws and glue to assemble the unit and fix it in position. The same idea can be adapted to make a rack for food processor blades.

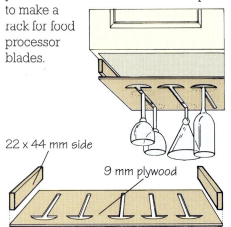

Organizers

Stow-aways
The space under kitchen cupboards is either unused, or has hooks screwed into it for storing coffee mugs and cups. Use this space even more profitably: make up a flat tray using 6 mm plywood mounted on a frame of meranti or SA pine and subdivide it if you wish. Fix it to the underside of the base as in the illustration using two 30 mm hinges at the rear and two chains of a suitable length to retain it at the front. It is kept up by a toggle catch mounted on the cupboard frame. Use the tray to store spices, small utensils and other items.

Mobile work island
You can give new life to an old bedside table by adding casters to the base and converting it into a mobile work island that goes where you need it. If it is too low, increase its height by adding a storage section to the base. Cover the top with a heat-resistant surface.

A rack with a difference ▶
A hanging rack is easy to make and provides storage space just where you usually don't have it—in the centre of your kitchen. Make the rack from lengths of 32 x 32 mm meranti. Paint or varnish it and hang it from hooks screwed through the ceiling and into the roof trusses.

Stair-step shelves
Bring order to a messy cupboard: store its contents on step shelves so you can easily see items at the back. Make up a selection of small versions of the Add-a-shelf (see p 107) for a neater cupboard with boosted storage capacity (store smaller items under the shelves).

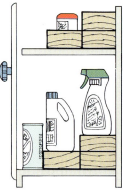

Bulletin board ▲
Use recycled wine corks to create a message centre by glueing them with a hot-glue gun onto plywood. Glue the corks lengthwise to the wood; start in a corner and position two corks vertically, then two horizontally. Continue the pattern until the plywood is covered; frame the board with strips of moulding.

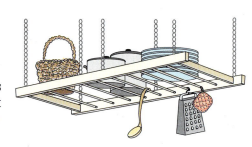

A different slant

If you buy tinned food or drinks in packs, this handy shelf automatically feeds tins toward the front each time you remove one. Hooks and brackets (mounted a little lower than the hooks) support wire shelving mounted upside down and at an angle. Tins roll forward as those in front are removed and the lip holds them in place until needed. ▼

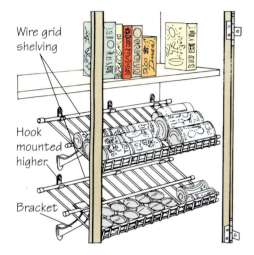

More kitchen organizers

▷ A pull-down cookbook rack that mounts on the bottom of a standard wall cabinet, similar to the stow-away rack shown on the facing page.
▷ A full-circle lazy susan for mounting in a base or wall corner cabinet.
▷ Wire racks installed on the inside of cabinet doors for keeping small items within easy reach.
▷ A pegboard or wire grid wall organizer (see p 127).
▷ A heavy-duty rack for hanging pots and pans from the ceiling or wall.

ISLAND LIFE

Create a practical kitchen storage and eating area by mounting an inexpensive countertop on refurbished base cabinets (surplus units are often available at giveaway prices when people refit their kitchens). The island shown here uses two cabinets, but you can use any number. Choose cabinets to fit your needs and which you can restore without too much outlay.

To anchor the cabinets, screw 44 x 44 mm timbers to the floor around the cabinets' interior perimeter line. Place the cabinets over the timbers and use wooden shims to level them. Then fix the cabinet kickboards to the timbers with screws and remove the shims. Use veneer to hide the screwholes or fill them and paint the boards.

Before building the countertop, work out the optimum overhang. If you're using ceramic tiles, size the counter to accept an even number of them in order to avoid cutting. (Remember to allow space for the grout.) Attach the countertop to the cabinets with screws coming up through the base cabinets' top rails.

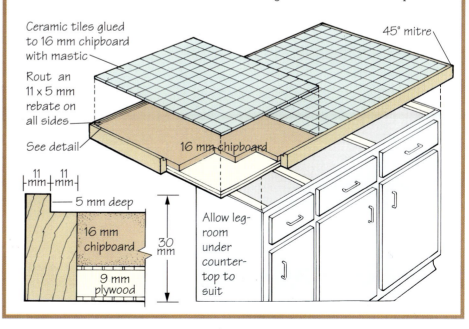

BATHROOMS

Shelves and racks

Out of the linen cupboard

For a colourful decorative touch, store towels on open shelving in the bathroom. The wall over the toilet is a good place. You can also use the space to store rolls of toilet paper or other bathroom supplies.

Easy-reach towel

If you're installing a new bathroom cabinet or redoing an old one, consider creating a recess that will keep a towel right where you need it most, below the sink. Make the niche about 60 mm deep, line it to match the surrounding cabinets, and fit it with a towel bar. Set the bar 10 mm back from the front of the cabinet. ▼

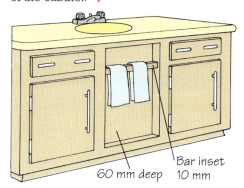

Recessed repository ▲

In a home with drywall interior walls an appliance cabinet can be installed within easy reach of the basin in the bathroom or near the sink in the kitchen. In the example shown above, a cabinet has been built into the space between wall studs. A roll-up door has been used for greater convenience.

Private library

A plastic magazine file makes a handy holder for bathroom reading materials. If you cannot buy a file at a shop dealing in office supplies, make one up from 3 mm plywood and attach it to the toilet wall.

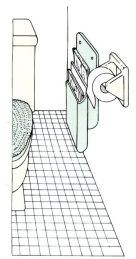

Over your head

The area above bathroom windows and doors is often wasted. Put the space to work by installing a decorative shelf or vinyl-coated wire shelving. Use these out-of-the-way shelves to store extra towels or items you wish to keep out of the reach of children.

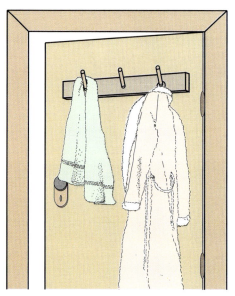

Door-mounted rack ▲

Take advantage of every bit of bathroom space with a door-mounted towel and robe rack. Take a length of 22 x 44 mm timber about 600 mm long and drill holes at regular intervals for 10 mm dowels. The dowels should be at an angle so that items won't fall off. Glue 75 mm lengths of dowel into the holes and attach the rack to the back of the bathroom door with toggle bolts if the door has a hollow core.

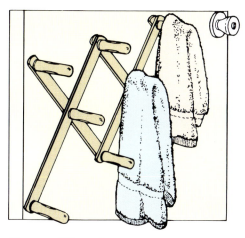

For small fry ▲
To encourage children to hang up their towels, make sure racks are accessible to them. If you have space on your wall, mount one or more towel racks below an existing rack. Or make a rack like the door-mounted version opposite and fasten it to the wall. An expandable wooden mug rack also makes a handy hanger. Make sure, however, that no rack is attached at a height that might cause an eye injury.

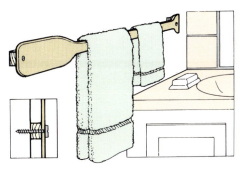

Paddle bar ▲
Make an eye-catching towel rack from an old wood canoe paddle varnished with several coats of clear polyurethane. Mount the paddle on the wall with screws driven through spacer blocks.

Organizers

Shower caddy
Shower caddy units with shelves and racks are easy to install in the corner of a bath or shower and provide a place for many items. They are available from bathroom accessory shops.

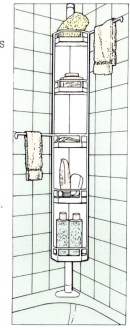

Soap, shampoo, conditioner
Organize your bath products, avoid spills and make more economical use of shampoos and so on with a push-button dispenser mounted on the wall. ▼

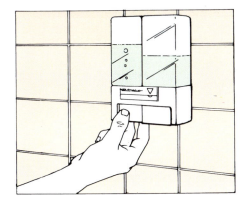

Not for kitchens only
Many of the cabinet accessories designed for kitchens (p 108) can also help bring order to your bathroom cabinets. A case in point is the lazy susan. Check the space inside the cabinet carefully, making allowances for pipes and fittings, and then buy the unit that best suits the space. If unable to find a suitable model, why not make one out of two discs and a base of 9 mm plywood, and 12 mm dowels. ▼

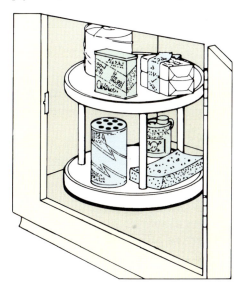

Under a pedestal
One way to increase storage space in a bathroom equipped with a pedestal basin is to hang a skirt just below the rim and use the newly created space to store paper goods and cleaning products. Make the skirt out of a heavy washable fabric. Sew a Velcro strip to the top inside edge of the skirt and glue another strip to the basin rim with a waterproof adhesive. Adding a shelf will increase storage space even further.

LAUNDRY AREA

Hidden boards

Now you see it...

Kitchen renovators and suppliers of storage systems offer many different space-saving options to suit every need. These include a variety of options to cater for your ironing needs. The three shown on this page are super space savers and can be brought into action in seconds. They are ideal for situations where space is at a premium. Adapting a standard ironing-board to fold away should not present a problem for the home handyman.

...Now you don't

The door-back ironing-board hooks on to a door and folds down. If, however, you cannot buy such an item in your area, adapt a standard board—and whether you decide to buy, or adapt a board, reinforce the door and hinges if necessary.

Bins and racks

Ironing organizer

This rack to hold an iron, a freestanding ironing-board, and other items can be made up from part of a washing-up rack. Mount the rack on a laundry room wall or in a cupboard near where you do your ironing. ▼

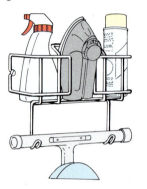

Laundry rack

This simple washer/dryer shelf rack is very useful where you may not wish to attach shelves to the wall. The unit is made out of SA pine or meranti and assembled using 50 mm screws. To avoid having to disconnect the washer's hoses, slide the shelf rack into place before screwing the bottom brace to the sides. On one side attach a rack on which to hang clothes as you take them out of the dryer.

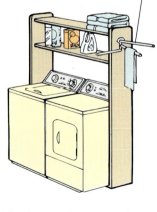

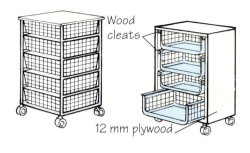

Order out of chaos ▲

Sorting bins are essential for any laundry room. Home centres offer a variety of sorting systems, such as the units shown here, or you can make your own. Build a frame out of 12 mm plywood, and attach pairs of wood cleats to the sides to support pull-out plastic or wire baskets. You'll need at least three baskets: for whites, colours, and permanent press; if you can fit a fourth bin, use it for towels and work clothes.

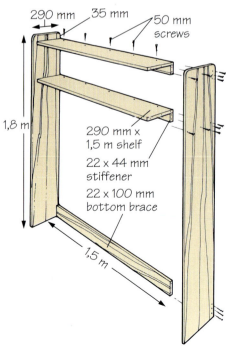

112 / Household Storage

HOME OFFICE

Found spaces

Guest room office

Most home offices borrow space from an existing room. Here a small guest room does double duty as a home office thanks to the addition of a compact wall unit equipped with shelves, drawers, desk, a computer centre, and a variety of slide-out and pull-down work surfaces. ▼

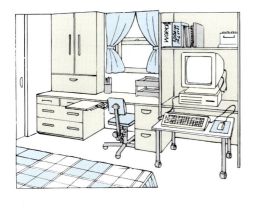

Under the stairs

If the area under a stairway can accommodate shelves (see p 126), odds are it can also serve as a small work station. You can leave an under-the-stairway office exposed or conceal it behind doors when not in use. In the example shown here, a folding door serves as a screen, providing a bit of extra privacy while you work.

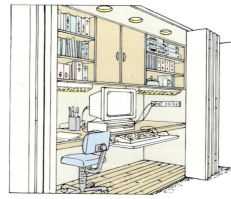

Office in a cupboard ▲

An important feature of a good home office is a sense of separation from other household activities—which is exactly what this converted cupboard provides. Good lighting and electrical outlets have been added, and books and equipment are within easy reach. Folding doors hide the clutter at day's end.

In the attic

The awkward space under eaves is ideal for storing boxes of seldom-used files or other household items. A solid-back bookcase mounted on casters and extending up to the sloped ceiling not only conceals the stored boxes (while allowing access to them), it also serves as a convenient backdrop for an attic office. ▼

Cook's corner

Don't overlook the kitchen as a possible location for a home office. Below are two suggestions for getting more use out of an under-utilized kitchen nook. At a pinch, even a tight galley (top) can do double duty as a makeshift office. Make use of swing-out shelves and other means to move office items out of the way when they're not in use. In the larger kitchen shown at bottom, an area once devoted to cabinets has been turned into a work centre. ▼

Household Storage / 113

SHELVES

Open shelving

Shelves to go
These notched knock-down shelves are ready to move any time you are. The posts are 44 x 69 mm meranti and the shelves are 12 mm plywood. Cut the notches with a jigsaw, spacing them about 300 mm apart on the posts and at least 600 mm on the shelves. Keep all notches at least 50 mm from the end of the piece. ▼

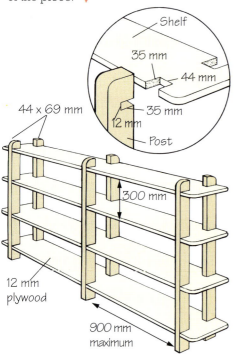

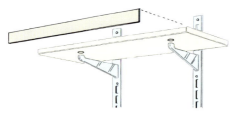

Out of sight ▲
Shelf brackets will be a lot less noticeable if you buy them 25 mm or so shorter than the shelf depth. Drill holes a few millimetres into the shelf bottom to accommodate the bracket tips. Adding moulding along the edges of the shelf and painting the standards and brackets the same colour as the wall also help camouflage shelf hardware.

Let the sun shine in
Always trying to squeeze another plant onto the windowsill? Turn your window into a miniature greenhouse with everyday shelves. Attach metal shelving standards to each side of the window, insert shelf brackets, and add acrylic or safety glass shelves. (Don't use standard glass; it might break and injure someone.) ▼

BUILT-IN SHELVING

A built-in shelving unit can bring a bleak wall to life. Available space and the type of items stored will determine a unit's dimensions. For shelves 250 to 300 mm deep and liable to have to bear heavy loads, space vertical supports no more than 750 mm apart.

Materials. Use either solid timber 22 mm thick or 9 mm plywood doubled up and glued together. Paint or varnish the shelves as required. Finish the plywood edges with moulding or iron-on veneer tape, shown at right.

Assembly. Line up the sides and vertical partitions, and install one of the two types of adjustable shelf supports shown at right. Then glue and screw the full-length top and bottom pieces to the sides. Attach the mounting cleat and vertical partitions. Assemble the base, level it with shims, and set the case on it. Screw the cleat to the wall. Cover gaps along the ceiling edge with cornice. Attach meranti or SA pine quadrant, varnished or painted, to finish the sides and cover any gaps where the unit meets the walls.

Swinging standard
To install a metal shelf standard without a level, mount it loosely to the wall through the top screw hole. Then lift it to one side and let it swing like a pendulum. The standard will be vertical when it comes to a stop.

Assembly

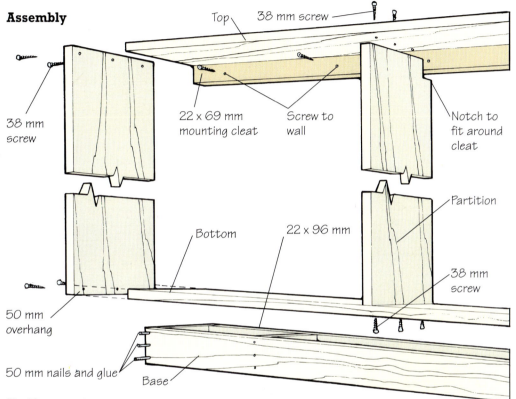

Edgings

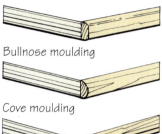

A wide variety of mouldings and edgings of assorted shapes, sections and widths is available. Cut veneer edging with a utility knife; use a dovetail saw on moulding. Score the surface first to stop chipping.

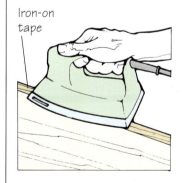

Iron-on tape, sold by most timber outlets, is another edging alternative. Heat the tape in place, and trim it with a utility knife.

Shelf supports

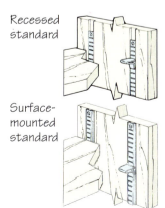

Standards with snap-in clips look best when set into grooves routed in the vertical supports (top) because the shelves fit snugly against the supports. But surface mounting (lower) is easier.

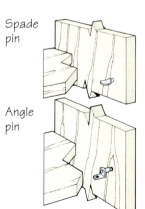

Plug-in pins require two rows of regularly spaced holes on each vertical support (for drilling tips, see p 72). A shelf rests flat on straight spade pins (top) but angle pins (lower) offer a little more support.

SHELVES

Book ends

A weighty trick
Do book ends keep sliding off your desk or shelves? Replace the felt on their bases with pieces that extend under the books for several centimetres. The weight of the books on the felt will keep the book ends firmly in position.

Bookkeeper with a difference ▶
To keep books from falling off open-end shelves, install two cup hooks on each shelf end and run dowels through them. Stain the dowels to match the shelves. Pinch the hooks on the bottom shelf to hold the dowels; the other hooks should allow the dowels to slide through. If necessary, join the dowels with sleeves made of clear plastic tubing.

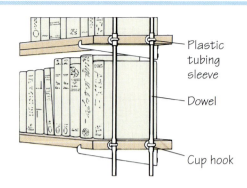

Cabinets

The eyes have it
Want to add another shelf to a cabinet to hold lightweight items? Insert two or more small screw eyes in each side of the cabinet and rest the shelf on them. Make the shelf out of a piece of plywood sized and finished to suit the cabinet.

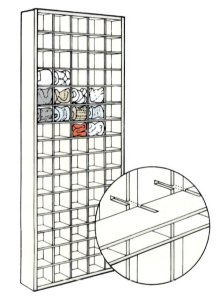

Storage grid ▲
This wall-mounted cubbyhole cabinet holds a variety of small items and protrudes only about 100 mm from the wall. The unit consists of a 22 x 96 mm frame fastened to the wall and a grid made out of 90 mm-wide slats of 6 mm plywood. The slats are notched halfway through at 90 mm intervals, then interlocked in cross-lap joints. Scale the cabinet and vary the cubicle size to suit your needs.

On display
Create a china cabinet or collectibles display case by adding sliding glass doors to a shelving unit—either a built-in (see pp 114–115) or a ready-made bookcase. Buy sliding-door tracks and glides from a glass and mirror store, and have them cut to size. The store will also cut glass for the doors. To allow room for the doors, trim the middle shelves so that they are set back from the front. ▼

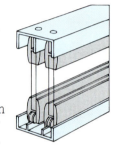

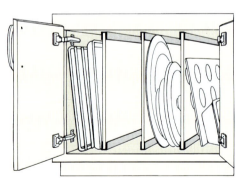

Long division ▲
Vertical dividers in a cabinet make it much easier to store items such as trays, baking pans, and magazines. To make the dividers, use 6 mm plywood or acrylic; install U-shaped wood moulding or metal channels to hold them in place.

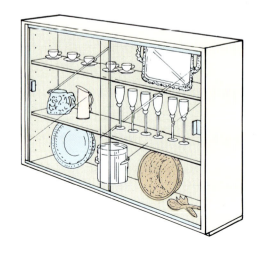

TYPES OF WALL FASTENERS

Whenever possible, if you have drywalls, attach heavy items directly to wall studs (p 135) or to a board secured to studs. Use one of the special fasteners below when you want to secure a light to moderately heavy load to wallboard or plaster, or when you need to attach an object to a masonry wall. For a drywall, use a fastener whose shank length matches the wall's thickness. On brick walls, it's usually best to attach to the mortar joints. (To drill into masonry, see p 10.)

FASTENER	USE	HOW TO INSTALL
Plastic anchor	Very light load on wallboard, plaster, or masonry	Drill hole slightly smaller than anchor, and push in anchor. Attach object with sheet-metal screw.
Hollow-wall anchor (Molly bolt)	Moderate load on wallboard or plaster	Drill hole same diameter as anchor. Insert anchor, and tighten bolt to collapse sleeve against wall. Remove bolt and use to attach object.
Toggle bolt	Moderate load on wallboard or plaster; heavy load on hollow-core concrete block	Drill hole large enough to let bolt's folded wings pass through. Attach object to bolt, then insert in hole. Tighten bolt to pull wings against interior.
Plastic toggle	Moderate load on wallboard or plaster	Drill hole same diameter as anchor. Squeeze wings together and insert in hole. Push nail through screw hole to pop open wings. Attach object with screw.
Metal drive-in anchor	Moderate load on wallboard or plaster	Hammer into wallboard. Predrill 3 mm starter hole in plaster or thin panelling.
Screw-in anchor	Light load on wallboard. Speeds installation of many fasteners	Screw anchor directly into wall with screwdriver or variable-speed drill. Attach object with screw.
Plastic nail anchor	Moderate load on masonry	Drill hole same diameter as anchor, and insert anchor. Attach object with supplied drive-in/screw-out nail.
Lead shield	Moderate to heavy load on masonry	Drill hole same diameter as shield, and insert shield. Attach object with lag bolt.
Expansion shield	Heavy load on masonry	Drill hole same diameter as shield. With object attached, insert shield in hole and tighten bolt to draw wedge into sleeve.

Household Storage

CUPBOARDS

Space savers

Quick sorts
You don't need to revamp your entire cupboard to gain more space. A three-tiered wire basket or pot-plant holder hung from the cupboard ceiling makes a great receptacle for socks and other small items. Use a cardboard drum or a tall plastic bin to hold canes, umbrellas, or sports equipment. ▼

Basket drawer
Add a drawer or two for socks and underwear by mounting a small plastic basket on U-shaped aluminium channels underneath a cupboard shelf. ▼

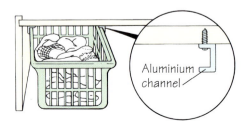

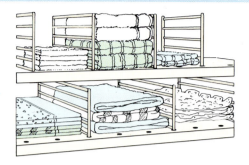

Dowel dividers ▲
Make up cupboard dividers using 20 mm dowels for the uprights and thinner 10 mm dowels for the crosspieces. They slot into 20 mm holes drilled in the shelves at 200 mm centres and keep everything neat.

Inner space
When installing a cupboard system, keep these basic spacing guidelines in mind:
▷ A standard cupboard is 600 mm deep, with the clothes rod placed 300 mm from the back wall; each hanger requires 25 mm of rod space (bulky winter clothes require 50–75 mm).
▷ Allow 1,6 m from the floor for full-length clothes; 2,05 m for double-hanging space (place the bottom rod 1 m above the floor, the top rod 2 m).
▷ For standard storage, use 300 mm deep shelves, spaced 330 mm apart; use 400–500 mm deep shelves for bulky items.
▷ Don't plan on using the floor space underneath double-hanging garments. The above guidelines allow for 50 mm between the garments and the floor for easy cleaning.
▷ For extra storage space, you can install a slide-in shelf (see p 107).

Central tower
This handy organizer divides the one-rod side of the cupboard from the two-rod side. Make the shelf tower from 300 mm wide 12 mm chipboard, sized to fit between ceiling and floor or between a shelf and the floor. Install the rods 1,6 m from the cupboard floor on one side and 2 m and 1 m from the floor on the other side. ▼

Doors with a difference

Roller blinds used instead of doors on this built-in wardrobe not only save space but add colour to the room when they are pulled down. You can build the wardrobe frame from 12 mm plywood, much like a built-in bookcase (pp 114–115). Make the unit 600 mm deep, and use the dimensions on the facing page as a guide for positioning clothes rods and shelves. ▼

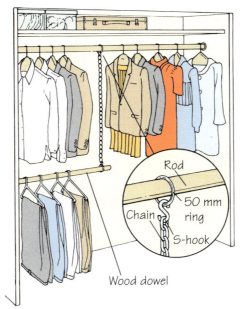

Trapeze bar ▲

A cupboard with a single clothes rod wastes space. An easy way to convert a cupboard to multilevel storage is to suspend a second rod from the first by means of steel rings, S-hooks, and two lengths of chain.

Put 'em in chains

Yet another way to increase cupboard storage is to secure a chain to the clothes rod. Then just hook clothes hangers onto the chain links.

A stronger hanger

Weak wire hangers can support winter coats and other heavy clothes if you tightly tape two (or more) together.

Belt organizer

To turn a wooden hanger into a handy belt rack, simply screw cup hooks into the bottom bar of the hanger and hang your belts from the hooks.

Hangers and rods

Muscle rod

Is your wooden cupboard rod giving way under the burden? Create a sag-free rod from a length of galvanized pipe. For a more finished look, insert the pipe into an equal length of PVC pipe. Remove any lettering on the plastic pipe with lacquer thinner, or by gently rubbing it with steel wool.

A new angle

If your cupboard is about a metre deep, double its capacity. Install two clothes rods in the space now occupied by one. Cut shallow notches in the rods as shown so that the hangers are held at a 45° angle. Place the clothes you wear most frequently in the front; store other garments on the rear rod. ▼

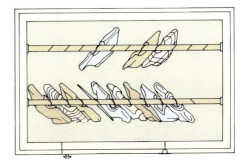

Shoe storage

Shoe-in

When designing shoe storage, plan to use shelves 300–325 mm deep. Allow at least 160 mm between shelves for regular shoes, more for boots. Allow 230 mm of shelf width for each pair of women's shoes, 250 mm for men's.

Hang-ups

Doorstops screwed into the back of a cupboard door make a convenient shoe storage system.

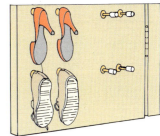

Household Storage / 119

CUPBOARDS

On the inside

Linings that enhance

Lining the interior of a large cupboard with lengths of tongue-and-groove pine or meranti strips can enhance its looks if the walls are uneven and unattractive. This is especially true of a large cupboard or walk-in pantry—which could be lined to match a kitchen's theme, if you wish. Lining a cupboard this way also makes the addition of shelves far easier as the need for drilling into masonry can be avoided. Attach the strips to evenly spaced lengths of 19 x 19 mm pine fixed vertically to the wall. Varnish or stain the completed finish as desired and attach your shelves to the lining. Complete the revamp by attaching a matching lining to the inner surface of the door. A lining like this can transform a large cupboard—if you're turning it into a mini work station, for example. ▼

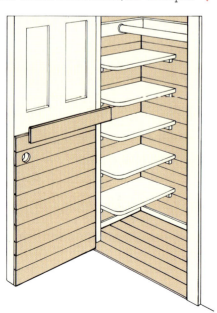

Sheet lining ▲

Here's an alternative to strips—and it can be cheaper and easier as well: put plywood or decorative sheets on the interior walls. In this case, the battens may be attached horizontally. For easy installation, cut the sheet 10 mm shorter than the floor-to-ceiling height, wedge the sheet against the ceiling as you nail, and cover the gap along the base with skirting board.

Wiring made easy

One of the advantages of lining a cupboard this way is that wiring for a light or computer (if you are converting a large cupboard into a work station) can be run behind the lining. If you do this, make a note of where the wires are, so that when you attach shelves or other items to the unit, you'll know where to work. **Caution:** *It is illegal for any persons other than qualified electricians, or persons authorized by legislation, to work on the fixed wiring of any electrical installation. Don't do any electrical work unless you're absolutely sure of what to do and how to do it. If you're not, call in a qualified and licensed electrician.*

INSTALLING A WIRE

If cupboard clutter is driving you to distraction, a vinyl-coated wire cupboard system may be the answer. Not only are these systems efficient organizers, they keep clothes fresher by allowing air to circulate around them. Typically, ready-to-assemble cupboard systems rely on basic components: wire baskets in freestanding or built-in frames; shelving designed for clothes hangers and shelved items; and racks for smaller items such as shoes, socks and ties. Versatility is further enhanced by the availability of separate basket runners and casters. The runners

CUPBOARD SYSTEM

enable you to use baskets in existing cupboards, while the casters convert basket units into trollies which can be moved where needed. The system components are available in a variety of sizes. This allows you to tailor the system you buy to your storage needs.

Before buying a cupboard system, obtain full details of each system which appears to suit your requirements. Then measure the height, width, and depth of your cupboard and sketch your plan on paper so that you can visualize what the system will look like. Experiment with layouts until you find one that works for you. (For more on cupboard design, see p 118.) When selecting a system, try to choose one that will give you the most adaptability: your needs may change.

Illustrated at right are step-by-step instructions for mounting just one type of a typical built-in shelf or linen rack.

Each system, whether free standing or built in, has its own recommended hardware and fasteners; be sure to use the recommended items and follow kit directions carefully. If attaching runners directly to a drywall, for example, using the correct fasteners will enable the unit to be loaded to its maximum without damage to itself or the wall. By mounting runners in an existing cupboard (see p 118), you will be able to increase its storage capacity. In a deep cupboard, you may be able to insert narrow baskets two deep, but sideways, for even greater versatility.

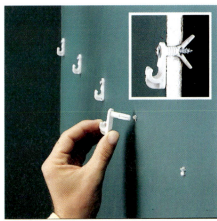

1 Mark a level line for the length of the shelf at the desired shelf height. Drill a 6 mm hole every 250 mm, and insert a fin-back clip into each hole. Insert and tighten the screw, while holding the clip to keep it from spinning.

2 Slip an end-mounting bracket over the shelf lip next to the wall. Set the shelf in the clips and hold the end bracket against the wall. Make sure that the shelf is level front to back and side to side, and then mark the screw locations on the wall.

3 Drill 6 mm holes for the end bracket and insert the anchors. Then screw the end bracket to the wall. If the shelf runs from wall to wall, attach an end bracket at the other end of the shelf the same way.

4 Attach a support brace at least every metre along the length of the shelf. Secure the top end of the brace to the shelf; fasten the bottom end to the wall, using a plastic anchor and screw.

Household Storage / 121

CHILDREN'S ROOMS

Toy storage

Stacking bins

Toy clean-up is a breeze with this set of five interlocking bins made from 9 mm plywood. Cut all parts as shown. Using the dimensions given below, you can cut all five bins from one 1,22 x 2,44 m sheet of plywood. Sand the edges and assemble the bins with glue and 40 mm panel pins. Attach 50 mm casters to one or more bins. For durability, paint the bins with an oil-base primer and top coat. ▼

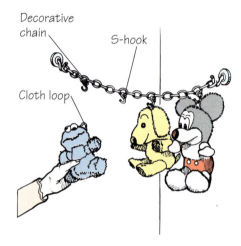

Chain gang

Stuffed animals can be kept clean and out of the way with a length of decorative chain. Simply attach the chain from wall to wall near the ceiling. Stitch a loop of hem binding to each stuffed animal, and suspend each one from the chain with S-hooks. ▼

A tisket, a tasket

Instead of being kept in a traditional toy box, toys can be sorted into brightly coloured laundry baskets—the open weave allows children to see what's inside, and they don't have to pull everything all over the floor to get the toy they really want. The baskets are also light and won't hurt a child when they topple over.

Toys to go

A good way to get children to round up toys that stray from their rooms is to keep a bright red wagon on hand. Wheel out the wagon and watch your children race to clean up; afterward, it's easy for even small kids to pull the whole load back to where it belongs.

Kiddie combos

A bed and more

With the right furniture, two kids can share even a small room comfortably. A bunk bed is one way to free up floor space. An alternative is to buy (or build) platform beds that rest on drawers, like the one shown here. ▼

Double-duty desk

When the toy bins are rolled out, this storage chest doubles as a desk. Use 16 mm plywood for the sides, back, top, and lid of the desk; 9 mm plywood for the base of the divided tray; and lengths of 22 x 96 mm pine for the tray frame. Assemble the pieces with glue and wood screws; then finish with colourful enamel. Make roll-out bins as shown at left or buy them ready-made. ▼

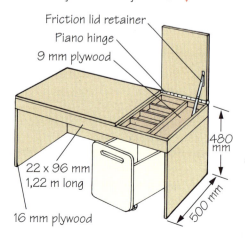

122 / Household Storage

SPORTS EQUIPMENT

Bicycles

A real hang-up
To eliminate clutter and save floor space in the garage, hang your bicycle from large plastic-coated hooks that are screwed into ceiling joists or walls. Bicycle hooks are available at hardware stores and cycle shops. ▼

A better bike rack
Here's a convenient two-bike rack that's easy to make. Three stakes anchor the rack, which is made from 22 x 44 mm SA pine. To accept the wider wheels of mountain bikes or the thinner ones of racing bikes, use spacers to alter the width of the slots. To prevent rotting, treat the stakes with creosote before setting the rack in position. ▼

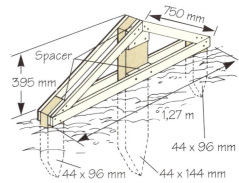

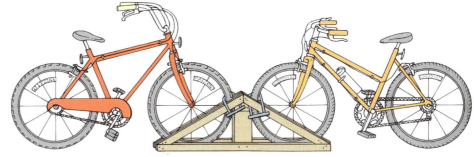

Other gear

Golf rack ▶
This handy organizer can be made out of 5 mm steel bar, painted and hung on two of the large plastic-coated hooks mentioned above. Adapt the design to your needs and use it to keep your golf shoes and bags organized. Mount it on a garage wall or in a cupboard.

Keep fishing rods safe and sound
Put the space between the exposed ceiling joists in a garage to work. Nail lengths of scrap wood across two joists at 1 m intervals. You'll be able to stow fishing rods and other long lightweight items. For a sturdier ceiling rack for holding timber, see p 61.

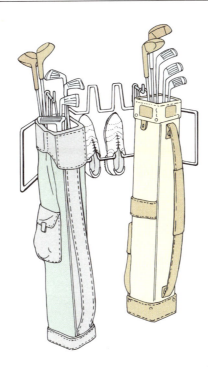

Batter up
Stow baseball equipment in this corner organizer. Cut a triangle from 12 mm chipboard. Drill 35 mm holes for the balls; cut the bat slots with a coping saw. If you wish, add a hook or two for the mitt and a cap, and nail the unit to cleats fixed to the wall.

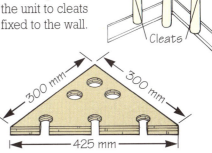

Household Storage / 123

ATTIC AND GARAGE

Overhead storage

Over-the-car rack
This garage rack hangs over your car, so it won't take up any floor space. Use lengths of 22 x 69 mm timber for the end supports and shelf cleats and 12 mm plywood for the shelving. The depth and vertical spacing of the shelves depend on your needs. Use 40 mm drywall screws to assemble the frame and attach it to overhead beams with 60 mm lag bolts. ▼

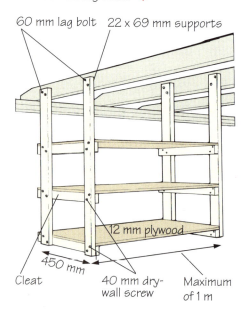

Reel 'em in ▶
To avoid the annual untangling of Christmas lights, store them on empty electrical wire spools (electricians and computer cabling companies may have some spare). For easy access, slide several spools onto a length of 20 mm diameter PVC pipe, then mount the pipe between the joists in your garage.

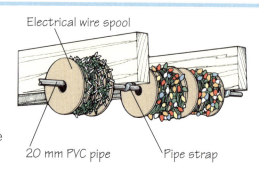

Overhead bins
Overhead storage bins are a great way to put wasted space to work. Construct them from 22 mm planks, plywood or chipboard, and assemble them with 50 and 38 mm drywall screws. Make sure that one side of each bin extends to attach to a ceiling joist; fasten the other end to the adjacent bin. Mount the top-opening doors with butt hinges and provide a hook and eye to hold them in the open position. ▼

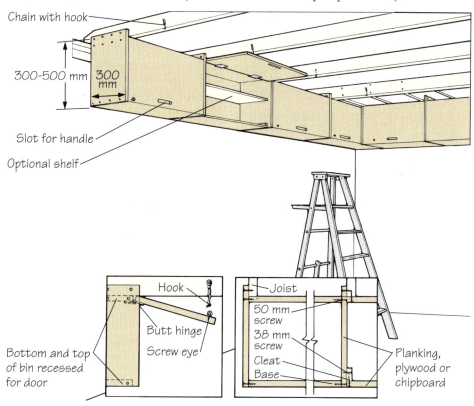

Flying carpet
Store a rolled-up rug by suspending it from two old belts attached to the garage rafters. To deter insects from nesting inside, seal the ends with heavy paper and tape.

Hanging around

Here's another way to put the space over your car to work. String a hammock from screw eyes fastened to joists and use it to store sports equipment, exercise mats, and other light bulky items. ▼

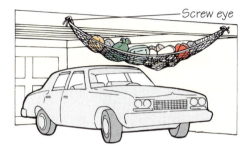

Storage loft over the car ▶

Store patio and pool furniture on this sturdy loft. Use 44 x 96 mm timbers for the frame and wall cleat, 96 x 96 mm posts to support the front and 12 mm plywood for the top. Bolt the cleat onto the wall. Assemble the frame with framing anchors (joist hangers at joist-cleat connections; framing angles at post-frame connections). For greater security, anchor the posts to the floor with post base brackets bolted to the floor.

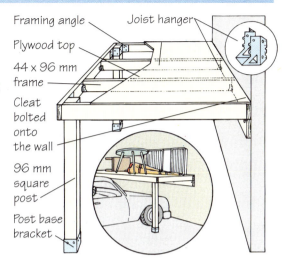

More racks

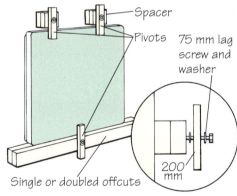

Card table rack ▲

Need to store a card or game table? Try this easy-to-make rack. Fasten an offcut (thick enough to accept the table—or join two thinner pieces as in the illustration) to the wall. Mount two blocks of offcuts above this base timber, allowing 10 mm clearance. Use 75 mm lag bolts or screws to attach the 200 mm pivots of 22 x 44 mm offcuts to their mounts. Washers will prevent the pivots binding.

Cushion station

This handy wall-mounted rack is great for storing unwieldy patio furniture cushions and similar items indoors. By keeping them off the ground, the rack also helps prevent mildew. Above a shelf about 300 mm wide by 1,8 m long, bolt a pivoting frame to two timbers fixed to the wall. ▼

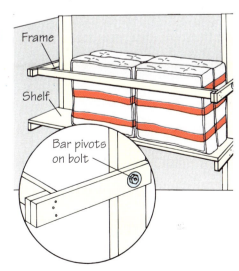

Furniture racks

Keep garage or attic clutter under control with this simple space saver. Just fasten ordinary shelf brackets or L-brackets to the wall and use them to hang folding chairs, recliners, and other lightweight outdoor furniture. If you don't have any L-brackets, you can make supports out of oversize nails, vinyl gutter brackets, or wood dowels fitted into predrilled holes in the wall. Arrange the supports in pairs to suit the pieces to be stored.

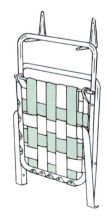

Household Storage / 125

ATTIC AND GARAGE

Utility shelves

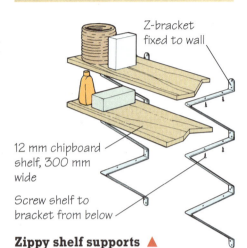

Zippy shelf supports ▲
Use 3 mm steel bars about 20 mm wide to make these Z-brackets for a shelfing system in your garage. Use 12 mm chipboard for the shelves. They will support light loads as shown, or can be reversed and will then have greater load capacity.

Under the eaves
Turn wasted space under the eaves into a convenient storage area with this handy shelving system. Fix 44 x 44 mm uprights and 22 x 44 mm cleats securely to the rafters; use nails to attach 12 mm chipboard shelves to the cleats. ▼

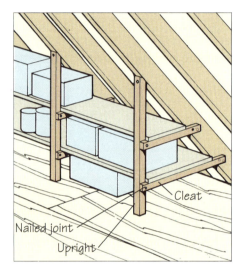

◄ Stacking cases
These flexible modules allow you to change or add to your storage unit as needed—they're very useful when stacked against a peaked attic wall. The boxes are made of 12 mm plywood or chipboard. Since there is no stress on the joints, case parts may be glued and nailed together rather than screwed. Double 44 x 44 mm lengths form the base for the assembly.

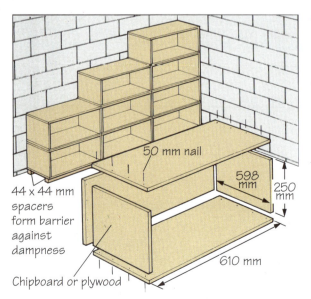

Double-duty stairs

Roll it away
This roll-out bin is designed to make the most of the wasted space under the lower end of a stairway. Use it to store awkward items ranging from cleaning supplies to boots and sports equipment. The bin is a simple box made of 12 mm chipboard, assembled with screws and glue and mounted on casters. The corners are reinforced with 22 x 22 mm battens as shown. To cut the front, back, and filler pieces at the correct angle, trace the slope of the stairs on a piece of cardboard and use it as a template for marking the wood. Allowing for casters, the bin's front and back should clear the stairs by 5 mm; the filler panel fits flush. For easy access, install a handle on the front of the bin. ▼

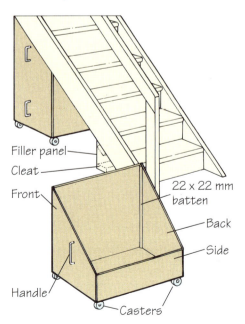

INSTALLING PEGBOARD

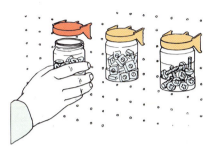

Pegboard, short for perforated hardboard, is an excellent solution to a variety of storage problems, both in and out of the workshop. Brightly painted and edged with moulding, it makes a great kitchen wall organizer. In addition to the standard S-hooks and hangers, a variety of shelves and containers designed to attach to pegboard allows you to customize your storage system.

Available at home centres and hardware outlets, pegboard panels are easy to install. On an unfinished drywall, screw the panels directly onto the exposed studs. (To keep screwheads from sinking all the way through the pegboard, use washers, or drive screws through the flush surface, not through the holes.) Attach pegboard to wallboard by driving drywall screws through the panel, then through a rubber or plastic spacer (short sections of PVC pipe, each about 15 mm long, work well) and directly into a stud (see right). The spacers hold the panel away from the wall, allowing clearance for the hooks. Mount pegboard on masonry walls with mounting strips, as shown below.

On wallboard and drywalls

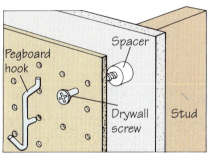

To mount pegboard onto wallboard or a drywall, first locate the wall studs by tapping the wall or using a stud finder (p 135). After placing the panel in the desired position, drive 50 mm drywall screws through the flush surface of the panel, then through the spacers and into the studs. Position screws at intervals of 300 mm vertically and at every stud along the top and base of the panel.

On masonry

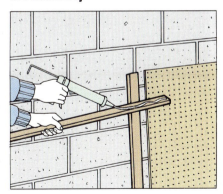

To install pegboard on a masonry wall, cut lengths of 22 x 44 mm mounting strips equal to the height of the pegboard panel. Then apply panel adhesive to one side of each strip.

Fasten the mounting strips to the wall with 50 mm masonry nails. To make sure the pegboard panels are properly supported, place the strips no more than 1,2 m apart.

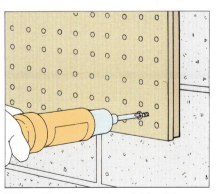

Position the panel, and drive 20 mm drywall screws through the panel's flush surface into the strips at 300 mm intervals. No spacers are required—the mounting strips provide clearance.

HOME IMPROVEMENTS

WALL REPAIR 129
WALLBOARD INSTALLATION 132
WALL TRIM 134
WALL FRAMING 135
WALL PANELLING 136
CEILINGS 137
FLOORS 138
FLOOR COVERINGS 140
CERAMIC TILES 142
WINDOWS 144
DOORS 146
SOUNDPROOFING 148
WEATHERPROOFING 150
WALLS, FLOORS AND COLUMNS 156
CLADDING AND WOOD PRESERVATION 158
WALLS 160

WALL REPAIR

Small jobs

Caulking gaps
Fill gaps between a wall and its trim or between a wall and masonry with paintable latex caulk. Apply the caulk with a caulking gun; smooth and seal the newly caulked joint, using one of the techniques described on p 150. Use caulking that matches the colour of the wall, or paint it to match.

Flatten a popped nail ▲
Usually caused by shrinking framing, popped nails are the curse of wallboard interiors. To fix one, drive a drywall screw into the stud 20 mm below the popped nail, sinking the head just below the surface (p 132). Then scrape away the loose paint and compound around the popped nail, and drive it back into place. Finish with three layers of compound.

Anchors away
To remove a regular plastic wall anchor from wallboard or plaster, just insert a tight-fitting screw and wiggle it out.

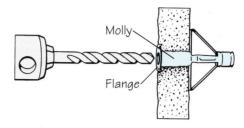

Goodbye molly
To remove a molly wall fastener (p 117), you have to drive it into the wall cavity. The resulting hole will be much smaller if you use a drill bit slightly larger than the screw hole and drill just enough to cut off the flange. Then push the rest of the molly into the wall.

Quick standard patch
To fix a small hole in wallboard or plaster, apply the self-adhesive film used for covering wide cracks in masonry. Complete the repair with a couple of coats of compound (p 131).

Press-on patch
An even quicker and neater way to repair a small hole in wallboard is with an iron-on polymer fabric repair patch. When applying the patch, be careful not to scorch or blister the surrounding paint. Paint the patch and let it dry. Then lightly sand the edges to feather them, and apply a second coat of paint. ▼

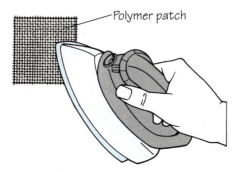

Many layers are better than one
For other minor wall repairs, the best choice is a lightweight premixed filler compound. If the hole to be filled is quite large or deep, apply a number of thinner layers rather than one single amount. Fill the hole until the filler stands slightly proud of the surrounding surface and then sand and paint it.

Smooth ruler
When patching a hole that's wider than your putty knife, don't use the putty knife to smooth and remove compound. You'll just gouge it. Instead, use a wide smoothing tool, or, if you don't have one, a metal ruler. Hold the ruler on edge and wipe it across the area.

Blow dry
On damp days, filler or joint compound can take forever to dry. To speed the process, use a hairdryer. Set it on a low temperature and keep moving it back and forth over the area so that the compound doesn't dry too quickly and begin to crack.

Invisible wall patching
Even on a flat, untextured wall, patches can stand out as smooth spots after you paint. To mimic the texture of the surrounding wall, let the patch dry; then before painting the wall, lightly spray the patch with water and brush the surface gently in a circular motion with a small scrubbing brush. After it's painted, the patch won't show.

WALL REPAIR

Patching wallboard

Mesh makes sense
To patch a large hole, attach a backing of suitable steel mesh, slightly smaller than the hole, to a piece of fibreglass about 30 mm longer on each side. Glue the patch over the hole and spread a layer of filler over it. Sand the surface to a smooth finish and paint. ▼

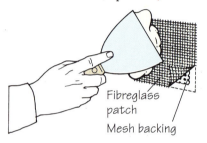

Look, no back support
Here's how to fix a hole up to 200 mm wide without backing the patch. Square the hole with a utility knife and cut a wallboard patch 20 mm larger on all sides than the hole. Score and break it along the back to the hole size. Peel off the backing and gypsum along the edges, leaving a border of facing paper. Lightly sand the border's undersurface to feather the edges, apply joint compound, set the patch in place and finish the seam using the flap as tape. ▼

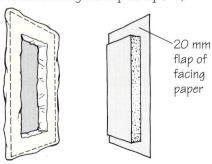

Patching a corner
To patch a badly chipped outside wall corner, use a long, flat trowel as a form. Holding it even with the edge on one side of the corner, fill in the area on the other side with compound or plaster. Then slide the trowel away from the corner, being careful not to lift it until it is clear of the patched area.

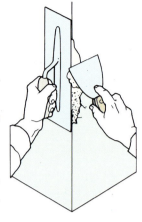

Plaster repair secrets

Thump it like a melon
When you repair a plaster wall, always remove the plaster down to its soundest layer before attempting a repair. Sound plaster makes a solid, snappy noise when you thump it; loose plaster produces a hollow, dull sound.

Give it a grip
When patching plaster which meets a wooden frame for a door or window, drive screws into the wood, leaving the heads sticking up. This gives the new plaster something to hold on to.

Work your way to the top
When replastering, start from the base of the damaged area and work your way to the top—so that each amount you apply, rests on the one below it.

No-sag plastering
To fix a large hole in plaster, use patching plaster (mixed with perlite); it's less likely to sag than joint compound. For the plaster to adhere well, dampen the old surface well or apply a latex bonding agent. Apply the plaster in layers no more than 9 mm thick. Crosshatch each layer with the corner of a putty knife as it starts to set. Let it dry; then wet it before applying the next layer.

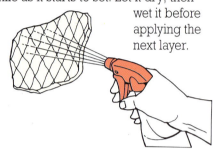

A new type of bar clamp
Repairing damaged plaster on the end and both sides of a wall can be eased greatly by clamping two planks to the wall. The clamps are two lengths of 8 mm steel bar bent into circles and then opened far enough to clamp the planks in position. You can use bars of all sorts of lengths to apply pressure to surfaces quite far apart, but in such cases, bend the ends only. ▼

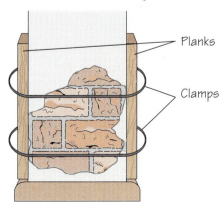

FIXING DAMAGED WALLBOARD

A hole may have been caused by a doorknob, furniture movers or peeling tape resulting from humidity. Whatever the cause, damaged wallboard is easy to repair. If you encounter a stud when you are removing a damaged section, cut the wallboard back to the centre of the stud and secure one edge of your patch to the stud. If the damage to a wall is extensive, cut the wallboard back to the middle of the stud on each side, and secure the patch directly to the two studs.

When finishing a patch or a joint, apply thin coats of joint compound; let each coat dry and then sand it lightly with fine-grit paper. Each time you apply compound, broaden the area covered with the compound until the patch blends with the surrounding wall.

Retaping a joint

1 Remove all loose tape, including tape that is only partially loose; don't try to salvage old tape. Sand away loose tape remnants and rough edges.

2 Apply a coat of joint compound and embed new paper tape in it. Then apply two thin coats over the tape, feathering the edges. Sand smooth.

Patching a hole

1 Cut out the damaged section, using a drywall saw (or a utility knife). Square up and enlarge the area you cut out to make it easier to repair.

2 Cut two boards a few centimetres longer than the hole. Slip them into the hole at top and bottom and secure them with 30 mm drywall screws.

3 Cut a wallboard patch 3 mm smaller on all sides than the hole. Insert the patch into the hole and attach it to the boards with drywall screws.

4 Cover seams with crack-sealing film (p 129) and then apply three thin coats of joint compound, sanding the compound smooth after each coat.

WALLBOARD INSTALLATION

Installing wallboard

X-ray walls
Before putting up new wallboard, take photographs of the wall construction, including plumbing and electrical lines. Later, when you need to know what's in there, you'll have a record. Take the picture as straight on as possible, and include a stretched-out tape measure.

Take it all off
Even with the most careful finishing, it's hard to hide crushed edges and corners and nailhead tears on wallboard. Instead of trying to salvage the damaged facing paper, you'll get a much better finish if you tear off the loose paper and apply the compound directly to the gypsum.

Cutting edge
When cutting wallboard a utility knife blade quickly becomes clogged and blunt. To prevent this, keep a small piece of fine sandpaper handy and periodically rub the blade with it to remove the chalk buildup.

Across, not up and down
In a room with a low ceiling, install wallboard horizontally, using sheets with lengths equal to or greater than the height of the ceiling. You will find horizontal seams are easier to tape, and the long sheets reduce the number of vertical seams, or even eliminate them totally, by spanning the room from wall to wall. Start at the top of the wall, and work from one side to the other. When installing the lower tier, make sure any vertical seams are staggered. Start with a half sheet if necessary. ▼

Making a point
To mark the position of an electrical box on wallboard, put machine screws, whose heads have been cut off, into the holes for mounting the receptacle or switch.

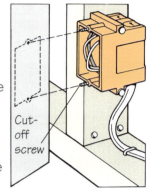

Then position the wallboard panel and press it against the screws. To outline the cutout on the wallboard, just place a spare electrical box over the holes made by the screws. If a box is wired, be sure to turn off the power to it at the main distribution board first.

Smooching wallboard
Another, quicker way to mark an electrical outlet's position on wallboard is to coat the edges of the box with lipstick and press the wallboard in place. Then remove the panel and cut along the "kiss marks" on the back.

Fold for carrying ▶
Getting wallboard around stairway turns (or other obstacles) isn't easy. Instead of cutting the sheets apart, score the back of each panel at the stud location, fold it as shown, and carefully carry it up the stairs. To install the sheet, simply unfold it and mount it, double-nailing at the scored seam.

A useful warp ▶
When installing decorative wallboard, avoid unsightly fasteners along vertical seams by bowing the sheets. Stack the sheets face up overnight, with the centres on the floor and the ends propped up on timbers. To attach a sheet, apply adhesive to the studs and fasten the sheet at top and bottom. The bow in the sheet presses its centre against the adhesive.

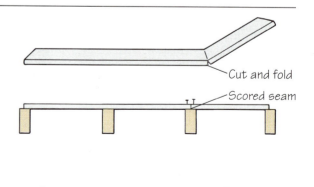

Don't rip it out

Need to take down a wallboard panel you just installed? If you haven't finished the joints yet, you can reuse the panel. Sharpen one end of a short length of 20 mm copper tube with a file. Place the tube over each nailhead, and strike it sharply with a hammer to cut through the wallboard. Then lift off the panel. To replace the piece, fit it back on the studs, placing the cutout holes over the old nails. New nails are driven in about 20 mm or so from each old nail. ▼

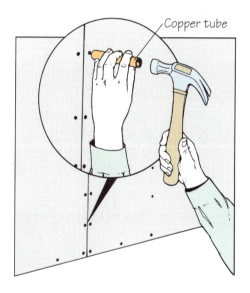

Dust-free smoothing

Sanding wallboard patches and seams can stir up a dusty mess. Instead of sanding, try using a damp sponge to remove excess compound after it dries. Select a large, fine-textured sponge, and rinse it regularly in a bucket of water. With practice, you can get perfectly smooth seams that may need a light sanding at most. You can also keep the dust down by using a sanding sponge, an abrasive-surfaced sponge.

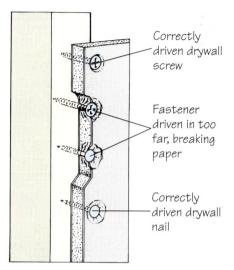

Gentle touch ▲

When driving nails or screws into wallboard, the trick is to set the fastener just below the surface so that it can be hidden with compound. If you drive it in too deep, so that it breaks the paper or crushes the wallboard, you compromise the fastener's holding power.

Compound tricks

Saving leftovers

Do you buy filler compound in large containers, use some, and a few weeks later find that the rest has turned lumpy? Here's how to stop this happening: before it dries, scrape all the excess compound off the inside surfaces of the container and wipe the surfaces clean. Level the compound, and pour 100 ml of water over it. Rinse and replace the plastic that was over the compound when you opened the container, then put the lid on tightly.

Stick 'em up

Installing wallboard with panel adhesive reduces the need for fasteners, which means fewer need be hidden with filler and there will be fewer popped nails later on. Apply adhesive to each stud with a caulking gun. Then press the wallboard in place, and secure it with drywall nails or screws every 400 mm around the edges and once in the centre. Follow all safety warnings on the adhesive; it's highly flammable. ▼

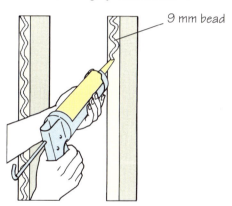

Give it a stir

To mix or thin compound, use a paint mixer attachment on a 9 mm variable-speed drill running slowly. To avoid making a mess, use an old lid with a cutout for the mixer and for adding water or powder.

Easy cleanup

When working with dry compound, mix it in a flexible plastic container. When the job is done, let the leftover compound harden. Then flex the container. The material will break away; throw it out and wash the container.

WALL TRIM

Skirting and quadrant

Easy indicator

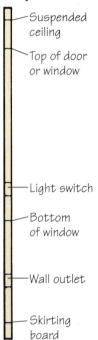

If you're planning a lot of building or remodelling, use any light, rigid length of wood to make yourself a story pole. This handy tool, basically a rod with frequently used measurements marked on it, reduces the time you spend measuring and helps ensure that you put trim and other items in the same place—in one room and in all the others.

Easy-off quadrant

Remove quadrant without damage to it or the skirting: slip a putty knife between the quadrant and the board and put a piece of 4 mm plywood on the skirting. Then carefully prise the quadrant off the board. Do this a little at a time in a number of places to avoid breaking the quadrant.

No-one will ever know

If you can't find quadrant that matches what you already have in the home, lift a piece from behind units that won't be moved—such as TV wall units and built-in units. Where necessary, replace it with closely matching stock and use the old matching quadrant in areas where it will be seen more often.

Skirting and quadrant saver

You can reuse trim if you pull each nail through the wood from the underside. This won't mar the finish or splinter the top surface. When reusing the trim, use slightly bigger nails (for a firm hold) driven through the same nail holes.

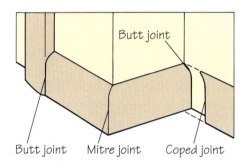

Corner ins and outs

Here are some rules to help you when you're installing skirting boards and quadrant:
▷ Fit outside corners first, joining the pieces with a mitre joint.
▷ On an inside corner, butt one piece against the wall and cut the other to fit around it, making a coped joint (p 79).
▷ When trim runs into a door frame, make a butt joint.
▷ When cutting skirting or quadrant to fit a mitre joint, cut it about 2 mm too long and trim to obtain a perfect fit.

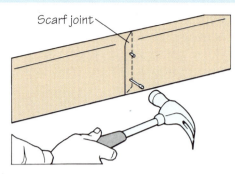

Joining on the angle

When joining straight lengths of skirting, cut the end of each piece at a 45° angle and splice the pieces together. A scarf joint, as this is known, is less noticeable than a butt joint, particularly if shrinkage occurs.

Easy on the cornice

Installing cornice is quite difficult at the best of times. It will be greatly eased, however, if you make a template that duplicates the cornice's bearing points. Put the cornice on a framing square and measure the points. Then make a template by nailing two wood blocks together. Use it every metre or so to mark the positions of the cornice bearing points on the wall and ceiling.

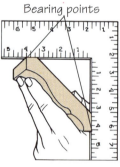

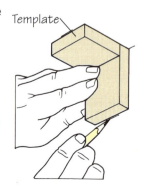

WALL FRAMING

Wall studs

Solid toehold
When installing wall studs, accurate toenailing—driving nails at an angle to join a stud to the soleplate—is essential. To keep a stud from shifting as you hammer, place the head of a large common nail against the opposite side of the stud and tap it into the plate. Or if you are installing several studs, cut a spacer to fit between them and use it to hold each stud in place as you nail. It also helps to bend the end of the nail slightly so that the nail curves as it goes into the wood. ▼

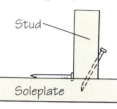

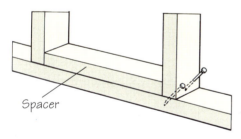

Amicable separation
Need to separate two studs or beams that are nailed together? Insert the flat ends of two pry bars as shown, and push the angled ends towards the centre. Start near one end of the studs and work along to the other end.

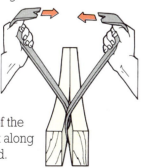

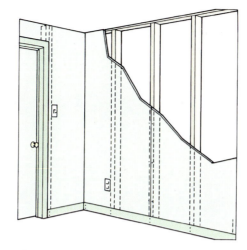

Detective work ▲
Trying to find wall studs can frustrate the homeowner. Here are two clues as to what to look for: nails securing skirting boards to the wall go into studs, and electricity outlets are attached to studs (turn off the power at the main distribution board before probing next to a box). Also look for wallboard seams and nailheads (you may see them when you angle a bright light across the wall). Once you've found one stud, you should be able to find the others as they will be spaced at regular intervals, measuring from the centre of one stud to the centre of the next.

Sensitive stud
When nailing or screwing into a stud, don't use a fastener that penetrates more than 20 mm into the timber. The centre third of a stud is often used by plumbers and electricians for routing pipes and wiring. Secondly, always try to hit the stud's centre. If you're too far off centre, the fastener may go through the side and lose holding power.

STUD FINDERS

An electronic stud finder is a handy battery-powered device with a sensor that detects differences in wall density. To use it, you press a button and pass the finder over the wall. A light goes on when the finder reaches the edge of a stud and goes out when it passes over the other edge. Some electronic stud finders are self-calibrating; others have to be calibrated to a wall's density before you can use them.

The simpler magnetic version contains a magnet that swivels like a compass needle when it passes over nails in a stud. It works best when used just below the ceiling or just above the floor, where the studs are nailed to top beams and soleplates.

Both types of stud finders may be misled by pipes, metal cables, foil-backed insulation, and other framing members. And neither may work well on plaster walls.

Home Improvements / 135

WALL PANELLING

Installing panelling

Period of adjustment
Panelling tends to shrink or expand with changes in humidity in the first few days after you get the panels home. To minimize problems after installation, let the panels adjust to their new home first. Separate them after delivery and stand each one up in the area where you plan to install them. Over the course of two or three days, they will adjust to the room's humidity and you can install them without worrying about shrinkage.

The perfect panel
The key to perfect panelling is getting the first panel straight—the rest will follow suit. Align the first panel against a corner, and tack it into place with a single nail centred in the top. Use a level to make sure the panel is straight and plumb. If the plumbed panel doesn't fit snugly against the adjoining wall, use a compass to scribe the panel edge next to the wall (p 71), copying the slant of the wall onto the panel. Remove the panel, and trim it to fit. Then secure it in place.

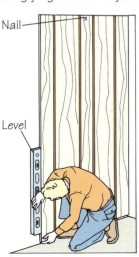

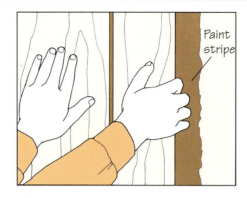

Concealing gaps ▲
When you're putting up panelling, it's almost inevitable that there will be some space visible between panels. This can be a real problem when you're installing dark panelling on light-coloured walls because the wall will peek through the open joints. To avoid this, brush a broad stripe of paint—the same colour as the panel joints—on the wall behind each seam before installing the panels. Use a small roller or a tin of spray paint to speed the work.

Warped panels
Even fresh-from-the-factory panelling may be warped. As long as the problem isn't too severe and the warped panels aren't more than 6 mm thick, you can mount them successfully using both panel adhesive and panelling nails. (Panel adhesive is made specifically for installing panelling and wallboard.) If the panelling is thick or badly warped, however, you'll be better off returning it.

For a firm, clean job
Before securing panelling to bare studs or to mounting strips on masonry walls, install wallboard panels first. Of course, it will be more expensive but you'll get a stiffer and far more substantial wall with no bowing or warping. You'll also avoid nail holes, since the panels can be attached with panel adhesive alone. For economy and ease of handling, use 9,5 mm wallboard. And even though the joints won't show, tape them to reduce air infiltration.

Nail disguise
To camouflage nails in panelling or trim, try to place them in a natural blemish or in the darker lines of the grain pattern.

Finish now, fill later
If you will be staining and varnishing your panelling, fill the nail holes after you stain and varnish the wood. This allows you to match the putty colour to the finished look of the wood. If you fill the nail holes before staining, the putty will absorb the stain differently than the wood, causing the holes to stand out. ▼

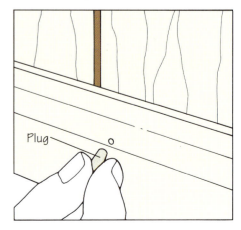

CEILINGS

Ceiling tiles

An appealing ceiling
To keep ceiling tiles clean while you're installing them, dip your fingers in cornflour before handling each tile—the powder will shield the tiles from being smudged. A little extra powder in one pocket of your tool apron will save you lots of trips up and down the ladder.

Tongue tapped ▲
Tongue-and-groove ceiling tiles often don't fit together snugly when installed. To ensure a good fit, cut one tile in half and use it as a striker panel to coax the other tiles into place. Butt the tongue of the cut panel into the groove of the tile being fitted; a light hammer tap on the cut tile will nudge the full tile into place without damaging it. When the striker panel becomes worn, throw it away and use another half tile.

Graceful grid ▶
You can't eliminate the metal grid supporting a suspended ceiling, but you can soften its visual impact. Mount decorative cornice around the perimeter of the room to give the ceiling a more elegant, finished look.

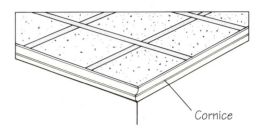

Patching wallboard

The cardboard butler
If you have to cut into a wallboard ceiling, do it from the attic if possible. You'll avoid the risk of cutting unseen wires (you'll also keep dust out of your face). Reduce cleanup by putting a cardboard box on the floor below to catch debris.

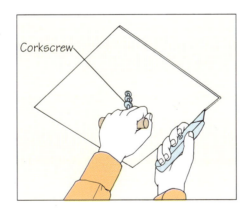

Corkscrew handle ▲
If you can only cut into a wallboard ceiling from below, twist a corkscrew into the centre of the waste area first; then use it as a handle to keep the piece from landing on your head. For smooth, easy-to-patch edges, cut with a utility knife. Always turn off the power to any ceiling light at the main distribution board before making a blind cut into the ceiling.

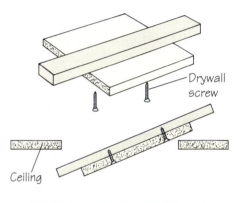

Hole fixes ▲
To patch a hole of moderate size in a wallboard ceiling, trim and square up the damaged area, and cut out a wallboard patch that's slightly smaller than the opening. Then screw (or glue) a wood cleat to the back of the patch. Make the cleat about 150 mm longer than the patch so that it extends about 75 mm on each side. Tilt and drop the patch into position, and screw the cleat to the ceiling. Finish the seams with tape and compound. For a large hole, trim the opening to the centre of the ceiling joists on either side and secure the patch to the joists. Repair a small hole with a patching kit as you would fix a hole in a wall (p 129).

FLOORS

Squeak solutions

Shim to the rescue

Squeaking is one of the most annoying floor problems. The cause is usually wood rubbing against wood or a nail. To stop a squeak caused by the movement of the subfloor against a joist, tap a wood shim between the joist and the subfloor in the vicinity of the squeak. Don't force it in too far, though, or you'll cause more problems than you solve. Dab a little glue onto the shim before installation so that it stays in place. ▼

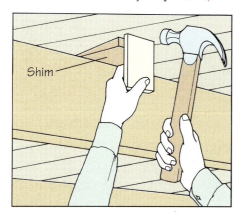

Squeak end work

Carpet replacement time offers a great opportunity to track down and eliminate squeaks in an unfinished floor that's otherwise always covered. After the carpet is up, walk over the entire area to find the squeaks. Wherever there's a problem, drive 50 mm drywall screws through the floor and subfloor into the joist below. A line of existing nails is the best clue to the location of a joist.

Stop a squeak ▲

Sometimes you fix a squeak in one place only to find that it has moved to another spot. One squeak-stopper you can quickly apply to large areas of a floor is construction adhesive. Put a tube in a caulking gun and run a bead along both sides of a joist, right where it supports the subfloor. The squeaks should be gone for good.

Sneaky squeak stoppers

The best fix for a squeaky floor is to eliminate the usual culprit: the rubbing of wood against wood. But if this isn't possible, try lubricating the squeak. Any number of lubricants have been known to work, including talcum powder, furniture wax, penetrating lubricant spray, graphite, and liquid soap. Sometimes linseed oil dribbled into the cracks between floorboards will expand the wood enough to tighten the flooring.

Mind your step

Squeaky stairs? Screw metal shelf brackets to the underside of the stair to silence offending treads. The brackets needn't be large, but make sure the screws don't poke through to the top.

Braced for action

Squeaky floors are often caused by floor bridging that has worked loose over the years, allowing the joists to move a bit when the floor above them is walked on. The solution is easy: just reattach the bridging with nails. ▼

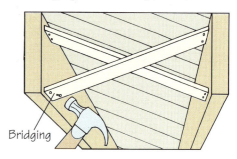

Repairing strip flooring

A fix from below

Sometimes you can pull loose flooring back into place by running screws into it from below. Make sure that the screws are shorter than the combined thickness of the flooring and the subfloor. Weight down the loose strips or have someone stand on them. ▼

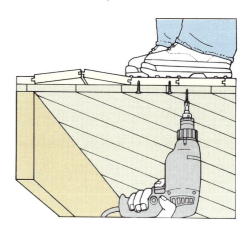

Wayward board

Before you go to the effort of replacing a warped floorboard, try this solution: strip the finish from the offending board and cover it with a damp cloth for a couple of days. If the moisture solves the problem, secure the board with countersunk wood screws before it dries and springs back.

Removing a damaged board

Taking out a damaged portion of a floorboard calls for some care and precision. Whenever possible, remove an entire board or at least the part of the board from the damaged area to the closest joint. If you have to make a crosscut, use a carpenter's square as a guide to mark the cut line. Then bore several overlapping holes just inside the line. Split the board with a chisel, and prise out the pieces carefully, centre piece first. Finally use a wide chisel to square off the opening, using the cut line as a guide.

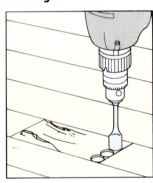

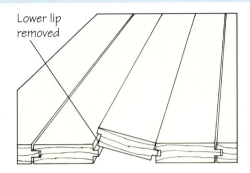

Replacing damaged boards ▲

Once you've removed boards from a strip floor, replacing them is simply a matter of lining up the tongues and grooves and nailing the boards in place. Simple, that is, until you get to the last board. The trick to fitting it is to chisel off the lower lip on the board's groove side. With the lip gone, the board will fall easily into place. You'll have to nail through the surface of the board to secure it. Use a little filler over the countersunk nails to conceal your work.

Nailing tip

Whenever you use nails to secure strip flooring, drive them into the floor at an angle. An angled nail is less likely to work itself loose later on.

Save your knees

A large block of rigid polystyrene foam from a discarded appliance carton makes a great kneeling pad when you're working on the floor. It is easy on the knees and it won't scratch the floor finish. Another knee-saver is a pair of pads of foam wrapped in carpet offcuts and tied to your knees with tapes.

Structural remedies

Floor stiffeners

The bounce of an old floor is often due to tired or undersize floor joists. If the joists are accessible from below, here's an inexpensive fix. Attach a 2,4 m length of 12 mm plywood—at least 200 mm wide—to one side of each joist, securing it with adhesive and two rows of 50 mm nails spaced about 150 mm apart. Adding these braces to the centre of each joist should stiffen the floor noticeably. ▼

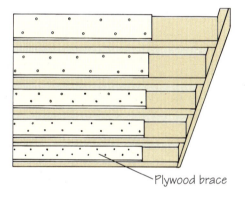

Removing a subfloor

Pulling out nails one by one to remove boards in a subfloor makes for a long day. You can sometimes speed the work by cutting the floor into sections with a circular saw. Set the saw blade to a depth just short of the thickness of the subfloor; then run it down the length of a joist (just to one side of the nails). With any luck you may be able to prise entire sections of the subfloor loose, nails and all. The trick works just as well when removing old strip flooring.

FLOOR COVERINGS

Carpeting tricks

Pile plugs
To patch small burns or stains in a carpet, file the end of a short length of copper pipe into a sharp cutting edge. Put the sharpened pipe over the carpet and hit it with a mallet to remove a plug around the damage. Follow the same procedure on a matching carpet scrap or hidden section of carpeting to create a replacement plug. Dab some adhesive on the replacement plug, align its fibres with the surrounding carpet, and set it in place; you'll never see the patch.

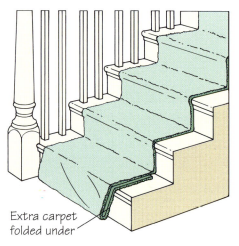
Extra carpet folded under

Carpet retreads ▲
If you're replacing the runner on the stairs, buy an extra 500 mm. When you install the carpet, fold the extra length at the bottom of the stairs. When the carpet begins to wear—usually along the projecting nose of each tread—just untack the runner, shift it up a few centimetres, and reattach it. You should be able to do this at least two or three times over the life of the carpet.

Good brews for removing glue
Here's a mixture you can use to remove dried carpet adhesive from a floor. Mix one part vinegar with three parts water, and apply the mixture to the floor. Let it stand for 30 minutes or so, and then scrape up the adhesive with a wide, stiff putty knife. Sometimes you can get away with using hot water instead: the heat alone may be able to soften the dried adhesive enough for you to remove it.

Carpeting at the threshold
Fastening carpet at the threshold between two rooms can be tricky. If the finished floor in one room is more than 10 mm higher than the floor to be carpeted in the other room, use a tack strip to hold the carpet down near the threshold, just as in the rest of the room. But if the difference between the two floors is less than this, you'll have to staple the carpet directly to the floor. Cut the carpet pad back about 25 mm from the edge of the threshold. Then simply tuck the edge of the carpeting under about 25 mm to cover the area that isn't padded. Spread the carpet pile apart with one hand and staple through both layers of carpet into the floor. ▼

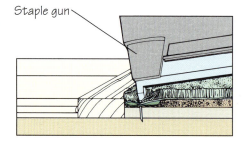
Staple gun

Removing vinyl tiles

A pressing solution
Heat is usually the key to removing vinyl floor tiles. If you need to remove a damaged tile, place a cloth over it and move an iron, turned to a medium setting, across the cloth with slow, even strokes. The heat will soften both the adhesive and the tile, making it possible to prise up the tile with a putty knife. ▼

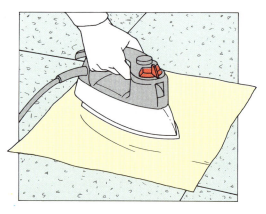

Shiver your tiles
If heat doesn't help remove a tile, try cold. Place dry ice on the tile (but be careful not to touch the ice directly). Once the tile is cold enough, a smart rap with a hammer should shatter it.

Second-hand tiles
If you want to reuse loose, undamaged floor tiles, you'll have to remove the adhesive clinging to their backs. You can scrape it off with a paint scraper, but it's much easier to soak the tiles in water overnight to soften the adhesive and then remove it with a putty knife.

Repairing vinyl floors

Clear cover

A scrape or heavy scuffing that removes the clear top layer on vinyl flooring can result in the quick deterioration of the layers below. To repair such damage, coat it with vinyl seam sealant (sold by flooring outlets and hardware dealers). If the flooring has a deeper gouge, replace the tile or the section of sheet vinyl (see right).

Bursting bubbles

Water leakage can cause a sheet vinyl floor to bubble. The repair is easy once you've eliminated the source of the problem and allowed the floor to dry thoroughly. Cut a slit in the centre of the bubble with a utility knife. Then use a plastic sauce or mustard bottle (with a pointed tip) or a glue syringe to squirt vinyl floor adhesive through the slit. Work it under the bubble with a narrow putty knife. Then press the bubble down with a rolling pin, wipe up any excess adhesive and leave a weight on the area until the adhesive has set. ▼

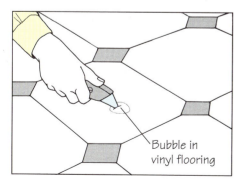
Bubble in vinyl flooring

FLOORING PATCH

To patch a damaged section of sheet vinyl flooring, use a piece left over from the original job or "stolen" from a hidden place, such as the floor under the refrigerator. The patch should be 25 mm larger all around than the damage. Whenever possible, plan for the patch seams to follow a pattern line in the flooring.

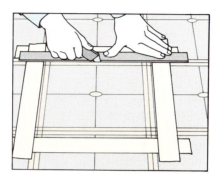

1 Place the patch over the damage, align it with the pattern, and secure it with duct tape. Use a sharp utility knife guided by a straightedge to cut through the patch and the flooring. Then prise out the damaged material and scrape out all the old adhesive.

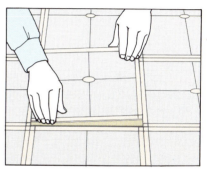

2 Spread vinyl floor adhesive on the back of the patch, fit it into place, and wipe off any excess adhesive with a damp cloth. Weight the patch overnight until the adhesive sets. Then apply vinyl seam sealer to the seams around the patch to bond it to the flooring.

Laying sheet vinyl

Strong-arm flooring

Sheet vinyl covers large areas quickly. But before installing it, you must flatten and trim the rolled material to fit the room. Getting it to stay flat right off the roll can be daunting. If the weather is warm, spread the sheet outside in the sun to relax it. In winter, try covering the sheet with an electric blanket to warm it and get out the curls.

Nick relief

If you nick or tear vinyl flooring while laying it, disguise the damage with bath and tile caulk in a closely matching colour. Dab a little into the damage and wipe off the excess with a damp cloth.

Procrastinators, this one's for you

To remove floor adhesive from your tools, put them in the freezer overnight. In the morning you'll be able to chip off the hardened adhesive. Wear goggles to protect your eyes from flying shards.

CERAMIC TILES

Working with tile

Mixing tiles
By the time you have to replace a tile, you may not be able to find an exact match. If that is the case, remove some extra tiles to form an interesting pattern and replace them with new tiles of a contrasting colour or design.

Thinking ahead
When purchasing tiles for a new project, buy a few extra for future repairs. Wrap them carefully to prevent breakage, and mark the package with the date, the name of the store they came from, and the room to which they belong. Save some matching grout, too.

Chipped tile?
You can repair nicks or chips in ceramic tiles with appliance touch-up paint. It dries to a hard, glossy surface and is available in a variety of colours.

Marking tile
During nearly any tile job, you'll have to cut tiles into odd shapes. To mark a cut line, use a felt-tip pen or a grease pencil; if you need a really precise line, scratch it with a drywall screw.

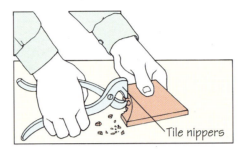

Nibble a cut ▲
When using tile nippers to make a cutout, start at the edge in the centre of the waste area and work toward the cut line. To avoid ragged edges, keep the jaws parallel to the cut line and place no more than two-thirds of the jaw surface on the tile for each bite. Smooth the edges with 80-grit carbide sandpaper.

You've got this job taped
For a neat caulking result, run masking tape along both sides of your planned line of caulk, apply and smooth the caulk, and then carefully lift away the tape. You'll get a caulk line with crisp, straight edges. To avoid messing your hands, put plastic shopping bags over them, remove the tape and turn the bags inside out and discard them. ▼

◀ Shape shifting
Fitting tiles around irregular projections can be tricky. If you have several to do, make your own contour gauge by clamping lengths of coat hanger wire between scraps of **6 mm** plywood. Fit the wires into saw kerfs in the bottom piece, spacing the kerfs to suit the degree of accuracy you need. (The more wires used, the more accurate the tool will be.) Fasten the pieces together with machine screws and wing nuts. To use the gauge, push the ends of its wires up against an obstruction until they take on its shape; then move the gauge to the tiles or to paper and trace the cut line.

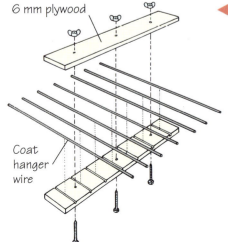

Picking between tiles
When replacing a tile, make sure your new tile is squarely aligned. Pieces of round toothpicks make perfect spacers for holding the tile in place while the adhesive sets (see step 4, facing page).

Grout match
Matching new grout with existing grout can be tricky. To increase your chance for success, buy a small amount of grout first, mix up a sample batch, and let it dry for three days or so. You'll get a much better idea of how the colour will compare with the existing grout.

REPLACING A CERAMIC TILE

Ceramic tiles are durable and stain-resistant, but sooner or later one might crack and need replacement. Fortunately the job isn't that difficult. You must remove the surrounding grout, chip out the damaged tile and replace it with a new one, and finally regrout the area around the new tile. If the damaged tile is in a bath or shower surround, the repair is one you shouldn't postpone. A cracked tile allows water to seep behind it, and over time this will damage the wallboard or other material under the tile. Eventually the moisture will multiply your problems by loosening surrounding tiles. Here's how to get the job done quickly.

1 If the tile is over the bath, use cardboard or an old blanket to protect the bath surface and keep debris out of the drain. Remove any fixture that is covering the tile, such as the spout shown here.

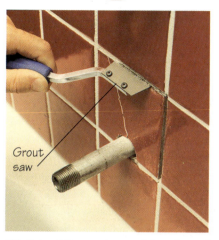

2 Cut out the grout around the edges of the damaged tile with a grout saw, or scrape it free with the tip of an old screwdriver. Work carefully to avoid chipping the edges of the surrounding tiles.

3 Wearing safety goggles, use a sharp cold chisel and a ball-peen hammer to crack the tile in an X-pattern. Tap lightly to avoid damaging other tiles. Prise out the pieces, and chip out the old adhesive.

4 Shape the new tile as needed (facing page). Spread 3 mm of tile adhesive on the back, press it in place, and use tape or spacers to hold it. Scrape excess adhesive from joints, and wipe clean.

5 When the adhesive cures, press grout into the joints and smooth it. Wipe off excess grout with a damp sponge. Use a dry cloth to burnish off any haze that forms on the tile surface.

WINDOWS

Quick fixes

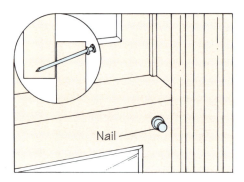

Nail order ▲
Here's a cost-effective security measure for double-hung windows. Drill a hole through the inner sash and halfway into the outer sash. A nail slipped into the hole prevents anyone from pushing the sashes open. If you angle the hole, a nail can't be jiggled out. Use a nail long enough to protrude a few millimetres so that you'll be able to remove it easily.

Lazy guard
Nearly any sliding window or door can get a simple security boost. Cut a dowel or a board to fit flat in the window track. This will prevent the sash from sliding open even if the lock is jimmied. ▼

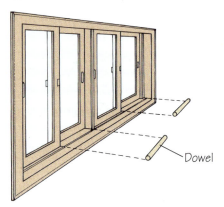

Stubborn sash?
A window may stick for any number of reasons—including warped or swollen wood or accumulated dirt or paint. So, before undertaking major repairs, try lubricating the channels with candle wax, soap, paraffin, or silicone spray. ▼

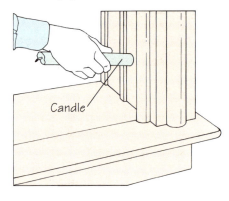

Stain be gone
Many windows feature vinyl or vinyl-clad frames to improve their weather-resistance. If you accidentally drip or brush stain or paint on the frames while working on the surrounding surfaces, do not use sandpaper or steel wool to remove it. Instead, dab off the stain with naphtha, mineral spirits, or turpentine. A slower method, but one that's easier on the vinyl, is to scrub it with a hand cleaner containing lanolin. Before using a cleaning compound, spot-test it on an unobtrusive portion of the frame.

Removing glass

Upright proposition
Always carry and store a pane of glass in a vertical position. Otherwise, the glass may break under the force of its own weight.

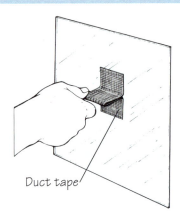

Handle on a roll ▲
Even a small pane of glass can be unwieldy when you're trying to manoeuvre it into place, so give it a handle. Fold a length of duct tape into a tab that you can grab. On a large pane use two.

Another glass carrier
To carry a sizable pane of glass safely and easily, slit two short sections of old garden hose and slip them over the top and bottom edges of the glass.

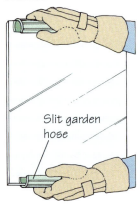

Safety strategies
Most injuries associated with repairing broken windows occur while removing the glass. If you remove the glazing putty first, the glass will be loosened enough for you to pull it easily from the window. Always wear canvas or leather gloves when handling broken glass.

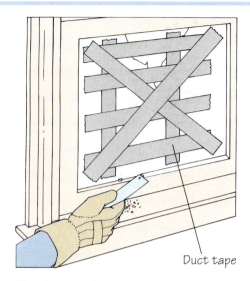

Duct tape

Combine and conquer ▲
Use wide duct tape to hold together all the pieces of a broken pane while you're removing the putty. When you've finished, just lift out the glass or press it out from the other side.

Pull, don't push
When removing broken glass, pull the shards toward you; if they break, any slivers will be directed away from you. Don't forget to wear gloves and goggles.

Installing panes

Don't be a pane killer
When you measure for the new glass, remember that a snug-fitting pane can easily crack when a wood window frame moves or shrinks. That's why glass should be cut about 3 mm smaller overall than the height and width of the actual opening. Cut the glass yourself (p 99) or have it done by the glazier.

Well-prepared rabbet
Before installing a new pane, scrape and sand the rabbet (the notch in the edge of the sash that the pane fits into). Then give it a coat of primer or linseed oil. This will keep the wood from absorbing the oil in the glazing compound.

Pane bed
To cushion the glass, even out wood irregularities, and create a weathertight joint, put a bead of paintable latex caulk on the rabbet of the sash before setting in the glass. Caulk, which goes on quickly with a caulking gun, is preferable here to glazing compound, which is often stiff and can break the glass when you press it in.

Tape for a neat border
Prior to installing a pane, dry-fit it to see where the putty will be applied. Then lay it on a flat surface and run masking tape around the perimeter at a suitable distance from the edge. When you repaint the frame later, you will obtain a neat border.

Clamp it
A batten clamped across the top of the window frame a few centimetres from the top will stop the new pane falling out should you need to be elsewhere for a few moments and cannot continue holding it in position.

Safety first
The film used to reduce solar heating of homes can also help prevent injury when applied to large, low windows in homes with small children.

Roll a rope
Applying the layer of glazing compound around a new pane is much easier if you roll a lump of compound between your hands to form a ropelike length. Then just press the rope along the joint and smooth it. ▼

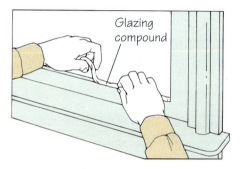

Glazing compound

Non-stick knife
When smoothing glazing compound, dip your putty knife blade in turpentine, mineral spirits, or paint thinner now and then; it'll keep the compound from sticking to the blade. ▼

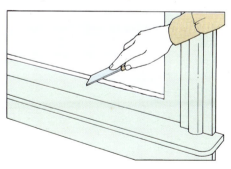

Take your time
After installing a new pane, wait about a week for the compound to cure before painting it. When you do paint, lap the paint just a bit onto the glass to seal the edge of the compound.

DOORS

Easy tune-ups

A good first impression
The wood threshold beneath an exterior door is a thing of beauty, at least until time and weather take their toll. To restore and protect a weatherworn threshold, first strip or sand off any remaining finish. Then apply a generous coat of boiled linseed oil, let it soak in for 30 minutes and then wipe off the excess. Repeat the process about 24 hours later. Let the threshold dry completely; then finish it with two or more coats of marine varnish.

Handing a door
Left-hand door or right-hand—which is it? Because some doors are bevelled to permit smooth opening in one direction, you'll need to know this if you're replacing one. Here's how you can tell the difference: face the door so that it opens toward you and you can see the hinge barrels. If the knob is on your left, the door is left-handed. If it's on your right, the door is right-handed. ▼

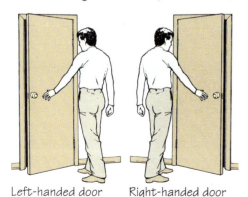

Left-handed door   Right-handed door

Ink a lock
To make sure the bolt of a deadbolt lock or a lockset aligns with the strike plate, mark the bolt with ink, lipstick or chalk, then close the door and rotate the bolt against the jamb to make an imprint. Use the imprint to align the plate.

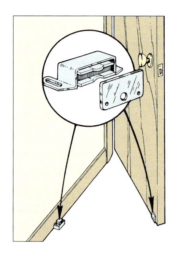

Open-door policy ▲
Are you bothered by an interior door that slams shut whenever a breeze blows or you walk by it? Screw a magnetic cabinet door catch to the floor, with its strike plate on the back of the door. Make sure the catch is far enough out from the skirting board to allow for the door handle. If necessary, mount it on a small block of wood to give the necessary clearance.

Finish it off properly
Many people forget to paint or finish the bottom and top edges of an entry door, and that's a big mistake. Unsealed edges provide access to moisture, which can cause swelling and warping, and peeling paint. Coat the edges with an exterior paint or penetrating sealer.

Taming slippery hinges
It's important to position the two leaves of a butt hinge so that they will match exactly. But it's hard to hold a hinge leaf in place as you mark around it because the pencil tends to follow the grain of the wood and cause the hinge to move. The trick is to use a sharp pencil and press lightly. Another solution is to temporarily screw the hinge in place or stick it down with double-sided tape while you trace around it.

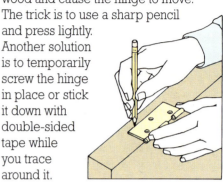

Pop goes the pin
You can remove many hinge pins without damaging the hinge barrel by slipping a nail into the hole at the bottom of the barrel, then driving the nail (and the pin) upward.

Securing the perimeter

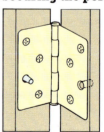

If its hinge pins are exposed, locking a door offers little security because the pins, and then the door itself, can be removed with relative ease. To make a break-in less easy, remove two opposite middle screws from a hinge. Run a long screw partly into the jamb side of the hinge, and cut off the screw's head with a hacksaw, letting the shank stick out about 6 mm. When you close the door, the shank will fit into the opposite hinge hole, securing the door.

INSTALLING A RIM DEADBOLT LOCK

It may be on the homely side, but a surface-mounted rim deadbolt is about the strongest door lock available. It's also easier to install than an in-the-door cylindrical deadbolt, making it a good choice for anyone short on skills or time. Locksmiths and well-stocked hardware stores carry good-quality rim deadbolt locks.

1 Cut the outline of the strike plate onto the jamb with a utility knife; then chisel a mortise for the strike plate. Attach the plate, using long screws that anchor it firmly to the door frame.

2 Tape the paper template that comes with the lock to the door directly opposite the strike plate. Use a nail to mark the centres of the holes you'll be drilling for the lock cylinder and housing screws.

3 Use a hole saw to drill the cylinder hole. (To prevent splintering, drill until the pilot bit pokes through the other side; then finish from the other side.) Drill pilot holes for the housing screws.

4 Mount the lock cylinder and backplate in the hole. The bolts for attaching the cylinder and the connecting bar are notched so that they can easily be cut to fit doors of different thicknesses. Use side-cutting pliers or nippers to cut them, and wear safety goggles to protect your eyes against flying metal pieces.

5 Slip the lock into place, and make sure the connecting bar in the cylinder meshes correctly with the lock. Check the fit of the lock by engaging and disengaging the deadbolt with the strike plate. If all's in order, drive the housing screws into place, and the job is done.

SOUNDPROOFING

Sound barriers

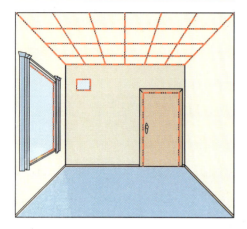

Seal that gap ▲
Sound is like a fluid: it will pass through any gap, no matter how small. So one of the basic aids to soundproofing a room is sealing every gap, no matter how small. Pay particular attention to gaps between doors and their frames and the floor. The same applies, of course, to windows. One way to seal these gaps is to use draught excluder sealing strips. They're available in a variety of widths from hardware dealers.

Try these
You may not be able to eliminate noise completely, but these tricks might help to keep irritating noise in check:
▷ Run noisy food appliances on foam rubber pieces to deaden their noise.
▷ Place a piece of foam against the wall behind a stereo speaker or TV. Ensure ventilation holes are not blocked.
▷ Hard surfaces reflect sound: rugs and carpets will deaden the sound of footfalls. The thicker the material, the better it deadens noise, by cushioning the impact between floor and footwear.

Stop that noise
If you don't wish to soundproof a whole garage or workshop, section off a part of it, or even half (preferably that which does not have windows or air bricks, as these will make sealing the area more difficult). The work area should be of sufficient size for the tasks you normally carry out in the workshop, but the larger it is, the better—you never know what future projects might entail. Ensure that you have adequate lighting and proper ventilation in the insulated area. Bear in mind, however, that the latter can be a source of sound "leakage".

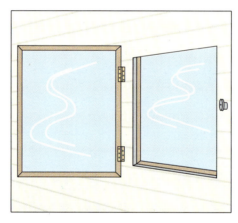

Workshop wonder window ▲
A single layer of glass, as in a normal window, may still allow a lot of noise to escape. Make up a large frame and put a pane of glass in it. Attach the new "window" to the inner or outer wall, hinged if necessary, and seal the gaps between the wall surfaces and frame with draught excluder tape. The double glass layer will make it more difficult for sound to pass. Adding foam or heat insulation fibre to the masonry surround and windowsill can attenuate the sound even further.

Beat that traffic noise
A screening wall between your home and passing traffic can work quite well, but the problem is compounded by the fact that the noise source is moving. To be as effective as possible, however, the wall must be high enough. In fact, it must rise a few metres above the line of sight between the noise source and your ear. It will not be effective if too low, but you will have to judge the probable noise reduction of a high wall against the probable loss of natural ventilation—cooling breezes during summer, for instance.

Sound results

Trees are for the birds
A line of tall trees planted around a property has a negligible effect on noise. So consider this option carefully before making a final decision.

Off the wall
Lining the inside of the walls of your home with acoustic tiles may succeed only in reducing the amount of reflected sound in a room.

And off the ceiling
Heat insulation material in the roof will not necessarily make a house quieter, but it could help. In a solidly constructed home, sound may pass into the roof space and bounce down into another room. But, in many houses, doors leak more sound than the ceiling. If heat insulation does reduce sound, consider it a bonus, but don't try to install heat insulation with sound reduction in mind until you have sealed every other leak.

INSTALLING A SECOND DOOR

Installing a second door on the same frame as the existing entrance to your workshop can be an effective measure to contain workshop noise.

As usual, of course, you should ensure that all gaps between the doors and their frames are sealed. The second door can simply be a 12 or 16 mm sheet of chipboard with a foam lining on the inner surface (an old foam mattress would be suitable), draught excluder sealing strips along each edge, and a simple catch.

Make sure you seal the base of the door where it meets the floor—even if you extend the inner foam lining to the floor, and opening the door requires a little effort. The noise reduction will be worth it.

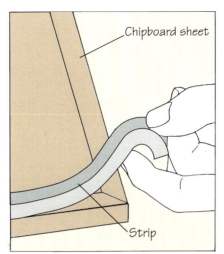

1 Cut the door to size so that it closes flat against the existing door's frame or the surrounding wall. Attach draught excluder strips along the edges.

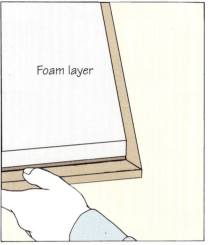

2 Glue the foam lining onto the chipboard with contact adhesive. The lining should be as big as possible so that it presents the largest possible surface.

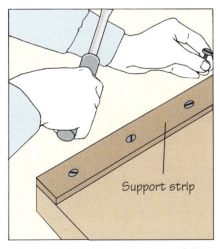

3 Attach the hinges to the door. If the foam is heavy (aim for a minimum thickness of 50 mm or so), you may need to attach a support strip to the door.

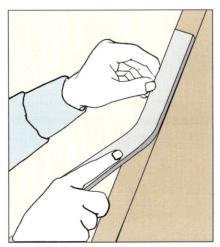

4 Attach the door in position and use extra strips of draught excluder to close the remaining gaps (a light shone from the far side will show up any gaps).

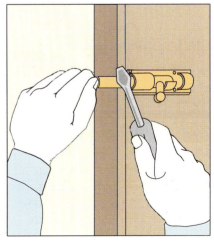

5 Attach the catch. This need not be substantial, as this door is not designed as a security measure.

WEATHERPROOFING

Caulking

Timing the job
The best time to caulk a joint outdoors is during the spring or autumn. That's when the width of the joint is halfway between its seasonal extremes.

Push or pull?
Even experts disagree about whether it's best to pull or push a caulking gun as you fill a crack. In fact, both methods work well as long as you force the caulk well into the crack. For the pull method, cut the caulk tube spout at a 45° angle, then hold the gun at a 60° angle as you pull it along the crack. For the push method, cut a double angle on the spout and hold the gun at a 45° angle as you push it along the crack. ▼

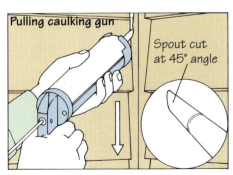

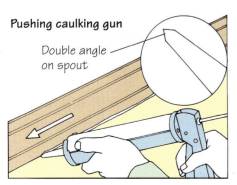

For better caulking
▷ Cut the nozzle opening slightly smaller than the bead you want. Keep the bead between 2 and 9 mm.
▷ To avoid jagged caulk lines, release and squeeze the gun again at a logical break, such as at a corner.
▷ Carry a rag to remove buildup on the nozzle as it can spoil the bead.
▷ If you're a first-time caulker, start on a seldom-seen part of the house. By the time you get to the front, you'll be a pro.

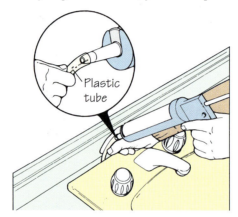

Reach out to caulk ▲
A plastic drinking straw, the sheathing of electrical cable or a length of plastic tubing makes a handy extension tube for caulking hard-to-reach places. Secure your extender with duct tape.

Get the last drop
To squeeze the last bit of caulk out of a tube, put a short length of dowel or old broom handle between the caulking gun plunger and the tube.

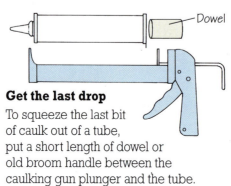

A lick of advice
Don't smooth caulk with your finger. Some caulks contain harmful chemicals, and some are hard to remove from your skin. Use a plastic spoon or an ice-cream stick; either of these will do a tidier job than a finger.

Ice-cube caulk smoother
To get an ultrafine, attractive finish on a bead of caulk, smooth it with an ice cube. Use the heat from your hand to melt the cube to the bead shape you want. Then run it over the caulk.

Caulk savers
The hardest part about sealing a partial tube of caulk is remembering—or taking the time—to do it. You can buy handy screw-on caps or use one of many home solutions:
▷ Insert a large rustproof common nail or machine screw.
▷ Cap the spout with a wire connector large enough to slip over the end of it.
▷ Skewer the spout with a stopper made from a piece of clothes hanger wire.
▷ Wrap a short length of duct tape around the end of the nozzle, ensuring an airtight seal.

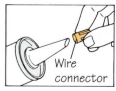

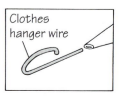

CAULK BUYING GUIDE

The caulks here will fill your home's exterior needs and some interior ones as well. Not listed is plain latex caulk, which is suitable only for interior jobs such as filling gaps around trim. When buying caulk, bear in mind that a 300 g tube will produce an average-size bead 12 to 15 m long—enough to seal about four windows or doors. If a crack is over 10 mm deep, first pack it with suitable material before applying caulk. Besides tubes for caulking guns, caulk comes in smaller squeeze tubes for little jobs. Expanding foam caulk in aerosol cans is available for filling extra-large gaps.

ACRYLIC LATEX

Best use: Timber walls; around windows and doors

Life: 5–25 years, or longer if blended with silicone

Strengths:
▷ Easy to apply, cures quickly
▷ Can be painted and comes in colours
▷ Water cleanup
▷ Good for interior caulking

Weaknesses:
▷ Not for high-moisture areas
▷ May not bond well to metal and non-porous surfaces

BUTYL RUBBER

Best use: Concrete block and brick, metal, flashing, chimneys

Life: 10–20 years

Strengths:
▷ Good flexibility
▷ Usable in high-moisture areas
▷ Can be painted and comes in colours
▷ Can be used for sealing around aluminium frames

Weaknesses:
▷ Stringy when applied
▷ Cures slowly; fairly high shrinkage
▷ Solvent cleanup

COPOLYMER*

Best use: Concrete, tile, brick, stone, glass, vinyl, wood, metal, tar

Life: 30–50 years

Strengths:
▷ Excellent adhesion
▷ Good flexibility
▷ Joins dissimilar materials
▷ Paintable and comes in clear and colours
▷ Resists tearing when abraded

Weaknesses:
▷ May be inflammable during application
▷ May damage polystyrene and other plastics

*May be labelled only as "new technology" caulk

POLYURETHANE

Best use: Concrete block and brick, wood, wood walls, metal, plastic, fibreglass

Life: 20–50 years

Strengths:
▷ Excellent adhesion and strength
▷ Good flexibility
▷ Resists weather, temperature, stress
▷ Works under water
▷ Paintable and comes in colours

Weaknesses:
▷ Solvent cleanup
▷ Higher cost
▷ Hard to find (try a builder's or marine supplier)
▷ Flammable and toxic when applied

SILICONE

Best use: Metal, glass, tile; smooth non-porous surfaces

Life: 20–50 years

Strengths:
▷ Good flexibility
▷ Least shrinkage
▷ Joins many dissimilar materials
▷ Can be applied at most temperatures

Weaknesses:
▷ Not for use on masonry
▷ Poor performance on some varieties of wood
▷ Not paintable
▷ Smelly and irritating to skin when applied

WEATHERPROOFING

Weatherstripping

Locating leaks ▲
Cold air entering a home can change a comfortable room into a cold one. Examine the edges of windows and doors. If you see any light, that's where air is coming in. Also run your hand, moistened to improve sensitivity, around doors and windows to feel for draughts. Or hold a tissue next to them to see if incoming air causes it to move.

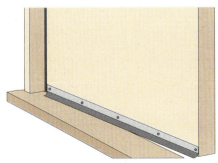

At the threshold ▲
Closing the gap at the bottom of a door is an important defence against heat loss and the seepage of rainwater under the door. A strip of rubber about 50 mm wide clamped under a 20 mm strip of 3 mm aluminium makes a neat and efficient barrier. Use 20 mm wood screws to secure the guard in position.

Some sticky advice
Self-adhesive soft foam rubber weatherstripping doesn't last forever, but it is easy to install and replace—and is inconspicuous when used on the inner edges of the frames of doors and windows. Use it in positions in which it will be clamped tightly between the frame and the door or window when the latter is closed. This type of barrier is available in a range of widths, lending itself to a variety of applications.

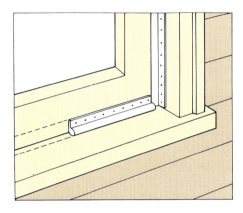

Get that gap with a gasket ▲
An easy, inexpensive way to weatherstrip a window or door is with keyhole canvas-and-rubber gaskets. Staple them on the opening's exterior so that as the window is closed, the gaskets are deflected and seal the gap. On a door, attach the pieces to the frame at the sides and the top. On a sash window, attach the vertical pieces to the trim at the sides and the horizontal pieces to its sashes as shown. These gaskets can also be used very effectively when sealing garage swing-up or roll-up doors—and sliding patio doors as well. There is a wide range of rubber gaskets available and they can be used in a large number of applications.

Working with insulation

Cover up—it's safer
Fibreglass particles can be harmful. When working with this material, wear goggles and a dual-cartridge respirator (p 65). To keep itchy fibreglass slivers off your skin, wear long pants, a long-sleeved shirt, gloves, and a hat. Tuck your sleeves into the cuffs of your gloves for extra protection. If you do get slivers on your skin, don't scratch them. Take a cool or tepid shower—hot water opens the pores, making the itch worse.

Cutting batt insulation
Trimming fibreglass insulation to length is not difficult if you use the squeeze-and-slice method. Place the insulation on a solid wood surface. Position a plank along the cut line and press it down with your knee, then cut through the fibreglass with a utility knife. It's important to use a sharp new blade to avoid tearing the insulation's paper facing or catching and dragging the fibres. ▼

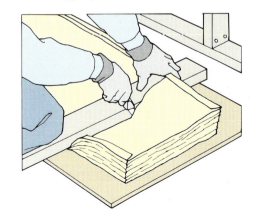

152 / Home Improvements

TYPES OF INSULATION

There is a variety of materials available in different forms for use in a number of situations: blankets, rigid foam sheets, foam and loose-fill, for example. Whatever type you select, however, insulation requires a vapour retarder to keep warm, moist air from condensing inside the wall or ceiling, causing damage. Always put it facing towards the wall's heated side.

INSULATION	BEST USES	PROS AND CONS
Fibreglass batts and blankets	Precut batts or longer blankets fit between joists or rafters in ceiling or open studs in new walls.	Economical, easy to install, and nonflammable, but allows heat loss through framing.
Loose-fill fibreglass	Poured loose into ceiling or blown into finished walls or ceiling with limited access.	Better coverage than batts over ceiling joists, but requires contractor.
Loose-fill rock wool	Poured loose into ceiling or blown into one with limited access. (Settles too much for use in walls.)	Better coverage than batts over ceiling joists, but requires contractor.
Loose-fill cellulose	Poured loose into ceiling or blown into finished walls.	Better coverage than batts over ceiling joists. Easy to install, but a dusty job.
Extruded polystyrene rigid foam sheet	For walls and foundations. Best choice for below-grade insulation of exterior wall or floor.	Resists moisture, but costly. Flammable; needs wallboard cover indoors.
Expanded polystyrene rigid foam sheet	Sheathing beneath exterior cladding, as core of foam-core panels.	Less costly. Not moisture-resistant. Flammable; needs wallboard cover indoors.
Polyurethane rigid foam sheet	Sheathing beneath exterior cladding, as core of foam-core panels.	Good resistance to heat loss, but costly. Flammable; needs wallboard cover indoors.
Urethane foam	Pumped into finished dry walls as a liquid, then solidifies.	Excellent insulating power and forms own vapour retarder, but requires contractor.

CELLULOSE FIBRE CEILING INSULATION

Cellulose fibre insulation is a general-purpose ceiling insulation which is installed using a hose connected to a blower. It can also be poured from a bag and raked to the desired depth. It is designed to give a light fibrous matrix with maximum air entrapment, and hence good heat-insulating properties. It can also be used in timber frame homes as an acoustic filling between studs in dry walls or between timber floors. Other benefits include durability, ease of handling and the practical protection it is claimed to afford against the spread of fire, and hence the reduction of fire damage.

SUMMER (HEAT FLOW DOWNWARDS)

Thickness	Reduction in heat flow
No insulation	—
40 mm	71%
50 mm	75%
75 mm	81%

WINTER (HEAT FLOW UPWARDS)

Thickness	Reduction in heat flow
No insulation	—
40 mm	77%
50 mm	80%
75 mm	85%

WEATHERPROOFING

Insulating walls

When in doubt, check
You can always check ceiling insulation by climbing up and taking a look. But how do you know if your house walls are insulated if you have interior dry walls?
▷ Turn off the power to the electrical outlets, remove the outlet covers and check if there's insulation around the electrical box.
▷ Find an unobtrusive spot, for example in a cupboard, and cut a small hole in the wall with a hole saw.

Flange mystery solved
Where do you staple the flanges on batts of insulation? Stapling them to the front of the studs is easier and creates a better vapour seal than stapling them to the sides. But if you plan to install wallboard with adhesive, the studs' fronts must be bare, and so you should attach the flanges to the sides. In either case, secure them tightly, leaving no gaps for water vapour to pass through.

See-through sealer
When you are installing a plastic vapour retarder over insulation, you may have to run it over electrical boxes and cut openings for them later. For a tight seal and fewer air leaks, cut the plastic 5 mm inside each box perimeter. Then carefully stretch the plastic around the outside of the box and tape any tears with duct tape.

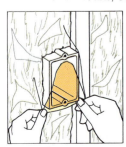

Insulating ceilings

Bridge repair
To add insulation to an already insulated ceiling, run batts over the tops of the joists at right angles to the existing batts. This covers any gaps in the first layer and insulates any heat escape routes created by the joists. When adding batts, work from the eaves towards the centre on a strong platform. Use unfaced batts. If the batts have a facing, slash it every few centimetres so that it won't trap moisture. ▼

Give yourself some rope
You've decided to add more insulation to the ceiling. Now, how do you get up there time and again if all you have is a ceiling hatch for access? Secure a stout rope to the rafter directly above the hatch. Then just grab the rope firmly to help pull yourself up. Some knots in the rope will give you a better grip and a stout platform next to the hatch will give you a firm foothold.

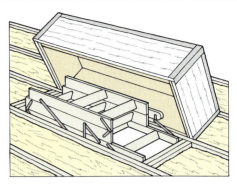

Box block ▲
Any ceiling opening, whether a fold-down stair or a simple hatch, should be insulated to keep heat from leaking from the house. Use self-adhesive foam or vinyl weatherstrips to seal any gaps around the opening's frame. To insulate, build a lightweight box that fits around the opening and cover it with foil-faced rigid foam insulation sealed with duct tape. Hinge the box, or simply lift it aside when you go into the ceiling.

Avoid fire hazards
Even though an insulation material such as cellulose fibre can withstand the heat from a blowlamp, it is as well to keep insulation and timbers well away from a metal chimney. The same applies to any ceiling-mounted electrical fixture that may produce heat. To contain loose-fill such as blown cellulose fibre, fix a board or a sheet-metal shield between the joists on each side of a fixture. ▼

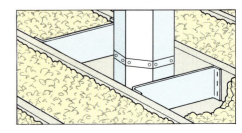

Hot-weather special

In a hot, sunny region, a shiny foil radiant barrier under the roof helps deflect heat and keep the home cooler. Staple the fibre-reinforced radiant barrier to the rafters with the shiny side facing down. ▼

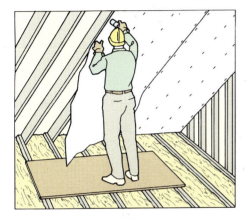

Above crawl spaces

Get a snug fit

If cross-braced bridging is used between floor joists, installing insulation can be tricky. To fit batts snugly around the bridging, cut the insulation to create a joint at the bridging. Then make short lengthwise cuts in the centre of the batt ends as shown. The resulting tabs will fit neatly around the obstruction. ▼

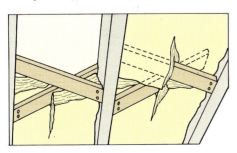

Old hangers never die ▲

Insulating a suspended floor above a crawl space presents a problem: with the vapour retarder of the batts facing up against the floor (as it should be), there are no flanges to hold the insulation in place. An easy solution is to jam wires—slightly longer than the width of the cavity—against the batts. Buy the wires or cut them from clothes hangers. Push them in every 600 mm or so, bowing them upward.

A simple leveller ▲

To avoid wastage and achieve optimum results, you have to ensure loose-fill insulation has a uniform depth. If you're doing the job yourself, make a leveller like the one above. You will get a perfect result all the time. The short handle makes reaching those awkward areas a little easier, but is not so long that the tool is difficult to manoeuvre.

Moisture barrier

Lay a ground vapour retarder in your crawl space to prevent moisture from damaging the floor insulation and from entering your house. Use sheets of 250-300 micron polyethylene, extending them several centimetres up the foundation walls and over-lapping the edges by at least 150 mm. You can secure the edges of the sheets to each other and the walls with duct tape or use bricks to hold down the seams. ▼

Hot, humid situations

In warm, humid climates, a vapour barrier can retard the infiltration of moist air into your house. Staple sheets of plastic insulation to the floor joists of a suspended floor. Seal the seams with duct tape. In cooler regions, however, putting plastic on the bottom of joists can cause the wood to rot. If you are in any doubt, consult the experts. ▼

WALLS, FLOORS AND COLUMNS

Repairs

Miner's hat trick

When you have to slither into a crawl space to repair or investigate something, pack a light where it makes the most sense: on your head. It'll leave both hands free. Models on an elastic headband are available from outdoor-living centres. These are great for any job that normally requires extra light.

Pipe it away

A simple solution to keep the area under a suspended floor dry is to direct water away, and there are two ways of doing this. Sloping the ground surrounding a home, away from it is, one way. You can also fit extensions to your drainpipes so that rainwater is carried well away from the home.

Make a moat

Reduce the amount of water collecting under a home on columns by building a shallow concrete-lined channel around the outer perimeter of the house—as is often done by campers to keep water from flooding their tents. It will lead water away and stop it pooling under the house. Planting a thick hedge a metre or so from the side of the house on the weather side will provide a barrier to some of the rain that would otherwise be driven in by the wind.

Run a test

Can't decide whether dampness under a suspended floor is outside water seeping in or an excess of house humidity condensing on the cool walls? Try this simple test: attach squares of aluminium foil to the walls—and floor if it is concreted—sealing the edges of each square with duct tape. Check after a few days. If beads of moisture have formed on the side against the wall or floor, that means seepage is occurring from outside. Beads on the outer surface mean there's interior condensation.

Mirror, mirror, on the ground

At caulking time, don't overlook cracks and gaps between the foundation and the siding—insects can get through them. To save wear and tear on your knees, use an old mirror to see under the timbers. It will make the job easy. ▼

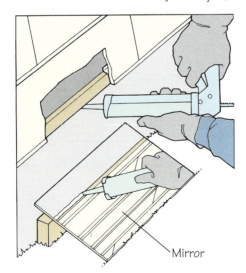

Use the underfloor area

Blissful batten bashing

If you have enclosed the area under a house on columns, mounting battens for built-in cupboards on brick walls is much easier if you do it like this. Start the nails in the batten so that they just poke through the back.

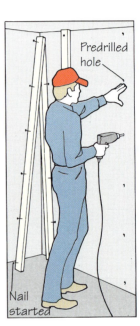

Then hold the batten against the wall, and tap the nails to mark their locations on the wall. Drill holes in the concrete with a 3 mm masonry bit; then nail the battens into place. The masonry won't chip and the nails will go straight in.

Save your breath

After drilling into masonry, don't try to blow debris out of the holes. Insert a thin tube into the hole and blow through it—but don't stand directly in front of the hole when you do so or you will get a faceful of dust.

Concealing rough walls

Concrete or block walls enclosing a space below a house on columns can be ugly. Consider plastering them in a smooth finish or a decorative texture.

Chill-free floors

Here's how to give a warm cover to a cold concrete floor. Clean the surface, and apply a coat of slightly thinned asphalt mastic. Lay 250–300 micron polyethylene sheeting, and press it down with a weighted floor roller. Next, embed pressure-treated 37 x 76 mm strips in rows of mastic. Finally, nail 16 mm plywood to the strips and lay your underfelt and carpet. ▼

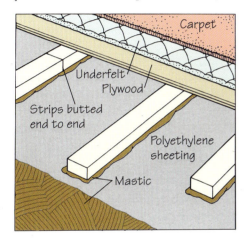

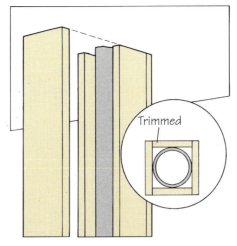

Boxed posts ▲

Improve the appearance of a timber home on columns by cladding the latter in timber as shown. Join the pieces as shown when attaching them to the columns. If the ground under the home becomes wet during the rainy season, attach the timbers so that their bases are sufficiently clear of the ground to remain dry. This will help prevent deterioration.

Building out windows

When you enclose the space under a home on columns, the windows you install should suit the overall theme of the home, particularly if you line the inner walls of the enclosed space with panels or wallboard. So, after the panel framing is in, build a timber box around each window as shown. Secure the box to the framing, and after installing the wallboard or panelling, trim it with moulding as you would a standard window. ▼

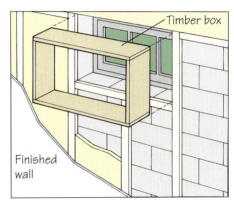

The gold mine below: keep it dry ▶

If you enclose the area under a home on columns and the house is on a slope, the wall on the upper side may have to act as a retaining wall to some extent. To keep dampness out, attach 300 micron polyethylene sheets to the outer wall from the grade level to floor level, and a second layer to the inner wall, as in the illustration, with dabs of adhesive. Let them extend about 150 mm onto the floor. Install your panelling frame on the wall, nailing the top plate to the joists above and securing the foundation beam to the floor with masonry nails. Drill a 10 mm vent hole in the top plate between each stud pair, press in unfaced fibreglass batts, and staple on more polyethylene sheets. Finally, fix your panelling or wallboard to the frame.

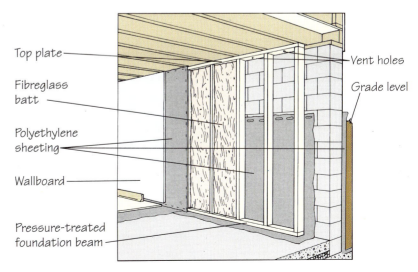

CLADDING AND WOOD PRESERVATION

Wood care and repair

Preventive survey
It's a good idea to take a walk around your house from time to time with a screwdriver and probe for areas of rotten wood. Why must you look for trouble? Because the rot will get worse if you ignore it. To repair minor damage, clean away the rotted wood and fill the excavation with car body filler. Polyester resin/styrene monomer motor vehicle body filler adheres well to clean, dry wood, and you can smooth, carve, or sand it to match adjoining areas.

Closing a split

To repair split cladding, prise out the bottom section of the damaged board, and insert a shim to hold it out. Apply waterproof glue all along the edge. Then remove the shim, push the section back into place, and nail both the upper and the lower sections. Wipe off the excess glue with a wet cloth.

Cladding sidekick
When replacing or installing cladding which does not have a rebate, measuring the exposed section of each course is tedious and leaves room for error. Here's a better way: make a gauge by nailing a cleat to a wood scrap as shown. Hold it against the bottom edge of the upper course and rest the next course on the ledge as you nail. ▼

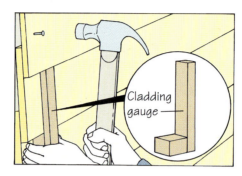

Preserve and protect

Under attack
The hazards wood faces in different situations are classified as follows:
▷ H6—timber in sea water: marine borers, decay fungi, wood-boring insects above the high-water mark.
▷ H5—timber in fresh water: all of the above, except marine borers.
▷ H4—timber in ground contact: decay fungi, termites, wood-boring insects.
▷ H3—exterior timber above ground: moderate decay, all wood borers, drywood termites.
▷ H2—interior timber above ground: wood borers and drywood termites.
▷ H1—interior timber above ground, completely dry: wood-boring insects.
Caution: Applications can differ widely. If in any doubt, consult an expert.

Standing room only
Stand posts in a large drum of creosote until you are ready to use them, even days later. The creosote will soak into the wood. Store the creosote in the drum for future use.

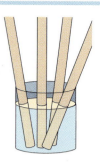

Preserve that colour
Boron and tributyltin oxide-lindane (TBTOL) preservatives don't alter the colour of a wood. Pentachlorophenol (PCP) and pentachlorophenol-zinc naphthenate (PCPZN) may darken the colour slightly. Consider using one of these preservatives when you wish to retain a natural wood finish. If used on wood surfaces that will be exposed to rain, all of them, however, should contain a water repellent to prevent leaching. CCA (copper-chromium-arsenic) compounds give the wood a greenish tinge, but no leaching occurs.

Top it off
Cut the tops of posts at an angle so that rainwater cannot pool and slowly seep into the wood—the sooner water is shed, the better. You could also cap each top with either a metal cap, or a wooden cap. If you use the latter, rout a shallow groove around the lower edge of the cap to stop water seeping under it and into the post. ▼

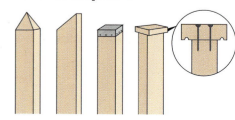

158 / Home Improvements

REPLACING DAMAGED CLADDING

Cladding comes in a variety of woods, profiles, and widths. But the steps for replacing damaged sections are the same for all. The bottom edge of each board is usually nailed to the underlying sheathing or studs every 450 mm or so. The top edge is pinched in place by the nails of the board above. When removing more than one section, work from the top down. Take a damaged board to a timberyard to find a match.

1 If you can see nails, use a nail set to drive them through the damaged cladding. Also drive them through on the undamaged board above it to release the damaged piece's top edge.

2 If you can't locate the nails under multiple paint layers, gently pull up the cladding and slip the blade of a mini-hacksaw under the cladding. Feel for the nails and cut them.

3 Cut out the damaged cladding, using a keyhole saw with the blade reversed. Make sure that the cut is square and that the seams in the succeeding courses don't line up.

4 Working from the bottom up, install the replacement boards, using galvanized cladding nails. Apply caulk at seams and where new cladding abuts window, door, or corner trim. Prime and paint.

Wet won't work

Prior to applying a preservative to any surface, make sure the wood is dry. If it is not, check the instructions carefully or contact the manufacturer or dealer before applying the preservative. You may be able to dry an area of wood to be treated by using a heat gun. Dry a far larger area than you plan to treat, but repeat the treatment when the whole surface is dry after a long sunny spell.

Plastic power ▶

Put the end of a post into a plastic bag and wrap the bag around the post. The wood preservative you have used will be contained for longer and the wood will be protected from damp.

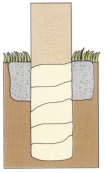

Protect yourself

Creosote, and the CCA and PCP/PCPZN range of preservatives are very toxic. TBTOL is moderately toxic, and boron has a low toxicity. Treat them all as toxic, however. Wear rubber gloves when handling them, and wear an old sweatband. If creosote, for example, is flicked into your hair, it will be assisted into your eyes as you perspire on a hot day. Discard the sweatband after use.

WALLS

Brick walls

Mortar quick draw
Use an old caulk tube to fill mortar joints: push the bottom out by slipping a dowel through the spout. Clean the tube and load it with mortar. Then replace the bottom, cut the tip to the width you need, and put it in a caulk gun.

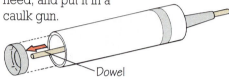

Making mortar match
"Age" new mortar joints to match old ones by patting them with a wet tea bag. Or add colourant (from a builder's supply outlet) to the mortar as you're mixing it. Experiment to get the right shade.

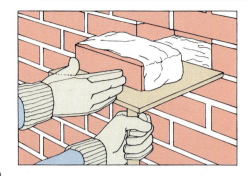

Brick replacement ▲
To replace a damaged brick, chisel out the mortar around it (Step 1, facing page), being careful not to chip the surrounding bricks. Then chip the brick apart with a chisel, and pull out all the pieces. Dampen the opening. Spread mortar on the base of the cavity and on the top and ends of a damp new brick, and insert the brick. Add or remove mortar as needed.

Thumbprint test
When to finish a mortar joint—a process known as tooling, jointing, or striking—depends on the mortar mixture and the temperature. The mortar needs to set long enough so that it can take an impression but not so long that it becomes hard. Use the traditional builder's test: mortar is ready for tooling when it will show a clear thumbprint. ▼

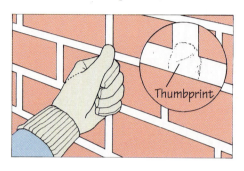

Getting the right shape
If you need to shape a mortar joint and don't have a special rake or jointer tool (Step 3, facing page), improvise your own. Use an ice-cream stick or piece of pipe, for example, to make the common concave joint. Or carve a scrap of wood or grind an old spoon to the profile that matches the joints on the surrounding bricks.

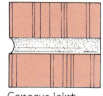

Concave joint

New meets old
It's not always possible to get a perfect match when adding new brickwork to old. Here are some tricks to minimize the difference.

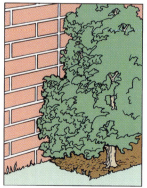

Plant shrubs or climbing vines where the old work meets the new, or hide the area with a trellis.

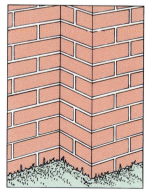

Build a small offset into the wall, putting the new bricks on a different plane from the old ones.

Place a window at the juncture of old and new work so that the only visible disparity will be low on the wall.

Stains

Shade-side solution

Whether you have brick or wood walls, patches of mould or mildew in shaded areas are distressing. Commercial stain removers are available, but you can do a good job with a 50/50 mixture of household bleach and water in a plastic spray bottle. After an hour, flush well with water. Wear goggles and rubber gloves, and take care not to damage plants. If you'd rather not use bleach, scrub with pure vinegar—it takes elbow grease but works well.

In the first place

The best way to prevent mildew staining on wood fittings is to use a stain or paint that contains a fungicide or mildewcide.

Spot removers

Here's how to remove some common stains from bricks and other masonry. Test any cleaner on an inconspicuous spot first. Scrub with a nylon bristle brush (wire may damage the surface). Wear goggles and rubber gloves when working with solvents or caustics.
▷ Fresh paint: blot up; then wipe with the solvent recommended for the paint.
▷ Dried paint: scrape off; then remove residue with paint remover as directed.
▷ Rust: mix 500 g oxalic acid crystals in 5 litres of water and brush on. After 3 hours, scrub and rinse.
▷ Tar: scrape off, and scrub with scouring powder. Apply a paste of talc and kerosene, allow to dry, and scrub again.
▷ Smoke and soot: scrub with scouring powder; rinse well. Apply talc mixed with bleach to stubborn areas.

REPOINTING BRICKS

The most common masonry repair is repointing—replacing damaged mortar joints between bricks. The tools you'll need are a joint or cold chisel (no wider than the joint), a 1 kg sledgehammer, a trowel, a pointing tool (to push mortar in), a wheel rake or brick jointer (to shape the mortar), and a whisk broom. For convenience, use ready-mix mortar. Add water gradually, mixing the mortar until it's a uniform stiff paste that you can shape into a ball. Let it stand for 10 minutes; then stir it briefly with a trowel before using. If the mortar becomes too stiff to use, don't add water—mix a new batch. Wear work gloves.

Joint chisel

1 Wearing safety glasses, chisel out loose and cracked mortar to a depth of 20 mm, or until you reach sound mortar. Do not chip the brick itself. Brush away debris, and dampen the brick with a fine spray of water.

2 Place some mortar on your trowel, hold it close to the joint, and push some in with the pointing tool. If a gap is 20 mm or deeper, add the mortar in 5 mm layers. Allow each to become thumbprint hard before adding the next.

3 Once the final layer is thumbprint hard, use a brick jointer or wheel rake to smooth the joint to a shape that matches the existing mortar joints. Brush away any excess mortar from the face of the bricks after it has stiffened.

ROOFS

Gutters

Gutter scoop
Make a great gutter-cleaning scoop from a rectangular motor-oil container. Cut away the bottom portion, and it's just the right size to fit into the gutter. The spout gives you a hand grip. ▼

White-glove service
Are your gutters filled with mucky, rotted leaves and who knows what? Use a pair of old kitchen tongs and you won't have to touch the stuff. The tongs reach nicely into tight spots, and their pincer action helps you grip debris.

Gutter buddy ▶
An inexpensive plastic bucket can be a handy gutter cleaning aid. Cut the wire handle in half, bend the ends to form hooks, and hang the bucket on the gutter. Slide the bucket along as you work your way along the length of the gutter. If you don't wish to cut the handle, however, make a hanger from thick wire. It will be in the shape of a flattened "M", with the ends turned up as hooks and the top corners turned down to grip the gutter rim.

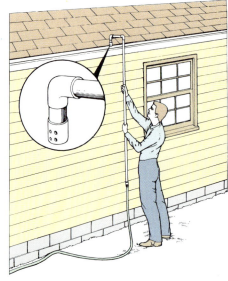

I'm just fine down here, thanks ▲
If you're not keen on climbing to clean gutters, this hose extension will let you flush them out while keeping your feet planted on terra firma. Make it from 20 mm PVC plastic pipe, two elbows, a garden-hose coupler, and a cap. Drill four 2 mm holes in the cap. Weld the parts together with PVC cement.

Trouble sign
A depression in the ground underneath a gutter is a sign that the gutter is dripping water. Look for a sag or leak in the gutter. Check for a clogged downspout that's causing an overflow.

Give a gutter a lift
You can realign a gutter that has sagged because the fascia board to which it's attached has warped. Simply loosen the screws of the supporting brackets nearest the warped section and glue wedges under their lower ends. Then retighten the bracket screws. ▼

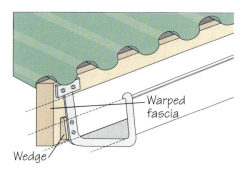

Prevention is better than cure
Plastic mesh (used for supporting climbing plants) keeps a gutter clear of most debris—which means no more drainpipe blockages. ▼

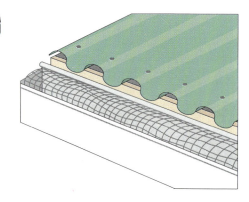

Checking and protecting

Remote is easier
Make a habit of regularly checking your roof for loose or damaged tiles or any other problem areas requiring attention. But keep your ladder in the garage. Make the initial check from the ground—with a pair of binoculars.

Can your roof pass this test?
Here's how to establish if you'll soon have to install a new asphalt roof:
▷ Pinch off a corner of a shingle. If the inside is black, it still has life; if it's grey or crumbly, you'll have to replace it.
▷ Shingles should be flexible and resilient on a 20° C day. If you bend back a few corners and the shingles crack or seem brittle, they won't be doing their job much longer.
▷ Discoloration or streaking on shingles indicates that the granular top coat is deteriorating.

Vent guard ▲
To prevent plumbing vent pipes from becoming clogged with leaves, cover the openings with a piece of 10 mm welded mesh. Secure it with a wire collar or dabs of roofing cement.

Pull through
Thread a length of nylon rope down a drainpipe and allow about a metre extra, secured out of sight in the gutter. The lower end should be in the downpipe shoe. If the pipe becomes blocked, release the top end, tie a hook to it to catch the blocking debris and pull it through the pipe from the lower end.

Think like a drip
Don't just assume that a leak in the roof is directly over a stain in the ceiling. Water may flow along the ceiling for quite a distance before dropping. Next

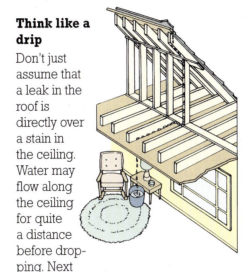

time there's a heavy rain, go into the roof and search carefully. Once you find the leak, measure to a couple of landmarks—a wall, a chimney or a vent pipe. Repeat your measurements on the roof, and you'll have a good idea where to look for damage.

A clean cure
Where a wall is plastered to ground level, mud splashes often cause ugly stains. A solution is to lay a bed of large stone chips against the wall on the weather side of the house. Make the bed about 100 mm deep and 1 m wide. Spray it well to wash away any soil, prior to repainting the wall.

CARE UP THERE
Climbing onto a roof can be hazardous. Here are some precautions you should take:
▷ Work on a dry, mild, windless day after the dew evaporates.
▷ Use a sturdy extension ladder that reaches at least 600 mm above the eaves. The distance between the ladder's feet and the wall should equal one-quarter of the ladder's height. Tie the feet to stakes in the ground. If possible, tie the top—to gutter supports, for example.
▷ Sweep the roof lightly before you start, and keep the work area clear of debris you could slip on, such as loose shingles.
▷ Wear heavy rubber-soled shoes and long pants.
▷ Keep yourself and your ladder well away from any power lines or telephone lines.
▷ Pull up loads with a rope. Don't carry a load up by hand. Use both hands to grip the ladder.
▷ Place tools and shingles where they won't slide off the roof.
▷ Keep other people far away.
▷ For maximum security, wear a safety harness tied tightly to an immovable object such as a tree on the opposite side of the roof.
▷ Avoid steep roofs (over 30°) and houses over two storeys high.
▷ If you're uncomfortable on a roof, hire a professional.

ROOFS

Repairing a roof

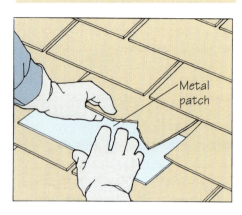

Metal backup ▲
You don't always have to remove a damaged shingle or slate to repair it. Cut a square of sheet aluminium, coat one side with roofing cement, and slip it under the damaged area, cement side down. Then dab roofing cement on top of the patch and embed the shingle or slate in it.

Seal breaker
Lift a shingle by slipping a heavy-duty masonry trowel under the edge and gently tapping on the trowel's edge with a hammer. You can use a trowel to lift a slate or asbestos roof tile as well, but be careful not to crack surrounding tiles. ▼

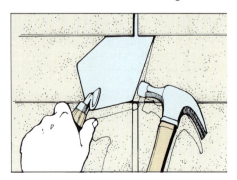

Undercoated valley
It's not always easy to find the exact location of a leak in a valley. Rather than replace all the flashing, coat it with a waterproof coating—the repair is quick and easy and can be used for other flashing and metal gutters. You will also achieve a uniform finish, without unsightly patchwork.

Copper cure
Troubled by moss and fungus on your cement tiles? Put a copper lightning conductor across the ridge of a roof. It will inhibit the growth of moss. If fixing the conductor to the ridge cannot be done, attach a length of copper wire under the lip of the top row of tiles. Bend the wire into a series of spurs and push them under the tiles. A slight downward kink at their ends will help keep them in place. Don't forget to treat the roof's hips in the same way. ▼

Steep slope safety
For added security when working on a roof, tie a stout rope to a ladder laid flat on the tiles. You will have a firm foothold and something to grab on to. The ladder will also spread your weight over more of the roof's surface, reducing the risk of cracked tiles.

Skid stopper
Next time you get a package, save those sheets of soft plastic foam packing. They're great for keeping hand tools from sliding off the roof. ▼

Roof replacement

Flat roof leak?
If you have a leak-prone flat roof, talk to a contractor about replacing it or covering it with a single-ply membrane. This rubberlike material is flexible enough to allow for roof movement and covers most home roofs in one seamless sheet.

Just keep rolling along
Repaint a roof with ease: extend your reach like this. Push the end of a broomstick or the handle of an old spade into the roller handle. You'll paint large areas quickly and easily.

Keep it clean

Painting or cleaning the roof of a house, particularly one without eaves, could result in the walls below the work area getting dirty. To control the mess, secure the top and sides of a canvas tarpaulin or large plastic sheet to a timber frame, and put it hard up against the wall below the gutter. If necessary, add a couple of supports between the two outer ones. You can also use this trick when cleaning gutters. ▼

Sliding course guide

Professionals use chalk lines to align rows of shingles. If you want some extra help, make this simple guide by nailing a cleat to a suitable plank. When you butt the cleat against the bottom of one course of shingles, the plank's top edge will form a ledge on which you can rest the next course. You can use a similar guide to align new cladding (p 158).

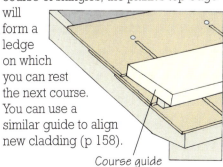

REPLACING SHINGLES

Replacing a few shingles that have missing or broken tabs (the visible flaps) is easy. Each shingle usually has three tabs and is held in place with six nails (or staples) under the tabs of the two rows of shingles just above. Some roofing supply outlets or home centres sell shingles in small quantities as well as full bundles. Take a broken shingle along to find a close match. To avoid cracking the shingles, work on a warm day when they are pliable.

1 Gently lift the three tabs in the row above the damaged shingle and the three in the row above that. Before lifting a tab, slide the bar under its full length to break the seal.

2 Remove the nail from under each of the tabs that you lifted in the two rows above the damaged shingle. This will release the latter, allowing you to slide it out.

3 Slide the new replacement shingle under the rows of tabs above, and secure it with six galvanized roofing nails, putting one under each of the tabs that you loosened.

4 Put a couple of dabs of roofing cement under the tabs of the new shingle and under all the other tabs that you loosened. Press the tabs down firmly into the roofing cement.

CHAPTER 6
PAINT AND WALLCOVERINGS

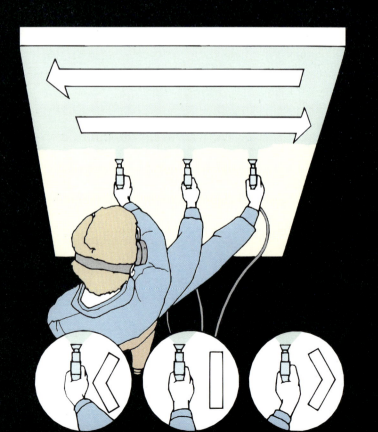

WORKING WITH PAINT 167
BRUSHES 170
ROLLERS AND SPRAY GUNS 172
CHOOSING AND BUYING PAINT 174
PREPARING A ROOM FOR PAINTING 176
PAINTING WALLS AND CEILINGS 179
WINDOWS, DOORS, AND STAIRS 180
DECORATIVE PAINTING 182
PAINTING A HOUSE EXTERIOR 184
PAINT CLEANUP AND STORAGE 188
PREPARING TO HANG WALLCOVERINGS 190
HANGING WALLCOVERINGS 192

WORKING WITH PAINT

Mixing it up

Power-stirring
A power drill mixing attachment is handy for PVA and enamel paints, but don't use the attachment to stir lacquer, epoxy paint, shellac, or any finish that says "Do not shake" on the label. You won't want to do battle with the bubbles that power-mixing stirs up. Instead, stir these paints and finishes by hand; they'll stay fairly free of bubbles.

Spatter shield
Stirring full tins of paint with a drill-driven mixer splatters paint everywhere. One way to contain the mess is with a large plastic coffee tin lid. Drill a hole in the centre of the lid and slip it onto the mixer shaft before inserting the mixer into the drill chuck. Hold the lid tightly on the tin while mixing the paint and run the drill at a low speed. By doing so, you'll find you have better control, particularly when the mixer head hits the side of the tin. You will also have far less splattering and fewer bubbles in the paint.

Clever container
Cut off the top of a clean 2 litre plastic milk container and use it for mixing (or holding) small amounts of paint or stain. The corner of the container makes a good pouring spout and you can throw it away when you've finished.

Newspaper collar
Here's another way to reduce the mess when stirring a full tin of paint. Increase the height of the tin by taping a newspaper section around it. The paint will splash onto the paper when you stir it with a paddle or a power attachment.

Homemade mixer
For small jobs you can make your own power mixing attachment by using a beater from an old kitchen mixer in your electric drill. This makeshift attachment works well in smaller tins, but the shaft is too short to reach the bottom of large tins. To avoid splattering paint, use a plastic lid as shown at left and hold small tins firmly—they tip over easily if the side is struck.

Blending for colour
If the job you're working on requires two or three 5 litre tins of paint, mix the paint from all the tins together to get a consistent colour. To do this, find a clean container and open all of the paint tins. Pour half of the paint from the first one into the extra container. Then pour some paint from the second and third tins into the first. Move to the extra container and pour in some more paint from the second and third tins. Then pour the contents of all four containers back and forth several times. When the paint is mixed, return it to the original containers and seal the lids tightly. A quicker alternative is to mix all the paint in a 20 litre container.

The super stirrer!
A paint stirrer is more effective if it has several holes along its length. With each stroke the paint flows back and forth through the holes, allowing for faster, more thorough blending. To make one, drill 6 mm holes at about 25 mm centres in a length of batten about 450 mm long. Rinse the paint from the holes to stop them becoming clogged with dried paint. As an alternative to a wooden batten, you could use a length of aluminium or thin-walled pipe flattened for part of its length. Leave 100 mm as is for a handle.

WORKING WITH PAINT

Special remedies

Say "Cheesecloth"
Strain the lumps from paint by pouring it into a container covered with cheesecloth. Hold the cheesecloth in place around the perimeter of the tin with a sturdy rubber band, tape, or string.

Screen old paint
Here's another way to deal with lumps in old paint: use fine-mesh screening, available from hardware dealers. Cut a circle with a diameter 6 mm smaller than the diameter of the paint tin. Bend the screen a little so it will fit inside the rim, and drop it onto the surface of the paint. Push the screen slowly to the bottom with a paint stirrer. As the screen travels down, it will carry the lumps of dried paint with it. Even if the brush touches the screen on the bottom of the tin, the bristles won't pick up any lumps.

Stocking filter
A clean pantihose cut off near the ankle also makes a good paint strainer. Stretch the pantihose around the rim of the tin and secure it with a rubber band. Dip a brush into the tin to force the pantihose toe into the paint. The paint rising through the mesh will be finely strained.

Handling fumes
The fumes of some paints and primers persist even in a well-ventilated room. To reduce the odour, add a few drops of vanilla extract to the paint—up to a tablespoon per 5 litres. The extract won't affect the way the paint performs, and the wet paint won't be so smelly. Note, however, that good ventilation is still required to combat the physical side effects of the noxious solvents.

Paint tin handlers

Tin holder
One way to keep a work surface clean and to avoid accidental spills is to place your tin of paint in an old saucepan. It catches runs and provides a brush rest. The handle of the saucepan doesn't collect messy paint drips and makes it easy to carry the tin from place to place.

Nail holes
No matter how neat you try to be, paint still tends to accumulate in the lid groove of a paint tin, creating puddles of paint that squirt out when you seal the tin. To drain the paint back into the tin, use a nail to punch several holes in the groove before you paint. When you reseal the tin, the lid will cover the holes and form a tight seal. ▼

Pour neatly
If you don't have a funnel on hand to help you pour paint neatly, hold a pencil over the opening of the pouring tin. The paint will follow the pencil to its end and from there flow into its new container without any mess.

168 / Paint and Wallcoverings

Plate catcher

Attaching a sturdy paper plate to the bottom of a paint tin makes it easier to keep the floor or other work surface clean. The rim of the plate catches and contains paint runs better than newspaper. Use a little putty or adhesive to make the plate stick to the tin. If you do use newspaper under a paint tin, put a piece of wax paper between it and the newspaper so that it won't stick to the tin.

Brushwork

Grip and load

Applying paint successfully begins with a proper grip on the brush. Hold the metal band, or ferrule, between your thumb and fingers. This grip gives you the most control, especially if you switch the brush to your weaker hand. Dip the bristles about 50 mm into the paint, and then press the brush lightly against the side of the tin. Do not drag the bristles against the rim, as that will cause bubbles to form. Let the paint pool on top of the bristles, but don't overload the brush.

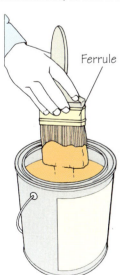
Ferrule

Even strokes

To spread paint evenly with a brush, use a few zigzagging strokes (1). Then spread the paint out to cover the gaps as in (2). To finish an area, raise the brush so that just the tips of the bristles lightly smooth the painted area (3). This is called tipping or feathering off and removes any unsightly lap marks. ▼

1

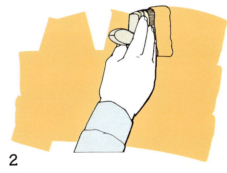
2

3

Less is better

You'll be less likely to overload a brush if your paint tin is only partly filled. The extra free space near the top makes it easier for you to neatly slap the brush against the side of the tin to remove the excess paint.

Wire tap

Bend a piece of coat hanger or other heavy wire as shown, and tape it securely to one side of a paint tin. Use the wire, instead of the rim of the tin, to tap the excess paint from your brush. The wire will keep paint from getting into the lid groove and stop it dripping down the side.

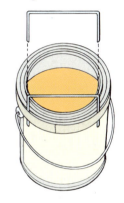

Brush rest 1

If you'd like an easy way to make a temporary resting place for your brush, just lay an ordinary paint stirrer across the rim of the paint tin. Position the stirrer so that it forms a bridge near the middle of the tin. That way it will offer a steady support for the wet bristles while the brush handle rests on the (cleaner) rim of the paint tin.

Brush rest 2

Two small screw hooks driven into one side of a paintbrush allow it to be hooked onto the rim of a paint tin during breaks in painting.

BRUSHES

On the job

Make your own disposables
Disposable foam brushes are handy for touch-ups and other small painting jobs. Instead of buying disposable brushes, you can save trips to the paint or hardware store, and some money as well, by making them yourself. You'll need some scrap 20 mm foam rubber and a bag of clothes pegs. Cut the foam to size with a utility knife, angling the tip as shown. Snap on a clothes peg handle and you're ready to paint. For really fine work, cut the foam to a point. ▼

Tape protection
Your paintbrush will be easier to clean if you wrap masking tape around the ferrule and the base of the bristles, extending the tape about 10 mm over the bristles. Rather than drying and hardening on the bristles, paint will collect on the tape. When it's time to clean up, remove the tape and clean the wet paint that remains on the bristles. ▼

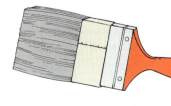

Comb-out
Stray bristles that fall onto a wet paint surface can mar a job. To remove loose bristles before you begin painting, groom the brush. Either use a brush comb bought for the purpose or a pocket comb or a pet's brush.

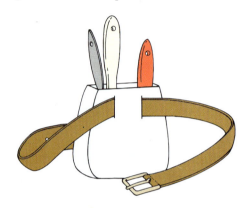

Belted caddy ▲
If you plan to use more than one size of brush during a paint job, you'll want to keep those brushes handy, especially if you are working on a ladder. You can make a reusable brush holder that attaches to an ordinary belt. First, find a clean rectangular plastic container that is wide enough to hold your brushes but sufficiently narrow to keep them upright. Fabric softener or shampoo bottles and some lubricating oil containers would be suitable. Cut off the top of the bottle and make two slits in one side for your belt. Thread the belt through the loops on your pants and through the slits, positioning the brush caddy on one hip. Not only will you have the brushes at your fingertips, you'll have just one container to clean when the job is done.

Between coats

Freezer wrap
If you are working with oil-base paint and know that you will be using the brushes and rollers the next day, there's no need to clean and scrub them at the end of the day. Just wrap everything in plastic bags or foil and stick the packets in the freezer. The cold temperature will keep the paint from hardening. When you are ready to paint again, thaw the pieces for about 45 minutes. You can repeat this procedure for as many coats of paint or varnish as you need. However, if you are using water-base paint, you'll have to wash your brushes and rollers each night.

Wire hang-up
Here's a way to park your brush during a break. Attach a small wire hook to the neck of the handle by twisting a piece of wire around it. Hang the brush on the edge of the tin so that its bristles will stay in the paint and not dry out, but don't let the brush sink too low in the paint or rest on the bottom of the tin.

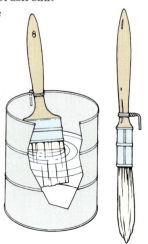

Two coffee tin ideas

A coffee tin with a plastic lid makes a good holder for your brushes while they soak (briefly) in paint thinner or water. Cut slits in the lid, and insert the brush handles in the slits so that the bristles clear the bottom of the tin by about 10 mm. If the tin has no lid, use a rubber band to attach a stick to the handle of each brush. This will keep the bristles off the bottom of the tin.

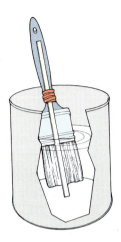

Easy wiper solution

A container for moisturizer tissues also makes a great holder. The slit in the top that dispenses the towelettes will hold the handles of most brushes. The bristles should stay about 10 mm above the bottom of the container—to prevent them from bending and to keep them out of the settling paint debris. Don't allow a brush to soak too long. It is not a substitute for thorough cleaning.

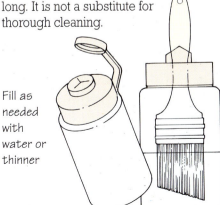

Fill as needed with water or thinner

When the job's over

Newspaper story

Looking for a place to wipe your brush when it's time to clean up? Instead of a piece of scrap wood or cardboard, use a thick section of newspaper. Place the bristles between several layers of pages. Then as you remove the brush, squeeze the bristles.

Bristle work

The best way to get a brush clean is to scrub the bristles against wire mesh. You can submerge an old kitchen strainer in a coffee tin filled with water or paint thinner. Another option is to cut a circle out of 10 mm welded mesh. Bend the material to form a lip around the edge. Place the mesh on the bottom of a coffee tin and fill it with solvent. The mesh provides a surface for the brush to work against and allows paint sediment to collect on the bottom of the tin.

Go for a spin ▶

Remove excess water or thinner from a clean brush by spinning it back and forth between the palms of your hands. To protect yourself from the spraying liquid, hold the brush inside a paper bag.

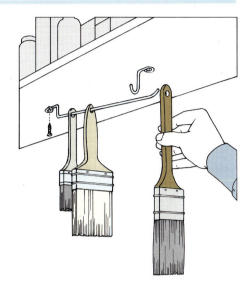

Drying hanger ▲

After cleaning your paintbrushes, hang them up to dry on a three-arm metal towel rack. Or make your own rack out of a wire coat hanger, using a wire cutter and pliers to shape the hanger and fashion the hooks. Mount the hanger with two screws, and provide a drip catcher underneath.

Long-term storage

Store brushes in self-seal plastic bags. To keep the bristles supple, add a teaspoon of vinegar to each bag if water-base paint was used, or a teaspoon of paint thinner if oil-base paint was used.

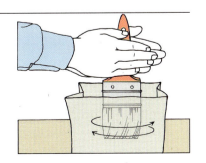

ROLLERS AND SPRAY GUNS

Easy rolling

Bucket brigade
Roller trays are not ideal for large jobs unless you happen to be working on a ladder. They don't hold very much paint and it's easy to step on them, spilling the contents. Instead of using a roller tray, do what the professionals do and take the paint directly from a large bucket. To remove excess paint, run the roller against a section of expanded metal screen, cut to fit the container and with its ends bent so that it can hang off the rim of the bucket.

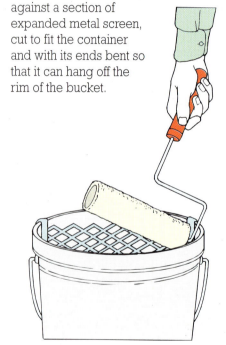

One liner
You can avoid having to clean your roller tray if you first line it with aluminium foil. Overlap all four sides, being careful not to puncture the foil as you fit the corners. When the job is done, return any excess paint to the tin; then peel the foil up carefully and discard it. (For more on discarding paint, see p 39.)

Another mess manager
Here's how to remove a paint-filled roller cover without getting paint on your hands: pull a plastic bag over the end of the roller and pull the cover off. Seal the bag and discard it (p 39).

Clean and dry

Hanger helper
The hook of a wire clothes hanger makes a great tool for removing the excess paint from a roller cover. To shape the hanger into a cleaning tool, bend the "wings" of the hanger so that they can be held together as a handle. Start at one end and pull the hanger hook down the length of the roller several times, turning the roller slightly with each pass.

Dangling dryer

Drying a clean roller on its side flattens some of the nap and ruins the cover's smooth rolling action. Instead, tie a small piece of scrap wood to one end of a string and drop it through the cover. Hang it up where it can dangle freely and not be covered by dust. You can also store it this way.

Another hanger trick
This rack helps to keep a roller cover round and paintbrush bristles flat as they dry. To make it, cut near the bottom of a wire hanger at one end;

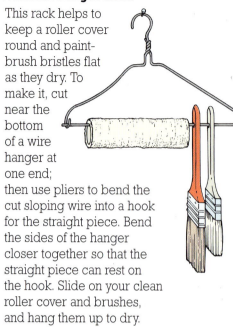

then use pliers to bend the cut sloping wire into a hook for the straight piece. Bend the sides of the hanger closer together so that the straight piece can rest on the hook. Slide on your clean roller cover and brushes, and hang them up to dry.

Using a spray gun

Safe operation
An airless sprayer forces paint out of its nozzle with a lot of pressure—so much so, in fact, that paint can become embedded in the skin. Therefore it is essential to wear long sleeves, gloves, a mask approved for use with a paint sprayer (not a dust mask), and goggles.

Cleaning up
To clean a gun, spray the appropriate solvent through the machine to flush the hoses and the body of the gun. (Collect the solvent in a bucket.) Then remove the nozzle and soak it in solvent to clean its orifice and tip.

How to handle a sprayer

It's crucial that each spray coat be thin and even, so overlap your passes a little. Keep your body parallel and your arm perpendicular to the surface. Bend your wrist as you move your arm (insets). This keeps the spray nozzle the same distance (150 to 200 mm) from the surface during the pass. Begin moving your arm before you press the trigger and keep moving it after you release it. Keep clear of the cord and ensure it's long enough when painting a long item: jarring can ruin a job.

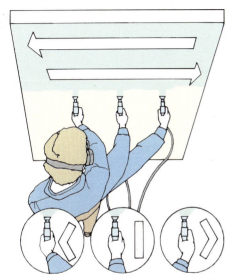

Inside corners ▶

To avoid paint buildup in a corner, turn the gun 90° so that the spray fans out horizontally. Then move the gun from the top to the bottom of the corner.

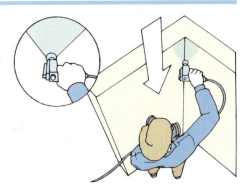

Outside angles ▶

Stand directly facing the edge of an outside corner. Begin at the top and move the gun from side to side, overlapping the strokes as at left. In order to cover both surfaces and the edge, bend your wrist (insets at left).

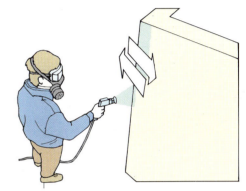

PAINTING TOOLS

TOOL	USE	WHAT TO LOOK FOR
Brushes	Use 75 or 100 mm brushes for wide surfaces. Use 35 or 50 mm brushes for trim and panelled doors. Use 20 or 30 mm brushes for around glass, etc. For PVA paint, choose nylon or polyester bristles (natural bristles absorb water and lose their shape). For oil-base paints, use natural bristles.	Flagged ends give good paint retention and smooth coating. Tapered bristle body helps paint flow evenly and aids cutting in (see p 179). Look for fullness and variety of bristle lengths for smooth painting results.
Rollers	Rollers are an excellent choice when painting interior or exterior walls, masonry, and stucco. When painting with enamels use blended polyester/wool covers. When using water-base paint, use synthetic-fibre covers (which won't absorb the water in the paint).	Construction of roller frame should be sturdy: either professional-quality compression or slip-on type. Avoid types with wing nuts or end caps. Check that the roller cage moves freely.
Paint pads	Use for cladding on timber houses, shingles and wood fences. To store, place fibre side up.	Pads that have fibre applicators are preferable to those made of foam.
Sprayers	Useful on large areas or rough surfaces. Speed and ease of application are the main advantages. Also useful on more intricate jobs, such as burglar bars, but the amount of paint used will most likely be more than if a brush is used.	You may be able to hire one from a rental company. Consult the dealer to ensure the sprayer matches your needs. For example, don't select a unit with a small container if you need to do large-volume work.

CHOOSING AND BUYING PAINT

The right colour

Tried and true
The best way to determine whether a certain colour will suit a room is to hang a swatch of it on the wall where it is to be and leave it there for 24 hours. Observe how the colour looks as the light changes, under artificial light, and at the times when the room is used the most. To make a swatch, either tape a number of paint cards together or coat a thick piece of porous paper, such as poster board, with the paint. ▼

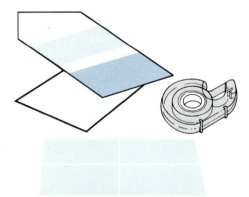

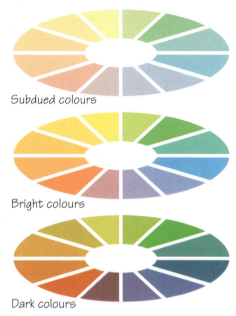

Subdued colours

Bright colours

Dark colours

In the mood ▲
You can use colour to create a mood. Dark colours will absorb light and lend a quiet, intimate feeling to a room. But be careful—too dark a room can be depressing. Bright colours are generally exciting; subdued ones are relaxing and restful.

Lighten up
When choosing a strong, bold colour for your walls, consider going one or two shades lighter. You'll find that a colour seems to darken and intensify as you spread it across walls. If you select one that's too strong, you may end up with more colour than you really wanted.

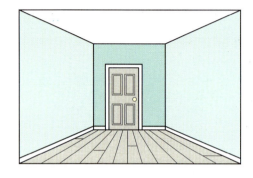

Room makeovers ▲
If you want a long, narrow room to look wider, paint one or both of the short walls a bright or dark colour and the other walls a pale colour. If a room is square and lacks a focal point such as a large window, paint one wall a rich accent colour such as maroon.

Check the exposure ▶
Rooms that face south, southeast, or southwest receive little or no sunshine during the day, making them dark and uninviting. You can lend some cheer to such rooms by choosing from a palette of warm colours—yellow, red, orange, and brown. Likewise, you can make sunny rooms seem cool with blues, greens, greys, and lavenders. But beware of those cool shades if you live in a colder area: research shows that people feel colder in rooms with cool colours. If you are committed to off-white, choose either a warm or a cool tint of that neutral colour.

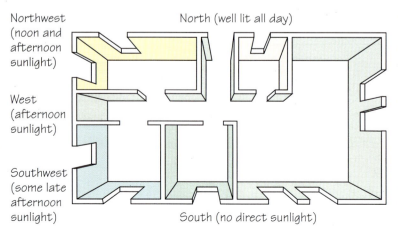

Moving the walls

Colour can also create optical illusions. For example, light colours reflect light and make a small room seem larger. Warm colours seem to advance and "fill" space, whereas cool colours recede. A white ceiling will seem higher; a dark ceiling will appear lower.

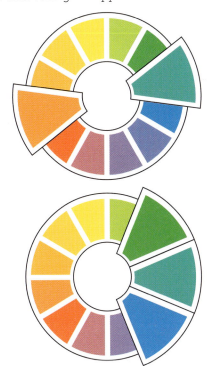

Wheel of colour ▲

While a favourite colour or object often determines the main paint colour for a room, you may wish to consult a colour wheel for a secondary or contrasting shade. The colours that are opposite each other are called complementary colours. These hues will enhance each other in a colour scheme. The hues on either side of a given colour are related colours and form the basis for a co-ordinated look to a room.

What to buy

Nothing but the best

You'll get the best results if you buy a premium-quality paint recommended by a reliable paint retailer. Buying a cheaper paint won't really save you money, since it will cover fewer square metres and isn't likely to wear as well as a better-quality paint.

Exact calculation

If your room has an irregular shape or is very large, you may want to calculate exactly the area you need to cover. First, measure the length of each wall or section of wall, including any alcoves and other irregular shapes. Add up the figures and multiply by the wall height. Subtract the area of any doors and windows and add the ceiling area. (You can often use the floor dimensions instead, multiplying length times width.) Finally, multiply that last number by the number of coats you think you're going to need. Don't try to buy too little and stretch it—rather buy a little extra for touching up afterwards (p 189). ▼

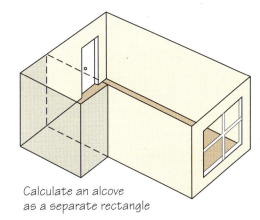

Calculate an alcove as a separate rectangle

Estimating rules

As a rule of thumb, 5 litres of paint will provide one coat for four 2,4 m walls in a 3,6 x 4,6 m room. (You'll need more for rough-textured walls.) Work on another 2 litres for the ceiling.

Buy a little extra

To avoid running out of paint in the middle of a job, always buy a little more than you think you'll need, and buy it in 5 litre instead of 2 litre tins. You may find that the cost of purchasing five 2 litre tins exceeds the amount you will have to pay for two 5 litre containers.

Instant blackboard

If you're planning to paint a child's room, a playroom, or a kitchen, consider brushing a couple of coats of blackboard paint on a section of the wall. Attach a moulding to frame it and as a chalk rest. Not only will this be a safe place to draw on the wall, it will also be a convenient place for the rest of the family to write messages.

Buying that special colour

If you buy a quantity of paint specially made up to a specific colour, buy what you need in one purchase. If another batch has to be mixed a few days later, there's a chance it could be a slightly different shade and this could ruin the effect you're trying to achieve. Secondly, if your order has had to be put in more than one container, mix the contents of all of them together before starting the job. Your order may have taken a while to make up—and could have been made up in more than one batch. This means the contents of each container could be slightly different in colour.

PREPARING A ROOM FOR PAINTING

Removing paint

Say when
If the trim in a room already has three to five coats of old oil-base paint, you can probably add another one or two coats of oil-base paint, but it's not a good idea to apply that many layers of PVA paint. Use a heat gun or chemical stripper to remove the old paint before applying a new coat of PVA. And no matter what kind of paint has been used on it, wood trim often looks best if all the built-up paint is removed first.
Caution: Before removing paint, check its lead content (see facing page).

Scraping by ▲
To remove a rough section of built-up paint, try wrapping some metal window screening (not fibreglass) around scrap wood and using it just as you would a sanding block. This improvised scraper removes paint quickly and won't damage the surface.

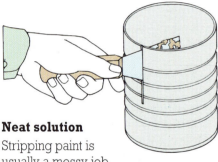

Neat solution
Stripping paint is usually a messy job. Here's a way to contain the globs of paint and stripper as you clean your putty knife. Use tin snips or a hacksaw to cut a slot in a large coffee tin. The slot should be a little wider than the thickness of the blade of the putty knife, and a little deeper than its width. To clean the blade, insert it into the slot at the handle and pull the knife towards you. The edges of the slot act as a double-edged scraper and catch the residue neatly in the tin. Cutting the slot about halfway down the tin will be sufficient even for broad putty knives (For more on stripping finishes, see pp 242–245.)

More prep steps

Degreasing
Greasy and oily stains show through newly painted surfaces, especially if the paint is PVA. Before you paint, check the surfaces for these stains. If the spots are few and small, rub them off with cotton wool or a cloth saturated with rubbing alcohol (coat larger stains with a stain-blocking sealer or primer). As you rub, you'll find that paint will come off too, so be sure to wear rubber gloves to keep your hands clean.

Crayon and ink marks
Children find it hard to resist drawing on walls, and unfortunately crayon and ink will show through a fresh coat of paint. To remove crayon marks, put on rubber gloves and rub the areas with a cloth dipped in paint thinner. You can remove ink stains in the same way, using either paint thinner, as for crayon marks, or household bleach.

Wash the walls
Before you get out the paintbrushes, it's a good idea to wash the walls and ceiling. Choose a cleaner that doesn't require rinsing. To keep water out of the electrical outlets, tape over them and squeeze excess water out of the sponge before cleaning around them. ▼

Attack those cracks
Don't rely on paint to hide thin cracks in plaster. You have to take a trip around the room and fill them first. You should open up each crack a little before filling it (an old bottle opener works well). Do not use a putty knife, as you could damage the blade. Use this tool only for filling the cracks: the blade will last longer and produce better results.

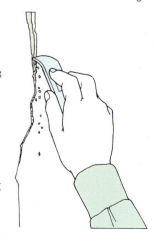

Fill 'er up

Once you have removed all the loose plaster, use a putty knife to fill the cracks with filler, leaving the surface slightly proud of the surrounding area. After it dries, sand the filled area until it is smooth and then apply primer to seal the repair. (For more tips on repairing walls, see pp 129–131.)

Safe outlets

When it's time to remove the outlet covers, switch off the power to the circuit at the main distribution board and only then remove the outlet covers. To keep track of the screws, reseat them in their holes or tape them to the backs of the covers. Paint the area around and below the outlets first, so that you can replace the covers sooner and switch on the power again.

Cover-ups

Door protection

An easy way to protect a door from paint is to slip an "envelope" of plastic over it. To make the cover, staple two large pieces of plastic together on three sides. When you are measuring and cutting the film to size, don't forget to add a little extra to accommodate the doorknob and to make the cover easy to slip on.

PAINT PROBLEMS

Lead paint

Lead is a toxic metal that, if inhaled or ingested, can cause neurological damage (particularly in children), and paints manufactured in this country often contain the metal.

Bright red, orange and yellow paints generally have higher levels of lead than paints of other hues. This means that the very colours more likely to be used on a child's toys and in the bedroom—bright reds, oranges and yellows—are those that tend to have more lead.

No lead-base paint should be ingested and any that is peeling and cracking is even more hazardous. (Lead-base paint that is intact does not present a problem, unless it is chewed and ingested.) Another danger comes from less visible sources: the lead dust that rises when you sand this type of paint and the lead fumes created when using a heat gun to remove paint. If old paint is deteriorating, or you are planning even a minor renovation, take a few samples for testing and analysis to a laboratory.

Check with your local health authority for laboratories that can analyze paint samples for lead content or contact one of the major paint manufacturers for advice. If a test shows lead in your paint, seek advice as to the best way to safely remove and dispose of it.

Ventilation and protection

Working in a ventilated area makes good sense because the fumes from some paints could irritate your throat, sensitive nasal passages and your eyes. Even if there is no lasting harm, being comfortable can mean you will complete the job properly without rushing it. Always wear goggles and respiratory protection.

Tape and drape ▶

The next time you need to protect a wallpapered wall, panelling, or any other large surface from paint, try this: tape a large dropcloth to the edge of the surface to be protected. If necessary, apply two layers of tape—the first one being your edging tape to achieve a fine finish. The second tape is laid over the first and holds the dropcloth in position. You should be able to remove the latter tape immediately you complete one area and move it on to the next.

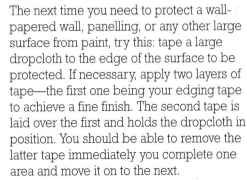

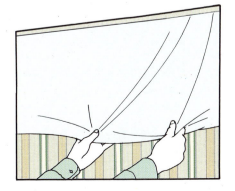

PREPARING A ROOM FOR PAINTING

More cover-ups

Dropcloth options
You can never have too many dropcloths. While professionals use heavy canvas ones because they absorb paint spills, provide nonslip footing and won't stick to your feet, many DIY'ers rely on inexpensive plastic dropcloths. To make plastic cloths function more like canvas, cover them with thick sections of newspaper, to absorb paint and provide a nonslip surface. And if you need an extra cover, use an old plastic shower curtain.

Go wall-to-wall
Strips of old carpeting can also serve as dropcloths when you are painting or doing messy repairs. The weight of the strips makes them stay in place, and they can be used over and over again. The strips should be about 3 or 4 m long and wide enough so that all four legs of a stepladder will rest on the carpet at one time. Place the strip with its nap side up or down, as you wish. After use, let any wet spots dry; then vacuum the strip if necessary. If you don't have any used carpeting on hand, carpet dealers may have offcuts and remnants available for sale.

Press-on tape

Have you peeled away masking tape only to find that paint has seeped underneath it? Masking tape protects a surface only when the seal is perfect. To make sure the tape does its job, press it in place with the flat side of a 50 mm putty knife.

Foiled again
A good way to protect doorknobs, telephones, electrical switches, taps, handles, and other items that you want to keep paint-free, is to cover them with aluminium foil. Crimp the foil to fit the shape; it will stay there until you have finished painting. It's also a good idea to keep some plastic sandwich bags handy. Use them as makeshift gloves to protect telephones and doorknobs from paint-splattered hands.

◀ **Protection for hardware**
For best results, you should remove all hardware before painting. But if you can't or don't want to do this, you can protect hardware by applying a thin coating of petroleum jelly. After painting, just wipe the metal clean.

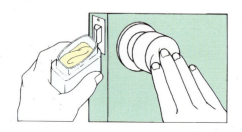

Shoe saver
To keep paint off your shoes, slip an old pair of socks over them. The cotton will absorb splatters and save you the work of cleaning up. ▼

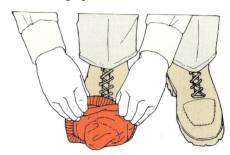

Step by step

Work order
Few things are as frustrating as finding you've dripped paint on a newly painted surface. To keep the mess to a minimum, work from the top down. Here's a step-by-step work plan for painting a room: after the prep work is done, paint the ceiling. Next, prime the walls and the trim. Then, give the walls a final coat. Finally, give the trim a final coat, saving the skirting board for last.

Primer versus sealer
A sealer is used to coat stains and keep them from bleeding through the fresh paint. A primer helps new paint adhere better and helps keep the colour and the sheen uniform. If you are changing colours and planning on two coats, make the first coat a primer that's tinted to match the final coat. If you are repainting a room with the same colour, you need to prime only the areas that have been repaired or sealed.

PAINTING WALLS AND CEILINGS

Painting large areas

Cutting in
Use the narrow edge of a brush to edge, or cut in, a swath of paint equal to the width of your paintbrush along the perimeter of the walls and the ceiling. Begin in a corner and put just enough pressure on the brush to flex the bristles. To minimize lap marks, always work from a dry section back into a wet one. If you are working with a non-matt paint, put two people on the job—one cuts in with a brush while the other fills in with a roller. If you are working alone, cut in a section and then fill it in with the roller. ▼

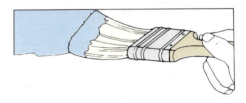

Paint catcher
When you are painting a ceiling, wrap an old dishcloth or paper towel around the handle of your brush and secure it with a rubber band. This absorbs the inevitable paint drips and helps keep your hand clean.

Find a stopping place
What should you do if you have to halt a project before you've finished applying a coat of paint—or if you find that you're running low on paint? Try not to stop in the middle of a wall—rather finish it and then stop. You'll avoid obvious lap marks and if you have to buy more paint (specially mixed or not), a slight difference in shade won't be as noticeable.

ROLLING PAINT

After a painstaking job of preparing a room, it's rewarding to see how quickly a roller can cover the walls and ceilings with paint. Begin by saturating a clean roller in the paint, rolling it over the tray ridges or wire grating (see p 172). Then dip the roller in the paint. (To avoid drips, don't overload the roller.) Spread it as shown.

Paint small areas (2 or 3 square metres) at a time. Begin painting a ceiling in a corner, and work across the narrower dimension of the room. Start painting a wall in an upper corner, and work from top to bottom and left to right. If possible, work in natural light—you'll find it easier to see any gaps.

1 Apply the paint in zigzag strokes. Use an "N" or "M" stroke on walls, as above, and a "W" pattern on ceilings.

2 Move the roller horizontally to even out the paint, and work back into the wet edge of the previous area.

3 To remove roller marks and even out the texture, use light up-and-down strokes. An extension handle on the roller really helps here.

Paint and Wallcoverings

WINDOWS, DOORS, AND STAIRS

Neat edges

Pane protection

Beginners may wish to cover the edges of the windowpanes to reduce the amount of cleanup that's needed. One way is to mask each pane (p 178). However, this takes a long time and removing the tape can be a chore, thereby defeating the initial goal. Instead, try rubbing soap or lip balm around the edges of the glass next to the trim. Any paint marks or splatters on the glass will be easy to remove when the paint is dry.

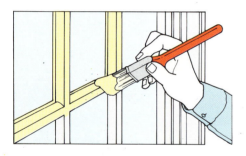

Going steady ▲

If you have a steady hand, you can paint the trim around windowpanes without masking them. You'll find that you have the most control if you use an angled sash brush and hold it as you would a pencil. Always work from the glass edge outward. As you do so, be sure to leave a thin paint line on the glass so you will seal the paint to the glass—and keep moisture from invading the paint film, causing the paint to peel. When the paint is dry, scrape off any paint that is beyond the paint line. See p 188 for hints on scraping paint off window frames and trim.

Work order

Door stops ▶

When painting a door, begin with all four edges (1). Next, paint the trim around any glass panes and all wood panels, whether raised or recessed (2). Then paint the door body, beginning at the top and proceeding down the sides (3 and 4). Finish the job by painting the door frame from top to bottom (5). As you paint the frame, work from the door towards the outer edges of the frame. For more on door edges, see the facing page.

Mask or remove hardware

Steps for a window

Here's the best sequence of steps for painting a sash window. First, pull the top sash three-quarters of the way down and push the bottom sash three-quarters of the way up (below, left). Paint the entire bottom rail (1) and half of each side rail on the top sash (2). Slide both sashes back into place, stopping a few centimetres from their closed positions (below, right). Then finish painting the top sash (3 and 4) and paint the entire bottom sash, working from top to bottom (5 and 6). To finish the job, paint the top of the trim (7), then the sides (8), and finally the bottom (9). ▼

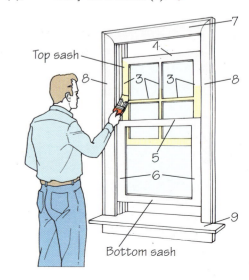

On edges

Connecting colours

When a door connects two rooms that are different colours, what shade should you paint the door edges? Here's the rule of thumb: the latch-side edge should be the same colour as the room into which the door opens. The hinge-side edge, which is visible when the door is open, should be the same colour as the other room.

The bottom line

If you are not going to remove the door before painting, you can paint the underside with a scrap of carpet. Why bother with an edge that no one will see? Paint helps to seal the end grain, preventing the wood from absorbing moisture and expanding. ▼

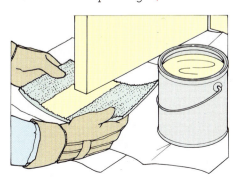

Steps for steps

Painting stairs

Here are two ways to paint stairs and still keep foot traffic moving. You can paint every other step, let the paint dry thoroughly, and then paint the rest. Or you can paint half of the width of each step, wait for the paint to dry, and then finish the job.

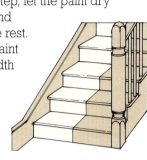

Reaching high places

Painting a stairwell may involve erecting scaffolding. You can either rent it or make your own. If you rent, ask the dealer to show you how to set it up correctly. If you are going to build your own, first analyze the space to determine what combination of stepladders, extension ladders, and planks you need. (Three typical situations are shown below.) When you are erecting the platforms, be sure to clamp, nail or securely tie the planks to their supports, and open or lock any doors that might accidentally knock into the scaffolding. Allow the planks to overhang at least 300 mm on either side. ▼

Glove action

Do you have a decorative railing and baluster in need of a coat of paint? Try using a paint glove. It does a great job of reaching the tight spots and crevices of metalwork motifs, and it makes short work of slender banisters, whether they're wood or metal.

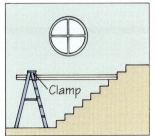

Place a stepladder so the plank will be level when it is placed on a ladder step (no higher than the next-to-top one). If the span between supports is more than 1,5 m, use two planks.

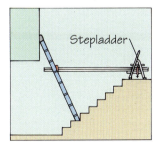

When the method on the left won't give you enough reach, brace an extension ladder at an angle. Select a step that lets you reach the points you have to and ensure the ladder's feet are level.

If there isn't enough space for a stepladder to open completely, you'll need to brace it in position with a cleat. To make the cleat, nail a board securely to the landing at the base of the stepladder.

DECORATIVE PAINTING

Stencilling

Make your own stencil

You can easily turn a favourite drapery or upholstery pattern into a stencil. Just photocopy a length of the original fabric, enlarging or reducing it as desired. Then place a piece of thick plastic sheet on top of the photocopy, tape it securely in place, and cut out the design with a craft knife. Try mixing designs.

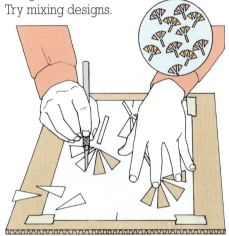

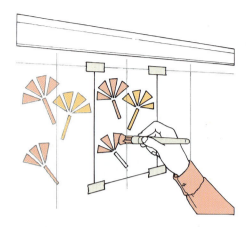

A light load ▲

Successful stencilling begins with loading the brush properly: dip a stencil brush only about 5 mm into the paint (use a fast-drying PVA paint). Then distribute the paint on the bristles by dabbing the tip lightly on a section of newspaper. The brush will appear dry when it is ready to use. Dab the paint into the stencil openings with short in-and-out strokes, keeping the brush perpendicular to the stencil.

Design ideas

Floor it

Fancy paint effects need not be limited to walls and ceilings; they can be used on floors if a protective coating is also applied. New non-yellowing super-hard polyurethanes are ideal for the job; they will protect a painted decoration with a rugged and almost invisible shield.

Ordinary objects

Professional decorative artists use tools other than sponges, rags, and brushes. They may use a piece of cork, a nail, a bottle top, a broom, or even their gloved hands to create a special effect. Here, a piece of cork and a nail have been used to simulate a knothole design.

Repeating designs ▶

In any stencilling job, patterns rarely repeat evenly across a surface. Some designs can turn a corner in mid-pattern, but often the design will end awkwardly on a wall. In such cases, plan to either stretch or overlap it a little on each wall, whichever is easier. To determine how much adjustment is needed, divide the length of the pattern into the distance to be covered on each surface. Then, when you are painting the pattern, work from opposite corners toward the centre of the wall. To make your adjustments less visible, overlap or stretch several repetitions by just a little bit. If you opt to stretch the design, fill in the gaps by hand.

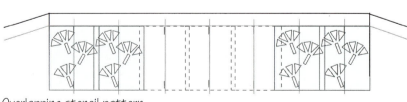

Overlapping stencil pattern

Stretching stencil pattern

TEXTURING TECHNIQUES

Sponging, rag-rolling, and stippling techniques add a wonderful dimension of pattern and texture to a routine paint job. These effects are easy to create, and they dress up a room while adding little to the cost.

To prepare a surface for any of the three techniques, apply a base coat and then cover it with a compatible glaze. Use either all PVA or all oil-base products; never apply one over the other.

You can make your own glaze in any colour by simply diluting paint. If you are using PVA paint, mix 3 parts water into 1 part paint. For a translucent PVA glaze, make the mix 4:1. If you're working with oil-base paint, begin with equal parts of semigloss paint and solvent. Try out the glaze and the tool you'll be using on a scrap board, thinning the paint little by little up to a 2:1 ratio. To ensure that the colour and effect will be uniform, mix as much glaze as you'll need at one time. Practising on the scrap board will also help you to decide on the pressure to use.

Sponging is an additive technique: you dab the glaze onto a dry base coat. It is the only one of the three techniques shown here that can be done with fast-drying PVA. Use only natural sponges torn into manageable pieces.

Rag-rolling and stippling are subtractive techniques in which you apply glaze and then partially remove it, and so it is important that the glaze dries more slowly. Fabrics commonly used for rag-rolling are worn cotton bedsheets, gauze, nylon netting, and sacking. To see various patterns, use different rags. Stippling brushes, made for the purpose, give the base coat a freckled effect; softer brushes create a mottled look.

1 Sponge on the first colour glaze over a dry (rolled-on) base coat with firm strokes. If you're adding a second colour glaze, be careful not to use too much of the first colour. When a sponge gets filled with glaze, switch to a fresh one.

To stipple a surface, apply an oil-base base coat; let it dry. Apply an oil-base glaze with a pad applicator or wide brush. Press the bristles of a coarse brush into the wet glaze. As the bristles become loaded with paint, clean them with a dry rag.

2 When you apply the second colour glaze, you can vary the effect by patting, dragging and twisting the sponge. If you're using PVA glaze, clean the sponges with water; if you're applying oil-base glaze, clean them with mineral spirits.

To rag-roll a surface, prepare the surface as for stippling (above). Then roll a crumpled rag across the wet surface. When the rag becomes saturated, switch to a fresh one. You can also wrap a crumpled rag around a roller core.

PAINTING A HOUSE EXTERIOR

Colour scheming

Find co-ordinates
When you are choosing the colours, begin by deciding on the main shade. As a rule, it should be a light to medium tone that complements or contains some of the colour of the roof. For the trim, choose a light shade—an off-white or if you have your colours custom-mixed, the same shade as the body but one-quarter of the colour formula. Next, choose an accent colour for any features that you would like to stand out, such as the front door and the window shutters. This accent colour is usually darker than the main colour, with a moderate contrast (see below). If you are painting entry steps or a porch, choose a neutral hue that echoes the roof colour.

Make a statement ▶
Your choice of an exterior colour scheme can affect the look of your house from the street. Light and warm tones (see pp 174–175) seem to advance and make a house stand out from its surroundings. Dark and cool hues recede and make a house seem less obtrusive. If your house is small, you can make it seem larger by using an accent that is lighter than the main colour. Stay away from the bold contrast of a light main colour and dark accent shade. The result will likely be a chopped-up appearance.

Light main colour stands out

Dark main colour recedes

Light accent on darker main colour seems larger

Dark accent on light main colour looks chopped up

Time and weather

Choosing sides
Who says you have to paint an entire house at one time? The job will seem much more manageable if you plan to paint just one side a year. If this idea appeals to you, take a trip around your house to determine which side has weathered the most. The north side usually receives the most sun; other sides may face prevailing winds and rain. Or if you prefer, begin with the most visible facade. After all, that's what you and your neighbours see every day.

A job for two seasons
The best time of year to paint the outside of your house is either in the spring or in the autumn, when air temperatures are not too hot or too cold. Not only will you be more comfortable, but the paint will stay wet longer, allowing more time for brushing out. What's more, many plants and trees will be either bare or losing their leaves and so will be less bothered by paint drips or spray.

Follow the shade
No matter what season it is, schedule the job so that you will be painting in the shade. Direct sunlight makes the paint dry too fast. Fast-drying paint is harder to work with and tends to blister, creating a soft paint surface that is easily damaged. You'll also avoid the eyestrain caused by sun glare reflecting from the paint, a problem that occurs especially with light colours.

Getting started

Making an estimate

To calculate how much paint is needed, calculate the area to be painted as you would for an interior (p 175). If your house has a gable, compute its area by multiplying its width times its height; then divide that number by 2. Keep in mind that exteriors require more paint than interiors. Add about 10 per cent to your total if you have timber home with cladding, 20 per cent for rough or porous surfaces, 30 per cent for corrugated material, and 50 per cent for a first coat on concrete or concrete block.

Power washing ▶

As with interior painting, the secret to a successful job is proper preparation. First, check for peeling paint, mildew, and cracked paint, and make repairs (see chart). Then wash the house with a no-rinse cleaner, working from the bottom up. Use a power washer to remove dirt and blast off any loose or flaking paint. (Wash bevel cladding with the power wash nozzle pointed downward—you don't want any water to get under the surface.) If you don't have a lot of dirt and loose paint to remove, or if the surface of your house is plastered, you are probably better off with a garden hose fitted with a spray nozzle—a power unit could damage plaster, which should have any cracks repaired before being washed.

Caution: The pressure from a power washer can be dangerous. Keep the nozzle pointed away from you and others and away from windows; there's enough power to break glass.

COMMON EXTERIOR PAINT PROBLEMS

PROBLEM	CAUSE	CURE
Peeling paint	Paint applied over dirty or mildewed surface	Wash exterior with scrubbing brush and detergent to ensure a dirt-free surface. Remove mildew with a mixture of 1 tblsp dry detergent, 1 litre chlorine bleach, and 3 litres warm water. Scrub with a wire brush. Rinse well with clear water. Remove any loose paint. Prime all bare wood. Use high-quality PVA paint; it "breathes" and won't trap unwanted humidity.
	Moisture penetrating cladding, plus inadequate venting or caulking around windows, doors	Install adequate venting in roof, attic, soffits, and cladding, or add caulk where needed.
	No moisture barrier in exterior walls	Apply oil-base primer/paint to interior side of exterior walls.
Mildew	Dirty, moist, or warm surfaces support growth of spores (mildew is a fungus)	To test "dirty" spots for mildew, wash with 3:1 water and bleach solution. If it's mildew, spots will disappear. Or remove with bleach/detergent mixture as for peeling. To prevent mildew, each spring apply detergent to house exterior with hose; spray nozzle removes dirt that supports mildew growth. Or apply a primer and paint with a fungicide additive.
	Too much shade permits moisture buildup.	Trim trees and shrubbery to allow air and sunlight to reach affected area.
	Inadequate venting in soffits, porch ceilings, or cladding permits moist conditions	Install vents in areas where mildew recurs.
Cracked paint	Many coats of paint on an old surface, or paint applied over improperly prepared surface	Sand, scrape, or burn off old paint.
	PVA applied over gloss oil paint	Sand glossy surface to dull finish. Use proper primer under PVA.
	Inferior cladding material	Replace cladding.

PAINTING A HOUSE EXTERIOR

More on preparation

Scrape and feather

To remove loose paint from timber cladding, use a heavy-duty scraper, sandpaper and a putty knife and be careful not to gouge the wood. Once the loose paint is off, you should feather (smooth out) the rough edges of the remaining paint. Start with an extra-coarse grade of sandpaper and progress to a medium grade, until the surface is evenly feathered. Use a putty knife to remove paint from the lower surfaces of the timbers of bevel cladding.

Filling out

After scraping and feathering, you'll still find places where the bare wood is much lower than the old bonded paint. Fill these areas with exterior filler, using a putty knife. Allow the compound to dry and then sand it smooth.

Of trim and wood cladding

The joints where cladding meets window and door trim may develop large gaps. These gaps not only look bad, they also allow the entry of air and moisture which could possibly create further problems in the future. Scrape out the old caulk and recaulk the joints with a paintable caulk.

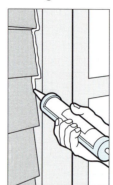

When it's rot

Check wooden posts, columns, balusters, and storm windows for rotting areas. Fill these spots with wood restorer/filler, and sand them smooth.

If rot covers a large area, you may need to build a form. Replace any wood that is too rotted to be repaired.

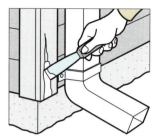

Techniques

Good spray-painting coverage

It's crucial to coat all the edges and surfaces of bevel cladding and other rough textures such as plaster. If you don't, moisture will seep into unsealed areas and cause problems. If you spray-paint, choose a windless day (even a 5 to 8 km/h breeze will blow overspray everywhere). Apply three light coats: (1) Spray from below so that the paint coats the underside of each timber. (2) Spray at a downward angle and cover the face of each timber. (3) Spray straight into the surface. Or instead of step 3, back-roll or back-brush—go over the wet paint with a roller or a brush to force the paint into the surface pores.

Scaffold setup ▶

The safest type of scaffolding is a steel pipe system, which is available from rental outlets. It gives you a stable support and a wide, safe work platform. If the surface around your house is firm and level, rest the scaffolding on casters for easy mobility. If you feel the scaffold will move when resting on a concrete or paved surface, have casters on one end only—you'll still be able to move it easily. If you have to work on quite a substantial slope, don't use casters at all. Rather use adjustable baseplates on all four legs. Don't try to use scrap wood to level it.

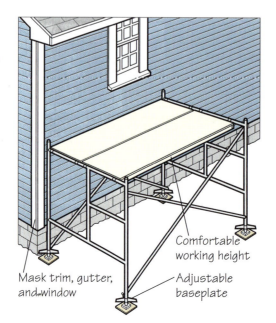

186 / Paint and Wallcoverings

Get a neat finish

When painting with a pad, glue narrow strips of thin plastic to both sides and the leading edge to provide a little clearance between the pad and wood trim such as a door frame. You will be able to achieve a very neat finish. Add more layers for more clearance. ▼

Help high up

Paint caddy

When you are painting on a scaffold or on a ladder, a brush that's parked on top of the paint can may fall off. What's more, the can may tip over, creating a huge mess and wasting paint. To prevent this, put the paint can and brush in a bucket and hang both the bucket and the brush from paint can hooks. If the bucket is large, you'll also have room for your paint scraper, putty knife, a rag, and any other painting tools you need.

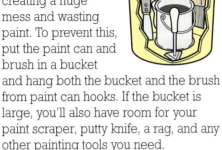

High roller pan

If you want to work with a roller from an extension ladder, here's a handy way to mount a roller tray. Drill two small holes at the top rear of the tray; then form two hooks from wire coat hangers and attach them to the tray. Position the tray on one of the ladder's rungs, and bend the hooks around a higher rung until the tray sits flat. The flanges at the front of the tray will hold it in place.

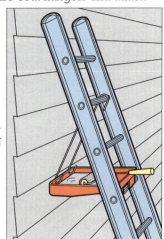

Order of work

Paint plan

When everything is washed, scraped, sanded, filled, and caulked, you're ready to paint. Begin by priming all the bare wood spots; then paint the walls (see right). Next do the trim and windows (see p 180); then move to the doors, along with any posts and balusters. If you intend to paint the entry steps or a porch, do it next. To finish the job, paint the shutters (if you have them). It may be easier to remove them and remount them when the paint is dry.

Achieve a uniform finish

The walls are the most visible part of a paint job so it's crucial to achieve a uniform finish. Work in the shade, brushing from a dry section into a wet one. Instead of working from top to bottom in vertical sections, keep to one level (see the numbered sequence in the illustration). If you are using a scaffold, you can keep it set to one height before setting it for the next level. Work from top to bottom and, if you are right-handed, from left to right. Follow a similar sequence for painting the trim. You may well find on going around the whole house that by the time you complete one circuit, the paint will be dry and you can immediately paint the trim at that level.

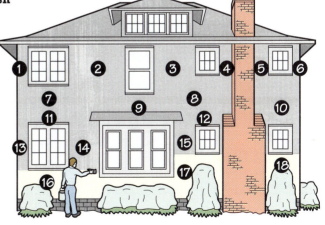

PAINT CLEANUP AND STORAGE

Flaws and spills

Clean line for trim
When painting around trim, have a screwdriver or putty knife and a cloth dampened with the proper solvent handy. If you get a bit of paint on the trim, fold the cloth around the tip of the tool and wipe the paint away. ▼

A clean scrape
Here's an easy, accurate way to scrape paint from windows. Place a 100 mm putty knife blade against the putty or wood moulding. Slide a razor-blade scraper against the knife blade to make a perfect line without damage. ▼

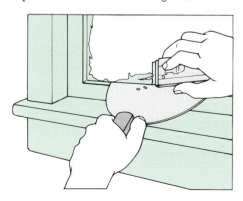

Unmasking
If possible, remove masking tape as soon as the paint is dry enough that it won't run or smear. As you remove the tape, clean away any paint that has seeped under the edges. If for some reason you've had to delay this job, soften the adhesive first by blowing hot air on the tape with a hair dryer.

Handling drips and runs
What should you do if you discover a flaw—a drip, a run, or a stray bristle—when the paint is too dry to brush it out? Don't be tempted to overpaint it—rather get rid

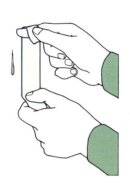

of it. If the paint is hard, either sand or scrape it down. If it is still tacky, hold a piece of masking tape at both ends, press the tape gently over the flaw or bristle, and then pull it straight off. Then when the paint is hard, sand the area smooth and touch it up with fresh paint.

Touch up
Even though paint is dry to the touch, it may not have hardened completely. Because a newly painted surface is still fragile, be careful not to scuff it when you are moving furniture back into the room. Keep a small brush and some extra paint on hand so you can easily repair any marks that you accidentally make.

Wash out
Be sure to wash a water-base paint spill out of clothes while it is still wet; once a stain dries, it becomes permanent. Your best bet is to wear a painter's smock that completely covers your clothing, including collar and cuffs, or to wear old clothes that you won't mind staining.

Skin treatment
To clean water-base paint from your skin, all you need is some hot soapy water. With oil-base paints you'll need something more. You can rub on some waterless hand cleaner, available at hardware stores, or try a little salad oil. (If paint gets in your hair, dip a piece of cotton or tissue in the oil and rub it gently over the painted hair.) You can also use a rag or paper towel soaked in mineral spirits. If you use mineral spirits, however, expose your skin to as little as possible, avoid breathing in the fumes and wash with soap and water as soon as possible afterwards.

Wrapping up

Keep your spirits
You can reclaim the mineral spirits that you've used to clean your painting tools. Put the dirty spirits in a covered coffee tin and set it aside (away from heat) for a few days to allow the paint to settle. Then carefully pour the clean liquid into a new container, leaving the paint sediments in the tin—if necessary pass it through a clean cloth held across the tin's rim to trap any particles of paint that might be stirred up when you pour.

Switches for matching

It's always a good idea to record the brand of paint, as well as the type (such as semigloss or matt) and the names of the colours used for a room. One way to do this is to mark a piece of masking tape with this information and mount it on the back of a light switch cover before you screw it back on. When you have used a special colour mix, write the details of its formula on the tape so that a colour match is possible.

Storing paint

Draw the line

When storing leftover paint, mark a line on the outside of each tin to indicate how much is left in it. Later, you'll be able to tell at a glance if you have enough paint for a job.

Sealing the tin

When you reseal a tin of leftover paint, any paint residue that has collected in the rim can prevent an airtight seal. What's more, it usually squishes out, making a mess. To minimize the build-up, punch holes in the rim (p 168) or wipe the rim clean before you close the tin. To improve the seal, stretch a piece of plastic wrap over the rim. Then tap the lid into place, using light hammer blows on alternate sides of the lid.

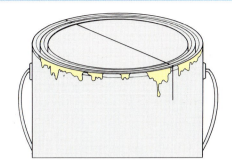

Resealing leftover paint ▲

Have you ever struggled to reseal a tin of leftover paint? Breaking a seal that is coated with dried paint leaves uneven surfaces on both the lid and the rim, making it difficult to reseat the lid the next time. So if you need to work from such a tin, mark the exact position of the lid as it sits in the rim—before you open the tin. To do this, draw a line across the lid and the rim at two places. When you replace the lid after using the paint, simply align the marks and press the lid down for a quick and easy seal.

More on leftovers

When you store leftover water-base paint in its original tin, you often get rust and paint flakes in the paint. To avoid this, pour the paint into a plastic or glass container with a screw lid. Rub a little petroleum jelly on the threads prior to pouring the paint—if you spill any on the threads the top won't be jammed, even when the paint is dry.

Leftovers again

You can also keep leftover paint fresh by pouring it into a plastic bag. Squeeze the air out before you seal the bag tightly; then put the bag into the original paint tin and tap the lid closed.

Wax paper barrier

Because a large air space will dry up a small amount of paint, you should put leftover paint into a smaller container (and a smaller air space) if the original tin is less than half full. Or cut a circle of heavy wax paper that is the same diameter as the interior of the tin and float it on the paint surface. The wax paper acts as a barrier, reducing the interaction of the oxygen and the paint.

Avoiding paint skin

Even if a tin of leftover paint is sealed tightly, a skin will form on the surface of the paint after a while. Removing the skin before you begin to paint is a messy job at best. To avoid this floating paint skin, store the tin upside down. Then when it's time to open it, turn it right side up. The skin will be on the bottom of the tin, leaving the fresh paint on the top.

No oil-base skin

Spreading a thin film of mineral spirits over the surface of oil-base paint before sealing the tin will keep a skin from forming. To apply the film, put the solvent in a small sprayer. Use very little—only a teaspoonful to a half-empty 5 litre tin of paint. To keep the film intact as you seal and store the tin, handle it very carefully without jarring it.

PREPARING TO HANG WALLCOVERINGS

Smart strategies

Cover tests
If there's only one layer of untextured wallcovering on the wall—and it's still adhering tightly—you don't have to remove it before hanging a new one. (More than two layers, however, is more weight than the adhesive is meant to support; the layers are likely to pull away from the wall.) Test the old wallcovering by running your fingertips over it. If you hear a crackling noise, the covering is loose and should be removed. You should also check the edges and corners by prising them up with a putty knife. If large sections lift off, continue the removal job.

Covering old coverings
If the old covering passes the crackle and corner tests (above), glue any loose areas with white glue or wallcovering paste (p 197). Then wash the surface with detergent or a mild solution of household bleach and water, and apply a primer made for use under wallcoverings. Beware, however, if the old layer is vinyl, foil, or plastic film. Covering these materials doesn't work very well. You're better off removing them instead.

Mess management
Removing wallcoverings is a messy job. Old sheets and bedspreads make first-rate drop cloths. You can either throw them away or use them again. As you work, pick up the globs of stripped paper before they dry. Otherwise they'll make your footing slippery and stick to the drop cloths and your shoes.

Razor's edge
If it's in good condition, plaster is tougher than wallboard. (Old plaster may be crumbly.) You can reduce the amount of soaking needed on a plaster surface by using a sharp razor scraper to remove wallcovering. The blade will slip easily between the paper and the plaster without damaging the wall.

Don't be stubborn
If a section of wallcovering backing just won't soak off, use a palm pad sander and 120- or 220-grit paper to sand the edges (only) of the area. Be sure that the backing is dry before you sand. Continue until the transition between the wall and the backing is smooth. Wear a dust mask when sanding.

Soaking solutions

Break it up
To break the surface film on vinyl or painted wallcoverings so the remover can penetrate the covering and soften the paste, use a sanding block fitted with coarse sandpaper, a wire brush, or a scoring tool made for the purpose. Take care not to gouge the wall as you work.

Scoring tool

Spray time ▲
Think twice about renting a steamer; they work very slowly. Brushing or sponging on chemical remover is also a time-consuming, messy job. You can speed the process considerably if you put the remover in a pressurized garden sprayer, hold the nozzle half a metre or so from the surface and spray it liberally. Allow the remover to soak in; the paper should almost fall off the wall. Respray any resistant areas. Before you fill the sprayer make sure it is absolutely clean and wear goggles and gloves when handling chemical removers.

Adhesive cleanup

Use a window squeegee to remove old, wet wallcovering paste from plaster walls. Dip it into very hot water, run it across the wall for about half a metre, wipe the paste off the blade and repeat the process until the wall is clean. ▼

Homemade mix

A mixture of 1 part vinegar and 10 parts water makes a good paste softener. To apply the mixture, use a sprayer (pump or pressurized). The smell, while non-toxic, is irritating, so ventilate the room.

After stripping

Wash and dry

Wash newly stripped walls with clean, hot water and a little household bleach 1/4 cup of bleach to 10 litres of water). Let the walls dry thoroughly—usually a few hours, but if it's humid possibly several days. Prepare the walls as for paint (pp 176–178); make sure the surface is smooth.

Greasy job

Kitchens and bathrooms are often painted in a glossy paint, which is likely to be coated with a film of grease or soap. Wash these walls with a heavy-duty detergent. Then prime them with an undercoat suitable for non-porous walls. If the primer beads up, there's still grease on the surface and you will have to wash the walls again.

Fill in the bumps

You can make a textured wall surface suitable for wallcovering with primer and drywall compound. Seal the wall with a water-base primer; then smooth drywall compound on with a metal float or broad knife. Apply another coat of primer, and you're ready to hang.

Planning the job

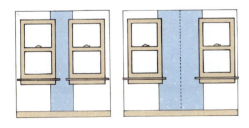

Two window treatments ▲
If you start a project between two windows, consider both the width of the covering and the space between the windows when deciding how to waste as little wallcovering as possible and how to avoid working with narrow strips. In a narrow space you'll probably need to centre the strip (left). In a wider space, try centring the seam (right).

Focal point strategies ▶
If you are hanging a large pattern that would look best centred on a main wall, or if the room has a focal point, such as a fireplace or a window, you'll need to centre the first strip, then work away from one side. Stop the first side when you get to an inconspicuous place for the mismatch. In the illustration, this is the area of wall above the door—well above eye level and relatively small. Then go back to your starting point and continue hanging the covering from the other side of the centred strip until it meets your first side at the mismatch spot.

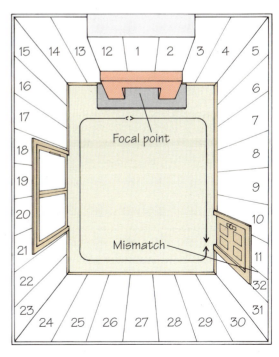

Paint and Wallcoverings / 191

HANGING WALLCOVERINGS

Strip tips

Put the top up
Many patterns are almost—but not quite—mirror images top and bottom. If there's a chance that you might accidentally hang your wallcovering upside down, mark an X on the top of the pasted side of each strip as you cut it off the roll. Note that you should do this with identical diamond and striped patterns as well—the shading may vary.

Reverse for one colour
With solid-colour textured (no-match) coverings, you'll get a more uniform result if you reverse every other strip.

Pressure point
When wetting the strips, don't apply too much pressure with the roller or pad applicator—you could remove some of the paste and end up with serious adhesion problems.

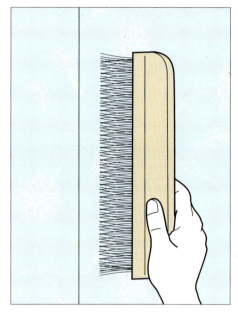

Brushing flock ▲
Never use a seam roller on flocked or other raised wallcoverings. Instead, gently tap the seams with a soft smoothing brush. That way you won't damage the raised pattern.

All the trimming
When you are trimming wallcovering at the ceiling junction or along the skirting board, always hold a broad knife between the cutting tool and the paper. This ensures a straighter cut and keeps the knife from damaging the paper if your hand slips. ▼

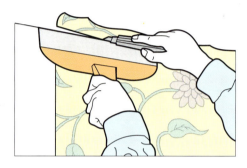

Keep an edge
Keep a sharp blade in your knife (and keep it away from children). A dull blade makes jagged cuts. To store all those used blades safely, pop them into an empty cooldrink can.

Water trays

Go soak it ▶
You may prefer to use a water tray to wet prepasted coverings. If you do, "backroll" the strip so that the pattern faces in and then soak the rolled-up covering in clear water to wet the paste. Then proceed with the booking process. This is the relaxing procedure (see step 3 on opposite page).

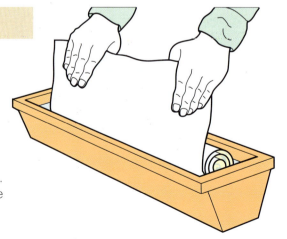

Include the kitchen sink
You may not have to bother with a water tray if you are covering kitchen or bathroom walls. A good-size kitchen sink or a bath will do the job.

One more tray idea
Here's a way to ensure that the strip is submerged uniformly and is thoroughly wet. When you are backrolling the strip, wrap it around a long medium-weight cylinder, such as a length of clean metal pipe or a heavy rolling-pin.

HOW TO HANG PREPASTED STRIPS

If this is your first wallcovering project, choose a pattern that needs little or no matching. Do a bedroom or a living room—they are easier than kitchens and bathrooms. Start off in a room with no alcoves or recessed windows, so you won't have to cut and match a lot of odd-size pieces.

You'll need a ladder, a utility knife and blades, a large flat work surface, sponges, a bucket, a paint roller, clean tepid water, levels, a pencil, a tape measure, scissors, a plastic smoother or smoothing brush, a seam roller, an apron, drop cloths, clean towels and refuse bags.

1 Use a level to strike a plumb line where the first seam will fall. If it is near an inside corner, position it so the strip will extend 3 mm beyond. (It should go 5 to 10 mm beyond an outside corner.)

2 Cut a strip the height of the wall plus 50 mm at the top and at the bottom. Use a roller dipped in tepid water to wet the back of the strip thoroughly, until the paste becomes milky.

3 Book, or relax, the strip by folding it pasted side in; make the first fold two-thirds of the sheet, the second, one-third. Roll the folded strip up loosely and let it rest as per maker's instructions.

4 Hang the strip. Begin at the top and align the right or left edge with the plumb line. Release the folds gradually. The strip must overlap both ceiling cornice and skirting board by about 50 mm

5 Flatten the strip against the wall, using a plastic smoother or smoothing brush. Start at the centre of the strip and push out. Small bubbles that remain will disappear as the strip dries.

6 Hang the next strip (without a plumb line), matching the pattern. After the third strip is hung, lightly roll both sides of the first seam with one pass. Wash off excess paste with a damp sponge.

HANGING WALLCOVERINGS

Paste

Enhancing the paste
Some prepasted coverings adhere better than others. To see how well a prepasted covering will stick to your wall, do a wet test: Wet a 150 mm piece of the pattern, place it on the wall, and let it dry. If you have any doubts about its adhesion, just roll some wallcovering paste activator on the pasted side before hanging it. (The activator looks and applies like wallcovering paste.)

Mildew stopper
Mildew, ever the enemy in bathrooms and kitchens, can easily find its way to the dried paste beneath a wallcovering. When it does, the bond weakens. While the pastes of some coverings have been treated to resist mildew, others have not. If you have chosen one of the latter, you can treat the paste side of the covering as you hang each strip. Before proceeding, however, test the preparation on a patch to be sure that it won't affect the pattern dyes.

Now you see it
When you are spreading clear paste on a wallcovering, it is hard to see if you're coating the surface completely and evenly. If your covering has a background other than white, you can add a few drops of food colouring to the paste to make it more visible. Pour it in drop by drop, just until it has a very light tint. Too much colour will bleed through the paper.

Table talk
Instead of renting a pasting table, use a large sheet of plywood or chipboard as a work surface. Use a relatively thick sheet so that it is sufficiently rigid.

Less mess
When you are ready to paste, put a drop cloth under the table to catch the inevitable drips. After you've pasted each strip, wipe the table clean (especially the edges). That way you'll keep the pattern side free of glue.

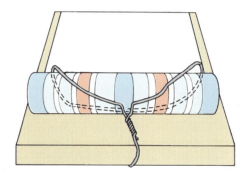

Hanger hold ▲
To keep a strip from rolling up when it's laid out on the pasting table, use this improvised holder. Simply bend a wire coat hanger into the shape shown, fit it over the roll, and secure the hooked end to the edge of the table.

Ceilings

When to do it
If you are papering a small room—such as a bathroom or a guest bedroom—consider covering the ceiling as well as the walls. It'll give the room a feeling of intimacy as well as a finished look.

Choose the direction
When you're covering a ceiling with the same material as the walls, remember that you'll be able to match the ceiling pattern on only one wall. Pick the most prominent wall in the room or, if the room is small, the wall opposite the most frequently used door. In the latter case, the pattern will seem to draw you into the room.

Ceiling strategy
If you plan to cover a ceiling, do so before you do the walls—and be sure to get someone to help you. Cut the strips of covering so that the ends will extend 10 mm down the wall. Then book the strips accordion-style, and you're ready to go. ▼

Neat edges

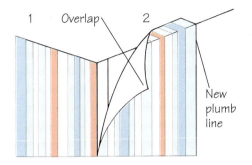

Turn the corner ▲

When covering an inside corner, you must overlap the strips. Never try to bridge a corner with one strip. Measure three spots (top, middle, and bottom) from the edge of the last strip to the corner. Use the widest measurement and add 3 mm. Cut the strip to size, knowing that the overlap will vary, and hang it. To finish the corner, strike another plumb line and hang the other cut piece.

Outside wrap

Outside corners are very visible—and seldom plumb, so you shouldn't wrap a single strip around the corner. Instead, treat the corner as you would an inside corner. Leave a larger overlap of 5 to 10 mm and smooth both strips carefully into place.

Arch comments

If you are not going to cover the underside of an arch, you'll want to leave a crisp edge of wallcovering around the archway. Leave about 25 mm of covering untrimmed. Allow the glue dry, and then trim the excess paper with a single-edge razor blade.

Odds and ends

Take a recess

When you are covering a recessed area (as for a casement window), start with full-width strips and allow extra for an overlap on each side. Snip the corners before smoothing the overlap (above). Cut strips to fit each side, and finish the job (below). ▼

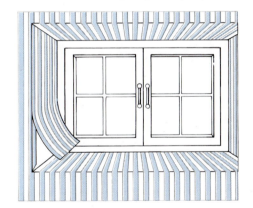

Smooth curves ▶

To cover the underside of an arch, follow a method similar to that for recessed areas. When it's time to smooth the overlap around the curve, snip relief cuts at frequent intervals. Cover the overlap with one strip, if possible. Cut the strip slightly narrower than the width of the arch to avoid any peeling edges.

Get behind a wall unit

You don't have to shift a heavy wall unit to hang wallcovering behind it. Position a full-length strip, smoothing it from the ceiling down to the top of the unit. Smooth the rest of the strip behind the unit with a length of wooden dowel or a measure. Then crease the trim line into the strip with a blunt long-handled knife. Pull the strip up from behind the wall unit and trim along the creased line with scissors. To complete the job, reposition the bottom of the strip and smooth it down.

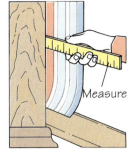

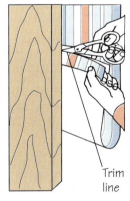

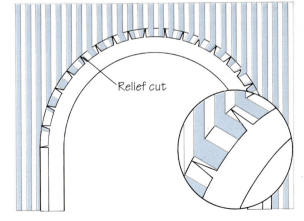

HANGING WALLCOVERINGS

Borders and accents

More is better
Putting up a border is an easy, inexpensive way to dress up a painted room. But if the room is quite large, you shouldn't economize too much. As a rule, the larger the room, the more border motifs you'll need. For example, a single border at the ceiling or at eye level tends to make a room look unfinished. Consider adding more borders and accents to unify the room.

Ceiling frame
In a room where the ceiling gets some attention, such as a dining room with a chandelier or a bedroom, put a border on the ceiling. Depending on the size of the ceiling and the effect you want to achieve, you can place the border frame 60 mm—or 600 mm—from the wall.

More frames
Brighten up a boring window or door opening by framing it with a border motif; then add co-ordinated drapes to complement the look. On a large wall you can create rectangular panels for a formal look. You can also frame a mirror, such as the one on a medicine cabinet in a bathroom.

Unexpected places
Looking for ways to accent a room without investing in a border covering? You can hang strips of wallcovering on the rear wall of open or recessed shelving or cover a wastebasket. If you're doing a bathroom, covering the inside of the medicine cabinet will dress up that typical eyesore and if you have a wooden container for your washing, try covering it. Without going too far, you can transform some eyesores while achieving a co-ordinated look.

Ganging together
You can combine several borders of various widths, or cut sections from a border and glue them on both sides of a main border motif, to create a decorative stripe around a room.

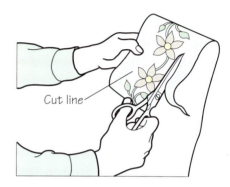

Create a stencil effect
Make a stencil effect with a wallcovering border: cut the edging from both sides; then hang the interior motif. It will look very much like a painted design.

Hiding imperfections

Plumb problems
If a room is badly out of plumb, the variations will show around the doors, windows, the ceiling cornice and the skirting board. Try selecting a random pattern, a floral, or a pattern with a vine motif. It is best to avoid geometrical patterns and stripes because they emphasize irregularities.

Border camouflage
One way to hide an uneven ceiling line is to hang a covering and add a co-ordinated border. Place the border so that half of it is on the wall and half is on the ceiling. Book the border, crease it in half, and hang it. At the corners, follow the steps below. This "half-and-half" approach neatly wraps the room, giving it a finished look. ▼

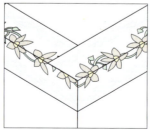

For an inside corner: 1. Butt two border pieces at the wall, overlapping the ends on the ceiling.

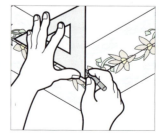

2. Cut a mitre through both layers on the ceiling. Remove the waste and smooth the rest.

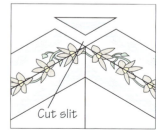

At an outside corner: Slit the ceiling side of one piece and wrap the piece around. Cut a patch to fill the gap.

When things go wrong

Too wet
If a pasted strip becomes too wet, book it and let it sit a little longer than you normally would. The extra moisture will evaporate. (Don't let it dry too much.)

Too dry
If for some reason you've been delayed and allowed a strip to dry out too much, you may be able to salvage it. Carefully place the dried book on the table; take care not to bang the strip as you do so. Spray a mist of clean water over the strip to relax it. Gently unfold the book; then reroll with paste and book again.
▼

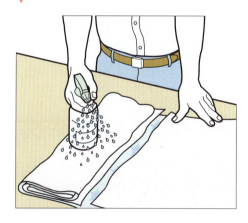

Free advice
While rolls of wallcovering come with a set of general instructions, they may not specify the particular needs of the wallcovering you have chosen. If possible, buy your covering from a local distributor who employs a trained and certified consultant. Such a person should be able to advise you if you run into problems.

Making repairs

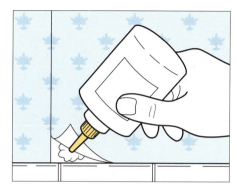

Mist those curls ▲
You'll have an easier time getting curled-up edges to stay down if you mist the repair area with clean water. With the curl in a relaxed state, it will lie in place when the glue is applied.

Tear it up
When a tear occurs, one side has the backing and the other has the pattern. To repair the tear, place the backing side down first and cover it with the pattern side. (Otherwise, the backing will be visible.) Where the two sides meet, you will see a small ridge. Gently smooth it down with your fingertip, the eraser end of a pencil, or the tip of a toothpick. If the repair area dries as you work, mist it with clean water. ▼

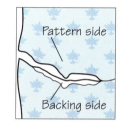 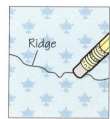

TROUBLESHOOTING WALLCOVERING PROBLEMS

PROBLEM	CAUSE	REPAIR	PREVENTION
Seams pull apart	Wallcovering shrinks after it is hung	Remove the strips and hang new ones.	Buy high-quality wallcoverings; prepare the wall properly; book according to maker's instructions; overlap seams 1 mm or less; add a paste activator when wetting.
Edges and seams curl when dry	Too much rolling	Apply seam adhesive or vinyl paste to edges.	Don't roll seams immediately—wait until several strips have been hung; roll seams just once.
Air bubbles	Overworking the covering	Slit the paper over the bubble, and glue down with seam adhesive or vinyl wallcovering paste.	Smooth the paper without overworking (small air bubbles that you see when the wallcovering is wet should disappear when it's dry).
Dried paste	Not washing paste off before it dries	Some may be picked off; use a paste remover, or wash paste off with an all-purpose cleaner If in any doubt as to how to go about it, seek advice from an expert.	Rinse off excess paste with warm water and clean sponges as you hang each strip; dry with clean towel.

CHAPTER 7

HOME SYSTEMS

ELECTRICAL TOOLS AND TESTERS 199
SAFETY FIRST 200
ELECTRICAL SYSTEM BASICS 202
WORKING WITH WIRING 204
EXPANDING CIRCUITS 206
LAMPS AND FIXTURES 208
LOW-VOLTAGE AND FLUORESCENTS 210
PLUMBING BASICS 211
PIPES 212
VALVES AND TAPS 214
BATHS, SHOWERS, AND MORE TAPS 216
TOILETS AND DRAINS 218
GEYSERS 220
SOLAR POWER 222
HOME COOLING DEVICES 224
HOME SECURITY 226

ELECTRICAL TOOLS AND TESTERS

Down to basics

Electrician's toolbox

A toolbox that contains a pair of long-nose pliers, a pair of side cutters, a standard straight-tip screwdriver, a small long-shank straight-tip screwdriver, and a Phillips screwdriver has most of the tools used for electrical work. You may also need a wire stripper to remove the insulation from the wires, and linesman's pliers if a cable is too thick for your side cutters to handle. Or buy a multi-purpose tool that measures, strips and cuts wire, cuts bolts and crimps wire connectors. ▼

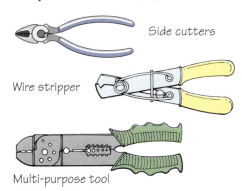

Side cutters

Wire stripper

Multi-purpose tool

Shocking screwdriver

The greater part of the shank of an electrician's screwdriver is covered in plastic to protect the user from shock. If you plan to use an ordinary screwdriver, here's a precaution you can take. Simply wrap insulation tape around the shank from the base of the handle to the tip; make sure the layers of tape overlap. Tape over any exposed metal parts on the handle too. And remember that the only real protection is to *always* turn off the power at the main distribution board before you work on that circuit.

TESTING EQUIPMENT

A voltage tester indicates the presence of voltage. It is most commonly used to make sure the power is off at a switch, outlet, or fixture, but it can also be used to locate incoming live wires and to test for earthing. A continuity tester detects shorts and other wiring flaws in sockets, switches, appliance and extension cords and fuses. A volt-ohm meter, or multitester, is a versatile instrument that does everything the other testers do—and more. Instead of simple yes/no readings, it provides actual measurements. It can be used to test resistance, direct or alternating current and voltages. They are available in analogue and digital versions.

Voltage testers are equipped with a bulb and two probes—but not a power source. When the neon light bulb lights, voltage is present. Check all the possible combinations of wires.

Volt-ohm meters, or multitesters, test for continuity, power on or off, and earthing. They measure high and low voltages (battery and household), current, and resistance. Whether analogue or digital, they have a selector which allows the user to select a function, and a range of values within that function. For example, the AC voltage function may offer a choice of 10, 50, 250 and 500 volts. Where you are unsure of the voltage or current to be tested, always set the selector at its highest range, and work down. These instruments operate off a battery when testing electrical resistance, so it is as well to periodically check your battery level and replace it as necessary. One basic step: always ensure the instrument is zeroed before use.

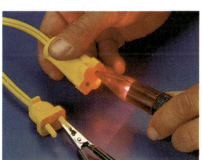

Continuity testers are battery-powered devices with a light bulb, probe, and crocodile clip, and indicate a complete circuit when the bulb lights.
Caution: Use it only with the power off.

SAFETY FIRST

Rules and regulations

The electrician's code
The South African Bureau of Standards code of practice for the wiring of premises is a set of regulations for safe electrical installation. The code requires that all wiring be done by or under the supervision of a registered and licensed electrician. The code is revised every year. So, even though you can purchase ceiling fans, for example, installing them will call for new wiring or for adding to existing wiring. Before installing the unit, make sure you contact your local electrical contractor so that you are fully aware of the latest requirements. If in any doubt whatsoever as to the execution of the job, call in a contractor to do it—one mistake could mean your own execution! Or that of a member of your family or a visitor.

Paperwork
It is required by the South African Code of Practice that all houses sold be issued with an electrical compliance certificate from a registered licensed electrician. Should you make any additions to your home, for instance, it is in your interests to ensure that all electrical work be done by a suitably qualified and licensed electrician.

What's in a label?
The South African Bureau of Standards mark (SABS) on any electrical device or component certifies that the product has been subjected to the bureau's exacting testing procedures and has met its very demanding safety standards. Play safe—go with the mark.

Avoiding hazards

Leave a sign

Before doing any work on a circuit, *always* turn off power to the circuit at the main distribution board, by either turning off the circuit breaker or removing the fuse that controls the circuit. Once you've turned off the power, make sure you put up a sign at the panel warning others to leave the power off.

Hand behind your back
When doing any work at the main distribution board, work with only one hand if possible. Keep the other behind your back. If you don't, and one hand comes into contact with electricity and the other an earth (such as a metal pipe), the electricity may travel from one hand to the other—with your heart in its path.

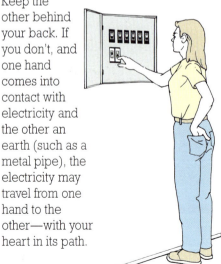

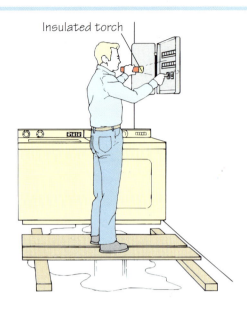

Insulated torch

Do away with puddles ▲
Before you do any work at the main distribution board, don a pair of sturdy shoes with non-conductive rubber soles. Even a dry concrete floor can be a good conductor of electricity. Keep a heavy rubber insulating mat near the board, or stack a few planks nearby where they will remain dry. Stand on the mat or dry planks while at the board. Never do any electrical job while standing on a wet floor.

Where stronger is NOT better
Always replace a fuse with one of the same amperage. A higher-amperage fuse will allow wires to overheat, which can create a short circuit and start a fire. Do not replace a fuse until you've solved the problem that made it blow in the first place. Keep a supply of fuses of the correct amperage near the main distribution board so that, if one blows, you'll have the right replacement handy.

Be certain—test it

Until you've tested an earth, don't take for granted that it's really earthed. To test an earth, clamp a 1 mm single-conductor wire to the earth wire, a metal pipe, or other bare metal on the main distribution board. Then run the wire to the outlet. Attach the crocodile clip of a continuity tester to the wire and touch the probe on the earth—either a bare earth wire or a metal water pipe. If the tester lights, you'll know that you have proper earthing.

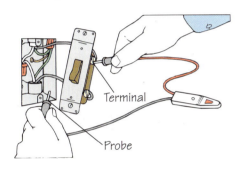

Is it live? ▲

Before working on a switch, remove the cover plate and check that the power is off by using a voltage tester. Place one probe on the outlet's metal box or on the earth wire conductor. Place the second probe on each terminal screw. If the power is off, the bulb will not light. At an outlet with one or more sockets, insert the probes into all the holes. If the tester does not light, carefully remove the cover and outlet; touch the probes to each terminal screw and a known earth. If the bulb still does not light, the power is off.

Metalproof

Be careful not to touch plumbing pipes or fixtures while working on wiring or repairing an appliance. Also avoid all metalwork—structural steel, metal gutters, and so on. Don't touch other electrical appliances.

Hand protection

Whenever you work with electricity, make sure your hands are completely dry. If you do come into contact with live equipment, dry hands can reduce the intensity of the resulting shock. If they become sweaty, dry them frequently.

In an emergency

Seeing sparks

When an appliance or power tool gives off sparks, unplug the cord without touching the body of the appliance. Or turn the power off at the main distribution board. If the sparks come from the cord or plug or if the cord is hot, turn the power off at the mains board. If you see sparks at a wall fixture, use a nonconductive item to turn the switch off before turning off the power at the main board. Call your electrician if the sparks are at the main distribution board.

Soaked

Do not touch a small appliance that's under water. Making sure you and the plug are dry, pull out the plug without touching anything metal. If a large appliance is surrounded by water, turn the power off at the main distribution board. If it is in a flooded area, however, have the power turned off by Eskom.

Outdoor power lines

Downed power lines are extremely dangerous. Do not try to move them—not even with a piece of wood. The voltage in these wires is high enough that wood can be a conductor. Do not go near the lines; call Eskom, your local protection services or electricity department. If the line falls on a car while you're in it, stay in the car until help arrives.

Helping a shock victim

If you find someone in contact with a live circuit, don't touch him. If the main distribution board is nearby, turn off the main power to the house. If not, use a nonconductive item, such as a wooden chair or wood or plastic broom to separate the person from the live wire. Or carefully loop a sweater or some other garment around the victim and pull the person away. If the victim does not have a heartbeat, apply cardiopulmonary resuscitation (CPR) if you've been properly trained in this procedure. Check the victim for burns and, if he or she was touching metal, also check for shards in unshielded eyes.

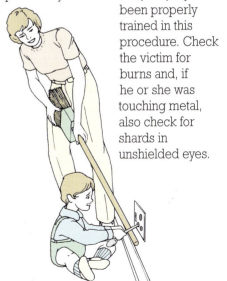

Home Systems / 201

ELECTRICAL SYSTEM BASICS

Circuits

Turn up the volume
Here's a way to quickly establish which circuit an outlet is on, even without a diagram. Plug a radio into the outlet, turn it on and turn up the volume. Even if it's in another room, you'll hear the silence when you switch off the right breaker or unscrew the right fuse. This is also a good safety tip—when working on a circuit, plug a radio into an outlet and turn the volume up. If someone turns the power on, the sudden racket will alert you to the danger.

At the main distribution board
If you can't see the imprinted number on the circuit breaker, rub chalk over the end of the toggle switch; then wipe away the excess. The chalk remaining inside the imprint will show the number.

Make a map ▶
To help solve electrical problems, map your electrical system. First make a sketch of your floor plan. For each room mark the location of every switch, light, and outlet, and code them as shown. At the main distribution board, switch off the first circuit and mark a "1" by it. Walk through the house, turning on lights and plugging in a radio at each outlet. If a light or the radio doesn't go on, you know the switch or outlet is on that first circuit. (Don't forget the garage and any outdoor outlets.) Write a "1" on your map at each outlet or light affected by that circuit. At the main board, label the location of the circuit—for example, "bedroom outlets and lights". Some dedicated circuits may power only one heavy-duty appliance, such as an oven or hob. Repeat for the other circuits. Keep a copy of the map in a plastic sheath at the board.

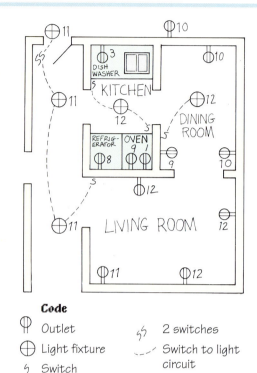

Code
- ⌽ Outlet
- ⊕ Light fixture
- ⌇ Switch
- ⌇⌇ 2 switches
- ---- Switch to light circuit
- 10 Circuit number

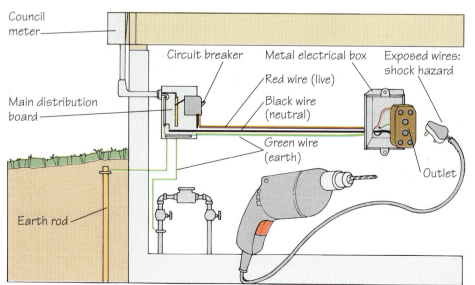

◀ A closed route
A safe electrical system routes electric power from the main distribution board through circuits of insulated wires and closed boxes. The system is essentially a closed one, in which there is no easy way for you to get to a live wire. A fault within the system, caused by a faulty outlet, a break in a wire, or frayed insulation, can blow a fuse or trip a circuit breaker. When this happens, only the circuit is protected. If the fault is outside the system where you may come into contact with it, you may get a shock. In this diagram, the potential leak is at the drill cord. Before using the drill again, replace the cord.

Power control

How you turn off all the power to your house depends on the type of main distribution board in your home. The "main" switch may be labelled: "In case of accidental contact or leakage, switch off this mains switch immediately". ▼

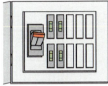

A circuit breaker panel will have one or more main breakers at the top. To turn the power off, flip the breakers to the Off position.

Circuit breaker panel

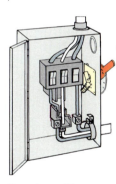

The older type of fuse box will have a lever switch on one side of the box; to cut the main power, simply push the lever to the Off position. Or you may find the lever switch in a box by itself, usually a few metres from where the wires enter the house.

Fuse box with lever switch

Reach out

Often the main distribution board is positioned high on a wall. Make up this simple aid: notch the end of a suitable length of 20 mm dowel so that it will fit loosely over the end of a switch. Keep the dowel near the board so that as and when the power has to be turned off or on, even the shortest member of the family will be able to do so without having to stand on a ladder. This can save valuable time in an emergency.

Fuses and breakers

Telltale signs

Plug-type fuse: when overloaded, metal strip melts

When a circuit draws too much current, a metal strip inside the fuse melts and breaks, stopping the current flow. An overload or a short circuit will cause a circuit to blow. An overload melts and breaks the fuse's metal strip but leaves the glass window clear; a short circuit discolours the window.

Earth leakage units

An earth leakage unit can protect you from a dangerous electrical shock that can occur if you become part of an electrical circuit. Suppose you touch a frayed cord on a power drill while standing on a wet floor. The resulting current running through you may not blow a fuse or trip a circuit breaker, but it can give you a nasty, perhaps fatal, electric shock. An earth leakage unit, however, will sense the misdirected current. In a split second it will shut off the circuit before the current can harm you. Many older installations are not equipped with an earth leakage unit. If that is the case, have one installed on your main distribution board by a licensed electrician. To ensure you are protected and that the unit is working properly, make a habit of testing the unit periodically by pushing the "Test" button. If it does not "trip", cutting off the circuit, call in a licensed electrician and have the unit replaced.

Breaker breakdown

When overloaded, parts inside a circuit breaker can be damaged. Signs of damage are a deformed plastic case or persistent shut-off. Because replacing the breaker means removing the panel cover, call in a licensed electrician.

Troubleshooting

To solve an overload problem, turn off an appliance or plug it into another circuit. If the circuit blows again right after you reset the breaker or replace the fuse, check for a short circuit. Turn off the main power. Unplug all of the appliances on that circuit, and look for damaged plugs and cords; repair or replace them if needed. Then, before replugging the appliances, reset the breaker or replace the fuse and turn the power on. If the circuit fails right away, the short is in the house wiring. Call a licensed electrician. If the short occurs only when you turn on a specific appliance, that's where the problem is.

Borrow a fuse

Has the fuse blown, and you're missing the big game on TV because you don't have replacement fuses? Simply replace the blown fuse with one of the same amperage from another circuit that won't be required for a while.

Keep them handy

Keep a multitester with the other tools you may need—a set of insulated screwdrivers, insulated pliers and so on—near your main distribution board so that the necessary tools are always to hand. Include a torch—but ensure the batteries are always fresh. Rummaging around for a light at night wastes time.

WORKING WITH WIRING

Stripping and splicing

How much is enough?
Don't get caught short of cable after stripping its ends. After measuring the length between the power source and the outlet, add 250 mm for each connection; then give yourself room for error by adding another 20 per cent to the total length. For instance, if the distance between the source and an outlet will be 6 m, add 500 mm for connections at both ends, giving you 6,5 m. An additional 20 per cent is about 1,2 m. For this job, you should allow a total of 7,7 m of cable.

The right connection

Wire inserted into connector

To join two wires, remove about 6 mm of insulation from the wire's end. Insert it into one end of the connector block, ensuring that all exposed wire is fully contained in the block. The wire should penetrate only halfway into the block so that there is space for the wire being inserted from the other side. Tighten the screw to ensure the wire is firmly connected but do not overtighten it as this could strip its thread and lead to a loose connection. Repeat the process for the other wire and then test the connection by giving the wires a gentle tug. If either one comes loose, reconnect it or use a new connector block. There is a range of blocks for different-size wires. Ensure you use the right size for the wires you're joining.

Make it stick
Moisture and stray wires from other connections are two potential causes of short circuits. To keep them out of a splice, wrap three turns of insulation tape around the spliced wires and the wire connector. Then dab a little PVC pipe cement under the end of the tape to stop it unravelling.

Finding a home for the splice
An exposed wire splice is a fire hazard. For your safety, the South African Bureau of Standards requires that all splices be kept inside an accessible junction box.

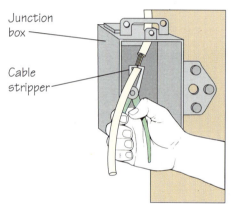
Junction box
Cable stripper

Cable exposure ▲
Not sure how much cable to expose for a junction box? Allow 50 or 60 mm for the depth of the junction box, then add another 150 mm for the cable outside the box. To strip the sheathing of the cable, use purpose-made wire strippers as in the illustration, or make a shallow cut down the length of the cable with a utility knife—taking care not to damage the insulation over the conductors. Peel back the sheathing and cut it off with the utility knife or side cutters. Don't forget to remove the wrapping or filler around the wires.

Stagger it
Joins can be made far safer if you stagger the splices so that, even should the insulation tape deteriorate or be damaged, there is less chance of the conductors coming into contact with each other.

Caution: Any join compromises the integrity of a cable or flex: avoid them if you possibly can—and if you do have to join cable or flex, make sure you connect the wires correctly: earth to earth, live to live and neutral to neutral.

Switches and outlets

A terminal situation
When connecting wires to an outlet, make sure that you attach them to the appropriate terminals. The neutral wire goes onto the terminal marked "N" (this wire bypasses the switch), the live wire goes onto the terminal marked "L", and the earth wire goes onto the terminal with the symbol for earth.

Pigtails
When you connect multiple wires to a terminal, a connector with a short wire (a pigtail) attached to it will make the task easier.

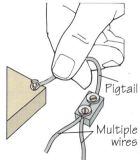
Pigtail
Multiple wires

Twist it

When connecting a wire, twisting the strands will keep them together and ensure that the screw in the connector gets a good grip. The insulation you are removing is a handy aid when twisting the wire: roll it through your fingers to twist the strands as you pull it away.

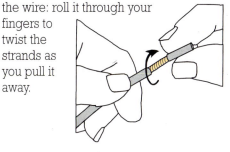

Make your own insulated tools

If you don't have insulated tools to hand when you need them for electrical work, try this: surgical tubing is available in various sizes from some pharmacies and suppliers of surgical requisites. You will be able to make your screwdrivers far safer to use by covering most of the shaft, apart from the tip, with tubing of a suitable diameter. A single length, slipped over both grips of a pair of pliers, will insulate the grips and will also help keep the jaws closed—which turns your pliers into helpful holders.

Time to unwind

Unwind an extension cord completely before use. If you don't, the conductors could get hot and cause an insulation breakdown. The same applies to cord that you have run from an outlet to an appliance or light: if you have made the cord quite long so that the unit can be used in more than one place, don't coil any excess when the unit is used close to the outlet. Spread it out loosely, out of the way, where no-one will trip over it.

SHOCKS: FIRST AID

Electric shocks can produce a range of injuries, including burns and asphyxiation. They can also kill.

The severity of the injuries depends on the strength of the current, the length of time the victim was exposed to the shock, and the degree of insulation the victim had against the shock.

Another factor is the victim's state of health.

Standing on a wet surface is very likely to increase the severity of a shock.

The first action to take is either to turn off the power, or break the contact between the victim and the source if you can do so safely and quickly (see p 201).

Then smother any burning clothes with a blanket or towel and immediately check that the victim is breathing and has a heartbeat.

If either has stopped, loosen any tight clothing around their neck and chest and immediately apply artificial respiration and cardio-pulmonary resuscitation.

Once the victim is breathing normally, lay him in the recovery position (below) and check for any burns.

Cool any burns with cold water, then bandage them or dress them with material such as linen.

As soon as the victim is stable, call for medical help if you have not already done so.

Lay the victim in the position shown, with upper arm and upper leg and thigh raised, the head tilted up and the near arm in front of the head.

EXPANDING CIRCUITS

At the box

Making everything fit
When working on an old box, you may find that the wires are crammed into it, leaving little room for working. More important, the wires can be damaged, creating a fire hazard. For your safety, the SABS code for the wiring of premises dictates the maximum number of wires that can be run into conduits and boxes of specific sizes. The size of the wire also determines the number of wires allowed in the box (the thicker the wire, the fewer in the box). In addition, if you have other devices in the box, such as switches, an outlet or earthing conductors, you'll have to deduct a certain number of wires from those allowed in the box. After making deductions, if you find you can no longer run enough wires for the job into the box, use a larger box. Check with your local licensed, registered electrician to confirm the size of the box that will be suitable.

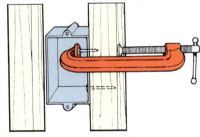

Hammer-free nailing ▲
To nail a box to a stud where there's not enough room to swing a hammer, use a G-clamp. By tightening the clamp you can squeeze nails through the holes in the side of the box and into the stud.

Running cable

Suction power
Fish cable through conduit or a pipe with knitting yarn and a vacuum cleaner. Tie one end of a length of yarn to the wire and suck the loose end through the conduit or pipe with the vacuum cleaner. Then pull the wire through.

Going fishing?
You can make fishing for a cable less frustrating. Tie a powerful magnet to the end of a fishing line, and lower it down to the new outlet's location. Push a straightened wire coat hanger (bend the end into a hook if you wish) through the hole at the new location. When the magnet locks onto the wire hanger, guide the magnet through the hole. (Alternatively, tie a magnet to the coat hanger and tie some metal object, such as a chain, to the line.) Then simply pull your electric cable through the wall, using the fishing line as a leader.

Elusive line
Sometimes grabbing the dropped line is difficult. To increase your chances, tie a plastic bag to the end of the line. The bag is bulkier and easier to grab.

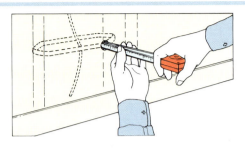

Fishing through a tiny hole ▲
Here's one way to grab a cable through a small hole: drill a 20 mm hole where you want the cable to exit. Extend a retractable tape measure, fold it at the halfway mark, and push it into the hole as far as it will go. The tape will conform to the space behind the wall—between the studs and the back of the opposite wall. Drop the cable from above, and pull the tape out, hauling the cable out as well.

Hidden!
When installing an additional outlet in a room, you can save yourself the trouble of chasing the wall if there is a built-in cupboard already installed. Drill a hole in the ceiling on the inner rear corner of the cupboard, and corresponding holes in each shelf. Pass conduit down from the roof and mount the outlet on the side of the cupboard.

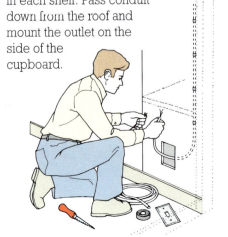

Doing it the easy way

The easiest path for a new cable in an existing home is through the ceiling space. To get the cable to an opening for an electrical box in a dry wall, you may have to "fish" the cable from holes cut in walls, ceilings, or floors. Use an electrician's fish tape to pull the cable through the spaces between studs or joists. Hook the tape to the cable, and wrap the connection with insulation tape. Have a helper push the cable through while you fish it out.

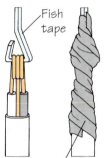
Fish tape
Insulation tape

Avoiding obstructions

When checking for existing wiring and other obstructions before running new cable through walls, do not assume the wiring goes vertically down to an outlet. It might not. Switch off the power, take the front cover off each outlet and confirm the position of the conduit. If necessary, check in the roof as well.

Getting around the corner

Cable being pulled around a corner can get snagged. One solution is to hold a paint roller against the cable at the trouble spot. As you pull the cable up, the rotating roller will keep it moving.

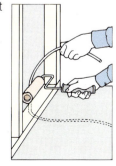

CHASE THAT WALL

An angle grinder makes short work of wall chasing when you are installing a new outlet in a brick wall. Just bear in mind that the job produces a great deal of fine dust, so seal the door to prevent dust getting into the rest of the house, and wear goggles. It is also a noisy task—so wear ear protection too.

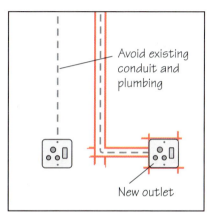
Avoid existing conduit and plumbing
New outlet

1 Boldly mark the intended route after having checked extremely carefully that it will avoid other electrical conduits and water pipes.

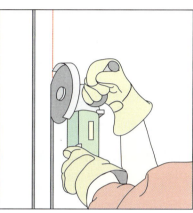

2 Cut the wall to a depth of about double the diameter of the cable you are installing. You will have to cut to a depth of 50 mm or so when cutting the position of the outlet.

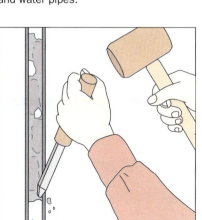

3 Chip out the channel and the space for the outlet. Wear eye protection and use a large dropcloth: some of the chips will fly out when struck.

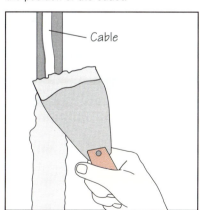
Cable

4 Install the cable and outlet, and fill the channel. Hot glueing the cable into position at every 300 mm or so will keep it in place as filler is applied.

Home Systems / 207

LAMPS AND FIXTURES

Incandescent bulb

Reaching the bulb
Most homes have a light bulb that is out of reach. Instead of climbing on a ladder, fasten a clip from a lampshade to a 1,2 m long, 20 mm diameter dowel or broom handle. For a better grip on the bulb, wrap insulation tape around the clip.

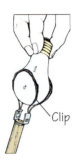

A raw deal
If a bulb breaks off in the socket, unplug the lamp or turn off the power at the main distribution board. Then press half a raw potato into the broken glass and turn it carefully. Or unscrew the socket using needle-nose pliers.

Revamping lamps

Missing the light?
If a lamp flickers or doesn't light, first replace the bulb with one that you know works. If that bulb fails to light properly, disconnect the lamp and inspect the plug and the cord. Look for bent or corroded prongs, a missing insulating disc, or cracks or fraying in the cord. If the plug or cord is damaged, replace it (see right). Check the socket for dirt. If it needs cleaning, wrap a piece of fine-grit sandpaper around your finger and scrape off the dirt. Also prise the metal tab at the bottom of the socket up a little to make sure it can make proper contact with the bulb.

Switch to a crutch
The small round switches on some lamps and fixtures can be hard to turn but there is a way around the problem. Fit a hard rubber ferrule (one that fits snugly) over the switch. You'll find it is easier to grip.

Give it new life
When replacing a cord inside a folding-arm lamp, unplug the lamp and remove the bulb. Cut the old cord 100 mm from where it passes into the channel of the lamp. Splice the new cord onto it. Now cut the old cord just short of the lamp head. Pull it at the elbow until the splice appears and pull through sufficient of the new cord to reach the lamp head with enough to spare for connection to the terminals. Then pull the old cord through the upper channel until the splice appears. Undo the splice before feeding the new cord into the lamp head. Attach the wires to the terminals, but make sure the live wire, indicated by an internal thread, is connected to the switch terminal screw. Reassemble the lamp and attach a plug.

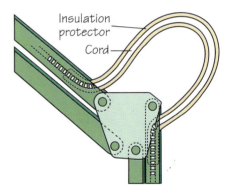

What's in a plug?
When replacing a plug on a lamp with exposed metal parts, ensure that the connection to the plug has the correct polarity. The live of the plug must be connected to the live wire, identified by an internal thread in the case of a flat cord, or by the brown in the case of a sheathed cord. The neutral of the plug must be attached to the other wire, or the blue in the case of a sheathed cord. In the case of a three-core lead, ensure that the earth wire (green-and-yellow) is also connected to the plug. (See p 24 for the correct wiring of a three-pin plug.)

Protect that wire ▲
The channels through which the wires run in a folding-arm lamp, like the one on the left, sometimes have sharp edges. Over the years, the continual flexing of the arms can lead to the cord's insulation being worn through. Just slip a short length of aquarium air-pump pipe over the cord at those spots where it rides on the channel edges. The pipe will protect the cord's insulation. You can use this same technique in other lightweight applications like this to give a little extra protection—the clear pipe is an unobtrusive but effective insulation protector.

REPLACING A LIGHT FIXTURE

Of the many varieties of light fixtures, a double-bulb fixture that mounts to a ceiling box is one of the easier types to install. Even a more complicated light fixture can be installed without too much difficulty if you follow the manufacturer's directions.

First, at the main distribution board or fuse box, turn off power to the circuit you'll be working on. When you take the old fixture out, you may find that it wasn't earthed. By adding the mounting strap, you'll have a place to secure the earth wire. Make sure you use wire connectors of a size that corresponds with the wire size and check for the correct-wattage bulb or bulbs.

Using a higher-wattage bulb than that for which the unit was designed, might cause a fire.

1 Switch off the power to the old fixture's circuit. To remove the fixture, loosen the mounting screws, then twist it slightly and pull down on it (carefully, so that you don't cause any damage). Disconnect the fixture wires from the mains wires.

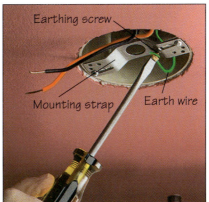

2 Secure the new fixture's mounting strap in position. Once it is in place, fasten the earth wire, which will be inside the junction box, to the earthing screw. (If the unit is heavy, try putting a length of timber in the ceiling and fixing the strap to it.)

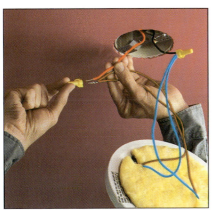

3 Use connectors to join red (live) wires or black (neutral) wires. The fixture wires may be brown for live, blue for neutral. If so, join mains red to fixture brown, and mains black to fixture blue.

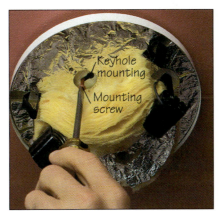

4 Install the new mounting screw. Slide the keyhole slot in the new fixture base over the screw and rotate the fixture until it locks in place. Tighten the screw.

5 Fit light bulbs of the proper wattage, then push the cover over the spring-loaded clips, which will hold it securely in position.

Home Systems / 209

LOW-VOLTAGE AND FLUORESCENTS

Lines and chimes

No more staples or saddle clamps
Low-voltage wiring, such as telephone, thermostat, home security, and doorbell wires, can be secured to walls and ceilings (even concrete and cement blocks) with hot-melt glue. Simply run a bead about 20 mm long, and press the wire into place for a few seconds. Repeat the process at intervals of 300 mm or so.

Slip it through a straw

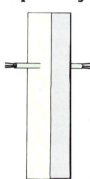

Fine low-voltage wires threaded through a brick wall can get caught in the holes. Slip an ordinary drinking straw through each hole to guide the wires. Do the same when running low-voltage wires through a drywall.

Low-voltage hideaways
A safe place to hide low-voltage wire is under wall-to-wall carpeting between the skirting board and the tack strip. Use masking tape or glue to keep it in position while you replace the carpet—if it moves at all it could be damaged if it lies across the tack strip. ▼

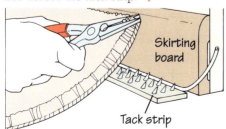

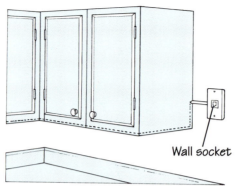

Hide it in the cupboards
Low-voltage wires can be hidden by running them through bathroom or kitchen cabinets. You can run them along the back of the cabinet or, for an invisible job, inside the front edge of the cabinet's face frame. Drill 5 mm holes between cabinets where needed.

Can't hear the doorbell?
If the doorbell won't ring, remove the button cover and check for low voltage at the button. Sand the contacts; then prise them up. If it still won't ring, disconnect the wires and touch the ends together. If the bell rings, replace the button.

Ring those chimes
If the chimes or doorbell won't sound and the button is OK (see above), the plungers or clappers may be dirty. Use alcohol and a cotton swab to clean a mechanical chime unit's plungers or clappers and the gong. Do not clean electronic chimes.

TROUBLESHOOTING FLUORESCENT LIGHTS

If your fixture isn't working up to par, check below for the cure. Before replacing a tube, make sure it's of the correct wattage; check the ballast for the size.

PROBLEM	CAUSE	CURE
Light blinks on and off	Indicates a tube near the end of its life	Replace it with another tube. If this doesn't correct problem, shut power off; check for loose wires.
Tubes hard to start	Defective or old starter for starter-type fixture; bad ballast in rapid- or instant-start fixture	If starter has reset button, press it. Replace starter with one of equal rating (twist out old starter). Replace ballast with exact match. To remove it, shut off power; untwist nut connectors and screws.
Swirling or flickering light	A new tube or cold temperature	Leave new tube lighted for several hours to stabilize it. Install cold-rated tube in cold rooms.
Orange glow at tube ends	From end filaments, which heat gas	If they don't shut off after a few seconds, replace the starter.
Black tube ends	Tube nearing end of life	Replace the tube.
Loud humming	Fixture parts vibrating, or ballast shorting	Tighten all screws; wedge vibrating parts in place. Replace ballast.

PLUMBING BASICS

Before you start

Licence to plumb
You can do simple plumbing jobs, such as replacing a washer in a tap or unclogging a sink, as the need arises, but you may need a permit or licence for larger jobs, such as adding lines for a new bathroom. Check with your local municipality before attempting a big job.

Wired pipes
In many older homes the electrical system is earthed to a steel cold-water pipe. Before splicing plastic pipe into the line, make sure the line doesn't function as the conductor. If you do remove any earthing wires in the course of making a plumbing repair, reattach the earth wire to an appropriate conductor.

Sorting out your pipes
Home plumbing involves two systems: the water-supply system and the drain-waste-vent (DWV) system. Water enters the house through a main service pipe; near the point of entry you may find a water meter and you should find the main shut-off valve. Inside the house the water travels under pressure through cold-water supply pipes, and attached air chambers cushion the pressure-driven water when a tap or appliance is turned off. The larger DWV pipes carry used water and waste out of the house. Waste pipes carry water, and soil pipes carry discharge from toilets. A trap at each fixture keeps foul air from seeping into the house. Vents allow sewer gas to escape, thus balancing the air pressure in the system and stopping the water in the traps from being siphoned out. ▶

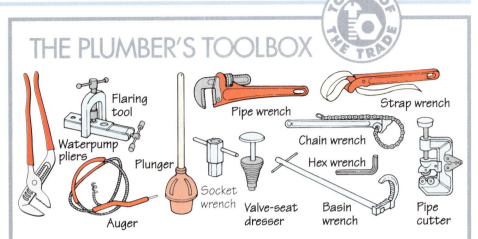

THE PLUMBER'S TOOLBOX
TOOLS OF THE TRADE

A hammer, chisels, and a hacksaw will supply many of your plumbing needs but keep these additional tools on hand for specific jobs: two pipe wrenches for working on pipes and a pair of waterpump pliers for turning large nuts. Tap repairs may require hex and socket wrenches, a basin wrench for reaching up under the sink, and a valve-seat dresser. Strap and chain wrenches can grip large-diameter pipes. An assortment of pipe cutters is handy for cutting copper, steel, and plastic pipes. A flaring tool helps to join flexible tubing. A plunger and an auger can help clear blockages. If you have rigid copper pipes, you will need soldering tools. Finally, keep some pipe-joint compound or pipe-thread tape and plumber's putty on hand.

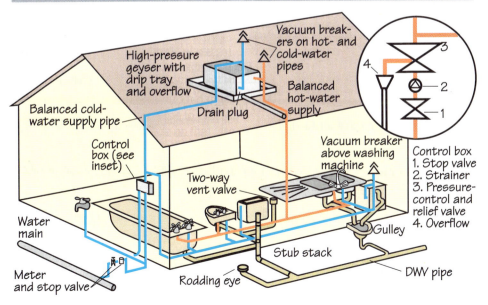

Home Systems / 211

PIPES

Metal pipes

Know your pipes
Copper, brass and galvanized pipes are rust-resistant, so they are used for water pipes. Copper piping is usually installed between the mains pipe and the home. It is also used for a home's hot-water systems, as its strength will remain uncompromised when heated.

Sizing the pipe
Before replacing threaded pipe or adding it to a pipe, be sure you buy enough. When estimating the length of pipe you'll need, remember to allow for the overlap at joints. You should add 10 mm per threaded end for 15 and 22 mm pipe, and 15 mm for larger diameters of pipe.

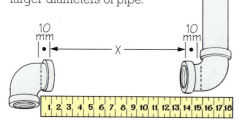

Strong grip
To remove or attach threaded pipe, hold the fitting in place with one pipe wrench; turn the pipe with another. If it's a fitting that you want to attach or remove, reverse the order. Work carefully to avoid breaking any other connections in the pipe.

Say no to dope
Instead of old-fashioned pipe dope (joint compound), use thread sealant tape on threaded pipes. The tape helps seal the joint and it lubricates the pipe threads, making it easier to install and remove the pipe. To keep the tape from unwinding as you install the pipe, wrap it in the opposite direction of the pipe threads. Start the tape at the first thread, and wrap it around the threads three to four times. Be especially careful not to overtighten the pipe.

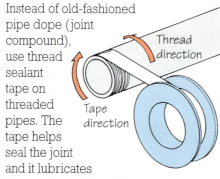

Fitting solution
You can't simply unscrew a section of pipe from the middle of your plumbing system. As you unscrew the joint on one end of the pipe, the joint on the opposite end will tighten. To repair a leak or add a T-fitting for a new fixture, you'll have to cut and remove a section of the pipe, and then reconstruct the section by installing two short pieces of pipe and a union—a fitting that lets you screw in a section of pipe without unscrewing its opposite end.

No more kinks
If you need to bend a copper pipe and you don't have a special tubing bender or bending spring, block one end of the tubing with tape and fill it with dry sand. The sand will stop the tubing walls from kinking. Thoroughly wash out the sand before installing the tubing.

Bread stuffing
If every drop of water isn't removed from an existing copper water supply pipe, soldering a joint can be an exasperating job. As the torch heats the water, the water turns to steam and pushes the solder out of the joint. To avoid this, push a piece of soft white bread about 200 mm or so back into the pipe. The bread will absorb the water. When your soldered joint is complete, turn on the water and the bread will break up and disappear. ▼

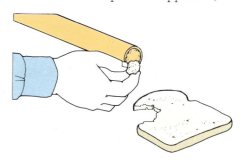

Plastic pipes

It takes all types
Aren't sure which type of plastic pipe to use for a specific job? Polycop pipe (a terracotta colour) can be used for the water supply. White PVC pipe is used for drainage and vent systems. Look for these designated letters imprinted on a pipe to identify it and use the same type of pipe throughout a plumbing project. Never try to cement together two different types of plastic pipe. As usual, if in any doubt whatsoever, or merely to confirm you have chosen correctly, consult a licensed plumber for advice.

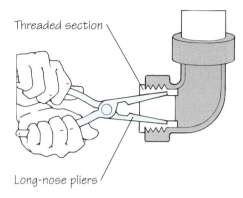

Threaded section
Long-nose pliers

Get the threads out ▲
Sometimes when you're unscrewing a plastic pipe, the threads stick in the joint and the pipe breaks off. To remove the threaded section, use a gas torch to heat the jaws of a long-nose pliers. Insert the pliers into the threaded section and slowly push the pliers handles apart until the hot jaws make grooves in the plastic. Remove the pliers and let the plastic harden; then reinsert the pliers and twist them to unscrew the pipe.

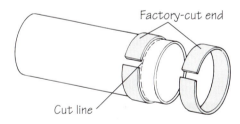

Factory-cut end
Cut line

On the mark ▲
This guide will help you make accurate handsaw cuts on PVC pipe. Cut a 25 or 50 mm piece from the factory-cut end of the pipe. Then cut a slit through it so you can slide it onto the pipe being cut. Use the factory-cut edge as the guide for all your own cutting.

Pipe repairs

Leak control
Here are a few strictly temporary fixes to stop minor leaks: in a PVC drain fitting, tighten a motorcar hose clamp around the hub of the fitting. For a small leak in a waste pipe, force a toothpick into the hole and break off the end. Then wrap three layers of duct tape around the leak, making sure you overlap each turn by half the width of the tape. For a stronger repair, secure a slit rubber hose around the pipe with several hose clamps or twisted wire. ▼

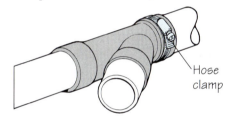

Hose clamp

Frozen solid
To thaw frozen water in a metal pipe (but not a plastic one), close the shut-off valve, open a tap, wrap rags around the pipe, and pour boiling water over the rags. (Place a container under the pipe to catch the hot water.) Be sure to work from the tap to the frozen area so that any pressure that builds up escapes through the open tap instead of bursting the pipe. Repeat the process until the ice thaws.

If you're careful, you can heat the pipe with a hair dryer instead. You should keep the dryer moving and the pipe cool enough to touch. To help prevent the pipe from freezing again, install pipe insulation or wrap the pipe with strips of foil-faced fibreglass batts, foil side out, and secure the batts with duct tape. (Wear gloves when handling the fibreglass.)

An end to water hammer
Don't despair if a water pipe bangs when you turn off a tap, even though you have an air chamber to stop the banging (called water hammer). Sometimes the air dissipates and water fills the chamber. If you can't unscrew and drain the chamber to let air in, you can always drain the system. Turn off the water at the main valve, open the taps in the highest and lowest parts of the line, and let all the water drain out. Then close the taps and turn on the water.

Drain pipe noise control
The best time to muffle the noise of drain pipes inside the house is when you remodel. Wrap scraps of carpeting around the pipes and secure them with duct tape. In hard-to-reach areas, stuff the scraps around the pipe. Or slip a slit garden hose around a pipe to reduce vibrations between a strap and the pipe.

VALVES AND TAPS

Shut-off valves

Stuck stem
When a shut-off valve isn't used for a long time, the packing inside the packing nut can dry up or become corroded. Instead of forcing the valve and risking a leak, put a few drops of light oil around the stem near the packing nut. Loosen the nut about one turn, then retighten it by hand. After letting the packing absorb the oil for a few minutes, you should be able to turn the valve without a problem. ▼

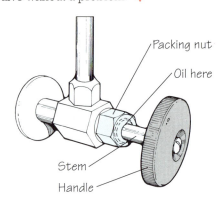

The great valve search
In some houses a shut-off valve may not have been installed at each fixture. If this is the case in your home, you'll have to search for the nearest valve along the plumbing pipe whenever you need to turn off the water to make a repair. After making the repair and before turning on the water, install a shut-off valve near the fixture for future repairs. This involves cutting out a section of pipe and installing an inexpensive shut-off valve. Use a fitting at each end of the valve to join it to the pipe.

Taps

Stubborn seat

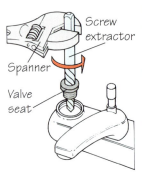

If you need to remove the valve seat from a tap but the threads are worn, try this. Insert a screw extractor into the valve seat and gently tap it tight. With an adjustable spanner, turn the extractor anticlockwise, forcing it tighter into the seat. Or you can try tapping and turning the extractor. The seat will twist out.

Stem extractor
Is the cartridge in your single-handle bath tap hard to remove? Drill a 25 mm hole into scrap plywood. Place the scrap against the wall with the hole over the stem. Starting with a washer large enough to cover the hole, slip a stack of progressively smaller washers onto the stem; add a snug-fitting nut. Insert a screw into the hole in the end of the stem. Turn the nut with a spanner to back out the stem. Stop the screw turning by holding it with a screwdriver. ▼

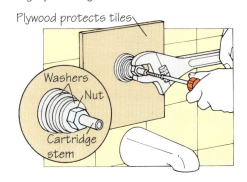

Keep the cold out

To keep an outdoor tap from freezing in the winter, turn the water supply off. If there is no shut-off valve inside the house, cut a hole in the lid of an empty plastic tub for margarine or butter. Place the lid over the tap, and screw or glue it to the wall. Wrap fibreglass pipe insulation loosely around the tap, securing it with masking tape. Push the tub over the wrapped tap and snap it onto the lid.

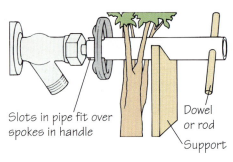

Extension handle ▲
Here's one way to reach a handle on an outdoor tap that is blocked by shrubbery. In a suitable pipe, make slots on one end large enough to fit over the spokes in the tap handle. At the other end drill holes through the pipe. Slide a metal rod or wooden dowel into the holes, and use it as a handle. If you need a support for this extended handle, you can make a V-notch in a piece of scrap wood which is then driven into the ground. The pipe is rested in the notch.

REPAIRING A CARTRIDGE TAP

You can repair a cartridge tap by replacing worn parts. Plumbing centres and hardware dealers sell replacement kits for major brands. Directions for installing one type of tap are shown here, but models vary—so read the kit's instructions carefully before attempting any repairs.

The parts that wear out and need replacing are the cartridge and the O-rings. Drips from the spout or improper mixing of hot and cold water indicates a worn cartridge. Leaks around the base of the spout indicate worn O-rings.

Begin by turning off the shut-off valves on the hot- and cold-water pipes and opening the tap. Plug the drain so that parts aren't lost, and protect the basin's surface from scratches. Take the tap apart, laying the parts in a row so that you'll know how to reassemble them. Replace the O-rings or the cartridge, as needed, and reassemble the tap.

1 Pull off the cap to expose the handle screw. Remove the screw; then lift off the handle lever and handle assembly.

2 Unscrew the retainer pivot nut with pliers. Be careful not to scratch the body of the spout.

3 To remove the spout, swing it from side to side and lift it up at the base. If you have a sprayer, lift off the diverter.

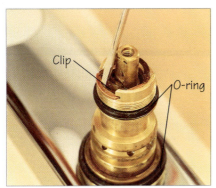

4 Prise off the retainer clip. Set the clip aside for reinstalling later. Remove or replace the O-rings.

5 Place the plastic cap from the kit over the old cartridge, and twist it in both directions to release the cartridge.

6 Pull up the stem with pliers to remove the cartridge. Remove debris inside the body before installing a new cartridge.

BATHS, SHOWERS, AND MORE TAPS

Bath and shower

A sneaky leak
If water seeps out from under your bath or shower, it is not necessarily leaking. Water could be entering the wall from around the tap. Remove the tap handles, escutcheons, and spout. Caulk around the openings in the wall; then replace the fittings. Also check the seam between the tiles and the bath or shower, and recaulk if necessary.

A quiet, warm bath
Before installing a new bath, attach fibreglass insulation to the bottom and sides of the bath with duct tape. This will reduce the level of noise when water is run into it, and it will also keep the water warm for a longer period of time.

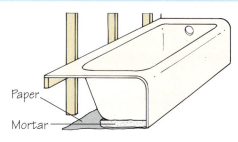

A firm bottom ▲
When installed, some lightweight fibreglass baths feel as though they are not capable of supporting you, even if you, too, are lightweight. Before installing one of these baths, make a cradle so that it feels more solid. Staple building paper to the subfloor. Then pour onto the paper just enough mortar or plaster for the bath to rest on, and install it. Not only will it feel solid, but the mortar or plaster will also help retain the heat of the water.

On skids ▶
Bringing in a new bath (or taking out an old steel one that can't be broken or cut up) takes muscle power. To make the job easier, slide two boards under the bath. Then place two more boards at the ends of the first two in the direction you plan to move the bath, butting the ends of the pairs together. With the aid of a helper, slide the bath from one pair of boards onto the other; then pick up the free pair and move them to the other end of the occupied boards. Repeat to continue moving the bath.

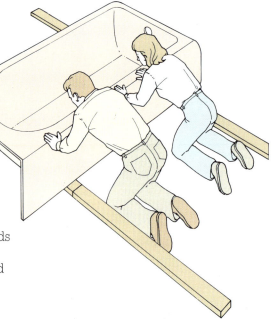

Bag it
You can clean a chrome-plated shower head that has become clogged with mineral deposits without taking it apart. Put some vinegar in a small plastic bag, then secure the bag around the shower head with duct tape or wire. Let the head soak overnight. Do not try this on brass or brass-plated fixtures.

Foam filler
Here's one way to solve the problem of loose pipe straps behind a shower wall. Pull the flange or escutcheon away from the wall (if a tap is attached, remove its handle). Tape the pipe into position, and spray aerosol foam insulation into the wall cavity. Don't overfill it if you're working on a drywall, or the foam may damage the wall when it expands. Once it is dry, it should be hard enough to securely hold the pipe.

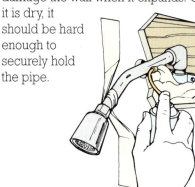

BALL TAPS

The ball-type tap is easy to repair. If the spout drips, the rubber seats and springs are worn. If the spout base leaks, the O-rings are worn.

For any type of leak, disassemble the tap and replace all the parts at one time. Replacing only some of the worn parts may mean you'll have to open the tap again later.

Begin the repair job by turning off the water shutoff valves and plugging the drain to keep dropped parts from falling in. Then disassemble the tap as shown, replace the old parts with new, and reassemble the tap in the opposite order you took it apart. There's only one trick to reassembly: Before you tighten the adjusting ring with the special tool, turn the water back on; then tighten the ring until no water leaks around the stem. Make sure you don't overtighten the cap or the adjusting ring. You should be able to easily move both the handle and the spout.

1 Loosen the setscrew with the hex wrench, and lift off the handle. The wrench is included in the replacement kit.

2 Release pressure on the ball by loosening the adjusting ring with the special tool. Unscrew and remove the cap.

3 Remove the ball assembly by grasping the protruding cam and lifting it up. Lay the pieces aside.

4 Gently lift out the rubber seats and springs, using a screwdriver. Install the replacement parts.

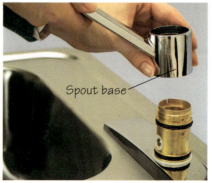

5 Work the spout off by swinging it back and forth while lifting it up from the base. It may be stubborn, but keep at it.

6 Replace the two O-rings. If necessary, cut them off with a utility knife. Clean all rubber debris from the tap body.

Home Systems / 217

TOILETS AND DRAINS

Toilet trouble

Hand-bag retriever
You can easily and hygienically retrieve an item that your toddler dropped into the toilet. Just slip your hand into a plastic bag for protection. Grasp the item and pull it out of the toilet, then turn the bag inside out. The wet item will be in the bag and your hand will remain dry and clean. ▼

Detective work
If your toilet runs continuously, water is probably leaking out between the ball or flapper and the valve seat. To detect a leak, add a little food colouring to the water in the cistern but don't flush it for a while. If the water in the bowl changes colour, the valve is leaking. You can temporarily stop the leak by adjusting the lift chain or wire. And while you're doing so, check the cistern ball or flapper. If it's cracked and dried, replace it.

Flush valve revival
You can sometimes revive an old ball or flapper by rubbing it with petroleum jelly or spraying it with a silicone spray. The rubber will become more supple, allowing the ball to seal the valve.

Getting out of a jam
The lift wire between the trip lever and the toilet valve may jam and stop the valve returning to its proper position. When this happens, try replacing the wire with a length of chain.

Use a little muscle power
The water level in a toilet cistern should be about 20 mm below the overflow tube outlet. To increase the amount of water used in each flush, bend the float rod upwards, a little at a time, until the correct water level in the cistern is achieved. Make sure that you keep a firm grip on the ballcock end of the rod while doing this, so that the ballcock is not subjected to any strain.

Bottled water
If you want to save water when flushing your toilet, try this: Fill a 1,5 or 2 litre cooldrink bottle with water or sand (to weigh it down) and seal it with a tight cap. Position the bottle inside the toilet cistern where it won't interfere with the movement of the parts. With its bulk, the bottle will displace water that would normally flow into the tank. However, if the smaller amount of water doesn't remove all the waste, change the container to a smaller size to allow more water into the tank. If you ever replace the toilet, buy one that flushes on less than 10 litres of water.

Replacing a perished seal
The toilet outlet pipes in some older homes fit over the toilet outlet and are sealed by a large plastic seal that fits over both. If this perishes, replace it with a dense foam rubber seal, sold by hardware dealers. When doing so, make sure the ends of the new seal are at the top of the pipe and that the seal is pushed well into the pipe.

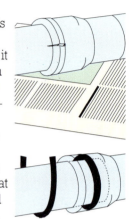

Removing unsightly stains
The pan of a toilet might sometimes become stained by surface deposits of calcium or lime. Remove them gently with a rounded-off putty knife. Be careful not to score the enamel when doing this. Finish off by rubbing off the last of the deposits with a plastic scourer and scouring powder.

Jet lag
To remove deposit buildup at the siphon jet hole, unbend a wire clothes hanger and carefully scrape the deposits out of the hole without scratching the finish. ▼

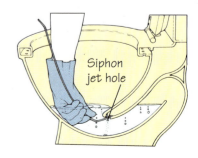

Siphon jet hole

Unblocking drains

Hot grease
The kitchen sink can become clogged by grease buildup in the drain. To keep the drain grease-free, every two weeks put a few tablespoons of baking soda into the drain. Fill the sink with hot water; then let it flow freely down the drain. If you suspect that grease is starting to clog your drain, try melting the grease by heating the trap with a hair dryer, then running hot water down the drain. But if grease has already clogged the drain, bail the water out of the sink, pour one cup each of baking soda and vinegar down the drain, and plug it with a strainer or rag. Let the mixture bubble for 20 minutes; then unplug the drain and flush out the debris with hot water.

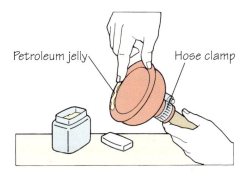

A better plunger ▲
Your plunger can become a more effective tool with the aid of a little petroleum jelly. Just smear some jelly around the edge of the suction cup. The jelly will create a better seal between the sink and the cup. If the handle on your plunger is loose and easy to pull out of the cup, use a hose clamp to secure the cup to the handle.

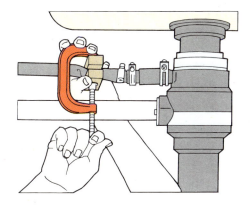

Seal all openings ▲
When unclogging a drain with a plunger, plug or seal the overflow opening in a washbasin or bath, or the second drain in a double sink. This allows you to develop the necessary suction and pressure to free the clog. If you can't block off any opening properly, try clamping the hose—if it's soft rubber—that leads to it, as in the illustration. You will be able to achieve a tight seal.

Go fishing
If your bath drain is still clogged after using a plunger, try dangling a three-prong fish-hook on a piece of fishing line down the drain (if you can remove the plug-hole grille). If the clog hasn't gone beyond the trap, you might be able to hook it and pull it out.

Unclogging the toilet
You can see if the blockage is at the entrance to the drain of a toilet by placing a small mirror in the drain hole. Shine a light on the mirror and adjust the mirror until you have a view of the channel. If you can see the blockage, try using a straightened wire clothes hanger to remove it. For a blockage further up the channel, use an auger (snake). If that doesn't work, try working from outside. Remove the cover at the point where the toilet drain leaves the wall and clear the drain in both directions. ▼

It's not really in the drain
Does the water still run out slowly, although you've tried to unclog the drain? If it is definitely clear, check the vent pipe on your roof. You may find a bird's nest perched right on top of the pipe. Remove the obstruction, and the water should drain efficiently.

Unpleasant odour
The pan of a toilet is designed to hold water to block sewer gas from entering the room. If the fixture has not been used for several months, the water can evaporate, letting the gas escape. To get rid of the offensive odour, flush the toilet to fill the pan.

GEYSERS

Getting hotter water

Noisy deposits

Mineral deposits in the water settle to the bottom of a geyser. Deposit buildup can create rumbling noises, decrease the amount of heat that reaches the water, and reduce the storage capacity of the unit. To remove these harmful deposits, turn off the electricity and close the cold-water inlet valve to the geyser. Open a hot-water tap. Then attach a garden hose to the drain valve at the bottom of the geyser, and drain the water through the hose into a floor drain or sink, or to a safe place outside the house. (This may take hours.) Once the tank is drained, reopen the cold-water valve and run water through the tank until it drains clear. Finally, close the drain valve and hot-water tap, and switch on the geyser again.

Before the buildup

To stop mineral deposits building up, periodically flush them from the drain valve through a garden hose or into a container. If you have soft water, drain about 3 litres of water two to four times a year. For harder water with a high mineral concentration, you may have to drain water monthly. ▼

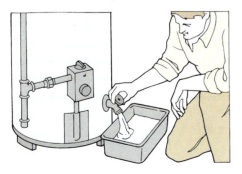

Lukewarm ▶

If you have a geyser with a plastic cold-water fill pipe and the water being produced isn't hot enough, the fill pipe may have broken near the top of the geyser. This lets the incoming cold water mix with hot water near the top. To replace the pipe, turn off the electricity and the water to the geyser. Unthread the fitting, replace the pipe, and screw the fitting back into place. If the ceiling is too low to manoeuvre the pipe into the geyser, disconnect the hot- and cold-water pipes, and tip the geyser over. (If necessary, leave the broken pipe in it.)

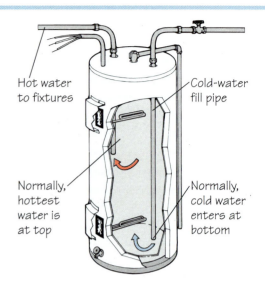

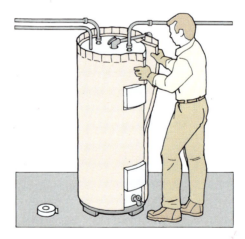

Under wraps ▲

A geyser that feels hot when you touch it is losing heat. If it doesn't void your warranty, keep the escaping heat under wraps by covering the tank with an insulating fibreglass blanket or another cover that will help to contain the heat loss. By doing so, you will reduce your electricity bill. Take the opportunity to lag the outlet pipe as well—the water will arrive at the taps somewhat hotter.

Waiting for hot water

When a plumbing fixture, such as a kitchen sink, is far from the geyser, a lot of standing water must run through the pipe before hot water reaches the tap. That means a lot of clean, unused water goes down the drain, literally. Consider installing either a small geyser or an "instant" water heater. If you place one of these separate auxiliary heaters near the fixture (such as under the sink), you'll get hot water right away without first running the water. Some units use electricity as the power source and others use gas. These heaters are of even greater benefit during times of water restrictions.

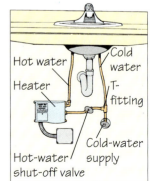

Conserving energy 1

If you want to conserve energy and lower your electricity bill, turn your geyser off at night when you aren't using it and back on in the morning in time to provide hot water for the earliest risers. If you're going to be away for more than a day or so, turn it off. Another way to save energy is to turn the thermostat down to provide hot water at a suitable temperature that is comfortable for all members of the family. Providing water that's almost boiling is a waste of energy and water (cold water usually has to be added to make it bearable), and in a home with small children, water that could scald them is dangerous.

Conserving energy 2

During the summer months not only do many of us bath more often, but we end up using more cold water because we often prefer a cooler bath when the weather is hot. Take advantage of this trend and turn your geyser thermostat down during the hot summer months. You could achieve a big saving in water usage and electricity costs.

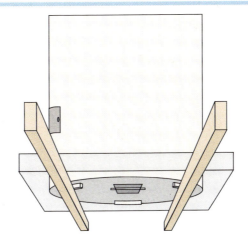

Leak test ▲

Sometimes it's hard to tell whether a puddle of water on the floor indicates a leak in the geyser or merely dripping due to condensation. Here's an easy test: wearing gloves to avoid burning your hands, attach a small piece of glass (or a small mirror) to the underside of the tank with tape—leaving some of the glass exposed. Remove the glass after a few hours. If its exterior is wet, the moisture is from condensation, not from a leak in the geyser.

Ready for the big chill

Draining the house

During freezing weather, you might consider taking the following steps if you have an extended power failure or if you're planning to leave your house for a prolonged period.
▷ Turn off the water supply at the main shut-off valve.
▷ Flush all the toilets, and empty the bowls with a siphon or by bailing them out and sponging up excess water.
▷ Open every tap in the house, and those outdoors.
▷ Drain the geyser (facing page).
▷ If your water is from a well, drain both the above-ground pump lines and the tank. Switch the pump off and drain it.
▷ Pour a mixture of antifreeze and water into all toilet bowls and into the trap of every sink, washbasin, shower stall, bath, and floor drain. Prepare the antifreeze for the lowest temperature expected in your area. (Be sure to keep children and pets away from it.)

Emergency: what to do

A leaking geyser

▷ Turn off the power supply to the geyser at the main distribution board, or, if your hot water is fire-heated, put the fire out and call a plumber.
▷ Turn off the stopcock on the inlet pipe to the geyser.
▷ Turn on the hot-water taps to drain the geyser as much as possible.
▷ Call a plumber.
Caution: Turn the stopcock on again before turning the power back on.

Tread softly—and safely

If you are going to periodically adjust your geyser's thermostat as suggested above, lay a rough platform on the joists next to the geyser. You will then have a safe place to stand, without the danger of falling through the ceiling, as you might do if you have to balance on the joists. Trim the planks to a suitable length and nail them securely to the joists. Avoid any overhang greater than a few centimetres: if you place your weight on long, unsupported planks the nails could pull out and allow the plank to tip up, causing an accident.

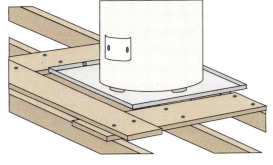

SOLAR POWER

Some do's and don'ts

Do your sun sums first

Before you have a solar water heater installed, consider the following:
▷ The present annual cost of heating your water, divided by 12 to give an average monthly cost. (Your municipal electricity department will be able to tell you what proportion of your bill can be apportioned to the geyser.) If your geyser consumes 3 000 watts and is on for 2 hours a day, the monthly cost of running it will be:
3 000 x 2 hours x 30 days = 180 000 watt-hours. This is 180 kW or 180 units, as electricity is sold. So, multiply 180 by the cost per unit of electricity in your area and you will have your average monthly cost for hot water.
▷ Ascertain the total cost of the system, including installation.
▷ Ascertain the guarantee period, what maintenance may be required after the guarantee has expired, and its cost.
▷ Have your water tested. Many solar water heaters are stainless steel, but if there is more than 100 mg of dissolved chlorides per litre of water, the steel could be damaged. Investigate the cost of alternative materials.
▷ Add up the costs and divide the total by your monthly water-heating bill. Bear in mind that having a solar heater will not eliminate the need for a geyser—on overcast or cloudy days and at night, for example. But, in this country with its abundant sunshine, a solar heater could save you a lot of money in the long term. If you can recoup your costs within 10 years or so, a solar water heater could be a worthwhile investment.

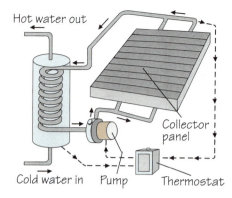

Keep it close ▲

Ensure your solar water-heater panel is sited as close a possible to the geyser to keep pipe lengths between the panel and the rest of the system as short as possible. The system should also be as close as possible to the main area of consumption—the bathroom and kitchen, for example.

What's your angle?

The panel must be angled to catch the maximum number of solar rays, for as many hours as possible during the day. This angle is latitude, plus 10°. The angle for Cape Town is about 44°, for Gauteng about 36° and about 33° on the Limpopo River. It should also face true north, or be within 15° either side of it. Here's a quick way to find true north with sufficient accuracy for preliminary planning: keeping the timepiece horizontal, point the 12 of an analogue watch at the sun. True north is midway between the 12 and the hour hand. Repeat the exercise later to confirm your findings.

Keep it out in the open

Shade will severely limit a panel's efficiency. Ensure no tree or other obstacles will shade the panel at any time of the day, particularly between midmorning and midafternoon, when the sun's radiation is at its strongest. ▼

No more 5 o'clock shadow

A solar panel does most of its work during those hours of the day when the sun's rays are shining down directly on it. In the early morning and late afternoon, the rays strike the panel at an oblique angle and are less effective. To ensure your system works as efficiently as possible, consider having one or more of the following features in your solar heating system:
▷ A tracking system. This may be expensive, but as the sun moves across the sky, automatic adjustments ensure your system receives maximum sunlight during the day.
▷ Reflectors, which direct the sun's rays onto the panel over a greater part of the day.
▷ A selective coating on the panel's absorber surface. This provides for a heating effect ostensibly 25 to 30 per cent more efficient than ordinary matt black paint.

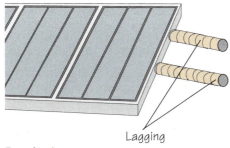
Lagging

Lag it ▲
The less heat lost, the better. Lagging a system's pipes will pay dividends. Lag the inlet pipe to the panel as well—heat lost on the way to the panel will decrease the system's efficiency—the higher the inlet water temperature, the closer the outlet water from the panel will be to optimum temperature.

Avoid mixing metals
Do not use different metals in a system. Copper and brass are compatible, but an electrolytic action can occur if copper and steel, for example, are used in the same system.

Windproof that panel
If you live in an area prone to high winds, consider having your solar panel mounted in the roof, rather than on it, if the design permits this. You will have a panel that is immune to any wind or gale, and it will be less noticeable. ▼

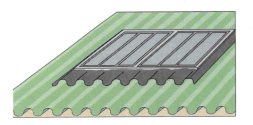

Make sure there's enough hot water
Ensure, when having a system installed, that it will be big enough to handle the normal hot-water needs of the household. Going too small may well prove a waste of time. Only about 67 per cent of the water in any geyser is immediately available as hot water. Work on 35 litres per day per person and ensure the solar heating tank will be sufficient.

Something for those winter days?
During winter, when the sun is at a lower angle, its rays are less effective. Mounting a polished plate at an angle above the panel will direct more rays onto the panel when they're needed. In summer, when the sun is high in the sky, the reflector will have little effect. As usual, check with the manufacturer of the panel to confirm that the reflector's action will not detrimentally affect the panel's operation in the long term. ▼

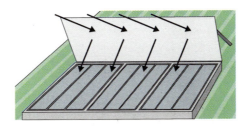

Electricity from the sun

What about later?
If you want a small solar electricity system installed, make provision for further expansion when you have it installed. The initial cost might be slightly higher, but upgrading the system later on will be much easier.

It's the size that counts
Solar power systems are available in three basic sizes:
▷ Small: sufficient to power lights, radio and TV. These systems usually work on 12 volts DC.
▷ Medium: sufficient for all of the above, plus ceiling fans, refrigerators, food blenders and other appliances with a low-power requirement. These systems usually operate on 12 or 24 volts DC, but can also incorporate a 220 volt AC supply via an inverter for appliances requiring such power—a colour TV, for instance.
▷ Large: usually 220 volts 50 Hz, single-phase AC via a large inverter (3-phase is possible, but expensive). A large system will power all of the above, plus washing machines, vacuum cleaners, power tools and toasters. Stoves, geysers, air conditioners and items requiring similar or greater power cannot be operated on a solar system.

What about cloudy weather?
Investing in a small generator will take care of those times when the sun simply refuses to shine for days on end, and the battery power is low.

Keep those batteries clean
Batteries must be housed in a well-ventilated area as close as possible to the solar panels and control panel, and they must be kept clean. A simple frame with a shadecloth cover will help keep them clean and free of dust. But you must ensure that, whatever materials or design you employ, there is still enough circulation of air around the batteries. Check with an expert if in doubt.

HOME COOLING

Creating a breeze

Window trick 1
If the air is cooler outside than in, you can bring the cool air into your house. Because hot air rises, open upstairs or attic windows to let it out, and open downstairs windows to let in the cool air. However, if it's hotter outside than inside, be sure to tightly seal up the house by closing doors and windows, and by closing curtains and blinds.

Window trick 2
If you're having a home built, have a window installed in a position that allows you to take advantage of the prevailing winds in summer. It will help to maintain a cooling breeze throughout the house during the hottest months.

Watch the surrounds
Sunlight baking down on bare slasto, concrete or asphalt, or reflecting off a swimming pool, can make a room unbearably hot. Lawns and trees around a house will help keep it cooler.

Vibrating ceiling fan ▲
Follow this troubleshooting checklist to discover why a ceiling fan is vibrating or oscillating—and stop it.
▷ Clean the blades. Accumulated dirt can throw the fan off balance.
▷ Check for loose screws on the blades.
▷ One or more blades might be warped. Remove them and lay them on a flat surface. They should lie flat. If a blade is warped, replace the entire set. (Blades are matched as a set by the manufacturer.)
▷ Examine the blade mounting brackets for defects. They are set at the factory at an angle of about 12°. Stack them on top of one another. If you find one that does not match the others, bend it to the same angle or replace it.
▷ Check the fan motor. With the blades and brackets removed, turn the fan onto the fastest setting. It shouldn't wobble. If it does, send the motor in for repair. Look in your owner's manual for the closest authorized centre.
▷ If you still haven't found the problem, balance the blades on the reassembled fan by taping small coins or washers to the tops of the out-of-balance blades. Once the blades are balanced, glue the weights into place (using as little glue as possible). For a four-bladed fan, balance two opposite blades at a time.

In the shade
Even if your house is superinsulated, you can benefit from a deciduous broad-leaved tree if it's by a window. The tree will keep hot sunlight from entering the window in the summer, and, after the leaves fall, sunlight can pass through and warm the room in the winter. If you're planting trees for future shade, plant them on the north, east and west sides of the house, where the summer sun hits the windows the hardest. For an immediate way to shade a window, add an awning, porch roof, trellis, or arbour, or install an outside shade or indoor blind. ▼

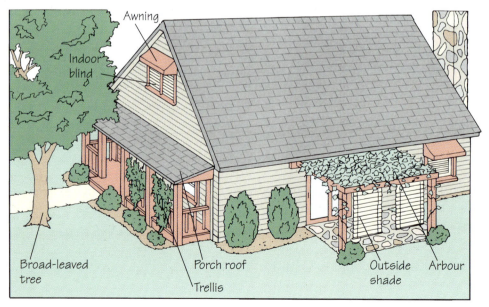

Room air conditioners

For the best cooling
Because cold air falls, the higher a room air-conditioning unit is placed, the better it can cool a room. Install the unit in the wall that gets the least amount of direct sunlight—usually the southern wall. But if you'd like to place the unit where the sun is normally strongest, consider if there is an obstruction blocking it. For example, a tree or a building may block the sun from a northern wall.

Filter reminder
During the air-conditioning season, clean the filter weekly or, depending on the type of air-conditioning unit you have and the filter it uses, clean or replace the filter monthly. To jog your memory, note with a grease pencil the date you should attend to the filter on the unit's control panel. Each time you adjust the unit, you'll see the reminder.

Bending fins
Bent condenser and evaporator fins in room units can obstruct the efficient flow of air. If you remove the front panel and filter, you can then straighten the fins with a plastic spatula or with a small section cut from a pocket comb. ▼

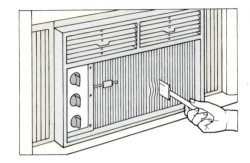

Cold-weather care
Covering the exterior of a window air conditioner with a sheet of plastic does more than reduce cold drafts on windy winter days. It also serves to keep the condenser coil and fan clean. Make sure you remove the plastic in the spring—before the hot weather comes.

Musty-smelling conditioner
A clogged drain hole under the barrier between the evaporator and the compressor, or in the channel under the evaporator, may emit a musty smell. To clean the hole, unscrew and remove the front panel. On some models you may have to pull the chassis out a little. Clean the hole with a bent wire coat hanger, or flush the channel with a water-filled bulb baster. Dust the unit and take out any debris.

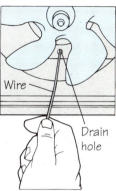

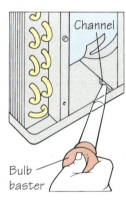

Too much racket? ▶
The racket created by a window air conditioner can occur because of several reasons. By following the steps given here, you can soon run your unit with less noise.
Note: To reach the fan on some models, you have to remove the chassis completely from the housing.

1. With the unit running, press your hand on the window sashes. If the noise stops, insert small wood shims between the sash and the frame. If the glass rattles, reputty it; as a temporary fix, stick cellophane tape tightly between the edge of the glass and the frame.

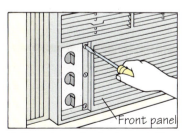

2. Press in on the front panel. If the unit's noise ceases or if the pitch changes, tighten any loose panel fasteners. If the panel won't fit snugly and quietly against the cabinet, secure it to the cabinet with duct tape.

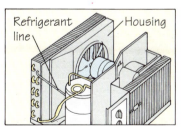

3. Unplug the unit. Slide the chassis partially out of the housing; rest one end on a stool. Spin the fan blades. If a blade hits the cage, bend it slightly for clearance. Jiggle the chassis; if the refrigerant line hits the fan's housing, gently bend it away from the housing.

HOME SECURITY

Simple steps

Smooth and difficult
The walls surrounding your property can act both as a deterrent and as a benefit to an intruder, because once he is in, a high wall can shield him. So, do not build the wall too high, and make its outer surface as smooth as possible, with a rounded crest to make it much harder to scale. You could also mount an electrified wire along the top as a further deterrent. Another alternative is a concrete palisade wall: it is difficult to scale and can be seen through, thus denying the shielding a solid wall would provide. **Caution:** If you want to install any electrified barrier, check with your municipality or local authority first.

Trapped! ▲
Trap mats, which close an alarm circuit when stood upon, should be laid in front of windows, and in those areas an intruder would have to pass through—passages and doorways, for instance. They can also be placed in front of the TV set, VCR and cupboards. Cover the mats with rugs to hide them.

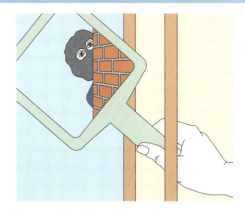

Upon reflection ▲
If you cannot get a clear view through a barred window or a door with a security gate on it, use a hand mirror to check those spots you otherwise cannot see.

Use your head
Telephones can give criminals useful information. Show your domestic how to respond to questions about you, your family, your whereabouts—and make sure you and your family also follow the rules. If you are asked to take part in any survey, watch any answers which concern you and your spouse's work habits, items you may own, whether you own a dog, and so on. Be wary of calls about home-security systems. Usually it's a legitimate call from a reputable security company trying to attract new business. But it may not be... Avoid giving your number if it is asked for by a stranger: some nuisance callers dial randomly and don't know what they dialled. Keep emergency numbers prominently displayed by the telephone.

Safe and sound
There is a wide range of safes available to suit every purpose, but for the home-owner, a small wall safe is adequate for the storage of jewellery, documents and perhaps a firearm. If possible, mount the safe in the wall, behind a picture or a mirror. If you cannot do that, mount it in a corner, bolting it to both walls. If you can bolt it to the floor as well, so much the better. You can also disguise it: put a couple of dummy switches onto a fake panel with cables leading from it, and label it "Pool light" or something equally innocuous. This can fool an intruder. Whatever route you take, keep quiet about the fact you have a safe. You should also try to keep friends and servants unaware of it, if possible—they might innocently pass some information on to a potential intruder.

Room with a view
Most of us prefer to have homes that are light and airy, but open curtains can help tempt an intruder into breaking in if he sees valuable items ready for the taking. Consider having tinted solar film installed: not only will it afford greater privacy, it will also make it more difficult to break through the window's glass. ▼

Dogs as deterrents

Avoid poisoning
A watchdog is one of the most effective deterrents, but it can be neutralized if given drugged or poisoned food. Don't train it to accept food from only certain people (which can be a problem if they are absent). Train it to take food only from a specified place or bowl, far from the property's boundary. Then anyone can feed it, but it's less likely to be poisoned or drugged, because an intruder is most likely to toss food over the wall and wait for the dog to eat it and the poison or drug to take effect.

Clever kennelling
Put your dog's kennel in the area most at risk—the secluded back of the house, or near an unbarred sliding door, for example. Those are the areas a potential intruder is more likely to target, not the part of the house that is in full view of the road or neighbours.

Give him the run-around
Giving any dog the freedom to run and wander where it wishes takes first prize, and should always be your main objective. If, however, your property is unfenced but you still want a watchdog, consider this: buy a steel cable that encircles the whole house. The ends must be joined smoothly (splicing may be best) to allow a large shackle to pass the join easily. Attach a lead or second cable to this link, and clip the dog's collar onto that. This setup allows the dog access to the entire perimeter of the house. Remove any plants or obstacles within the cable's reach.

IS YOUR HOUSE SAFE?

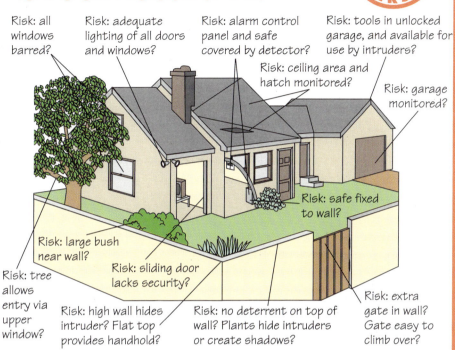

Risk: all windows barred?
Risk: adequate lighting of all doors and windows?
Risk: alarm control panel and safe covered by detector?
Risk: tools in unlocked garage, and available for use by intruders?
Risk: ceiling area and hatch monitored?
Risk: garage monitored?
Risk: safe fixed to wall?
Risk: large bush near wall?
Risk: tree allows entry via upper window?
Risk: sliding door lacks security?
Risk: high wall hides intruder? Flat top provides handhold?
Risk: no deterrent on top of wall? Plants hide intruders or create shadows?
Risk: extra gate in wall? Gate easy to climb over?

Don't become paranoid, but you should think like a criminal when it comes to making your home—and family—as safe as possible against crime. The more difficult you make things for a potential intruder, and the more visible some of the steps you have taken, the less likely you are to become a victim.

For example, trim any plants that produce shadows large enough to hide a body, and ensure that large items such as rubbish bins are not left near doors or windows where someone can use them for cover.

Don't make the message on your telephone answering machine a clue as to your absence. Instead of saying "We're not at home now…" rather say "We're not available now…", as the latter leaves the potential intruder in some doubt as to whether or not you are actually at home.

Caution: Any steps you take that could result in injury to an intruder—or his death—could land you in court. Obtain legal advice if in any doubt whatsoever as to whether or not a measure you wish to take is lawful. For example, check with your local authorities if considering electrified fences, razor wire or other deterrents that are designed to cause pain or shock to an intruder, and, if you install such systems, keep them in proper working order and do not attempt to adapt them for greater effectiveness.

HOME SECURITY

Doors

A simple card-stopper

To prevent the bolt being opened with a credit card, cut a groove 2 or 3 mm deep, about a third of the way along the curved part of the bolt of a night latch. The edge of the card will be caught in the groove. ▼

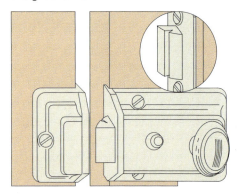

A new type of door jam

A length of 22 x 76 mm timber, notched at one end to fit under a door handle, will prevent the door being opened, even if it is unlocked. Cut the timber to a length so that it stands at an angle of about 70° when the notch is jammed under the handle. For added security, tack a strap across the top of the notch so that the timber continues to jam the door even if the foot is moved.

Angle of about 70°
Strap

Bolt with a difference

If you intend leaving your home unoccupied for a while, here is a very useful security measure for application on some exterior doors. Drill four 12 mm holes, to a depth of 120 mm, into both sides of a solid door, and then drill matching holes in the frame. Cut a 1 m length of 10 mm coarsely threaded rod into eight equal sections, each of 125 mm long, and insert each section into the door—the ends must protrude 4 or 5 mm (hence the need to drill the hole to a depth of only 120 mm). When the door is closed, a knife blade is used to shift the threaded rods halfway into the frame, securely locking the door. A gap of about 5 mm between its frame and the door's edges on both sides will be sufficient to insert a blade. Assuming the gap is 5 mm, ten "flicks" will move the rod 50 mm into the frame, leaving 70 mm or so in the door.

Reinforce that door ▶

When installing exterior doors, consider fitting a burglar guard to the inner surface. Attach it to the door frame so that even if the centre panels are flimsy, the door will still be a strong barrier, particularly if this measure is combined with the hint above. It is particularly useful on a kitchen door in which you may wish to mount a swinging flap for a pet—position it to fit between the bars.

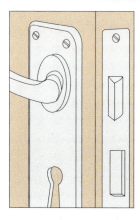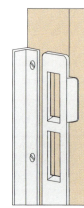

A new angle on securing doors ▲

A length of "L" angle iron down the outer edge of a door frame will stop the lock being forced. Make sure the angle iron butts up tightly against the door so that there is no gap into which the tip of a crowbar can be slipped.

Secure the interior

A security door mounted in a passage between the sleeping and living areas provides added protection, particularly if the living area has doors or windows that make it vulnerable. Ensure a key is hung on a wall near the door, but not where it is visible from the other side of the door, nor where it can be reached.

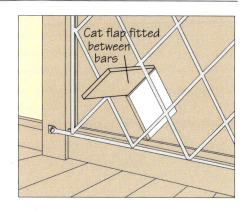

Cat flap fitted between bars

Bolt it

Stop a sliding door being moved—or removed—by fitting a loose-bolt anchor to the frame at floor level.

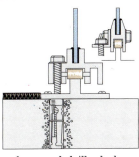

Close the sliding door and drill a hole for the bolt at a suitable point along the inner frame—a bolt of about 6 to 8 mm diameter is ample. (If the door frame's design doesn't lend itself to a bolt, attach a length of angle iron as shown in the illustration.) Slide the door open and drill a hole in the floor for the shield anchor. After checking that the two holes are absolutely aligned, slide the door aside and insert the shield. Seat it in the hole by bolting a scrap piece of timber to it. (Do not use the door frame to seat the shield as it will distort.) Remove the bolt and discard the timber scrap. When the door is closed, you will be able to bolt it shut for total security, even if the bolt is finger-tight.

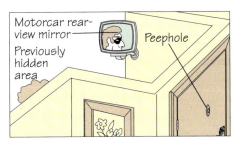

Mirror image ▲

Fit a convex rear-view mirror opposite your door's peephole so that any areas otherwise hidden from view can be checked. This is very useful if a front door is in a vestibule or in any other situation where the view is restricted.

Self-tapping trick

A self-tapping screw in the top member of a sliding door's frame will stop anyone lifting the door off its tracks. Leave the head of the screw far enough out so that it protrudes beyond the track.

Windows

A sticky solution

Glue the panes of a louvre window into their frames to make it more difficult for an intruder to remove them. The frames are easily bent so he will still probably be able to take the panes out, even if more slowly; so burglar guards are still your best security measure.

Sash solutions 1

A bolt, screw or nail driven through both frames of a sash window is a quick and effective security measure,

or you can drive the screw or nail into the frame, as shown here. This will allow the window to open only a little, if you wish, or you can prevent it opening at all. For a more secure result, drive them in on both sides of the frame.

Sash solutions 2

Many sash windows are secured with a simple butterfly catch—which can be easily opened with a knife blade

pushed between the two sliding frames. Drive a screw into the frame next to the catch so that the latter can't be opened.

Block it up

Why not replace a seldom-opened window, in a lounge, for example, with glass blocks? They admit light, provide a secure barrier and, in the right situation, will enhance a room's appeal.

Air-conditioned security

A window-mounted air conditioner must be firmly attached to its mounting brackets with bolts so that it cannot be removed, and the brackets should be welded to the window frame.

Easy movers

Try fixing a burglar guard in place with mirror screws and apply hot glue after screwing the decorative chrome-plated caps tightly into the screwheads. The glue will make it even more difficult to remove the caps, which are difficult to grip anyway. When you wish to remove the guard for painting, heat each screw cap to melt the glue and release the bond, before unscrewing it.

Don't forget the floor

If you have a home with a suspended floor, make sure any ventilation window serving the underfloor area is properly barred. An intruder could break his way in—up through the floor. Include this window if having alarm sensors fitted.

A guard for security—and safety

Have a burglar guard on one of your windows adapted by attaching heavy-duty hinges to it so that it can be swung open in the event of an emergency, such as a fire. Keep the key nearby, though out of sight and reach of a potential intruder. Select a smallish window in an easily accessible area for this purpose.

HOME SECURITY

Alarms

Cover the key areas
When deciding on the positions of alarm sensors, make sure the system's control panel is covered by a beam so that an intruder will trigger the alarm if he tries to turn it off. Try to cover all areas through which he would have to pass or where he is likely to go—down a passage, near a safe or cupboard, for example. Every unit has a particular range and any movement beyond that will remain undetected, so put sensors in vulnerable areas, and in "bottle-necks" where the beam can't miss the intruder. Ensure sensors are not masked by pot plants or ornaments, for instance.

Put a handle on it
Trying to keep someone out of the home while simultaneously trying to press the panic button is difficult, if not impossible. Mount the panic button on the inside wall next to the door handle and firmly attach a sturdy handle to the wall next to it. Hanging on to the handle will stop you being pushed back and away from the button. Make sure the handle and button are so placed that the arrangement is suited to everyone in the home.

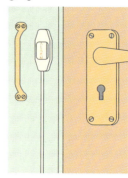

Hit the button
Have panic buttons placed on the lock side of the exterior doors—not the hinge side, where they could be difficult to reach. Secondly, if you tend to move about a lot in the home, a button in an area through which you frequently pass will be a useful addition to those in the bedroom, study and kitchen. If there are children in the home, place the buttons at a height they can reach (like a second peephole for them in a door). Test panic buttons—fixed and portable versions—at least once a month, by arrangement with the monitoring company. Keep portable panic buttons in established spots when not on your person, so that if you have to rush for one, you don't have to think about where you left it.

Types of sensor
Some types are better suited to particular applications than others. Points to bear in mind are those such as whether you own a pet (which could trigger the alarm if the beam extends to floor level), your home's design, and the sensors' range.

When buying a system, also consider installing sensors to cover your driveway, gate and some areas in the garden, or buy a couple of the economical units sold in supermarkets. Choose ones with two lights so that if one bulb fails, the other will still provide some light.

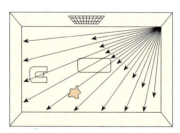 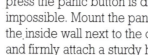 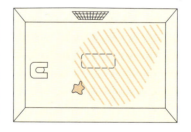 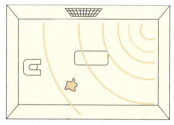

1. Infrared
There are two types of infrared beam. The narrow finger beam between transmitter and receiver (like those used to open doors to banks) sets off the alarm when it is broken. The passive type has the transmitter and receiver in the same unit. A series of finger beams are sent back and forth and any movement is detected.

2. Microwave: separate units
These beams are cigar-shaped—narrow at source and receiver and ballooning out between them. This means it may be possible to pass below the beam at either end. Transmitter and receiver must therefore be positioned so that this possibility is reduced to a minimum or eliminated altogether.

3. Microwave: single units
In this type, the transmitter and receiver are in the same unit, so the beam is narrow at the unit and balloons out and away from it. Position the unit so that its "blind" area can be reached only by passing through the beam—for example, by aiming the unit down a flight of steps.

4. Ultrasonic
This type sends out a series of high-frequency sound waves. They are too high to be audible to the human ear so an intruder will be unaware of them. The waves bounce off objects in the room and any movement within their range alters their pattern and activates the alarm.

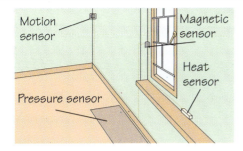

Multiple deterrents ▲

Any sensor or system has its pros and cons. Use different types of each for full protection. For example, magnetic sensors on windows backed up by motion and heat sensors inside, plus pressure mats, will be difficult to beat.

Deception

An open and shut case

Arrange to have at least some of your curtains closed every night and opened every morning. Barred windows can also be opened. Your home must give the appearance of being occupied.

Take note

Avoid leaving notes on your door, but if you have to do so, even if you live alone, use "We", not "I", on the note and add a fictitious name to reinforce the message.

Look who's talking now

As well as leaving a radio or television set on while you are out, play back a recording of the family at dinner, for example. The effect will be more lifelike and you can use timer switches on the tape recorder, radio, television set and lights to simulate varied activity for hours. Close the curtains properly to prevent your ruse being discovered.

BE SECURE AWAY FROM HOME

▷ **Leaving home:** Get into the habit of checking that toys, bicycles and other items are put away before you leave the house and that valuable items such as radios have been moved away from windows. The former, if left lying in the garden, may attract a trespasser on impulse; the latter leads him to break in. Avoid leaving garden tools out—they could be used to break in.
▷ **On public transport:** Avoid being alone in a railway carriage or on the top deck of a double-decker bus. Sit near other people or an official.
▷ **Avoid being mugged:** Don't walk close to a building when passing an alley, and avoid passing too close to a parked car, refuse bin or shrub: it could be a cover for a mugger. Get into the habit of watching which shops are open or if a traffic or police officer is nearby. If you often go walking, vary the routes and times. Never carry a lot of cash or wear too much jewellery.
▷ **On the road:** Drive with your doors locked and windows up. Loop your bag's strap through your safety belt if driving an open vehicle. If anyone makes signals indicating something is wrong with your car, but all appears fine to you, don't stop—drive to the nearest garage. If something does seem wrong with your car, stop—but stay in it with the windows open just enough to talk to the other driver. On long trips, rent a cellular telephone.
▷ **Defensive measures:** Carry a whistle and/or a self-defence spray or siren. A firearm is also useful—but only if you know how to handle it safely and legally. The best defence, however, is prevention.
▷ **Returning home:** You are vulnerable when out of the car to open the gate. Drive past your home if suspicious of anyone nearby, or stop at a neighbour's home and hoot until they come out and can keep an eye on you.

Snakes alive!

▷ While on holiday, ask your neighbours to put some of their refuse bags outside your home for collection. It is just one further indication to anyone on the prowl that there is someone at home.
▷ A notice on your front gate, to the effect that there are snakes on your property (and therefore possibly in the house) can deter a burglar.
▷ Have a neighbour, friends or family frequently leave their car in your driveway to imply that the home is occupied.
▷ A shut-up home with a neglected garden is a giveaway. Arrange to have your garden tended while you are away for any length of time.

CHAPTER 8
HOUSEHOLD REPAIRS

REPAIRING FURNITURE 233
FIXING FURNITURE SURFACES 238
STRIPPING FURNITURE 242
VARNISHING AND STAINING FURNITURE 246
PAINTING AND ANTIQUING FURNITURE 248
SPRAY-PAINTING FURNITURE 250
APPLIANCE REPAIR TIPS 252
REFRIGERATORS AND FREEZERS 256
DISHWASHERS AND STOVES 258
WASHING MACHINES AND DRYERS 260
ELECTRONIC EQUIPMENT 262

REPAIRING FURNITURE

Drawers

No-turn knobs

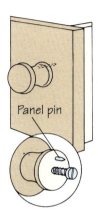
Panel pin

To anchor a wood knob on a drawer, drill a hole in the base of the knob. Clip a small panel pin in half, and insert the lower half into the hole with the point outwards. When the knob is put back on, the point will bite into the wood, anchoring the knob.

Dry out a balky drawer

Drawers often stick simply because humidity has swelled the wood. When a drawer sticks, take it out and dry it in a warm place. After a couple of days, test it for fit and sand or plane any areas that still stick. Then seal all wood surfaces with a coat of clear polyurethane to retard future moisture absorption.

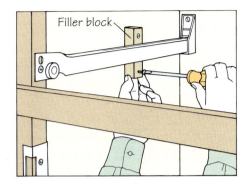
Filler block

Staying on track ▲

On kitchen cabinets, metal drawer slides often bow to the side with use, letting the rollers on the drawer slip out of the track. To fix this, mount a block of scrap wood on the side of the cabinet to hold the track parallel to the drawer.

Smooth sliding

A quick way to improve the action of a drawer on wood runners is to remove the drawer and spray the runners with aerosol furniture polish. The wax in the polish will reduce the friction.

Sand 'n wax

Here's another way to help a wood drawer slide more smoothly: lightly sand the bottom edges of the drawer sides and the tops of the runners with 100-grit sandpaper. Then wax them with a candle stub.

Spill preventer

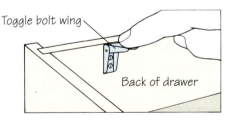
Clipped nail

To keep a drawer from pulling out all the way, install a 50 mm nail as a stop on each side, about 30 mm in from the back. Drill a hole 35 mm deep, its diameter being slightly larger than the nail's. Clip the nail so that it's high enough to catch the top edge of the face frame when the drawer is pulled open. Slip the drawer into the cabinet and reach inside to insert the nails.

Toggle bolt wing

Back of drawer

Toggle stop ▲

You can also make a drawer stop with the wings of a toggle bolt. Drill two holes in one wing and screw it to the inside face of the drawer back, with the other wing projecting above the edge. Hold down the top wing to remove the drawer; it will automatically spring back when the drawer is replaced. A turn button (pivoting wood block) also makes a great drawer stop (p 56).

Fast fix for droopy drawers

When a drawer begins to stick and scrape, its bottom edges and the frame they ride on are often worn. A simple solution is to tap a large drawing-pin into the front of the frame just under the drawer's edge on each side. This provides a new low-friction sliding surface and raises the drawer to the proper height.

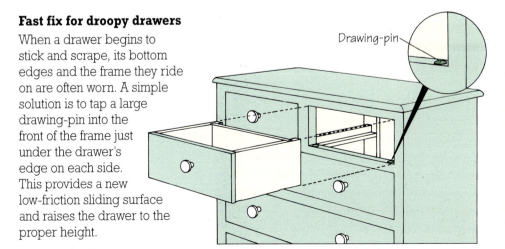
Drawing-pin

Household Repairs / 233

REPAIRING FURNITURE

Doors

Open-and-shut solution
Sticking cabinet door? To locate the areas that are binding, hold a sheet of carbon paper between the door and the cabinet frame, with the carbon side toward the door, then close the door. The carbon will smudge the high spots, showing you where the door needs to be sanded or planed. Move the paper along the edge and repeat as needed. ▼

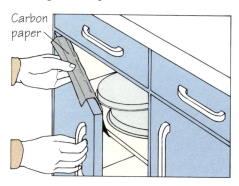

Door lift
If loose hinges are causing a cabinet door to bind, take out the hinge pins and make a slight bend in the centre of each one. The pins will fit tighter, lifting the door and making it operate more smoothly. ▼

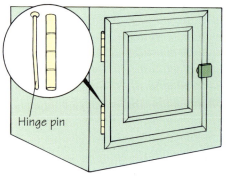

Upholstery

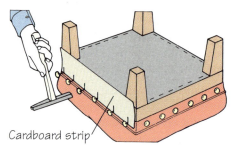

Cardboard strip

All straight in a row ▲
Getting a row of upholstery tacks straight and evenly spaced is not as easy as it looks. One solution is to pin a dressmaker's tape measure just above the line where the tacks go. Another is to mark the spacing along the edge of a lightweight cardboard strip and press the tacks into it. After driving all the tacks most of the way in, tug on the strip to pull the edge free.

Getting a better hold
Is an old chair frame so chewed up with tack holes that tacks for a new fabric won't hold? Apply a strip or two of muslin to the damaged surface with white glue and let it dry thoroughly. This will give grip to the surface and let you attach fabric more securely, especially if you use staples instead of tacks.

For future use
Put leftover material from a reupholstery job in a large envelope or plastic bag, and staple it underneath the chair or sofa. Also store extra decorative tacks there. Tap them in far enough so they won't fall out. Later, if you need a patch or want to cover an additional area, you'll find fabric and tacks available.

Ripped heavy materials
Sewing a tear in leather, vinyl, or certain heavy fabrics may do more harm than good. Try glueing on a patch instead. Use a razor blade to cut a neat circle or square around the rip and glue a backing of similar material behind the hole. Then trace the hole on paper and use it as a pattern to cut a patch to glue to the backing. Cut the patch from an inside or underside area of the upholstery if necessary.

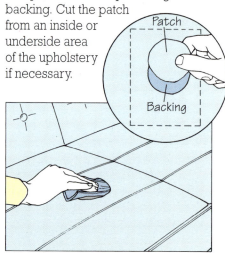

Chairs

The old-fashioned way

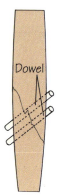

Broken chair leg or rung? If the parts still fit snugly, fix the break with dowels. Glue and clamp the parts together. After the glue has dried, remove the clamp and drill angled holes for dowels through both parts. Glue the dowels into the holes and trim them. For more tips on using dowels, see p 79.

Spring action

To replace a broken spindle in a chair back that's difficult to take apart, cut off the top tenon of the new spindle. Drill a hole in the top of the spindle and insert a small spring and a dowel. Then glue the tenon you cut off into the hole in the top of the chair back and drill a matching hole in it. Apply glue to both ends of the spindle, and set it in place. As you do, press the dowel down and let it pop into the top hole. ▼

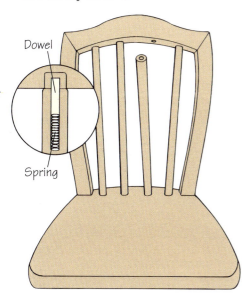

Bridge that spindle break

You can make a strong hidden repair by very accurately fitting a dowel about one-third of the spindle's diameter down the centre of each half so that the break is bridged.

Raising cane

To take the sag out of a cane chair seat, soak it well with hot, soapy water. Then rinse and leave it to air-dry. The cane will shrink and pull taut.

Leg problems

Get a leg up

To build up a tubular metal table leg on an uneven floor, put furniture leg tips on all four legs, adding washers inside the tip of the leg you want to lengthen.

Even keel

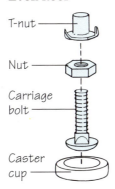

Uneven floor got a piece of furniture wobbling? Put this easy-to-make furniture leveller on all four corners. For each leveller, use a carriage bolt with a mating T-nut and regular nut. Drill a hole and tap the T-nut over it; then screw in the bolt with the nut on it. After you level the piece, tighten the nut against the T-nut to keep the bolt from moving. Put a caster cup under each leveller to protect the floor. ▼

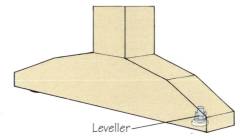

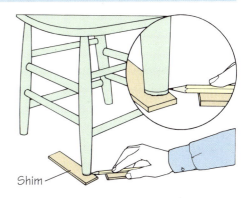

Cure for the wobbles ▲

If a chair or table wobbles because one leg is shorter than the others, put the piece on a flat surface and shim the short leg until the wobble stops. Then mark around each leg with a pencil held flat on a thin wood block slightly higher than the shim. Finally, trim the legs with a small handsaw; they will all be exactly the same length.

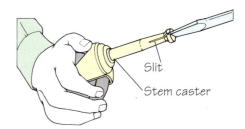

Faster casters ▲

To keep stem casters from falling out of loose sockets, wrap the stem with steel wool. Or, for a more permanent solution, cut a slit in the top of the stem with a hacksaw. Then spread the slit with a screwdriver just enough so that the caster will not drop out. If you can remove the metal housing from the leg, do so and bend the tongues in slightly so that the rim at the top of the stem is gripped more tightly.

Household Repairs / 235

REPAIRING FURNITURE

Taking it apart

Avoid a jigsaw puzzle

When you take a chair apart to reglue it, it's often difficult to tell one leg or rung from the other. Before starting, put masking tape labels with numbers or letters and alignment marks on each joint. Then putting the chair back together will only be a matter of matching markings. You can peel the tape off without damaging the finish.

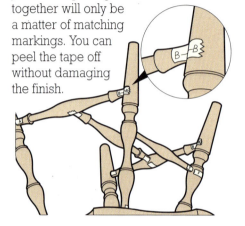

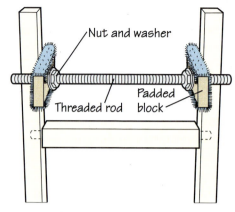

Homemade joint popper ▲

Here's a simple device for opening stubborn chair joints. All it consists of is a threaded rod (with two nuts and two washers) going through two blocks of wood padded with carpet. Use it to apply outward pressure slowly and evenly to the joints to force them open. To do this, just alternately tighten the nuts on either side a little bit at a time.

Old cabinetmaker's trick

After taking apart a piece of furniture for regluing, dab or brush hot vinegar on the joints to loosen and remove the old glue. It usually works in minutes, but loosening a thick glue buildup could take up to an hour. The vinegar won't harm any finish, leaving only a white film that you can easily wipe off.

Ream it out

To sand off the old glue in a round mortise, use sandpaper wrapped around a wood dowel. Use a narrow chisel to remove built-up glue from the bottom of the mortise.

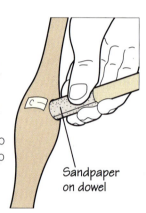

Don't break a leg ▶

When removing the spreaders or rungs on a chair, it's easy to accidentally break one of the chair's legs. To avoid this, support the chair so that the leg rests lightly on a carpeted surface. Then tap straight down on the leg with a rubber mallet. This will loosen the bond and let you pull the spreader or rung out without any damage to it or the leg.

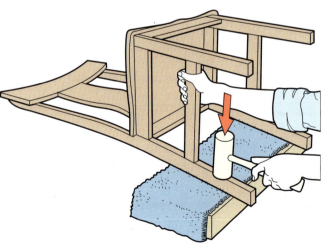

Putting it together

Five commandments

Here are some basic rules for reassembling or repairing furniture:
▷ Don't use nails, L-brackets, or mending plates. Use glue and, if necessary, dowels or splines. Use screws only where they were used before.
▷ Remove all the old glue so that the new glue can adhere to the wood fibres.
▷ Use the right wood glue. Avoid epoxy; future disassembly is nearly impossible.
▷ Always keep the parts of a glued joint clamped together until the glue dries.
▷ Never apply paint or varnish until the glue is completely dry.

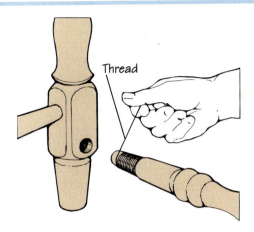

Loose joints 1 ▲
If a furniture joint you are reglueing is only slightly loose, you may be able to rely on the glue itself to bridge the gap. If it is so loose that it's wobbly, however, here is one trick to try: coat the tenon with glue, and wrap it tightly with cotton thread. After the thread dries, glue the tenon into the mortise.

Loose joints 2

If a round tenon is too small for a hole, glue a thin wood shaving around it before you glue it into the mortise. The advantage of this filler is that you get a joint that's all wood. Make sure the shaving has an even thickness so that the tenon is accurately centred in the mortise.

Loose joints 3
If a rectangular tenon is too small, glue thin pieces of veneer to all four sides. When the glue dries, use a utility knife or sandpaper to fit the enlarged tenon into the mortise. You can also use this method to centre a tenon—by applying the veneer strips to only some sides.

Loose joints 4
Wrap strips of thin porous or absorbent fabric (cheesecloth, pantihose, or cotton sheeting) around a loose tenon. Use as many layers as you need, and soak each with glue. Allow the glue to harden; then sand and trim the tenon for a tight fit.

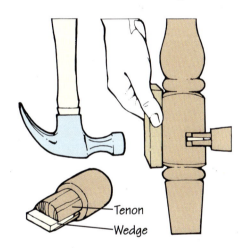

For a really loose joint ▲
Make a slot in the tenon, cutting at a right angle to the grain on the end of the tenon. Cut a wedge that will be driven tightly into the new slot when the joint is reassembled. Experiment to get the wedge the right length. Don't make it too thick because it may split the rung. Put glue on the wedge and the slot as well as on the rung and in the mortise before reassembling and clamping.

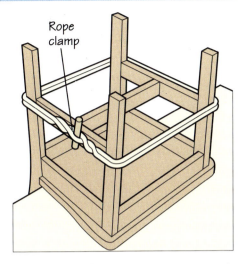

Quick chair clamp ▲
If you don't have bar clamps, the easiest way to secure chair legs while the glue is drying is to wrap two turns of rope around the legs. Then insert a stick between the turns and tighten the rope like a tourniquet. You can also use elastic cords to hold the legs (p 86).

Out of glue? Raid the pantry
If you run out of wood glue and there's no hardware dealer open, make your own. Ordinary household gelatine used by housewives is a good substitute for workpieces that will be painted or varnished, or be used indoors—this glue is not waterproof. Make up a mixture of 10 parts glue to 1 part water and keep it simmering away at a temperature of about 60°C. You can apply the glue with a brush or spatula. Simply leave the applicator in water and the glue will soak off. As with any home remedy, experiment a little before mixing up a large batch. When you have arrived at the ideal mix, make a note of it for the future.

FIXING FURNITURE SURFACES

Scratches

Use your nut
You can actually hide a fine scratch on furniture by rubbing it with the meat of a pecan or other oily nut or with a little peanut butter. But if that sounds a bit too nutty or smelly, there are alternatives. It's actually the oil in the nut that's doing the job, and olive or vegetable oil will work even better—without the danger of further damaging the finish by rubbing too hard. Rub the oil in well with your thumb, and polish the surface using a clean soft cloth.

An instant solution
For a brew that will obscure scratches on a dark furniture finish, mix 1 teaspoon of instant coffee in 1 tablespoon of water or vegetable oil. Don't use this on shellac or a valuable antique.

More home scratch eliminators
Several other common household items can hide small scratches on finished wood. Here are some to try, but test them in an inconspicuous spot first and make sure that when you do apply them, you keep your coverage to the smallest possible area:
▷ Iodine works on mahogany and other reddish finishes.
▷ Liquid and wax shoe polish come in shades that match wood finishes.
▷ Felt-tip markers in brown, red, and yellowish hues let you match a range of wood tones, although some may require two or more markers.
▷ Crayons in similar colours also work if warmed slightly first to soften them.

Basic scratch removal
Simply applying wax polish and buffing will often eliminate fine scratches. For more pronounced marks, sand with the grain using superfine wet-or-dry sandpaper lubricated with mineral oil (or baby oil). To get an even shine and a satin finish, rub the area with superfine steel wool lubricated with oil soap. For a higher shine, wax and buff. But don't wet-sand older veneer pieces; they often have tiny high spots where the finish will wear off.

Wear and tear

Marker magic
Worn finish on a chair arm or table edge can be fixed with special touch-up pens—available from wood-finishing suppliers—that seal and refinish worn spots and scratches. Wipe the area with mineral spirits and scuff it with superfine sandpaper. Then draw over it with a pen of the appropriate colour. Feather out the repair by rubbing it gently with your finger. Repeat several times to build up the new finish. ▼

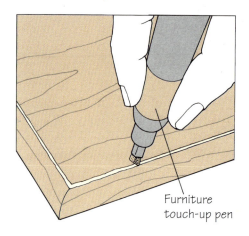
Furniture touch-up pen

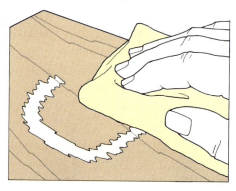

White rings ▲
A white ring left by a sweaty beverage container will often disappear if you just wipe up the moisture and wait a couple of hours. If the ring persists, try passing a hair dryer set on low heat back and forth over it, but keep the nozzle at least 150 mm away and allow the wood to get warm but not hot. If a trace still remains, rub it vigorously with boiled linseed oil (or olive or vegetable oil); then buff with your palm to create friction. Wipe clean.

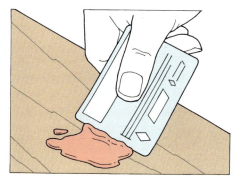

Spilled nail polish ▲
Don't wipe it up! The solvents in nail polish soften most finishes, and wiping may take off the finish. Instead, let the polish dry completely; then gently scrape it off with a credit card. Wax the surface, using superfine steel wool.

Pearly and plaque-free

To brighten a dulled lacquer or varnish finish, mix a little regular non-gel toothpaste with water and rub it on with a cloth. If necessary, blend in a pinch of baking soda to make it more abrasive.

Scorched surface

To remove a surface burn, rub it with a paste made of fine fireplace ash and lemon juice. Then wipe the area clean, and touch it up with the same kind of finish that is already on the surface. To determine the finish type, see p 242.

Burn marks

To treat burns that go into the wood, mask closely around the area with tape, and scrape out the charred wood using a craft knife with a rounded blade. If necessary, stain the bare wood to match the finish. Mix equal parts of clear nail polish and acetone-base nail polish remover; apply one thin coat at a time until you fill the hole, letting each coat dry before applying the next. Sand the surface with extra-fine paper, and then remove the tape. If a burn goes through a veneer, patch the veneer (p 241). ▼

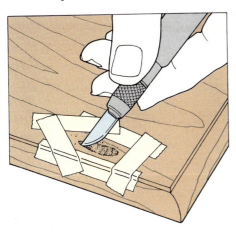

Deeper damage

Soft fill

To hide nicks and gouges on a table leg or cabinet side, use a wax (or putty) furniture filler stick and dark furniture wax (available from larger hardware stores). First clean the area with mineral spirits. Fill the larger gouges with filler from a stick matching the lightest shade of the wood. Smooth the filler and buff it lightly with superfine steel wool. Then use the dark wax a little at a time to fill the small scratches and even up the colour. The repairs are not durable enough to withstand hard use, so don't try this on a tabletop—the first time you write a cheque, you'll poke your pen into the filler. ▼

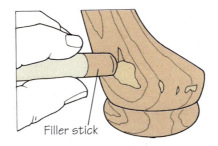

Filler stick

Swell solution ▶

A dent can often be fixed by swelling the compressed fibres back to their normal size. Prick the finish in the dent several times with a fine pin so that moisture can penetrate into the wood. Then cover the dent with a pad of wet cloth, put a metal bottle cap on top to spread the heat, and apply an iron on a high setting for a few minutes. Be careful not to scorch the finish. Afterwards, fill the pinholes with a thin coat of varnish.

Shellac stick

Burn-in knife

Hard fill ▲

A more solid way to fill deep scars on furniture is with a shellac stick. Get one that closely matches the colour of the finish. Apply it using a curved burn-in knife (or a grapefruit knife) heated on a smokeless heat source. Reheat the knife often, press it against the stick and melt shellac into the hole a little at a time to fill it just above surface level. Use the hot knife to smooth the shellac. After the patch cools, carefully sand it level with superfine wet-or-dry paper and a little mineral oil. Remove any excess shellac with alcohol. This procedure takes skill, so practise before trying it on antiques.

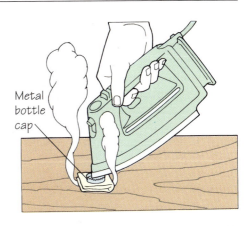

Metal bottle cap

FIXING FURNITURE SURFACES

Veneer

The last straw
Reglueing old, brittle delaminated veneer is tricky. Try this: cut a length of plastic drinking straw and flatten it. Fold it in half and fill one half with carpenter's glue, dripping the glue in from above very slowly in tiny drops (this requires patience). Slip the filled half under the veneer and gently blow in the glue. Wipe off any excess, cover the area with wax paper and a wood block and clamp overnight. ▼

Just a sliver ▷
A blister in veneer usually results when the veneer swells too much to fit its original area. Use a sharp craft or utility knife to cut a thin sliver (about 1 mm wide) from the centre of the blister. Cut with the grain for the length of the blister, tapering the cut's ends. Work carpenter's glue under the veneer with a straw (see hint at left), clamp or weight the area and leave it to dry.

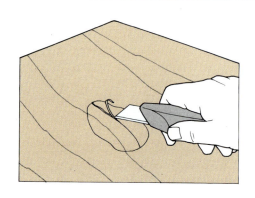

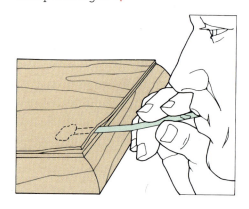

Older means easier
Flattening blistered or peeled veneer on an older piece is often easy because heat and moisture will soften the type of glue commonly used to bond veneer before the 1940s. Lay a damp towel over the area and carefully heat it with an iron set on *Low*. Then press the veneer flat with a rolling pin and clamp it or weight it down overnight. One caution: don't wet and heat a shellac finish unless you plan to refinish the piece. To test for shellac, dab some alcohol on a hidden area; if the finish is shellac, it will dissolve or cloud.

Plastic laminate

Counter countertop peeling
When laminate comes loose, it's usually along an edge. To reattach a loose edge, scrape away the old glue, brush contact cement on the surface of the base under the laminate and coat the lower surface of the laminate by pressing it down on the base surface and quickly pulling it away. Prop it up with toothpicks or nails until the adhesive is almost dry. Then press it into place and roll with a rolling pin. ▼

Frying pan burn the counter?
Rubbing toothpaste on the laminate may remove a slight surface discoloration, but a deeper burn can't be removed. If you don't want to replace the laminate, glue some ceramic tiles over the spot and use them as a pot rest. Or put in a heatproof insert comprising a varnished frame with tiles glued to a plywood or chipboard base. ▼

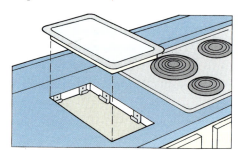

Hot separation
To remove plastic laminate from a surface, heat one edge with an iron or a heat gun to soften the adhesive. Slide a putty knife under that edge to lift the laminate. Then work your way across the length of the piece, heating and pulling the laminate free as you go.

PATCHING VENEER

Replacing small damaged sections of veneer is not difficult but the patch must be carefully fitted so that it is as unobtrusive as possible. Get a piece of veneer from a hardware store (or try a furniture manufacturer). You will also need a tube of contact cement.

Replacing a large area of veneer, such as an entire chest top, is also simple. But for large areas, use the thinner water-base cement, which spreads with a roller and won't become lumpy or uneven when applied. Also, let the new veneer's edges overhang on all sides, and trim them with a utility knife after mounting. Don't stain a large section of veneer until after you mount it.

1 Use a utility knife to remove the damaged veneer and to straighten the edges of the cut-out section. When possible, cut with the grain to hide the seam. Scrape or sand off any old glue.

2 Sand the new veneer smooth, and test stains on it until you get a good match. If the new veneer is thicker than the original, sand it down on the back to the proper thickness.

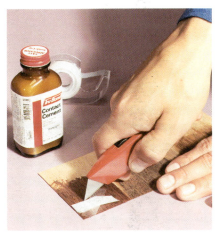

3 Outline the missing area on paper by rubbing with the side of a pencil lead. Cut out the paper, and use it as a template to cut an exact copy of the area from the new veneer.

4 Test-fit the patch, and trim it if necessary. Carefully apply contact cement to the back of the patch and to the base wood, and allow it to dry. Then press the patch into place.

5 Finish the patch with oil or varnish to match. Then hide the seam using a furniture touch-up putty stick in a matching colour. Use the touch-up stick last because finish won't adhere to the putty.

Household Repairs / 241

STRIPPING FURNITURE

Before you strip

Clean up your act
Sometimes all that's needed to make that grimy garage sale bargain look like new is a good cleaning. Mix equal parts of boiled linseed oil and mineral spirits. Warm the mixture slightly in the top of an old double boiler, and rub it on with cheesecloth, sacking, or superfine steel wool, depending on how dirty the surface is. After removing the bulk of the dirt, buff with a soft cloth.

Fast new finish
If a surface is basically alright there's no need to expend a lot of time and effort on it. You may be able to remove minor blemishes by rubbing them gently with steel wool. If you prefer to treat the entire surface, you could use a furniture restorer or amalgamator (available from specialist stores). These products work by dissolving a thin layer of the old finish. You get a reworked surface that's lighter in colour than the old one, with scratches and dirt removed. Restorer won't, however, change the basic colour, rescue a thin, flaky finish, or repair deep stains and gouges. ▼

Cheaper fast finish
You can sometimes rejuvenate a grimy but otherwise solid finish with a solvent that softens it. Work out what that solvent is (see below), brush it on, let it stand until most of it has evaporated and then rework the finish with fine steel wool. It will take more elbow grease than using a commercial refinishing product, but it costs a lot less. Always test a hidden area first and be prepared to strip and refinish the piece if this doesn't work.

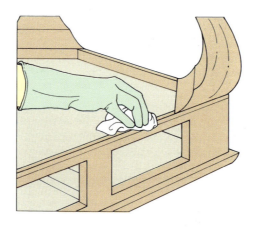

What finish is it? ▲
Clear finishes are difficult to tell apart, but it's important to know what you're working on. Finishes with a low sheen and very little surface thickness are likely to be penetrating-oil finishes. To identify other types of finish, moisten a cloth with alcohol and vigorously rub a hidden spot. If the finish softens, it's shellac. If it doesn't, try the test using lacquer thinner. If the finish softens, it's a lacquer-base finish. If neither product affects the finish, it's probably a varnish. You'll find a list of finishes and their solvents on p 246.

Tips on stripping

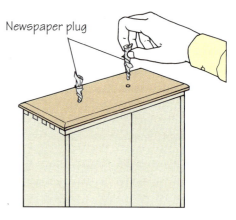

Newspaper plug

Plug up first ▲
After removing the hardware to prepare a piece for stripping, fill key and screw holes with twisted bits of newspaper before applying the stripper. The paper will keep the holes from getting clogged with stripper sludge, which is difficult to remove after it dries and hardens.

Bits and pieces
Take the tedium out of stripping hinges, knobs, and other hardware. Fill an old coffee tin with enough stripper to cover a couple of pieces; then tie a string to them and lower them into the tin. Cap it with the plastic lid, leaving the string hanging over the rim. After the suggested time, pull the pieces out and clean them. The stripper can be used several times.

Concealing scratches in mahogany

Iodine can be used to stain and conceal scratch marks in mahogany and other dark woods such as imbuia and teak. Apply the iodine with a fine artist's brush or with the end of a toothpick wrapped in cotton wool.

No drip

The best way to avoid having stripper run off vertical surfaces is to use semi-paste stripper or to keep turning the piece so that the surface being stripped is horizontal. But if you need to keep liquid stripper from running, sprinkle it with some sawdust.

Recycle those tuna tins

Put a shallow tin under each chair or table leg to catch stripper drippings. You'll not only control the mess but you can save the drippings and reuse any that are still clear, for a second coat. You can also drive a nail into the base of each leg to keep the foot clear of the tin's base. This allows all of the stripper to drop off the wood and speeds drying later. Leave the nails in place when finishing the unit: you will be able to achieve a much neater finish. ▼

Shallow tin

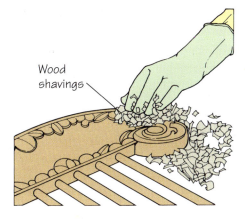
Wood shavings

Waste not ▲

Wood shavings from a planer or jointer are great for scrubbing loosened finish out of carvings and other finely detailed areas, and as an added benefit, they absorb the sludge. If you don't have enough shavings from your own workshop, ask a local woodworker or cabinetmaker for some. Sawdust will also work, but not as well as shavings.

Absorb the mess

On a messy stripping job, the sludge will be easier to remove if you add a material that soaks up some of the softened finish. Use sawdust or cat litter.

Stripper helper

If you're removing a heavy coat of paint, cover the stripper with plastic—food wrap, a refuse bag or a large plastic bag from a shop. The plastic keeps the stripper from evaporating so that it can work longer. Placing a piece of scrap cloth over the area and soaking it with the stripper helps to keep the surface wet and prevents runoff. An old T-shirt is ideal. Wring it out into a tin after use so that you can reuse the leftover stripper again.

STRIPPING RISKS

If a product is strong enough to remove paint, you don't want to breathe it into your lungs or get it on your skin or in your eyes. But some strippers require more precautions than others. This is especially true of ones containing methylene chloride. Methylene chloride is fast-acting, but it is flammable and is a skin and eye irritant. Inhaling high levels of it causes dizziness and headaches and reduces the body's ability to absorb oxygen. Long-term repeated exposure is associated with cancer in laboratory tests in the United States of America. Do not use methylene chloride if anyone in your family is pregnant, has heart or lung problems, or is sensitive to chemical fumes.

The wisest course is to use a water-base stripper whenever possible. It takes hours to work, and raises the wood grain, but is much less noxious. Even so, take care when working with any paint remover. Wear long sleeves and long pants, safety goggles, solvent-resistant gloves and a respirator with an organic-vapour filter. Work in a well-ventilated area—outdoors is best. Consider using a heat gun to remove a heavy buildup of old paint.

Dispose of the old finish and leftover stripper safely (p 39).

STRIPPING FURNITURE

Stripping tools

Scratch prevention

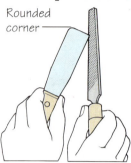

Rounded corner

Prepare a putty knife for removing finish by gently rounding the corners with a file. Remove any burrs from the edge with fine sandpaper.

For an easy-to-clean putty knife
Lightly coat your putty knife with non-stick cooking spray, and the stripper residue won't adhere to it.

Super spatula
With its flat, flexible blade, an old plastic kitchen spatula makes a great scraper for removing stripper. Hold the spatula upside down and push it along as shown for a clean pickup. ▼

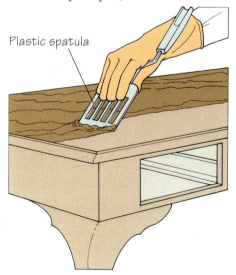

Plastic spatula

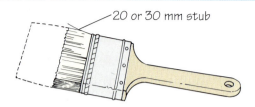

20 or 30 mm stub

Stub brush ▲
An old paintbrush is a good tool for removing softened finish in hard-to-reach areas. Just trim the bristles to a stiff stump about 20 or 30 mm long. Dip the brush in water (for water-base stripper) or turpentine (for solvent-base) and use it to flush the old finish out of carvings, turnings and grooves.

Cut-off section

The little brush that can ▲
To reach into curves and crevices when stripping furniture, cut two rows of bristles off a stiff-bristle scrubbing brush. Use the cut-off piece to work stripper into the areas and later to rub off the loosened finish.

No-mess scoop
Here's a way to remove loosened finish with less mess: cut an aluminium plate in half, using heavy scissors, and put the halves to work as scooper-scrapers. The metal is rigid enough to scrape up the loosened finish and hold it too.

Snappy solutions
To remove softened finish on turned legs, twist a piece of sacking or old pantihose and move it back and forth across the surface as you would a shoeshine cloth.

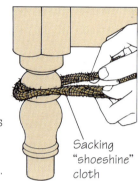

Sacking "shoeshine" cloth

On fine turnings and grooves in furniture legs, remove the sludge with coarse twine or with medium-grade steel wool wrapped around a string. If you need to get old finish out of a really tight groove, use a toothpick or cocktail stick.

Save that old fishing rod
Bamboo is a great material for making tools that remove stripper sludge. You can quickly cut it to whatever shape you need, and it's soft enough that it won't mar most woods.

Other ways to strip

Press it off
Remove a heavy buildup of varnish or other clear finish with an old steam iron. Put several layers of damp cheesecloth over the surface to absorb the finish, and press with the iron on a medium steam setting. Often this will remove most of the finish, leaving only a thin layer to be removed with stripper or with the appropriate solvent.

REMOVING AN OLD FINISH

Before starting, remove all hardware from the piece and put cardboard or thick newspaper layers under it. Apply stripper with an old paintbrush that you can dispose of afterwards. To avoid rust spots, don't use steel wool with water-base stripper.

Caution: When using stripper, wear an organic-vapour respirator and protective gloves, goggles and clothing. Handle stripper containing methylene chloride with special care (see box, p 243).

1 Brush on a heavy coat of stripper in one direction; back-and-forth strokes reduce the stripper's potency. Let it work for the recommended time. If solvent-base stripper starts to dry, apply a little more.

2 Rub lightly with a sponge scrub pad or medium steel wool to loosen the finish. Then use a wide, flexible putty knife to remove finish on flat surfaces. If needed, apply another coat of stripper.

3 Remove finish along edges and corners with a brass-bristle brush—the type sold for scrubbing pots. It works better than a toothbrush and won't damage the wood the way steel will.

4 Clean finish out of narrow grooves and creases with an awl or toothpick. Use light strokes to avoid damaging the wood. For more intricate areas, see the hints on the facing page.

5 Wash the entire area to remove any residue of the stripper. Use mineral spirits to remove the remains of solvent-base stripper and plain water to remove the remains of water-base stripper.

It's not just for ovens
Use oven cleaner to strip paint and varnish. It's cheaper than stripper, sprays on, and doesn't sag much on vertical surfaces. But use it only on non-valuable pieces you plan to paint, as it darkens the wood. Neutralize the stripped surface with vinegar, wash it with water and let it dry thoroughly before painting. Wear gloves and goggles.

Out of the ashes
You can strip the finish from hardware with this home brew: 250 g of wood fireplace ash mixed with 10 litres of water. This mild caustic solution will loosen paint on hardware that is soaked in it overnight. Even though the solution is mild, wear rubber gloves when you put your hands into the bucket.

Sour milk
Does the paint on an old piece resist every stripper you try? It may be milk paint from the mid-19th century. If so, household ammonia will take it right off. On the other hand, if the milk paint is in good condition, the piece is probably more valuable with the paint on than it would be stripped and refinished.

VARNISHING AND STAINING FURNITURE

Before varnishing

Quick preview
Want to know what a wood surface will look like with a clear varnish finish? Just dampen a cloth with mineral spirits and wipe it on an area. If you like the effect, go ahead and varnish the wood; it will look almost the same as the wet wood. If you don't like the look, apply stain before varnishing.

Mineral spirits wiped on

Banish black water marks ▲
Black water marks on stripped tabletops disappear like magic when you apply oxalic acid (sold in hardware stores). Wearing protective gloves and goggles, make a solution with boiling water and brush it carefully just on the stain. When the stain is gone, neutralize the entire surface with distilled white vinegar, assessing any colour differences while the wood is wet. Touch up an overly light area with stain.

Bleach it off
After you strip wood, you sometimes find that the old stain has penetrated so deeply that it won't come out. Ordinary chlorine bleach will often lighten a stain. Apply it generously and evenly and give the piece several days to dry. Neutralize the bleach with a white vinegar wash. Bleach will also remove many types of spots from stripped surfaces.

Staining wood

Instant patina
Getting new wood to match the old on repaired furniture is tricky. On light-coloured pieces, give new wood a coat of golden oak stain before staining and finishing it. The stain's amber hues approximate the effect of aging, so the new wood should finish the same as the old.

COMMON FINISHES FOR FURNITURE

For best results, apply a finish following label directions and observe any precautions about safe handling or flammability. Lacquer, polyurethane, and most varnishes come in satin, semigloss, and glossy finishes.

FINISH	SOLVENT	CHARACTERISTICS	HOW TO APPLY
Penetrating oil	Mineral spirits	Soaks into wood fibres for natural-looking finish. Tung oil is most durable type.	Wipe or brush on, let stand for about 30 minutes, then rub vigorously. Apply two or more coats.
Shellac (white or orange)	Denatured alcohol	Thin, lustrous clear or amber surface film. Wears well but is easily marred by spills.	Brush on two or three thin coats. Easy to spot-repair. Also use to seal wood for other finishes.
Lacquer	Lacquer thinner	Thin, hard film. Very good spill and wear resistance. Used on commercial furniture.	Spray on two or three coats; brush on slow-to-dry type. Don't use over other finishes.
Acrylic varnish	Water (before the varnish dries)	Thin, hard film with no amber tones. Moderate resistance to wear and spills.	Spray or brush on two or three thin coats. Usually comes in a spray can.
Oil-base varnish	Mineral spirits	Hard, warm-toned film. Moderate to good resistance to wear and spills.	Brush on two or three coats. Easy to recoat but hard to spot-repair. Sand between coats.
Polyurethane	Turpentine, mineral spirits	Very hard, warm-toned film. Excellent resistance to wear and spills.	Brush on two coats. Hard to spot-repair. Recoat within specified time. Don't use over shellac.

Blotchiness tamer

Some softwoods absorb stain unevenly with very blotchy results. The same is true for dark stains on some hardwoods, maple for example. To prevent this, before staining the wood, seal it with a very thin coat of shellac (1 part shellac to 5 parts denatured alcohol). Leave it to dry for 30 minutes and then sand it with very fine paper. If you select an alcohol-base stain, make sure you apply it quickly and sparingly, or the alcohol will liquefy the shellac.

Tidy stain applicator

Here's an efficient way to apply stain: use a hacksaw to cut an ordinary nap paint roller into three equal sections. Hold a roller piece in your hand to wipe on stain. The roller absorbs more stain than a brush and applies it more evenly than a cloth. After the stain soaks in, wipe off the excess with a cloth.

Paint-roller section

Mix-and-match stains

Need a special colour wood stain to match an existing piece? Any colour stain can usually be mixed with any other of the same brand and type. Pick the stain that comes closest to the shade you want. Then work out what tone is missing and add some stain in which that tone predominates. For instance, adding mahogany or cherry boosts red tones, while adding oak enhances yellow. Test your mix on a hidden spot.

A NATURAL FINISH

BACK TO BASICS

Before staining and varnishing a piece, make sure the surface is clear of traces of stripper or old finish. Sand it smooth, and fix any defects. Filling the surface before varnishing (Steps 2 and 3) is optional but is often done to close the large pores on open-grain woods (oak, mahogany, walnut) and produce a smooth finish. Use a neutral-colour paste wood filler, thinned as directed. Add a tinting colour or stain to make it match the stain's shade. Test the stain and filler colours on an unobtrusive spot. For accurate results, sand, stain, fill, and varnish the test patch. Work in a well-ventilated space; wear a respirator. (For tips on using filler, see p 90; for selecting a brush, p 92.)

1 Stain and seal the surface in one operation by using a stain that contains sealer. Or apply stain, leave it to dry as directed and then apply sealer.

2 On open-grain wood, apply a generous wet coat of wood filler and brush in thoroughly (left). Let it dry until dull and flat (right) but not rock hard.

3 Wipe off the excess filler with sacking, going across the grain. Rubbing with the grain tends to pull the filler out. Let the surface dry overnight.

4 Sand lightly with very fine sandpaper and wipe with a tack cloth. Apply three coats of varnish; sand and wipe again between coats.

PAINTING AND ANTIQUING FURNITURE

Painting furniture

Slick finish

To get a supersmooth paint finish, work in a dust-free area and give the paint a chance to flow out and lose the brush marks. Here are some tips:
▷ Apply two coats of enamel undercoat as a primer.
▷ Use an oil-base enamel paint with a slow drying time (about 24 hours).
▷ Use a paint additive to increase penetration and drying time.
▷ Strain paint (even fresh paint) through a filter, and thin it by up to 10 per cent.
▷ Paint surfaces horizontally when possible—if necessary, turn a piece on its side. Lay a door flat.
▷ Use a good natural-bristle brush.
▷ Put on a thin coat of paint, applying three or four coats.
▷ Paint the surface across the grain first. Then make light full-length strokes with the grain, using just the tip of the brush.
▷ Sand thoroughly with fine paper and wipe with a tack cloth between coats.

Disposable mini-applicators

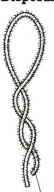
Pipe cleaner

For small touch-ups and tiny tight corners, apply the paint with a cotton swab. You'll get neat, accurate results, and you can throw the applicator away when you're through. For hard-to-reach spots, use a pipe cleaner. Simply bend it in half and twist its ends together as shown, forming a loop of the size you need.

Push-pin helper

The next time you paint a cabinet, press a few push pins into service. Put one on a cabinet door lip to keep the door and frame from touching while the paint dries. Also use pins as temporary drawer and door handles. The holes will be covered later by the knobs.

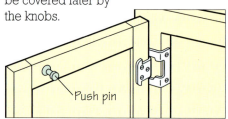
Push pin

Antiquing

Home-brewed finish

Antiquing can magically transform an old (or unpainted) piece of furniture and you don't need a kit to do it. Just give the piece a base coat of satin or semigloss enamel and let it dry for at least a day. Then make a transparent glaze by mixing clear wood sealer or thinned varnish with a dark tinting colour. Apply the glaze and then wipe it off, leaving flat surfaces lighter than grooves and recesses in order to simulate natural wear. Experiment on wood scraps first. ▼

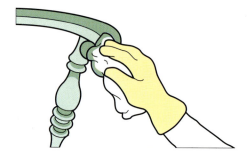

Fake that finish

Before antiquing a new piece, you may want to "distress" it. Round corners and edges slightly by sanding or filing. Dent edges with a ball-peen hammer, and mark flat surfaces with a bunch of keys. Make worm holes and irregular scratches with an awl. But don't go overboard; a little damage goes a long way. It helps to examine naturally worn pieces. Sand the distressed areas.

Age spots

To mimic worn areas on a piece you're making look old, use a small stick to apply paint stripper to the base coat in little irregular patches. Then wipe the stripper off gently when the paint has the look you want—ranging from a simple crackling effect to total removal of the paint. Neutralize the stripper with water or solvent as directed and let it dry before applying the glaze.

Crackling paint on purpose

Try this to create areas of crackled paint in your imitation antique finish: before applying the base coat of enamel paint, brush on a coat of white glue thinned with water and let it dry thoroughly.

Deep-down old

Before painting a piece you're antiquing, stain the wood a dark brown. When you remove paint to simulate wear, the wood underneath will look old and dark.

Other fake finishes

Fine freckles

One way to enhance the effect of glazing is to splatter specks of a very dark colour on the surface after wiping off the glaze. Make some of the glazing solution deeper in colour, dip a toothbrush into it and flick it over the surface. The effect varies depending on how close you hold the brush to the surface and how quickly you move it. ▼

Ersatz wood grain

You can simulate wood grain with the glazing process used for antiquing. Apply a base paint that matches the lightest tones in the wood you're imitating and a glaze that matches the darkest. Create grain by wiping the glaze lightly, first with steel wool and then with a dry brush, in a wavy pattern. You can also try dragging a feather, a carpet scrap or a soft-bristle brush over the surface.

AN ENAMEL FINISH

Back to Basics

You don't have to strip furniture in order to paint it. But for paint to adhere, the surface must be free of grease and dirt and any gloss must be dulled by sanding. Either oil-base or water-base enamel will provide a tough finish if you apply at least two coats over primer, but three is better. Oil-base enamels have a wet look when dry (see "Slick finish", facing page); water-base enamels are more satiny. Wear a dust mask when sanding and a respirator when painting. Work in a well-ventilated space.

1 Wipe the surface with mineral spirits on a rag. Sand off the shine with medium-grade paper. If the surface is still rough, sand again with fine paper.

2 To fill nicks and gouges, apply wood filler with a putty knife. Let it dry as directed, then sand smooth. Wipe the surface clean with a tack cloth.

3 Prime the surface with an oil-base primer, which brushes on easily, dries quickly, and provides the best undercoat for oil- or water-base enamel.

4 Apply two or three coats of enamel. Let each dry thoroughly; if finish is glossy, sand with very fine grit paper and wipe with a tack cloth between coats.

SPRAY-PAINTING FURNITURE

Spraying techniques

Spray booth
Want to spray-paint a piece of furniture but fear the mess? Use a large cardboard appliance shipping box as a spray booth. A furniture store may have one available.

Flip and paint
It's easier to paint a chair if you turn it upside down and spray the legs and rungs first, spraying their insides before their outsides. Then turn it right side up and spray the back and seat. This works with a small table as well. ▼

Spray inside first

Corners first and last
When spray-painting the outside of a piece of furniture, spray the corners first, aiming directly at each and coating both sides evenly. But when spraying the inside of a cabinet, it's best not to spray into the corners. Instead, just spray straight onto the flat surfaces, doing the back first, then each side.

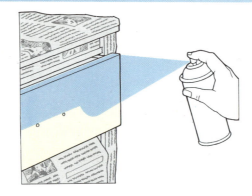

Just a crack ▲
To spray-paint a drawer front, leave it in the cabinet. Mask the cabinet around the drawer; then pull the drawer out about 15 mm. This will let paint cover the drawer edges without getting inside it. After the drawer dries, remove it to paint the cabinet case.

Get an angle on it
With open-weave material, such as cane, you'll get a finer, more even finish if you hold the spray can at about a 45° angle above the material. On wicker, spray first from one side at a 45° angle, then from the other, to penetrate the weave as much as possible. ▼

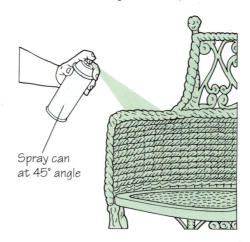

Spray can at 45° angle

Not the way you think
When spray-painting a flat surface, such as a tabletop, begin on the side nearest you and work toward the opposite side. This may seem a little strange, but when you spray a flat surface you hold the can at a slight angle, causing it to send some overspray ahead of it. By starting nearby, you cover up that overspray as you progress across the surface. If you did it the opposite way, the overspray would leave a pebbly texture on the areas you had already painted.

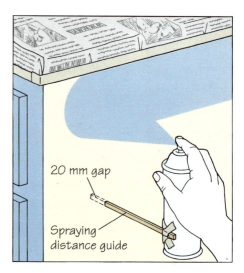

20 mm gap

Spraying distance guide

Keeping your distance ▲
For an even finish, you must keep the spray nozzle the same distance from the surface the whole time you are spraying. After working out the best distance for spraying with a can, tape a stick to it as a guide. Make the stick about 20 mm shorter than the distance so that you won't scrape it across the paint. You can also use a drinking straw and, if you're not going to be passing the guide over a newly painted surface, a small feather will provide a low-friction "foot".

Clean lines

If you want to leave some parts of a piece of furniture unpainted, use masking tape and newspaper to protect the areas. For a clean line along a tape edge, direct the spray so that it is blowing over the tape rather than toward the tape edge.

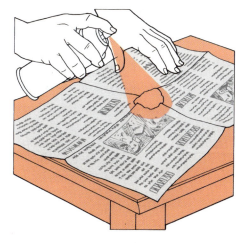

Instant feathering ▲

To touch up a small spot, try this: fold a newspaper in quarters, and then unfold it and cut a hole in the centre the size of the spot to be touched up. Place the newspaper over the spot, with the folds in the paper peaked up slightly. Then make several quick passes over the hole with the spray can. Moving quickly prevents paint buildup, and the raised paper at the folds lets the paint feather out around the spot to blend in with the rest of the surface. Prop up the paper with a couple of scraps if you have to, but make sure they are well out of the way and won't affect the way the paint feathers. Perfect your technique on scrap before working on a good piece of furniture.

For better spraying

Elusive last drops

No paint comes out of the spray can, but you can still feel paint sloshing around inside? The paint pickup tube may be on the side of the can opposite the direction you are spraying. Give the nozzle a half turn and try again.

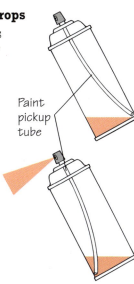

Cowboy sprayer

Stop your airless spray-painter dripping on your clothes and on the floor. Make a bandanna out of an old workshop towel and wrap it around the sprayer just below the nozzle. The rag will catch any drips and make cleaning up easier. ▼

Sure shot

To clear a clogged nozzle on an aerosol paint can, remove the nozzle and put it on the end of the spray tube on a can of penetrating lubricant. Blast a shot of lubricant through the nozzle. ▼

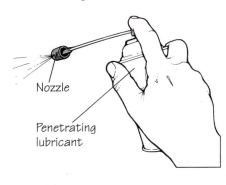

More clog busters

If an aerosol spray-paint can nozzle is clogged and you don't have penetrating lubricant, don't give up—try these tips:
▷ Soak the nozzle in lacquer thinner or mineral spirits overnight.
▷ Save the nozzles of discarded spray cans to use as instant replacements for clogged ones. Store them in a small jar filled with solvent.

Clog prevention

There is a simple way to keep a spray-paint can nozzle from becoming clogged in the first place. After spraying, turn the can upside down and press the button briefly. It will emit a short blast of plain propellant, which will clear the nozzle. If you are concerned about wasting too much propellant, put the nozzle on an insecticide can and clear the nozzle. Clean it properly before putting it back on your spray-paint can.

APPLIANCE REPAIR TIPS

Parts protocols

Parts on ice
Keep track of small parts while making repairs. As you disassemble an item, put the parts into prenumbered compartments of a plastic ice-cube tray. Reverse the procedure for reassembly. An egg carton works just as well. ▼

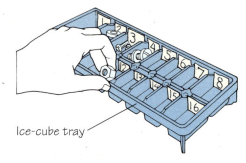
Ice-cube tray

All in a row
Tape can keep parts in the right order. Attach some tape, adhesive side up, to your bench top and stick the parts onto the tape in sequence.

Parts saver
While waiting for new parts to arrive, don't leave small parts and screws just lying around. Put them in resealable plastic freezer bags so that you won't lose them.

Grease bag
Here's another use for those resealable plastic bags: they can keep your hands from getting all messed up when you have to grease bearings or other parts. Just put some grease in a bag, add the parts, seal the bag, and work them around in the grease. Plastic shopping bags also work well—and they're free.

Metal paint tray

Parts washer ▲
Use a metal paint tray to wash small parts. Fill the deep end with solvent and soak the parts in it. Then use the upper end as a work area for brushing and wiping the parts after they've soaked.

Oops!
Dropped a part and can't find it? Turn off the lights and close the curtains. Then turn on a torch, hold it close to the floor, and move it in a circle. Like a searchlight, the beam raking across the floor causes a small object to cast a large shadow, making it easy to find.

Thrifty parts sources
Need a three-speed fan switch? Try pawnshops or garage sales in your area. You can often find appliance parts or old appliances from which you can salvage parts. You can also strip down your own appliances that aren't worth repairing. Save the parts you know are sound, and dump any that are suspect.

Electrical fixes

Won't wiggle off
When joining wires in an appliance such as a vacuum cleaner, use a crimp-on connector. You can buy sets of connectors with their crimping tool from chain stores and hardware dealers. Strip the wires, slip each one into a connector and crimp each end to fix the wires in place.

Outer plastic insulation
Crimped
Inner aluminium connector

Vital spray
Keep a spray can of electrical contact cleaner handy for appliance repairs. A quick burst of this cleaner is often all you need to cure a sticky switch or push button. It is sold by hardware dealers and motor-spares stores. ▼

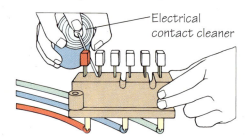
Electrical contact cleaner

USING A MULTITESTER

A multitester, or volt-ohm meter (VOM), is a battery-operated tester that can tell you whether an electrical part, such as a power cord, switch, or heating element, is good or defective. The tester may look complex, but most tests are simple.

The most common test is for electrical continuity. A continuity test can locate shorts or open (interrupted) circuits. You can also test for resistance to electricity flow, which occurs in heating elements and other parts. Both tests are made using the ohm (Ω) scale (usually set for RX1 on a non-autoranging model). A reading of zero or near zero (less than .05 ohms) signals a complete circuit. The circuit is incomplete when the reading is infinite resistance—infinity (∞) on an analogue (non-digital) meter, or a flashing number or other indicator (check the manual) on a digital VOM.

The DC volt scales let you check a battery voltage or a low-voltage system such as a doorbell. The AC volt scale can measure house current, but it's safest not to do this.

To set up a multitester, insert the red lead into the appropriate positive (+) jack and the black lead into the negative (–) jack. "Zero" an analogue meter (p 199): touch the probes together and turn the adjustment knob until the needle is on zero.

These testers are available from hardware dealers.

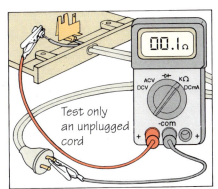

Check a power cord one wire at a time. Set the meter for ohms (Ω). Touch one probe to a disconnected lead and the other to each plug prong in turn. A zero or very low reading on only one prong shows continuity. There is an open circuit if both prongs show infinite resistance, a possible short if both read zero or near zero.

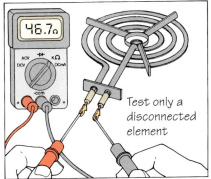

To test a stove element for resistance, set the meter for ohms (Ω). Touch the probes to the element's two terminals. The reading should be between 20 and 100 ohms. If it's much higher, the element is defective and may have an open circuit. If lower, it may have a short. Test also for an earth fault (below, left).

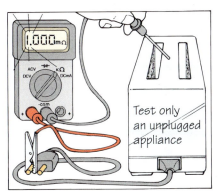

Always check a repaired appliance for an earth fault—a dangerous current leakage. Set the meter for ohms (Ω). Touch one probe to a metal part on the body and the other to each plug pin in turn. The meter should show infinite resistance on both short pins. The earth pin should read zero or near zero.

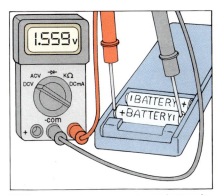

For greatest accuracy, test a battery's voltage while it's powering a device. Select a DC volt setting slightly higher than the battery's rating, and touch the probes to the battery's terminals (red to + and black to –). If the DC volt scale reading is much below the battery's rating, replace or recharge the battery.

APPLIANCE REPAIR TIPS

Gaining access

Nameplate coverup
Have you taken out every visible screw from a small appliance and it still won't open? Look for screws hidden under the manufacturer's nameplate. Remove the plate's mounting screws, or if the plate is glued on, carefully prise it off with a screwdriver. Stick-on labels or metal facings may also conceal screws. Rub your fingers over them to find the screws. If you feel one, lift a corner of the label and peel it back. ▼

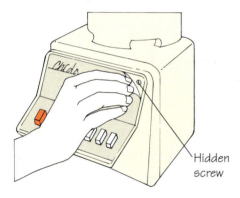

Secret screws
Sometimes an access screw is hiding under a plastic plug set flush with the surface of an appliance's housing. Insert the tip of a small screwdriver into the seam around the plug to prise it out.

Underfoot screws
Also look for screws hiding inside an appliance's feet, especially rubber or plastic feet that fit into holes on the housing. Often you can pop them out with your fingers or a small screwdriver. ▼

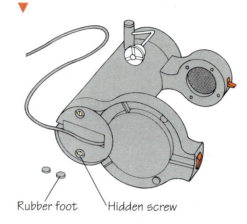

Interlocked
No signs of a screw? The plastic covers on some small appliances are held together by interlocking posts and holes. Look for the tops of posts projecting from one part through another. Prise open a nearby seam to pop the posts out of the holes. ▼

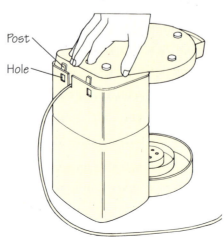

Tough to crack open
Tabs and notches just under the seam often hold small appliance housings together. Pressing the tab side of the seam inwards will often free the tab from the notch. If necessary, slip the tip of a small screwdriver into the seam and gently prise the pieces apart. If there are several tabs, work your way around the seam, opening one tab at a time. ▼

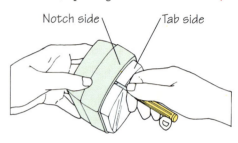

Taking things apart

Easy does it
When disassembling appliances with moving elements, remember that nuts and bolts on rotating parts may have left-hand threads. If a part doesn't loosen when turned in the normal anticlockwise direction, try turning it clockwise. Forcing it the wrong way will strip the threads.

Back off a minute
If you are having trouble getting a screw to go back into an item, don't force it in. Instead, stop and very lightly turn the screw anticlockwise until you hear a click or feel the screw drop slightly. Gently turning a screw in the wrong direction like this is often the easiest way to literally get it back in the groove. After that, it should go in easily.

Paper clip to the rescue

Switches often have self-locking terminals that clamp onto a wire when it is inserted. To free a wire from this type of terminal, just insert a straightened paper clip and pull the wire out.

Quick disconnect

Don't pull off a quick-connect terminal; you're likely to damage the wire. Push it off with a screwdriver instead. ▼

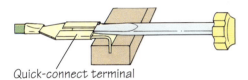

Small appliances

Save your sole

Got an iron with a dull soleplate? As long as it's not aluminium and doesn't have a nonstick coating, you can revive it. Mix 2 tablespoons of salt with enough water to form a paste. With the iron unplugged, rub the paste on the soleplate with crumpled newspaper; then wipe it clean with a damp paper towel. ▼

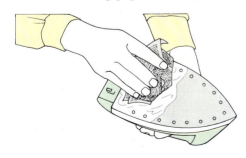

SHOCK-FREE REPAIRS

Worried about getting a serious shock from an appliance you have just repaired? Keep it from happening by testing the appliance for an earth fault (a current leakage, as when a bare wire touches a metal housing). With a large appliance, it's easiest to use a multitester (p 253). But you can test a more portable appliance using a test light with crocodile-clip leads. Before plugging in the appliance, connect one lead of the test light to a bare metal spot on the appliance, and the other lead to an earthing element—a metal cold-water pipe, for example. With the appliance still unplugged, switch it on. Then plug it in. If the test light glows, the appliance has an earth fault and is dangerous. Pull the plug out—do not touch the appliance's on-off switch.

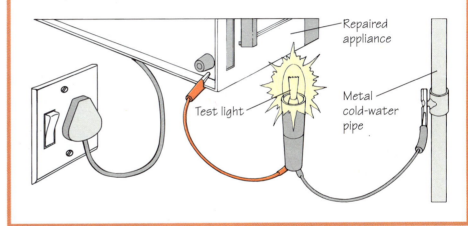

No greasy shower

After you oil a fan, put a paper bag over it and turn it on for a few minutes. Any oil the fan throws off will hit the bag instead of being flung around the room.

Don't slam it against the wall

Is the whirring of an electric clock driving you mad? Turn it upside down for a few hours. Or unplug it and put it in a slightly warm oven (under 65°C) for an hour. Either action will help redistribute the lubricant in the clock, quietening it.

Icy coil insight

If your air conditioner's coils get frosty, chances are you're running it when the temperature is below 20°C. You could try to get a new unit with a control to stop it icing up. Meanwhile, plug your present unit, which in all likelihood doesn't have this control, into a timer. Set it to switch the unit on and off. For example, let it run for 4 hours and stay off for 1 hour—or whatever other combination works for you. The pause gives the ice time to melt.

REFRIGERATORS AND FREEZERS

Refrigerator problems

Shaken up
Your refrigerator won't run after you've moved it around? It's probably just a loose wire. Unplug the power cord, remove the back service panel, and systematically check each wire. When you find one that's fallen off a terminal, simply reattach it.

On the level
To work at its peak efficiency, a freezer or refrigerator should be as level as possible. Some models have adjustable feet, but if your unit doesn't have them, put it on a sheet of plywood or chipboard about 12 mm thick, cut to fit neatly under the unit. Jam small wood wedges between the board and the floor to level the unit. Paint the board to match the unit.

Light leaks
To see if a refrigerator door gasket is forming a tight seal, put a 150 W outdoor floodlight in the compartment and shine it toward one side at a time with the cord coming out near the opposite side. With the door closed and the kitchen lights off, look for light leaks. ▼

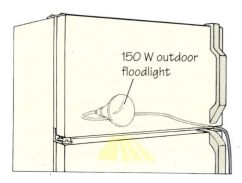

Gasket fix-up
You can often fix a single small crack in the gasket around a refrigerator door with silicone caulk. Roll the gasket open (see Step 1, facing page) and apply the caulk to the inside of the gasket, being careful not to apply too much. Use only caulk whose label's fine print indicates it's safe for contact with food.

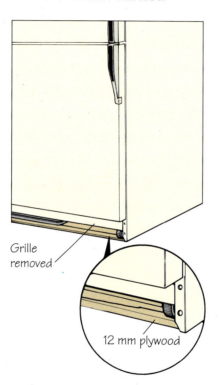

Open and shut ▲
Do your kids always leave the refrigerator door slightly ajar? Put a piece of 12 mm plywood under the front feet. The board won't show behind the grille, and the tilt is too small to be noticeable, but still enough to shut the door. However, don't do this if you have an automatic ice maker, which requires the unit to be perfectly level.

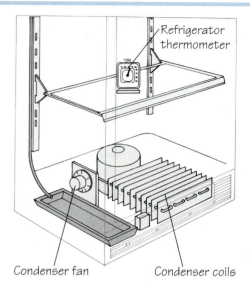

Fridge under the weather ▲
Food not keeping well in your refrigerator? Put a refrigerator thermometer in the centre of the food compartment and leave it overnight. It should read between 1°C and 5°C. If you can't maintain this temperature by adjusting the refrigerator's thermostat, check for clogged condenser coils under the unit or on the back of it. Also look for an obstructed or defective condenser fan underneath.

Another use for ice cream
To check a freezer's temperature, put a refrigerator thermometer on top of a carton of ice cream or frozen food and leave it for a day. Look for a reading around -18°C. Actually, ice cream alone can tell you if a freezer is at the right temperature. If the ice cream is firmly solid without being rock hard, the temperature is fine.

Slippery ice cubes

Do ice cubes stick to the tray of your automatic ice maker? Take out the tray, and wash and dry it well. Then lightly coat the inside with nonstick cooking spray, and wipe off any excess. The cubes will slide right out, and there will be no aftertaste. It lasts longer than vinegar, which is often recommended as a solution to this problem.

Frosty tubes

If there's frost on one of the tubes running into your fridge's compressor, it probably melts regularly, leaving a messy puddle. The solution is to cover the tube with a foam sleeve or wrap-around insulation. Try air-conditioning companies for this material. The tube is the suction line from the evaporator coils inside the unit. Its location may vary from unit to unit. ▼

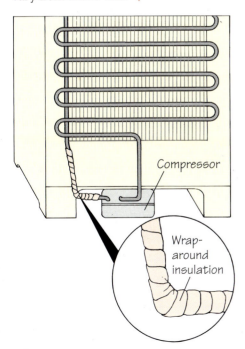

NEW DOOR GASKET

A damaged refrigerator door gasket wastes energy but replacing one is easy. Order the gasket ahead of time. Your local appliance store may not stock one for your refrigerator model but can order it for you. Most gaskets are held by a retainer strip and screws, although some simply slip under a retainer and others are held only by screws. When installing a new gasket, don't overtighten the screws; they can crack the plastic door liner. Tighten the screws slightly, then close the door and gently twist it if necessary to conform it to the cabinet; then tighten the screws properly.

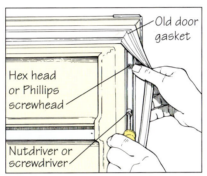

1 Roll the gasket back and loosen—but do not remove the screws. Slip the gasket from under the retainer. Before installing the new gasket, inspect it. If it is crimped, soak it in hot tap water for a few minutes.

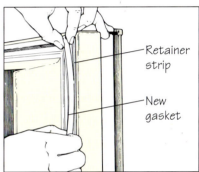

2 Position the new gasket over the retainer corners at the door top. On each side, start at one corner and slide the gasket under the retainer. Carefully tighten the screws at each side's centre, then do the corners, then in between.

Preventing emergencies

Safety light

A tripped circuit breaker could turn the food in your freezer into a soggy, spoiled mass before you discover it. To avoid this, put a low-wattage night-light in the same wall outlet as the freezer. You'll be able to see immediately when the power is off. An electric clock can also serve to give notice of a failure.

Avoiding a meltdown

If your area has power failures, keep your freezer full, packing empty spaces with cool-box freezer packs or plastic bottles of frozen water. If there's a prolonged failure, 10 kg of dry ice will keep a large freezer cold enough for about three days. The Yellow Pages "Ice Distributors" category lists sources of ice and dry ice. Put layers of newspaper between your food and the latter, and wear gloves when handling it.

Household Repairs / 257

DISHWASHERS AND STOVES

Dishwashers

Rusty rack fix
Is the plastic coating peeling off the racks in your dishwasher? Cover them with pieces of flexible, clear plastic tubing. For most racks, tubing with an outside diameter of 6 mm and an inside diameter of 3 mm works well. Cut it into 10 mm lengths and slip them over the rusted rack ends. ▼

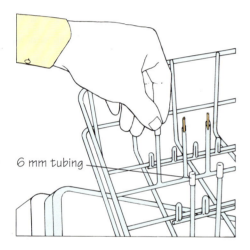
6 mm tubing

Another rack saver
You can also touch up a rusty dishwasher rack with paint, but unless you remove all the rust, it will simply crack the paint again and continue spreading. Treat the rusted areas and those where the paint is even slightly cracked with a rust inhibitor (available from hardware dealers) before repainting with at least two coats of a good-quality enamel. Use a rust inhibitor that actually coats and seals the bare metal areas. After you have repainted the rack, slip lengths of tube over those parts of the rack that will take a beating.

Rusty machine
Iron in the water is the usual cause of blotchy yellow or brown stains in a dishwasher. To remove the stains, let the empty machine fill, add a cup of citric acid crystals, and run it through a cycle. For a permanent solution, put an iron filter on your water supply.

Chalky chaser
To remove the chalky mineral deposits on your dishwasher's interior, let the empty machine fill, put in a cup of white vinegar, and run it through a cycle. Then add detergent and run it through another cycle. But don't do this too often; vinegar is an acid, and excessive use of it could damage the enamel.

Don't be a mug
If the part of the rack for glasses, cups and mugs is level, you will find that the concave base of each will hold water, so you will still have to dry each one. Bend the supports slightly so that these items are held at an angle—no water will be trapped and the items will dry properly.

Black marks
If your dishes have mysterious black smears, it may be the result of metal, especially aluminium utensils, rubbing against them. Separate pots and dishes when you load the dishwasher, but don't put in throw-away aluminium items. The thin aluminium coating breaks down under the heat, and marks dishes.

Beware
Certain plastics, ivory and finishes can be damaged by hot water. Wash these items separately, turning the temperature down to avoid damaging them.

Replacing parts

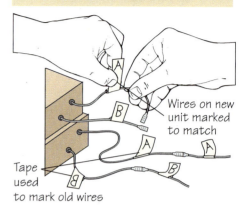
Wires on new unit marked to match
Tape used to mark old wires

On your marks, go for the tape ▲
One of the biggest mistakes you can make when replacing any defective part is mixing up the wiring, which can have expensive, if not deadly, consequences. So, mark each wire *and* its associated terminal with dots, lines, symbols or numbers *before* removing the old part. Then check the new part carefully against the old, ensuring it's identical (a newer version may have rearranged components), and transfer the markings on the old part to the corresponding components on the new. Now, connecting the new part is simple: match the marks. If, however, the replacement part has a new arrangement, and you are in any doubt as to what goes where, call in a qualified and licensed electrician. ▼

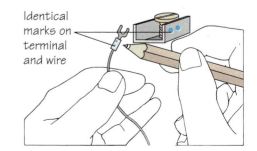
Identical marks on terminal and wire

Electric stoves

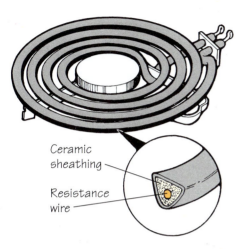

Hot spot ▲

If a stove element develops a spot that glows brighter than the rest of the coil, the ceramic insulation sheathing has broken down, exposing the Nichrome resistance wire inside. The element may continue working for a while, but it's best to replace it at once. The hot spot could damage your cookware.

Forget foil

Covering the floor of your electric oven with aluminium foil to catch drips may sound like a good idea, but don't do it. Foil reflects and intensifies heat, which can cause the baking element to burn out prematurely. Don't cover a rack with foil either. This traps heat in the bottom of the oven and keeps it from reaching the heat sensor near the top. The overheating in the bottom could damage not only the element but the oven lining and the oven-door glass as well. It can also affect cooking times.

OVEN ELEMENTS

Having a burnt-out element in an electric stove replaced can be expensive, but takes only a few minutes to do yourself. Buy a new element for your stove model from the service agent for that make of stove, or from an electrical dealer. If your oven has a door that lifts off, remove the door, if necessary, to gain easier access to the interior. Switch off the mains power and only then start work. Before disconnecting any wire, mark it and its terminal (p 258).

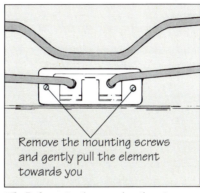

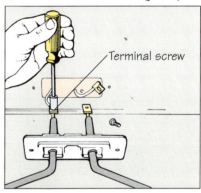

1 Before starting, unplug the stove or switch off the circuit at the main distribution board. Remove the mounting screws and pull the element out until the terminals are accessible.

2 Disconnect the wires from the terminal screws or slip-on clips, noting which wire goes onto which terminal. Attach the wires to the new element, and screw the bracket into place.

Avoid fuss with fuses ▶

When you buy an electric stove, make it one of your first duties to see where the fuses are situated. Then buy a spare for each fuse and store them in a nearby drawer or, if there is space, next to the existing fuses. If a ring or hotplate on your stove suddenly stops working, the problem is most likely to be a blown fuse—and the replacement will be right there. Make sure you replace the blown fuse with one of the same rating. If it immediately blows again, turn the stove off and have it checked by a qualified and licensed electrician.

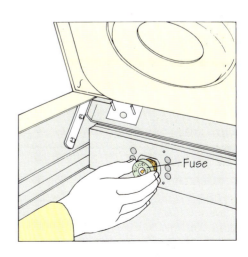

Household Repairs / 259

WASHING MACHINES AND DRYERS

Washing machines

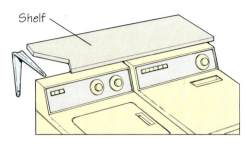
Shelf

Bridging the gap ▲
Are you always dropping or spilling things into the no-man's-land behind your washer and dryer? There's no way to eliminate the gap; the machines must stand away from the wall because of the washer hoses and the dryer vent. An easy solution is to cover the space with a shelf mounted on brackets. As an added bonus it'll give you a place to put detergent boxes, bleach bottles and other laundry-room clutter.

Lint trap
To avoid plugging drains with lint from the washer, secure an old thin sock or pantihose foot to the end of the drain hose with a strong rubber band. When the washer drains, the sock will collect any lint in the water. Turn the sock inside out to clean it. ▼

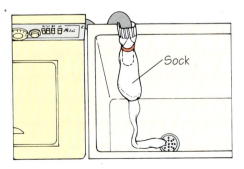
Sock

Fabric snagger
Is there something in your washing machine that's catching on your clothes? Rub an old pantihose over the spindle and the tub surface. Smooth any rough spot you find with very fine sandpaper.

Car tool to the rescue
If you can't remove the cap holding your washer spindle, try turning it with an automotive oil-filter wrench. This tool has a flexible strap that can be adjusted to fit a round object snugly. ▼

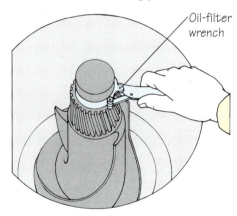
Oil-filter wrench

Beat that rust
Some washing machines have metal feet that eventually rust because the floor they rest on is often awash or damp. Cut four squares of wood 16 or 22 mm thick and about 50 mm along each edge and apply two or three coats of marine varnish or white enamel paint to each. Attach them to the feet of the washing machine with glue or screws—paint the screws and the holes in the washing machine's metal as well. Your washing machine will be level and the feet will be kept clear of water on the floor, which will prolong their life, and your machine's.

Dryers

Thermostat sizzle test
A defective thermostat may prevent a dryer from heating. Test the unit first at room temperature: unplug the dryer, disconnect a lead from a terminal on the unit's thermostat and hold a multitester's probes to the thermostat's terminals; the meter should read zero or close to it. Next, remove the thermostat and place it in an electric frying pan. Heat the pan to just above the temperature (stamped on the thermostat) at which the contacts should open, or until the thermostat clicks. Put the probes on the terminals. Look for a reading of infinite resistance or infinity (∞).

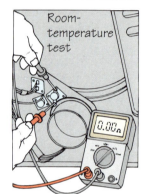
Room-temperature test

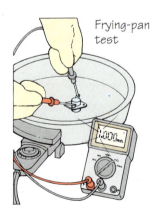
Frying-pan test

Stop grumbling
If the dryer drum makes a "grumbling" noise while rotating, it may only be bearing on the front housing. A couple of wedges to raise the front of the unit slightly may fix the problem.

REPLACING A DRYER DRIVE BELT

Most dryers' drums are turned by a drive belt that wraps completely around the drum. A worn belt will produce a thumping noise while the dryer is running. A broken one will not turn the drum at all. In either case replacement is in order, and it's an easy job. Buy a manufacturer's replacement belt from the service company; order it using the model number of your dryer—the metal plate giving this and other details is usally fixed to the back of the unit.

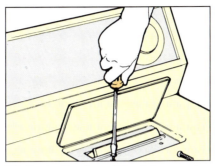

1 Unplug the dryer. If the lint screen is on the top, remove it and unscrew the screen housing. Then remove the screws fixing the top to the unit.

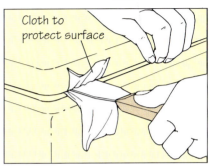

2 Slip a putty knife under the top about 50 mm from a front corner. Push it in as you pull up to unclip the top. Do the other corners in turn and prise the top off.

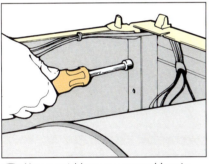

3 Use a nutdriver or a screwdriver to remove the fasteners holding the front panel. If there is a toeplate, remove it by taking out its clips or screws.

4 Remove the old belt. Using the wear marks as a guide, put the new belt around the drum with the ribbed side innermost against the drum.

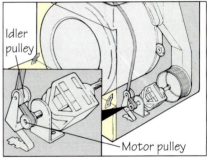

5 At the motor, slide the belt under the idler pulley and around the motor pulley. If the old belt broke, the spring-loaded idler will have popped out of position.

Keep hot air safely flowing ▶
If your dryer is under a shelf or counter, moisture may cause the wood to deteriorate, and corrosion of metal fittings. Install a duct of rectangular PVC so that moist air from the dryer is vented away from it. Make sure the duct is at least as large as the vent on the back of the unit. Attach it to the vent and side with glue or screws.

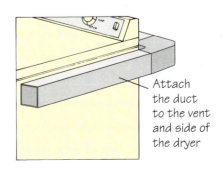

On the move
If there's no space for a duct, as on the left, try fitting casters to the feet of the dryer. When operating the unit, just roll it out from under the countertop and push it back in once the job is done. The tumbling motion of the drum is not vigorous enough to cause the unit to wander.

ELECTRONIC EQUIPMENT

Setting up

The art of concealment
Transform that jungle of wires behind your TV, VCR, decoder or stereo into a neat, attractive cable. You can use a variation of the Cord Hanger (see p 51): cut short lengths of hose (about 50 mm long), slit them diagonally and slip them over the cords. Another method is this: just clip the plugs from an old coiled telephone cord and wrap the coils around the wires.

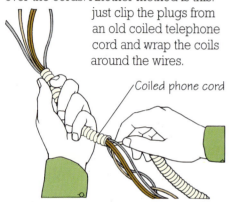
Coiled phone cord

Cool it
In theory, putting a VCR on top of a TV set is a no-no, because heat from the TV could damage the VCR. But if there's no other convenient spot for the VCR, cut four small spacers from 6 mm plywood, paint them flat black and put one under each VCR foot. They'll be practically invisible on cabinets of any colour and will let the TV heat escape.

Underfoot fire hazard
When laying speaker cord from one side of a room to another, or between rooms, attach it to the top of the skirting board. Don't lay it under carpets—you will tread on it. Eventually the insulation may break, you will need new wires and fire is likely to be a major hazard.

Have your cake and eat it too
It often happens, particularly in this age of VCRs and satellite (plus a variety of channels), that a number of members of the family each want to watch different programmes. This often causes a great deal of strife in the home. A solution is to link a second or third television set (if you have more than one in the house) to the system. The path is: from the aerial to the decoder, decoder to VCR, VCR to set. Plug in a splitter connector between the VCR and the set and run a cord from it to a second set. You will now be able to watch a video while another family member watches the news on the other set in another room. Run the cables through the ceiling space to hide them. Don't try to split the signal to too many sets—the quality of the signal received by all the sets can be affected. ▼

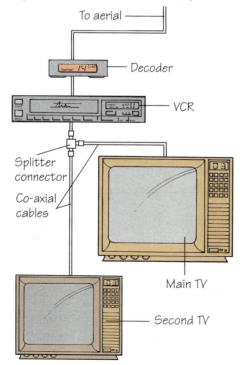

Improving quality

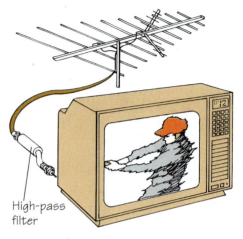
High-pass filter

Ham problem ▲
If your TV develops wavering lines occasionally for no apparent reason, the cause may be a ham radio operator, especially if it happens on VHF channels and not on UHF ones. To correct the problem, install a high-pass filter—sold by electronics dealers—between the set and its aerial wire. If possible, try to borrow a filter to confirm that it will solve the problem, before going to the expense of buying one.

Mind your head
The easiest way to clean VCR heads is to use a video cassette cleaning tape. The "wet" type requires you to place a few drops of cleaning solution on the tape. Run it through the machine like a regular cassette and it will do the job in about 30 seconds. How often? After 40 to 50 hours of use. That's every month if you watch five movies a week; every six months if you average one movie a week. Be sure to allow enough time for the heads to dry properly afterwards.

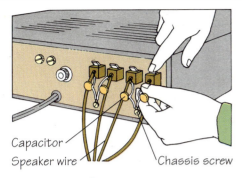

Capacitor
Speaker wire
Chassis screw

Not so good, buddy ▲

If your stereo picks up someone's CB radio, install capacitors on the speaker outlets. Get four 0,01–0,3 microfarad (mfd) disc capacitors at an electronics dealer. There are usually four outlets, two for each speaker. With your stereo unplugged, insert one capacitor wire into each outlet along with the speaker wire lead. Attach the capacitor's other wire to a chassis screw to earth it.

Wide receiver

If you need better radio reception in a room with a suspended ceiling, attach the bare end of the aerial wire to the metal gridwork supporting the ceiling.

Moving computers

Computer wrap

If you have to move a computer any distance, pack it into the original cartons, if possible. Otherwise, pack it as snugly as you can into other cartons, using crumpled paper on all sides to cushion the units. Never wrap a computer in plastic. Condensation can form on the inside of the plastic and damage the computer.

Always back up

Moving a personal computer can be a tricky business, especially because you risk losing any valuable information stored in it. Even if it's handled carefully, a computer hard drive can be damaged by being jarred in a moving van or truck. To lessen the chances of losing data, copy whatever is stored on your hard drive onto backup disks and carry them separately to the new location.

Making repairs

Save a cassette ▲

Has a favourite irreplaceable audio cassette tape snapped? Fix it with a splicing kit from an electronics dealer. If either end of the tape is inside the cassette and the cassette case can't be unscrewed, get an empty cassette case. Then carefully prise apart the old case, transfer the tape to the new case, splice the broken ends and snap the new case shut. Now might also be a good time to make a copy of the tape and use that, while keeping the old tape as a master copy. The same procedure can also be followed with valued video tapes.

Mini probe

When using a multitester to check a circuit, you may sometimes find the instrument's probes are too large for tiny contacts. The solution is to put a crocodile clip on the multitester probe and use a sewing needle in the clip to reach the contacts and terminals. ▼

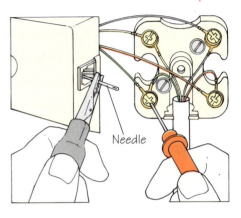

Needle

Torn speaker

To fix a ripped speaker cone—for a while, at least—take it out of the cabinet and cut a patch from a paper coffee filter—but don't make the patch too big. Coat one side of it liberally with rubber cement. Holding the back of the cone with one hand, gently apply the patch to the front and rub lightly to smooth it. Let the cement dry before reinstalling the speaker. If the tear is very small, however, you could try using the cement only.

Coffee filter patch

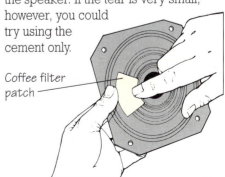

CHAPTER 9
YARD AND GARDEN

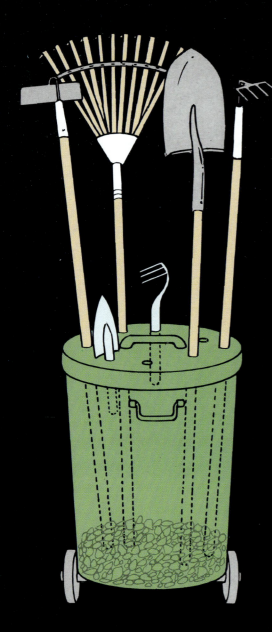

PLANTING A GARDEN 265
LANDSCAPING 268
HANDLING WEEDS, INSECTS, AND ANIMALS 270
EASIER GARDENING 272
ESTABLISHING A LAWN 273
LAWN CARE AND MAINTENANCE 274
TREES AND SHRUBS 276
YARD AND GARDEN TOOLS 280
OUTDOOR POWER TOOLS 282
SETTING POSTS 284
BUILDING AND REPAIRING FENCES 286
BUILDING AND RESTORING DECKS 288
MASONRY AND CONCRETE 290
REPAIRING MASONRY AND CONCRETE 292
GARDEN IMPROVEMENTS 293
SEASONAL CHORES 297
SWIMMING POOLS 298

PLANTING A GARDEN

Breaking ground

Making a bed the easy way
Take a break: let a cover crop prepare your new vegetable beds. The autumn before you intend to plant it, clear the bed, rake it level and sow it with lucerne, cowpeas or agricultural lupins. When this cover crop matures—but before it sets seed—cut it down and dig it into the soil. As it rots, the crop will enrich the bed, while its roots will have already loosened the soil. You can do the same with flower beds, if it doesn't detract too much from your garden.

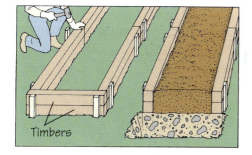

On the rocks ▲
If you'd like a lush garden on a rocky or other inhospitable site, build a raised bed. It can be as long as you like and any shape, but it must be narrow—about 1,2 m across, so that you can work on it from both sides without stepping on the soil. That would compact it and ruin the aeration. Install edging, such as railway sleepers or concrete wall panels. You can make irregular shapes using plastic or timber edging (these are available as rolls of short lengths of decorative timber wired together). Fill the bed with compost-rich topsoil. The drainage will be good and the plants will develop healthy root systems.

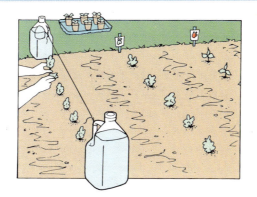

Setting things straight ▲
To establish straight rows in a garden, fill two plastic bottles with water and set one at each end of the row. Then stretch a line between them and move them from row to row. It is easier than driving stakes for the string.

Seedlings

Greenhouses from bottles
Start seeds in 2 litre plastic cooldrink bottles. The type with the black base simply has it removed, the bottle section cut in half and inverted into the base. In the case of the one-piece type, simply cut two in half and tape the one onto the other. The clear lid allows light to pass through, holds moisture in and lets you keep an eye on the sprouting seeds. ▼

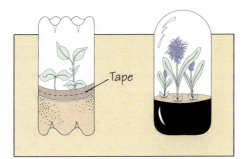

New life for yoghurt cups
Plastic yoghurt cups make handy mini-pots for starting seeds indoors. Punch drainage holes in the bases of the cups. For easy carrying, put the cups on a tray. Fill them with soil and place them on a sunny windowsill. Now they're ready for your seeds. ▼

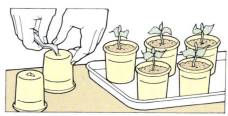

All-weather ID
This inexpensive plant label will always be readable. Cut tags from an old aluminium container or foil pie plate. Put them on a soft surface, such as a towel or some newspaper and use a ballpoint pen to write the plant names on them. Attach them to stakes. The imprints will last for ages.

Quick cover
On chilly nights, protect seedlings from frost (and set the stage for an extra-early crop of flowers or vegetables) with this simple structure. To build it, you need only construct a frame of PVC pipe and cover it with shade cloth or with the plastic sheeting pictured here. This light, sturdy greenhouse can be moved from spot to spot as the need arises, and it is easy to store at the end of the season, particularly if you can disassemble it after use.

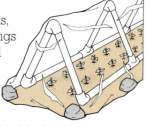

PLANTING A GARDEN

Edgings and trainers

Border posts

Wood edging is attractive, economical and practical as a border around your garden beds. Treat the pieces with a wood preservative and then set them in an overlapped alternating pattern. Drive them into the ground with a protective block of wood and a mallet. ▼

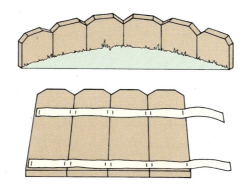

Stay flexible ▲

If you have a curved garden bed that needs a decorative edging, join some wood edging planks by stapling to their backs a couple of heavy-duty plastic strips or wire, such as you might see on a commercial edging. If it is a big bed, assemble about 2 m of edging at a time, leaving a few centimetres of extra wire or plastic at the end of each section. Treat the wood with a preservative, place the sections in a shallow ditch, level them and fill in the ditch with soil.

Movable trellis

Would you like to brighten the side of your house with a vine *and* retain easy access to the wall behind it for painting and repairs? Make up a movable trellis out of a section of concrete reinforcing wire or galvanized fencing and hang it on hooks screwed into the wall. When it's time to work on the house, gently unhook the trellis and rest it on a support such as the stakes shown here. ▼

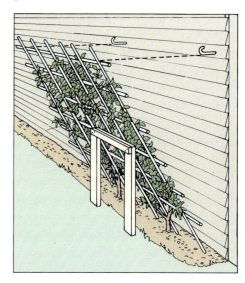

Tongue-and-grooving ▶

You can also use pine tongue-and-groove planks, available from hardware dealers, as an edging. To make them easier to drive in, cut the bottom edges of the planks at a 45° angle. The length of the planks should equal the depth of the roots that you're containing, plus 60 mm for the above-ground section and about 100 mm for the length of the 45° cut. Treat the pieces. Then use a protective block of wood and a mallet to drive the tongue sections into the grooves.

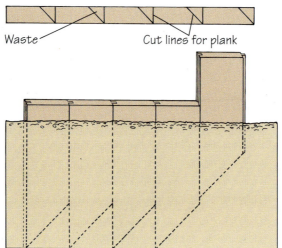

Lampshade support

The metal frame of an old lampshade makes a great freestanding support for top-heavy plants such as carnations. Collect various sizes for plants both large and small.

Making compost

It's in the bag
Rather than fussing with bins and heaps, why not do all your composting in a bag? First fill a heavy-duty rubbish bag with refuse such as grass clippings, leaves and organic kitchen scraps. Add a spadeful of soil and about 30 g of high-nitrogen fertilizer, such as a 3:2:1. Moisten the mixture thoroughly. Seal the bag and set it in a sunny place; roll it over twice a week, taking care not to tear it. In two months (or less) the contents will have turned to humus that will enrich the soil.

Blending in
An easy way to speed up the composting process is to put your collection of fruit and vegetable peels, eggshells and other easily biodegradable scraps in a blender along with a cup of water. (Don't use meat or dairy scraps, as they tend to attract animals.) Purée the scraps and pour the mixture onto the compost pile. The mush will decompose quickly—usually in a few weeks. To minimize the mess, collect the scraps in a small plastic bag and purée them every few days.

Small wonder
If you have a compact garden and don't need a lot of compost, you can use a household plastic laundry basket as a compost bin. Choose one that's an attractive colour and has perforations on the sides. A removable hinged lid will make it easy to add to the pile.

Vegetable gardening

Slinging melons
To make room for more eatables in a small garden, train melon vines on a trellis. As the fruit becomes heavier, support it in a sling made from a cloth or pantihose. Tie the ends in a knot or fasten them together with a safety pin.

Instant shade
Lettuce thrives in cool conditions, but summer heat makes the leaves start to taste bitter. To help prevent this, build a portable shade structure. Connect eight lengths of PVC pipe with four three-way fittings, and cover the frame with 40–50 per cent shade cloth, available from nurseries and hardware stores. The cloth keeps the plants cool as it filters the sunlight. Fold the cloth and take the frame apart during winter. ▼

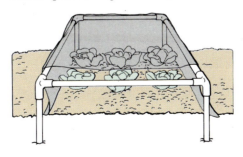

Nourishing nightcap
If you water leafy greens in the evening and then pick them the next morning, they'll be crisp and full of flavour.

THE RIGHT PLANTS FOR THE RIGHT SOIL

The pH scale is used to measure the acidity or alkalinity of the soil, on a scale of 1 to 14. A reading below 7,0 (the neutral point) denotes acidic soil. The lower the reading, the more acidic the soil. Readings over 7,0 denote alkaline soil, and the higher the reading, the more alkaline the soil. Most soils are in the range of 4,5–5,0 and most plants thrive in slightly acid soils, with a pH of 6,5. Most vegetables, however, do best in soils which are slightly alkaline—with a pH level of 7,5. Here are just some examples of plants and the pH levels to which they are best suited:

pH level 4,0–5,5: ajuga, arbutus, blue hydrangea.
pH level 4,5–6,0: azalea, erica, gardenia, potato, rhododendron.
pH level 5,0–6,5: apple, chicory, fuchsia, iris, parsley, violet.
pH level 5,5–6,5: basil, carrot, clematis, pansy, pepper, rose.
pH level 5,5–7,5: aster, cauliflower, garlic, lupin, marigold, parsnip, rhubarb, thyme, zinnia.
pH level 6,0–7,0: abelia, apricot, artichoke, beetroot, broccoli, cabbage, celery, dahlia, lettuce, lobelia, onion, pea, pear, radish.

LANDSCAPING

Planning the garden

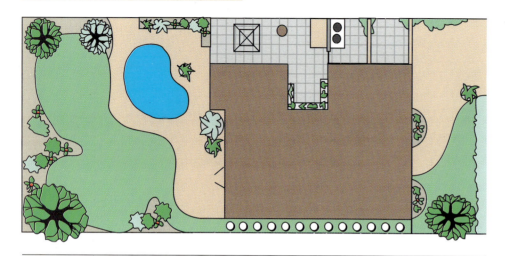

SOME BASIC DO'S AND DON'TS

Perception is reality
▷ Smaller gardens can be made to appear bigger by having larger plants closer to the house and smaller ones nearer the fence. This exaggerates the effect of perspective by making the fence seem more distant.
▷ The starkness of a concrete wall can be relieved by lining it with small plants. But avoid having large plants against a wall—they tend to make the property seem smaller.
▷ Try to make the lawn area as big as possible to give an impression of space.
▷ Terracing on a sloped property can be used to hide a perimeter wall or fence when viewed from the house. This will enhance the impression of space, even in a small garden.
▷ When planting a new lawn on a new property, make it somewhat bigger than planned so that you can adapt its shape and character with greater ease.

Water wonderlands
Like every other garden feature, the shape and surrounds of a fish-pond should suit the general tone of the garden. Try to visit other residences of similar size to your own, with ponds, to obtain an idea of the best size and features to select: a waterfall or fountain can really enhance your pond.

Snap—what an idea!
Taking a few photographs from vantage points can help you plan a garden. They can also help you decide on the best method to hide an ugly building, for example. Take some photographs from different angles and lay clear plastic over them. Draw the various options realistically on the clear plastic. You will have a better idea as to how a tree, trellis or other alternative will achieve the result you're seeking.

Grand plans

A mower-friendly lawn
Mowing will be faster and easier if you eliminate the grass peninsulas and islands that require a lot of turning manoeuvres with the lawn mower, and add to the trimming time. Use your lawn mower to draw a new perimeter that you can mow without a stop. Fill the areas outside the line with mulch, ground cover, and shrubbery.

A low-water landscape
If water is scarce or if your water bills are high, here's how to conserve water.
▷ Landscape with drought-tolerant plants. Ask your local nursery for ideas.
▷ Reduce the lawn area to a minimum. Turf grass is a heavy water-user, so wherever possible replace it with mulch or a drought-tolerant ground cover.
▷ Make pavements permeable. Bricks set in sand let rain soak through to roots below; tarred and concrete surfaces send water to the storm drain.
▷ Group plants with similar water needs.

A visual trick
Give a small yard the illusion of greater space by "forcing the perspective", a technique known to architects. Just angle the plantings towards each other as they extend to the far end of your property.

FOUNDATION PLANTINGS

When you are devising a planting scheme, try several different combinations on paper first. Using graph paper, make a scaled master plan of your house. Include all existing trees, features and other landmarks, all of course to the same scale as the main plan. Use removable (and perhaps colour-coded) stickers to help you mark the plan.

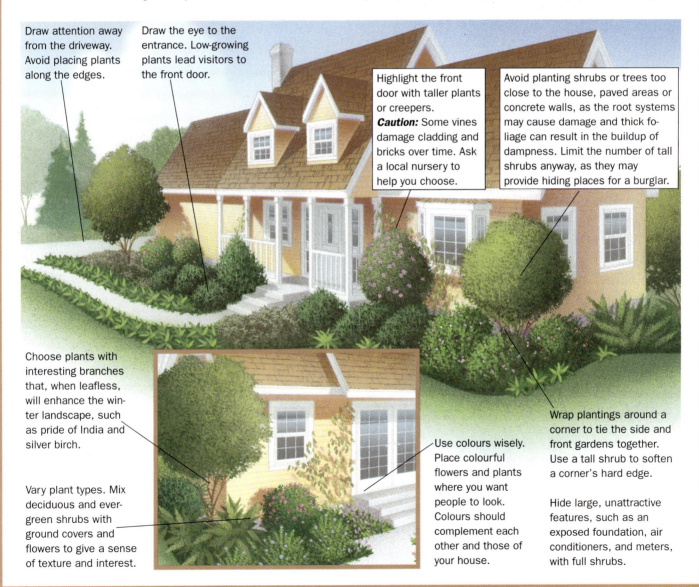

Draw attention away from the driveway. Avoid placing plants along the edges.

Draw the eye to the entrance. Low-growing plants lead visitors to the front door.

Highlight the front door with taller plants or creepers. **Caution:** Some vines damage cladding and bricks over time. Ask a local nursery to help you choose.

Avoid planting shrubs or trees too close to the house, paved areas or concrete walls, as the root systems may cause damage and thick foliage can result in the buildup of dampness. Limit the number of tall shrubs anyway, as they may provide hiding places for a burglar.

Choose plants with interesting branches that, when leafless, will enhance the winter landscape, such as pride of India and silver birch.

Vary plant types. Mix deciduous and evergreen shrubs with ground covers and flowers to give a sense of texture and interest.

Use colours wisely. Place colourful flowers and plants where you want people to look. Colours should complement each other and those of your house.

Wrap plantings around a corner to tie the side and front gardens together. Use a tall shrub to soften a corner's hard edge.

Hide large, unattractive features, such as an exposed foundation, air conditioners, and meters, with full shrubs.

Yard and Garden / 269

HANDLING WEEDS, INSECTS, AND ANIMALS

Weed attack

Weed whacking ▲
You can use a long-handled weeding fork to rid your lawn of dandelions and other weeds. But if you don't have one on hand, whack and grab the pests with the claw of an old hammer and then pull them out, roots and all. The deeper you can grab the roots, the better.

Customizing a hoe
To turn a regular hoe into a versatile tool, file a deep notch into the right side of its blade. With this sharpened V you can delicately snip weeds off at their base, even in the most hard-to-reach corners, by simply levering the handle to the left.

When to weed
Timing can be a great help in your war against the weeds. Wait for a sunny day; then pull out or hoe the weeds (without seed heads) in the morning and leave them lying on the surface of the soil. The sun will wither the weeds and transform them into beneficial organic mulch.

Weeds in concrete
Use piping-hot water to kill weeds that sprout through concrete joints and brick paving—without endangering yourself or wildlife. Boil water in a kettle, pour it into the cracks, and watch the weeds wilt. If you have a lot of weeds, use a watering can or bucket, but be careful not to splash the hot water on yourself.

Pest preventives

Gardening helpers
▷ Landscape with plants that are naturally insect- and disease-resistant, such as lavender. Ask at your nursery or garden centre about varieties that do well locally.
▷ Always plant grass types and other plants that are suited to your area. Plants which are not climatically suited to your garden will be more prone to pests, diseases and other problems.
▷ Reduce soil-borne diseases by varying your flower and vegetable plantings. Rotate the crops, changing the type of plant and its location each season.
▷ Keep your garden free of weeds, dead leaves, and brush—these provide a refuge and breeding place for insect pests and plant diseases.

Mole deterrent
Moles can wreak havoc in the garden. However, though they have poor eyesight, they have a very good sense of smell. Rags soaked in strong-smelling substances such as creosote, or wrapped around old fish heads, and pushed into the runs or holes will discourage them.

Keep them off
If pets, especially cats, are turning your garden into a litter box, sprinkle the area with mothballs. You can also cover the soil in plant pots or small garden beds with chicken mesh. Cats cannot dig through it and they don't like walking on the mesh. Use small stones to keep it clear of the soil surface.

Safe stoppers

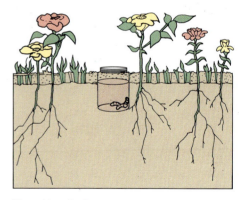

Slug it out ▲
Snails and slugs love beer. Put a small amount in a bottle, tin or jar and seat it in the ground with the rim slightly exposed. The pests will crawl in for a sip and drown. Coarsely crushed eggshells strewn in areas prone to slugs also act as a deterrent.

ATTRACTING THE GOOD GUYS

While many gardeners strive to rid their gardens of insect and animal pests, others go to great lengths to entice visitors from the animal kingdom to their gardens. Below is a sample of who is invited, how they are encouraged to come, and why.

ANIMAL TYPE	SHELTER AND ENVIRONMENT	FOOD AND WATER	BENEFITS TO GARDEN
Birds of all types	Build nesting boxes; leave dead trees in place for nests; offer protective shelter of large shrubs, hedges and trees; provide sources of drinking water.	Plant berry-laden bushes, fruiting vines, and trees that produce nuts and berries; set out bird feeders with seeds, suet, and peanut butter and maizemeal balls; provide small pools of water.	Eat insects; provide nature-watching opportunities.
Butterflies	Leave areas of tall grass and some small indigenous weeds; install windbreak in warm sunny spot; provide large, flat rock for sunning; keep birdbaths and bird feeders at a distance; grow plants that attract butterflies, such as plectranthus, daisies and salvia.	Plant milkweed, rue and wild peach for them to feed on; use butterfly attractant plants such as mint, borage, buddleia, thyme and catmint.	Offer nature-watching opportunities; enhance beauty of the garden.
Earthworms	Create soil rich in organic matter; refrain from using pesticides.	Mix organic matter into soil; add a layer of mulch to keep soil moist.	Burrow constantly into soil, tilling and aerating it; ingest organic waste and deposit humus-rich castings in soil.

Easy wasp control

The smell of vinegar attracts wasps. To cure a wasp problem, put 50 mm of vinegar in a long-necked bottle. They'll crawl in and won't be able to crawl out.

Go for garlic

Strong-smelling garlic can make a useful homemade spray for aphids, snails, caterpillars and cabbage moths. Roughly chop up three large heads of garlic, put them in a blender with six teaspoonfuls of medicinal paraffin oil, or rub them through a grater. Put the pulp in a bowl and leave it for 48 hours. Then melt one tablespoonful of oil-base soap in 500 ml of warm water and mix it with the garlic pulp. Mix two tablespoonfuls of the solution with two litres of water and spray plants thoroughly every three to four days.

Oily spray

Mixing vegetable oil and non-detergent liquid soap makes another effective, inexpensive, and nontoxic spray that is fatal to aphids, spider mites, scales, mealy bugs, and some caterpillars. Mix 1 cup of cooking oil with 1 tablespoon liquid soap; then dilute it, using 1 teaspoon of oil-soap mixture for each cup of water. Spray the leaves as for soap spray, but only when air temperatures are below 30°C. If it's hotter than that, the oil can damage some foliage. The spray is effective against eggs as well as adult insects.

Wash away

Many smaller pests, such as aphids, can be dislodged with a jet of water. Spray both surfaces of the leaves. Water also helps to deter red spider mite.

Insect allies

Some insects are on your side. Dragonflies and spiders eat thousands of harmful insects, including mosquitoes, and consume great numbers of other insects, such as aphids. ▼

EASIER GARDENING

Lifesavers

Latex liners
Your cloth gardening gloves protect you from thorns, but they don't help much against cold and damp. To boost their insulation value, slip your hands first into a pair of lightweight latex gloves. These will keep your hands warm and dry, and you'll hardly know they are there.

Keep those nails clean
Stop dirt and grime getting under your nails when you are engaged in tasks that are difficult when wearing gloves. Pull your fingertips over a bar of cheap soap so that it lodges under your nails. No dirt can get in, and cleaning up is quick and easy.

Knee protectors
Much of a gardener's work is done on the hands and knees, and that can cause joints to ache. To combat the problem, make a kneepad out of a piece of rigid foam insulation about 450 mm square and 30 to 40 mm thick. Wrap the pad in a plastic refuse bag. The foam not only serves as a cushion, it also reflects body heat and protects your knees against the cold. ▼

Child's play
Another device that can save you from the discomfort of squatting or kneeling is your child's tricycle. Turn it around so that you are seated on it backwards and you'll find yourself at exactly the right level to get your fingers down into the dirt. And when you've finished weeding or planting one patch, you can push yourself along to the next one.

Circle gardens
A further way to minimize bending and kneeling is to confine your most work-intensive garden beds to small-diameter circles, say 600 mm to 1 m. You'll be able to reach the entire garden without a lot of effort and do most of the work sitting down.

Kinder tools

A blister-proof rake
Does leaf raking leave your hands raw with blisters? The cure for that is to pad the handle with ordinary pipe insulation—use the type designed for 20 mm copper pipe. Coat the rake's handle with contact cement, cut the insulation to length, and slip it on.

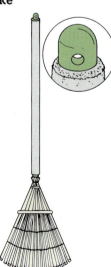

Tall tools
Be good to your back by standing up while weeding and planting bulbs. All you'll need are a few tools with long handles, which are available at garden centres and hardware dealers.

A back-saving sledge ▶
Heaving a heavy weight into a wheelbarrow or garden cart can strain your back badly. The next time you need to move a big rock, tree, or shrub, make a simple sledge out of a scrap piece of 6 mm plywood. Drill a pair of holes in one end of the plywood and attach a loop of rope. Roll your load onto the sledge and pull. You'll find that it will slide easily across the lawn without damaging the grass—or your back.

Softer stepping
To cushion your foot as you dig, slip a piece of old garden hose over the shoulder of the shovel where you step on it.

ESTABLISHING A LAWN

Better spreading

Sowing in the wind
Even a moderate breeze scatters seed as it drops out of the spreader, and that means gaps in your new lawn. Try mixing the seed with barely damp, clean sand. The weight of the sand will help shield the seeds from the wind and enable them to fall where intended.

Crisscross coverage
It is crucial to spread seed and fertilizer evenly. Try setting the spreader application rate at half of what is recommended on the package and then make twice as many passes. Work back and forth across the whole lawn from left to right; then turn and repeat the process at a right angle to the first passes. This is a bit more work, but you'll eliminate gaps and surpluses in your spreading. ▼

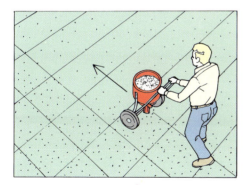

Flour power
It's often hard to tell which areas have been covered with fertilizer or seed. Mixing some kitchen flour with the product before you spread it will mark what you've covered without harming the lawn or the wildlife, and it will disappear with the first rain or watering.

Nourishing thoughts

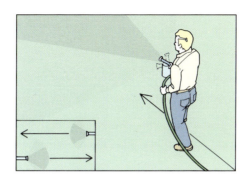

Spray 'n walk ▲
Spraying a liquid fertilizer greatly reduces the likelihood of fertilizer burn. All you have to do to avoid burning your grass is to wet the lawn before you spray, or water it immediately afterwards. To apply the fertilizer, connect a sprayer to a garden hose. Walk in a straight line fairly slowly and move the spray nozzle back and forth.

Lawn planting

Sods versus seed
Using grass sods rather than grass runners will provide an "instant" lawn that will be ready for light traffic in a couple of weeks. It is not surprising, then, that grass sods are expensive. If you do the job yourself, expect to pay about twice as much per square metre as for runners or seed, and hiring a professional to do it will double the cost again. Whatever your choice, prepare the soil well. For sods, loosen it to ensure the roots can get a good grip.

A quick pickup
Pause in your passes with the spreader for a moment, and it will probably dump a fertilizer overdose that kills the turf below. To quickly remove the spill before it does any harm, use your workshop vacuum cleaner. If it's grass seed you spilled, clean out the vacuum canister first; then you can retrieve the wasted seed.

Aerating shoes
Aerate your lawn the easy way: make up a pair of attachments as shown, using doubled-up 6 mm plywood with 50 mm nails through the lower sections. Glue these to their matching upper sections. Tapes are used to tie them to your work shoes. As you walk, you work. ▼

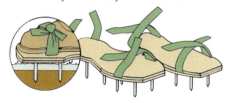

Rolling out the carpet
Sod is delivered in strips that are rolled and stacked. As you roll out your new lawn, stagger the ends of the strips, the way you would for bricklaying. In addition, make sure that the edges of each strip butt tightly against the previously laid strip. A snug fit will minimize any gaps in the lawn and will keep the strips from drying out too quickly.

Make a stand
If you stand on a board or piece of plywood as you lay the strips, you won't disturb the soil you've worked so hard to prepare.

LAWN CARE AND MAINTENANCE

Mowing

Clippings controversy
To remove lawn clippings after mowing, or leave them on the lawn, is a hotly debated issue. If you mow your lawn frequently, so that there is never a large amount of clippings, they could be left on the lawn. If, however, mowing is infrequent, the layer of clippings should be removed as they can build up into a thick "thatch" which can harbour pests and fungal diseases.

Working against gravity
Cutting the grass on a slope or bank can be a dangerous business—one slip and your foot may end up in the lawn mower. Mowing across the slope, rather than up and down, minimizes the danger. And to be extra-safe, why not put on a pair of cleated golf or sports shoes first?

Push a reel lawn mower
Consider a manual reel lawn mower rather than a powered model. Today's versions look like the mowers of ages past but in fact are much improved. New models are lighter, self-sharpening, and more manoeuvrable. They also cut the grass blades cleanly and quietly—so you have little risk of disturbing your neighbours—which means you can mow at virtually any time. But because you have to push this quiet cutter, you'll be happier if your lawn is not too large to handle and relatively level.

That blade is blunt
If the grass develops a straw-coloured tinge a day or two after mowing, it's a signal that your lawnmower blades need sharpening. Look closely and you'll find that the tips of the grass blades have been shredded rather than neatly sliced. Those ragged ends not only look bad, they provide easy entry for turf diseases. For hints on sharpening garden tools, see p 281.

Patching

Seasonal seeding
In areas where the common lawn grasses go dormant in winter, you can spread lawn seed mixtures to cover the spaces and give you a green winter lawn. The same applies to shady areas where the lawn dies down in cold or wet weather.

Set the height ▶
Mowing by the calendar won't help your lawn; it doesn't care how many days it's been since the last cut. You'll work less and have a healthier lawn if you let the grass decide when to mow. Set the lawn mower to the right height for the grass: usually 10 to 20 mm for couch grasses, and about 30 to 40 mm for coarse grasses and cool-season varieties. Cut often enough so that you never remove more than one-third of the grass blades. Taking more will shock and weaken the root system.

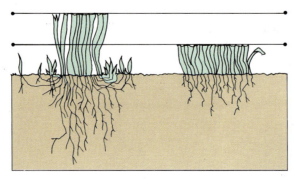

Correct mowing height, with healthy root growth

Closer mowing height, with shallow roots that need more food and water

Coffee tin spreader
When it's time to reseed bare spots you may find seed goes everywhere, with only a fraction landing on target. For precision seeding, you can fashion a spot seeder from an empty 750 g coffee tin and a pair of plastic lids. Into one lid drill or punch holes large enough to let grass seed pass and snap this into place when reseeding. Keep the other, unpierced lid snapped over the tin's bottom. When you have finished the job, reverse the lids and you'll seal in the unused seed for safe, waterproof storage for when you next need it.

Guides for watering

Watering and your soil ▶
Turf guides recommend giving a lawn 25 mm of water with each irrigation—no matter what type of soil you have. What does vary with the soil texture is the frequency of irrigation. Use the chart at right to find out how often to irrigate and how deeply 25 mm of water will penetrate. If you don't know what kind of soil you have, do the test below.

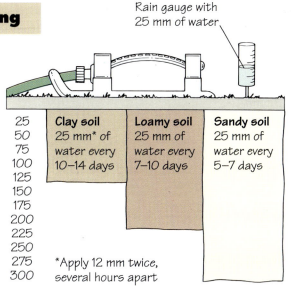

*Apply 12 mm twice, several hours apart

A custom hose
A soaker hose is a precise way of delivering water right where the garden needs it—but not if the hose is too long. With an old G-clamp or spring clip, though, you can shorten the hose to match the length of the bed or lawn. ▼

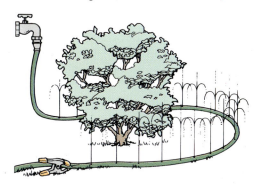

The squeeze test
To determine your soil's texture, use a trowel to extract several small samples from the turf's root zone (75 to 100 mm below the surface). Shake these up together in a bag, extract a tablespoonful, and squeeze it in your fist. If it makes a ball that stands up to a poke, the soil is clay. A ball that cracks with a poke or two is loam; a ball that crumbles easily is sand. Use the chart above and the test below to determine if you have watered your type of soil deeply enough.

Dig deep
An old screwdriver makes a good tool for double-checking the effectiveness of your lawn watering. After you've finished sprinkling, push the tool through the sod. It will penetrate wet soil easily and will register resistance when it encounters the dry zone below.

Waste not
On a sunny, breezy day, as much as half your sprinkler's droplets may evaporate before they reach the ground. But nothing could be simpler than reducing this kind of waste: all you have to do is switch your watering to early-morning hours, when the air is still and the sunlight less intense.

Sprinklers and hoses

Testing a sprinkler
How fast does your sprinkler sprinkle? Surrounding it with empty tins will give you the answer. Run the sprinkler for exactly 1 hour, and then measure the depth of the water in each tin. This test will let you determine not only the sprinkler's average output, but also if there are any gaps in its sprinkling pattern.

Cutting out those cut corners
A hose tends to cut the corners as it follows you around the garden, and in the process it may flatten prized flowers or vegetables. To protect your plantings (and reduce the wear on your hose), install a permanent guard at the outer corners of each bed. Drive a stake into the ground and drop a short length of PVC pipe over it. The pipe will also tend to rotate as the hose passes, making it easier to pull.

TREES AND SHRUBS

Good buys

Weather beaters ▶

A belt of evergreen trees set between your house and the prevailing wind makes an effective windbreak. Because these trees provide shelter to a distance five times their height, you can set tall-growing varieties such as wild olive or wild silver oak well away from the house. To provide even more protection for flower beds, plant a mixed border of shrubs in front of the trees.

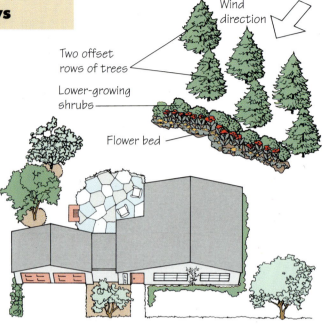

Two offset rows of trees
Wind direction
Lower-growing shrubs
Flower bed

Symptoms of good health

Clues to vigorous plants are compact growth and dark green, unblemished leaves. Avoid seedlings with roots coming out of the punnets.

Beware of bogus bargains

Tall trees and shrubs in small bags are often on sale at bargain prices. They may look quite good, but on closer examination you will usually find that they are completely rootbound. They also often have roots protruding from the bottom of the bag. If these roots have grown into the ground, they will have to be broken off before you can move the plant. You may find that, even after being planted out, your purchases remain stunted and fail to thrive. A plant in a larger container is a better choice.

Protective measures

Gentle staking

Stake a large tree firmly when you plant it, so that it will develop a strong, straight trunk. But wire or even plastic ties can damage the bark, so slip a piece of hosepipe over the wire to cushion it.

Keep it protected

Bark protects trees from infection and disease, so avoid chaining bicycles or other potentially damaging items to a tree. Nailing or wiring signs, such as a yard sale notice, to a trunk or branch may also cut or bruise the bark. Rather try using cotton string to hang signs.

Lethal lines

Edging power tools that use nylon cord or blades to cut do a great job but can damage trees and other plants. You can protect the bark of a sapling from damage by slipping a sleeve of PVC drainpipe over the stem. A length of about 150 mm, slit vertically so that you can slip it on and off as needed, will be sufficient to protect the young stem.

Stripping a circle

Keeping the soil around young trees and shrubs stripped of grass and weeds increases the amounts of water, air, and nutrients that reach the roots, and keeps the trunks from being damaged when you use an edge trimmer on the lawn. Here's how to dig out a circular patch: loop a rope around the trunk and your spade. Adjust the loop so that when pulled outward, the spade reaches the desired radius. Move around the plant, digging as you go.

PLANTING A TREE OR SHRUB

Before you buy a young specimen, envisage the size and shape of the mature plant. Review your landscaping goals (pp 268–269): will it grow fast, provide shade, add colour?

Don't put plants too close to drains, water pipes or electrical conduits. Apart from the danger of hitting them when you're digging the hole, the roots could cause damage later on. Don't dig a hole that is too deep and then backfill it. The weight of the tree will likely sink the root ball below ground level.

Improve the soil, if needed (below), but don't overdo it. Have compost and a preplanting fertilizer handy to improve the soil. Use a high-phosphate fertilizer such as bone meal or superphosphate or 2.3.2 to encourage plenty of new growth.

1 Dig a hole that is about 150 to 200 mm wider and deeper than the plant's container. Loosen the soil in the bottom of the hole, add some fertilizer and cover it with soil.

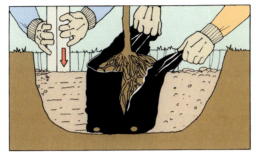
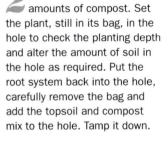

2 Mix the topsoil with equal amounts of compost. Set the plant, still in its bag, in the hole to check the planting depth and alter the amount of soil in the hole as required. Put the root system back into the hole, carefully remove the bag and add the topsoil and compost mix to the hole. Tamp it down.

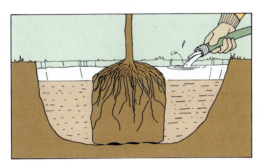

3 The level of the soil in the bag must be level with that of the surrounding soil. Carry on adding the topsoil and compost mix, ensuring that the plant remains upright. When the mix is about 50 mm below the surrounding soil level, water it well. (Support the plant so that it settles properly.)

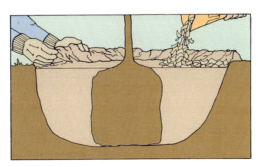

4 After the soil/compost mix has settled, top it up until it's almost at the same level as the surrounding soil. Then use some extra soil for a shallow water-retaining "saucer". Finally, add a 100 mm layer of mulch, being careful to keep it away from the trunk. Water it thoroughly once again.

TREES AND SHRUBS

Pruning

When to prune?
The best time to prune most flowering shrubs is right after the season of bloom. An earlier trimming removes buds that provide that year's show, while a late pruning may interfere with the production of buds necessary for the next year's blossoms. An exception is shrubs that bloom repeatedly throughout the growing season, such as hybrid roses. Prune them in late winter.

Treatment for a neglected shrub ▶
When you are bringing an overgrown shrub back under control, remember the three D's: remove all dead, diseased, or damaged branches. Next, remove the weaker of each pair of crossing branches—branches that rub against each other. Finally, thin the bush by removing several of its oldest branches at their base. Be sure while you are doing this, though, to leave a framework of healthy, younger branches to fill in as replacements.

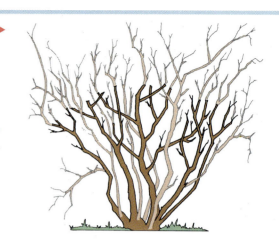

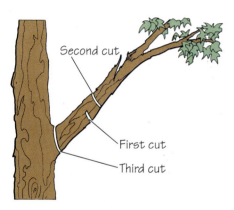

Removing a storm-damaged limb ▲
If you just slice a cracked or splintered limb off at its base, it's liable to tear a strip of bark off the trunk when it drops, which means you've done more harm than good. To avoid this mishap, use only a sharp bow saw or pruning saw and amputate in three steps. First, undercut the limb 300 mm away from the trunk—cut up from the bottom no more than halfway through the limb. Remove the branch with a second cut 100 mm or so further out along the limb and down from the top. Remove the remaining stub in one cut from top to bottom, just outside the "collar".

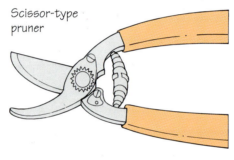

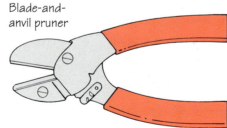

The kindest cut ▲
You'll make the cleanest, easiest cuts with scissor-type secateurs—in which the blades slip past each other with a scissor-like action. Blade-and-anvil pruners are less expensive, but they require more strength to use—and they crush as they cut, leaving a ragged wound that's an invitation to disease.

Pocket holder
A long-handled lopper is a handy tool for pruning high branches, except that it takes three hands to manage one properly. Create an extra hand by putting on a carpenter's apron and resting the end of the lopper's pole in one of the pockets. This leaves one hand free to steady the pole and one to pull the line. ▼

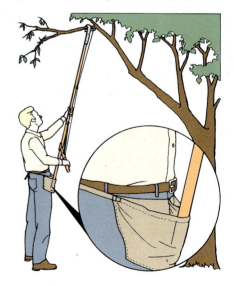

278 / Yard and Garden

Watering wisdom

Do-it-yourself sprinkler
Make a few holes in one side of a plastic 2 litre bottle and attach it to a hosepipe (a 25 mm hose connector fits onto a 2 litre bottle). Put the bottle on its side and turn on the water. Make holes as required until the spray has a suitable arc.

Put the water where it's needed
Water given to large plants may not soak deeply enough into the soil to reach the main root system—which is where it will do the most good. Place a large-diameter PVC or metal pipe into the ground 500 mm from each trunk. Fill it when watering the garden, and the plant's roots will get water without any wastage. Drilling a few small holes near the base of the pipe will make drainage more efficient.

WASTE NOT

The sparing use of waste water from some domestic sources can help a garden survive a drought. But excessive use, and that from other sources, can cause severe damage.

Do's
▷ Use all waste water sparingly.
▷ Use biodegradable detergents.
▷ Use water from the bath and shower, but not if it contains bath salts or bath oil.
▷ Use only the final rinse-cycle water from a washing machine.
▷ Add plenty of compost and organic material to your garden. It helps break down chemicals.

Don'ts
▷ Don't use dishwasher water. The detergents are very concentrated and toxic to plants.
▷ Don't use waste water from the kitchen sink if it contains fatty material or strong detergents.
▷ Never use any waste water on pot plants or outdoor containers, as chemicals will build up rapidly.
▷ Don't use waste water only. Use tap water as much as you can, to prevent the buildup of chemicals.
▷ Use waste water mainly on your lawn: grass is less likely to be affected by chemicals than many other plants.
▷ Use detergents with a low potassium level to help slow or prevent a buildup of this element.

BE A WATERWISE GARDENER

Droughts and water restrictions can cause havoc in a garden, but there are ways in which you can use water more effectively. This reduces the amount of water you will need to keep your garden looking healthy and attractive.

Have a system	Install an efficient irrigation system: these systems can be an effective and economical means of watering beds and borders. If the system is planned properly, the water is applied only where it is required—it does not spray out over paved areas, into a neighbour's garden, or over your own lawn. The sprinklers are also usually set low or protected by surrounding shrubs, so water droplets are not blown away in the wind. A few systems of shorter length give you more flexibility: plants in one area may not require watering as much as those in another part of the garden.
Timing	Early mornings are among the best times to irrigate a garden. The water has more time to soak into the soil, and mornings are often calm, so any tendency for droplets to be blown away is minimized.
Grouping	Grouping plants with similar water needs will help you make more effective use of your water resources.
Suitability	Plants indigenous to your area thrive on the natural rainfall and require less extra water than species foreign to your area.
Limit lawns	Lawns require a lot of water to maintain their condition and appearance. If you live in an area prone to droughts, limit your lawn areas and make use of stone chips, pebbles and other surfaces and features to make attractive contrasts in your garden.

YARD AND GARDEN TOOLS

Improvisations

Protecting the lawn
Clearing twigs, stones, and other non-leaf debris from a lawn is easier if you use a steel rake with inflexible tines rather than a flexible leaf rake. Stop the sharp rigid teeth digging into the lawn by driving sewing thread spools over the rake's two outside teeth. You'll find that the rake will ride smoothly as it cleans up the lawn.

Digging measure
Mark commonly used depths on the handles of your digging tools. That way you can gauge just how deep you've gone without interrupting your digging. For more on posthole diggers, see p 285.

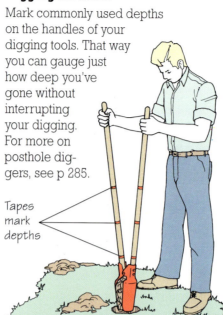

Tapes mark depths

D is for dibble
Here's a job for an old D-handled tool that you don't use anymore (or better yet, a broken one). Saw off the business end if necessary, and sharpen the wood handle to a point. You will then have a dibble—a digging tool for planting seeds and bulbs.

Step on it
To increase the amount of pressure you can put on a digging tool, such as a fork or a shovel, have a short length of angle iron welded to the shoulder of the tool. It will also be kinder to your foot.

Wheelbarrow extender ▶
Your wheelbarrow will hold more leaves if you add a lightweight extender to it. Staple chicken wire to a frame of 22 x 22 mm SA pine or meranti. Don't make the frame so high that loading the leaves will be difficult. When it's time to rake the leaves, hold the frame in place with some elastic tie-down cord while you fill and empty the wheelbarrow.

22 x 22 mm SA pine or meranti frame

Elastic tie-down

Tool tips and totes

Dirty business
Tools last far longer if you clean and oil them after every use. This is very important for digging tools, whose protective coatings wear away through use. Scrape off the dirt with an old putty knife (hang one on a nail where you store your tools). To oil your tools, keep a bucket of oil-soaked sand on hand. Clean the tool, then drive it in the sand.

Bright IDea

Small gardening tools are easy to lose in the yard, but not if you paint at least part of the handle a bright colour (other than green). As a bonus, if someone borrows one of these personalized tools, you'll be more likely to get it back.

Tool caddy

If you have an old, unused golf bag, give it a new life as a carrier for your garden tools. Store long-handled tools where you used to keep your woods and irons, and stash your work gloves and small tools in the zipper pockets. If the bag has a pull-cart attachment, use it to roll your tools around the yard.

Rubbish bin stand

Here's another neat way to store long-handled tools: make a holder out of a large rubbish bin, preferably one with built-in wheels so that you can cart your tools around the garden. Use a 38 mm spade bit to drill holes in the lid to accept the tool handles. Then drill a few small holes in the bottom of the bin to allow water to drain away. To help hold the tools in place, add some coarse gravel to the bottom of the bin.

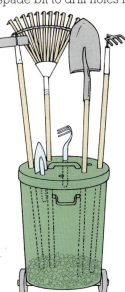

KEEP TOOLS SHARP

For rough sharpening jobs, use a bastard (coarse) or a second-cut (medium) file to re-establish the bevel. To create a sharp digging or cutting edge, use a smooth (fine) file or a sharpening stone. Depending on the garden tool, use a toe-to-heel stroke, a straight stroke, or a sweeping motion. Always clamp the tool firmly in a vice. For more on files and sharpening techniques, see pp 20 and 22–23.

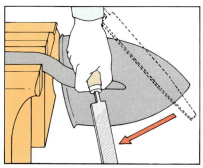

Sharpen a shovel by holding the toe of the file on the bevel at a 45° angle. Push the file diagonally in one direction, ending the stroke at the heel of the file. Work from the centre out on one side; repeat on the other side.

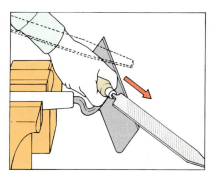

Hoes are bevelled on the outside surface of their blades. Hold the file as for the shovel, but begin with the toe at the near end. Push the file diagonally away from you, ending near the heel.

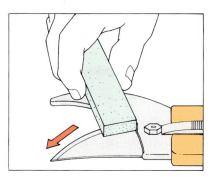

Renew the cutting blade of pruning shears with a small, flat stone. Place the stone on the bevel at the edge of the blade, and rub the cutting edge with several sweeping strokes.

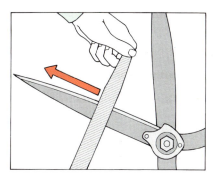

Give hedge clippers a fine cutting edge with a smooth single-cut file. Hold the file perpendicular to the cutting edge. Use straight pulling strokes without any side-to-side movement.

OUTDOOR POWER TOOLS

Lawn mowers

Sharpening and balancing a blade
Before sharpening a rotary blade, disconnect the spark-plug wire and remove the blade, following the manual's instructions. Put the blade in a vice and sharpen both ends equally. Use a bastard file and a toe-to-heel stroke (p 281) to restore the original bevel, usually a 30° angle. Don't try to remove deep nicks, as you'll remove too much metal and unbalance the blade. As you work on the blade, check its balance occasionally by hanging it on a nail driven partly into a piece of wood. If one side persists in dropping lower, resharpen that end to remove more metal. ▼

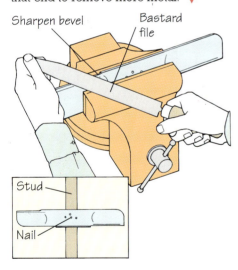

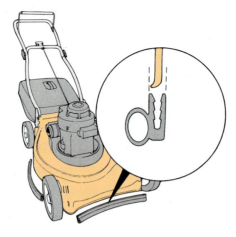

A bumper for trees ▲
If grass grows right up to your trees, there's a danger that your lawn mower could bang into the trunks and damage the bark. As a safeguard, slip a pair of inexpensive plastic car door guards onto the front of your lawn mower. A length of hosepipe will also work. The bark of your trees will stay healthy.

Preparing for winter
Your lawn mower will last longer if you clean it thoroughly at the end of the season. Run it until all the petrol is out of its system, and change the oil. Remove the spark plug and squirt a little oil into the hole. To distribute the oil within the hole, pull the starter cord a couple of times and replace the plug. To finish off, oil the height-adjustment mechanism and the blade.

Petrol pointer
Using up the remaining petrol at the end of a season can take a long time. So use a discarded turkey baster to remove most of the petrol and run the engine to use up the rest.

Put a guard up
Mowing will be safer if you install a rubber guard at the back of your lawn mower as a protection from flying rock fragments. Cut the guard from a narrow piece of 3 mm rubber, and pop-rivet it to the bottom edge of the lawn mower's deck. The rubber guard will yield with the contours of the lawn and won't hinder the manoeuvrability of the lawn mower. ▼

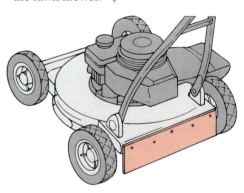

Spray 'n clean
Remove the grass buildup around the blade of a mower by flushing it out with water—a sprinkler slipped under the lawn mower will do the job. To dry the blades, run the lawn mower for a few minutes. **Caution:** Don't attempt this on an electric lawn mower.

Don't cut the cord
You'll be less likely to mow over the cord of an electric lawn mower if you wrap a spiral of colourful tape down the length of the cord. It'll be more visible as it snakes around the lawn. Or use a bright orange exterior extension cord.

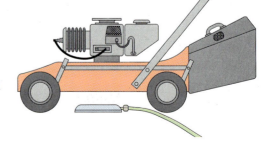

Edge trimmers

Don't be sloppy
Wear a pair of stout shoes when using an edge trimmer. If you wear sandals or slip-on footwear with open toes, you could be injured by the trimmer's line.

Simple skid for stylish edges
Edge trimmers have a blade on the guard to trim the line to the right length. However, the guard is often cut away at the front so that you can work more effectively on stubborn plants. The problem, of course, is that you might sometimes cut too deeply when edging. The answer is to pop-rivet a simple skid of scrap aluminium to the front of the cut-out section of the guard. Arrange it so that the cutting arc of the line is level with the skid. You'll get a perfect cut every time you use the trimmer. ▼

Always at the ready
Tie a roll of cutting line to the handle of your edge trimmer so that you always have line spare. When you finally roll it onto the spool, buy another spare roll at your earliest convenience, so that you never run out of line.

Chain saws

Out of chips
A chain saw needs sharpening when it starts to produce sawdust rather than chips. A resharpened chain saw runs faster and smoother. It's safer, too.

Mixing two-stroke fuel
Chain saws run on a mixture of petrol and oil, but the exact ratio varies, so check the tool's manual before proceeding. Then mix a few litres and store them in a sealed container in your garage—adhering to the usual precautions. You will always have sufficient on hand for even the lengthiest job. Just give the container a shake before topping up the chain saw's tank, to ensure the petrol and oil are properly mixed.

Shake it up, baby
If the chain saw has been idle for a while, shake it for at least a minute before you use it. This redistributes the oil within the tank.

Starter-rope savers
▷ Always pull the rope straight, rather than at an angle, so that you avoid chafing it on the saw's housing.
▷ Always use a nylon rope (not a cotton one) that is the same length as the original. A shorter cotton rope will wear out and break sooner.
▷ If there is an engine problem, sort it out as soon as possible—an engine that's hard to start forces you to use the rope more often. This increases the wear on the rope.

BE CAREFUL OUT THERE

▷ Before a cleaning or repair job, turn off the motor, remove the ignition key, and disconnect the spark-plug wire, securing it away from the plug.
▷ Store fuel in a red petrol tin well away from the house, flames or sparks, and children.

Lawn mowers and trimmers
▷ Wear leather shoes and long pants, even in hot weather.
▷ Keep away from moving parts.
▷ If you leave a tool, turn it off.
▷ Before mowing, clear away all obstructions.
▷ Know where the kerbs are.

Chain saws
▷ Retrofit an older chain saw with a bar tip guard and an anti-kickback chain.
▷ Wear hearing protection, a face shield, high-traction steel-toed shoes, and Kevlar gloves (a cut-resistant material).
▷ Brace the saw on the ground or on a log when starting it.
▷ Stand uphill from the work.
▷ Maintain secure footing. Grasp the saw with both hands. Never hold it more than chest-high.
▷ Turn off the saw if you have to walk with it.
▷ Let a professional do a job that requires any climbing.
For more on tool safety, see p 24.

SETTING POSTS

Down-to-earth advice

Don't dig your way into danger

Unless you know for certain the routes of water pipes, drains and electricity supply cables, be wary of digging holes in your garden for plants or posts. If you are in any doubt, check with your local authority. Also confirm the routing of any pipes or cables serving neighbours. Once the routes of cables and pipes are known, dig no closer than 600 mm from the route. That way you won't cut a service to your house and end up with an expensive repair bill—or worse, injure yourself.

Rooting around

If you encounter a root that's too large to remove with a shovel or post-hole digger, use a pruning saw or shears. But make sure you're not killing a tree by severing a main root, and ensure it's a root, not a pipe or cable (see above), before you chop away.

Work on one cylinder

Sometimes loose soil caves in as fast as you can dig it out, leaving you with a crater rather than a cylinder. If that happens, make a tube of a piece of stout cardboard or scrap hardboard. Dig inside the tube and wiggle the tube down as you work. Once the post is ready to be placed, the tube will also hold the concrete or dirt fill. If the hole is not going to be too deep, an old 25 litre paint container or large bucket will also work well.

Ready, get set

Add a second level ▶

If you are setting many posts, consider buying a tool that has two levels mounted at a 90° angle to each other. When it's time to plumb a post, have someone hold the post in place while you place the tool against it. Adjust its position as necessary and secure it with braces as shown.

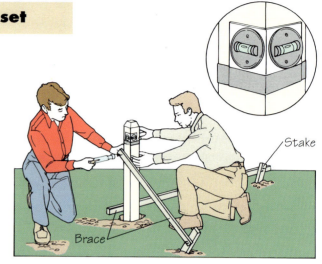

Rock-solid post anchor ▲

Gate posts, clothesline poles and handrail posts need a firmly anchored footing. You can do this without a ton of concrete: dig the hole for the concrete footing and drive three or four lengths of old pipe or angle iron, each about 600 mm long, down into the surrounding soil. Their ends must protrude into the hole so they will become embedded in the concrete when you pour it. This added bite will prevent the entire footing from shifting under stress.

Nail holder

Another way to reinforce a post in its footing is to drive nails into the post before you set it in place. The nails provide a gripping surface for the concrete when it is poured into the hole. For best results, use 150 mm nails. Stagger them on all sides up and down the post, driving each one about halfway into the wood. ▼

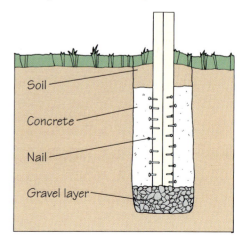

284 / Yard and Garden

TOOLS FOR POST HOLES

Digging a deep cylindrical hole calls for an arsenal of tools that can help you handle rocks and soil without fear. The tools shown on this page will help you dig the post holes for fences as well as the excavations for pier footings. (To avoid the network of underground pipes, drains and cables, see the facing page.)

Clam shell digger. You can use this digger in all types of soil. Simply plunge its open jaws into the hole, spread the handles to make the jaws bite the soil, lift it out, and push the handles back together to release the soil. Loosen rocky or clay soils by stabbing with it. The deeper you dig, the less you'll be able to move the jaws.

Hand auger digger. The twisting motion used to power this tool works well in soft ground but not in rocky soil. The cutting teeth can churn soil up into the space between the jaws, but they are powerless against rocks.

Power auger digger. This petrol-powered tool (usually rented) is ideal when you need to dig many holes in loose soil. (It isn't very useful in rocky ground.) The corkscrew auger, varying in size from 150 to 300 mm, pulls itself into the hole and spins the dirt out onto the ground. However, the tool is heavy and its weight can be hard on your back. Use one only if you're fit, or operate it with an assistant. (Several models are intended only for two-person use.)

Trenching shovel. This type of shovel has a narrow curved blade that will flare the bottoms of holes for concrete footings. A smaller one can be used to finish the bottom of a clam shell-dug hole.

Heavy-duty bar. This is a must-have tool for clays or rocky soils. It dislodges large rocks, breaks up rocky ledges and loosens clay soil. One that is 1,5 m long and weighs more than 10 kg can do most jobs around the home.

BUILDING AND REPAIRING FENCES

Picket fences

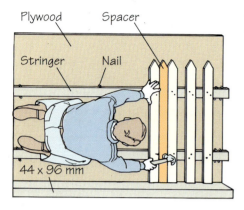

Spaced out ▲
Spacing the pickets evenly on the horizontal members, or stringers, is a major task, but there is an easy way to do it: make a spacing guide with a sheet of plywood 1,22 x 2,44 m and a 2,4 m length of 44 x 96 mm timber. Nail this timber to the bottom of the plywood—this will align the pickets evenly. Next, drive nails into the plywood at intervals to hold the stringers in position. To assemble the fence lengths, lay the pickets next to each other and nail every alternate one. (The intermediate unnailed pickets act as spacers.) Remove the spacers and continue to the end.

Design your own
If you'd like to try designing your own picket fence, use more than one picket style and vary the spacing between the pickets. Begin with pencil and paper, and experiment with various repeating patterns. Once you've settled on one, make a spacing jig (as shown above) to help you assemble the fence lengths.

Removable fence sections ▶
Building a fence with light, removable sections makes a lot of sense. It lets you open the space for a party, move large objects on and off the property, and run the lawn mower between the fence posts instead of having to trim beneath the pickets. To make fence sections removable, support the stringers on joist hangers instead of fastening them permanently to the posts. You can purchase joist hangers from hardware stores. You'll need four for each fence section. Position the hangers where the stringers are to align, and fasten them to the posts with screws. To assemble the fence, rest the stringers in the hangers.

Working with boards

◀ Nailing jig
Use a jig to ensure fence pickets are in perfect alignment and at the correct height. The jig shown here is made of a board with two spacer blocks; one block rests on top of the upper stringer while the other marks the top of the fence. Starting at a post, position the first picket with the jig next to it. Nail the picket to the top stringer, and then repeat the process with the next picket, and the next. When you reach the second post, check that the gap between it and the last picket is uniform at both top and bottom. Then go back and nail all the pickets in the section to the bottom stringer.

◀ Cutting scallops
You can give a picket fence a decorative, finished look with the help of a strip of 6 mm hardboard. Here's how: for each post-to-post section, tack one nail to each post just at the top of the pickets, and tack a third nail in the middle of the fence section 150 mm down from the other nails. Bend the hardboard strip between these nails and trace a smooth curve. Cut out the curve with a jigsaw, finishing the end of the cut with a coping saw. Smooth the cut edges of the pickets with a rasp.

FENCE REPAIR

Before you tackle any single repair, inspect the entire fence. If one post has a severe lean to it, give the others a firm shake to see if they're wobbly too and if one picket is rotten, probe others with an old screwdriver to see if they're spongy as well. If most of the framework seems solid, go ahead and perform the repairs and maintenance shown here. But if the framework is falling apart or if half the posts are rotten, consider building a new fence.

Realigning a sagging gate

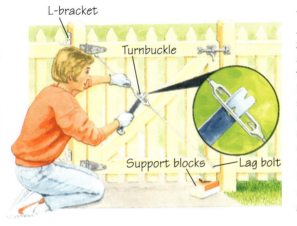

Push a sagging gate post back into place and reconnect it to the horizontal members with two L-brackets and screws. If the gate itself is sagging, tighten the hinge screws. If they no longer grip, replace them with longer screws or fill the holes and refasten the hinges (p 14). Next, raise the gate on support blocks; open a turnbuckle fully and install it diagonally with lag bolts. Depending on the turnbuckle, tighten it with a short bar or a spanner. Finally, resecure any loose pickets with some galvanized screws.

Replacing a post

Pull the nails that secure the fence sections on each side of the vertical post. Swing the sections out of the way, propping their free ends up on scrap boards.

Prise the old post out of the ground while a helper pulls it at an angle to keep it from slipping back into the hole. Position the new post; then reposition the two fence sections and nail them in place. Brace the post to hold it plumb, and pour in the concrete. (For more on setting posts, see p 284.)

Yard and Garden / 287

BUILDING AND RESTORING DECKS

Planning

Outdoor room
A deck is an outdoor living room, and as such it needs a sense of enclosure. You can achieve this with a simple perimeter railing or by edging it with a few low benches or planters. **Caution:** For safety's sake, put a slatted railing around any deck raised 600 mm or more above ground level.

On the beams
When building a deck, don't go too small on the beams. Undersize beams, even if they satisfy building regulations, also make a deck feel soft underfoot since they bounce rather than remaining rigid. It will be worth the extra cost to increase the dimension of the beams by one timber size. You'll end up with a deck that is sturdier and safer.

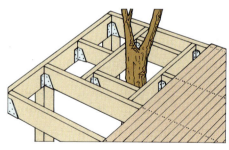

Built-in tree ▲
If you want to design a deck around a tree, plan to box the tree in with short joists. These short lengths compensate for the interruption in the joist system. Be sure that the box is large enough to let the tree grow. If children are going to be playing on the deck, it's best to build a small fence around the tree opening as a safety measure.

Building

Joist leveller
To hold long joists and beams in place for levelling, secure one end of the timber and support the body of the piece with a scissors car jack. Adjust the jack to level the piece as necessary; then secure or support the other end at just the right position. You'll find that the jack is a strong and helpful partner.

Do your level best
Before you cut posts to their final height, tack-nail the beams in position, using a level as you go. Then, with the beams in place, check your work by placing a carpenter's or mason's level on a straight beam that's been laid diagonally across the deck. Repeat in the opposite direction. Adjust the position of the beams as needed, and then cut the posts.

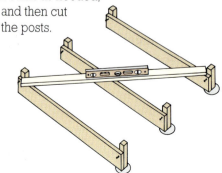

Erosion barrier
Before you build your deck, determine if rainwater seeping through the boards will erode the soil. This is likely to happen if the ground slopes. If you decide that erosion could be a problem, all you need do to keep the soil in place is cover it with a generous layer of gravel before you build the deck.

Spaced-out boards
It's easy to space deck boards evenly. Just drive nails into several pieces of scrap wood. Push the nails down between adjacent deck boards, and then fasten the boards in place. ▼

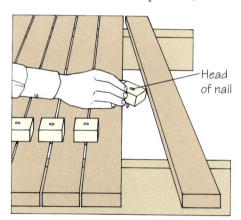

Fasten-ating problem
While headed nails are often used in deck building, they may not be the best fastener. The hammer blows needed to drive them flush dent the surface, marring it, and the heads become very hot in summer. A better choice is galvanized deck screws. As you seat these screws with a power driver, they countersink themselves below the surface. The spiral threads won't allow them to back out (as nails tend to).

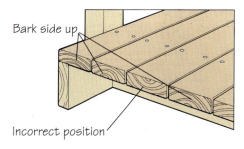

Direction of the board ▲

When placing a deck board, always place it bark side up. To tell which is the bark side, check the annual growth rings on the end of the board; the convex side is the bark side. Putting this side facing up (and the concave side down) means that it'll be less likely to cup, or warp, and you'll also avoid feathering, or splitting along the annual rings, which results in long spearlike splinters. Put the bark side down only if that side has a bad knot or splits.

Drive it straight

You can straighten a crooked deck board as you nail or screw it down by wedging it into position. First, screw a length of scrap wood to the top of the joist closest to the end of the problem board. Drive a wedge between the end of the scrap and the board until the board is properly spaced, and then fasten it to the joist. Repeat at other joists as necessary. ▼

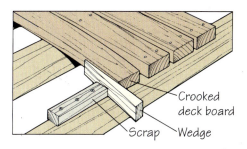

Movable deck umbrella

A deck umbrella is more useful if you can move it around as needed. To help you get it in the right spot, mount pairs of galvanized plumbing pipe straps on the deck posts or railing in key places. (The straps should be slightly wider than the umbrella pole.) Then just slip the umbrella pole through the straps, until the pole rests on the deck. ▼

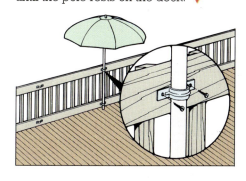

Finishing up

True grit

Don't slip on wet deck steps: if you intend to paint them, mix 1 part fine, clean white sand with 4 parts paint. If not, glue down nonslip strips with an exterior adhesive. Either way, the gritty texture will provide traction.

Wait to paint

Unless the pressure-treated wood you use for your deck was kiln-dried after treatment, be prepared to wait a few months before painting it. The pressure-treating process saturates the wood with chemicals and usually leaves it too wet to accept paint or stain well. Kiln-dried wood can be painted immediately.

Instant weathering

If you are replacing a portion of a deck, you can give it an "instant" weathered appearance. Apply a solution of 1 cup of baking soda and 4,5 litres of water to the new portion, allow it to dry, and rinse it off. When the area is dry, apply a water sealant. The sealant forms a moisture barrier beneath the surface of the wood, allowing the deck to continue to weather gradually.

Spray-on sealers

Choose a windless day to spray on a wood sealer. Using a pump garden sprayer, you can apply the sealer between the deck boards without any trouble. To clean a water-base sealer from the sprayer, spray water until it is clear. (For an oil-base sealer, soak the sprayer parts in paint thinner.)

Restoratives

Waterproof test

Over time, moisture takes its toll on a deck. An easy way to tell if you need to reseal your deck is to pour a glass of water on it. If the water beads up, the deck is waterproof. But if the surface absorbs the water quickly and turns a darker colour, it's time to reseal.

Speedy deck cleaners

Deck cleaners and restorers do a great job of bringing your deck back to life, but if the deck is very dirty, you may have to do some heavy scrubbing. If so, consider renting a high-pressure washer; it will make the job easier.

MASONRY AND CONCRETE

Mortarless helpers

Getting edgy
Use steel reinforcing rod, cut to lengths of about 400 mm, to hold the edging bricks of a mortarless path or patio of concrete pavers or bricks in place on soft or sloping ground. The rod is available in long lengths and is an economical way to keep edging bricks in place. Drive them down flush with the top surface of each brick. ▼

Even edgier
When laying the edging for a path with parallel sides, take care to keep the sides evenly spaced; it will make life easier when you screed (smooth and level) the sand and lay the masonry.

A day's work
Lay down and screed only as much sand as you can cover with pavers in one day, and then throw a tarpaulin over the sand pile. Uncovered sand is guaranteed to be disturbed by wind, rain, kids, or a stray cat who thinks he's found the world's biggest litter box.

Dry idea
Before you sweep sand between newly laid paving, be sure it's dry. Wet sand will bridge the gaps rather than fill them. To ensure the gaps are filled completely, wait a few days and then sweep sand into the gaps a second time. This is important because the sand helps solidify the paving and also fills any spaces where dirt might enter and provide a mini planting bed for weeds.

Saving your paving ▲
The best way to lock paving into its sand bed is to use a power vibrator, but be careful with this heavy machine. Don't let it stay in one place too long, or the bricks could settle unevenly, or crack. Some operators place large sheets of plywood on the paving and run the vibrator over them; the plywood helps distribute the weight of the machine.

Go ahead—be a blockhead ▶
Want an easier way to build a retaining wall? Drive a series of thick reinforcing rods into the soil so that at least half their length is in the soil. Angle them backwards as in the illustration and space them so that the concrete blocks can be slipped over them. Use this method only for low walls, as no mortar is used in its construction. Fill the spaces in the blocks with soil. Then plant flowers and small bushes in the wall for a really attractive and easily maintained garden feature.

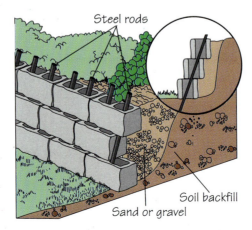

Stone paths

Make sand stay put
If your flagstone path has fairly wide joints, you may find that the sand tends to wash away. If you get around to resetting the stones, set them in sand as before, but change your approach to the joints. Mix a little dry cement with the sand and pack the mixture firmly between the stones. Then, to set the filler, sprinkle the joints with a little water. You'll find the sand will stay put.

Put the design on paper ▲

Working with flagstones is like solving a giant jigsaw puzzle. Some stones fit together without cutting, but others need to be cut to fit. An easy way to find the best candidate to fill any given space is to make a template out of brown paper. Just lay the paper over the void and fold back the edges until it fits (don't forget to leave room for the sand joints). Take the template over to your stockpile of stones and choose one that's closest to your needs. Mark any cut lines. Place the stone on sand, and score along the cut lines with a stone chisel and a club hammer. Strike the stone.

Flour power

Before you dig any holes for a stepping-stone path, place the stones on top of the grass and space them so that the strides between the stones are comfortable. Take a couple of practice walks. When the placement looks and feels right, sprinkle flour over the path. Then lift the stones out of the way and use the outlines to dig holes for the stones.

Pattern making

If you'd like a path that has a random pattern but isn't as irregular as the one at left, use paving slabs that have been cast to 450 x 450 mm, 450 x 600 mm and 600 x 600 mm. If you cast your own slabs, you can dye some of them for a very different effect. ▼

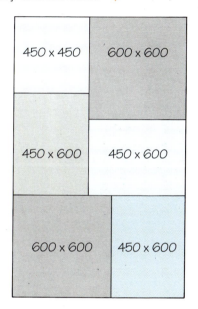

Some concrete secrets

Using leftovers

When you have a concreting job, you will often have some left over. So, plan ahead: make a few moulds for paving slabs and put them onto heavy plastic sheets. Pour the leftover concrete into the moulds. (When making them up, lightly nail the corners so that they can be pulled apart for easy separation from the slab.) Slabs 44 mm thick and about 450 mm along each edge will be suitable for most applications.

Concrete connection

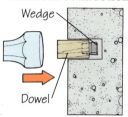

To securely mount a screw, hook, or nail in a solid concrete surface, create a solid base for the fastener. First drive a steel tool-handle wedge partly into the end of a length of dowel, and then use a masonry bit to bore a hole in the concrete the same diameter as the dowel. Drive the dowel into the hole, wedge end first. As you hammer it in, the wedge will expand the dowel, creating a super-tight fit.

Flagstone fake

Next time you pour a concrete path or patio, you might want to try a decorative finish for it, such as the flagstone effect shown here. While the smoothed concrete is still wet, use a brick jointing tool to carve the outlines of joints between the simulated flagstones. For best results, plan your design ahead of time and work quickly (you have to complete the task before the concrete sets). Go over the surface again with a trowel, and then use an old paintbrush to remove particles of concrete and smooth the edges of the design. ▼

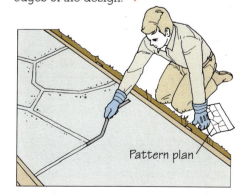

Yard and Garden / 291

REPAIRING MASONRY AND CONCRETE

Patios, walks, and steps

Concrete shock absorber
Pounding a chisel to remove loose material from a crack in concrete can make your hands and arms tingle. Reduce this excessive shock by punching a hole into a sponge-rubber ball and pushing the chisel through it. When you pound the tool, hold onto the sponge rubber. You won't feel the vibrations as much. (**Note:** Don't forget to wear eye protection for this job.) ▼

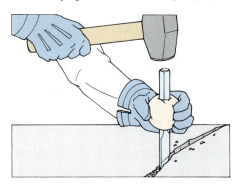

Hold your chips
When chipping away at concrete, keep the pieces from scattering all over the place, including into your face. Push the chisel through a square of fine mesh. Wear safety goggles, just in case.

Wobble fixer
A wrought-iron railing column may rust and become loose in its concrete foundations. If you cannot remove the column, stabilize the rust by pouring some rust inhibitor into the channel. Leave it for a few days to evaporate, then repack the channel with a strong concrete mix. Tamp it down well to firmly anchor the column.

Railing against the weather
Prevention is better than cure, so stop moisture seeping into the space between a wrought-iron column and its concrete base by  using copolymer caulk (see p 151) to fill any gaps between the iron and the surrounding concrete.

Patio paver puller
You may find that some bricks or paving slabs in a sand-base paved area may need relevelling. How do you get the brick or slab out? Make two pullers from stout wire, like the ones shown below. Slip them into the gaps on either side of the slab, turn them a quarter turn, and pull it up. For large slabs, make four pullers and get a second person to help you. Use a piece of scrap wood to slip under the slab once it's up. ▼

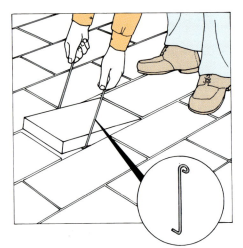

No more moss
Moss thrives in warm, damp climates, growing almost everywhere. Not only is it unsightly, it makes concrete and brick steps, patios, and walks dangerously slippery. To get rid of it, mix 1 part household bleach with 3 parts water in a plastic wateringcan, apply it to the mossy surface, and then scrub with a stiff-bristle brush.

Driveway fixes

Fresh stain
Cover a fresh oil or grease spot on your tarred or concrete driveway with baking soda or cat litter. If you use the latter, grind it into a fine powder with a brick  (there's no need to bear down hard). Let the soda or litter stay there for a day or so; then sweep the area clean.

Stubborn spots
If the baking soda or cat-litter treatment (above) won't remove an oil or grease stain from a concrete driveway, saturate the spot with carburettor cleaner. Or use a commercial degreaser.

Push grooming
The next time you clean your concrete or tarred driveway, tape a garden hose to the handle of the broom. The nozzle will direct water in front of the broom as you push it over the surface.

GARDEN IMPROVEMENTS

Layout and staking tips

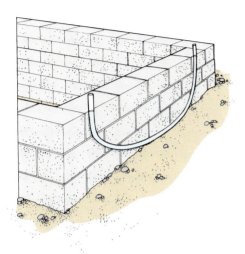

Long level line ▲
Use this simple tool to maintain a level line over a long distance. Almost fill a length of 15 mm diameter clear plastic tubing with water. The water will seek identical levels at each end, giving you an accurate levelling device for laying out projects such as decks and fences. For long distances, attach a metre or so of clear tubing to the ends of hosepipe.

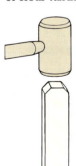

Don't split the stakes
When wood stakes split, it's usually because you've struck them on the corners, instead of in the centre. To solve this problem, cut off the upper corners. Then you'll have no choice but to hit each stake in the centre, and it will go into the ground with minimal splitting.

Lighting up

Take a dimmer view
If you have a dimmer switch installed on your exterior spotlights or floodlights, you'll be able to produce diffused light at the touch of a dial, creating the ideal mood for a party on your patio or in the garden. Ensure it's a heavy-duty dimmer designed for exterior use. To avoid the annoying hum that many dimmers cause, choose one with a filter. For safety tips and information on working with electricity, see pp 199–210.

Sand in your socket
If the lamp socket of a garden light is corroded, you can clean it out with the type of emery board used for fingernails. First, turn off the electric power and disassemble the light to gain access to the socket. Brush out any grit, sand it clean with the emery board and reassemble the light.

TYPES OF OUTDOOR LIGHTING

Light can be used many ways: to set the stage for an outdoor party, add a dramatic touch to a garden, or boost the security of your home. Here's a brief sampler.

TYPE	TECHNIQUE	COMMON USES
Backlighting	Places a light fixture behind an object.	To silhouette a shape and cast shadows beyond it.
Contour lighting	Focuses two or three beams at different angles around an object. (To deepen the contrast of light and shadows, make one light more intense.)	To draw attention to trees, statues, fountains, and other items of sculptural interest.
Cross-lighting	Mounts two beams of equal intensity on opposite sides of its objective.	To make an object or area prominent.
Diffused light	Sets several nondirectional lights, on posts and in the ground.	To soften the contrast between light and shadow and set a mood.
Downlighting	Directs light from a tree or roof to a specific area.	To outline paths and driveways or to increase security around the house, often with a movement sensor.
Grazing	Brushes light beams across a surface.	To emphasize the texture of plants, vines, rock gardens, and plaster.
Moonlighting	Beams light from a high position such as a tree or roof.	To enlarge the area of diffused light, as for a large outdoor party.
Uplighting	Directs (usually) one light beam upward from the ground.	To draw attention to bushes or trees.

Yard and Garden / 293

GARDEN IMPROVEMENTS

Furnishing the outdoors

Takeaways with a difference
This is an easy way to move your picnic table around the garden. Install a pair of fixed casters at the bottom of the legs at one end of the table. (Wheels of about 200 mm diameter navigate a lawn well.) Then when it's time to follow the shade, mow or rake underneath the table, or make room for other activities, just lift one end of the table and go.

Cloth control
Wind wreaks havoc at a picnic—napkins and paper plates fly away and the tablecloth yearns to set sail. To anchor a cloth to the table, glue spring-type clothes pegs to the underside of the table with epoxy. You'll need about eight for an average table. Space them around the table, and tape them in place until the adhesive dries.

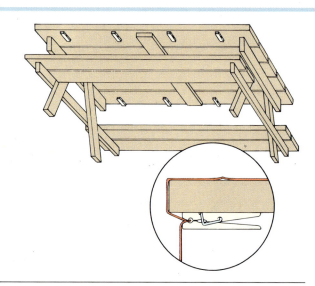

Metal protector
Patio furniture with metal feet usually comes with protective plastic or rubber tips. Over time, the metal cuts through the tips and starts to rust and scratch the floor. To lengthen the life of these plastic protectors, fit a metal washer inside the bottom of each one.

Lawn chair medic
To clean dirty aluminium frames, use steel wool and a little turpentine. If the metal is pitted, rub the areas with aluminium cleaner. Finally, protect the frames by spraying them with clear acrylic finish.

Lawn chair revival
Don't discard a perfectly good lawn chair just because the fabric is ruined. Replace the covering with wooden slats. You'll find it easier if you finish the slats, including painting or sealing them, prior to attaching them to the frame with pop rivets—use each slat as a template when drilling the holes in the frame. ▼

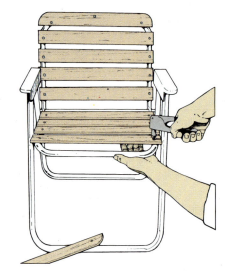

Make holes in one
The water that pools in the contoured seats of metal lawn chairs invites rust. A solution is to drill several drainage holes in the seat. Be sure to deburr their edges. Then paint the chair (and the holes' edges) with rust-preventive paint. Drilling holes also works for plastic chairs—but instead of controlling rust, it just helps the plastic dry faster.

Something for the kids

Go for bolts
Protruding bolt ends on play structures are dangerous. Remove them (filing down any rough edges) or countersink them into the wood. There should be no sharp edges on any play equipment.

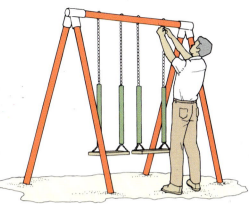

Swing easy ▲
Chains on a child's swing can cut into small fingers. To make the chains more comfortable to hold, slit lengths of foam pipe insulation or a garden hose and slip them over the chain.

Now birds can't just drop in
To stop birds leaving droppings on a swing set, attach a corner bracket near each end of the top rail of the set. Run a broom handle (or long dowel) between the brackets and attach it to them, using a nail in each end. It must be able to rotate very freely: whenever a bird tries to land on the swing set, the broom handle will revolve. The bird can't perch there—so it won't leave its droppings on the swing set either. ▼

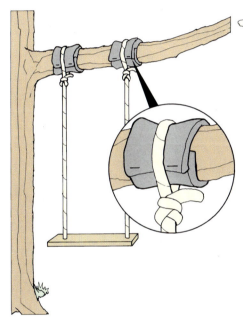

Branch saver ▲
A tree swing is fun for the kids, but not so healthy for the tree branch. The sawing action of the rope cuts the cambium layer just under the bark, killing the branch. To prevent damage, make a protective sleeve out of tough rubber, such as an old car tyre. Tack it to the tree with staple nails, and tie the rope around it.

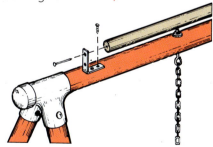

PLAY SET RULES

A play set, whether it's home-built or store-bought, can be a safety hazard. A 200 mm layer of cushioning material under the play set is vital. Use foam, sand, gravel, or an organic material such as shredded bark. Don't rely on grass. It will soon wear off, and soil is extremely hard. Clean or replenish the cushioning material as needed. Once the set is up, inspect it periodically and correct any problems immediately.

The safest play sets will have:
▷ Handholds at strategic points, easy for small hands to grip.
▷ A slide slope of no more than 30°, with a level section at the end to slow a child's exit speed and a soft surface to receive them if they go right off the end. (Watch the orientation of any wood grain or joins between metal panels.)
▷ Securely fastened side guards at the top of the slide.
▷ Swings spaced 600 mm apart, with the seats at least 750 mm from the frame.
▷ A solid or slatted enclosure at least 1 m high safeguarding any platform more than 750 mm above ground. The slats must be tightly spaced.
▷ Rounded corners and edges to prevent injuries.
▷ Recessed or covered hardware (see hint at top left).

GARDEN IMPROVEMENTS

For the birds

Slide-out feeder

If you want to attract birds to a hanging feeder near a second-storey window, you'll need to hang the feeder out from the house but still be able to safely reach it easily for restocking. Mount an old runner for vertical blinds on a length of timber. This, in turn, is attached to a roof truss. Hang the feeder from one of the movable eyes. You'll be able to fill it and slide it back out so the birds can see it, and when it rains you'll be able to move it under the eaves.

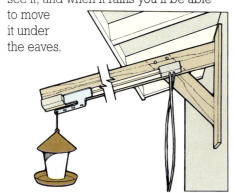

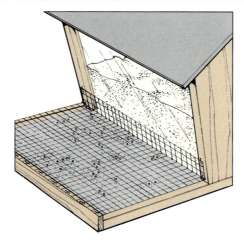

Keeping seed in its place

When birds search through a feeder for the perfect seed, a lot of rejected food ends up on the ground. Add a lip to the edge of the feeder's tray, and stretch a piece of 10 mm welded mesh over the tray with enough clearance for the seeds to spread out under the wire. Staple the wire to the lip and the frame of the feeder. The birds will be able to eat, but they won't be able to scratch the seeds away.

Clotheslines

Laundry basket hang-up

Here's a simple slide-in shelf that will hold your laundry basket at waist height on a post. Just cut a notch for the post in a 295 x 450 mm length of 22 mm board. Nail a slot made of 22 x 44 mm blocks to the post, and slide the shelf into the slot. To hold the basket in place, add a top bracket (locate the position of the bracket by measuring the depth of your basket). You'll have to tip the basket to fit it under the top bracket.

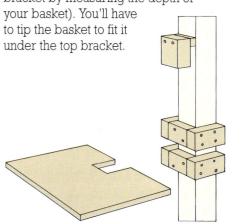

Clothes-peg storage

If you want a sheltered home for your clothes pegs, build a covered box with a hinged lid out of 12 mm plywood. Drill holes in the bottom and ends for drainage, and attach the box to a post.

Hang it all

When you run out of space on a clothesline, hang small items, like socks, on wire coat hangers—you'll be able to fit a great deal more washing on the line. Not only that: if you need to take in the washing in a hurry, you'll be able to just grab the hanger—socks and all.

Postboxing

Painting boxes

If you'd like to dress up your galvanized metal postbox with a coat of paint, it'll stick better if you first wash the exterior with some vinegar. (The mild acid removes much of the oiliness from the surface and helps the paint to grip better.) To paint the box, apply a coat of a primer formulated for galvanized metal, and follow with a coat of paint.

Pipe dream

Avoid having your newspaper ruined by being jammed through the slot of your postbox—or by being dumped on the ground. Attach a 400 mm length of PVC drainpipe to a support next to your postbox. It looks neat, too. ▼

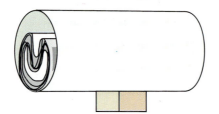

296 / Yard and Garden

SEASONAL CHORES

Firewood

Splitting wood
For strenuous bending and lifting activities, such as splitting wood, wear a wide leather weightlifter's belt. Its support reduces fatigue and helps to prevent lower back pain. You can find these belts in most sporting goods stores.

This end up
You'll split a log more easily if you chop into its true top end. How can you tell which end should be up? Check the diameter at each end of the log. The smaller end is almost always the top.

Tyre holder ▲
Here's an easy way to hold logs for splitting: stack a couple of old car tyres and put one log at a time into the opening. The tyres will keep the split halves from falling and will protect the axe blade if you miss the log.
Caution: Beware of bouncing blades.

On the chopping block
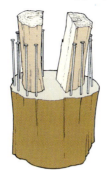
Prevent your chopped wood from falling to the ground each time it's split. Drive some 200 mm nails around the edge of the chopping block, leaving an opening at the front and back so that your axe is clear. The nails act like a fence to catch the pieces and save you a lot of bending over.

Handle saver
If you split a lot of wood, you've probably missed the mark enough times to damage the axe handle. A good way to prevent this is to tape a 150 mm piece of rubber hose to the underside of the handle, next to the axe head. This will triple the life of the handle and take the sting out of the misses.

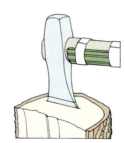

Cleaning up that mess

Do the board walk
A major problem when painting outdoors is the threat of a sudden gust of wind blowing your dropcloth up against the newly painted surface. Rather use a sheet of old hardboard (old cupboard backing, for example). It's easier to control than a dropcloth and in a gust of wind it won't fly up and ruin the job.

Good brooming
If your driveway or pavement is covered with only a little mud, try sweeping it away instead of lifting it off with a spade. It will save wear and tear on your back. And if you're apt to encounter stubborn patches of mud, screw a scrap of angle iron to the top of the broom head; you'll be able to flip the broom over and scrape at the mud.

Easier verge cleanup
If your local municipality is about to dig a trench past your house, cleaning up afterwards will be far simpler if you peg down strips of shadecloth about 1,5 m wide (available at garden centres) in the area they plan to dump the spoil. Then, when they fill in the trench, cleaning up will be easy and your verge will soon be back to normal.

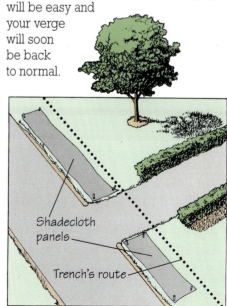

SWIMMING POOLS

Planning and building

Take a look
Visit a few pool owners in your neighbourhood before you decide on a pool builder or the features you think you should incorporate in and around your pool. You will get a good idea of how various designs, features and motifs look "in the flesh" and a better idea of what's available. You can also use these visits to find out more about builders serving your area.

A pretty picture, but…
Get at least three quotes and ask for references when deciding on the firm to build your pool. Don't rely on pictures: they might lie! Talk to people who have had pools built by the firm in question—recently as well as a few years back. You will need to know how the workmanship has stood up to the test of time and if standards are being maintained. Reputable firms will be quite happy to supply you with the necessary names and details. Take the time to actually look at these pools.

Make a plan
Draw your property to scale on graph paper and experiment with different positions, shapes and sizes of pool. Draw them on tracing paper overlays.

Don't plan yourself into a corner
When you design your pool, bear in mind that some pool cleaners may get stuck on steps or trapped in a corner. Some cleaners negotiate these features better than others do, but do take ease of cleaning into account in your design.

Avoid the slippery slope
Use railway sleepers or a wooden pool deck as a pool surround to combat the effects of soil subsidence around a pool built on a slope. Even compacted ground may subside and this leads to a cracked pool surround. But loosely laid sleepers can be shifted or have soil packed under them as and when needed, and a pool deck, with its foundations in undisturbed ground, will be immune to subsidence.

The big buildup
You can use the soil from the hole being dug for a pool on a slope to make an entertainment area. Compact it as you go, and slope the surface up at a slight angle. Then, as the soil subsides (no matter how much you compacted it), the surface will approach dead level. You can also stabilize the slope to some extent by driving a number of posts into the embankment and then planting shrubs and ground cover to bind the soil with their roots. ▼

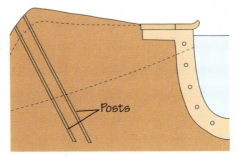

Colour me cool
Light-coloured marble plaster tends to result in cooler water, whereas darker finishes will tend to result in a higher water temperature. That means in hotter areas of the country, a white finish may be a better choice, and in cooler areas such as the Cape, a dark finish will help provide a longer swimming season.

Banish backwashing blues
A 100 mm PVC pipe is a great way to get dirty backwash water away without any mess. Just make sure you follow local bylaws as regards disposal of backwash water, and ensure that none flows onto a neighbour's property. ▼

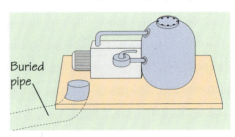

Don't be stumped by a tree
Get rid of a problem tree as follows. Remove the branches, using a block and tackle attached to the trunk or other branches, to lower the bigger pieces to the ground. Use the same method to get the trunk down. Once the stump has been cut off at ground level, drill large holes into it and fill them with diesel fuel. This will kill what's left.

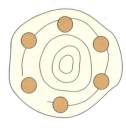

298 / Yard and Garden

Pipes and pumps

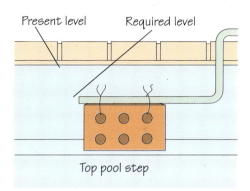

Simple siphon ▲
When heavy rain overfills your pool, try this siphon stunt instead of using your pool pump to backwash water out of your pool. Fill your hosepipe with water and tie one end to a brick—this end must be at the final desired water level. Putting your thumb over the other end of the pipe, pull it to a lower level and allow the water to flow out. The pool water will be siphoned out until it drops to the required level—when the top end of the hose will be exposed. Air will break the siphon effect and the flow will stop—at exactly the right level.

Waste not, want not
Water restrictions and pools don't go well together. Save water like this: backwash your pool water into one 210 litre drum, and rinse into a second one. Leave both for a few days for sediment to settle, then gently siphon as much water as possible back into the pool. Avoid any disturbance of the sediment. Clean the drums out afterwards, ready for the next backwash. This method will help you keep wastage to a minimum.

Don't push your pump too hard
The pump you select for your pool must be able to handle the volume of water and it should be sited reasonably close to the pool—usually within 3 m or so. You will also find that no amount of backwashing will completely clean the filter medium, and debris will build up. Make a point of opening the filter and thoroughly cleaning the medium, and topping it as required. Carry out this task once a year or so, but watch your pump's pressure gauge, if it has one—if the pressure reaches about 100 kPa, clean out the medium. The operating pressure is usually about 45–80 kPa.

Quick fix for cracked pipes
When a pool-cleaner pipe cracks, wind insulation tape tightly around the break, followed by a length of 2 mm fence wire, ensuring it goes into the grooves. The repair will last until you buy a new pipe. This trick also works when a pipe has been twisted and its wall strength impaired—the wire "corset" supports the pipe's wall. **Caution:** Turn the ends of the wire inwards and take the pipe out of the pool while people are swimming. ▼

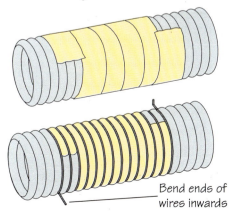

Before backwashing...
Disconnect your pool cleaner and clear the leaf trap of debris before you backwash. For greatest efficiency, the water flow must be unimpeded.

Pool equipment

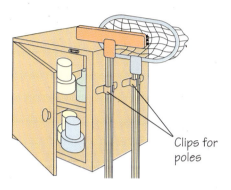

Keep it where you need it ▲
Mount an old bedside cupboard on a wall near the pool and screw clips to the sides to hold pool brush cleaners and other items.

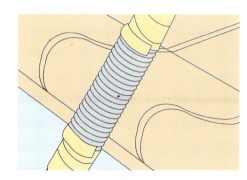

Care for your coping ▲
Slip a length of old pool-cleaner pipe over the pole of the pool brush or vacuum and tape it into position. Both the pool coping and the aluminium pipe will be protected.

Yard and Garden / 299

SWIMMING POOLS

Problem solving

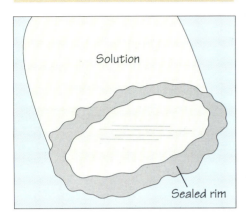

Algae away ▲
Get rid of algae by giving a patch a blast of concentrated algaecide. Cut a plastic 2 litre cooldrink bottle in half and run Prestik around the rim. Completely fill the bottle with a strong algaecide mix and place a plastic bag over the open end. Gently lower the bottle into the water and position it over the patch. Remove the plastic bag slowly, to prevent too much mixing of the solution with the surrounding water. Push the rim of the bottle hard against the pool surface and seal the rim. The highly concentrated solution will be largely confined to where it is needed.

Now see here
Need to see some detail below the surface of the water? Put a glass bowl or glass into the water and you'll get a very clear view through its base.

Clean, but green
Before you use any copper-base algaecide in your pool, check the instructions carefully or consult the manufacturers. The copper component in the formula may turn the pool surface green. It might also turn hair green.

Keep it crystal clear
Pools sometimes turn green more readily following a rainstorm, or when they have been used a lot. When rain approaches, give your pool a little extra boost of chlorine beforehand, and a further small boost after heavy use.

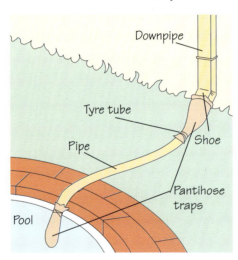

Water when you need it ▲
During water restrictions, make the most of every downpour. Slip the foot section of an old pantihose over each gutter downpipe shoe. Over that, firmly tie a section of car-tyre tube. Slip the other end over the end of a pool-cleaner pipe and, if you wish, put a second piece of pantihose over the end of that, where it goes into the pool. When it rains the pool will be filled, and the pantihose will trap leaves and debris.

Is it leaking?
Place a 210 litre drum in the pool and fill it to exactly the same level as the water in the pool. (Put the drum on a plastic sheet to prevent any rust marks.) Leave the drum open so that the water in it can evaporate at the same rate as the pool water. After a week, check the levels. A difference of 10 mm or more could indicate there is a leak.

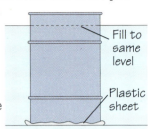

Don't lose your marble
Marble plaster will deteriorate if exposed to sunlight, so keep the water level above the lower edge of the tiles. If water restrictions make this impossible, however, cover the entire pool with shadecloth. This will protect the marble plaster from direct sunlight to some extent. Top the pool up to the correct level as soon as possible. ▼

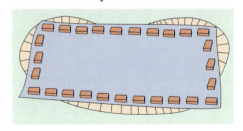

Call the experts
Contact your local office of the National Spa and Pool Institute of South Africa. The NSPI will be able to advise you on a number of factors which may influence your decision as to pool builder, site and design of your pool, and type of construction, for example.

Pool safety

Ban it!
Ban anyone from swimming alone, no matter what their age or sense of responsibility. Accidents do occur—people trip, slip or bang their heads, and if they're alone, there could well be a tragedy.

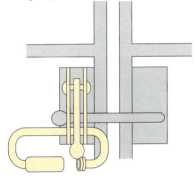

Quick release ▲
A pool gate should always be of the self-closing type and it should also be kept locked when the pool is not in use. If you have to get into the pool area in a hurry, however, every second counts. You should padlock the gate and keep the key nearby, but out of reach of children. Or you could consider locking the gate with a firmly tightened quick link that small hands cannot undo.

Planks for pets
Varnish a couple of planks, about 1,5 m long and 300 mm wide and leave them in the pool while you're out. They will give any pet a better chance of survival if it falls into the pool. In addition, wildlife such as lizards and frogs will have a refuge—which means your pool cleaner won't get blocked.

EMERGENCY!

Pool accidents are sometimes minor, but often they're tragic. Make sure you know what to do in an emergency: seconds are vital and can mean the difference between life and death. The following information is a guide only. If you own a pool, it is advisable for at least two members of the family to take a course in CPR (cardiopulmonary resuscitation). If only one person knows the procedure and he or she is the victim, a tragedy could result.

Follow the three major steps:
A: Air passages: remove any matter blocking the air passage.
B: Breathing: give artificial respiration if victim is not breathing.
C: Circulation: give external chest massage if there is no pulse.
Give the first four breaths as quickly as you can to stimulate breathing. Then give them at regular intervals of 5 seconds apart for adults, and 3 seconds apart for children. Alternate breathing with chest massage (at a rate of 80 times a minute). Check for a pulse every 15 seconds or so and cease chest massage as soon as a pulse is detected. To check, use your middle three fingers only—not your thumb (its own pulse could mislead you). Take the pulse by feeling at the side of the victim's neck, the temples or the underside of the arm near the armpit.

2 If the victim is not breathing, turn their head to one side and remove dentures or food from their mouth. Now tilt their head back to open the airway.

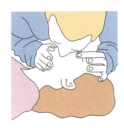

3 Holding their head back, close the victim's nostrils, open their mouth and blow into it. With children, cover the mouth and nose with your mouth.

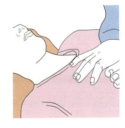

4 To stimulate circulation, push the lower half of victim's sternum 80 times a minute. Stop when pulse starts. Continue (3) until breathing starts.

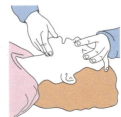

1 To open the airway, tilt the head back. Should breathing begin spontaneously, roll the victim over into the recovery position.

When pulse and breathing are present, cease CPR. Roll victim into recovery position (also see p 205) and request medical assistance.

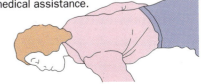

Yard and Garden / 301

CHAPTER 10

CAR AND GARAGE

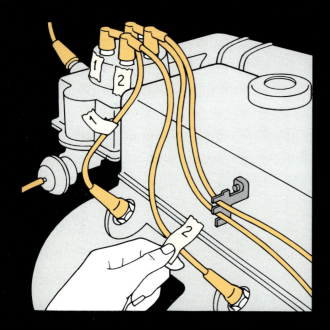

TOOLS AND EQUIPMENT 303
CHANGING THE MOTOR OIL AND OIL FILTER 304
TUNE-UP 306
COOLING AND EXHAUST SYSTEMS 308
TRANSMISSION, STEERING, AND SUSPENSION 310
TYRES 312
WHEELS AND BRAKES 314
ELECTRICAL SYSTEM 316
FUEL SYSTEM 318
PAINT TOUCH-UP 319
KEEPING UP APPEARANCES 320
STORAGE, RESTRAINTS, AND SECURITY 322
WINTER TIPS 324
GARAGE 326

TOOLS AND EQUIPMENT

Handling tools

Handy hose helper
If you start threading a spark plug or nut in a spot that's hard to reach, it's likely you'll scrape your knuckles. To keep your skin intact, get things going with a short length of rubber fuel line, motor-car vacuum hose, or garden hose. The hose should fit snugly over the nut, or spark plug insulator. Slip the hose into the tight area, and twist it to start threading on the part. If you need a grip for twisting, insert the blade of a short screwdriver into the open end of the hose and turn the hose that way. Tighten the nut or plug as normal with a spanner.

To the point
When removing a stubborn six-sided nut, don't be tempted to use the wrong tool, such as pliers or a spanner that "almost fits". It can round off the points on the nut without removing it—and then you'll have to take a hacksaw to it (p 96). Instead, spray a penetrating solvent on the nut and let it soak. (If a solvent isn't available, use a cola cool drink.) Then pick a spanner that fits tightly; a six-point version is best, but if you have a plumber's pipe wrench, it will also work.

Burn rubber
Working on a car usually means your hands end up oily, and slippery. Wind a few large rubber bands around a spanner's handle for a better grip. This works particularly well on screwdrivers. The bands greatly improve the force you are able to apply to the tool.

Garage equipment

Seat relief
It's tiring to squat or kneel while you work on the brakes or suspension. Give your knees a rest by making a combination seat and tool caddy. Bolt together two pairs of wood strips with one side of a sturdy plastic crate or wooden box sandwiched between them. At each corner, attach casters to the bottom strips. As long as you aren't on the heavy side, you can sit on the crate, roll into position, and remove and store tools and parts inside the crate all at once.

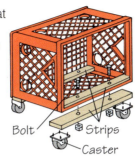

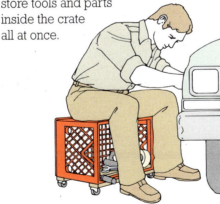

Cheap creep
Is your mechanic's creeper too tall for a job? Place a large scrap of vinyl flooring on the floor or driveway; then you can easily slide under the car on its slippery surface. In addition, it's easier to remove spilled oil or grease from the flooring rather than from concrete, tar or paving.

FIRE CONTROL

Keep a fire extinguisher rated for petrol and electrical fires in the garage, and another in your car. Store the latter within reach of the driver—under the seat is ideal.

A fire extinguisher, however, will not help much if it's windy. You can try to smother a small fire with a heavy tarpaulin or blanket. But if the fire is out of control, get away from it and call the fire brigade immediately.

Keep all flammable materials such as fuel, paint, thinners, gas bottles and lubricants, near the door so they can be removed from danger rapidly and easily. Storing them on platforms with casters will allow you to move them out very rapidly. Make the platforms out of scrap chipboard.

CHANGING THE OIL AND OIL FILTER

Motor oil

Leak lookout
Leaking fluids are often the first sign of car trouble. Check under your car at least once a week for leaks. To identify them, spread a length of white paper under the car, secure the corners with heavy weights, and leave it overnight. The colour and location of the leak will identify it: clear water near the front seats is usually harmless condensation from a running air conditioner. Green or yellowish liquid with a sweet smell under the engine or radiator is anti-freeze. Red or brown fluid with a strong odour under the engine is power-steering fluid; under the transmission, it's transmission fluid. Brown or black slippery liquid under the engine is motor oil. A colourless oily fluid near the wheels or engine could be brake fluid. A colourless or nearly colourless watery liquid under the engine compartment could be leakage from the washer reservoir—the location varies from car to car. Repair any leaks, and check the appropriate fluid reservoirs for low levels.

Squint saver
Oil dipsticks can be made easier to read. Drill small holes through the dipstick at the "Full" and "Add" marks. Make sure you clean off all the metal filings before you reinsert the dipstick.

Safety first ▶
If you have to work under your car, jack it up and lower the chassis or axles onto steel jack stands. Never work under a car supported only by a jack, no matter how sturdy it seems. Be sure to apply the handbrake, put the transmission into *Park*—or first gear for a manual transmission—and chock the wheels that remain on the ground. Metal chocks are available at car spares outlets. Wear safety goggles when working under a car. You never know when muck will be dislodged!

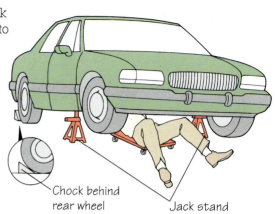

Keep it pure oil
Be sure to remove the plastic lock ring that sometimes clings to the neck of an oil container after you remove its cap. If the ring falls into the engine while you're pouring in oil, it can cause big problems. If you use a funnel, make sure you first wipe off any debris.

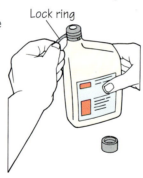

When to change
The cooler oil is, the more viscous it is. The warmer it is, the easier it flows. So, speed things up by running the engine for a couple of minutes to warm the oil prior to draining the sump. Then remove the drain plug—the oil will flow out faster than it otherwise would have. Just make sure none goes near the exhaust pipe and keep your hands clear of the pipe or manifold, too: it will be very hot.

Don't dump that old bucket
Cut down an old plastic bucket to a height of about 200 mm. It will make an ideal container to catch the oil when draining the sump.

Diversionary tactics
If the drain hole on your engine is angled in such a way that oil pours all over the chassis rail as it drains, try this: make a funnel by cutting the bottom off an empty plastic bottle that has a handle. After you've loosened the plug, position the funnel between the chassis and the drain hole. Once the funnel is in place, remove the plug. ▼

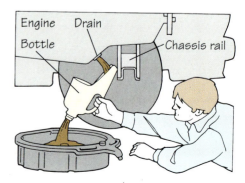

304 / Car and Garage

DISPOSING OF AUTOMOTIVE WASTES

Local regulations governing the disposal of harmful substances, such as automotive waste materials, may vary from one area to another. Make a point of checking product labels for suggested methods of disposal and contact your municipality for details of their disposal requirements.

Generally, you can dispose of a small amount of antifreeze, coolant, or windscreen-wiper fluid by diluting it with plenty of water and pouring it down a drain. But if you have a septic tank or large amounts of these materials, recycle them or treat them as hazardous wastes.

Used oil from your vehicle should be handed in for recycling (ask your local garage for details), and battery manufacturers recycle old batteries. Old tyres are retreaded or disposed of by tyre dealers.

Other materials may have to be recycled at special centres or treated as hazardous wastes. These include automatic transmission fluid, brake fluid, diesel fuel, engine degreaser, paint, and power-steering fluid.

Municipal dumps are often split—garden refuse being kept separate from metal, concrete and other non-organic rubbish. Separate your rubbish into the relevant types and dump it as required.

Don't burn waste materials unless your local authority suggests this method of disposal: you will simply contribute to air pollution.

Oil filters

Slippery business
Can't get a grip on a slippery oil filter? Fold a strip of sandpaper in half lengthwise with the grit side out. Place the sandpaper between the filter and the wrench. With the sandpaper grit gripping the wrench and the filter, it will be off in a jiffy.

From kitchen to car
If you have a small car with a cramped engine compartment and don't have a specialized filter wrench on hand, try one of those rubber disc jar openers to remove the oil filter. You probably have an opener in the kitchen.

Piercing problem
Sometimes an old oil filter can't be budged with any wrench. If this is the case, use a hammer to drive a large screwdriver right through the filter, about 50 mm from the engine block. Then turn the filter anticlockwise, using the screwdriver handle as a lever. Once it budges, remove the screwdriver and spin the filter off. Keep a tray under the filter to catch the oil that will leak out.

Screwdriver
Oil filter

Keep it clean
Here's one way to eliminate oil spills and mess when you're removing the oil filter: after loosening the filter, place a plastic bag around it. Once you've removed the filter, simply let it drop into the bag without any oily mess coming into contact with your hands.

Fill 'er up!
When you first start the engine after changing the oil, it takes a few seconds for the oil pump to move the new lubricant through the engine. If the filter screws on vertically or at an angle, you can speed up the oil flow by filling the new filter with fresh oil before you screw it in place. Of course, you can't try this on a horizontally mounted filter or one mounted upside down.

TUNE-UP

Spark plugs

Heads up!
While working on the engine you can accidentally bang your head against the latch under your car's bonnet. To avoid this painful situation (and a large lump), cushion the blow by cutting a slot in an old tennis ball and slipping the ball over the latch.

Flip-flop stop ▶
When using a plug socket spanner with a universal joint to install a spark plug, the joint may be too floppy to reach its target. Try supporting it with a few wraps of sturdy tape. The joint will still be flexible enough to turn.

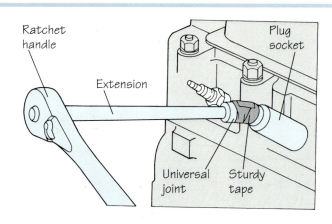

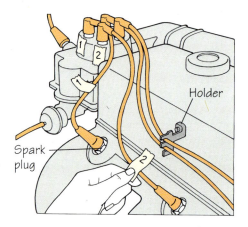

Every spark has its place ▲
You should always reconnect a spark plug wire to the correct spark plug, or the engine will misfire. To avoid a mix-up, remove one wire and plug at a time and replace them before going on to the next one. Or if you want to remove all of the wires and plugs at the same time—which can be more convenient for some jobs—first identify them. Wrap a piece of masking tape around each wire, and place a piece of the tape by each distributor socket. Mark the corresponding number on the tape for each wire and plug. When replacing a wire, make sure it follows the same route previously used, including through the holders that separate the wires.

Gap facts
Spark plugs are not always gapped correctly as they come out of the box or when they are removed from the engine. Before installing a plug, check the gap against the specifications for your car, using a feeler gauge. To adjust the gap, bend the side electrode on the plug with the gapping tool on the gauge, or tap the plug lightly on a hard, flat surface. Never bend the electrode with pliers, you could damage it. ▼

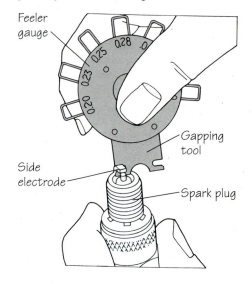

Head ache
A cylinder head can be damaged if you strip its threads while installing or removing a spark plug. To prevent damage to the head, let the engine cool down before removing a plug. Before installing a new plug, brush just a little antiseize compound on the threads. It will make removal easier later on. To avoid cross-threading (when the plug goes in crooked), turn the plug by hand until you feel it seat; then tighten it to the car maker's specifications.

Other tune-up hints

Timing is everything
If your car has an engine with a timing mark, you'll be able to see the mark better if you highlight it with white chalk or paint. Or put a piece of light-coloured tape on each side of the correct timing mark, spacing the pieces about 3 mm apart. When the engine is running, the dark line between the pieces of tape will be even easier to see than a paint or chalk mark.

Filter fixes

A clogged air filter can cause an engine to run poorly or stall. To see if the filter is clogged, remove it and shine a light or torch through it. For a rectangular filter, place the light against one side. If the light barely shows through, the filter is dirty. Replace it. If you don't have a new filter at hand, reuse the old filter by tapping it sharply on the pavement, thus removing some of the dirt. Put in a new filter as soon as possible.

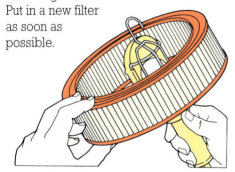

Plugged on purpose

For some tune-up procedures, you have to remove and plug a vacuum hose. (Clamping the hose won't give complete blockage.) Instead of using tape to plug the end, which doesn't always provide an airtight seal, try a golf tee. The tee's tapered shape makes a perfect plug. ▼

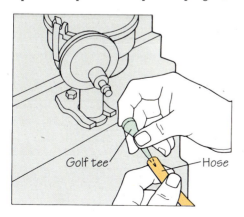

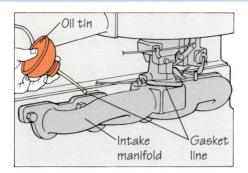

Leaky manifold

Does your car idle roughly without a sign of the standard problems? There could be a leak in the intake manifold. Try squirting some oil along the gasket lines. If there's a leak, the oil will momentarily plug the hole and the idle speed will change. When the oil is sucked through the leak, the rough idle will resume. Try tightening the retaining nuts or bolts to the manufacturer's specifications, using a torque wrench. If that doesn't work, replace the gasket.

PCV leak

If you don't find the reason for a rough-running engine and leaking noises after checking all the vacuum lines, try the PCV (positive crankcase ventilation) line. There may be a crack close to the bottom of the line, where it's exposed to high temperatures.

Wake-up call

Has the starter in an older car given up? You may be able to knock some sense into it if the solenoid clicks but the starter won't turn over. This can be a sign that a worn brush is wedged sideways. A sharp blow on the starter housing with a wooden or rubber mallet may dislodge it. But have the starter repaired as soon as possible.

Fuel injection

Cold start

Traded in your carburettor-equipped car for a new one with electronic fuel injection? Don't floor or pump the accelerator before turning the key to start a cold engine. If the engine doesn't catch immediately, some manufacturers suggest depressing the accelerator pedal about 30 mm as you crank the engine again.

Hot tempered

Trying to restart a hot fuel-injection engine on a hot day can leave you hotter than the motor. If the engine will crank but not start, you have vapour lock. Here's the solution: turn the ignition key on and off for about 3 seconds without cranking the engine. After several on-and-off cycles, crank the engine without pushing the accelerator; if that fails, press the pedal down about 30 mm.

Leaky injector

On an engine with port fuel injection (one injector for each cylinder), air leaks can occur around the O-rings on the fuel injectors. If you can reach them with your fingers, try to rock each injector body side to side, then fore and aft. Any movement will be very slight, but if there is a change in idle speed, the O-ring seal is leaking and needs replacing.

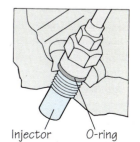

COOLING AND EXHAUST SYSTEMS

Coolant and radiator

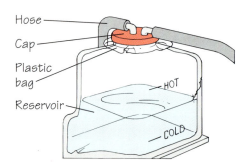

It's in the bag ▲
If the motor is not installed at its base, you can temporarily repair a leaking plastic coolant tank (or windscreen washer tank). Place a clean, sturdy plastic freezer bag inside the tank. Fill the tank to the proper level; then replace the cap and trim off any excess bag, if necessary. Replace the tank or have it repaired as soon as possible.

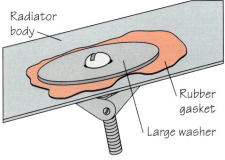

Plug it! ▲
When rust causes a hole in a radiator body, you may be able to temporarily slow the leak. Slip a large washer and rubber gasket onto a suitable toggle bolt. Push the toggle into the hole and tighten the washer and gasket against the body of the radiator. Have the hole properly repaired as soon as possible.

A pinch in time
You may be able to make a temporary quick-and-dirty fix if a radiator tube springs a leak. Wait until the radiator and coolant cool down, or put on a pair of heavy gloves. Then use pliers to bend away the fins near the damaged tube and to pinch the leaking tube closed on both sides of the leak. This will cause more damage than the original leak, but it could keep the car going long enough to get you as far as a garage. ▼

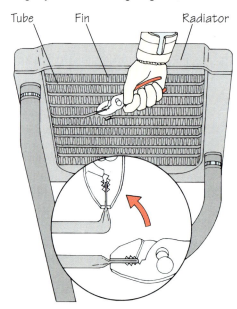

Sweet poison alert!
Antifreeze is very poisonous, but its sweet taste can be alluring to children and animals. Ensure you always store it in a securely closed container and clean up or hose away any spills—no matter how small they may be. When you drain any antifreeze/coolant mixes, you should drain them into a container and dispose of them properly (p 305).

Hoses

A hose in time
A burst coolant hose usually means a stranded car. To avoid breakdowns on the road, make a habit of checking all the coolant hoses, such as the radiator, heater, and bypass hoses, every month or so and replace them as necessary. Check again before going on holiday.

Hot tip
If you must repair a hose leak around hot engine parts, you can protect your hands from burns by wearing kitchen oven mitts. Of course you can't do much fine work with the mitts on. It's better to let the engine cool off if possible.

Hose taming
If a stiff radiator hose is difficult to install, soak it in hot water for a few minutes to make it more pliable.

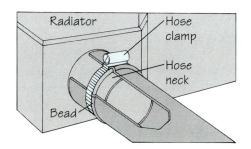

Clamp cramps ▲
When installing a hose clamp, make sure that it's positioned between the radiator and the bead on the hose neck. The clamp should be snug against the bead. If the clamp is on the wrong side of the bead, the hose can leak. If the clamp is too far from the bead, pressure and sediment can build up in the void.

Belts

Chirp, chirp, chirp

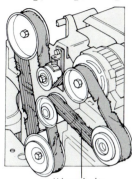
Worn belt

Does your car make a chirping noise? You don't have a nest of birds under the bonnet, but you do have a drive belt that needs attention. The chirping may be caused by a belt that is cracked, frayed, glazed (has a slippery, shiny look), or oil-soaked. A suitable lubricant can reduce the noise, but the belt should be replaced.

Stifle that scream

If you hear squealing noises when you start the engine, a fan belt might be slipping. Check for a loose belt while the engine is cold by pressing the tip of your finger against the belt midway between pulleys on its longest run. You should be able to push the belt in only about 10 to 15 mm, but check this result against those recommended in your vehicle's manual. If you adjust the belt, don't overtighten it. A tight belt is just as bad as a loose one: it won't slip, but the bearings of the pulleys it serves will be subjected to greater wear, leading to earlier replacement.

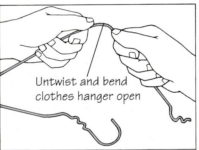
Fan belt

EXHAUST DRAG

The sound of a dragging tailpipe or silencer calls for immediate action. It's dangerous to keep driving. The offending pipe or silencer could wedge itself under your car, or it could break free and end up in the path of another vehicle. If the problem is due to a broken support, you can temporarily secure it until it is properly repaired. Wear thick gloves or use layers of rags to protect your hands while touching the hot tailpipe.

Glove — Rag — Broken support

1 Drive carefully up onto a kerb so that one side of the car is raised. Never work under any vehicle that's supported by a jack. Take a look at the situation. Remember that the tailpipe will be hot.

Untwist and bend clothes hanger open

2 You can use heavy wire, such as a straightened coat hanger, to temporarily support the silencer or pipe. Look for one of these in your car, in roadside trash, or at a nearby business.

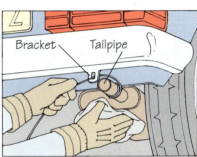
Bracket — Tailpipe

3 Wrap the wire around the end of the tailpipe at least 150 mm from the end and slip it through a bracket while supporting the tailpipe; then twist the ends of the wire support together.

Alignment check

Misaligned pulleys are often responsible for belt noise, erratic operation of belt-driven accessories, belts jumping off pulleys, and uneven belt wear. With the engine running, look at the pulleys from the side of the engine compartment. If you can see a pulley wobbling, it's misaligned and needs adjustment.

Don't trust your eyes

Here's another way to check for pulley alignment, as long as there is adequate space in front of the belts and at least two outer pulleys are in line. With the engine off and cold, place a straight-edge across the pulley faces. If it won't rest on the faces and there's more than a hairline gap, the pulleys are not aligned.

Car and Garage / 309

TRANSMISSION, STEERING, AND SUSPENSION

The transmission

Fluid check

Good automatic-transmission fluid should be translucent and odourless. If it's cloudy or opaque and smells burned, the fluid is in bad condition. To check the condition of the fluid, pull out the transmission dipstick and let a little fluid drip onto a paper towel. After a few minutes, good fluid will form an even red, pink, or tan circle. Burned fluid will form a bull's-eye that's darker in the centre than at the edges.

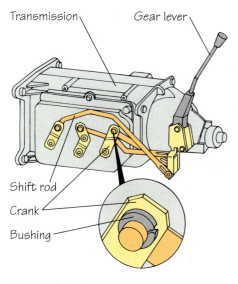

Loose link ▲

A loose shift linkage can make a manual transmission difficult to shift; it can even make the transmission jump out of gear. An experienced do-it-yourselfer can test the linkage by getting underneath the car and wiggling the shift rods back and forth. If there's play at the ends of the rods near the cranks, check for worn bushings and replace them.

Magic mushroom

When you remove the oil sump from an automatic transmission to replace the fluid and filter, don't be surprised if you find a loose mushroom-shaped plug in it. The plug keeps debris out of the transmission during factory assembly and is knocked into the transmission at the last minute. Just toss it out.

Steering and suspension

Stop and go

If the power assistance on your steering seems to stop and start as you turn the wheel around a corner, look for a loose or worn V-belt (p 309) on the power steering pump. If you find one, adjust or replace it. A slipping belt cannot supply constant hydraulic assistance.

Shimmy solution

Steering-wheel shimmy that increases with speed is usually caused by an out-of-balance front wheel. But before the wheels are balanced, check the inside of the wheel rims. An accumulation of grease from a nearby fitting, dried mud or other material can throw the wheel out of balance. Removing the material may be all that you need to do.

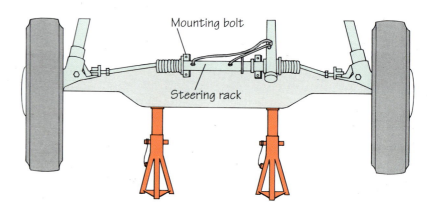

Lost control ▲

Erratic steering may indicate loose parts in the steering linkage. To check for excess play, wiggle the steering wheel while a helper watches the front wheels. There should be less than 6 mm of steering-wheel play before the wheels move. If there is too much play, check for loose steering-rack mounting bolts: place the car on jack stands and chock the rear wheels (p 304). Then move the front wheels while watching the steering rack; the rack shouldn't move. If it does, tighten the bolts.

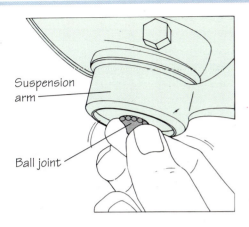

Ball-joint wear ▲

When you replace a ball joint, check the suspension arm it's mounted in for excess wear. Insert the new ball joint into its housing; then try to wiggle it from side to side. If it can wiggle, you'll have to replace the suspension arm too.

Fitting grabber

You can remove a broken grease fitting by tapping a rectangular concrete cut nail into the remaining portion of the fitting, then twisting the nail with pliers. It's painless, effective, and can be performed on the vehicle. ▼

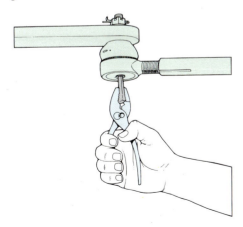

Strutting out

MacPherson struts, used at the front of many front-wheel-drive cars, can be bent if the car hits a kerb or a deep pothole. Check for a bent strut under the bonnet by loosening the nut on the strut rod in the centre of the strut tower. Rotate the strut rod exactly 360°. If the top of the tyre moves in and out, the strut is bent and should be replaced. ▼

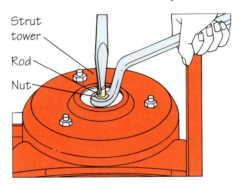

Nothing to boot about

A car owner needs to add one more check to the maintenance list when it comes to a front-wheel-drive vehicle with constant velocity (CV) joints. If you look under the front of your car, you'll see a pair of accordion-ribbed rubber boots by each front wheel. The CV joints are housed inside these boots and are packed with grease. A CV joint will last for years as long as the boot remains sealed. The boot itself may split from fatigue, especially in cold-weather areas, and rocks and potholes can also cause damage. Inspect the boots every three months. Look for grease outside the boot or sprayed onto nearby components. The sooner you have a damaged boot replaced, the better are your chances of keeping the repair bill down.

Down in the valley

Here's another way to spot CV-joint boot failure: the first place that a boot usually cracks is in the valleys between the ribs. To get a clear view for inspection, have a helper turn the steering wheel all the way to one side and back.

Noisy warning

A clicking or clunking noise from the drive shaft as you turn or accelerate is a late warning that the CV joint is on the road to certain failure. The noise indicates a lack of grease in the boot and contamination from road grit. Have the joint replaced as soon as possible.

Snappy service

The mounting nut on a shock absorber often rusts on tight. When it's time to replace the shock, the nut may be difficult to remove. If you can snap off the mounting stud, you can remove the old shock. Place a deep socket spanner with a long extension over the stud and nut. Then rock the stud back and forth steadily until it breaks. The rubber bushings will protect the frame. ▼

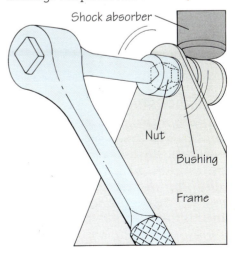

TYRES

The valve

Leak detector
A slow leak may be caused by a faulty valve. To check the valve, remove the cap and wet the end of the valve with a solution of soapy water. If bubbles appear, the valve is leaking. Deflate the tyre fully; then unscrew and replace the valve core. If that doesn't work, have the whole valve replaced.

Cap extractor
Some valve caps are buried deep within fancy wheel covers. You can remove them by using the cap from a felt-tip marker. Push the marker cap over the valve cap until it sticks; then unscrew both caps.

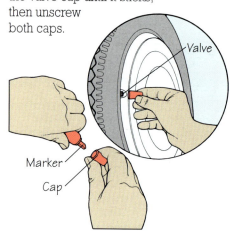

Reach that valve
Extra-long valves (about 20 mm longer than its shorter stablemate) can be fitted by a tyre dealer to wheels with covers. These sometimes make the valves hard to reach but that extra 20 mm or so will often make all the difference.

The treads

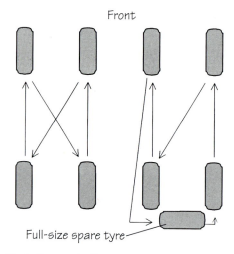

Rotation notation ▲
Car manufacturers recommend rotating tyres from position to position periodically to equalize tread wear. Rotate your tyres as shown above, or check the owner's manual for your car. A good time to rotate the tyres is when you have your vehicle serviced, every 10 000 km or so. So you'll know the previous positions of the tyres, use nail polish or paint to note the relevant information on the rim next to the valve. Small marks such as RF, LF, RR, LR and S (for spare) are sufficient.

Don't just glance at them
Improper tyre inflation and worn treads can cause an accident. Don't rely on visual inspection alone to check the inflation of a radial tyre. A radial's sidewalls normally bulge where the tyre meets the road, making it difficult to determine when they're bulging too much. Use an accurate pressure gauge at least once a month.

Depth perception
The minimum amount of tread allowed on a tyre, over at least 75 per cent of its road-bearing width (but over its entire circumference), is 1 mm. Don't, however, allow any one of your car's tyres to reach that stage—start making plans to have them replaced when the tread reaches the depth of a matchstick. Break one in half and put a piece into a tread groove—do the test in a few positions around the tyre's circumference. If you can feel the matchstick standing proud of the surrounding surface of the tyre, in any area, take action.

Reading treads
The wear patterns on your car's tyres tell a lot about the car's suspension, how well you maintain the tyres, and your driving habits. If a tyre exhibits any of these signs, have the problem fixed. ▼

A worn centre points to an over-inflated tyre.

Wear along both edges tells you that the tyre was underinflated.

Feathered tread edges indicate incorrect wheel alignment.

A single worn spot shows that you've skidded with the brakes locked.

A scalloped, or cupped, wear pattern means that the wheel is unbalanced, suspension or steering parts are worn, or the wheel bearings are faulty.

CHANGING A TYRE

Tyre changing is a basic skill every driver should have—not only in case of a flat, but in order to rotate the tyres from wheel to wheel (see facing page). The best time to practise tyre changing is during free time in your garage or driveway—not along the side of a busy highway or on an isolated road in the rain.

Make sure you always keep a spare tyre, jack, jack handle or screwdriver, wheel spanner, rubber mallet, and tyre pressure gauge in the boot. You should also carry a couple of blocks of timber for use as chocks. (A piece of 22 mm plank, about 250 x 250 mm, is also a good addition to the list.) Make a point of regularly checking your spare's pressure—finding it's flat when you have a puncture can be annoying.

Park on firm level ground and turn off the engine. Set the handbrake, and put the transmission into park (or a manual transmission into reverse). Make sure everyone is out of the car before you start changing the tyre. If the ground is soft, put the piece of plank under the jack to stop it sinking into the ground. If necessary, set out a reflective triangle between yourself and oncoming traffic. After changing the tyre, don't forget to remove the chocks and return your tools and equipment to the boot.

If your spare tyre is a "temporary" type, observe the precautions set out in your owner's manual.

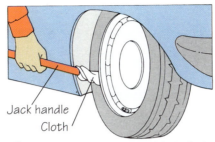

1 Remove the wheel cover with the jack handle or a screwdriver wrapped in a cloth. Some covers have special locks. Check your owner's manual if the cover can't be prised off.

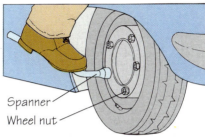

2 Loosen the nuts two or three turns. If one won't budge, set the spanner horizontally and push down on its handle with your foot. Most nuts are loosened in an anticlockwise direction. In an old car, you may have to turn the nuts clockwise.

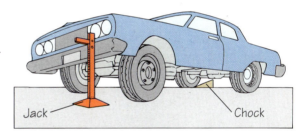

3 Put chocks (p 304), wood blocks, or stones under the wheel diagonally opposite the flat tyre. Following the car maker's directions, position the jack and raise the car until the flat is 50 mm off the ground. Remove the jack handle.

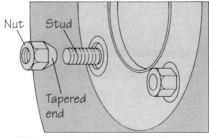

4 Remove the wheel nuts, and remove the wheel. Mount the spare tyre on the studs. Press against the wheel, and thread on the nuts by hand, starting at the bottom. The tapered part of the wheel nuts should face the wheel.

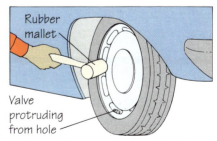

5 Lower the car and remove the jack. Tighten the nuts in a crisscross pattern (p 314). Align the hole in the cover with the tyre valve. Tap the cover into place with a rubber mallet.

Car and Garage / 313

WHEELS AND BRAKES

Getting wheels on or off

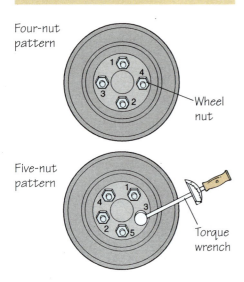

Four-nut pattern

Five-nut pattern

Nut cracker ▲
Always tighten the wheel nuts in a criss-cross pattern—not in a circle. Overtight wheel nuts can crack the wheel or warp disc-brake rotors. Use an inexpensive torque wrench to tighten the wheel nuts to the car maker's specifications, but do so progressively. For example, tighten all the nuts to 5 kg, then 10 kg, and so on until the suggested torque is reached.

Torque talk
The power tools used by some tyre dealers speed things up, but often the nuts are so tight you may have difficulty if you ever have to change a wheel. Have the dealer use a torque wrench instead, and be there when the wheels are put back on the hubs to ensure they are torqued down properly. If in any doubt, loosen each wheel nut at home and retighten each one to the correct torque.

Spanner spinner
Cross-type wheel spanners work well, but spinning one on the palm of your hand can raise painful blisters. To spin the spanner easily and without damage to your hand, make a holder from a 200 mm length of 40 mm PVC pipe, and cement a cap to one end. When you're ready to use the spanner, slide the pipe over its end and spin away. After you've finished the job, you'll find your palm is blister-free. ▼

Bust it loose!
A wheel can rust onto the brake drum or hub and be hard to remove, even when the wheel nuts are off. To remove the wheel, don't yank on it while the car is jacked up—the car could fall off the jack. Instead, put the nuts back on finger-tight, then loosen them two turns. Lower the car to the ground and rock it from side to side. If that doesn't free the wheel, drive backwards and forwards for a couple of metres, applying the brakes hard.

Not just a pipe dream
Carry a length of pipe to slip over your wheel spanner. It's a useful aid when changing a wheel. Women, especially, may need the additional leverage.

Rust and rattles

Rust alert
If you mount new tyres on old rims, make sure they are rust-free. Rust at the hub can weaken the wheel and if it's on the rim, it can cause slow air leaks from tubeless tyres. Remove any rust with a wire brush; apply a rust-arresting fluid and, when it dries, rust-resistant paint.

Easy off
The next time the wheels are off the car, flush the studs and wheel nuts with a penetrating oil. Avoid getting any oil on the brake surfaces and other parts. To be absolutely sure the studs won't corrode, coat them with an antiseize compound before replacing the nuts.

Rattle traps
Wheel covers and hubcaps can sometimes cause annoying rattles. To isolate the culprit, remove one wheel cover at a time and go for a short test drive. Then try these cures:
▷ Look for a pebble or loose wheel nut rattling around behind the wheel cover.
▷ If a loose emblem is rattling, tighten it, glue it down with epoxy, or remove it.
▷ If a wheel-cover clip is loose, readjust it so that it grips the rim tightly.

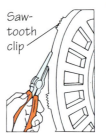

Saw-tooth clip

Brakes

Braking awareness

Quite a few cars on the road have brake problems. If you feel, see, or hear any of the following conditions, it's time for repairs—don't delay.

▷ Rhythmical vibrations or pulsations in the brake pedal (unless your car has an antilock braking system, where these are normal) could mean the brake rotors or drums are warped.

▷ Pay attention to that brake warning light on the instrument panel. If it stays on after the engine is started, the brakes could be unsafe.

▷ Brakes that pull the car to one side, grab suddenly, lock up prematurely or drag, are dangerous. Check for any hydraulic fluid leaking onto the brakes, sticking disc brake callipers, or wheel-cylinder problems.

▷ An occasional squeak or squeal from disc brakes when braking lightly is OK, but any loud screeching, grinding, or shuddering may mean worn-out brake pads or brake shoes that are scoring the rotors or drums.

▷ Changes in the feel of the brake pedal may also indicate trouble. A pedal that is high or difficult to press down could be a sign of a power-brake problem. A too-soft pedal that goes nearly to the floor may be caused by poorly adjusted drum brakes or a serious brake system failure. A spongy-feeling brake pedal often means that air is trapped in the brake system.

▷ Beware of brake pipes passing close to panel joins or other sharp edges. A leak may result if they vibrate against the edge. Bend the pipe out of the way.

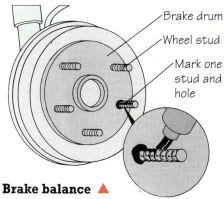

Brake balance ▲

If you remove a drum to do work on a drum brake, be sure that you reinstall it in its original position. As a guide, mark one stud and the hole it goes through with chalk, paint, or a felt-tip marker before you remove the drum.

Wheel wobble ▲

An annoying vibration that feels like an out-of-balance wheel could also be caused by a warped brake drum. To check if the drum is straight, remove the wheel and lay a straightedge across the drum's mounting surface. Check four sides of the drum, in a square pattern. If you see daylight under the straightedge, replace the drum.

Hang it up

When you remove a brake calliper to do work on a disc brake, don't let it hang on the rubber brake hose. Use a length of coat hanger or other heavy wire to hang the calliper from the suspension. This will ensure a secure resting place for the calliper where it won't get knocked about, which can cause damage to the hose. ▼

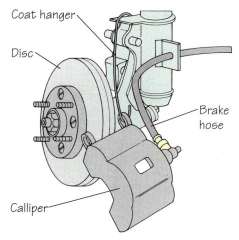

Taking up the slack

If the handbrake cable has stretched so much that you can no longer adjust it, try using a cable adjuster to take up the slack—but first ensure there is enough exposed cable and room to fit in the adjuster, even after slacking off the cable. If the cable is frayed, kinked, or corroded, it must be replaced. ▼

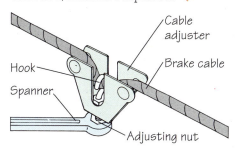

ELECTRICAL SYSTEM

The battery

Positively shocking

When disconnecting battery cables, always start with the negative cable. If you start with the positive cable (on the post marked POS or +, or painted red) and your spanner accidentally touches another metal part, the battery will be short-circuited, sparks will fly, and you'll receive a shock. The spanner may also weld itself to the metal part. ▼

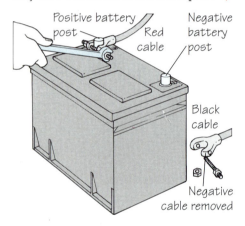

Damage control

If your battery is fully discharged, it will have to be jolted with a special high-voltage charger. Before using a charger (or letting a mechanic use one on your car), make sure the battery cables are disconnected. Otherwise, the charger can blow fuses and damage electrical components from clocks to computers.

A swipe in time

Dirt and grit on a battery can form a path for a slow electrical drain, more so in damp weather. Whenever you check the oil, clean off the top and sides of the battery with a damp cloth.

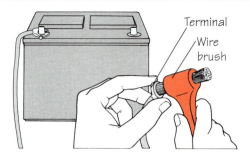

Terminal treats ▲

Many car owners know that a light coat of petroleum jelly will reduce corrosion buildup on the top posts of batteries. Trickle a warm solution of bicarbonate of soda (a teaspoon or two in a cup of water) over the corrosion. It will bubble and when this ceases, wash it off with water. Clean the post with a wire brush or terminal cleaner, reattach the cable clamp and lightly coat that and the post with petroleum jelly. Make sure you coat the underside of the clamp and post.

Secret vents

A maintenance-free battery has an extra electrolyte inside, so it may take years of water evaporation to affect the battery's output. When that time comes, however, a flat sealed-top battery will have to be replaced. But if your model has disguised vent caps, you may be able to extend the battery's life. Try prising the vent caps off carefully, without breaking or cracking them. If you can do this, you can replenish the water in the battery.

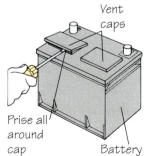

Space filler

Most batteries in this country are sized to meet car manufacturers' specifications, but you may purchase a battery that is too squat to be securely anchored by its J-bolts or hold-down clip. If so, buy a spacer, or use a piece of an interlocking plastic floor mat.

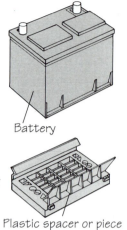

Electrical connections

Disconnected

Many electrical problems are caused by loose, corroded, or faulty connectors. When you trace a fault to a particular connector, look for signs of corrosion or damage, and check that the two parts still fit together tightly. If they don't, adjust them so that they do, then spray them with a contact cleaner and reconnect them.

Lube job

When you open an electrical connector, you may find that it has a special grease inside to help keep out moisture, retard corrosion, and dissipate heat. In most cases, it's silicone dielectric grease (check the service manual for the car, or call the service department of your car dealer). This grease is available from motor spares dealers. You should never apply ordinary grease.

Lights

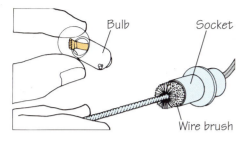

Can't be too clean ▲

If a light refuses to work, it doesn't necessarily mean that the bulb is faulty. Corrosion in the socket can prevent electricity from reaching it. Use a wire brush to clean out the socket.

Slippery fingers

When handling a quartz halogen bulb, keep your fingers off its glass. These bulbs burn so hot that the oil on your fingers will crack the glass. If you do accidentally touch the glass, clean it with alcohol.

Drain stopper

If you need to keep the car door open for a long time and you can't switch off the roof light independently, wedge a tennis ball between the door and the light switch. It will keep the light off and reduce battery drain. If you don't have an old ball, cut a triangular wedge of scrap wood and pad it with a cloth.

A NEW AERIAL

Replacing a car radio aerial is a common 30-minute repair that most people can do themselves. But yanking all the old parts out without noting the way the cable is routed can turn the job into a few hours of frustration.

Before routing the new cable through the car, make sure it's long enough: measure the old cable where it's visible and calculate, as accurately as you can, the length out of sight behind the bodywork. When you have removed the old cable, check the replacement against it for length. If it is any shorter, beware. If it's a little longer, you have more freedom of action.

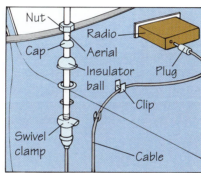

1 Unplug the old cable from the radio jack. Tape a length of sturdy string to the cable plug. Free the cable from any clips or brackets. Remove the nut at the aerial; slide other parts off.

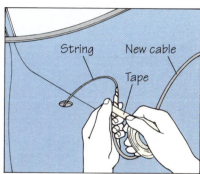

2 Push a screwdriver through the hole down one side of the clamp; pull the aerial and old cable out. Tape new cable to string end; pull it through. Plug in new cable; attach new aerial.

Aim to please ▶

After having your headlights adjusted by a professional, park the car at the entrance to your garage. Mark the outline of the patterns made by both the high and the low beams on the back wall of the garage. Also mark the position of the front wheels on the garage floor. If the headlights go out of alignment, use these marks to check and readjust them. To do this, remove any trim to reach the adjustment screw above the light.

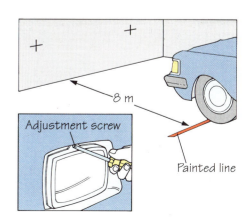

Car and Garage / 317

FUEL SYSTEM

Petrol in the car

Never let your car have too much

Alcohol is often used as a petrol additive. More than 10 per cent alcohol can cause a rough idle, stalling, and power loss in your car. If the rest of the fuel system is OK, siphon some petrol out of the tank. Tape a photocopy of a metric rule to a glass jar and pour in 50 mm of water. Very slowly add the same amount of petrol without mixing it with the water; the petrol will float above the heavier water. Seal the jar with a lid, and shake it. The alcohol will separate from the petrol and mix with the water. Let the jar stand for five minutes; then check the new levels. If the volume of the water (on the bottom) has increased by more than 10 per cent (over 60 mm), there is too much alcohol in the petrol. Switch to another brand.

Cap keeper

After filling the petrol tank, have you ever driven away without replacing the petrol cap? Glue a magnet to it so that when you fill the tank, you can stick the cap in view so you won't forget it. You can also fix a line to the cap, connecting the other end to the car. Even if you fail to replace the cap, it won't be lost.

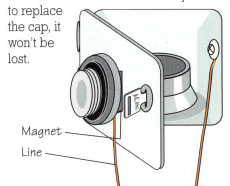

Magnet
Line

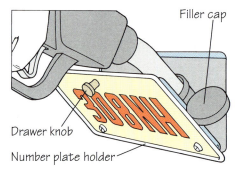

Filler cap
Drawer knob
Number plate holder

Filler flap ▲

Some cars have their petrol filler hidden behind a hinged, spring-loaded number plate holder. To make it easier to open, drill a hole through the plate and install a small drawer knob. Once you remove the petrol cap, wedge it behind the holder to keep it open while you insert the petrol nozzle.

Saving fuel

Most drivers are familiar with the time-tested advice for improving petrol consumption: avoid "jackrabbit" starts and avoid speeding. Here are a few additional tips that should be observed:
▷ Check the tyre pressure often. Fuel consumption will increase if your tyres are markedly underinflated.
▷ Have the wheel alignment checked periodically. Wheels that drag increase fuel consumption.
▷ Have the brakes checked regularly. Brakes that drag increase consumption.
▷ Remove excess weight from the boot: the more the engine has to move, the more petrol it has to use.
▷ Don't remain stationary to warm the engine. It's better to start on your trip, driving relatively slowly to warm the engine. Progressively increase your speed as the engine gets closer and closer to its operating temperature.

Leak stopper

You can temporarily plug a small leak in a petrol tank with bubble gum! Chew the gum until all the sugar is gone, then press it into the leaking area. The petrol will harden it into a hard mass that should hold long enough for you to drive to a garage.

Don't choke on it!

If your engine often stalls immediately after being started, the choke may be opening too much. If your car has a specified opening gap (not an angled gap) between the choke plate and the carburettor barrel, you can check the opening with a drill bit that is the same size as the gap (a 9 mm bit for a 9 mm gap). On a warm day, while the engine is cold, remove the air-filter cover, start the engine, and the instant the choke opens, insert the bit. It should slide in and out with a light drag. To avoid dropping it into the carburettor, stick a piece of masking tape around its end. If the bit is a loose fit, have the choke adjusted, but as it opens quickly, don't hold the bit in place to retest—the result won't be accurate. ▼

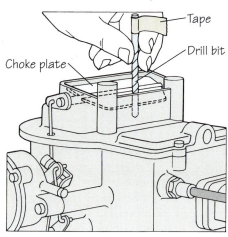

Tape
Drill bit
Choke plate

PAINT TOUCH-UP

Applying paint

Rust arrester
After scraping or sanding rust from a chip or scratch, apply a rust converter. This product transforms rust into an impervious black coating that prevents further rusting under the paint. Follow the instructions on the label to apply two thin coats. Let the converter dry for 48 hours before applying paint.

To prime or not
Acrylic latex automotive paints require an undercoat of a solvent-base primer or sealer. Lacquer and enamel paints don't. Check paint labels for primer recommendations.

Fill 'er up
It may take several coats of touch-up paint to fill a chip up to the original paint surface. Dab on the coats with a small artist's brush, a cotton swab, or an ear bud. Allow each dab to dry before applying the next.

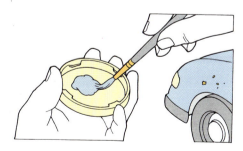

Spray away ▲
Want to touch up a small chip or two but the matching colour of touch-up paint is available only in an aerosol can? Shake the can well. Spray some paint into a jar lid or paper cup; apply it with a brush.

PAINT PROBLEMS

Before using a primer or paint, do a test in a hidden spot, such as under the bumper. When painting, always work in a well-lighted area. Here are a few problems encountered with spray-paints, and ways to deal with them:

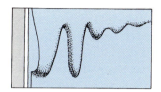

Drips and runs happen when paint is sprayed on too thick. Let the paint dry completely; then smooth the area with wet, fine sandpaper (200 grit or finer). Clean the area and repaint it.

Orange peel, as the name implies, resembles the rough skin of the citrus fruit. It's caused by spraying too thin a coat or by paint that's improperly mixed (not enough solvent). Wet-sand, clean, and repaint the area.

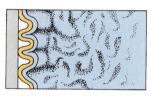

Wrinkling or lifting occurs when paint is applied over an incompatible primer. Sand down to the bare metal, and start the job over using a compatible primer and paint.

When silicone or wax isn't completely removed, small spots, called fish eyes, let the old surface show through. Wipe off the wet paint with a lint-free cloth and thinner. Clean the area with alcohol or a precleaning solvent, and start from the beginning.

Mask task ▶
When painting small areas with an aerosol spray-paint, use this trick to avoid the hassle of masking off the surrounding surface: cut a 30 mm hole in the centre of a piece of cardboard. Hold the cardboard a few centimetres from the car, and spray through the hole with the nozzle about 30 mm from the hole. This confines the spray without leaving behind the ridges you get when masking tape is removed.

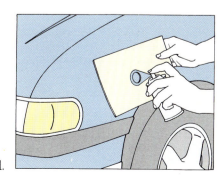

Car and Garage / 319

KEEPING UP APPEARANCES

Car wash, etc

Foaming seat
You can give your vinyl car upholstery a fresh, clean look by scrubbing it with a mixture of 30 ml of liquid dishwashing detergent in 2,5 litres of hot water.

Hair of the dog
Don't pour leftover stale beer down the drain (or worse yet, down your throat). You can use it to clean off the leather upholstery in your car. But don't do this on the road—and leave the car to air for a while. You don't want a traffic officer to misinterpret the situation, do you?

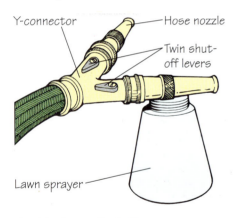

Double-barrelled ▲
For convenience, attach a Y-connector with double shutoff valves to your garden hose. Screw a hose nozzle onto one side of the Y and a lawn sprayer holding concentrated liquid car soap to the other side. With this setup, you can switch from soapy water for washing to clear water for rinsing at will. All it takes is the flick of a finger.

Bug beater
Here's a remedy for removing dead bugs from your car: spray the car with a mixture of 1/2 cup baking soda and 2 cups warm water. Wait 2 minutes; then respray the car and sponge off the bugs. The baking soda neutralizes the acid in the bugs, making them easy to remove, but it won't damage the car's finish.

Sapped
Remove dried tree sap from your car by following these steps: carefully break off lumps of sap, using a plastic kitchen spatula to avoid scratching the paint. Soak a soft cloth in a mixture of laundry detergent and hot water. Wearing heavy plastic or rubber gloves, rub the sap residue with the cloth as hard as you can. Continue rubbing and breaking off lumps until the sap disappears; then rinse the area with cold water. When the surface is dry, treat the spots with a car polish and then rewax the whole car.

Don't be stumped by stickers!
To remove a bumper sticker, heat it with a hairdryer until the glue loosens, then carefully peel it off. To remove a dealer emblem, heat it with a hairdryer and then prise the emblem off using a putty knife with its blade wrapped with tape. After removing a sticker or emblem, get rid of any remaining adhesive by rubbing it with your thumb. If it doesn't ball up, apply alcohol or rubber cement thinner with a paper towel.

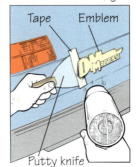

Cheap scrubbers
A small scrap of a deep-pile carpet makes a good car scrubber. An unused dust-mop head is also handy—just stick your hand into the pocket and scrub.

Hot wheels ▲
Your brakes can heat parts of the wheel to 150°C or more. Never apply a cleaner to such a hot wheel. The mild acids contained in these cleaners can do damage at high temperatures. Cool off the wheel with a garden hose before applying a cleaning solution.

White-washed
For the reappearance of white lettering hidden under the dirt on your tyres, tackle the dirt with a soapy pot scrubbing pad from the kitchen.

A repelling thought
Apply a thin coat of one of those clear plastic-protecting-and-enhancing sprays to alloy wheels to help keep tar flecks, insects, grease, dirt, and other debris from staining them.

Stubby to the rescue!
To remove dried polish from the seams and crevices on your car's bodywork, trim a paintbrush's bristles to 20 mm, then brush away the deposits.

The windscreen

Clear clogs, confirm connections

Don't simply buy a new pump if your windscreen washer unit fails: check the electrical side first—wiring, switches and connections. If the washer refuses to spray, even though the tank is filled with fluid and there are no leaks in the system, look for clogs. The bottom of the tank must be clean: if not, the inlet pipe may be blocked. If the tank's fine, disconnect the hose from the nozzle at the windscreen. If the hose is clear, the nozzle is clogged. Clear it by carefully probing it with a small safety pin, fine needle or thin wire. ▼

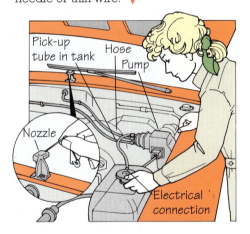

More solutions

A few drops of liquid dishwashing detergent in your windscreen washer water helps in the removal of debris and dirt from your windscreen. The problem of haziness on the inner surfaces of a window can be caused by vapours from vinyl. So, wash vinyl surfaces, using the mixture recommended for upholstery: 30 ml of liquid dishwashing detergent in 2,5 litres of hot water.

WIPER WOES

Replace your windscreen wipers as soon as they begin to lose their effectiveness, but read the hints in this panel first. A simple solution may solve the problem, saving you the expense of buying new wipers.

Straighten a bent arm with the wiper at mid-stroke. Using two pairs of pliers, carefully twist the arm until it's parallel to the glass. But if the tip is bent, take the whole assembly off to straighten it.

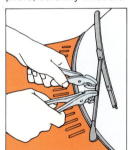

Water beads indicate a buildup of grease, wax, oil, or grime. Try increasingly stronger cleaning solvents. Cover the car when it's parked outdoors to protect it from air pollution.

Smearing is a sign of a dirty windscreen or wiper, a worn blade, or a poor mix of washer solution. Clean the wipers and windscreen, and replace the solution; if this fails, replace the blade.

Smearing in only one direction often occurs when the blades are the wrong size or when they harden from cold weather or old age. If they're cold, let them warm up; otherwise, renew them.

Chattering is caused by a bent wiper arm or a frozen blade on a cold day. Straighten the arm (see above left), thaw out or replace the blade, or replace the wiper arm and blade.

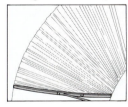

Demister deflector

Temporarily block the demister vents on the passenger side of the car. More air will be forced through the vents in front of the driver, clearing that side of the windscreen more quickly. The sooner the driver has a clear view of the road ahead, the better.

Glass repair

You can polish out shallow scratches in a clean windscreen with jeweller's rouge and a small polishing pad on an electric drill set at a low speed. Polish the glass, using several passes if necessary and clean off the rouge with soap and water.

STORAGE, RESTRAINTS, AND SECURITY

Everything in its place

Valuable papers
Keep a plastic A4 document sleeve in a safe place in your car to hold valuable papers such as guarantees: you'll always have the necessary documents handy. You can also keep a list of dates for tune-ups, oil changes, and tyre rotation in the sleeve as a handy reminder.

Pocket protector
Make this storage bag out of strong cloth; it's ideal to keep maps and other items organized, particularly on long trips. Use Velcro strips or tape to hold the bag against the seat back and at the base.

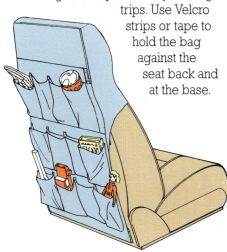

Mat tact
Does your floor mat refuse to stay in one spot, or do the corners flip up all the time and get in the way of your feet? Use Velcro tape at each corner of the mat to keep it and the corners in place.

Visor advisory
Here's another way to put Velcro tape to use: apply it to a drooping sun visor to hold it up and out of the way.

Containment policy
Be prepared for an emergency. Wrap tools and warning triangles in a blanket, and secure the bundle in the boot with a rope or an elastic cord. The blanket keeps the items together, stops them rattling, and it comes in handy if you have to crawl under the car.

Carpet capers 1
Carpet remnants are useful for lining the boot of your car. They protect your luggage and stop the contents rattling.

Carpet capers 2
Rest a bakkie's cargo on an old carpet: you'll be able to move it about without scratching the bakkie's bed.

Kneepads
Storing and retrieving items from the bed of a bakkie can be tough on the knees. To protect them, pad the top of the tailgate with carpeting. Attach a sheet of hardboard to the tailgate with self-tapping stainless-steel screws. Then glue the carpeting to the hardboard with contact adhesive. ▼

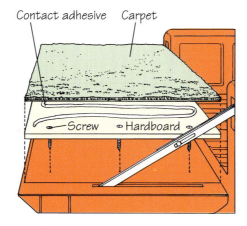

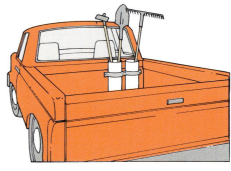

Tool caddy ▲
You can carry tools such as rakes and shovels upright in a bakkie bed by making holders from 1 m lengths of 150 mm diameter PVC pipe. Secure the pipe to the inside of the bakkie bed with galvanized pipe straps and stainless-steel self-tapping screws. You can attach several pipes, but make sure that your view from the driver's seat won't be restricted and that items don't protrude beyond the bakkie bed.

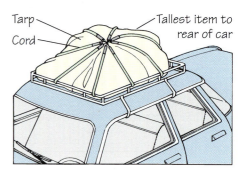

Beat the wind ▲
Planning to carry a load on a roof rack for a long trip? Spread a large tarpaulin over the rack; then load it, with the tallest items to the rear of the car. Wrap the tarpaulin over the items, and secure the bundle with crab-style elastic cords. The streamlined shape will offer less wind resistance and the tarpaulin will provide protection from the weather.

Roof padding

When hauling items on your car's rooftop, protect the paint by placing a partially inflated blow-up bed or a scrap of carpet padding under the cargo.

Aiming devices

Here's how to line up your trailer and hitch for an easy hookup:

▷ On a car: mount a small mirror on the trailer, facing your car, and adjust it so that you can see the trailer's hitch from the driver's seat. Manoeuvre your car using the view in the mirror.

▷ On a bakkie: place a strip of brightly coloured vinyl tape over the top of the tailgate, directly above the hitch, and a second piece on the trailer above its hitch. Keep the two pieces of tape aligned as you back up to the trailer.

Keys and locks

Backup key

Avoid the hassle and expense of locking yourself out of your car. Have a duplicate key cut, then wire it out of sight under the vehicle or behind the grille. There are plenty of places where you can hide it completely (without any security problem) yet where it will still be accessible when you need it. ▼

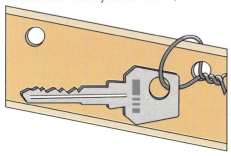

Stuck in the boot

Boot lock cylinders may become jammed, in some cases because of an unsuccessful theft attempt. If you can't get at your prized possessions inside your boot, drill through the keyhole with a large bit (such as 10 mm), then insert a narrow screwdriver to release the latching mechanism. Replace the lock, but remember that you'll have to use a separate key just for the boot from now on, as the door key will no longer fit. To avoid confusion and possible damage to the door or boot locks, mark the new key very clearly.

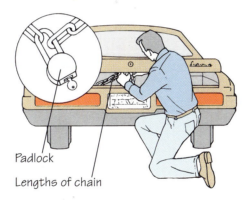

Padlock
Lengths of chain

Linked ▲

Thieves can force your boot open with a crowbar. Take this step to foil them: bolt a few links of chain inside the boot lid, and anchor a second length to the boot floor; then connect the free ends of the two chains with a padlock. The chains should be just long enough to let you fit your hands inside to open or close the lock, but not long enough to let luggage or valuables be removed. Cover the chains with pieces of rubber hose to keep them from rattling or damaging items stored in the boot.

Two for the price of one

If you own two cars of the same make and they use double-cut keys with identical notches on the top and bottom, a locksmith can make you one key that fits both cars. Starting with a blank key, have the locksmith cut one side each to fit each car. Then have a notch cut into the side for the car you drive most often, so you can tell which side is up. ▼

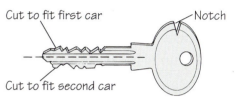

Cut to fit first car — Notch
Cut to fit second car

Jammed latch

A door that bounces back open after you swing it closed may have a jammed latch. Inside the U-shaped opening in the side of the door is a rotating latch with a pair of prongs. If it's flipped to the closed position, the door won't shut. To unjam the latch, pull, lift, or push the exterior handle as if to open the door. If the latch doesn't rotate to the open position, hold the handle open and move the latch downward with your finger or a screwdriver. ▼

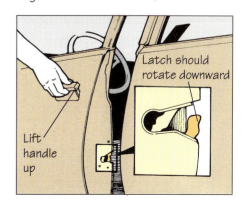

Latch should rotate downward
Lift handle up

WINTER TIPS

Preparing for the cold

Lighten up
Lighter-viscosity motor oils (5W30 or 10W30) make a car easier to start in cold weather than heavier-weight oils such as 10W40. Check your owner's manual to see if lightweight oils are recommended for your car. If so, switch to one when cold weather threatens.

Heat cure
A warm battery produces more cranking power than a cold one. If you live in an area that gets very cold in winter, give a feeble battery a helping hand: put a small fan heater near it and turn it on first thing in the morning, before you prepare for work. By the time you are ready to depart, an hour or so later, the battery should be warmed up.

Faster starts
The colder your motor oil is, the thicker it gets and the harder it is for the engine to crank over. In cold weather, immediately you have parked your car in the garage, place a thick blanket (try some leftover heat insulation batts or dog blankets) over the car's bonnet. This will retain the heat of the engine for a while at least. You can also reinforce this measure by having a small bar heater positioned on the garage floor below the engine compartment. Switching this on at the same time as covering the engine can slow cooling to such a degree that in the morning the engine will be easy to start.
Caution: Ensure that the bonnet cover is secured in place and cannot fall on the heater—tape loops fitted over the wing mirrors will hold the cover in place.

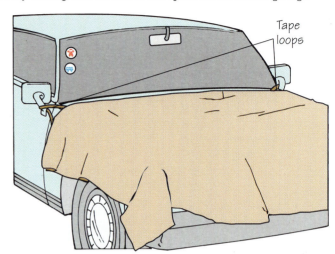

Jumper cables

Jumper bump-up
Buy the longest and thickest jumper cables you can find. Short cables limit the distance and positioning of the two cars and cables that are too thin won't carry enough current to boost a dead battery—especially in cold weather.

Too hot to handle
If, however, you have only thin cables, first use them to charge the dead battery for a few minutes. Trying to start the second car at once puts an extra load on the cables, causing them to heat up. Charging the battery eases the load.

Avoid tangles
To keep jumper cables from getting tangled, lay them side by side and wrap plastic insulation tape around the pair in three or four places. But don't tape them together within 1 m of either end. ▼

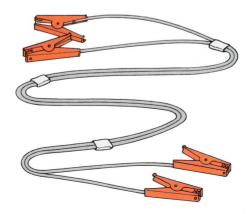

Snow and ice

Traction aid
Going up to the mountains to see the snow? A couple of rolls of half-round timber edging, available from nurseries, could be useful. Roll out the edging with the rounded surfaces uppermost, and drive out of trouble. When spring comes, use the edging in your garden as intended.

Gritty aid

Keep a bag of cat litter or a few large plastic bottles filled with sand in the boot. In rear-wheel-drive cars, they will add extra weight for better traction. If you do get stuck in mud or snow, you can pour the sand or litter under the drive wheels to get going again.

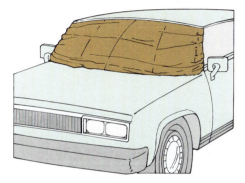

Labour saver ▲

Instead of scraping frost from the windscreen on a winter morning, try one of the following: the night before, cover the windscreen with a heavy-duty plastic refuse bag that's been cut open along the edges. Close the doors on the edges of the plastic sheet to keep it from blowing away. Or cover the windscreen with a piece of old carpet (pile side up) that's been cut to fit. In the morning, peel off your cover, shake it to remove the frost and drive away.

Emergency scraper

If you use your windscreen washer in very cold weather, the spray may freeze on the glass. A credit card will remove all but the thickest buildup, but take care not to damage the black magnetic strip that runs along the back of the card.

Chilled out

Frozen door locks can ruin the better part of a winter day. Here's what you can do to prevent or cure the problem:
▷ Cover the locks with tape before going through a car wash or whenever precipitation is predicted.
▷ Keep lock cylinders lubricated by squirting in penetrating oil, a water repellent, or cigarette-lighter fluid.
▷ Place a drinking straw in the key slot and exhale into it until the lock thaws.
▷ Heat the key with a lighter or matches, then slowly work it into the frozen lock. Be sure to wear thick gloves so you don't burn your fingers. ▼

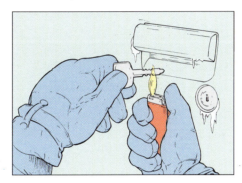

Car heater

Finding the heat

On a bitterly cold day, it often seems that it takes too long for your car to heat up. If it really does take too long, there could be an inadequate flow of heat. To analyze the situation, stick a meat thermometer into an interior heater vent. With the engine warmed up, the heater set on *Hot*, and the selector on *Vent*, the thermometer should read 38°C or more. If it does, all is well.

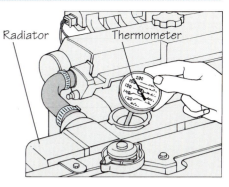

Thermostat out of whack ▲

To isolate a faulty thermostat (another reason for poor heat), warm up the engine with the radiator cap removed. Stick a meat thermometer into the coolant. If it reads at least 80°C and the upper radiator hose is hot to the touch (watch out for the fan), the thermostat is OK. If not, replace the thermostat.
Caution: Never remove the radiator cap from a hot engine!

Hot hands

With the heater on, carefully touch both heater hoses (they could be hot). If they're not hot, have a mechanic check the water control valve or heater core.

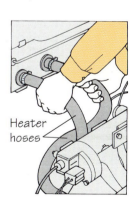

Final test

Check each selector setting (*Vent, Floor, Defrost*, etc.) inside the car. If air isn't flowing to the correct outlet, or if the air flow changes speed or location as you accelerate, have a mechanic look for vacuum-control or linkage problems.

GARAGE

Keep out the elements

Seal it up
Keep rainwater, rodents and debris out of your garage by installing a foam draught excluder on the bottom of the garage door. It's available in rolls and in a variety of widths. Simply peel off the cover strip and press the excluder into place.

Even it out
If your garage floor is uneven, you can still create a good seal between the bottom of the garage door and the floor. Simply tack a length of ordinary garden hose to the bottom of the door. If it is slit along its length, you will find it easier to attach to the door. The slit will also allow the hose to conform more readily to the contours of the floor. Have the slit side on the inner surface so that a neat result is apparent when viewed from the outside. But remember that a well-sealed garage means a greater danger of carbon monoxide buildup. Never run an engine inside a closed garage.

Moisture barrier 1
Do you have a multipanel wood garage door? Protect its vulnerable bottom section from moisture by running paintable caulk along the joint where the bottom horizontal rail joins the panels. ▼

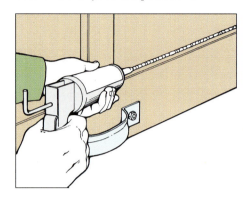

Moisture barrier 2
You know what a mess rainwater makes on your garage floor when you park your car. Confine the water to the area beneath the car by glueing three strips of rubber garage-door bottom seals or draught excluder to the floor. Most of the garage floor will stay clean and dry, and the water will be channelled out to the driveway. ▼

Parking

Things that go bump
Judging how far is far enough when parking your car in the garage is often tricky. Save your car and the garage wall from damage by hanging a tennis ball, or a sponge rubber ball, from the ceiling to use as your guide. To install it, park your car exactly where you want it. Then mount a screw eye in the ceiling, positioned so that when the ball hangs, it touches the windscreen on the driver's side. No more guesswork!

Front and centre
Have you parked your car only to find you could barely get out because of lack of space on the side? End the frustration by painting a bright stripe the width of your car on the back wall of the garage. You'll centre your car with ease.

Stay within the lines
Keep bicycles, garden equipment and other items out of the way by painting white lines on the garage floor, outlining a space for each item. As long as all the items are returned to their designated spots, you won't have to get out of the car to move them before you can park in the garage. You can also paint a border down each side of the floor, say 1 m from each wall; all items must stay within the borders.

Door protection
Avoid damaging your car door: attach a piece of carpet, padding or foam-rubber insulation to the wall where the door makes contact.

Door-to-door barrier

Parking one car next to another in a two-car garage often leads to damaged doors on both cars. Avoid scratches and dents altogether by creating a cushioned barrier. Cut equal lengths of swimming-pool cleaner hose and a thin wooden dowel. Put the dowel through the hose, and secure a screw eye on each end of the dowel so that the hose is securely attached to the wood. Suspend the barrier from the ceiling with rope tied to each screw eye. Hang it so that it meets the car doors just below the handles. ▼

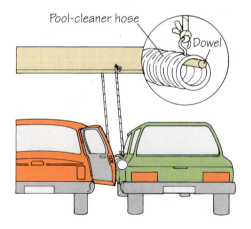

Mirror, mirror in the corner

Before you get out of your car at night, you can quickly and easily check to see if all its lights are functioning. Install a mirror at an inside front corner and another one in a back corner of the garage. Be sure that the two mirrors are positioned so that when you are sitting behind the steering wheel and looking in the side- or rear-view mirror, you can see the headlights in the front mirror and the taillights in the back one.

Garage doors

Garage-door opener safety

Mark your calendar with reminders to periodically inspect your automatic garage-door opener. Follow the owner's manual, and keep in mind the following:
▷ Every month check the safety features for proper operation. Check that the manual disconnect works properly.
▷ Every 3 months adjust the open and closed settings, if necessary. Check that the door opens and closes properly.
▷ Every 6 months see that the door and door hardware operate smoothly. Lubricate if necessary. Check the tension on the chain/cable or the opener.
▷ Every 12 months tighten all the nuts and bolts. Check the fasteners on the garage door and the door opener.

Add a button

Consider installing two buttons instead of one when you put in an automatic garage-door opener. Place one by the door to the house and the other inside the garage, right by the garage door. When you need to take something out of the garage, there will be no need to race to beat the closing door.

Clamp it

When working on a manual garage door, set it at a comfortable height by securing a G-clamp or locking pliers on the door track. This is safer than propping the door with a chair or other object.

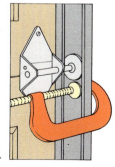

Spring safety

Roll-up overhead garage doors use tightly coiled springs. If one snaps, it can injure you and damage nearby items. Take the time to install a safety cable or rope. Pass it through the centre of each spring when the latter is fully extended. Tie the ends securely to the spring attachment points at each end. The cable or rope will not interfere with the action of the door or springs, but it will prevent a broken spring from whipping around if it breaks. ▼

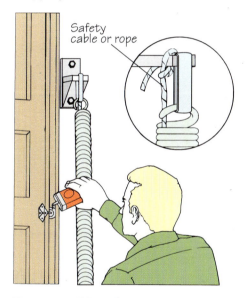

Keep on rolling ▲

Doors move sluggishly because of inadequate lubrication in the roller bearings. Periodically apply a thin film of lightweight oil to the rollers and hinges. Go easy, though; too much oil will collect dirt. Keep the tracks clean by wiping them occasionally with a cloth dampened with oil.

HOUSEHOLD HINTS

CURTAINS AND BLINDS   329
PICTURE FRAMES   330
PICTURE HANGING   331
CHILDPROOFING YOUR HOME   332
ELIMINATING HOUSEHOLD ODOURS   336
PETS   337
CONTAINER GARDENING   338
FRESHLY CUT FLOWERS   339
BRAAIS   340
FIREPLACES   341
CHRISTMAS DECORATIONS AND WRAPS   342
CONTROLLING HOUSEHOLD PESTS   344
MOVING HEAVY OBJECTS   345
HOUSEHOLD MOVING   346
SIMPLE SOLUTIONS   350

CURTAINS AND BLINDS

Hang it up

Easier curtain hanging
You needn't have an extra hand to install curtain rods without trouble. Simply use masking tape to hold the brackets in place while you work. Not only will you free up your hands for marking, drilling, and attaching the brackets, you'll minimize arm strain as well.

Wrong way up
Is your window rounded or oddly shaped at the top? If so, try mounting your blind upside down. To do this, install the brackets at the base of the window and attach a small pulley at the top. To raise and lower the blind, secure a cord to the edge of the blind and run it through the pulley.

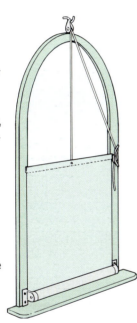

A new life for blinds ▲
Instead of discarding worn blinds, give them a face-lift. Choose a fabric to complement your decor, and cut it to fit the blind. Apply a thin coat of rubber cement or spray-on adhesive to the blind; then attach the fabric. Carefully smooth the fabric to eliminate air bubbles, which could cause wrinkling when the blind is rolled up.

Like-new blind
If the bottom of a blind is badly stained or worn, don't throw it out. Turn the blind upside down and attach the damaged end to the roller. First, unroll the blind and take out the staples holding it to the roller. Then remove the pull and slat at the bottom, open the hem, and staple that end to the roller; make sure the blind's long edges are at a perfect right angle to the roller. Sew a new hem for the slat, and reattach the pull. ▼

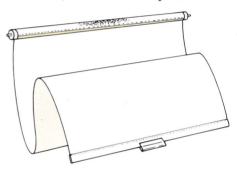

Blind renewal
Replace a frayed venetian blind lift cord without taking down the blind by using the old cord to pull the new one into place. Remove the buckle on the lift cord, and clip off the cord a few centimetres above the loop. Tape the ends of the new cord to the cut ends. Then open the bottom of the blind and pull on the knotted ends of the old cord to draw the attached new pieces through the blind. ▼

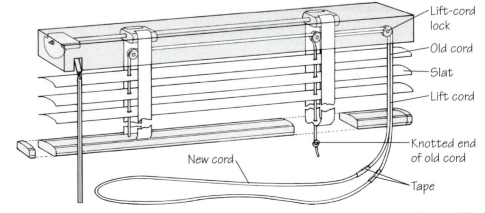

Just like new

Quick patch
Small tear on a blind? Fix it before it grows. Stick a piece of masking tape on the back and coat the front with clear nail polish.

PICTURE FRAMES

Making the frame

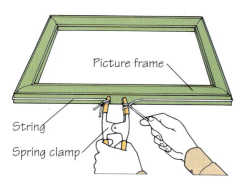

A picture-perfect clamp ▲
You can hold picture-frame joints together until the glue sets by using only a spring clamp and some string. Cut a piece of string to fit around the perimeter of the frame. Tie one end of the string to a jaw of the clamp, and run it around the frame. Then squeeze the clamp open and tie the other end of the string to its other jaw. Release the clamp to pull the string taut around the frame.

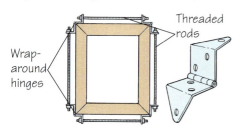

Handy hinge clamp ▲
For larger frames, make a clamp from four threaded rods and four wrap-around hinges. Drill holes for the rods at the ends of the hinge leaves; then bend each leaf 90°. Push the rods through the holes in the hinges, forming a square larger than the frame, and screw a nut onto each rod end. Twirl the nuts to tighten the clamp around the frame.

Clickety click, this does the trick
When framing a larger picture, gently clamp it down to a firm level surface, to keep it flat, and then pass the loop of a ratchet tie-down around it. Protect each corner of the frame with a piece of cardboard and then tighten the tie-down until sufficient force is exerted.

Quick finish
To tint and protect raw wood picture frames easily and inexpensively, use a coat of brown wax shoe polish. Give the polish a few minutes to soak into the wood, wipe off any excess, and then buff the surface with a soft lint-free cloth.

Wiring the frame

Wiring like a pro
Make your own picture hanger with a length of 1 mm stranded wire, two eye hooks, and two 10 mm pieces of small-diameter copper tubing. Attach the eye hooks to the picture frame. Slip the pieces of tubing onto the wire, loop the wire through the eye hooks and back through the pieces of tubing. Crimp the tubing down over the wire with pliers to complete the job. ▼

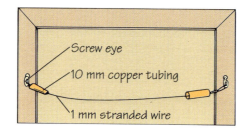

Go fish
Super-strong nylon fishing line (monofilament) is practically invisible, making it a great material to use when hanging pictures from ceiling mouldings.

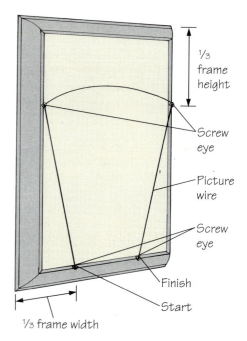

Stress stopper ▲
A heavy load can cause the joints of a large wooden picture frame to separate. To prevent this, rig the picture wire to support the frame at the bottom. Attach screw eyes to the frame as shown; then fasten one end of a length of braided picture-hanging wire to one of the bottom screw eyes. Thread the wire through the two side screw eyes, and fasten it to the other bottom screw eye. Pull the wire taut before fastening it to the last screw eye.

PICTURE HANGING

Hanging the picture

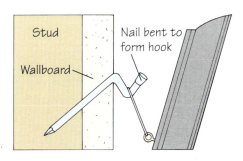

Quick hanger ▲
To make an inexpensive picture hanger, grasp the shank of a 50 mm nail in the jaws of a vice; then, using round-nose pliers, bend it as shown. To start the nail into the wall, tap its head lightly with a hammer. Then use a punch, positioned at the bend, to drive the nail home into the wall stud.

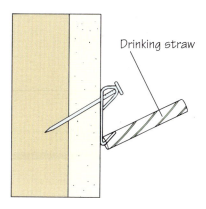

In good position ▲
Slip a section of drinking straw over a picture-hanger hook to help position the picture wire over it. Remove the straw once the picture is in place.

A dent marks the spot
Avoid hit-or-miss. With this handy tool made from a wire coat hanger, you can create a small indentation in the wall, showing you exactly where to mount your picture. Cut a 250 mm piece of wire from a hanger, and file one end to a point. Using pliers, bend the wire as shown, forming a hook at the pointed end and a finger-size loop at the other end. To use the tool, insert the pointed end under the picture wire. Position the picture on the wall, holding it by the looped end of the tool, and gently push the point into the wall to mark the spot.

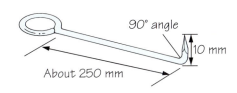

Wallcovering coverup

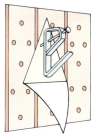

Don't damage wallcoverings with picture-hanger holes. Instead, install the hanger underneath the wallcovering. Slit a tab in the wallcovering where you want to install the hanger; moisten the area, and very carefully peel down the tab. When it's time to rearrange your pictures, disguise the hole by glueing the tab back into place.

Keeping it straight

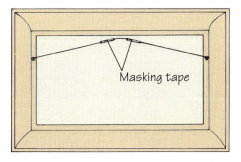

No-slip picture ▲
Keep your pictures hanging straight by wrapping bits of masking tape around the picture wire on both sides of the wall hanger or hook.

Tacky trick
Another way to keep a picture straight, on a drywall, anyway, is to use a drawing pin gripper on the lower corners of the frame. Push them through short pieces of masking tape from the sticky side, and stick them on the frame. Their points will hold the frame in place without penetrating the surface of the wall. ▼

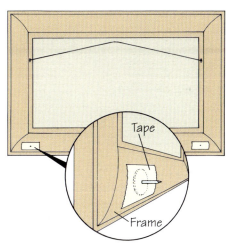

Household Hints / 331

CHILDPROOFING YOUR HOME

Household menaces

Cures for the common cord

Pulling on a dangling power cord can result in a countertop appliance falling and causing an injury. Playing with a long window-blind cord can result in the child's pulling the blind off the wall or in accidental strangulation. Keep all cords out of reach of children by clipping them into self-adhesive electrical cord holders, available from hardware dealers. ▼

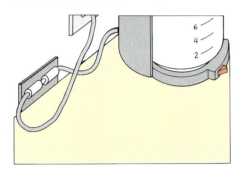

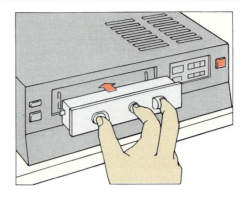

Open wide ▲

Children are fascinated by the way VCR's seem to swallow up video tapes. Keep your machine from "eating" other items by either placing the VCR out of reach or by putting a protective cover over the slot. To make your own version, build a box out of 6 mm plywood and fit it over the entire unit.

Finger saver

Keep your tot's fingers from getting caught in a door with a simple stop made from 19 mm quadrant and a 150 mm length of coat hanger wire. Drive one end of the wire into the end of the quadrant, and bend the other end to form a hook. Slide the wire over the top door hinge, making sure the stop is positioned between the leaves of the hinge. Just remember to remove it before you try to close the door. ▼

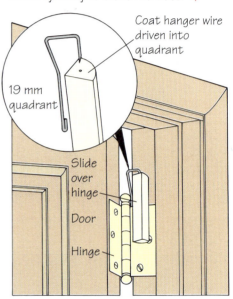

Prop it up

It's easy to catch little fingers under the lid of a piano keyboard or a chest. To avoid this, glue blocks made from corks to the edge of the lid; on some pianos, you can use small suction cups to hold the lid either open or closed. ▼

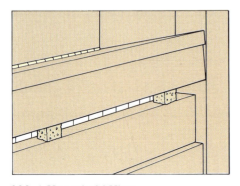

Windows and doors

Door ajar

Keep a room off limits to children but still allow for ventilation by installing a hook with a spring clasp near the top of the door. Be sure to screw the eye as close to the edge of the door as possible. When it's latched, kids won't be able to enter but the door will stay slightly ajar.

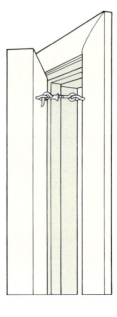

Window safety

A child can fall out of a window in the twinkling of an eye and can be injured as a result. If you have casement windows, a small G-clamp, fixed tightly onto the sliding rod, will stop the window being opened beyond a certain point. If the window frame is wood, fix one screw eye to the frame and another, on the same level, to the window section. A strong cord between them will stop the window opening too far.

Seeing spots
To a child in motion, a closed sliding glass door can easily appear to be open. Prevent painful accidents by attaching colourful decals to the glass just below the child's eye level.

Stair safety

All fenced in
Because kids can squeeze through even tiny openings, make sure deck rails and stairway balusters are child-proofed. An easy solution is to attach heavy-duty plastic mesh fencing to the inside of the railings. Feed the fencing through thin dowels top and bottom and tie it in place with strong string. ▼

Safe stairs
With crawlers and toddlers in the house, a safety gate is a must at the top and bottom of every staircase. Select one-piece gates or the type with sliding sections—a child's head can easily get caught within the bars of an accordion-type gate.

Garage

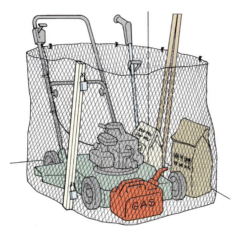

OK corral ▲
Enclose dangerous tools and toxic substances in your garage in a child-proof cage made by attaching standard-width chicken wire to the walls. Staple a beam to each sharp, cut end and install screw eyes on them for two padlocks.

Open Sesame
Make sure that your garage door's operating switches and remote devices are out of a child's reach. And if your automatic garage door is old, replace it with a newer model that reverses if it touches anything while closing.

SAFE AT HOME
Keep your child safe and prevent accidents by following some basic rules and by using your common sense.
▷ Never leave a child unattended in the bathroom or in the kitchen.
▷ Install safety covers on all unused electrical outlets.
▷ Store household cleaners and other chemicals in a locked box kept out of reach of children.
▷ Remove the doors from any discarded appliance, regardless of where it is stored.
▷ Place a thick, soft rug underneath your baby's cot in case the baby climbs out and falls.
▷ Run cold water into a baby's bath, then run hot water to bring it to the required temperature. By running the hot water first, you increase the possibility of inadvertently scalding the child.
▷ When cooking, turn pot handles in towards the wall.
▷ Prevent a child from closing and locking a door by draping a thick towel over the top of the door.
▷ Keep houseplants out of reach by hanging them from the ceiling.
▷ Constantly look for potential danger areas in the home and eliminate them immediately.
▷ Talk to your children about household dangers and the importance of keeping safe.

CHILDPROOFING YOUR HOME

Kitchen safety

Keeping company in the kitchen ▶

Kitchens pose many hazards, so reduce the risk of accidents by installing a stove guard or by removing the control knobs when the unit is not in use. In any event, you should not leave a child alone in the kitchen. Toddlers soon learn they can reach forbidden zones, such as a stove top, by pushing a chair into the desired position and climbing up. Even the best stove guard might not prevent a nasty accident. Remember, prevention is always better than cure.

Locks 'n latches ▲

Toddlers love to explore and investigate every corner. To protect your appliances and cabinets from your kids, and the kids from your appliances and cabinet contents, install childproof latches or locks wherever necessary.

Sit tight

Small children can easily slip on smooth wood or plastic high-chair seats, winding up with their heads under the tray. A rubber sink mat secured to the seat keeps baby in place.

Temporary solution

Kids are insatiably curious, especially when they get the chance to explore a new environment. When visiting a home that may not be childproof, temporarily "lock" accessible cabinets with heavy-duty string or thick rubber bands. Simply loop the string around the cabinet handles and knot it tightly; make sure it's secure enough to keep the child from pulling the door open and squeezing a hand inside. ▼

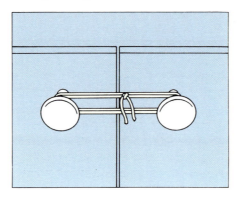

Anchored down

Any child who bounces on the open door of a freestanding stove or dishwasher, risks tipping the appliance over and becoming the victim of a serious accident. Prevent this by anchoring the appliance to the wall or floor. A ratchet tie-down, passed through two eye bolts in the wall and around the unit will be sufficient to keep it upright.

A safer bath

Nonslip grip

Water and soap residue can make baths very slippery; reduce the risk of falls by installing nonskid decals on the bottom of the bath and shower. To ensure a tight seal between the decals and the bottom of the bath, make sure that it is clean before sticking them into place.

No more bumps

Many accidents are the result of falling against a bath's taps. Protect your child from bumps by placing a protective cover over the taps. You can make one from a length of pliable rubber hosing (available at home centres). Slice the hose lengthwise and wrap it securely around the tap. If you have a very wide tap, you may need more than one piece of hose. Use ring clamps to hold the hose in place. For a more temporary solution, fold a towel lengthwise into quarters and wrap it firmly around the tap fitting. **Caution:** Taking these precautions is not the complete answer. Never leave a young child unattended in the bath.

No burns here

Temperatures that seem comfortable to adults can seriously burn a child's sensitive skin. Antiscald valves, which can be attached to standard taps and showerheads, prevent accidents by automatically stopping the water flow when the temperature exceeds a specified setting. An alternative is to turn your geyser's thermostat down to provide water at a lower temperature.

Don't add insult to injury

Bear in mind that if a child has got a little sunburnt, bath water should be a little cooler as their skin will be even more sensitive than normal.

In the nursery

Pets begone ▶

If a safety gate isn't enough to keep a curious pet out of the baby's room, replace the traditional solid door with a screen door. A screen will keep pets out and allow you to hear if the child cries or to peek in without disturbing the baby. Remember, pets should not be left unattended with newborns.

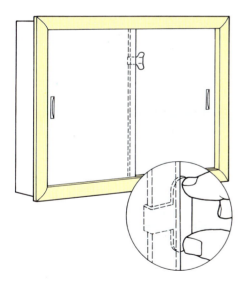

Medicine chest safety ▲

Keep that medicine cabinet securely locked—even if you think it is out of reach. Kids quickly become adept at climbing, and the typical medicine cabinet is full of hazards, such as razor blades, medications, scissors, and tweezers.

Child's play

Unlidded bins and boxes are the safest containers for toys—you won't have to worry about children pinching their fingers or getting trapped inside. But if your toy box must have a lid, drill some holes in the walls of the box to allow ventilation should a child get into it. (For more ideas on storing toys and sports equipment, see pp 122–123.)

Say no to plastic

To reduce the risk of suffocation, use a mattress pad instead of a plastic bag for the cot's mattress cover. Ensure the pad is always securely fastened to the mattress. Don't keep a pillow in the cot, and be sure that any toys left there are too big to fit into your baby's mouth. With regard to toys, take their parts into consideration as well: the toy as a whole may be too large for a baby to swallow, but if its arms, for example, can come off, your child could be in danger.

On the move

A bouncing toddler can "walk" a lightweight cot across the floor—and within proximity of something unsafe. Prevent this by securing the cot to the wall with a pair of heavy-duty hook-and-eye fasteners screwed into the wall. Use this same trick to keep a wooden high chair in place. ▼

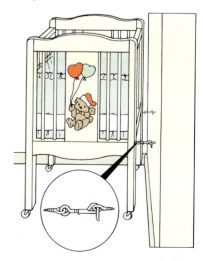

Household Hints / 335

ELIMINATING HOUSEHOLD ODOURS

Musty odours

Book freshener
To rid books of musty odours, store them for a few days in a paper bag filled with crumpled newspaper. The newspaper will absorb the smell. Repeat several times with fresh newspaper until the odour is completely gone.

Sweet linens
Freshen stored linens by tossing an unwrapped bar of scented bath soap in among them. Replace the soap with a fresh bar every few months. An added bonus: after a few months the soap will be dry, making it last longer in the bath.

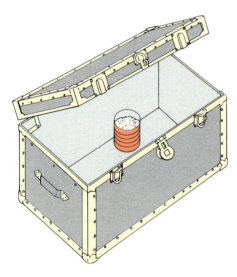

The cat's meow ▲
Here's a terrific way to deodorize a musty trunk. Simply pour cat litter into a large uncovered coffee tin, put it in the trunk, and close the lid. The next day the odour will be gone, and you may remove the tin.

Household odours

Odour begone
Cat litter can also be used to eliminate the smell of rubbish. Sprinkle it in the bottom of rubbish bins to keep them smelling fresh. Change the litter every week or whenever the bins get damp.

Eliminating mothball odour
The smell of mothballs can linger in an enclosed space for months. Restore a fresh scent by scrubbing every part of the space with a mixture of equal parts of white vinegar or lemon juice and rubbing alcohol. Repeat the procedure if the scent remains.

Whole-house deodorizer
If a bad odour has permeated the whole house, the solution is easy: put a couple of perforated containers of solid room deodorizer in front of a fan and turn it on. Place it facing away from an open window on the windward side of the house. The unpleasant odour will soon be driven out.

Home, sweet home
Sweet-smelling plants, near a window on the windward side of the house, is a simple way to give your home the smell of the country—always.

Fresh scent
For a unique air freshener, spray a bit of your favourite cologne onto a cool light bulb. When you switch it on, the heat from the bulb will release the aroma of the perfume, sending your favourite scent wafting through the room. ▼

Pet odours

A concrete answer
Concrete absorbs odours, and a urine-soaked concrete floor has a terrible smell that can permeate the entire house. To deodorize it, scrub the floor with a solution of half white vinegar and half water. Or put undiluted denatured alcohol in a spray bottle and spray the floor thoroughly.

A strong solution
Severe urine stains may require the application of a commercial pet odour remover (available at pet stores). Less severe problems can be sorted out with a spray bottle filled with a household disinfectant mix. Adjust the nozzle to give a wide coverage of the area.

PETS

The great outdoors

The run-around ▶

If you chain your dog to a stake, you know it doesn't take long for Fido to wind up in tangles. Keep him running free by building a pivoting tether. Remove and discard the wheel from a plate-type caster by cutting through the axle with a hacksaw. Sink a 96 x 96 mm beam, about 600 mm long, firmly into the ground, and screw the plate to the top of it. Make a pivoting arm by drilling a hole the size of the caster's old axle through one end of a strip of wood about 300 mm long. Secure the arm to the caster with a nut and bolt. Attach a screw eye to the opposite end of the arm, and hook the dog's tie-out chain to it.

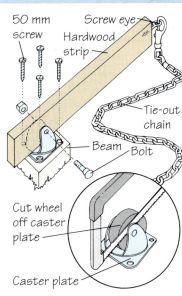

No-tip dish

To protect your pet's outdoor water supply from accidental spills, serve up the water in a large angel-food cake tin. Keep the tin in place by setting it over a wooden stake that's been firmly driven into the ground.

Have pet, will travel

You can have water available any time your pet wants it. Cut a circular hole in the centre of a bath sponge so that it is like a large doughnut. Put it in the pet's dish and top up the water. The sponge stops spills—and the hole in the centre allows your pet to quench its thirst.

Protecting houseplants

Scat, cat

Keep kitty from using potted plants as a litter box by burying a few mothballs in the soil.

Plant protection

This wire-mesh shield lets water into the soil but keeps animals out. Make a paper pattern the same diameter as the pot, and tape the pattern to a piece of wire mesh. Cut out the shield; then cut a straight line to the centre, and cut out a circle about 30 mm larger than the plant's stem. Coat the cut edges with clear nail polish, and slip the shield into place.

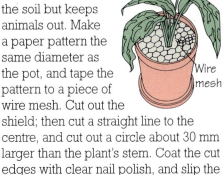

Bathing your pet

Pet prewash for super smell

For sweet-smelling fur, prewash your pet with full-strength tomato juice before washing with shampoo. Then rinse with a few tablespoons of ammonia mixed into 5 litres of warm water—but be sure to keep this solution away from your pet's eyes. Use plain warm water for a final rinse. If you don't have tomato juice on hand, try a solution of equal parts of vinegar and water. Rinse your pet with clear water; then repeat the process until the odour is gone.

Slip-sliding away

The slipping and sliding that usually accompany bathtime can frighten even stalwart dogs. Ease your pet's nervousness by providing a secure nonskid surface to stand on. When bathing your pet in a sink, cut a hole for the drain in a foam-backed place mat and position the mat, foam side up, for your pet to stand on. When bathing your pet in a bath, put down a nonslip rubber or vinyl mat.

Drain strainer

Prevent clogs when bathing a pet by covering the drain with an upside-down tea strainer or a nylon kitchen scrubber. Either will keep pet fur out of the drain.

Waterless wash

Need to give the dog a bath but can't get him near the water? Try a dry bath. Rub mealie-meal into your pet's fur, then brush it out. If a pet needs a deodorant, follow with a baking-soda rub.

CONTAINER GARDENING

Pots and repotting

Stand up straight
Does your flowerpot wobble when you set it down? Here's how to make flowerpots, planters, and boxes sit flat without scratching or slipping. Apply four evenly spaced dabs of silicone caulk to the bottom. Before the caulk dries completely, turn the pot right side up and place it on a sheet of wax paper. Once the caulk cures, the container will have four stable, level feet. ▼

The root cause of the problem ▶
If your flowerpot has holes, you may want to think twice before you automatically spread a layer of gravel beneath the soil. The last 50 mm or so of soil in the bottom of a pot remains saturated with water, whether there is a gravel base or not. Because saturated soil lacks oxygen, roots won't grow into this area; by adding gravel you reduce the growing area available to the plant roots. On pots without drainage holes, however, continue to add the gravel layer to collect excess water that has no way of draining out.

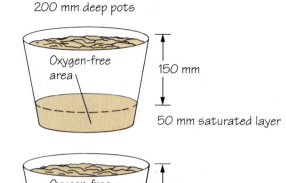

200 mm deep pots

Oxygen-free area
150 mm
50 mm saturated layer

Oxygen-free area
125 mm
50 mm saturated layer
25 mm gravel

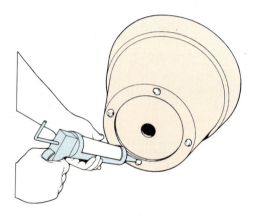

Room to grow
Repotting a plant is easy when you take advantage of the old pot. First, layer some potting soil in the bottom of the new pot. Place the old pot inside the new one, and pour potting soil in around it, gently tamping the soil with your fingers. Then remove the smaller pot and it'll leave a well that's the perfect size for your plant's root ball.

Keeping plants healthy

Too rich for me
Plants thrive in good soil. For a good, rich soil that drains well, try this recipe: combine equal amounts of loam, compost or peat moss, and perlite or coarse sand. Then stir in 2 teaspoons of superphosphate, 3 teaspoons of horticultural lime, and 2 teaspoons of all-purpose granular fertilizer for every 4,5 litres of soil. Your plants will love you for it.

A fungus among us
Combat fungus on houseplants with this baking-soda solution. First, trim off any badly infected leaves. Mix 1 tablespoon of baking soda into 4,5 litres of water; use a spray bottle to apply the mixture on the remaining leaves. Repeat this procedure every few days until all signs of the fungus are gone.

The brush-off
Recycle a soft toothbrush by using it to remove scale insects from leaves. Dampen the brush in a solution of 3 tablespoons denatured alcohol per 1,25 litres of water and gently scrub away the insects. Check the plant weekly, and repeat as necessary. If you find a toothbrush too cumbersome, use a soapless facial cleansing sponge or a soft facecloth. ▼

FRESHLY CUT FLOWERS

Stem treatment

Hardy harvest
Minimize moisture loss when cutting flowers by harvesting them on a cloudy day or early in the morning. Be sure to make clean cuts, using pruning shears or a sharp knife; don't break or tear the stems. To prolong the life of the freshly cut blooms, plunge the stems directly into tepid water after cutting.

Daffodil know-how

Newly cut daffodils secrete a milky substance that creates a seal when it mixes with water, preventing the stems from absorbing water. To avoid this, singe the cut end of the flower by briefly passing it through the flame of a match. Repeat every time you recut the stems.

Kind cuts ▲
Freshly cut flowers need water to survive. Encourage your flowers to drink up by recutting their stems every few days. When recutting green stems, first carefully cut a 50 mm slit running from the base of the stem up. Next, cut the bottom of the stem at a 45° angle. If possible, cut stems under water to eliminate air bubbles that could get trapped in the stem and block water intake. Let the flowers stand in deep water in a cool place for several hours before arranging them.

Whittling away wood
On woody plants, carefully scrape the bark from the last 50 mm of the stem with a sharp knife or florist's scissors; then slit and recut as described at left.

There's life at the bottom
Before arranging flowers, strip off all the lower leaves. If they are submerged in water, they'll rot and produce a gas that hastens wilting. If the flowers are tall, trim off the uppermost buds (which are unlikely to flower) to allow the others their share of water and increase their chances of blossoming. ▼

Water treatment

Straight up, no ice
If you've ever created an arrangement of cut tulips, you know that they tend to droop soon after cutting. Keep them standing straight by adding a few drops of vodka to the water.

Home brews
The best way to preserve cut flowers is to use a commercial preservative. But if you don't have any, mix 2 teaspoons of medicinal-type mouthwash into 4,5 litres of water—it'll be more effective than the old-fashioned options of aspirin or sugar. A tin of clear soft drink mixed with 4,5 litres of water can also help (because of the acid in the drink).

No wilting here

50 mm boiling water

Some flowers, including hollyhock, black-eyed Susan, gerbera, Queen Anne's lace, dogwood, and butterfly bush, will wilt unless you boil their stems before arranging them. As the hot water rises upward, it forces air down and out of the stems, eliminating the airlocks that prevent water from reaching the flower heads and foliage. Protect the blooms by securing plastic bags around the flowers with twist-ties. Carefully holding the flowers diagonally, place the stems in the boiling water for 20 seconds. Then plunge the stems into a bucket of tepid water and leave them for several hours before arranging.

Half fill bucket with tepid water

BRAAIS

Homemade braais

Quick & easy cooking
Do you have everything you need for the braai—except the actual braai itself? Don't despair; you can build a temporary one quickly and easily. Simply stack concrete blocks in a U-shape around a concrete stepping-stone or a bare patch of ground. Make the structure about 350 mm high. Top it with a grill and you're ready to cook. Face the open side into the wind. ▼

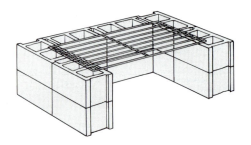

Just rolling along
When your guests can't come to the braai, bring the braai to them with this unique mobile grill. Transform an old metal-bed wheelbarrow by placing an oven rack across the top. ▼

Charcoal lighters

Carton starter
You can make a disposable charcoal starter by loading briquettes into an empty waxed milk or juice carton. To start the fire, just light the carton. An alternative is to use a large paper bag; you will have a no-mess fire starter. If a flimsy bag is put into another, it will contain the fire for longer.

Cleaning the grill

Burnt out ▲
Yes, even permanent briquettes in a gas grill need to be cleaned—but here's an easy way to do it. Simply turn the briquettes so that the greasy side is face down. Then light the grill, set the temperature on high, and close the cover. Let the fire burn for 15 to 20 minutes; your briquettes will be as good as new.

A safe start

A large coffee tin will serve as a reusable charcoal starter. Using a punch-type beverage opener, cut openings all around its base. Remove the bottom with a standard tin opener, and securely place the tin in your grill—be sure it doesn't wobble. Put a small wad of paper and scraps of dry wood in the tin; then fill it to the top with charcoal. Light the paper through the triangular openings at the bottom. Once the briquettes are burning, lift the tin off with tongs (it'll be red-hot) and spread out the briquettes.

Leave it for the morning
The worst part of a braai is the cleanup. Make it a bit easier by removing the cooled grill and dropping it on the grass, cooking side down. Let it lie there overnight, and in the morning wipe away the dew (and grease) with damp paper towels.

Overnight soak
For really tough baked-on grease, put your dirty grill inside a heavy-duty plastic refuse bag. Mix a solution of 1/2 cup of liquid dishwasher detergent in 4,5 litres of water. Pour the mixture over the grill and seal the bag with a twist tie. Let it soak overnight. The next day, use a stiff brush to remove the residue. Rinse the grill thoroughly.

FIREPLACES

A good fire

Getting started ▶

The best way to lay a fire is to create a pyramid out of the logs. For the base of the pyramid, use one large log and one medium-size log, keeping the smaller one in the front. Stuff newspaper and sticks into the gap between the two logs, and top off the pyramid with a small log. Always start a fire from the bottom by lighting the paper and sticks at both ends. Keep the fire going by replacing the logs as needed. As the rear log burns, use a fireplace poker to carefully roll the front log to the rear and then put in a new front log. Add other logs as required.

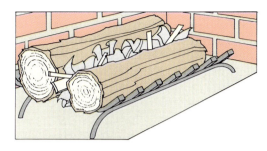

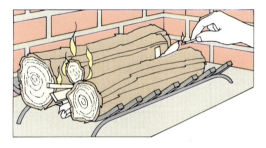

Open up

Fires need oxygen in order to burn, and often the only air supply is the warm air from the house. To stop heated air from rushing up the chimney, feed your fire fresh air from an open window. Just open the window a few centimetres; if you pick a window on the windy side of the house, you'll probably boost the fireplace's updraught and reduce smoking.

In the end

Because embers can smoulder even when there are no flames, you should be certain that the blaze is completely extinguished. Don't pour water on the flames; this can cause heavy smoking. Instead, put out the flames with baking soda, salt, sand or dirt. It's also smart to keep some baking soda close by in case the fire burns too rapidly and needs to be smothered.

A newsworthy start ▲

If you have trouble lighting wood fires, try this no-fail fire starter. Beginning at an outside edge, rip a section of newspaper into strips, stopping just shy of the fold. Tightly wedge the paper underneath the logs, add sticks, and then carefully light the ends of the strips.

Ash sifter

Fires burn longer when you separate the coals from the ashes. To do this, cut a piece of 10 mm welded mesh (available at hardware stores) and fit it over the grate. The openings in the mesh will let the ashes fall through and at the same time hold the coals up closer to the flames. ▼

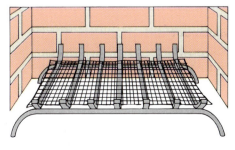

Glass doors

Recycle those ashes

It sounds odd, but smoke stains can be removed from glass fireplace doors with ashes. Just dip a damp cloth into cooled ashes and rub away the stains.

Unsmoked glass

If the smoke stains on your glass fireplace doors refuse to come off with ashes, as described above, use a foam-type aerosol oven cleaner. Simply spray on the foam, let it stand for a while, and wipe it off, following the manufacturer's instructions. Your doors will sparkle.

CHRISTMAS DECORATIONS AND WRAPS

Ornaments and garlands

Pretty blocks
Create your own Christmas tree ornaments by covering small cardboard boxes with scraps of fabric or wallcovering. Tie a ribbon around them to create a package. You can wrap scraps of wood as well. ▼

Not a thread out of place
After a couple of seasons, crocheted ornaments look tired and droopy. Perk them up with a few pumps of hairspray.

No butter, please
When making garlands of popcorn, pop the corn a week before you plan to string it. Stale kernels won't crumble when you pierce them with a needle.

Light fixtures
Having trouble securing lights where you want them on the tree? Tie them to the branches with green pipe cleaners.

Tending the tree

Tree test
To make sure that the Christmas tree you are buying is fresh, check it well, smell it, and handle it. A fresh tree will have a good green colour and a pleasant fragrance. If you lift the tree a few centimetres off the ground and slam the stump down, the needles shouldn't fall off in substantial numbers. As a final test, hold a branch about 150 mm from its tip between your thumb and forefinger and pull it towards you, allowing the branch to slip between your fingers. If the needles adhere to the branch, the tree is fresh; if they fall off, it's not.

Drink up
To fire-retard your tree and keep its needles green, mix a solution of 10 litres of hot water, 2 cups of syrup, ¼ cup of liquid bleach, 2 pinches of Epsom salts, and ½ teaspoon of borax. Saw a few centimetres off the bottom of the trunk, and let the tree stand overnight in a bucket filled with this mixture. Use this mixture in the tree stand, too.

It rings a bell
Children love a Christmas tree. To warn you of little hands reaching for the ornaments, tie a number of small bells to the lower branches.

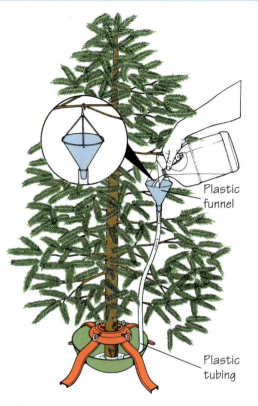

No more aching back ▲
Make this simple watering device and you'll never again have to squirm underneath the branches of a Christmas tree. You'll need a medium-size plastic funnel, a length of plastic tubing, and some straight wire. Punch three holes along the top rim of the funnel, thread a length of wire through each hole, and twist the wires together to form a hook at the top; hang it from a branch of the tree. Force the tubing over the small end of the funnel, put the free end of the tube in the water trough of the tree stand and secure the tube to the trunk. Next time the tree needs water, just use the funnel.

Stand tall ▶

Keep your tree straight and tall with this sturdy stand. Drill four equidistant holes around the rim of a 20 litre plastic container. Partly fill the bucket with sand; move it into place. Soak the sand with water, tamp it, and add more sand, leaving the holes exposed. Trim the lowest branches off the tree, and use a saw to cut an X into the bottom surface of the trunk. Insert the trunk into the sand, and stabilize the tree with four lengths of fishing line. Tie each line to a sturdy branch; then pass the lines through the holes in the bucket and tie them securely.

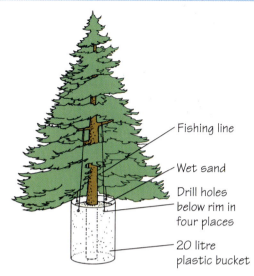

- Fishing line
- Wet sand
- Drill holes below rim in four places
- 20 litre plastic bucket

In the bag

Don't drag your dried-out Christmas tree through the house, leaving behind a trail of needles. Instead, take it apart one branch at a time. Using pruning clippers, cut the branches into little pieces and drop them into a black plastic refuse bag. When you have finished, all you'll have to carry is the bare tree trunk and a refuse bag. ▼

Faster fakes

If you're putting up a reusable artificial tree, here's a way to make the job easier: dip the ends of the branches in petroleum jelly before inserting them into the frame.

Gift wraps

Wrapping-paper resources

If you want an economical alternative to traditional wrapping paper, try scraps of unused wallcoverings, especially the shiny metallic kind. Or use aluminium foil and brightly coloured ribbons.

Emergency wrap

When you run out of wrapping paper on Christmas Eve and have a couple of items left to wrap, don't despair. Black-and-white newspaper tied with red ribbon or gold cord makes a wrapping that is more than acceptable.

CHRISTMAS TREE CARE

The fresh scent of a real fir tree puts people in the Christmas spirit; but a tree can be a serious fire hazard if it is used carelessly or allowed to dry out. Here are some tips for keeping a tree fresh and safe for several weeks:

▷ If you are storing your tree for a few days before decorating it, keep it outside in a cool area, away from the sun and wind.

▷ Help your tree retain moisture during storage by making a straight cut across the trunk, 30 mm from the bottom. Stand the tree in a bucket of water, making sure the water covers the cut.

▷ Prior to bringing the tree inside, make another cut across the trunk, 30 mm above the first.

▷ Use a stand that holds at least 5 litres of water, and ensure the water remains above the top cut.

▷ Position the tree away from fireplaces, television sets and other sources of heat.

▷ Don't use combustible decorations on the tree.

▷ Check all wires and connections; don't use lights with frayed cords; never use lighted candles.

▷ Always turn off all the tree lights before you go to sleep and before leaving your home.

CONTROLLING HOUSEHOLD PESTS

Creepy crawlers

Special delivery
The space behind the toekick and underneath the base of a kitchen cabinet provides a safe haven for all kinds of insects because it's difficult to reach. Deliver a straight shot of insecticide by drilling a 10 mm hole through either the toekick or the cabinet floor. After spraying, plug the hole with a furniture dowel button or a wood dowel plug. ▼

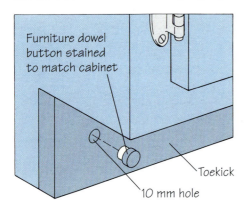

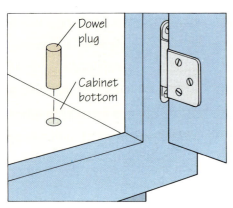

Keep ants at bay
Crumbled bay leaves spread on windowsills and across doorways, and put in sugar containers, will stop ants in their tracks. Replace the leaves every month. Also make a point of washing up soon after eating any sweet or greasy foods—ants will be attracted by even small amounts of these foods.

Not a "hair-brained" idea
If you don't have any insecticide on hand, use hairspray. It makes it difficult for the insect to fly, so it's easier to swat.

This has got the problem taped
Put double-sided tape across surfaces next to gaps pests use to enter the house: they will become stuck when trying to cross the sticky surfaces.

Furry house guests

No more fun and games
When mice or rats get into a house, they can do a lot of damage—by eating wiring insulation, for example. Block any gaps you can find and put out some mouse-repelling sachets. Make your own sachets by creating small bags out of discarded pantihose or scraps of fabric and filling them with crushed dried peppermint leaves. Tie the bags securely and toss a few under beds, into cupboards, inside the stove, and into the dishwasher.

Squirrels, scram
If squirrels invade your chimney or roof, reach for the aftershave. You may like the smell, but it's repulsive to squirrels.

Light the way
Flush bats from their hangout in your roof by leaving a small light burning in the dark areas for a week. Once all the bats are gone, prevent their return by sealing every opening. Crushing chicken mesh and jamming it into any opening will keep them out. Avoid late spring and early summer evictions, as bats breed at this time and you risk trapping a flightless bat pup inside.

It's a trap
These open-ended "valves" let bats out of your roof at night to feed but prevent them from coming back in to roost. Cut a piece of polypropylene bird netting wide enough to span the bats' entryway and long enough to hang a metre below it. If your home is timber, use staples and tape to secure the top and the sides of the netting to the house. If your home is brick, use battens lightly nailed to the wall. Be sure to leave the bottom open. Taper the netting so the bottom opening is no more than 350 mm wide. After several days the bats should be gone and you can seal the openings. ▼

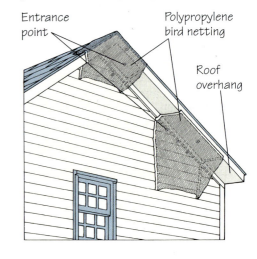

MOVING HEAVY OBJECTS

Damage control

Glass handles
When moving heavy mirrors or panes of glass, cover the edges with pieces of hose pipe. Slit a piece lengthways and cut it into pieces about 200 mm long. Slip them over the edges of the glass. They will protect your hands from injury and the floors and walls from gouges.

Magic carpet ride
If you have only a small piece of carpet available for moving a heavy appliance (see p 352), you may not be able to grip it easily. So, make a hole at each leading corner and pass a loop of rope through them. A second loop passes around the base of the appliance. Adjust the two loops so that they both apply equal force when you pull. Now carpet and appliance will move as one.

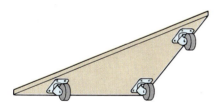

Hello, dolly ▲
Moving any four-legged piece of furniture or heavy appliance will be a snap if you slip a small three-wheeled furniture dolly under each leg. Make your own from 16 mm plywood and casters, available from hardware stores. Use larger casters rather than smaller ones: the larger wheels will mount bigger obstructions and their wider "footprint" spreads the weight more, so they're less likely to damage the floor.

Freewheeling
To keep heavy or unwieldy objects from falling and breaking during transport, wheel them around on a skateboard. You'll save your arm and back muscles.

Wide loads
Hand trucks are great for moving things around, but the lip just isn't deep enough to handle large objects. Remedy this by adding an extension made of 50 mm diameter PVC pipe. With a hacksaw, cut narrow slots into the pipe—the slots should fit snugly onto the truck lip, but if they're too tight, widen them slightly with a file. For added strength, glue the pipes together. Attach the assembly to the truck with a few taps of a rubber mallet; the extension is removable.

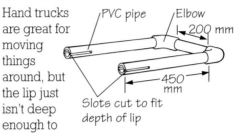

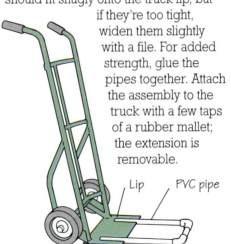

Protect resilient floors
Casters and dolly wheels can easily cut resilient flooring during a move. Instead of rolling the wheels directly over the floor, safeguard it by rolling them over strips of a thin, hard material (such as 6 mm plywood or hardboard).

SAVE YOUR BACK

Whenever you have to lift a heavy load, prevent back injury by following these steps:
▷ Position yourself as close to the load as possible.
▷ Always flex your knees; never bend forward from your waist.
▷ When leaning forward while lifting, keep your back perfectly flat; never arch it.
▷ When pushing heavy objects, bend your knees, keep your back flat, and power the push with your legs.
▷ If you need to turn while lifting or pushing, move your feet; don't twist your back.
▷ Never try to move a really heavy load by yourself—get help. A two-person lift is half the strain.

Household Hints / 345

HOUSEHOLD MOVING

Before the move

Moving checklist
Moving day is difficult at best, with all the last-minute details to take care of. Remove some of the stress and worry by completing the following chores in the weeks preceding the move:
▷ If necessary, have major appliances serviced. If you plan to drive to your new home, have your car serviced as well. If you are having your car moved by truck, make sure that the fuel tank is nearly empty.
▷ Empty all storage tanks of flammable fluids such as petrol and paraffin, and gasses such as propane and butane.
▷ Dispose of enamel paints and thinners.
▷ Drain petrol and oil from your lawn mower and any other power equipment.
▷ Drain water from all garden hoses.
▷ Dispose of flammable and caustic items such as matches, cleaning fluids, bleach, drain cleaners and acids.

Mapping out the territory
Draw an accurate scale plan of your new home. Indicate where you want to put each piece of furniture and other large items. This will save you having to move heavy pieces twice. ▼

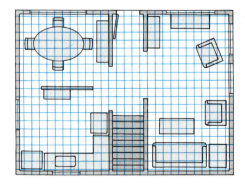

Moving by colours ▲
By assigning a colour to each room of your new house, you can eliminate much of the disorganization on arrival day. Here's how: as you pack up the contents of your old home, colour-code the boxes to the new rooms, using brightly coloured stickers or markers. On moving day, attach a colour-coded marker to each room's door frame to show the movers where to put the boxes.

Easy unpacking
Before packing up everything, select a dresser drawer to contain any linens and towels you'll need for the first night in your new home. Then, when you're exhausted at the end of the move, you won't have to conduct a frantic search for these necessities. It's also a good idea to use one box for a complete set of items you'll need if any delays occur at the trip's end. Fill it with a first-aid kit, change of clothing, basic foodstuffs, soap and shampoo, for example.

Boxes

As flat as a pancake
You can buy packing boxes from any major moving company or truck rental agency. But you can save money by using your own. Start collecting boxes from grocery and liquor stores a few months before the move. Rather than keeping the empty boxes open and letting them take up a lot of space, flatten them for easy storage by slitting open the bottom tape and collapsing the sides. Before filling the boxes, reseal their bases with strong packing tape.

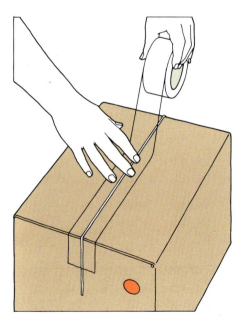

Zippy opening ▲
Before taping boxes closed, run a length of string along the seam. Place the tape over the string, leaving some of the string hanging off the end. When it's time to unpack, pull on the string to zip open the tape.

Protective padding

Bright spots ▲
Small items can easily disappear in the mounds of crumpled paper generated during unpacking. Keep little treasures safe by wrapping them in brightly coloured tissue paper. They'll be easy to spot and you won't accidentally throw them out.

Out of the linen cupboard
Save space by cushioning breakable items with towels, washcloths, sheets, pillowcases, and tablecloths. You'll also save money on paper, and you won't need to pack your linens separately.

Dishes and glasses

On the edge
Believe it or not, the best way to pack plates is on edge, rather than flat. Wrap the plates in bubble wrap (if you are using newspaper, place each dish in a plastic bag to save wash-up time later), and arrange them on their edges inside a sturdy carton. For the safest ride, layer 50 mm of folded paper between the plates and 75 mm of paper on the bottom of the carton.

Wrap up properly
Because of the dividers, liquor cartons are ideal for transporting cups and glasses—ask a local liquor store to save you some discarded boxes. But if you don't have any of these boxes on hand, you can still safely transport glasses and cups. Stuff your glasses and cups with crumpled paper before wrapping them in bubble wrap. Then nestle the wrapped pieces in the spaces between your other dishes. Don't nest any glasses that are unwrapped—they will bump together and chip.

Odds and ends

The bases are loaded
When packing table lamps, wrap the bases in paper or bubble wrap and alternate them end for end. Pack the shades separately, but don't wrap them in newspaper; the print can cause stains. Instead, use bubble wrap or unprinted paper.

Artful packing ▶
Small pieces of art can be placed between blankets or pillows for safe transport—don't use newspaper for padding because it can stain. Or use a collapsed cardboard box; slide in the item and seal the edges. Large, valuable artworks should be padded, wrapped, and crated by a professional.

Like clockwork
Before sending your grandfather clock off on a trip, take these steps to ensure a safe arrival. Remove the weights, pendulum, and finials, and pack them separately. Keep the hammers and weight chains from moving around by securing them to the case of the clock with strong string or tape. For long-distance moves, consult an expert—the works may need special protection against damage.

X marks the spot
Tape an X across each mirror with masking tape before wrapping it in paper or bubble wrap; if there's an accident, the tape will hold the shards in place. Small mirrors can be put on edge and packed in sturdy boxes, but large mirrors need to be shipped in special cartons that your mover can provide.

Packing in the knowledge
Pack books on edge in small cartons, and keep the weight of the carton under 15 kg or so, for easy handling.

HOUSEHOLD MOVING

Large appliances

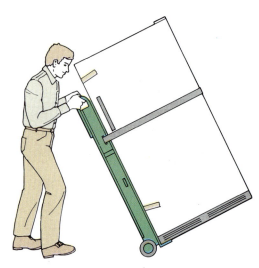

Upstanding appliances ▲
When transporting a refrigerator or an upright freezer, make sure the unit stays upright throughout the move. If it is put on its side, the fluid will flow out of the compressor and you'll have to let the unit stand upright for 24 hours before you can start it without damaging it. To help you keep a unit upright while moving it, rent a special heavy-duty dolly from the truck rental agency.

Clean machine
Before moving your refrigerator, thoroughly wash and dry the inside and let it air out for at least 24 hours. On moving day, toss in a sock filled with charcoal briquettes, fresh ground coffee, or baking soda to absorb moisture and odours. Tightly knot the neck of the sock so that its contents don't spill. Finally, seal the door shut with masking tape.

A different beat
Keep the drum of your washing machine from banging around inside the cabinet by stuffing towels between the drum and the housing.

On the carpet
A simple way to move heavy appliances over a wooden floor is by putting them on old carpet (pile side down) and pulling them along. The fibres in the pile provide a low-friction medium and the floor won't be scratched.

Rock 'n roll
Moving a large, heavy appliance? It's easy: put it on a stout board and roll it along on four steel pipes. Always keep at least three pipes under the board and take care on corners that you stop the appliance rocking back and forth.

Bulky beds

Restrain yourself
The day of the big move, don't forget to tie convertible sofa beds in place before transporting them to their new location. You don't want them opening up while in transit. ▼

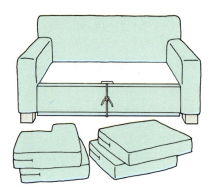

Electronics

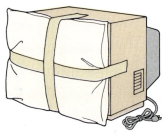

Unplugged ▲
Transporting a warm television set can cause severe internal damage. To make sure yours is at room temperature, disconnect it the day before you move. Also, to protect the screen while moving, tape a pillow over it.

No news here
Whenever possible, pack electronic equipment and small appliances in their original cartons. If you no longer have the original foam padding blocks, cushion the units with bubble wrap or crumpled paper. Don't use shredded newspaper; it can get into the machines and cause internal damage. (For hints on moving a computer, see p 263.)

Plant relocation

Keep them happy
Pack plants in cardboard boxes that are at least 30 mm higher than the tallest plant. To keep the boxes strong and dry, line them with large plastic refuse bags, and wrap clay pots with aluminium foil. Group plants of similar size, and stuff the spaces between them with bubble wrap or loose packing material.

LOADING A TRUCK

If you have a lot of muscle power at your disposal, you may want to rent a truck and do your own moving. Begin by parking the truck as close as possible to your home. Pull out the truck's loading ramp and place it on the highest front step, if possible. Then, following the guidelines shown below, load the truck one-quarter full at a time, packing everything solidly from floor to ceiling. Tie in each quarter securely, and fill any spaces with small boxes. Be sure to pack the truck snugly to make the best use of the space and to prevent damage to your belongings.

- Bring in the largest items first—generally large appliances and then furniture.
- Keep mirrors upright, and tie them in place or wedge them between a mattress and box spring. Never lay a mirror flat.
- Position long items, such as mattresses and box springs, tabletops, couches, and so on, along the sides of the truck and turn them on their edges.
- Roll up rugs and place them lengthwise in the centre.
- Fit odd-shaped items along the sides or on top of other items.
- Put heavy cartons at the bottom and lighter cartons on top. Stack heavy cartons on top of each other only if they are of nearly equal strength and weight.

Sleeves for leaves

Protect delicate foliage from crushing during transit with funnel-shaped plant sleeves. Make your own by rolling lightweight cardboard into a funnel and securing it with tape.

In your new home

In hot water

Upon arriving at your new home, turn on all the hot-water taps for several minutes. This flushes out any hydrogen gas that may have built up if the house has been empty for several weeks. Don't smoke or use an open flame when doing this; the gas is flammable.

Lighten up

The first items you should unpack (before it gets dark) are the lamps and other portable light fixtures. Place them around the house so that you will have ample light where you need it. Even though the existing lights may be working, you may need extra light—especially when rummaging around in boxes.

Household Hints / 349

SIMPLE SOLUTIONS

Keys

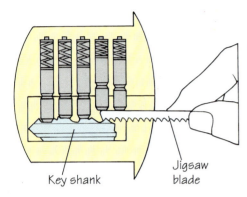

Key broken in lock ▲
If a key breaks off in a lock, try this. Use a jigsaw blade to push up the tumbler pins and grasp the broken key shank. Then, very carefully, slowly pull it out. Don't tug at the key shank, or you may damage the lock. If this doesn't work, call a professional.

Connect the dots
If you carry a lot of keys, it can be tricky to remember which one belongs to which lock. By colour-coding your keys and locks, you will be able to see at a glance which is the proper key. Simply place a colourful sticker on a key and a matching sticker on the lock to which it belongs.

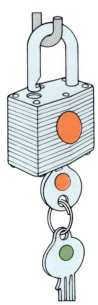

Mirror repair

It's all done with mirrors
Want to disguise damaged silver on an old mirror? Simply scrape off any peeling or discoloured silver, and then tape a piece of shiny aluminium foil over the spot on the back of the mirror.

Mirror image
Resilvering an antique bevel-edged mirror can be expensive. Instead, scrape all the old silver off the back of the mirror and have a new, inexpensive mirror cut to the exact size and shape of the old one. Sandwich the new mirror between the backing and the clear glass remaining from the old mirror. As the mirror is now heavier, reinforce the means of attachment, if necessary.

Book repair

Take a tip
To reattach a loose book page, cut a 15 mm strip of onionskin paper the length of the page and fold it in half lengthwise. Coat the back of the onionskin with white glue. With the crease toward the spine, place one half of the strip on the loose page and the other half on the following page. Push the strip into the spine and line up the pages' outer edges. Place wax paper across the strip, close the book, and let the glue dry.

All wet and soggy
Dry out a waterlogged book by placing it in a frost-free freezer for several hours. The freezer will draw the moisture from the book and separate the pages.

Scissors

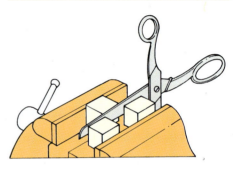

Bent out of shape ▲
Don't discard a pair of scissors if one of the blades is bent out of shape. Instead, place the blade in a vice between three evenly spaced blocks of wood. Tighten the vice slightly. This technique works with bent knives as well.

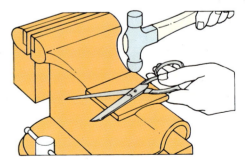

Wiggly scissors ▲
Loose scissors blades? If the pivot is a rivet or if tightening the pivot screw doesn't help, place the pivot head on a metal surface and hit the other end firmly with a ball-peen hammer.

Cutlery

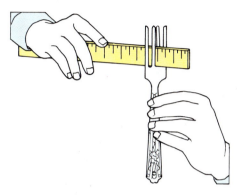

Pointing every which way ▲
Don't discard a fork simply because the tines are bent—straighten them. If the tines of the fork are bent towards each other, insert a wood ruler between them and force them apart. If they are bent outward, line a vice with soft cloth and gently tighten it to clamp and realign the tines.

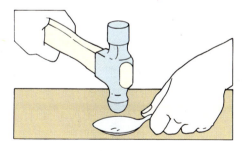

Lumps 'n bumps ▲
When a spoon gets dented, it usually bulges inwards. To fix it, place the spoon on a wood surface and gently tap it with a ball-peen hammer.

China

A clean fix
Before repairing a piece of china, make sure it is clean by soaking it in a solution of a 1/2 cup of household bleach and 2,5 litres of water, washing it, and letting it dry. To fill the crack, use epoxy, either alone or mixed with whiting or kaolin powder and a pigment. Fill the crack slightly higher than the surface, and smooth the area with a super-fine abrasive after the glue hardens.

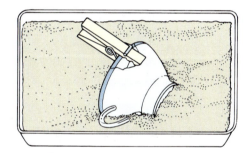

Like a day at the beach ▲
To repair a plate, cup, or even a figurine, bury the largest piece in a container of sand with the broken surface just protruding. Make sure the broken surface is horizontal so the other piece balances on it. If the piece isn't steady, hold it in place with a prop or with a simple clamp such as a clothes peg.

Sticky choice
Mend valuable china (or glassware) with a water-soluble adhesive, which lets you take a piece apart and fix it again. Use water-resistant epoxy to repair everyday pieces, but keep in mind that once it hardens you can't dissolve it.

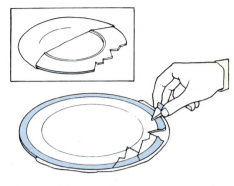

A way with wax ▲
Piecing the parts of a broken plate together is easier if you use a mould. To make one, heat candle wax until it softens, then pack it over the bottom of the unbroken side of the plate. After the wax has set, carefully arrange the mould under the broken side and fit the broken pieces in it. Glue only one or two pieces at a time.

Under pressure
To clamp the pieces of a mended plate together while the glue sets, drive nails in a circle slightly larger than the plate. Lay the plate face down within the nails, and stretch rubber bands over it. ▼

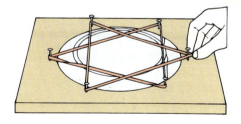

Timing is everything
To remove excess epoxy, wait until it begins to set, then slip a sharp knife-point under it and peel it off. If you try too soon you'll smear the glue; too late, and you won't be able to remove it.

SIMPLE SOLUTIONS

Boot cleaning aids

Kick up your heels ▲
Use a coat hanger to speed drying of rubber boots and other footwear. Bend the hanger to create two loops. Slide the boots through the loops, sole side up, and slip the assembly over a hook or nail. Hanging the boots this way helps them retain their shape and speeds drying by allowing plenty of air circulation.

The brushoff
Although this boot and shoe scraper is portable, it won't move around when you use it. Using screws, attach a large stiff-bristle scrub brush to a piece of plywood. Your weight keeps the plywood in place while you scrape your footwear on the brush. Wash the scraper with a hose, and store it out of sight when not in use. ▼

No more mud
Tired of scraping mud off your boots— or worse yet, off your floors? Prevent mud from coming into the house by providing a convenient boot scraper. Pick a location near the back door where there is no danger of someone running into it in the dark. Fill a 300 x 300 mm hole with concrete, and sink a spade 150 mm deep into it. When the concrete dries, you'll have a permanent boot scraper— complete with a handle you can hold for balance.

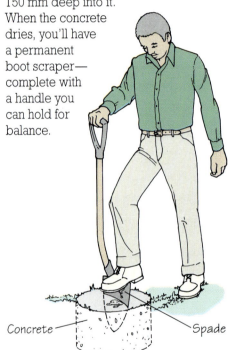

Chains and zippers

Tiny tangles
If a knot develops in a fine chain, don't try to pull it out; you may tangle it further. Instead, spread the chain on a piece of wax paper and place a drop of baby oil on the knot; use a couple of straight pins to slowly pick out the knot.

Easy gliding
Have a zipper that's hard to move? Keep it sliding easily by rubbing it with soap, candle wax, or pencil lead.

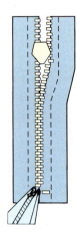 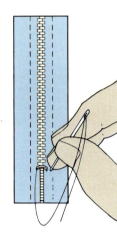

Restoring the zip ▲
If a zipper slider comes loose, prise off the bottom stop of the zipper with a pair of needle-nose pliers. Then move the slider to the bottom and carefully thread the loose track through the slider. Pull the slider up the tracks, and create a new stop by sewing several stitches at the bottom of the zipper.

Spectacles

Fog lifter
Coat both sides of your spectacle lenses with a thin film of soapsuds, let them dry, then polish them with a soft lint-free cloth. The transparent coating left behind won't impair your vision, but it will stop the lenses fogging up.

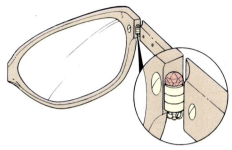

Where did it go? ▲
If you lose the screw that holds one of the earpieces to your spectacles, here's a temporary fix: insert a stud-type earring into the hinge.

No loose screws here
Do the screws keep working loose in your spectacles frame? Coat the threads with clear nail polish. When it dries, the screws should stay in place.

A better bath

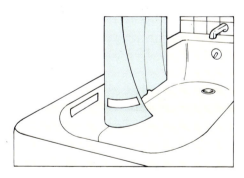

Curtain call ▲
Don't let your shower curtain attack you next time you enter the shower—keep it in place with Velcro tape. After cleaning the bath, simply attach the tape to both the side of the bath and the bottom hem of the curtain. Before turning on the water, secure the curtain to the tape.

No more nonslip decals
A 30-minute soak in laundry prewash makes it much easier to scrape off nonslip bath appliqués. Use a single-edge razor blade for scraping, holding it flat against the bath surface. Remove any excess adhesive by spraying it with aerosol lubricant/penetrant and scrubbing it with a terry-cloth.

Candle wax

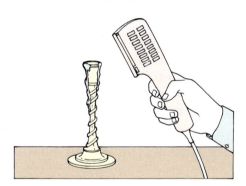

Hot melt ▲
Candle wax persists in dripping and hardening on candleholders, but cleanup can be easy. Remelt dripped wax with a hair dryer set on high heat; work a small area at a time and wipe off the wax as it softens. After cleaning the candleholders, mist them with a vegetable cooking-oil spray to make future wax removal easier.

Cool candlesticks
Another way of removing wax from candlesticks is to place them in the freezer for about an hour; the wax should peel off.

Sticky situations

Rejuvenate your tape
Age and weather conditions can dry up masking or insulation tape. Revive the adhesive by popping the tape into the microwave, set on high, for about a minute.

Saving postage
Often, when the weather gets warm, the glue on the back of postage stamps melts enough for them to stick together. When this happens, don't throw them out. Instead, toss the stuck-together postage stamps into the freezer until they become unstuck.

Photo finish
Heat and humidity often cause photographs to stick together. If your photos were taken within the past 10 years, it's probably safe to soak them apart. Place the photos in a shallow tray filled with tepid water. Every few minutes carefully try to separate them, but if there's even the slightest resistance, continue soaking. Change the water as often as necessary to keep it lukewarm. After separating the photos, dry them by hanging them from a clothesline. As with any untried procedure, first try this on a couple of less valuable photographs.

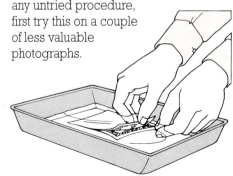

SIMPLE SOLUTIONS

Tape talk

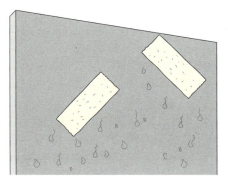

Save that silvering ▲
When you employ double-sided tape to attach a bathroom mirror to a surface, angle the lengths of tape so that water droplets flow off, rather than being dammed on the top edges of the tapes. The silvering will last longer.

No-mess tape-down
That beautiful flower arrangement will amount to a mess on the floor if the vase is blown over. A couple of lengths of double-sided tape on the base will stop the vase toppling in all but a strong gust.

A real pick-me-up
When an item falls down the back of a cupboard, fish it out with a little double-sided tape on the end of a dowel or ruler. If you don't have double-sided tape, attach a loose loop of ordinary sticky tape with the adhesive surface facing outwards.

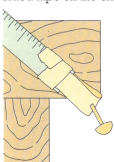

Straws

A loopy idea, but it works
Trying to reach a tiny item in an awkward spot? Push a crochet hook or thin wire down a plastic drinking straw and use it to pull a loop of cotton through the straw. Pull through enough to make a loop of sufficient size and use it to lasso the item. ▼

Safe and secure

Rent a box
The loss of valuable documents can lead to major complications in your life. Make copies of all your important papers, such as: retirement and annuity policies, your will, property records such as your title deed, birth and marriage certificates, shares certificates and papers such as airline tickets if you have bought them early. You should also make a list of all valuable items in the home and copy that too. Rent a safety-deposit box at your bank and store the originals in it. Get your copies certified at your local police station and keep them locked up at home. Use them as your reference material. You can also use the box at the bank for small items of jewellery, precious coins and so on.

The last straw
Cleaning small, hard-to-reach items such as electrical contacts need not be a frustrating and time-consuming task. Use a plastic drinking straw to blow away the worst of the dust. Then slip a cotton bud into the end of the straw, dip the bud into the cleaning solution and clean the item in question.

Reaching around corners
Whether cleaning an item, or lassoing something with a straw, you may find you have to reach around a corner. Simply push a length of stiff wire down the straw and bend it to the shape required. The straw will follow suit and you will be able to reach the spot you are seeking.

Keep it in a canister
The clear plastic canisters in which 35 mm films are packed, are airtight and waterproof. That makes them ideal for items that may tarnish or absorb moisture, and, as they are transparent, you can see what's in them. Use them to store items of jewellery, small quantities of touch-up paint, small fasteners and other items, and substances that may be tarnished by moisture, absorb it, or dry out. You can also use them for salt and other condiments if you go hiking. ▼

Doors

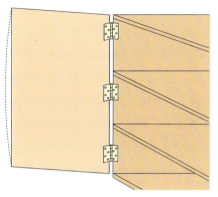

Get rid of that warp ▲
Adding a third hinge midway between the original two on a cupboard door will help correct a warp.

Slow release
Avoid mess when you oil a creaking door's hinges: tie a length of string quite tightly between the upper and lower hinges, looping the string around each hinge. Place a flat receptacle under the lower hinge to catch any overflow, then apply oil to the top hinge. Excess oil will not drop on the floor; it will soak into the string and then slowly seep down to the lower hinge. After a couple of days remove the string and discard it.

Safe removal
When removing an interior door, you may be able to knock out the hinge pins, thus separating the two halves of each hinge, or you will have to unscrew the hinges. Whatever method you use, always end with the upper hinge when removing the door, and begin with it when remounting it. If the lower hinge is the last to be unscrewed, or the first to be reattached, and the door topples, it will damage the lower hinge.

Flowers

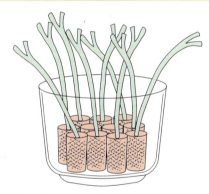

Rollers for roses? ▲
Here's a handy way to support the stems of cut flowers: tie a few hair rollers together with rubber bands and put them into the vase or bowl. Slip the flower stems into them. If you don't have any rubber bands, pack as many rollers into the container as you can.

Easy clean
Dried flower arrangements enhance any room in the home—until they get dusty. Use a hair dryer set to the lowest setting to blow dust off them. This way you won't damage the fragile blooms.

Vacuums

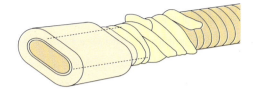

Protect the surfaces ▲
Stop a vacuum nozzle damaging the surface you're cleaning—such as cushions, for example. Tape a piece of foam securely around its end.
Caution: Ensure that the air flow is not impeded in any way. Not only might you damage your vacuum cleaner, but the slower the air flow, the less effective the cleaner's action.

Save that hose
The sharper the bend a vacuum hose has to make, the more likely it is to kink and collapse. Mount an old pram wheel rim on the wall. The hose will nestle in the rim and curve gently, without any stresses. This hint works for other hoses as well, such as pool-cleaner hoses. ▼

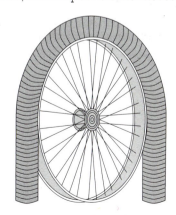

Household Hints / 355

CHAPTER 12
TRAVEL AND SPORTS

TRAVEL TIPS 357
SPORTS EQUIPMENT 360
BOATS 362

TRAVEL TIPS

Safe and sound

Give us a call
Hire a cellular telephone when you go on a long trip. That way, you will be able to contact home, hotels or anyone you may need to call in an emergency. They can be hired from the telephone-company kiosks at major airports. Consider going for the extra expense of hiring a plug-in car jack as well—as you travel, you can give the telephone battery a quick charge if necessary. ▼

Fight fatigue
Driver fatigue is a cause of many accidents, and a contributory cause in others. To fight drowsiness, avoid eating a big meal just prior to a trip and during the drive. You should also avoid drugs and alcohol. Analgesics, antihistamines and decongestants can make you drowsy. Alcohol, despite what some people may believe, is a depressant. During the trip, stop frequently and walk a little way along the road. Keep a damp cloth in the car to wipe your eyes every so often.

We've got your number
Make a list of useful numbers prior to going on holiday or a long journey. For example, important numbers such as those for the police, garages, traffic departments and accommodation in the various centres through which you will pass, will make it much easier to get help or arrange accommodation in a hurry.

Tricks on the trip

Do it in the daylight
When part of your trip takes you through a sparsely inhabited or remote area, or one with few repair facilities, plan that part of the trip for daylight travel. Should your vehicle experience problems, you will have a better chance of attracting help. Domestic stock and wildlife will also be easier to see, so that you can take avoiding action if they stray onto the road. In addition, garages will be easier to contact during normal working hours.

Stiff neck, aching arms?
Relieve those cramped muscles and aching limbs with a few simple exercises. For a stiff neck, rotate your head in a figure-eight pattern. Repeat the exercise a number of times. Loosen cramped leg muscles by stretching them out in front of you, clenching and unclenching your toes. Rotate your feet in one direction and then the other. Ease aching arm muscles by swinging your arms back as far as you can. Then let them dangle and shrug your shoulders a couple of times. Make a habit of doing these exercises regularly.

Essentials

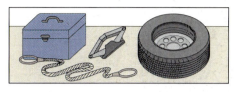

Take it with you ▲
A breakdown is no fun, so make sure the essentials you're carrying are fit for service:
▷ Check your spare tyre and have it pumped up if necessary.
▷ Check that the jack is in the car, is serviceable and that the wheelbrace and warning triangle are also present.
▷ Check that you have a full set of tools.
▷ Take a torch along (reverse one cell so that if the torch is accidentally turned on, it won't waste the cells).
▷ Pack a towrope and jumper leads.
▷ Take along an aerosol tyre inflator.
▷ Consult a motoring magazine and the Automobile Association for further advice. Rather two precautions too many than one too few.

TRAVEL TIPS

Trailers and caravans

Trailer tip
A padlock on your trailer's safety chain will stop anyone disconnecting your trailer and stealing it. Slip the chain over the hitch as normal and padlock two links together, as close as possible to the hitch, so that the resulting loop will not pass over the ball of the hitch. ▼

Forget that spare
Carrying a spare wheel for a trailer or caravan makes sense. But, if space is limited, a hub adaptor is a useful substitute. The adaptor has a set of wheel studs and holes. It is bolted onto the trailer's hub and the car's spare in turn is bolted onto that. Have the trailer or caravan's wheel repaired as soon as possible. The adaptor is available from outlets stocking caravan and trailer accessories.

Safe on the move
A small safe bolted to a caravan's floor is a useful repository for travel documents, jewellery and other valuables. The best place for the safe is under a bunk or in the bottom of a cupboard. Make sure the bolts pass through a chassis member so that the safe cannot be pulled out.

Towing with a difference
Bogged down while towing a caravan? Unhitch it, and get the car out onto firm ground. Then connect a towrope to the car and caravan. Lay planks under the jockey wheel or, if none are available, put heavier items towards the rear of the caravan to reduce the weight on the jockey wheel. Guiding the caravan from the sides or rear, slowly pull it onto firm ground. Stop as soon as it's clear, and hitch up as normal. **Caution:** Don't guide the caravan by holding onto the hitch—if the towrope breaks or the caravan suddenly rolls forward, you may be injured. Work only from beside or behind the caravan.

Stuck? Winch it out
The hand winches available from hardware and motor-spares outlets have a load capacity more than adequate for most situations. If stuck, get the towcar clear, as above, and then connect the winch between the car and caravan, and crank the caravan out of the mire. The same method can be used between one car and another.

Bags of chocks
Carry four small bags made of canvas or another strong material. Filled with tightly packed sand they make handy chocks, and they take up little space.

Turn over a new leaf
When parking your caravan in a resort that's new to you, take a look at the trees to get an idea of the prevailing wind direction, and position your caravan accordingly. You can also simply align your caravan with others in the resort. Sometimes aligning your caravan with the most scenic view might present problems when the wind starts.

What a bag 1
A couple of stout bags can have even more uses than simply as chocks. Fill some with sand and use them to help hold your caravan's awning down in high winds. These can be particularly useful when pegs will not grip properly in sand. ▼

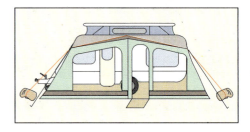

What a bag 2
Apart from use as chocks or hold-downs for a tent or awning, a couple of stout bags are a great help when you're stuck in mud or sand. Lay them down and drive out.

Get those gloves on
It's a good idea to keep a pair of old gloves or gauntlets in the car to keep your hands clean when you have to change a wheel or work on the engine.

Camping

Soft sand solver

Pegs may pull out of soft sand or wet soil, particularly if there's a wind blowing. Weld pointed plates 50 mm wide to four or five pegs. They will hold far better than they do in soft sand or mud.

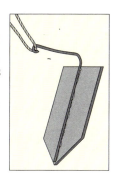

Double-duty plate

As an alternative to the above, make up a few anchors from 3 mm steel plates, about 300 mm by 300 mm. Drill a hole in the centre of each and attach an eye-bolt to the plate. These anchors work well in soft sand or mud when buried completely below the surface. Dig a trench for the rope so that the force on the rope is at right angles to the plate's surface. You can also use one as a base-plate for a jack when changing a wheel on soft ground. ▼

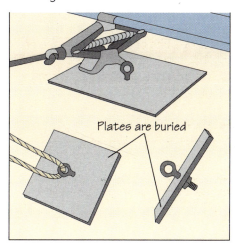

Plates are buried

On the road

Desert water source 1

Crossing a desert? Before leaving home, drain and rinse your windscreen-washer tank and fill it with clean water. Take ample water supplies anyway, but keep this water in reserve if travelling on a long stretch of road through a desert: a tank will often hold as much as 4 or 5 litres. It could be a life-saver. You could also consider using the radiator in the same way, but rinse it out thoroughly to ensure every trace of antifreeze or additive is removed.

Desert water source 2

Use a large sheet of plastic to make a solar still. Dig a hole about 1 m in diameter and half a metre deep. Put a container in the hole and surround it with plant matter. Place the plastic sheet over the hole, anchor the edges, and put a pebble in the centre, over the container. This will lead the water droplets to the centre. The water may not taste great, but it will help you to survive.

Punch it out

If a stone shatters your windscreen, punch out some of the glass in front of you so that you can see the road ahead.

A FIRST-AID KIT FOR THE CAR

Don't wait until the last moment to think about a first-aid kit for your car. Excellent kits are available, but you can make up your own, using a sturdy plastic container or fishing-tackle box. Label the kit's container boldly with paint, and keep it under a seat or in some other position where it will be readily to hand. Keep it out of the hands of children, however.
A basic kit will comprise:
▷ A selection of bandages, plus a number of safety pins.
▷ A selection of plasters.
▷ A selection of dressings and cotton-wool balls.
▷ Scissors, tweezers, eyebath, eyedrops and eyeshield.
▷ Acriflavine solution, sal volatile, toothache drops or gel, wound spray and disinfectant.
▷ Analgesic tablets, burn ointment and zinc and castor-oil cream.
▷ Any medicines required by the family—for allergies, for example.

SPORTS EQUIPMENT

Out in the wild

Here's a hot tip
If you're out hiking or camping and a bootlace breaks, don't curse and swear. Just replace the aglet and the lace will be as good as new. Using a match or a lighter, melt a scrap of nylon rope. Let the drippings land on the frayed lace end; then use a twig or a toothpick to shape the end. ▼

Handy oil
Usually the lantern or camp-stove plunger needs a bit of oil when there is none to be found. In a pinch, you can use a drop of salad or cooking oil as a substitute.

High and dry
Keep your topographical and trail maps from becoming water-damaged by coating them with a commercial wood and concrete waterproofer (available at hardware dealers). Spread the map out flat on top of some newspaper, and paint on the waterproofer with a foam brush. Once dry, your maps will stand up to even the worst weather.

Bright 'n shiny ▲
Soot accumulates quickly on camp-fire cookware. Keep your pots and pans bright and shiny by placing them in disposable aluminium plates when cooking. When these aluminium shields become black with soot, toss them out.

Light my fire
As a precaution, always carry a candle stub in the bottom of your waterproof matchbox. With its help, you'll be able to light a fire—even with damp material.

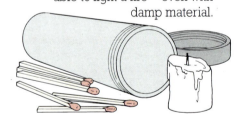

Inflation devices

A lazy solution
It's tiresome to inflate footballs, rugby balls, basketballs, and other such items by hand. If you have access to an air compressor, harness its power for the job. To adapt the compressor, simply fit a car-tyre valve extender onto an inflator needle and attach the two with silicone caulk.

Super-speed inflator
If you don't have an air compressor hanging around, you can create your own, easy inflation system using a wet-and-dry vacuum. Purchase a plastic pipe reducer to fit the air valve on the inflatable item, use it to connect the vacuum exhaust port to the valve, and let the blower do the work for you.

Fishing gear

Don't throw it out ▲
The next time a ballpoint pen runs out of ink, recycle it by removing the spring and ink tube and using the barrel to carry split shot whenever you go fishing. The pen makes a great dispenser—whenever you need a sinker, unscrew the barrel and let the shot roll out one by one. Clip the pen to your pocket for easy access.

Make it stand out
Various items of fishing equipment can be easily lost or left behind because they are not easy to see. Painting each one a bright colour, such as yellow or orange, will help even the smallest items stand out in long grass.

Get a grip

Hard-to-detach fishing-rod sections will be easier to pull apart if you provide yourself with a good grip. Here's how: buy two pieces of gum-rubber surgical tubing (available at pharmacies), cut them lengthwise, and place one on each side of the ferrule.

Just a teaspoon

Turn an old teaspoon into a spinner by sawing the bowl off the handle. Drill a hole into one end of the bowl, and wire a swivel onto it. Use it to enhance another lure, or drill a hole in the other end, attach a hook to it, and use it by itself. Don't toss away the handle; use it to make a minnow by drilling four small holes along its length and attaching a swivel to the hole at one end, a single hook in the hole at the other end, and double hooks in the other two holes. ▼

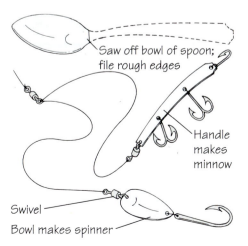

WATERSKI REPAIRS

Scratches and gouges might impair a ski's performance, but any damage certainly detracts from its appearance. You can easily repair a small gouge or screw hole in the base of a ski by using a suitable filler such as epoxy or fibreglass (depending on the ski's construction). However, leave major repairs to the professionals.

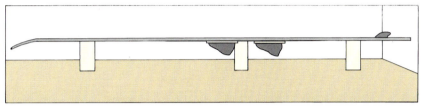

1 Place the damaged ski on wood blocks on a flat surface. For extra support, butt the tail of the ski against a wall. If you have a workbench, you can clamp the ski in a vice, but be sure to protect the ski from scratches by placing pieces of cardboard or wood between the jaws of the vice and the ski.

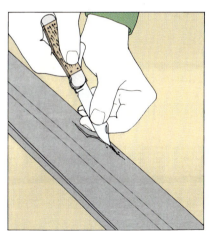

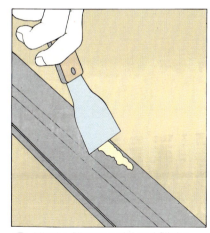

2 Using a knife or an old screwdriver, remove all traces of mud and dirt from the gouge. Also remove any flaked areas, which might become detached later—it's important that the filler material can adhere to a clean, solid base.

3 Mix the filler material and fill the gouge. If the gouge is deep, apply successive layers of filler, rather than a single one. Slightly overfill the gouge. Leave the material to set and then sand it down with fine sandpaper until the repair is flush with the surrounding surface, and then apply a final polishing.

BOATS

Canoe corner

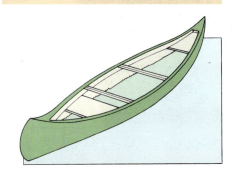

It's time to slim down
Paddles that have thick blades can be clumsy. To keep them slicing through the water, sand the edges of the blades to a thickness of about 3 mm; use a portable electric sander for best results. Varnish all sanded areas to keep the paddle from becoming waterlogged.

Noises off ▲
Glue scraps of carpeting to the undersides of coolers and tackle boxes to stop them knocking around in the bottom of a canoe (or other boat)—and to keep the noise from alerting fish and wildlife to your presence. Even better, pad the entire canoe bottom with carpeting. Keep the carpet clean by hosing off any dirt and hanging it from a tree limb or clothesline to dry.

Quiet, please!
Pad the gunwales with short lengths of foam-pipe insulation and your paddles won't bang on them. Because the insulation comes slit along one side, installation is simple—just cut the foam to the required length and press it into place on the gunwales.

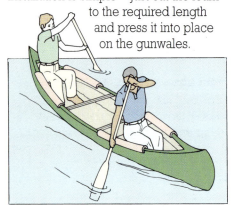

Trailer tricks

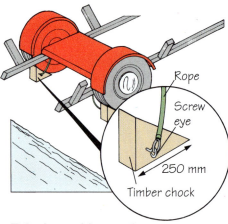

Take 'em with you ▲
Save time and aggravation at the launch ramp with these attachable chocks. Cut a 250 mm triangle from a piece of timber about 100 x 200 mm. Attach a screw eye to one side, and connect a length of ski rope to the eye. When you are ready to load your boat onto its trailer, place a chock behind each rear wheel and tie the ropes to the chassis of the trailer. Load your boat and drive away; the chocks will follow. Once you are out of the way of the other boaters, you can stop and detach the chocks. But keep them fastened to the trailer with the ropes so that they'll be ready for the next time.

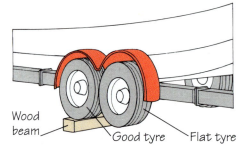

On the road ▲
In a pinch, a thick wooden beam makes a good temporary jack for a boat trailer that has a double axle (four tyres). Simply loosen the wheel nuts on the flat tyre; then ride the good tyre up on the beam. Be sure to place chocks behind the wheels on the other side of the trailer to prevent it from rolling. The flat tyre will be high enough for you to change it.

Put a leash on it
A couple of 25 mm nylon dog leashes will keep a boat from bobbing up and down during transit. Using an eyebolt, attach a tie-down with hooks on the ends to the front of the trailer. Slip the handle loops of the leashes over the cleats on the bow of the boat. Clip the leash hooks to the free tie-down hook and tighten the tie-down. Keep the winch strap attached as usual.

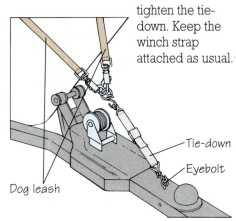

362 / Travel and Sports

Add it yourself

Not a puddle in sight
Rain can easily pool in a full-length boat cover, making the cover hard to remove without dumping at least some of the water into the boat. Encourage the rain to run off by propping up the cover with this homemade support. Cap both ends of a wood dowel with the rubber tips from a discarded pair of crutches. Place the support vertically where the water usually accumulates. ▼

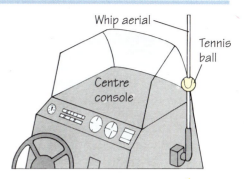

Follow the bouncing ball ▲
The tall whip aerial for the radio is often attached to a boat's centre console, where it can slap against the windscreen during rough weather. Protect both the aerial and any surfaces it may damage by installing a buffer. Just drill a hole that's slightly smaller than the diameter of the aerial through a tennis ball and slide the ball down onto the aerial.

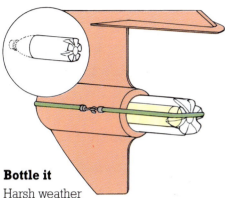

Bottle it
Harsh weather can wreak havoc with exposed metal parts. While the propeller is usually stored away separately, the propeller shaft is often left exposed to the elements. Protect it from corrosion with this handy cover made from a 2 litre plastic cooldrink bottle. Using a sharp knife, carefully cut off the neck of the bottle. Lightly grease the exposed propeller shaft, then slide on the bottle and hold it in place with a rubber cord.

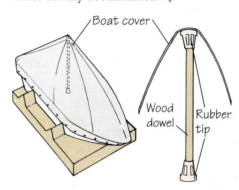

Anchors away
On a small-to-medium-size boat, the last couple of metres of anchor chain (or even the anchor itself) can bang against the bow as you haul it up—sometimes damaging the boat. To warn yourself that the anchor is close to the surface, tie a piece of brightly coloured yarn to the line a metre or so above the spot where the chain begins.

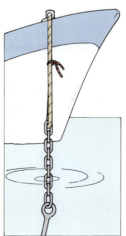

Easy maintenance

What a snap
One good tug on a dirty or rusty snap holding down a boat cover or canvas top may wind up tearing the material instead of opening the snap. Prevent sticking by smearing the snaps with a thin coat of petroleum jelly two or three times a year.

More absorbent than ever
It's nearly impossible to prevent oil from leaking into the engine trays, and every boater knows what a mess that can be to clean up. Make it easier by spreading an opened disposable baby nappy in each tray. The nappy will absorb the spills, making cleanup a breeze.

All aboard
If your boat has a recessed fishing-rod holder mounted on the stern, you can use it to rig a removable handhold. Cut a suitable length from a wood dowel and slide it inside a length of PVC pipe. Top off the assembly with a PVC pipe cap.

DIRECTORY

Manufacturers

Paints

Dulux
Bloemfontein 051-341525
Fax-051-435378
Cape Town 021-9513151
Fax-021-9513310
Durban 031-9121717
Fax-031-9121763
Johannesburg 011-8611000
Fax-011-8646701

Plascon and *Crown*
Bloemfontein 051-4481561
Cape Town 021-546151
Durban 031-4690841
Johannesburg 011-6161850
Kimberley 0531-829541
Pietersburg 0152-2921093
Port Elizabeth 041-434100

Vadek
Bloemfontein 051-471212
Fax-051-307144
Cape Town 021-5119330
Fax-021-5116667
Durban 031-7052766
Fax-031-7052726
East London 0431-435218
Fax-0431-438555
Johannesburg 011-3346130
Fax-011-3345308
Port Elizabeth 041-547603
Fax-041-571563
Pretoria 012-8042130
Fax-012-8041123

Tools

Atlas Copco
(*AEG, Dessouter, Kango,
Atlas Copco Air Tools*)
Cape Town 021-522073
Fax-021-5512947
Durban 031-7004575
Fax-031-7003464
Johannesburg 011-7414000
Fax-011-7414337
Welkom 057-3527365
Fax-057-3532353

Black & Decker
Bloemfontein 051-4470821
Cape Town 021-5110680
Durban 031-3053222
Johannesburg 011-4934000
Pretoria 012-3239542

Bosch/Skil
Cape Town 021-5118816
Fax-021-5117748
Durban 031-328535
Fax-031-328535
Johannesburg 011-6519600
Fax-011-6519825

Lasher
Cape Town 021-5119964
Fax-021-5115596
Johannesburg 011-8251100
Fax-011-8256822

Makita
Cape Town 021-544131
Fax-021-544144
Durban 031-252346
Fax-031-252013
Johannesburg 011-8731260
Fax-011-8731689

Metabo
Cape Town 021-5114914
Fax-021-5117954
Durban 031-230240
Fax-031-230271
Johannesburg 011-4341420
Fax-011-6834608

Ryobi
Johannesburg 011-4443320
Fax-011-4443565
Toll-free-0800-110221

Somta
Cape Town 021-5313126
Fax-021-5311968
Durban 031-9028134
Fax-031-9026850
Johannesburg 011-8258380
Fax-011-8732538

Organizations and Advisory Bodies

Automobile Association
Toll-free 0800 01 01 01
Bloemfontein 051-4483279
Fax-051-4308721
Cape Town 021-211277
Fax-021-4197691
Durban 031-329212
Fax-031-370867
East London 0431-439880
Fax-0431-435781
Johannesburg 011-4939313
Fax-011-4930736
Kimberley 0531-25207
Fax-0531-32882
Pietersburg 0152-2953051
Fax-0152-2953051
Port Elizabeth 041-573444
Fax-041-573445
Pretoria 012-3353850
Fax-012-3356561

Cement & Concrete Institute
Cape Town 021-5915234
Fax-021-5913502

Durban 031-861306/7
Fax-031-867241
Midrand 011-3150300/13
Fax-011-3150584
Port Elizabeth 041-532141
Fax-041-533496
School of Concrete Technology
011-3150300/13
Fax-011-3150300 x 206 (office hours) 011-3150584 (after hours)

Electrical Contractors' Association (ECASA)
Bloemfontein 051-4480331
Fax-051-4478381
Cape Town 021-4622690
Fax-021-456319
Durban 031-236313
Fax-031-230851
East London 0431-25279
Fax-0431-437276
Johannesburg 011-6141112
Fax-011-6145638
Port Elizabeth 041-571545
Fax-041-546048
Pretoria 012-3423242
Fax-012-3423455

HTH Pool Advisory Service
Toll-free 0800 022 240
Johannesburg Fax-011-619344

Institute of Plumbing
Bloemfontein 051-475542
Fax-051-478060
Cape Town 021-4685245
Fax-021-7824997
Durban 031-254288
Fax-031-252152
East London 0431-22531
Fax-0431-434889
Johannesburg 011-6731707
Fax-011-4774520

Port Elizabeth 041-311081
Fax-041-311302

Kitchen Specialists' Association
Johannesburg 011-7843438
Fax-011-7843411

Master Builders and Allied Trades' Association
Bloemfontein 051-471028
Fax-051-476436
Cape Town 021-214757
Fax-021-217385
Durban 031-867070/5
Fax-031-866348
Johannesburg 011-6141519
Fax-011-6183009
Kimberley 0531-811845
Fax-0531-21368
Port Elizabeth 041-311054
Fax-041-311676
Pretoria 012-3411508
Fax-012-3413111

National Spa and Pool Institute
Cape Town 021-7975591
Fax-021-7975097
Durban 031-824742
Fax-031-824742
Johannesburg 011-8860258
Fax-011-8861884
Port Elizabeth 041-354004
Fax-041-313381

SABS
Bloemfontein 051-4474408
Fax-051-4303485
Cape Town 021-6895511
Fax-021-6866375
Durban 031-289181
Fax-031-280519
East London 0431-462351
Fax-0431-461175

Pietersburg 0152-2973528
Fax-0152-2931365
Port Elizabeth 041-337748
Fax-041-332281
Pretoria 012-4287911
Fax-012-3441568

Security Association of South Africa
Johannesburg 011-8285314
Fax-011-8285495

South African Nurserymen's Association
(including *Landscapers' Institute; Interior Plantscapers; Turf Irrigation Association*)
Bloemfontein 051-4511314
Fax-051-4511314
Cape Town 021-7620345
Fax-021-7620345
Johannesburg 011-4641098
Fax-011-4641099
Pietermaritzburg 0331-425779
Fax-0331-944842
Port Elizabeth 041-332458
Fax-041-332458

Swimline Advisory Service
Cape Town 021-7977448
Fax-021-7974815
Durban 031-7004501
Fax-031-7003885
Johannesburg 011-8051711
Fax-011-8054189

Timber Frame Builders' Association
Cape Town 021-7854110
Fax-021-7854110

Wood Preservers' Association
Toll-free 0800 113 630
Johannesburg 011-9741061
Fax-011-9749779

INDEX

A

AA 357, 364
acoustic tiles 148
acrylic, working with 100, 101
adhesive tape *see* double-sided tape; insulation tape; masking tape
adhesives *see* glue and glueing
aerosol-can lids, uses for 10
aftershave, pest control and 344
air conditioners 225, 229, 255
air fresheners 336
alarm systems
    installation of 230
    telephone calls about 226
    trap mats and 226
    wiring of 210
aluminium
    caulk types for 151
    cleaning of 294
    dishwashers and 258
    working with 94
aluminium foil
    mirrors and 350
    ovens, in 259
aluminium-foil cutting strips 53
aluminium-oxide abrasive 80
aluminium plates 93, 244, 265, 360
amperage
    extension cords, of 43
    fuses, of 200
    power tools, of 24
anchors, wall *see* wall fasteners
animals
    gardens and 270, 271
    see also pets
antifreeze
    disposal of 305
    safety and 308
    water systems and 221
antiscald valves 335
appliances
    access to 254
    childproofing of 333, 334
    disassembly of 254
    earth faults in 253, 255
    moving of 345, 348
    noise reduction and 148
    repair of 252
    replacing parts in 258
aprons 64, 278
artificial respiration 301
ashes, smoke stains and 341
attics
    home offices in 113
    storage in 124
audio cassette tapes 263
augers 211, 219
Automobile Association 357, 364
awnings, anchoring of 358, 359
axes
    storage of 58
    use of 297

B

baking soda, uses for 219, 292
bakkies, cargo in 322
ballpoint pens, uses for 64, 360
balusters 181, 333
bamboo, removing finish with 244
band saws
    extension cords for 43
    safety with 31
    working with 77
banisters, painting of 181
bars, heavy-duty 285
basins, skirts on 111
baskets, in cupboards 118, 120, 121
bath mats, on workbenches 53
bathrooms
    safety in 333, 334
    storage in 110, 111
baths
    installation and repair of 216
    moving of 216
    safety and 333, 334, 335
battens, mounting of 120, 156
batteries
    car 316, 324
    disposal of 305
    solar power 223
    testing of 253
battery clips, as spring clamps 86
bay leaves, as ant deterrents 344
beaters (kitchen mixer) 167
bedrooms, storage in 104
beds
    platform 122
    storage space and 104, 105
beer, uses for 270, 320
beeswax, on nails, screws 12, 16
belts
    racks for 119
    uses for 22, 45, 58, 124
bench grinders 22, 23
bending brakes, homemade 96
bevels
    doors, on 146
    tools, on 22, 281, 282
bicycle handlebar grips 40
bicycle tubes, uses for 36
bicycles, storage of 123
bins
    bread 46
    overhead 124
    roll-out 122, 126
    rubbish 106, 281, 336
    sorting 112
    stacking 122
    swing-out 106
birds
    gardens and 271, 296
    swings and 295
biscuit tins, and saw blades 29
bits *see* drill bits; router bits
blinds
    cords of 329, 332
    wardrobes and 119
boats 362
body, as measuring tool 32
bolts (locks) 228, 229
bolts (nuts and)
    left-hand threads on 254
    storage of 60
    working with 19, 62, 96
book ends 116
books, repair of 350
boots, cleaning, scraping of 352
bottle openers, uses for 176
bottle tops, painting with 182
boxes
    cardboard 56, 61
    packing 346, 347
braais 340
brackets (wooden)
    making of 57
    see also shelf supports
brick jointers 160, 161
bricks *see* masonry
broom straws, oil spouts and 41
brooms
    customization of 297
    garden hoses on 292
    painting with 182
brushes
    care of 92
    wood finishing, for 92
    see also paintbrushes; wire brushes
bubble gum, petrol tanks and 318
bubble wrap, in toolboxes 46
buckets
    Christmas trees and 343
    digging holes and 284
    extension cords in 42
    gutters and 162
    heavy loads in 42
    ladders and 45, 187
    leaks in 42
    safety and 42
    tools in 47
builder's felt, stapling of 18
bulbs, planting of 280
bulletin boards 108
burglar guards 228, 229
burns
    electrical 205
    wood, on 239
butter tubs, on taps 214
butt joints
    cutting of 79
    drilling into 72
    strengthening of 79
    wall trim and 134

C

cabinets
    adding shelves to 116
    anchoring of 109
    bathroom 110, 111
    childproofing of 334
    china 116
    cubbyhole 116
    dividers in 116

electrical wires through 210
fitting of 71
kitchen 106, 344
location of 107
medicine 335
painting of 248, 250
pests and 344
racks under 108, 109
storage boxes above 106
towel racks on 110
wall studs and 110
wall-mounted 104
window seats and 104
see also cupboards
cables *see* electric cords; electrical wires
cake tins, uses for 29, 60
camphor, in toolboxes 47
camping 358, 359, 360
candle wax
   bucket leaks and 42
   lubrication with 20, 21, 28, 33, 144
   removal of 353
   see also paraffin
candles
   Christmas trees and 343
   lighting fires with 360
cane
   painting of 250
   pulling taut of 235
canoe paddles, as towel racks 111
canoes 362
canvas, staples for 18
caravans 358
carburettor cleaner, uses for 292
cardboard, corrugated 14
cardiopulmonary resuscitation 301
carpet remnants
   boats and 362
   cars and 320, 322, 323, 326
   contact cement and 38
   dropcloths, as 178
   heavy objects and 345, 348
   icy windscreens and 325
   joint openers and 236
   kneeling pads, as 139
   ladders, on 45
   noise reduction, for 50, 148, 213

BACK TO BASICS FEATURES

▶ Aerials on cars, p 317, "A new aerial"

▶ Built-in shelving unit, p 114, "Built-in shelving"

▶ Ceramic-tile replacement, p 143, "Replacing a ceramic tile"

▶ Cladding replacement, p 159, "Replacing damaged cladding"

▶ Cupboard systems, p 120, "Installing a wire cupboard system"

▶ Dryer drive-belt replacement, p 261, "Replacing a dryer drive belt"

▶ Exhaust repair on cars, p 309, "Exhaust drag"

▶ Fence repair, p 287, "Fence repair"

▶ Finishing wood, p 247, "A natural finish"

▶ Glass-cutting, p 99, "Cutting glass"

▶ Islands in the kitchen, p 109, "Island life"

▶ Landscaping a garden, p 269, "Foundation plantings"

▶ Light-fixture replacement, p 209, "Replacing a light fixture"

▶ Lock installation, p 147, "Installing a rim deadbolt lock"

▶ Multitesters, p 253, "Using a multitester"

▶ Oven-element replacement, p 259, "Oven elements"

▶ Paint texturing techniques, p 183, "Texturing techniques"

▶ Painting furniture, p 249, "An enamel finish"

▶ Painting with a roller, p 179, "Rolling paint"

▶ Pegboard installation, p 127, "Installing pegboard"

▶ Refrigerator door gaskets, p 257, "New door gasket"

▶ Repointing bricks, p 161, "Repointing bricks"

▶ Sanding a project by hand, p 81, "Hand-sanding"

▶ Second doors, p 149, "Installing a second door"

▶ Sharpening garden tools, p 281, "Keep tools sharp"

▶ Sharpening hand tools, p 22, "How to sharpen"

▶ Shingle replacement, p 165, "Replacing shingles"

▶ Spray-painting the car, p 319, "Paint problems"

▶ Stripping old finishes, p 245, "Removing an old finish"

▶ Tap repair on ball taps, p 217, "Ball taps"

▶ Tap repair on cartridge taps, p 215, "Repairing a cartridge tap"

▶ Trees and shrubs, p 277, "Planting a tree or shrub"

▶ Trucks and their loading, p 349, "Loading a truck"

▶ Tyre changing, p 313, "Changing a tyre"

▶ Utility shelving for the workshop, p 57, "Utility shelving"

▶ Veneer patches, p 241, "Patching veneer"

▶ Vinyl flooring repair, p 141, "Flooring patch"

▶ Wall-chasing, p 207, "Chase that wall"

▶ Wallboard repair, p 131, "Fixing damaged wallboard"

▶ Wallcovering basics, p 193, "How to hang prepasted strips"

▶ Water conservation and waste water, p 279, "Waste not"

▶ Waterski repair, p 361, "Waterski repairs"

▶ Windscreen wiper problems, p 321, "Wiper woes"

▶ Workbench to fit many needs, p 52, "An all-purpose bench"

Index / 367

INDEX

painting with 181
power-tool storage, for 58
sawhorses, on 54
toolboxes, in 46
workbenches, on 53, 82
carpet underfelt, staples for 18
carpets
    cutting of 29
    electrical wires under 210
    glue removal from 140
    laying of 157
    patching of 140
    runner 140
    stapling of 18, 140
    storage of 124
    thresholds, at 140
    workshop floors, on 49
cars
    aerials on 317
    air filters in 307
    batteries of 316, 324
    belts in 309
    bonnet latches of 306
    boots of 322, 323
    brakes of 315, 318
    breakdown essentials for 357
    choke gaps in 318
    cleaning of 320
    cooling system of 308
    cylinder head in 306
    demister vents in 321
    doors of 317, 323
    driver fatigue and 357
    electrical systems of 316
    engine timing of 306
    exhaust systems of 308, 309
    first-aid kits for 359
    floor mats in 322
    front-wheel drive 311
    fuel injection in 307
    fuel systems of 318
    heaters in 325
    hoses in 307, 308
    idling of 307, 318
    intake manifolds in 307
    keys for 323
    leaks under 304
    lights of 317, 327
    moving house and 346
    noises from 309, 311, 314, 315
    oil changes for 304
    painting of 319

PCV (positive crankcase ventilation) of 307
power loss in 318
radiators of 308, 359
roof padding for 323
roof racks on 322
security and 231, 323
spark plugs in 303, 306
stalling of 318
starting of 307
steering systems of 310, 312
stickers on 320
storage in 322
sumps in 304, 310
sun visors in 322
suspension systems of 310, 312
transmissions of 310
tune-up of 306
tyres on see tyres
upholstery in 320, 321
waste disposal and 305
wheels on see wheels
windscreen-washer units of 308, 321, 359
windscreens of 321, 325, 359
winter and 324
casters 235, 294, 337
cat food tins, uses for 97
cat litter 243, 292, 325, 336
caulk and caulking
    application of 129, 150, 151
    bucket leaks and 42
    buying guide for 151
    ceramic tiles, of 142
    cladding, of 186
    foundation, at 156
    fridge door gaskets and 256
    garage doors, of 326
    outdoor joints, of 150
    railings, of 292
    safety and 150, 151
    storage of 39
    window panes, of 145
caulk guns
    as clamps 86
    pulling or pushing of 150
caulk tubes 150, 151, 160
ceiling fans, vibration of 224
ceiling tiles 137
ceilings
    access to 154

drilling into 10
installation of 137
insulation of 153, 154
painting of 179
platforms on 221
repair of 137
sanding of 82
suspended 137, 263
wallcoverings on 194, 196
cellulose insulation 153, 154
cement see contact cement; rubber cement
centre lines 69, 70
ceramic tiles
    caulking of 142, 151
    countertops, on 109, 240
    cutting of 29, 142
    drilling into 9, 10
    grouting of 142, 143
    marking of 34, 142
    repair of 142
    replacement of 142, 143
chain saws 283
chains
    car boots, in 323
    clothes rods and 119
    drawing circles with 34
    knots in 352
    swings, on 295
    toys on 122
chairs
    clamping of 85, 237
    finishing of 93
    lawn 294
    painting of 250
    repair of 234, 235
    taking apart of 236
chalk
    files, on 94
    marking tool, as 34, 69
    screwdrivers, on 12
chalk line boxes, as plumb bobs 35
charcoal lighters 340
cheesecloth, as paint strainer 168
chemicals
    children and 333
    contact with 59
    disposal of 39
    see also flammable materials; hazardous waste

chest handles, for tool storage 58
chest lids, childproofing of 332
chest massage 301
childproofing 46, 332
children
    alarm systems and 230
    pets and 335
    towel racks for 111
    see also childproofing; play equipment
children's rooms
    painting of 175, 177
    safety in 335
    storage in 122
    see also playrooms
chimneys
    caulk types for 151
    insulation materials and 154
    pests in 344
china, cleaning and repair of 351
chipboard, finishing of 91
chisels and chiselling
    sharpening of 22, 23
    storage of 20, 46
    use of 73, 161, 292
chocks, construction of 362
Christmas decorations 342, 343
Christmas lights
    safety and 343
    securing of 342
    storage of 124
circle cutters 98
circles
    drawing of 34, 71, 100
    finding centre of 69
    finding diameter of 68
circuit breakers 202, 203
circuits see electrical circuits
circular saws
    binding kerf and 74
    blades for 28
    cleaning of 29
    extension cords for 43
    guides for 75
    lubrication of 28
    plywood and 74
    sharpening blades of 22
    storage of 29
    straight glueing edges and 79
    use of 28
cladding
    caulking of 186

gauges for 158, 165
houses on columns and 157
installation of 158
insulation of 153
painting of 173, 186
repair of 158
replacement of 158, 159
clamps
  band 37, 86
  bar 36, 37, 237
  do's and don'ts for 84
  edge 37, 84
  filing and 94
  G- *see* G-clamps
  glue and 84, 85, 87, 89
  handscrew 36, 85
  hose 86, 308
  improvised 86, 87
  mitre boxes and 84
  picture frames, for 330
  pipe 36, 85, 86
  planing and 73, 85
  plaster and 130
  plates, for 351
  pressure distribution with 84
  protecting surfaces against 36
  rust prevention for 36
  safety and 36
  solid-surface material and 101
  spring 86, 330
  tourniquet 87
  types of 37
  workbenches and 87
cleaning
  air conditioners 225
  aluminium chair frames 294
  bench grinders 23
  boat-engine pans 363
  candleholders 353
  cars 320
  china 351
  decks 289
  dishwashers 258
  doorbells 210
  drill bits 11
  driveways 292, 297
  electrical contacts 252, 354
  files 20, 94, 95
  fingernails 65, 272
  furniture 242
  grills 340
  gutters 162, 165

lawn mowers 282
light-bulb sockets 208, 293, 317
paintbrushes 170, 171
putty knives 176, 244
rollers 172
roofs 165
router bits 27
sanding belts 25
saws 21, 29
shoes and boots 352
shower heads 216
skin 65, 188
soldering irons 97
spray guns 172
switches 252
toilets 218
tools 24, 47, 280
upholstery 320, 321
VCR heads 262
verges 297
wheels 320
workshops 62
clippers, sharpening of 281
clocks, electric 255
clothes, for work 64
clotheslines 296
clothes pegs 294, 296
coat hangers
  air-conditioner cleaners, as 225
  boot dryers, as 352
  car-exhaust supports, as 309
  clotheslines, on 296
  contour gauges, as 142
  doorstops made with 332
  hooks, as 187
  paint tins and 169
  pictures and 331
  racks, as 103, 119, 171, 172
  rests, as 97, 315
  roller cleaners, as 172
  spring clamps and 86
  strengthening of 119
  tissue holders, as 59
  toilet cleaners, as 218, 219
  tube caps, as 150
  wallcoverings and 194
  wire fishers, as 206
coffee filters, uses for 263
coffee tin lids, as shields 167

coffee tins
  charcoal lighters, as 340
  cleaning brushes in 171
  cleaning knives in 176
  dust catchers, as 10
  mineral spirits in 188
  spot seeders, as 274
  string dispensers, as 59
  stripping hardware in 242
  trunk fresheners in 336
colours
  paint, of 174, 175, 177, 184
  plants, of 269
combs, holding nails with 15
compasses 34, 71, 100
compost 267, 277
compound *see* filler; joint compound
computers, moving of 263
concrete
  caulk types for 151
  drilling into 10
  fasteners and 117, 291
  flagstone effect on 291
  paths and patios of 290, 291
  repair of 292
concrete footings 284
contact cement
  application of 38
  storage of 39
  veneer and 241
continuity testers 199, 201
cookbooks, racks for 109
cooldrink tins, uses for 38, 46
cooldrinks, as lubricators 14, 303
copper tubing, pictures and 330
cords *see* blinds; electric cords; extension cords
corks
  blocks for lids, as 332
  bulletin boards of 108
  painting with 182
  tool storage and 11, 20
corkscrews, uses for 137
corner organizers 123
corners
  mitred joints on 87
  patching of 130
  squareness of 68
cornice 79, 134
corrosion
  car electrical systems, in 316

lights, in 317
  see also rust prevention
cotton buds, electrical contacts and 354
cots, safety and 333, 335
countertops
  construction of 109
  cutting boards in 107
  extension of 107
  laminating of 101
  sealing of 101
  swing-out 107
CPR (cardiopulmonary resuscitation) 301
crawl spaces 155
crayon marks, on paint 176
credit cards
  icy windscreens and 325
  measuring with 32
  opening doors with 228
creepers (mechanic's) 303
crocheted ornaments, droop in 342
crosscutting (sawing) 30
crutches, boat covers and 363
cupboard doors *see* doors
cupboards
  construction of 120, 156
  dividers for 118
  electrical systems and 206, 210
  home offices in 113, 120
  lining of 120
  playrooms in 106
  racks under 108
  retrieving items behind 354
  rods in 119
  space savers in 118
  spacing guidelines for 118
  staples for 18
  step shelves in 108
  see also cabinets; wardrobes
cupcake pans, uses for 56
curtain rods
  compasses, as 71
  measuring tools, as 33
curtains, hanging of 329
cutlery, repair of 351
cutlery trays, uses for 20, 46
cutting boards 107
cylinders, equal segments 69

INDEX

D

dampness 156, 157
decks
  building and restoring of 288
  childproofing of 333
  levels for 288, 293
  swimming pools and 298
dents, raising of 81, 239
desks, storage chests and 122
detergent boxes, manuals in 41
dibbles 280
diggers, types of 285
digging 272, 277, 280, 284, 285
dimmer switches 293
dipsticks 304
dish racks, uses for 56
dishwashers
  aluminium in 258
  childproofing of 334
  cleaning of 258
  repair of 258
  temperature in 258
dispensers, push-button 111
documents, storage of 354, 358
dollies (furniture) 345, 348
doorbells
  cleaning and repair of 210
  testing of 253
  wiring of 210
  workshops, in 49
doors
  catches for 146
  childproofing of 332, 333
  clamping of 85
  finishing of 93, 146
  glass 333
  insulation of 149
  jamming of 228
  laminating of 101
  left-hand or right-hand 146
  mounting of 355
  painting of 93, 146, 180, 181
  protection of 177
  reinforcement of 104
  removal of 355
  repair of 146
  second, installation of 149
  security and 144, 146, 228
  sliding 144, 229
  sticking of 234
  storage on 103, 104, 110, 112, 119
  warping of 355
  weatherstripping of 152
  see also garage doors
doorstops
  construction of 332
  shoe storage, for 119
double-sided tape, angling of 354
dowels
  chair repair and 234, 235
  chamfering of 79
  fasteners and 291
  fluted 79
  storage of 61
  test 79
drafter's rules 71
drain-waste-vent systems 211
drainage systems 211, 212, 213
drainpipes
  extensions to 156, 300
  unblocking of 163
drains
  trees and 277
  unblocking of 219
  washing machines and 260
draperies, stapling of 18
draughts see weatherstripping
drawers
  baskets as 118
  beds, under 105, 122
  compartments in 105
  counter space, as 107
  handles for 56
  knobs on see knobs
  painting of 250
  pull-out limits for 56, 233
  squareness of 68
  sticking of 233
drill bits
  auger 10
  brad-point 10, 11
  carbide-tipped 10
  cleaning of 11
  countersink 94
  Forstner 10, 11
  gauges for 9
  glass 98
  HSS (high-speed steel) 10
  masonry 10
  sharpening of 22
  spade 10, 11
  storage of 11, 46, 58
  testing of 10
drill chucks, replacement of 9
drill gauges, substitutes for 9
drills and drilling
  attachments to 25, 83, 167, 321
  buyer's guide for 11
  ceilings, into 10
  ceramic tiles, into 9, 10
  concrete, into 10
  cordless 11, 13
  extension cords for 43
  glass, into 98
  hammer 10
  masonry, into 10, 156
  metal, into 10, 94
  plaster, into 10
  plastic, into 100
  storage of 11, 59
  tubes, into 94
  use of 9, 72
  wood, into 10, 72
drive belts
  cars, in 309
  dryers, in 261
driveways
  cleaning of 292, 297
  landscaping of 269
dropcloths 177, 178, 190, 297
dryers
  repair of 260
  shelves above 112, 260, 261
drywalls
  insulation of 153, 154
  pegboard on 127
  wall fasteners and 117
dust catchers 10, 30
dustpans, magnets on 62
DWV (drain-waste-vent) systems 211

E

ear protectors 65
earrings, as spectacle screws 353
earth faults, testing for 253, 255
earth-leakage relays 51, 203
earthing
  pipes and 201, 211
  testing of 201, 253
earthing screws 209
eaves, shelves under 126
ECASA (Electrical Contractors' Association) 364
edging tools, use of 276, 283
edgings (garden)
  icy driving conditions and 324
  use of 265, 266, 290
edgings (wall) 115
egg cartons, uses for 252
eggshells, snails and 270
electric carving knives 100
electric cords
  concealment of 262
  hangers for 51, 332
  protection of 208
  replacement of 208
  safety and 51, 205
  testing of 253
  visibility of 282
  see also electrical wires; extension cords
electric frying pans, uses for 260
electric shocks 201, 205, 301
electrical boxes
  installation of 206
  sizes of 206
  uses for 60
  vapour retarders and 154
electrical circuits
  expansion of 206
  identification of 202
  open (interrupted) 253
  overload of 203
  shorts in 200, 203, 204, 253
  troubleshooting for 203
electrical compliance certificates 200
electrical conduits
  pulling wires through 206
  sizes of 206
  trees and 277
electrical contact cleaners 252, 354
Electrical Contractors' Association 364
electrical fixtures, insulation materials and 154

electrical outlets
    installation of 204, 206, 207
    removing covers of 177
    safety covers on 51, 333
electrical systems (household)
    basics of 202
    geysers and 221
    legal requirements and 120, 200
    pipes and 201, 211
    safety and 200, 255
    testing of 199, 201, 253, 263
    tools for 199, 203, 205
    turning off power in 200, 201, 203
    wallboard installation and 132
    water and 200, 201
    workshops, in 51
    see also energy conservation; solar power
electrical tools *see* power tools
electrical wire spools 124
electrical wires
    appliance repair and 258
    boxes, in 206
    checking path of 207
    closed systems, in 202
    colours of 209
    concealment of 262
    fishing for 206, 207
    joining of 204, 205, 209, 252
    length of 204
    low-voltage 210
    plugs, in 24, 208
    pulling of 206
    running of 120, 207, 210, 262
    staples for 18
    stripping of 204
    terminals and 204, 255, 258
    wall studs and 135
    see also electric cords
electrified barriers 226, 227
electronic equipment 262, 348
elements (heating) 253, 259
ELR (earth-leakage relay) 51
emery abrasive 80
emery boards 34, 82, 293
enamels 249
energy conservation
    geysers and 220, 221
    see also solar power
entrances, storage in 103

epoxy
    china, glass and 351
    furniture and 236
    mixing of 88
    removal of 351
    setting time of 38
equipment *see* tools
exercises, for stiff muscles 357
expansion shields 117
extension cords
    capacity of 43
    safety and 51, 205
    storage of 42, 58, 61
    use of 42, 43
    visibility of 282
eyes
    chemicals in 59
    protectors for 65

F

fabrics, repair of 64, 234, 329
face shields 65
fans
    ceiling 224
    oiling of 255
fasteners *see* wall fasteners
feather boards 31
feathering (paint) 169, 251
feathering (wood) 289
felt stripping, staples for 18
fences
    construction and repair of 286
    electrified 226, 227
    levels for 293
fertilizers 273, 277
fibreglass
    caulk types for 151
    insulation material 152, 153
file cards 20, 94
files and filing
    bastard 20, 281, 282
    cleaning of 20, 94, 95
    double-cut 20
    flat 20
    half-round 20
    handles for 20
    protecting work against 94
    round 20
    second-cut 20, 281

    single-cut 20
    small pieces, of 94
    smooth 20, 281
    soft metals, of 94
    square 20
    storage of 46
    strokes used with 20, 281, 282
    taper (triangular) 20
    types and uses of 20
filler
    application of 129, 176, 177, 239
    car body 158
    drying of 129
    mixing of 133
    storage of 40, 133
    wall panelling, on 136
    see also wood filler
filler sticks 239
film canisters 36, 84, 354
filters
    air 62, 307
    iron 258
    paint 90
    vacuum cleaner 63
fingernails, cleaning of 65, 272
finishes and finishing
    application of 90
    brightening of 239
    brushes for 92
    disposal of 39
    doors, of 93, 146
    drip catchers for 92
    drying time of 93
    glue and 89
    knobs, of 93
    non-toxic 91
    preparation for 92
    record of 93
    removal of 244, 245
    repair of 238, 239, 242, 243
    safety and 39, 91
    thresholds, of 146
    types of 242, 246
    wall panelling, of 136
    work sequence for 91, 136, 247
    work surfaces for 93
fire extinguishers 55, 303
fire hazards
    wires as 204, 262
    see also flammable materials

fireplaces and fires 341, 343
fires
    control of 303
    lighting of 340, 341, 360
firewood 297
first aid
    drowning victims, for 301
    electric shocks, for 201, 205, 301
first-aid kits 59, 359
fish tape 207
fish-hooks, blocked drains and 219
fishing equipment, tips for 360, 361
fishing line, pictures and 330
fishing rods, storage of 123
fish-ponds 268
flagstones 290, 291
flammable materials
    caulk as 151
    Christmas trees as 343
    disposal of 39
    finishes as 91
    fuel as 283, 303
    hydrogen gas as 349
    insulation materials as 154
    moving house and 346
    sawdust as 51
    storage of 55, 91, 283, 303
    vacuum fumes as 63
flaring tools 211
flashing 151, 164
flashlights *see* torches
flex, stapling of 18
floorboards 138, 139
floor bridging 138, 155
floor coverings 140
floor joists 139
floor tiles 140, 141
floor wax, uses for 12, 31, 36
floors
    insulation of 153, 155
    protection of 345
    repair of 138
    security and 229
    suspended 155, 156, 229
    warm covers for 157
    water under 156
flowerpots *see* houseplants
flowers (cut) 339, 354, 355
flowers (dried), dust on 355

INDEX

foam packing, uses for 164
foam rubber
    cutting of 100
    uses for 27, 148, 326, 355
folding rules, substitutes for 68
footings (concrete) 284
frames (picture) 330
freezers
    moving of 348
    problems with 256
freezing weather
    cars and 324
    locks and 325
    water systems and 213, 214, 221
friction boards, for routers 78
frost
    seedlings and 265
    see also freezing weather
fuel
    cars and 318
    disposal of 305
    storage of 283, 303
fuel-injection engines 307
fuel lines, uses for 303
fungus
    houseplants and 338
    roofs and 164
    see also mildew
furniture
    antiquing of 248
    basic rules for 236
    cleaning of 242
    distressing of 248
    moving of 345
    outdoor see outdoor furniture
    painting of 248
    repair of 233
    staining of 246
    stripping of 242
    surfaces of 238
    varnishing of 246
    wobbling of 235
furniture-leg tips
    hammers, on 15
    outdoor furniture, on 294
    table legs, on 235
furniture polish
    disposal of 39
    drawers and 233
furniture touch-up pens 238
furniture touch-up sticks 241
furniture wax, floors and 138
fuses 200, 202, 203, 259

G

G-clamps
    capping of 36
    deep-throat 37
    electrical boxes and 206
    use of 84
    windows and 332
garage doors
    childproofing of 333
    repair of 327
    weatherstripping of 152, 326
garages
    childproofing of 333
    heaters in 324
    insulation of 148
    parking guidelines for 326
    storage in 57, 61, 124, 126
    tools for 303
    weatherproofing of 326
    see also workshops
garden-hose remnants
    bucket handles, on 42
    carrying glass with 144, 345
    cord hangers, as 51
    garage doors and 326
    lawn-mower guards, as 282
    pipes and 213
    ropes and 42
    sanding tools, as 82
    shovels, on 272
    starting threads with 303
    storage, used for 21, 29, 35
    swings and 295
    tree stakes and 276
garden hoses
    brooms, on 292
    corner guards for 275
    double-barrelled 320
    extensions to 162
    levels, as 293
    soaker 275
    storage of 61
gardening
    container 338
    tips for 272
    tools for 272, 280

gardens
    animals in 270, 271
    birds in 271, 296
    furniture in see outdoor furniture
    landscaping of 268
    laying out of 293
    lighting in 293
    pests in 270
    planting of 265
    security and 230, 231, 293
    vegetables in 265, 267
    water conservation and 268, 279
    watering of 267, 275, 279
    weeding of 270
garlic, garden pests and 271
garnet abrasive 80
gas bottles, storage of 303
gaskets
    refrigerator door 256, 257
    weatherstripping and 152
gates
    safety 333
    sagging of 287
gauges
    cladding 158
    contour 71, 142
    depth 68
    drill 9
    feeler 306
    marking 70
    mitre 30, 76
    saws and 30, 74, 76, 77
    tyre tread 68
gelatine, glue made with 237
geysers
    costs of 222
    energy conservation and 220, 221
    repair of 220, 221
    water conservation and 220, 221
    see also solar power
glass
    carrying of 144, 345
    caulk types for 151
    cutting of 98, 99, 145
    drilling of 98
    glueing of 98, 351
    laminated 98
    marking of 34, 99

    safety 98
    sanding of 98
    tempered 98
    see also window panes
glass blocks, windows and 229
glasses see spectacles
glazes (paint) 183, 248, 249
glazing compound 145
gloves
    drip catchers, as 92
    gardening, for 272
    ladders, on 44
    pliers, on 19
    safety and 64
    sanding with 82
glue and glueing
    application of 88
    burglar guards, of 229
    caps on 38
    carpenter's 62, 240
    chairs, of 234
    china, of 351
    cladding, of 158
    clamps and 84, 85, 87, 89
    dispensing of 38
    disposal of 39
    furniture and 236, 237
    glass, of 98, 351
    hands, on 62
    homemade 237
    joints, in 89, 237
    low-voltage wires, of 210
    noise reduction, for 50
    plastic laminate, of 101, 240
    removal of 89, 101, 140, 141, 236
    setting time of 38, 88
    storage of 38, 39
    types and uses of 38
    veneer, of 240
    wallboard, of 132, 133
    water-base 88
    wood 237
    wood filler and 62, 90
    wood slivers, of 88
    see also epoxy; wallcovering paste
glue guns, storage of 39
golf bags, tools in 281
golf equipment, storage of 123
golf tees, as plugs 14, 307

grandfather clocks, moving of 347
graphite, squeaking floors and 138
gravy ladles, uses for 90
grease
  car electrical connectors, for 316
  drains, in 219
  driveways, on 292
  grills, on 340
  paint, on 176, 191
  parts and 252
  skin, on 65
  spills of 62
greenhouses 265
grills 340
ground faults see earth faults
grout 142, 143
guest rooms, offices in 113
gutters
  cleaning and repair of 162, 164, 165
  as shelves 61

hacksaw blades, uses for 53, 80, 88
hacksaws
  bolts, screws and 96
  cleaning of 21
  metal and 21, 94
  plastic tubing and 100
  use of 95
hair, paint on 188
hair dryers
  dust blowers, as 62, 355
  filler and 129
  glue softeners, as 188, 320
  grease melters, as 219
  stain removers, as 238
  wax softeners, as 353
hair rollers, cut flowers and 355
hairspray, uses for 342, 344
hammer tackers 18
hammers and hammering
  care of 16, 17
  carrying wood with 67
  customization of 16

hardwood, into 16
measuring tools, as 33
screws and 13, 14
storage of 17, 58
strip flooring, of 139
types of 17
use of 15
wall studs, into 135
wallboard, into 133
weeding with 270
hammocks, for storage 125
hand trucks, extensions to 345
handsaws
  cleaning of 21
  depth gauges for 74
  guides for 74
  lubrication of 21
  plywood and 74
  PVC pipe and 213
  sharpening of 22
  storage of 21
  types of 21
  use of 21
hardboard, perforated see pegboard
hardwood, hammering into 16
hazardous waste 39, 55, 91, 305
heavy objects, moving of 345, 348
hedges, as rain barriers 156
high chairs, safety and 334, 335
hiking 360
hinge pins 146, 234
hinges
  burglar guards, on 229
  loose 234
  oiling of 355
  position of 146
  strain on 104
  stripping of 242
hoes 270, 281
home offices 113, 120
home systems 198
homes
  cooling of 224
  improvements to 128
  odours in 219, 225, 336
  pest control in 344
  repairs in 232
  security in see alarm systems; security
  storage in 102

HEALTHY HOME FEATURES

▶ Disposal of automotive wastes, p 305, "Disposing of automotive wastes"

▶ Disposal of workshop materials, p 39, "Disposing of hazardous waste"

▶ Lead in paint, p 177, "Paint problems"

▶ pH values and plants, p 267, "The right plants for the right soil"

honing 22, 23
hooks 291, 332
hoses (garden) see garden hoses
house exteriors, paint and 184, 185
households see homes
houseplants
  care of 337, 338
  waste water and 279
houses
  columns, on 156, 157
  security risks of 227
  see also homes
HTH Pool Advisory Service 365
hub adaptors 358

ice see freezing weather
ice-cube trays, uses for 252
ice makers 257
inflators 360
ink marks, on paint 176
inner tubes 29, 44, 54, 300
insects
  gardens and 270, 271
  houseplants and 338
  houses and 344
Institute of Plumbing 365
instructions, working with 41
insulation
  baths, of 216
  ceilings, of 153, 154
  cladding, of 153
  climate and 155
  doors, of 149
  floors, of 153, 155
  foundations, of 153
  garages, of 148
  geysers, of 220
  pipes, of 213
  tools, of 205
  walls, of 153, 154
  windows, of 148
  workshops, of 49, 50, 148, 149
insulation materials
  cutting of 100, 152
  levellers for 155
  noise reduction and 148
  safety with 152, 154
  stapling of 18, 154
  types of 153
insulation tape
  rejuvenation of 353
  screwdrivers and 199
Interior Plantscapers 365
iron, stains of 258
iron-on tape 115
ironing-boards, storage of 112
irons
  raising dents with 81, 239
  removing finish with 244
  revival of 255
  storage of 112
islands, in kitchen 107, 108, 109

INDEX

J

jackets, as tool holders 46
jacks
   levelling decks with 288
   use of 304, 313, 359
jam tins, as tool pockets 46
jars, under shelves 61
jigs
   centre lines, for marking 70
   circle centres, for finding 69
   disc sanders, for 83
   drilling, for 72
   H-frame 87
   picket fences, for 286
   routers, for 78
   saws, for 75, 76, 77
jigsaw blades
   cleaning of 29
   extending life of 28
   lubrication of 95
   types of 29
jigsaws
   metal and 94, 95
   orbital action 29
   plywood and 74
   storage of 29
   use of 28, 75
joint compound
   application of 131
   drying of 129
   pipes, on 212
joints
   butt *see* butt joints
   caulking of 150
   coped 79, 134
   dado 72, 73, 78
   dovetail 73
   dowel 79, 89
   loose 237
   mitre *see* mitre joints
   mortar 160, 161
   mortise and tenon *see* mortise
      and tenon joints
   opening of 236
   scarf 87, 134
jumper cables 324
junction boxes 204

K

kerosene
   disposal of 39
   glass-cutting and 99
key rings, childproofing with 46
keys
   broken off 350
   cars, for 323
   colour-coding of 350
Kitchen Specialists' Association 365
kitchens
   cabinets in 106, 107
   counters in 107
   home offices in 113
   islands in 107, 108, 109
   organizers for 109
   painting of 175
   playrooms in 106
   pull-out tables for 107
   racks for 108, 109
   rubbish bins in 106
   safety in 333, 334
   shelves in 107, 109
   storage in 106
kneeling pads 139, 272
knives
   burn-in 239
   cleaning of 176, 244
   putty 176, 244
   repair of 350
   sharpening of 22, 41
   storage of 58
   utility 41
knobs
   anchoring of 233
   finishing of 93
   petrol tanks and 318
   stripping of 242
   temporary 248

L

labels 60, 265
laces, repair of 360
lacquer-base finishes 242, 246
ladders
   articulated 45
   buckets on 45, 187
   extension 44
   roller trays on 187
   roofs and 44, 163, 164
   safety on 44, 45, 163
   sawhorses, as 55
   scaffolding and 181
   storage of 45
   use of 44
laminate *see* plastic laminate
lamps 208
   see also lights
lampshade frames, uses for 266
Landscapers' Institute 365
landscaping, of gardens 268
lanterns, oil for 360
laundry 106, 112
laundry baskets
   compost in 267
   holders for 296
   storage in 122
laundry-detergent caps 47
laundry prewash, skin and 65
lawn mowers 274, 282, 283, 346
lawns
   care of 273, 274
   establishment of 273
   indigenous 270
   landscaping of 268
   mowing of 274
   watering of 275, 279
layout
   gardens, of 293
   projects, of 35, 70
lazy susans 109, 111
lead shields (wall fasteners) 117
leather
   cutting of 29
   patching of 234
   upholstery 320
levels
   decks and 288, 293
   drills, on 9
   improvised 35, 293
   posts and 284
   storage of 35
   testing of 35
light bulbs
   air fresheners and 336
   changing of 208
   quartz halogen 317
   wattage of 209
light fixtures, replacement of 209
lightning conductors 164
lights
   cars, of 317, 327
   checking of 208
   cleaning sockets of 208, 293, 317
   cords on 208
   fluorescent 210
   miner's 156
   outdoor 293
   plugs on 208
   power tools and 51
   switches on 208
   workshops, in 50
   see also Christmas lights;
      torches
line levels *see* levels
lines, straight 70, 75
linseed oil
   hammer handles and 17
   safety and 91
   screws and 12
   squeaking floors and 138
   thresholds and 146
   white rings and 238
lip balm, uses for 12, 16, 180
liquid rubber, ropes and 42
liquor cartons, glasses in 347
locks
   colour-coding of 350
   credit cards and 228
   drilling open of 323
   freezing weather and 325
   installation of 146, 147
   keys broken in 350
   reinforcements for 228
loppers, use of 278
lubrication
   cutting glass, while 99
   drawers, of 233
   drilling, while 10, 94, 98
   floors, of 138
   garage doors, of 327
   hinges, of 355
   locks, of 325
   nails, of 16
   planes, of 20
   sanding, while 98
   sawing, while 21, 28, 31, 95

screws, of 12, 13, 14
tape measures, of 33
wheels, of 314
windows, of 144
zippers, of 352
lunch boxes, as toolboxes 46

M

magnetic knife-holder strips 58
magnets
    clamps and 36
    fishing wires with 206
    measuring with 33
    metal dust and 40
    small parts and 16, 60, 62
    toolboxes and 46
main distribution boards 200, 202, 203
mains switches 203
mallets 17
manuals 41
maps, waterproofing of 360
marbles, as improvised levels 35
margarine tubs, on taps 214
marking 34, 69, 70, 71
masking tape
    drilling guide, as 72
    rejuvenation of 353
    use of 178, 188, 251
masonry
    caulk types for 151
    drilling into 10, 156
    laying of 290
    marking of 34
    pegboard on 127
    repair of 160, 292
    stains on 161
    wall fasteners and 117
Master Builders' Association 365
matchboxes, uses for 41
mattresses
    safety and 335
    uses for 149
measures and measuring
    centre lines, of 69
    circles, of 68, 69
    circular-saw cuts, of 28
    cylinders, around 69
    depth, of 68
    digging, for 280
    drafter's rules, using 71
    equal segments, of 69
    improvised 32, 33, 68
    insides of boxes, of 68
    plumb bobs, of 69
    sawhorses, using 54
    squareness, of see squareness
    story poles for 134
    transfer of 33, 68
    window panes, of 145
    wood lengths, of 75, 76
    see also gauges
measuring tapes see tape measures
mesh
    animal deterrent, as 270, 337, 344
    brush cleaner, as 171
    chisels and 292
    fireplaces and 341
    gutters and 162
    paint scraper, as 176
    stapling of 18
    tool holder, as 58
    vent pipes and 163
    see also screening
metal
    caulk types for 151
    drilling into 10, 94
    marking of 34, 96
    sawing of 21, 28, 29, 77, 94, 95
    working with 94
metal dust 40
metallic filings 62
methylene chloride, risks of 243
mildew 161, 185, 194
mineral deposits 218, 220, 258
mineral spirits
    cleaning hair with 188
    glass-cutting and 99
    reclaiming of 188
    sanding and 98
mirrors 350, 354
mitre boxes 79, 84, 100
mitre gauges 30, 76
mitre joints
    clamping of 87
    cutting of 77, 79
    wall trim and 134
moisturizer tissue containers 171
molly bolts 117, 129
mortar, and mortar joints 160, 161
mortise and tenon joints
    binding tests for 79
    glue and 89, 236, 237
    making of 73
    refitting of 237
moss 164, 292
mothballs
    cat deterrents, as 270, 337
    smell of 336
    toolboxes, in 47
motor oil
    changing of 304
    disposal of 305
    winter and 324
motor-oil containers, uses for 162
mould see mildew
mouldings
    cutting of 77, 115
    drilling of 72
    storage of 61
    tracing of 71
    types of 115
mousetraps, uses for 41, 86
moving, of heavy objects 345, 348
moving house 346
multi-purpose tools 199, 203
multitesters 199, 253, 260, 263
mustard bottles, and glue 38

N

nail polish
    spills of 238
    uses for 40, 64, 329, 353
nails
    caulk-tube caps, as 150
    concrete footings and 284
    decks and 288
    drywall 133
    electrical boxes and 206
    furniture and 236
    lubrication of 16
    mounting of 291
    painting with 182
    picking up of 16, 62
    picture hangers, as 331
    popped 129
    pulling of 16
    roofing 165
    starting of 15, 16
    storage of 60
    toenailing of 135
National Spa and Pool Institute of South Africa 300, 365
noise reduction
    air conditioners and 225
    appliances and 148
    baths and 216
    doors and 149
    hacksaws and 95
    houses and 148
    pipes and 213
    stereo speakers and 148
    traffic and 148
    windows and 148
    workshops and 50, 148, 149
nonslip decals, removal of 353
north, true, finding of 222
NSPI 300, 365
nuts
    keeping tight of 96
    left-hand threads on 254
    picking up of 62
    removal of 96, 303
    storage of 60
    threading of 19, 303

O

odours
    household 219, 225, 336
    pets, from 336, 337
offices, home 113, 120
oil
    camp stoves, lanterns and 360
    disposal of 39
    linseed see linseed oil
    machine 10, 94, 95, 99
    motor see motor oil
    olive 238
    penetrating 242, 246
    safety and 91
    spills of 62
    stains of 176, 292

INDEX

tung 91, 246
vegetable 65, 238, 271
oil filters (car), changing of 305
oil spouts 40, 41
outdoor furniture
    improvements to 294
    storage of 125
oven cleaner
    drill bits and 11
    router bits and 27
    saws and 21, 29
    smoke stains and 341
    stripper, as 245
ovens 259

packing (household) 346, 347, 348
pails see buckets
paint filters 90
paint gloves 181
paint pads 173, 187
paint and painting
    application of 169, 179
    banisters, of 181
    blackboard 175
    cars, of 319
    ceilings, of 179
    cleanup after 188
    clothes and 188
    colour consistency of 167, 175
    colours (exterior) 184
    colours (interior) 174, 175, 177, 181
    contact with 59
    cover-ups for 177, 178, 297
    crackling effect on 248
    decks, of 289
    decorative 182
    dishwasher racks, of 258
    disposal of 39
    doors, of 93, 146, 180, 181
    drying of 62, 93
    enamel 249
    feathering of 169, 251
    fumes of 168
    furniture, of 248
    glazes and 183, 248, 249
    glue and 88
    hair, on 188
    house exteriors, of 184
    lead in 177
    manufacturers of 364
    mildew and 185
    milk 245
    mixing of 167
    nonslip 289
    postboxes, of 296
    pouring of 168, 189
    preparation for (exterior) 185, 186
    preparation for (interior) 176
    problems with 185, 188
    quality of 175
    quantity of 175, 185
    railings, of 181
    record of 189
    removal of 144, 176, 186, 188, 243
    roller- see rollers and roller trays
    roofs, of 164, 165
    safety with 177
    sanding of 83
    skin, on 65, 188
    skins on 189
    spills of 62
    spray- see spray-painting
    stairs, of 181
    step-by-step guide to 178, 187
    storage of 55, 189, 303
    straining of 168
    supersmooth finish with 248
    texturing of 183
    tight corners, in 248
    tools for 173
    trim, around 188
    walls, of 179
    windows, of 145, 180, 188
paint removers, disposal of 39
paint scrapers 176, 188
paint stirrers 167
paint thinners, disposal of 39
paint tins
    digging holes and 284
    drip catchers for 167, 169
    holders for 168
    ladders and 187
    sealing of 168, 189
    storing paint in 189
paintbrushes
    cleaning of 170, 171
    disposable 170
    finish removers, as 244
    foam 170
    freezers, in 170
    holders for 169, 170, 187
    loose bristles on 170
    sash 180
    scrub brushes, as 40
    storage of 58, 171, 172
    types of 173
    use of 169
panelling, wall 67, 136, 157
panic buttons 230
pantihose
    filters, as 63, 260, 300
    finish removers, as 244
    melon supports, as 267
    paint strainers, as 168
    peppermint sachets, as 344
    smoothness testers, as 83, 260
    stain applicators, as 92
pantries 106, 120
paraffin
    clamps, on 36
    garden pests and 271
    plate moulds of 351
    window channels, on 144
    see also candle wax
parts
    finding of 252
    greasing of 252
    picking up of 62
    replacement of 258
    sources of 252
    storage of 60, 252
    washing of 252
passages
    security doors in 228
    storage in 103
paths 290, 291, 292
patio furniture see outdoor furniture
patios 290, 291, 292
patterns, working with 71
paving
    laying of 290, 291
    repair of 292
    water conservation and 268
    weeding of 270
peepholes 229, 230
pegboard
    drawing circles with 34
    hole-spacing template, as 72
    installation of 127
    protecting surfaces with 15
    storage, for 11, 25, 31
    workshops, in 56
pegs (clothes) 294, 296
pegs (tent) 358, 359
pencil sharpeners, uses for 79
pencils 34, 94
peppermint leaves, mice and 344
perforated hardboard see pegboard
pest control 270, 344
petrol, cars and 318
petroleum jelly
    car batteries, on 316
    glue tubes, on 38
    grease repellent, as 65
    plungers and 219
    toilet repair and 218
pets
    alarm systems and 230
    bathing of 337
    children and 335
    gardens and 270
    houseplants and 337
    odours from 336, 337
    tethers for 227, 337
    watchdogs as 227
    water dishes for 337
pH scale, plants and 267
phosphate, disposal of 39
phosphoric acid, disposal of 39
photographs, separation of 353
piano lids, childproofing of 332
picket fences 286
pictures, hanging of 330, 331
pie containers, saw blades in 29
pill containers, solder in 97
pipe cutters 100, 211
pipe dope 212
pipe insulation
    installation of 213
    uses for 272, 295, 362
pipes
    bending of 212
    electrical systems and 201, 211

376 / Index

frozen water in 213
lagging of 220, 223
loose straps on 216
metal 212
noise in 213
plastic 46, 211, 212, 213
polycop versus PVC 212
PVC see PVC pipe
repair of 213
replacement of 212, 220
rust-resistant 212
soil 211
soldering of 97, 212
storage of 61
trees and 277
unscrewing of 212, 213
wall studs and 135
wallboard and 132
waste 211
watering plants and 279
pitch, alignment of 35
planes and planing
　lubrication of 20
　sharpening of 22, 23
　storage of 20
　use of 73
plans, working with 41
plants
　butterfly attractant 271
　diseases of 270
　healthy signs in 276
　indigenous 270, 279
　insects and 270
　labels for 265
　landscaping of 268, 269
　moving of 348, 349
　pH levels and 267
　supports for 266
plaster
　application of 130
　clamps for 130
　drilling into 10
　painting of 186
　patching of 129, 130
　testing of 130
　wall fasteners and 117
plastic
　caulk types for 151
　working with 100
plastic bottles
　algaecides in 300
　funnels, as 304

paint in 167
paintbrushes in 170
parts scoops, as 62
propeller covers, as 363
seeds in 265
sprinklers, as 279
storage in 11, 60
string dispensers, as 59
toilets and 218
plastic laminate
　application of 101
　discoloration of 240
　drilling into 100
　reattachment of 240
　removal of 240
　sawing of 100
plastic sheets
　solar stills and 359
　stapling of 18
plastic toggles 117
plastic tubing
　cutting of 100
　dishwasher racks and 258
　level, as 293
plastic-wrap cutting strips 53
platforms see scaffolding
play equipment 295
playing cards, as sanding tool 82
playrooms, in cupboards 106
plectrums, uses for 90
pliers
　carrying of 46
　flat-jaw 99
　insulation of 205
　lineman's 99
　nail holders, as 15
　spanners versus 19
　torch stands, as 43
　use of 19
plugs
　connection of 24, 208
　safety and 51
plumb bobs 35, 69
Plumbing, Institute of 365
plumbing
　basics of 211
　see also pipes
plungers 211, 219
plywood
　carrying of 67
　cutting of 74
　storage of 61

pole sanders 82
polyethylene sheeting 155, 157
polymer repair patches 129
polystyrene
　cutting of 100
　insulation material, as 153
　kneeling pad, as 139
　storage in 20, 41, 58
polyurethane caulk see caulk and
　　caulking
polyurethane (finish)
　application of 246
　brushes for 92
　characteristics of 246
　disposal of 39
polyurethane insulation 153
pool furniture see outdoor
　　furniture
popcorn, as decorations 342
postboxes 296
posts
　decks and 288
　preservatives and 158, 159
　replacement of 287
　setting of 284
　storage of 158
　tops of 158
pot-plant holders, in cupboards
　　118
pot plants see houseplants
pot scourers see scourer
　　sponges
pouring, tips for 90, 168, 189
power, turning off 200, 201, 203
power failures, freezers and 257
power lines 201
power tools
　buyer's guide for 24
　cleaning of 24
　cords and 43, 51, 282
　lights and 51
　manuals for 41
　moving house and 346
　noise reduction and 50
　outdoor 282
　safety with 24, 49, 51, 64, 283
　storage of 58, 59
power vibrators, use of 290
power washers 185
pram wheel rims, uses for 355
preservatives see wood
　　preservatives

primers, versus sealers 178
pruning 278
pulse, checking for 301
punches, storage of 58
push sticks 26, 31
putty
　application of 90
　storage of 40
　see also wood putty
putty knives 176, 244
PVC pipe
　boat handholds, for 363
　clothes rods, on 119
　cutting of 213
　garden corner guards, for 275
　greenhouses, for 265
　hand trucks, on 345
　pegboard spacers, for 127
　polycop versus 212
　postboxes, for 296
　shade structures, for 267
　spanners, on 314
　storage, for 11, 17, 25, 61, 124
　tool holders, for 322
　vacuum cleaners, on 63
　watering plants, for 279

quadrant 134, 332

racks
　belts, for 119
　bicycles, for 123
　brushes, for 171, 172
　card tables, for 125
　cars, above 124
　cookbooks, for 109
　dishwashers, in 258
　doors, on 103, 104, 110
　golf equipment, for 123
　ironing equipment, for 112
　kitchen, in 108, 109
　linen, for 121
　outdoor furniture, for 125

Index / 377

INDEX

robes, for 110
rollers, for 172
shoes, for 103
tools, for 56
towels, for 110, 111
washer/dryers, above 112, 260
wood, for 61
radial arm saws
   extension cords for 43
   plywood and 74
   safety with 31
   storage of 29
   use of 77
radiant barriers 155
radio reception 263
railings
   painting of 181
   repair of 292
railway sleepers, in gardens 265
rakes 272, 280
rasps 20
razor blades, storage of 41
record album covers, uses for 29
recovery position (first aid) 205, 301
refrigerator-seal magnets 60, 62
refrigerators
   moving of 348
   problems with 256
refuse bags *see* rubbish bags
respirators 65
retaining walls 157, 290
right angles, checking of 68
ripping 30, 31, 76, 77, 100
rock-wool insulation 153
rods
   cupboards, in 119
   reinforcing 290
rollers and roller trays
   cleaning of 172
   ladders and 187
   running wires with 207
   storage of 172
   storage, used for 25
   use of 172, 173, 179
   wood stain and 247
roof tiles 164
roofing felt, stapling of 18
roofs
   cleaning of 165
   ladders and 44, 163, 164
   painting of 164, 165

pests in 344
repair of 163, 164, 165
roots, removal of 284
ropes, repair of 42
router bits
   ball-bearing 78
   cleaning of 27
   combination of 78
   insertion of 26
   sharpening of 22
   storage of 27, 58
   types of 27
routers and routing
   buyer's guide for 27
   dado jigs for 78
   extension cords for 43
   friction boards for 78
   guides for 26, 78
   problems with 78
   setting up of 26
   storage of 27, 59
   tables for 26
   use of 78
rubber, liquid 42
rubber balls, uses for 84, 292, 326
rubber bands
   clamps, as 86
   lock washers, as 19
   storage, for 20
   tools, on 18, 19, 43, 303
rubber cement, screws and 13
rubbish bags
   aprons, as 64
   compost in 267
   icy windscreens and 325
   vacuum cleaners and 63
rubbish bins 106, 281, 336
rulers 32, 33
runners (carpet) 140
rust prevention
   cars, in 314, 316, 319
   clamps, on 36
   dishwasher racks, on 258
   glass cutters, on 98
   outdoor furniture, on 294
   railings, on 292
   router bits, on 27
   screws, on 12
   toolboxes, in 47
   washing-machine feet, on 260
   workshops, in 49

rust remover, disposal of 39
rust stains 161

SABS
   contact numbers for 365
   electrical systems and 200, 204, 206
safes 226, 358
safety
   antifreeze, with 308
   buckets, with 42
   burglar guards, with 229
   caulk, with 150, 151
   clamps, with 36
   clothes for 64
   cutting glass, while 99
   electric cords, with 51, 205
   electricity, with 200, 255
   finishes, with 39, 91
   flammable materials, with *see* flammable materials
   grinding, while 22
   hazardous waste, with *see* hazardous waste
   home, at 333
   insulation materials, with 152, 154
   ladders, on 44, 45, 163
   lawn mowers, with 282, 283
   paint, with 177
   play equipment, with 295
   power tools, with 24, 49, 51, 64, 283
   preservatives, with 159
   roofs, on 163
   saws, with 28, 31, 283
   screwdrivers, with 12
   spray-painting, while 65, 172
   strippers, with 243, 245
   swimming pools, in 301
   wallcovering removers, with 190
   window panes, with 144, 145
   workshops, in 49, 51, 59
   see also childproofing
safety deposit boxes 354
safety gates 333

safety glass 98
safety glasses 64, 65
sand, paving and 290
sand bags, travel and 358
sanders and sanding
   belt 83
   bench grinders, as 22
   ceilings, of 82
   circular objects, of 83
   cleaning up after 25, 62
   curved shapes, of 25, 82
   disc 83
   drawers, of 233
   drum 25, 83
   extension cords for 43
   finishes, of 238
   glass, of 98
   hand, by 81
   hard-to-reach areas, of 25, 82, 83
   painted surfaces, of 83, 186
   power 25, 83
   protecting work while 82, 83
   random-orbit 25
   small parts, of 83
   smoothness tests for 83
   stands for 25
   storage of 25
   wallboard, of 82, 133
   wallcoverings, of 190
   walls, of 82
   wet- 80, 81
sanding blocks 81
sanding discs, recycling of 83
sanding sponges 81
sandpaper
   cutting of 80
   flexing of 80
   grades of 80, 81
   storage of 80
   strengthening of 25
   types and uses of 80
sap, on cars 320
sauce bottles, and glue 38
saucepans, paint tins in 168
sawdust
   air filters for 62
   cleaning up of 24, 30, 55, 62
   electrical outlets and 51
   safety glasses and 64
   uses for 62, 90, 243

sawhorses
   construction of 54
   substitutes for 45, 46, 55
   tool trays for 54
   working with 54
saws and sawing
   band *see* band saws
   bow 21, 278
   chain 283
   circular *see* circular saws
   cleaning of 21, 29
   coping 79
   dovetail 21, 115
   grout 143
   hack- *see* hacksaws
   hand- *see* handsaws
   hole 72, 147
   jig- *see* jigsaws
   mitre 76
   portable 28
   pruning 278
   radial arm *see* radial arm saws
   reciprocating 43
   scroll 77
   storage of 21, 29, 59
   table *see* table saws
   tenon 21
scaffolding 181, 186, 187
scissors
   repair of 350
   sharpening of 23
scourer sponges 47
scouring powder 12
scratches
   acrylic, on 101
   furniture, on 238, 243
   waterskis, on 361
   windscreens, on 321
screening
   stapling of 18
   uses for 47, 168, 176
screwdrivers and driving
   carrying of 46
   cordless 11, 13
   cross-tip 13
   electrician's 199
   improving grip on 303
   insulation of 205
   magnetized 12
   Phillips 13
   power 11, 13
   Pozidriv 13
   slot-tip 13
   storage of 12, 58
   torches on 43
   Torx 13
   types of 13
   use of 12, 13
   wall studs, into 135
   wallboard, into 133
screws
   appliance repair and 254
   brass 13
   caulk-tube caps, as 150
   cutting of 96
   deck 288
   drywall 13, 133
   earthing 209
   furniture and 236
   hammering of 13, 14
   lubrication of 12, 13, 14
   mounting of 291
   Phillips-head 13, 14
   picking up of 62
   removing and reseating of 14
   restoring slot on 14
   shellac and 13
   slotted 13
   square 13
   starting of 12, 13, 38
   storage of 60
   Torx 13
   types of 13
scrubbing brushes
   paintbrushes as 40
   uses for 244, 352
sealers
   application of 91, 289
   disposal of 39
   primers versus 178
   wood stain and 247
seats, tool caddies and 303
secateurs 278
security
   air conditioners and 229
   answering machines and 227
   cars and 231, 323
   deception and 231
   domestics and 226
   doors and 144, 146, 228
   houses and 227
   leaving/returning home and 231
   legal advice on 227
   muggings and 231
   outdoor lights and 293
   public transport and 231
   restricted views and 226, 229
   suspended floors and 229
   telephones and 226
   travel and 231, 358
   walls and 226
   watchdogs and 227
   windows and 144, 226, 229, 231
   see also alarm systems
Security Association of South Africa 365
seedlings
   frost covers for 265
   purchase of 276
seeds
   sowing of 273, 274, 280
   starting of 265
self-defence 231
   see also security
shade structures (plant) 267
shades
   hanging and repair of 329
   workbenches, on 53
shampoo, cleaning skin with 65
sharpening
   lawn-mower blades 282
   pencils 34
   tools 22, 41, 281
shears, sharpening of 22, 281
sheet laminate *see* plastic laminate
shelf liner, as marking tool 34

SAFETY FIRST FEATURES

▶ Appliance repair, p 255, "Shock-free repairs"

▶ Away from home, p 231, "Be secure away from home"

▶ Christmas trees as fire hazards, p 343, "Christmas tree care"

▶ CPR (cardiopulmonary resuscitation), p 301, "Emergency!"

▶ Electric shocks, p 205, "Shocks: first aid"

▶ Electrical risks in the workshop, p 51, "Avoid shock"

▶ Finishes and their hazards, p 91, "About finishes"

▶ Fire control in the garage, p 303, "Fire control"

▶ Fire prevention in the workshop, p 55, "Fighting fire"

▶ First-aid kits in the workshop, p 59, "First-aid kits"

▶ First-aid kits for the car, p 359, "A first-aid kit for the car"

▶ Heavy loads, p 345, "Save your back"

▶ Home safety, p 227, "Is your house safe?"

▶ Home safety, p 333, "Safe at home"

▶ Outdoor power tools, p 283, "Be careful out there"

▶ Play equipment, p 295, "Play set rules"

▶ Power-saw safety, p 31, "Power saws"

▶ Power-tool precautions, p 24, "Avoiding accidents"

▶ Protective clothing, p 65, "Protective gear"

▶ Roof work, p 163, "Care up there"

▶ Strippers and their hazards, p 243, "Stripping risks"

INDEX

shelf supports 57, 72, 114, 115, 121
shelf towers 118
shellac
    application of 239, 246
    characteristics of 240, 242, 246
    screws and 13
    sealant, as 247
shellac sticks 239
shelves
    addition of 116
    bathrooms, in 110
    beds, above 104
    built-in 114, 121
    drilling holes for 72
    eaves, under 126
    fold-away 104
    garages, in 57, 126
    gutters as 61
    jars under 61
    kitchens, in 107, 109
    knock-down 114
    laundry baskets, for 296
    open-end 116
    passages, in 103
    shoes, for 119
    slanted 109
    slide-in 107
    step 108
    utility 57, 126
    wall studs and 57
    washer/dryers, above 112, 260, 261
    windows, in 114
    workshops, in 57, 59
    Z-bracket system 126
    see also racks; wall units
shields (wall fasteners) 117
shingles 163, 164, 165
shipping tubes, uses for 61
shoes
    cleaning and scraping of 352
    protection of 178
    storage of 103, 119
short circuits 200, 203, 204, 253
shovels
    sharpening of 281
    trenching 285
    use of 272
shower caddies 111
shower-curtain rings, uses for 60

shower curtains
    securing of 353
    uses for 178
shower heads, cleaning of 216
showers, repair of 216
shrubs
    circles round 276
    landscaping of 269, 277
    planting of 277
    pruning of 278
    windbreaks, as 276
side cutters 199, 203
silica gel 47
silicone carbide abrasive 80, 98
silicone caulk see caulk and caulking
silicone sealant, uses for 42, 50, 64
silicone spray, uses for 21, 144, 218
sinks, shelves under 107
skateboards, heavy objects and 345
skin
    chemicals on 59
    cleaning of 65, 188
    protection of 65
skirting 134
slates 164
sledgehammers 17
sledges, gardening and 272
slides (play equipment) 295
smoke stains 161, 341
snow see freezing weather
soap
    garden pests and 271
    grease repellent, as 65
    linen freshener, as 336
    lubrication with 12, 13, 21, 144
    masking with 180
    squeaky floors and 138
socks, uses for 44, 178, 260
sofa beds, moving of 348
soil
    acidity or alkalinity of 267
    houseplants, for 338
    improvement of 277
    texture of 275
soil erosion 288
soil subsidence 298
solar heating, film 145, 226
solar power 222

solar stills, construction of 359
solder and soldering
    as contour gauge, wire 71
    pipe joints, of 97, 212
    use of 97
soldering guns, tips of 100
soldering irons
    cleaning of 97
    stands for 97
solid-surface material 101
solvents
    contact with 59
    disposal of 39
    finishes and 242, 246
    storage of 55
    see also thinners
soot stains 161
soundproofing 148
    see also noise reduction
South African Bureau of Standards see SABS
South African Nurserymen's Association 365
spades, as boot scrapers 352
spanners
    adjustable 19
    bucket handles, on 42
    improving grip on 303
    pliers versus 19
    plug socket 306
    universal joints on 306
    wheel 314
    see also wrenches
sparks (electrical) 201
spatulas, uses for 244
speaker cones, patching of 263
speaker outlets, capacitors on 263
speaker wires 262
spectacle cases, uses for 98
spectacles
    fogging up of 352
    pocket clips for 64
    safety 64, 65
    screws in 353
spirit levels see levels
splashbacks, laminating of 101
splicing
    tapes, of 263
    wires, of 204
sponge mops, as pole sanders 82

sponges, in water bowls 337
sports equipment 123, 125, 360
spray-painting
    cladding, of 186
    furniture, of 250
    problems with 251, 319
    safety and 65, 172
    techniques of 172, 173, 250
    touching up with 251, 319
sprinklers 275, 279
squareness, checking for 68
squares
    combination 35, 68, 69, 70
    framing 68, 69, 134
    try 68, 69
stacking cases 126
stain see wood stain
stains
    crayon 176
    grease 176, 191, 292
    ink 176
    iron 258
    mineral deposit 218
    nail-polish 238
    oil 176, 292
    paint 161
    rust 161
    smoke 161, 341
    soot 161
    tar 161
    water-mark 246
    white-ring 238
stairs
    childproofing of 333
    painting of 181
    space under 113, 126
    squeaks in 138
stakes 276, 293
stamps, unsticking of 353
staplers and staples 18, 140, 154
steel wool 40
stencilling 182
stepping-stone walks 291
steps 292
stereo sets 148, 263
stockings see pantihose
stone chips, at wall base 163
storage
    axes, of 58
    card tables, of 125
    carpets, of 124
    cars, in 322

chisels, of 20, 46
Christmas lights, of 124
clothes pegs, of 296
combination squares, of 35
cords, of 42, 58, 61
documents, of 354, 358
dowels, of 61
drills, of 11, 46, 58, 59
files, of 46
filler, of 40, 133
flammable materials, of 55, 91, 283, 303
garages, in 57, 61, 124, 126
garden hoses, of 61
garden tools, of 280, 281
glass cutters, of 98
glue and glue guns, of 38, 39
hammers, of 17, 58
household 102
ironing equipment, of 112
knives, of 58
ladders, of 45
laundry, of 106
levels, of 35
manuals, of 41
mouldings, of 61
outdoor furniture, of 125
paint, of 55, 189, 303
paintbrushes, of 58, 171, 172
parts, of 60, 252
pipes, of 61
planes, of 20
pool equipment, of 299
posts, of 158
power tools, of 58, 59
punches, of 58
putty, of 40
razor blades, of 41
rollers, of 172
routers, of 27, 58, 59
sanding belts, of 25
sandpaper, of 80
saw accessories, of 31
saws, of 21, 29, 59
screwdrivers, of 12, 58
shoes, of 103, 119
sports equipment, of 123, 125
stain rags, of 92
toys, of 122
tubes, of 39
wire coils, of 61

wood, of 61, 67
workshops, in 56
storage chests, desks and 122
storage lofts 125
story poles 134
stoves
  camp 360
  childproofing of 334
  repair of 258
straightedges
  checking edges with 68
  finding diameters with 68
  glass cutters and 98
  router guides, as 26
  saw guides, as 75, 77
straws
  caulk and 150
  electrical contacts and 354
  glue and 89, 240
  icy locks and 325
  measuring with 33
  picture wires and 331
  retrieving items with 354
  running wires with 210
  toilet repair and 218
string, dispensers for 59
strip flooring 138, 139
strippers and stripping
  application of 245
  cleaning up after 176
  contact with 59
  covering of 243
  disposal of 39
  drips and 243
  furniture, of 242
  hardware, of 242, 245
  home brews for 245
  milk paint, of 245
  preparation for 242
  safety with 243, 245
  tools for 244
studs *see* wall studs
subfloors 139
surgical tubing, uses for 205, 361
Swimline Advisory Service 365
swimming pools
  algae in 300
  backwashing of 298, 299
  builders of 298, 300
  cleaners for 298, 299
  equipment for 299
  expert help for 300

finishes on 298, 300
leakage tests for 300
planning of 298
rain and 300
safety and 301
siphoning of 299
surrounds for 298
underwater view of 300
water conservation and 299, 300
water level in 300
swings 295
switches
  cleaning of 252
  covers for 208
  dimmer 293
  disassembly of 255
  testing of 253
syringes, uses for 88

table saws
  accessories for 31
  blade alignment of 30
  extension cords for 43
  height gauges for 30
  mitre-gauge guides for 30, 76
  plastic laminate and 100
  plywood and 74
  safety with 31
  storage of 29
  straight glueing edges and 79
  use of 30, 76
tablecloths, anchors for 294
tables
  casters on 294
  clamping of 85
  finishing legs of 93
  fold-up 55, 125
  painting of 250
  pull-out 107
  wobbling of 235
tack rags 92
tackers and tacking 18
talcum powder 34, 94, 138
tape dispensers 59, 97
tape measures
  fishing wires with 206

improvised 32
lubrication of 33
notes on 33
sawhorses and 54
taps
  ball 217
  cartridge 214, 215
  covers for 334
  outdoor 214
  repair of 214, 215, 217
tar
  caulk types for 151
  stains of 161
teaspoons, uses for 361
telephone books, uses for 15, 93
telephones
  cellular 357
  security and 226
  wiring of 210
  workshops, in 49
television sets 148, 262, 348
tennis balls, uses for 15, 20, 31, 306, 317, 326
tenons *see* mortise and tenon joints
tents, anchoring of 358, 359
terminals, wires and 204, 255, 258
tethers 227, 337
thermostats
  cars, in 325
  testing of 260
  wiring of 210
thinners
  disposal of 39
  lacquer 242, 246
  pouring of 90
  safety and 91, 303
  see also solvents
thread sealant tape 212
thresholds 140, 146
tile nippers 142
tiles
  acoustic 148
  ceiling 137
  ceramic *see* ceramic tiles
  roof 164
  vinyl 140, 141
timber *see* wood
Timber Frame Builders' Association 365
tipping (brush strokes) 169

INDEX

tissues, holders for 59
toggle bolts 117
toilet-paper holders 59
toilets
    cleaning of 218
    leaks in 218
    odours from 219
    pipes from 211, 218
    retrieving items from 218
    unclogging of 219
    water conservation and 218
tongs, uses for 162
tool caddies, seats and 303
tool tables (fold-up) 55
toolboxes 37, 46, 47, 199
tools
    basics of 8
    care of 46, 280
    cutting, for 20
    digging, for 285
    electrical work, for 199, 203, 205
    garages, for 303
    gardening, for 272, 280
    holders for 46, 47, 58, 281, 303, 322
    identification of 47, 281
    ladders and 44
    manufacturers of 364
    masonry repair, for 161
    painting, for 173
    plumbing, for 211
    power see power tools
    roof, on 164
    safety with see safety
    security and 231
    shaping, for 20
    sharpening of 22, 41, 281
    storage of 46, 280, 281
    stripping, for 244
    wallcovering, for 193
toothbrushes, uses for 27, 92, 338
toothpaste, uses for 101, 239, 240
toothpicks, uses for 14, 88
torches
    finding parts with 252
    use of 43
touch-up pens 238
touch-up sticks 241
toy boxes, ventilation of 335

TOOLS OF THE TRADE FEATURES

▶ Brushes for wood finishes, p 92, "The right brush"
▶ Clamps, the handiest types, p 37, "User-friendly clamps"
▶ Digging tools, p 285, "Tools for post holes"
▶ Drills for everyday jobs, p 11, "Buying a drill"
▶ Electrical testing equipment, p 199, "Testing equipment"

▶ Hammers, types and quality, p 17, "Hammers"
▶ Handsaws for various jobs, p 21, "The right saw"
▶ Jigsaws and their blades, p 29, "Jigsaws"
▶ Plumbers' tools, p 211, "The plumber's toolbox"
▶ Routers and the various bits, p 27, "Buyer's guide"

▶ Screwdrivers and types of screw, p 13, "Screwdrivers"
▶ Vacuum cleaners in the workshop, p 63, "The workshop vacuum"
▶ Wall-stud finders, p 135, "Stud finders"

toys 122, 335
trailers
    boats and 362
    hookup of 323
    security and 358
    spare wheels for 358
trammels, substitutes for 34
trap mats 226
travel
    preparations for 221, 231, 308, 357
    security and 231, 358
    tips for 357
trees
    bark on 276
    circles round 276
    landscaping of 269, 277
    noise barriers, as 148
    planting of 277
    power tools and 276, 282
    pruning of 278
    purchase of 276, 277
    removal of 298
    shade from 224
    staking of 276
    swings and 295
    trimming of 21
    windbreaks, as 276
trellises 266, 267

triangles 35
triangulation 68
tricycles, gardening and 272
trim, wall 134, 176, 188
trucks, loading of 349
tubing
    copper see copper tubing
    plastic see plastic tubing
    surgical see surgical tubing
tuna-fish tins, uses for 97, 243
Turf Irrigation Association 365
turkey basters, uses for 90, 282
turnbuckles 287
turpentine, used in drilling 98
TV sets 148, 262
tweezers, as nail holders 15
tyre-tread gauges, woodwork and 68
tyres
    changing of 313
    disposal of 305
    inflation of 312, 318
    rotation of 312
    slow leaks in 312
    splitting wood and 297
    storage in 61
    swings and 295

tread on 312
valves on 312
wear patterns on 312

umbrellas, decks and 289
universal joints, on spanners 306
upholstery
    cars, in 320, 321
    leftover 234
    patching of 234
    tacking of 18, 234
urethane foam insulation 153

vacuum cleaners 63, 273, 355
vacuum hoses (car engines)
    plugs for 307
    uses for 303
valve-seat dressers 211
valves
    antiscald 335

shut-off 211, 214
tyres, on 312
vapour barriers
   climate and 155
   stapling of 18
vapour retarders 153, 154, 155
varnish
   acrylic 246
   application of 246
   brushes for 92
   characteristics of 242, 246
   disposal of 39
   glue and 88
   oil-base 246
   overnight in freezer 170
   preview of 246
   removal of 244
   safety and 91
   shaken, nor stirred 90
   wood stain and 91, 247
vases see flowers (cut)
VCR's 262, 332
vegetables, in gardens 265, 267
Velcro tape, uses for 82, 322, 353
veneer
   cutting of 77, 115
   repair of 240, 241
vent systems 163, 211, 212, 219
verges, cleaning of 297
vests, as tool holders 46
vices
   carrying of 37
   metal tubing and 94
   use of 36
   woodworker's 85
video recorders 262, 332
video tapes 263
vinegar
   brushes and 171
   glue remover, as 140, 236
   grease remover, as 219
   mineral deposits and 258
   preparation for paint, as 296
   stuck screws and 14
   wasps and 271
vinyl
   caulk types for 151
   coating 42
   cutting of 100
   frames 144
   patching of 234
   sheet 141

tiles 140, 141
upholstery 320, 321
voltage testers 199, 201
VOM's (volt-ohm meters) see
   multitesters

walks see paths
wall anchors see wall fasteners
wall fasteners
   installation of 117
   removal of 129
   types and uses of 117
wall framing 135
wall panelling 67, 136, 157
wall studs
   cabinets and 110
   finding of 135
   installation of 135
   pegboard and 127
   pipes in 135
   separation of 135
   shelves and 57
   wall fasteners and 117, 135
   wiring in 135
wall trim 134, 176, 188
wall units, in home offices 113
wallboard
   carrying of 67, 132
   ceilings 137
   cutting of 132
   damp prevention and 157
   glueing of 132, 133
   installation of 132
   insulation materials and 153
   patching of 129, 130, 131, 137
   pegboard on 127
   popped nails in 129
   retaping joints of 131
   reusing panels of 133
   sanding of 82, 133
   wall fasteners and 117, 133
   wall panelling and 136
wallcovering paste
   activator for 194
   application of 194
   mildew-resistant 194
   removal of 191, 197

wallcoverings
   arches and 195
   booking of 193
   borders and accents 196
   ceilings, on 194, 196
   Christmas decorations, as 342
   corners and 195, 196
   hanging of 192
   matching patterns on 192, 194
   mildew and 194
   pictures and 331
   planning of 191
   plumb problems and 196
   preparation for 190
   prepasted 192, 193, 194
   problems with 197
   re-covering of 190
   recesses and 195
   removal of 190, 191
   sanding of 190
   seams of 193, 197
   smoothing of 192, 193, 197
   testing of 190
   textured walls, on 191
   tools for 193
   trimming of 192
   wall units, behind 195
   wetting of 192, 197
   windows and 191
   wrapping paper, as 343
walls
   brick see masonry
   chasing of 207
   insulation of 153, 154
   mildew and 161
   noise barriers, as 148
   repair of 129, 177
   retaining 157, 290
   security and 226
wardrobes
   construction of 119
   see also cupboards
washers
   glue and 19, 38
   lock 19
   picking up of 62
   storage of 60
washing machines
   drain-hose filters for 260
   moving of 348
   repair of 260
   shelves above 112, 260, 261

waste disposal 39, 55, 91, 305
waste systems (household) 211
waste water, reuse of 279
watchdogs 227
water
   decks and 288, 289
   electricity and 200, 201
   iron in 258
   sources of 359
   under floor 156
   see also dampness
water conservation
   gardens and 268, 279
   geysers and 220, 221
   swimming pools and 299, 300
   toilets and 218
water hammer (in pipes) 213
water marks 246
water meters 211
water-supply systems
   description of 211
   draining of 213, 221
   freezing weather and 213, 214, 221
   pipes for 212
   turning on of 349
waterskis, repair of 361
wattage
   bulbs, of 209
   extension cords, of 43
wax see beeswax; candle wax;
   floor wax; furniture wax;
   paraffin
weatherproofing 150, 326
   see also insulation
weatherstripping 18, 152, 326
weeds 270
welding, protective gear for 65
wheel bearings, tread wear and 312
wheel nuts 313, 314
wheel rakes 160, 161
wheelbarrows 280, 340
wheels
   alignment of 312, 318
   alloy 320
   balance of 310, 312, 315
   care of 314, 320
   changing of 314
wicker, painting of 250
winches, stuck vehicles and 358
windbreaks, trees as 276

INDEX

window frames, vinyl 144
window panes
   carrying of 144
   installation of 144, 145
   removal of 144, 145
   safety and 144, 145
   solar heating film on 145, 226
window seats 104
windows
   childproofing of 332
   glass blocks in 229
   lubrication of 144
   painting of 145, 180, 188
   security and 144, 226, 229, 231
   shading of 224
   shelves in 114
   soundproofing of 148
   timber boxes around 157
   weatherstripping of 152
winter
   cars and 324
   lawn mowers and 282
   lawns and 274
   solar power and 223
   see also freezing weather
wire
   electrical see electrical wires
   razor 227
wire brushes 40, 47
wire coils, storage of 61
wire connectors
   caps for tubes, as 38, 150
   use of 204, 205, 209, 252
wire strippers 199, 203, 204
wood
   bark side of 289
   bending of 75
   burns on 239
   caulk types for 151
   drilling into 10, 72
   feathering of 289
   finishing of see finishes and finishing
   hazard classification for 158
   joining of 17, 79
   marking of 34, 71
   measuring lengths of 75, 76
   new 62, 90
   planing of 73
   preservation of see wood preservatives

purchase of 67
reuse of 67
rotting of 158, 186
sealing of see sealers
sizes of 67
splintering of 289
splitting (chopping) of 297
storage of 61, 67
warping of 67, 85, 91, 289
weathering of 289
wood filler
   application of 40, 90
   car body filler as 158
   chipboard, on 91
   making of 62
   stain and 90, 247
   storage of 40
wood grain, simulation of 249
wood preservatives
   application of 159
   chair legs, on 93
   colour and 158
   disposal of 39
   toxicity of 159
Wood Preservers' Association 365
wood putty
   application of 90
   mixing of 90
   storage of 40
wood shavings, uses for 243
wood stain
   ageing of 246
   application of 92, 247
   blotches in 247
   filler and 90, 247
   lightening of 246
   mix-and-match 247
   preparation for 92
   record of 93
   removal of 144
   stirring of 90
   varnish and 91, 247
workbenches
   bending brakes on 96
   catch-alls for 60
   construction of 52
   cutting strips for 53
   extension of 53, 55, 87
   grounding of 51
   lights on 50
   padding of 82

portable 87, 96
protection of 53
toolboxes as 46
workshops
   cleanup of 62
   electrical system in 51
   insulation of 49, 50, 148, 149
   lights in 50, 51
   rust prevention in 49
   safety in 49, 51, 59
   setting up of 49
   shelves in 57, 59
   skills in 66
   storage in 56
   vacuum cleaners in 63
   see also garages
wrapping paper 343
wrenches
   carrying of 46
   nuts and 303
   oil-filter 260
   plumbing jobs, for 211
   torque 314
   see also spanners

yoghurt cups, seeds in 265

Z-bracket shelfing systems 126
zippers 352

Acknowledgments

The editors wish to thank the following organizations for the assistance they provided:

AA Ball (Pty) Ltd
American Plywood Association
Atlas Van Lines, Inc
Building Centre
Carol Cable Company
Chapman's Hardware
DAP, Inc
Emperor Clock Company
Food and Drug Administration
Gem Electric Manufacturing Company, Inc
GE Wiring Devices
Gordons Power Tool Hardware
Halls Mica Hardware (Pty) Ltd, Amanzimtoti
Hardwood Plywood & Veneer Association
Institute of Plumbing
National Association of Canoe Liveries & Outfitters, Inc
National Glass Association
National Paint & Coatings Association
Nodak Farm & Home
North American Insulation Manufacturers' Association
Plascon Paints (Pty) Ltd
Ridgeway Clocks
Robert Bosch (Pty) Ltd
Rubbermaid Incorporated
Sligh Furniture Co
South African Bureau of Standards, Cape Town
South African Wood Preservers' Association
Tahran Paint and Decorating Centre
Timber Frame Builders' Association
WAP International
Wardkiss Homecare

Imagesetting by Unifoto (Pty) Ltd, Cape Town. Printing and binding by CTP Book Printers (Pty) Ltd, Cape Town.